Chaucer and the Challenges of Medievalism

STUDIES IN ENGLISH MEDIEVAL LANGUAGE AND LITERATURE

Edited by Jacek Fisiak

Band 5

PETER LANG

Frankfurt am Main · Berlin · Bern · Bruxelles · New York · Oxford · Wien

Chaucer
and the Challenges
of Medievalism

Studies in Honor of H. A. Kelly

Edited by Donka Minkova
and Theresa Tinkle

PETER LANG
Europäischer Verlag der Wissenschaften

Bibliographic Information published by Die Deutsche Bibliothek
Die Deutsche Bibliothek lists this publication in the Deutsche Nationalbibliografie; detailed bibliographic data is available in the internet at <http://dnb.ddb.de>.

Typesitting by **motivex**

ISSN 1436-7521
ISBN 3-631-51377-1
US-ISBN 0-8204-6478-3

© Peter Lang GmbH
Europäischer Verlag der Wissenschaften
Frankfurt am Main 2003
All rights reserved.

Printed in Germany 1 2   4 5 6 7

www.peterlang.de

Henry Ansgar (Andy) Kelly

Contents

Henry Ansgar (Andy) Kelly – *Curriculum Vitae*

Born: 6 June 1934, Fonda, Iowa, U.S.A.
Married: 18 June 1968, to Marea Tancred (Sydney, Australia)
Children: Sarah, born 1970; Dominic, born 1972

Education

1952-53: Creighton University
1953-61: St. Louis University: A.B. 1959 (Classics)
                                   A.M. 1961 (English Literature)
                                   Ph.L. 1961 (Philosophy)

1961-1964: Harvard University: Ph.D 1965
1964-66: Boston College: Weston College of Theology
                                   (1953-66: Jesuit Scholastic)

Employment

1967-69: Assistant Professor, UCLA
1969-72: Associate Professor, UCLA
1972- : Professor, UCLA
                (1986- : Above-Scale Rank)
1998- :Director, UCLA Center for Medieval and Renaissance Studies

Awards and Honors

1964-67: Junior Fellow, Harvard University of Fellows
                (1966-67: Resident Scholar, American Academy in Rome)
1971-72: Fellow, John Simon Guggenheim Foundation
1980-81: Fellow, National Endowment for the Humanities
                (1980-81: Visiting Professor, University of Sydney)
1986:   Fellow, Del Amo Endowment
1986- : Fellow, Medieval Academy of America
1986-88: Vice-President, Medieval Association of the Pacific
1987-90: Councillor, Medieval Academy of America
1988-90: President, Medieval Association of the Pacific
1996-97: Fellow, National Endowment for the Humanities
1996-97: UC President's Research Fellowship in the Humanities

List of Henry Ansgar Kelly's publications

Books

The Devil, Demonology, and Witchcraft: The Development of Christian Beliefs in Evil Spirits. New York: Doubleday, 1968 (137 pp.)

- *Towards the Death of Satan: The Growth and Decline of Christian Demonology*. London, Dublin, and Melbourne: Geoffrey Chapman, 1968 (137 pp.)
- *La morte di Satana: Sviluppo e declino della demonologia cristiana*. Trans. Lucia Pigni Maccia. La Ricerca religiosa: Studi e testi, no. 8. Milan: Bompiani, 1969 (168 pp.)
- *The Devil, Demonology, and Witchcraft. Revised Edition*. New York: Doubleday, 1974 (142 pp.)
- *Le diable et ses demons: La demonologie chretienne hier et aujourd'hui*. Trans. Maurice Galiano. Paris: Les editions du Cerf, 1977 (208 pp.)

Divine Providence in the England of Shakespeare's Histories. Cambridge, Mass.: Harvard University Press, 1970 (344 pp.)

Love and Marriage in the Age of Chaucer. Ithaca: Cornell University Press, 1975 (xii + 344 pp.)

The Matrimonial Trials of Henry VIII. Stanford: Stanford University Press, 1976 (xii + 333 pp.)

Canon Law and the Archpriest of Hita. Medieval and Renaissance Texts and Studies, vol. 27. Binghamton: SUNY, 1984. 203 pp.

The Devil at Baptism: Ritual, Theology, and Drama. Ithaca: Cornell University Press, 1985. 303 pp.

Chaucer and the Cult of St. Valentine. Davis Medieval Texts and Studies no. 5. Leiden: E. J. Brill, 1986. xii + 185 pp.

Tragedy and Comedy from Dante to Pseudo-Dante. Publications in Modern Philology no. 121. UCLA Center for Medieval and Renaissance Studies Cosponsored Publication no. 7. Berkeley: UC Press, 1989. x + 134 pp.

Ideas and Forms of Tragedy from Aristotle to the Middle Ages. Cambridge University Studies in Medieval Literature. Cambridge: Cambridge University Press, 1993. xvii + 257 pp.

The Monsters and the Neo-Critics: Proceedings of a Symposium Held at UCLA (1994), ed. Exemplaria 7.1 (Spring 1995) 1-98; "Introduction: Are the Middle Ages Theoretically Recalcitrant?" (pp. 1-7).

Chaucerian Tragedy. Chaucer Studies no. 24. Cambridge: D. S. Brewer, 1997. xii + 297 pp.

Inquisitions and Other Trial. Procedures in the Medieval West. Variorum Reprint Series. Aldershot: Ashgate Publishing, 2001. Ca. 300 pp.

Articles

"Consciousness in the Monologues of Ulysses", *Modern Language Quarterly* 24 (1963) 3-12.

"The Devil in the Desert", *Catholic Biblical Quarterly* 26 (1964) 190-220.

"The Deployment of Faith and Reason in Bacon's Approach to Knowledge", *Modern Schoolman* 42 (1965) 265-285.

"Demonology and Diabolical Temptation", *Thought* 40 (1965) 165-194.

"Demonology and Diabolical Temptation", *Theology Digest* 14 (1966) 131-136

"Canonical Implications of Richard III's Plan to Marry His Niece", *Traditio* 23 (1967) 269-311.

"Kinship, Incest, and the Dictates of Law", *American Journal of Jurisprudence* 14 (1969) 69-78.

"Death of the Devil?" *Commonweal* 93.6 (6 November 1970) 146-149.

"The Metamorphoses of the Eden Serpent during the Middle Ages and Renaissance", *Viator* 2 (1971) 301-327.

"Clandestine Marriage and Chaucer's Troilus", in *Marriage in the Middle Ages,* ed. John Leyerle, *Viator* 4 (1973) 413-501, Chapter 2, pp. 435-457.

"Occupatio as Negative Narration: A Mistake for Occultatio/Praeteritio", *Modern Philology* 74 (1976-1977) 311-315.

"English Kings and the Fear of Sorcery", *Mediaeval Studies* 39 (1977) 206-238.

"*The Genoese St. Valentine and Chaucer's Third of May*", *Chaucer Newsletter* 1.2 (Summer 1979) 6-10.

"Aristotle-Averroes-Alemannus on Tragedy: The Influence of the Poetics on the Latin Middle Ages", *Viator* 10 (1979) 161-209.

"Tragedy and the Performance of Tragedy in Late Roman Antiquity", *Traditio* 35 (1979) 21-44.

"Tillyard and History", *Clio* 10 (1980-81) 85-88.

"Chaucer's Arts and Our Arts", in *New Perspectives in Chaucer Criticism*, ed. Donald M. Rose (Norman, Okla. 1981), pp. 107-120.

"Gaston Paris's Courteous and Horsely Love", in *The Spirit of the Court: Selected Proceedings of the Fourth Congress of the International Courtly Literature Society* (Toronto 1983), ed. Glyn S. Burgess and Robert A. Taylor. Woodbridge, Suffolk: Boydell and Brewer, 1985. Pp. 217-223.

"Archpriests, Apostles, and Episcopal Epistles", *La Coronica* 14 (1985-86) 1-5.

"The Last Chroniclers of Croyland", *The Ricardian* 7.91 (December 1985) 142-177.

"Pronouncing Latin Words in English", *Classical World* 80 (1986-87) 33-37.

"The Non-Tragedy of Arthur", in *Medieval English Religious and Ethical Literature: Essays in Honour of G. H. Russell*, ed. Gregory Kratzmann and James Simpson. Cambridge: D. S. Brewer, 1986. Pp. 92-114.

"Heaney's Sweeney: The Poet as Version-Maker", *Philological* Quarterly 65 (1986) 293-310.

"The Varieties of Love in Medieval Literature According to Gaston Paris", *Romance Philology* 40 (1986-87) 301-327.

"The Devil at Large", *Journal of* Religion 67 (1987) 519-528.

"The Croyland Chronicle Tragedies", *The Ricardian* 7.99 (December 1987) 498-515.

"Juan Ruiz and Archpriests: Novel Reports". *La Coronica* 16:2 (Spring 1988) 32-54.

"Lawyers' Latin: Loquenda ut Vulgus?" *Journal of Legal Education* 38 (1988) 195-207.

"Dating the Accessus Section of the Pseudo-Dantean Epistle to Cangrande". *Lectura Dantis* no. 2 (Spring 1988) 93-102.

"A Juan Ruiz Directory for 1380-1382". *Mester* 16:2 (Fall 1988) 69-93.

"Chaucer and Shakespeare on Tragedy". *Leeds Studies in* English 20 (1989) 191-206.

"Inquisition and the Prosecution of Heresy: Misconceptions and Abuses". *Church History* 58 (1989) 439-451.

"Satan the Old Enemy: A Cosmic J. Edgar Hoover", *Journal of American Folklore* 103 (1990) 77-84.

"Croyland Observations". *The Ricardian* 8.108 (March 1990) 334-341.

"Shades of Incest and Cuckoldry: Pandarus and John of Gaunt", *Studies in the Age of Chaucer* 13 (1991) 121-140.

"Dual Nationality, the Myth of Election, and a Kinder, Gentler State Department", *University of Miami Inter-American Law Review* 23 (1991-92) 421-464.

"Medieval Relations, Marital and Other", *Medievalia et humanistica* n.s. 19 (1992) 133-146.

"Inquisitorial Due Process and the Status of Secret Crimes", *Proceedings of the Eighth International Congress of Medieval Canon Law* (UCSD 1988), ed. Stanley Chodorow. *Monumenta iuris canonici*, series C: *Subsidia*, vol. 4 (Vatican City, 1992), pp. 407-428.

"Interpretation of Genres and by Genres in Medieval Literature", in *Interpretations: Medieval and Modern*, ed. Piero Boitani and Anna Torti, J. A. W. Bennett Lectures, no. 7: Perugia, 6-8 April 1992 (Woodbridge, Suffolk: Boydell and Brewer, 1993, pp. 107-122.

"Sacraments, Sacramentals, and Lay Piety in Chaucer's England", *Chaucer Review* 28 (1993-94) 5-22.

"The Right to Remain Silent: Before and After Joan of Arc", *Speculum* 68 (1993) 992-1026.

"'Rule of Thumb' and the Folklaw of the Husband's Stick", *Journal of Legal Education* 44 (1994) 341-65.

"Cangrande and the Ortho-Dantists", *Lectura Dantis* nos. 14-15 (1994) 61-95.

"Reply to Robert Hollander", *Lectura Dantis* no. 14-15 (1994) 111-115.

"Joan of Arc's Last Trial: The Attack of the Devil's Advocates", in *Fresh Verdicts on Joan of Arc,* ed. Bonnie Wheeler and Charles T. Wood (New York 1996) 205-38.

"Manuscript Mores and the Libro de buen amor", *Comparative Literature Studies* 33 (1996) 187-97.

"A Neo-Revisionist Look at Chaucer's Nuns", *Chaucer Review* 31 (1996-97) 116 36.

"Statutes of Rapes and Alleged Ravishers of Wives: A Context for the Charges Against Thomas Malory, Knight", *Viator* 28 (1997) 361-419.

"Lollard Inquisitions: Due and Undue Process", In *The Devil, Heresy and Witchcraft in the Middle Ages: Essays in Honor of Jeffrey B. Russell*, ed. Alberto Ferreiro (Leiden: Brill, 1998), pp. 279-303.

"Meanings and Uses of Raptus in Chaucer's Time", *Studies in the Age of Chaucer* 20 (1998) 101-65.

"The Case Against Edward IV's Marriage and Offspring: Secrecy; Witchcraft; Secrecy; Precontract", *The Ricardian* 11.142 (September 1998) 326-35.

"Medieval Laws and Views on Wife-Beating", *Proceedings of the Tenth International Congress of Medieval Canon Law* (Syracuse University, 1996), ed. Kenneth Pennington. *Monumenta iuris canonici*, series C: *Subsidia*, vol. 11 (Vatican City 2001), 985-1001.

"Trial Procedures Against Wyclif and Wycliffites in England and at the Council of Constance", *Huntington Library Quarterly* 61 (1999) 1-28

"Bishop, Prioress, and Bawd in the Stews of Southwark", *Speculum* 75 (2000) 342-88

"The Pardoner's Voice: Disjunctive Narrative and Modes of Effemination", in *Speaking Images: Essays in Honor of V. A. Kolve*, ed. R. F. Yeager and Charlotte C. Morse (Asheville: Pegasus Press, 2001), 411-445.

Chaucer Encyclopedia: ca. 250 entries on religious subjects. (in progress)

Review Articles

Review of Birger Gerhardsson, The Testing of God's Son (Matt. 4.1-11 & Par.): An Analysis of an Early Christian Midrash (Lund 1966), *Theological Studies* 29 (1968) 528-531.

Review of Anges et demons, Points cardinaux 21 (Paris 1972), *Cahiers de civilisation medievale* 17 (1974) 391-392.

Review of Sandro Sticca, ed., The Medieval Drama (Albany 1972), *Classical World* 68 (1974-1975) 148-149.

Review of Rosmarie Thee Morewedge, ed., The Role of Woman in the Middle Ages (Albany 1975) and of Joan M. Ferrante, Woman as Image in Medieval Literature From the Twelfth Century to Dante (New York 1975), *Speculum* 52 (1977) 715-721.

Review of Peter Saccio, Shakespeare's English Kings: History, Chronicle, and Drama (New York 1977), *Journal of English and Germanic Philology* 77 (1978) 141.

Review of Roger Boase, The Origin and Meaning of Courtly Love: A Critical Study of European Scholarship (Manchester 1977), *Speculum* 54 (1979) 338-342.

Review of N. B. Smith and J. T. Snow, eds. The Expansion and Transformations of Courtly Love (Athens, Ga. 1980), *Studies in the Age of Chaucer* 3 (1981) 179-183.

Review of J. B. Russell, Satan: The Early Christian Tradition (Ithaca 1981), *Journal of Religious History* 12 (1983) 331-333.

Review of H. R. Coursen, The Leasing out of England: Shakespeare's Second Henriad (Washington 1982), *Modern Philology* 82 (1984-85) 204-206.

Review of Carlo Ginzburg, The Night Battles, Tr. John and Anne Tedeschi (Baltimore 1983). *Cithara,* 24.2 (May 1985) 61-63.

Review of Marjorie Curry Woods, ed., An Early Commentary on the 'Poetria nova' of Geoffrey of Vinsauf (New York, 1985), *Manuscripta* 32 (1988) 54-58.

Review of J. A. Burrow, The Ages of Man (New York 1986); Mary Dove, The Perfect Age of Man's Life (Cambridge 1986); Elizabeth Sears, The Ages of Man (Princeton 1988), *Speculum* 63 (1988) 630-634.

Review of Neil Forsyth, The Old Enemy: Satan and the Combat Myth (Princeton 1987), *Journal of American Folklore* 102 (1989) 107-110.

Review of Joseph Allen Hornsby, Chaucer and the Law (Norman 1988), *Speculum* 65 (1990) 429-432.

Review of The Welles Anthology: Ms. Rawlinson C. 813, ed. Sharon L. Jansen and Kathleen H. Jordan (1991), *Manuscripta* 35 (1991) 238-242.

Review of Katharina M. Wilson and Elizabeth M. Makowski, Wykked Wyves and the Woes of Marriage (1990), *Speculum* 67 (1992) 755-757.

Review of Piero Boitani, ed., The European Tragedy of Troilus (1989), *English Language Notes* 30 (1992-93) 78-80.

Review of Martin Camargo, The Middle English Verse Love Epistle (1991), *Speculum* 68 (1993) 482-485.

Review of John Dagenais, The Ethics of Reading in Manuscript Culture: Glossing the 'Libro de buen amor' (1994). *Comparative Literature Studies* 33 (1996) 187-97.

Review of Barbara Hanawalt, Chaucer's England: Literature in Historical Context (1992), *Envoi* 4 (1993) 51-62.

Review of C. W. Marx, The Devil's Rights and the Redemption in the Literature of Medieval England (1995), *Speculum* 72 (1997) 859-861.

Review of Judith Ferster, Fictions of Advice: The Literature and Politics of Counsel in Late Medieval England (1996), in *American Historical Review* 103 (1998) 866-867.

Review of Neil Cartlidge, Medieval Marriage: Literary Approaches, 1100-1300 (1997), in *Journal of English and Germanic Philology* 98 (1999) 340-343.

Review of J. M. M. H. Thijssen, Censure and Heresy at the University of Paris, 1200-1400 (1998), in *Speculum* 75 (2000) 729-731.

Review of Medieval Folklore: An Encyclopedia of Myths, Legends, Tales, Beliefs, and Customs, ed. Carl Lindahl, John McNamara, and John Lindow, 2 vols. (2000), in *Western Folklore* 60 (2001) 322-324.

Tabula gratulatoria

Christopher Cannon
Pembroke College, Cambridge

King-Kok Cheung
University of California, Los Angeles

Edward I. and Gail E. Condren
University of California, Los Angeles

Brian Copenhaver
University of California, Los Angeles

Roger Dahood
University of Arizona

Sheila Delany
Simon Fraser University

Robert Dent
University of California, Los Angeles

Kari Diehl
Western Washington University

Beatrice Dumin
University of California, Los Angeles

James M. Dunn-Smith
California State University, Fresno

Diane Favro
University of California, Los Angeles

John V. Fleming
Princeton University

Bernard Frischer
University of California, Los Angeles

John M. Ganim
University of California, Riverside

Linda Georgianna
University of California, Irvine

Piotr Górecki
University of California, Riverside

Christopher Grose
University of California, Los Angeles

Boris Catz, M.D.
UCLA CMRS, Council

Massimo Ciavolella
University of California, Los Angeles

Sr. Pegeen Connolly, SCRH
St. Bernard High School, Playa del Rey

Martha Cowan
University of California, Los Angeles

Vinton A. Dearing
University of California, Los Angeles

Luisa Del Giudice
Italian Oral History Institute

Peter D. Diehl
Western Washington University

Martin J. Duffell
Queen Mary, University of London

Dorothy Dunn-Smith
Immaculate Heart College
and Loyola Marymount University

Sigmund Eisner
University of Arizona

Christina Fitzgerald
University of California, Los Angeles

Reginald Foakes
University of California, Los Angeles

Lowell Gallagher
University of California, Los Angeles

Patrick J. Geary
University of California, Los Angeles

Marie Louise Göllner
University of California, Los Angeles

Tobias Gregory
California State University, Northridge

Curtis Gruenler
Hope College

Frances Gussenhoven, RSHM
Loyola Marymount University, Los Angeles

Karl Hagen
University of California, Los Angeles

Deidre Hall
UCLA CMRS, Council

Michael Hanly
Washington State University

Maryanne Cline Horowitz
Occidental College

Maria José Hulet
University of California, Los Angeles

Mark Infusino
University of California, Los Angeles

Andrea Jones
University of California, Los Angeles

Constance Jordan
Claremont Graduate University

Marea Kelly
UCLA CMRS, Council

Ann Kerr
University of California, Los Angeles

Sharon King
UCLA CMRS, Council

Gordon Kipling
University of California, Los Angeles

Stephen Knight
Cardiff University

V. A. Kolve
University of California, Los Angeles

Thomas Kren
The J. Paul Getty Museum

Carol Dana Lanham
UCLA CMRS

Barney Craig Hadden
University of California, Los Angeles

Thomas Hahn
University of Rochester

Christina Handelman
University of California, Los Angeles

Marvin and Betty Hoffenberg
UCLA CMRS, Council

Claude L. Hulet
University of California, Los Angeles

Michele Hutchins
UCLA CMRS

Eric Jager
University of California, Los Angeles

Leslie Ellen Jones
UCLA CMRS

Susanne Kahle
University of California, Los Angeles

Deborah Bochner Kennel
University of California, Los Angeles

Dorothy Kim
University of California, Los Angeles

Robert S. Kinsman
University of California, Los Angeles

Scott Kleinman
California State University, Northridge

Leonard Koff
University of California, Los Angeles

Barisa Krekic
University of California, Los Angeles

Efraín Kristal
University of California, Los Angeles

Ruth Lavine
UCLA CMRS, Council

Robert Lawton, S.J.
Loyola Marymount University

Jayne Lewis
University of California, Los Angeles

Bengt and Leena Löfstedt
UCLA and Helsinki University

Frank Lutz
President, L.A. Marketing Group

Sarah McNamer
Georgetown University

Ronald Mellor
University of California, Los Angeles

Peter Moore
University of California, Los Angeles

Caleb Kyu Na
University of California, Los Angeles

Carol Newlands
University of Wisconsin, Madison

Calvin Normore
University of California, Los Angeles

Anita Obermeier
University of New Mexico

Thomas P. O'Malley, S.J.
Boston College

Karen Orren
University of California, Los Angeles

James K. Otté
University of San Diego

Barbara Packer
University of California, Los Angeles

Mary Elizabeth Perry
Occidental College

Claudia Rapp
University of California, Los Angeles

Gail Lenhoff
University of California, Los Angeles

Kenneth Lincoln
University of California, Los Angeles

David Wong Louie
University of California, Los Angeles

Claire McEachern
University of California, Los Angeles

Ruth Mellinkoff
University of California, Los Angeles

Donka Minkova
University of California, Los Angeles

Katheryn A. Morgan
University of California, Los Angeles

Joseph Falaky Nagy
University of California, Los Angeles

John D. Niles
University of Wisconsin, Madison

Max and Estelle Novak
University of California, Los Angeles

Glending Olson
Cleveland State University

Ynez V. O'Neill
University of California, Los Angeles

Marijane Osborn
University of California, Davis

Aino Paasonen
Southern California Institute of Architecture

Derek Pearsall
Harvard University

Jonathan Post
University of California, Los Angeles

Peter Hanns Reill
University of California, Los Angeles

Florence H. Ridley
University of California, Los Angeles

Kevin Roddy
University of California, Davis

Alan Roper
University of California, Los Angeles

Richard H. Rouse
University of California, Los Angeles

Teofilo F. Ruiz
University of California, Los Angeles

Yona Sabar
University of California, Los Angeles

Catherine Sanok
University of Michigan

Paul R. Sellin
University of California, Los Angeles

Steve Sohmer
Lincoln College (Oxon.)

Curt Steindler
UCLA CMRS, Council

Robert Stockwell
University of California, Los Angeles

Marilyn Sutton
California State University Dominquez Hills

Paul Szarmach
Western Michigan University

Hovig Tchalian
University of California, Los Angeles

Emma Lewis Thomas
University of California, Los Angeles

Theresa Tinkle
University of Michigan, Ann Arbor

Tram Tran
University of California, Los Angeles

Mary Robertson
The Huntington Library

David Stuart Rodes
University of California, Los Angeles

Mary A. Rouse
University of California, Los Angeles

Karen E. Rowe
University of California, Los Angeles

Bianca Ryan
University of California, Los Angeles

Gayle Samore
University of California, Los Angeles

Victor I. Scherb
The University of Texas at Tyler

Paul D. Sheats
University of California, Los Angeles

Carmela Speroni
UCLA CMRS, Council

Stanley Stewart
University of California, Riverside

Blair Sullivan
University of California, Los Angeles

Geoffrey Symcox
University of California, Los Angeles

Paul Beekman Taylor
University of Geneva

Elizabeth C. Teviotdale
Western Michigan University

Norman J. W. Thrower
University of California, Los Angeles

Peter Thorslev
University of California, Los Angeles

Edward F. Tuttle
University of California, Los Angeles

Richard W. Unger
University of British Columbia

Nancy van Deusen
Claremont Graduate University

Patricia and Richard Waldron
UCLA CMRS, Council

Elizabeth Walsh
University of San Diego

Jim Walsh, S.J.
Georgetown University

Patricia Armstrong Warren
Getty Research Institute
and UCLA CMRS, Council

Robert N. Watson
University of California, Los Angeles

Scott Waugh
University of California, Los Angeles

Dora B. Weiner
University of California, Los Angeles

Herbert Weiner, M.D. †
University of California, Los Angeles

Stephen Werner
University of California, Los Angeles

Robert S. Westman
University of California, San Diego

Thomas Wortham
University of California, Los Angeles

Peter M. Wright
Alhambra, California

Pauline Yu
University of California, Los Angeles

Introduction

Donka Minkova and Theresa Tinkle

Henry Ansgar (Andy) Kelly's prolific scholarship ranges over a wide variety of topics: medieval and renaissance literature and history (in English, Latin, Spanish, French, and Italian, from Aristotle to Shakespeare – and Seamus Heaney), ecclesiastical history and theology, demonology, canon law and Church ritual, lay piety, drama, lexicology, philology, and contemporary academic and national politics. He is the author of twelve books and about a hundred articles and reviews; his learning is famously encyclopedic. The present volume of essays honors him but does not attempt to reflect, even partially, the astonishing range of his scholarship. In the interest of creating a reasonably cohesive and focused book, we have chosen to concentrate primarily on English and medieval literature, with several bows toward broader but closely related European and historical fields. The main goal of this volume is to enrich the medieval scholarly legacy by presenting fresh perspectives on texts and issues of current interest within the field, and by identifying questions likely to generate future research. The authors were selected from a list of the honoree's most distinguished and promising students, close collaborators, and intellectual opponents. Their essays showcase some of the latest and most stimulating developments in the area of medieval studies.

Theoretically and methodologically, this volume fulfills the dual task of taking stock and taking on the challenges now facing medievalism, a field of inquiry that has become extremely diverse. The traditional areas of strength in medieval studies have been Old English, philology, a few canonical authors, and national literatures. While these areas continue to attract scholarly attention and to yield surprising and exciting insights, other interests have emerged in recent decades. What medievalists consider a text, for instance, has changed considerably in recent years. Medievalist scholarship today, even if conducted out of an English department, has been broadened to include the study of material works, particularly marginalia, fragments, illustrations, and manuscript versions and compilations. Instead of focusing predominantly on such authors as Chaucer and the *Pearl* Poet, research now encompasses a broad variety of later Middle English texts, including noncanonical literature (ecclesiastical and secular works) and nontraditional texts (legal documents, city records, other archival sources). Latin literature has proven amenable to contemporary theoretical approaches, which has led to more complex arguments about the relations between Latin and vernacular literatures. As a consequence, considerable attention in English studies now falls on the relations among Latin, French, and English, with questions about the relative authority of each language at the center of interest.

At the same time, philology has expanded to encompass new approaches to texts, with increasing emphasis on interdisciplinarity, particularly on conjunctions between language and literature, literature and anthropology, religious studies, medicine, art history, and cultural studies. Increasing interest in material texts has led to thoughtful discussions of editing practice, new editing projects, and new methods of stylistic and metrical analysis. Studies of versification in this context have facilitated and reinvigorated neo-formalist approaches to literary texts, which now thrive alongside the historicisms that have dominated the field for many years. Finally, we have witnessed a breakdown in periodicity, with medievalists increasingly working between the traditional late Middle Ages (the fifteenth century) and the Renaissance (the sixteenth century), or between the late classical era and the high Middle Ages.

This volume both demonstrates these broad intellectual currents within the field and contributes valuable new perspectives to ongoing scholarly discussions. The essays collected here exhibit the tremendous appeal and rewards of redefining our understanding of medieval religion, studying material manuscripts and early print books, re-inventing and refining interdisciplinary and comparative approaches to literature, expanding our idea of what constitutes a text, and debating the precise nature of medieval versification. As is appropriate for a volume honoring the vast historical sweep of Andy Kelly's scholarship, the contributions range from Aristotle to Mary Wollstonecraft Shelley, though most of the scholarship centers on the twelfth through fifteenth centuries. Although the essays focus primarily on Middle English literature, in honor of Andy's wide interests and linguistic expertise, and in recognition of the comparative nature of medieval studies, they also deal with Latin, French, Spanish, Italian, German, Scandinavian, and Irish traditions. The reader will encounter a broad variety of "texts" here, from Chaucer's major works to Lydgate's mummings, folklore customs, manuscript illustrations and versions, early print works, and Romantic novels.

These essays fall under six major headings: the essays in Text, Image, Script investigate relations between verbal and visual (or other) texts, and develop rewarding interdisciplinary perspectives on literature; those in Text and Meter demonstrate the challenges of metrical analysis and the importance of that analysis to editing practices; contributions to Reception study the sometimes surprising evidence of how medieval works and manuscripts have been read, and suggest the complexities of aesthetic influence; essays on Chaucer propose stimulating re-readings and productive interdisciplinary approaches to several of his major works; those on Hagiography explore the difficult and fascinating translation of saints into texts; and those on Lay Piety and Christian Diversity offer important studies of medieval religiosity, concluding with a new edition and translation of a medieval work that describes diverse Christian groups at the close of the Middle Ages. In fact, each essay in this volume contributes to more than one of these headings: nine of the nineteen essays, for instance, concern Chaucer, and religious attitudes are viewed from numerous perspectives throughout the volume. The organization of the essays under these headings nonetheless signals what we perceive as their central research contributions.[*]

Text, Image, Script

Christopher Baswell's "King Edward and the Cripple" studies Matthew Paris's verse life of St. Edward the Confessor, *La Estoire de Seint Aedward le Rei,* which was written soon before the middle of the thirteenth century, and dedicated to Henry III's queen, Eleanor of Provence. Its surviving manuscript, the beautifully illustrated Cambridge U.L. Ee.3.59, is slightly later. At a structurally central moment of the *Estoire,* Edward performs his first miracle, the cure of a crippled man, by carrying him to the altar of Westminster Abbey. This essay examines the text and not-quite convergent illustration of that episode, and sees in it a destabilizing of identity and crossing of boundary analogous to Edward's unsettled (and politically unsettling) roles as king and chaste saint. Indeed, he argues, the cripple sparks a sacred progeny (Edward's cures, increasing holiness, and reconstruction of the Abbey) that fulfills, partly by verbal echoes of sexual contact, the unnerving absences of Edward's marital chastity.

V. A. Kolve in "Looking at the Sun" examines the two major dream images in Chaucer's *Troilus and Criseyde*: Criseyde's dream of a white eagle who sets his claws under her breast, tears out her heart, replaces it with his own, and flies away, heart exchanged for heart; and Troilus's dream of Criseyde lying in a forest in the arms of a wild boar whom she kisses over and over as he sleeps in the bright sun's heat. These extreme images, insistently enigmatic and symbolic, contrast with the imagery characteristic of Chaucer's mature art – narrative images embedded in the story, usually as setting or essential action, whose symbolic dimension is covered over by naturalistic detail, awaiting (but not insisting upon) discovery by the thoughtful listener or reader. Both kinds of image draw upon symbolic traditions widely current in literature and the visual arts of the time. And both kinds function as keys to large issues in the poem. But the two images examined here, naturalized only by the strangeness of dreams, conform as well to teaching concerning the art of memory in contemporary rhetorical treatises. According to those treatises, images of exceptional beauty or startling ugliness are most readily remembered, especially that which is monstrous, violent, sexual, and

---

[*] We are grateful to the authors for providing abstracts of their essays, which make up the remainder of the Introduction. We have slightly revised the abstracts for the sake of consistency in point of view and simplicity of reference, and we have made minor modifications in order to stitch them into an overview of the volume. Citations within the abstracts are linked to the list of works cited at the end of each essay.

vigorously engaged in action, whether noble or distasteful. These images, unusual in Chaucer's mature practice, fully qualify.

The symbolic potential of both dreams is explored in terms of Bestiary traditions concerning the eagle's keenness of sight, and the boar's fierceness and sensuality, traditions then set against four crucial lines of Antigone's song, comparing the power and mystery of romantic love to the power and brilliance of the sun. Shall we think the worse of the sun, she asks, because we cannot look at it directly? And shall we think the worse of such love, because it exceeds the capacity of many? Her song testifies (in the first person) to the possibility of experiencing such love fully, without being destroyed by it.

Chaucer uses the connection between these dreams and Antigone's song to interrogate the full mystery of love – from its most benign and exalted, when (in ideas borrowed from Boethius) it seems to participate in the very structure of the universe – to its most selfish and destructive (in the double sorrow of Troilus that furnishes the story of the poem). And it does so, structurally, in terms of vision – a much-extended version of what we these days call "the gaze" – including the way the lovers first see each other, the welcome darkness of the bedchamber, the dawn songs (*aubades*) that condemn the day's first light, the dimming of Troilus's vision, gazing over the walls of Troy awaiting Criseyde's deferred return, the brilliant mini-sun of the brooch that reveals to him Criseyde's betrayal, along with the view of the earth from the eighth sphere granted him at the end of his soul journey, and concluding with the view of Christ on the cross, who died for our love, communicated (from this earth) in the Palinode, at the close of the poem. Close attention to these three passages (the two dreams and the song), to Chaucer's modifications of his source (Boccaccio's *Il Filostrato*), and especially to his reading of Dante's *Commedia*, reveal a philosophical and religious coherence in the poem perhaps deeper and more comprehensive than has been suggested before.

Gordon Kipling concludes this section of the volume with an essay on "Lydgate: The Poet as Deviser". By virtue of seven poems, which variously describe themselves as "mummings" or "disguisings", John Lydgate has become a central figure in the history of English drama. For the first time, Lydgate seems to give us not just descriptions of dramatic performances but performance texts themselves. But what is the status of these texts? While many have attempted to read them as if they were theatrical scripts, if somewhat "primitive" ones, Kipling believes they are best understood as "devices", especially if that word is understood in a technical sense as referring to a particular kind of document, one which serves as the means by which the inventions of a "deviser" are communicated to the artisans who will execute the device described therein.

There is a long tradition of such devices being drawn up to govern the work of various artisans – poets, painters, architects, pageant makers, "sotiltie" decorators – who were involved in collaborative projects. Lydgate, too operates as just such a collaborative artisan. We can examine his "devising" for a variety of projects – a suite of tapestries, scriptures for banquet "sotelties", and a commemorative poem for a royal entry – all of which involve him composing suitable poetic material in response to a subject matter "device". Turning to an examination of his so-called "mummings", we can then examine them as literary material written in response to devices composed by others and also as verbal devices to introduce or otherwise accompany the mummers' performances.

There is every reason to suppose that Lydgate may have completed many of his tasks from his writing desk at Hatfield Priory or even at Bury St Edmunds. The device convention made it possible for him to complete such apparently collaborative commissions without actually working in the company of his collaborators. Indeed, the employment of such devices suggests that the various collaborators are not often, if ever, in personal contact, that they connect with one another only indirectly and primarily through the written device. Lydgate's texts are clearly not performance scripts, but merely literary devices which play a subordinate part in the mumming, which typically includes and extends beyond Lydgate's text.

Text and Meter

Martin Duffell studies comparative versification with "French Symmetry, Germanic Rhythm, and Spanish Metre". From the eleventh century onwards, French versification exerted a strong influence on its neighbors. This had implications that are of special interest to modern students of linguistics, because French verse is a clear example of the principle of fit. French metres are based upon three of the most salient features of the language's phonology: syllable timing, phrasal stress, and right-strong orientation (which enables phrasal stress to be reinforced by rhyme). Neighboring languages, however, have some of the phonological features that French lacks, such as word stress, stress timing, left-strong orientation, or full final vowels. One of those languages, Castilian, struggled from the thirteenth century until the sixteenth to come to terms with imported French metrics and, in particular, to accommodate its own strong word stress within a syllabic system. This article examines the conflict between stress and syllable in Castilian between 1200 and 1400 in folk verse, epic metre, *cuaderna vía*, and the *verso de arte mayor*. It concludes that the earliest verse composed in Iberian Romance had lines with a regular number of prominent syllables, or accents, rather than of syllables in total – exactly like the traditional verse of the Germanic languages. This accentual versification was still flourishing in fifteenth-century *cancioneros*, but by the middle of the sixteenth century it had been replaced by imported metres with a regular syllable count.

Donka Minkova and Robert Stockwell's study of "Emendation and the Chaucerian Metrical Template" reasserts the need to describe Chaucer's pentameter line in terms of syllable count, in spite of some authoritative pronouncements to the contrary. More specifically, they examine the arguments against syllable-counting put forward by Jill Mann in a recent essay in *Studies in the Age of Chaucer*. Their position is that Chaucer's metrical template is governed by two basic principles: regulated alternation of prominences and regulated syllable count per line. Emendations *metri causa* should respect these two regularities, and all those cited by Professor Mann do so. Minkova and Stockwell therefore have no empirical disagreement with the outcome of her editorial choices. But as a matter of theory, her suggestion that the number of stresses per line is the regulating factor confuses accidental fall-out (number of stresses) with governing principles (alternation and syllable count).

Reception

"A Franciscan Reads the *Facetus*", by Glending Olson, investigates the reception of an important Ovidian work. In his commentary on Aristotle's *Nicomachean Ethics*, the Franciscan Gerard of Odo discusses a number of terms that he says have been used to name one of Aristotle's virtues, the proper sort of pleasantness to observe in social conversations. Gerard argues that the usual terms for this virtue (*amicitia* or *affabilitas*) are not as good as *facetia*, which he discusses with reference to St. Augustine, Pseudo-Boethius on Parisian manners, and the twelfth-century poem known as *Facetus: moribus et vita*. Gerard's semantic excursus, subsequently adopted by John Buridan, not only documents the influence of the *Facetus* but indicates how Aristotle's virtue came to be read within the perspective of medieval ideas about (and nationalistic pride in) courteous, witty, and urbane behavior. It suggests that in some circles such behavior carried ethical import, and it may reflect one among a complex of attitudes lying behind Chaucer's socially "plesaunt" and "amyable" Prioress.

Theresa Tinkle examines Chaucer and fifteenth-century Chauceriana with "The Imagined Chaucerian Community of Bodleian MS Fairfax 16". Bodleian MS Fairfax 16 contains an extensive collection of Chaucerian poems of Cupid: Geoffrey Chaucer, F Prologue to the *Legend of Good Women* and *Parliament of Fowls*; Sir John Clanvowe, *Book of Cupid*; Thomas Hoccleve, *Epistle of Cupid*; John Lydgate, *Complaint of a Lover's Life* and *Temple of Glass*; "The Lover's Mass"; and "Parliament of Cupid". The compilation of this manuscript (*circa* 1450) was clearly governed by a strong interest in the "matere" of Cupid, and poets' diverse responses to this subject and to each others' treatments of it provide much of the anthology's interest. MS Fairfax 16, with all its rich intertextual resonances, therefore offers a stunning opportunity for us to advance our understanding of how the Chaucerians represent the literary community within which they fashion themselves as lovers and poets. Tinkle argues that the poems of Cupid in this manuscript context invent an "imagined community" of vernacular English writers and readers – a pre-national (and pre-print) alternative both to the Latinate clerical brotherhood and to the Gallic court. Although women are occasionally included in the imagined audience of these poems, this is a predominately masculine community. The reader of MS Fairfax 16 is repeatedly invited to enter into this community by participating vicariously in the homosocial bonds between men – by identifying with the masculine community of lovers, affirming their solidarity with one another, and acknowledging their strong emotional attachments to other men. This manuscript turns reading into an act of male bonding. By studying the material text, we can recognize the contemporary gender-specific appeal of the love visions. As significantly, we can perceive the homosocial bonds that constitute the imagined literary community of late medieval England.

John Ganim takes us into much later reception history with "Mary Shelley, Godwin's Chaucer and the Middle Ages". Ganim notes that Mary Wollstonecraft Shelley, the author of *Frankenstein*, is rarely thought of in the context of medieval revivals. Yet her father, William Godwin, wrote one of the most widely distributed biographies of Chaucer, and continued a lifelong interest in medieval English language and history. Mary Shelley herself wrote two novels, *Perkin Warbeck* and *Valperga*, and several stories set in the Middle Ages, as well as a number of essays on medieval Italian writers. Her interpretation of the Middle Ages is in dialogue with that of her influential father, as well as that imagined by the Romantic poets, eighteenth-century amateur enthusiasts, and Victorian historians. Mary Shelley extends the implications of Romantic medievalism to their logical political and personal conclusions, thereby offering yet another implicit critique of Romanticism.

Chaucer

Edward I. Condren begins this section by analyzing "The Disappointments of Criseyde". *Troilus and Criseyde* includes near its beginning an enigmatic scene initiated by the one character who would otherwise seem least likely to initiate anything. Now alone and a traitor's daughter, Criseyde lays her vulnerability before Hector to beg for his support. An enigmatic phrase in the narrator's spare summary of this interview, "she hym thonked with ful humble chere, / And ofter wolde, and it hadde ben his wille" (I.124-125), sets in motion a quintessentially Chaucerian multiple strategy. Hector's assurance that Criseyde is not a prisoner in Troy gives readers to understand that the later proposal to send her to the Greek camp serves no political purpose, yet results in the fatal return of Antenor to Troy. The scene also hints strongly of Criseyde's unspoken attraction for Hector, accounting for her deep interest in Pandarus's important news touching her honor. Criseyde knows that the game of love is her uncle's only subject and must therefore assume that this "news" concerns someone's romantic interest in her. The actual lines leading to the announcement of who loves her produce in her a crescendo of anticipation as she awaits the sound of the dear name Hector. That her admirer is not Hector but Troilus, a man she scarcely knows, renders her silent, challenging Pandarus to fill eighty lines with persuasive argument. The subtlest reach of Chaucer's strategy, flowing directly from this disappointment, prepares for a kind of second creation, requiring a rebuilding from nothing. Troilus was already depicted in Book I scoffing at love. But Criseyde too must be returned to a romantic null, uninterested in human love. As Pandarus reawakens her to the interest and joy of love, Chaucer introduces a new, darker strain to her character, closer to the methods of her father and Pandarus than to those of either Hector or Troilus. An artful, calculating use of language gains in strength and frequency, leading her disappointingly downward to the sad woman we see at the end of the poem.

John V. Fleming studies Chaucer's Prioress in "Madame Eglentyne: The Telling of the Beads". In the "General Prologue" to the *Canterbury Tales* Chaucer describes his Prioress as carrying a "peire of bedes" (rosary) with a decorative motto: *Amor vincit omnia*. A close textual investigation reveals that in conceiving her character – as also that of four other satirized ecclesiastics – Chaucer was considerably influenced by his reading of an extended passage in Jean de Meun's *Roman de la Rose* in which religious hypocrisy is a major theme. Specifically, the rosary was suggested by that carried by the false nun "Constrained Abstinence". Although Chaucer's satirical portrait of the Prioress is less overt and rhetorically striking than what we find in his treatment of Monk, Friar, Summoner, and Pardoner, the moral criticism it implies is not different in kind. In tracing a suggested path of Chaucer's poetic imagination elsewhere revealed in the "General Prologue", this essay adduces evidence from the material history of medieval rosaries, from iconography, and from philology, and reviews the opinions of earlier scholars. The connection between prayer beads and a festive garland, the token of amatory intermediation in the *Roman de la Rose*, is signaled by the word *chapel*. This thematic connection is richly confirmed by the history of the rosary and its complex literary associations in the late Middle Ages. Contextual congruence strongly argues that the motto *Amor vincit omnia* derives from Jean's citation of a line from Virgil's *Eclogues*, and that the Prioress's "courtesie" is to be connected with the personification "Courtoisie", who cites the line. The verbal and iconographic remembrance of Chaucer's text in Gower's image of a "peire of bedes" near the end of the *Confessio Amantis*, a poem obviously imitative of Jean de Meun, supports the principal claim of the essay.

Matthew Brosamer's "The Miller, the Cook, and Digestion" examines two Canterbury pilgrims – the Miller and the Cook – in terms provided by and associated with the medieval idea of the hell-mouth. It has long been noted that Chaucer's descriptions of the mouths of these drunkards may have been intended to evoke hell-mouth imagery in the minds of his readers, but this recognition has for the most part confined itself to the vantage point of iconography, in which the hell-mouth is simply a visually striking figure for the gateway to hell. This study details how the hell-mouth was far more than a simple image to Chaucer, embodying a great many associative ideas, derived ultimately from monastic theology, that can explain a great deal about the Miller and Cook. These ideas have more to do with ingestion, incorporation, and sin than with liminality. Innocent III's *De Miseria* is quite instructive in this regard. Its association with Chaucer is incontestable, and it devotes considerable attention to describing what exactly happens to the damned once they pass the threshold of hell. Many of these descriptions are alimentary in nature, and as such are clearly related to the idea of hell not only as a mouth, but as an entire digestive system. The Cook and Miller not only embody sin, but hell itself – a hell that has a stomach as well as a mouth.

Eric Jager's "The *Shipman's Tale*: Merchant's Time and Church's Time, Secular and Sacred Space" concludes the section on Chaucer. In the *Shipman's Tale*, Chaucer explores two temporal outlooks of the late Middle Ages that Jacques LeGoff famously dubbed "merchant's time" and "church's time". A fabliau about a monk who borrows money from a merchant to purchase sex from the merchant's wife, the tale mocks the materialism of the town-dwelling middle-class and the opportunistic clerics who preyed upon them. At the same time, the tale points to a pervasive confusion or disordering of the sacred and the secular. The satire includes not only the monk's obvious neglect of his religious vows in his quest for sensual satisfaction, but also a complex interplay of symbolic domestic spaces (garden, bedroom, and counting house) and certain temporal coincidences, such as the merchant's business trip during the monk's "Sonday" tryst with the merchant's wife. Double-entendres enrich the satire, from "creaunce" (financial credit or religious belief) and "good" (money or spiritual merit) to "thynges" – a term progressively applied to the monk's prayers, what a woman seeks in a man, and finally a merchant's sums. Even rhyme points up the sacred/secular contrast, as in the monk's well-known offer of "franks" for "flanks", and the merchant's devotion to his account books over a "mean time" that ends with "prime" – a pointed contrast between merchant's time and church's time. LeGoff's thesis, although its empirical basis has been challenged in recent years, helps to put Chaucer's satire of the rising middle class and its growing worldliness into a larger context that includes the Quentin Massys portrait (*ca.* 1500) of "The Banker and his Wife", where the woman's prayerbook, a sacred emblem meant to complement her husband's balance, coins, and other symbols of the secular life in the original painting, was replaced in some later copies by an account book.

Hagiography

Henry Ansgar Kelly's namesake, St. Ansgar (801-865), though not renowned for posthumous miracles, was an extraordinarily courageous teacher and missionary, guided by dream visions and idealism in the face of numerous hindrances. In a very apt contribution to this volume, George Brown studies the saint in "Ansgar, Pragmatic Visionary". Educated in the famed abbey of Corbie and then educator in the sister abbey of Corvey, Ansgar gave up his Benedictine vow of stability and the peaceful security of the monastery for the dangerous apostolate among the Scandinavians. His biographer and successor as archbishop of Hamburg-Bremen, St. Rimbert, traces Ansgar's difficult career as, at the request of the Emperor Louis the Pious, he accompanied King Harald Klak to missionize the Danes. His two year's work among the people and his education of youth was brought to an end by the expulsion of Harald. Bolstered again by a vision, Ansgar at the request of a politic Swedish delegation returned to Scandinavia. Undeterred by robbers who stole his supplies and books, he went on to proselytize in Birka. Appointed archbishop of Hamburg, and given the monastery of Torhout to support his work educating boys redeemed from captivity, he enjoyed only a short period of pastorate before he was deprived of Torhout by the division of the empire and deprived of his see by the Viking invasion of Hamburg. Provided a second see at Bremen, despite the objections of the Archbishop of Cologne, Ansgar in response to another powerful vision resumed missionary work in Denmark, with the support of Horic I, soon killed, and then of Horic II. Returned to Bremen, Ansgar resumed his scholarship and writing while continuing his often thwarted apostolate until his death. He did not die a physical martyr, as his early vision promised, but lived a martyrdom to the Truth.

Margaret Bridges takes us into the later Middle Ages with her study, "Uncertain Peregrinations of the Living and the Dead: Writing (Hagiography) as Translating (Relics) in Osbern Bokenham's Legend of St Margaret". The fifteenth-century translator of several holy women's lives (from the *Legenda Aurea* and other Latin sources) marks a long pause between his narration of St Margaret's death and that of the translation of her relics centuries later from Nicomedia to and through Italy, where a number of "accidents" govern the posthumous journey and prevent it from arriving at its intended conclusion. In his extended metaphor of the author as traveler, Bokenham foregrounds the contingencies to which the writer is subjected – contingencies that have a disruptive effect on the open-ended narrative, which is as incomplete as is the 500-year process of translation of the saint's relics. Beginning with Bokenham's self-representation in his *Mappula Angliae*, this paper focuses on the approximation of one mode of translation to another. Moving back and forth between story-time and the storyteller's time, the hagiographer-translator reflects on the polysemous nature of "translatio" in terms of who controls the translation process, who is the object of translation, the dubious efficacy of volition, and the uncertain legitimacy of translating from a venerated original linguistic or topographical context.

Anita Obermeier also addresses Bokenham, from a different perspective, in "Joachim's Infertility in the St. Anne's Legend". In the second-century *Protevangelium Jacobi*, the apocryphal parents of Mary, Anna and Joachim, are patterned after the barren couples of the Old Testament, but, unlike his male predecessors, Joachim grapples with his own infertility. Both medieval art and text privilege Anne over Joachim, endorsing a matrilinear genealogy of Christ. A series of texts, from Old Testament parallels, to the *Protevangelium*, to Jacobus de Voragine's *Legenda Aurea* (*Golden Legend*) (*ca.* 1260) and Osbern Bokenham's *Legendys of Hooly Wummen* (*ca.* 1443-1447), illustrates how medical, philosophical, and theological views deal with Joachim's admission of sterility, which marginalizes him in the conception of Mary, the Immaculate Conception. Since these concepts are intertwined with medieval theological fears of sexuality, and we are dealing with the birth of a divine being in Jesus, the powerful human male seed is now a tainting substance. Anne's and Mary's fertility and male infertility trade places, marginalizing the men. In essence, Anne, especially through her *trinubium* and supercharged fecundity, has returned us to Genesis and the pinnacle of fertility cults. Thus, the medieval Anne can be viewed as an ancient fertility goddess in her own right.

Lay Piety and Christian Diversity

Joseph Nagy takes on an intriguing folklorist problem in "A Pig for *Samhain*?" A fact often overlooked by Celticists and folklorists investigating the possible Celtic origins of modern Hallowe'en is that Irish customs and stories having to do with *Samhain*, a term referring to both the first day of November and the whole month, quite regularly feature pigs (from the vulnerable to the formidable), their slaughter, and their consumption. Pigs and the motif of animal sacrifice are also associated with St. Martin's Day (November 11), which presents its own intriguing mix of imported and native Irish traditions.

Michael Hanly offers a comparative study of French and English literary and historical relations in "Marriage, War, and Good Government in Late-Fourteenth-Century Europe: The *De regimine principum* Tradition in Langland, Mézières, and Bovet". The turmoil of the late fourteenth century engendered a number of writings intended to advise European rulers on the issues troubling the Christian West. Works by three authors – William Langland, Philippe de Mézières, and Honorat Bovet – participate in this *De regimine principum* ("Mirror for princes") tradition by exhorting their leaders to reform their realms in the service of various idealistic goals. The works under consideration in this essay deal with two topics, warfare and matrimony, and consider current approaches to these crucial issues as indicative of the era's corruption. Passages from Langland's *Piers Plowman*, Mézières's *Songe du vieil pelerin*, *Épistre au roi Richart*, and *Estoire de Griseldis*, and Bovet's *Apparicion maistre Jehan de Meun* demonstrate the authors' reactions to the chaos of their times as well as their commitment to effecting change through offering learned counsel to those in power.

Terri Bays investigates the relation between literature and religion in "'I xal excusyn þe & Ledyn þe & Bryngyn þe a-geyn in safte': Liturgy and Authority in *The Book of Margery Kempe*". In 1433, God commands Margery Kempe to go overseas. When Margery protests, God insists; with reluctance, Margery consents. Margery's journey, temporally centered on a pilgrimage to the holy blood of Wilsnack within the octave of Corpus Christi, appropriates the liturgical structures of a Corpus Christi procession. This paper explores the consequences of that appropriation for Margery's account. It focuses on Margery's use of processional structures to foster a renewed understanding of clerical prerogative, lay piety, and territorial boundaries. Margery's justification for her transgressions of clerical and lay boundaries involves appeals, both implicit and explicit, to the rituals of the Corpus Christi procession. So the divine provision of Margery's transportation expands and develops the notion of "bounds-beating" typical of such processions. As Margery elevates the "body of Christ" present in His people to the status it receives upon the altar, she challenges her readers to demonstrate the same devotion to the one that they already, and rightly, grant the other.

Thomas Hahn brings our attention to a thought-provoking religious text in "Christian Diaspora in Late Medieval, Early Modern Perspective: A Transcription of the Treatise *Decem nationes Christianorum* [*The Ten Christian Nations*]". This treatise, written in the fourteenth or fifteenth century, was published at least fifteen times between 1490 and 1516. The treatise presents a compact yet comprehensive survey of Christian diaspora, inventorying the differences – in ritual, belief, practice, language, geography – that mark world Christianity. Through its popularity in this interval – marked by the establishment of Asian trade routes, the encounter with the New World, and the Reformation – it articulates a distinctive perspective on the unities and divisions that shape late medieval and early modern Europe.

Text, Image, Script

King Edward and the Cripple

Christopher Baswell, UCLA

King Edward, gentle and debonair ("duz e debonaire", 1916), walks from his palace in courtly procession, surrounded by great ranks of knights, to hear mass at the chapel of St. Peter, in a church he has decided to restore in lieu of the pilgrimage to Rome which, as a young exile in Normandy, he had vowed to make if only St. Peter would protect him from his many enemies.[1] The stately progress of this aristocratic troupe is interrupted by a shocking if mundane spectacle.

Un povre sëet eu chemin,	A poor man sat in the road,
Cuntrait, mendifs e orfanin.	Crippled, needy and orphaned.
Guil Michel avoit cist nun,	His name was Guil Michel
E fu Irais de nacïun,	And he was Irish by birth,
Megres, cuntraiz, febles e las,	Thin, crippled, weak and weary,
Ki s'escrieit: 'Allas, allas!	Who cried out: "Alas, alas!
Jo sui ci un povre dolent	Here I am, a poor wretch
De ki nus hum pité ne prent,	On whom no man takes pity,
Ki tort sui e desfigurez.	I – twisted and disfigured.
Las, purquei fu jo unc nez?'	Alas, why was I ever born?"
La face avoit fruncie e teinte.	His face was wrinkled and dark.
Tut unt pité de sa pleinte.	All had pity for his lament.
Les pez out tortz, nerfs engurdiz,	His feet were twisted, his tendons numbed,
Gambes sanz brahun, engresliz,	His legs fleshless, emaciated,
Si ke dé genoilz la junture	And the joints of his knees
Au dos se tuert cuntre nature.	Turned backward, against nature.
Li pé besturné, flestriz,	His feet were back to front, withered,
As nages s'aerdent revertiz.	Grown stuck to his buttocks.
A uns eschameus feitiz	With cleverly made trestles
K'il teneit cuntre sun piz	That he holds against his chest
Se trait li povre frarin	The poor wretch drags himself
Par cel enboué chemin.	Along the muddy way.
	(ll. 1925-1946)

Guil Michel is not just visually disruptive, either. His voice calls from the social, even spatial margin, the muck of the road: "Alas, alas!" (1930). He singles out

---

1   I write this essay in honor of Andy Kelly not only as his recent colleague, but as the beneficiary for many years of his matchless scholarship. I am grateful for the help of Professors Jocelyn Wogan-Browne and Thelma Fenster, and an audience of their graduate students in Anglo-Norman at Fordham University; also to my colleague Prof. Scott Waugh, for sharing the manuscript of his forthcoming article.

Edward's chamberlain Hugo (elsewhere called Huges and Hugelin) and calls to him for help, appealing to his gentle blood, his pitying and frank heart. Guil Michel wants a message carried to the king: he has made six pilgrimages to Rome, but even there he learned he could be cured only if King Edward himself would carry him to the monastery. It is the will of Edward's own dear St. Peter.[2]

This encounter pulls the narrative, like the procession, to an abrupt and as it will prove an explosive halt. In a poem dense with martial violence, murder, and invasive attacks on royal lineage and dominion, the impoverished cripple is the most transgressive figure yet. No person in the story, it would seem, could be further from King Edward in rank or condition, even race. Guil Michel is the first poor man to emerge from occasional crowds of the dispossessed, to appear as an individual and receive a name; only one other commoner, also a cripple and the object of Edward's first posthumous cure, will be so forcefully depicted. The description has a certain incoherence, too, an irresolution that reflects the unstable, radical transformations it initiates. Guil Michel is crippled but geographically (even socially) mobile; he is weary and weak but has gone six times to Rome. No man takes pity on him, he says, but "All have pity for his lament". This long, even repetitive account of Michel's deformed body, and his strange if resourceful mobility, emphasize his extreme otherness. Yet he wants a ride on the back of his king; and Edward, already chaste and pious, will be translated by this encounter – "carried" paradoxically by Guil Michel – into public holiness and the saintly business of miracle cures. The bodily uncanny and the spiritual uncanny briefly conjoin. Indeed, King Edward and the cripple are already linked here by Rome, the patronage of St. Peter, and their movement toward Westminster itself. Further, the prayer leading to Edward's earlier pilgrimage vow ("Regard, duz Deu, a tun frarin, / Ki sul es pere a l'orfanin" ["Regard, sweet God, your wretch, / You who alone are father to the orphan"], ll. 754-755) is echoed in the cripple's description ("frarin", ll. 754, 1945, and "orfanin", ll. 755, 1926).

This episode comes from a long Anglo-Norman poem in octosyllabic couplets, *La Estoire de Seint Aedward le Rei*, probably written by the St. Albans historian and hagiographer Matthew Paris soon before the middle of the thirteenth century, and dedicated to Henry III's queen, Eleanor of Provence.[3] It is based loosely on the *Life* composed by Aelred of Rievaulx for Edward's canonization

---

2   Quotes are from *La Estoire de Seint Aedward le Rei*, ed. Wallace. All translations are my own. The only complete translation, by Luard (1858), is awkward and based on his very flawed edition.

3   Authorship, date, and provenance remain vexed issues, but Wallace's proposed date of 1236-1245 invites assent, as does the long-held association with Matthew Paris. See Vaughan (1958: 159-81); Wallace (1983): xvii-xxiii; Binski (1990: 334-335, 338-339); Binski (1995: 50, 57-60) (where he favors a date closer to 1245). Morgan (1988: 95-96, no. 123) questions the attribution to Matthew Paris.

and the translation of his remains to a new tomb, 1161-1163. As its title might suggest, though, the *Estoire* inserts that generically typical saint's life into a much broader secular framework of earlier Anglo-Saxon kings, the mechanics of war and royal dominion, and the civil strife that follows Edward's death, culminating in the triumph of William the Conqueror (Wallace: xxiii-xxix; Binski 1995: 55-60). The poem narrates Edward's exile in Normandy during the rule of several Danish kings, as they gradually kill off his siblings; his return as king and his increasing holiness, affirmed by his chaste marriage; his resolve to restore Westminster and the papal negotiations that ensue; an intermingled sequence of visions, prophecies and miracles both during his life and after; the social disorder after his death and its resolution in the Conquest; and finally the examination of Edward's uncorrupted corpse which further demonstrates his sanctity. Throughout the work, as in the episode of Guil Michel, Westminster Abbey itself is as much a presence as King Edward; key events repeatedly occur at the high altar.

The *Estoire* has been little read by literary scholars, though it has received considerable if sometimes tangential attention from art historians because of its unique manuscript. Cambridge University Library MS Ee.3.59 is among the most beautiful books surviving from the third quarter of the thirteenth century in England. If the poem is by Matthew Paris, this book is not his work but a copy made soon after mid-century, quite possibly produced for Eleanor of Provence's daughter-in-law and wife of Edward I, Eleanor of Castile (Binski 1990: 339-340). Its sixty-four large illustrated miniatures, pen drawn with delicate color washes, are probably the work of two artists, closely related and highly accomplished, whose drawings are remarkably complex and subtle in their evocation of gesture and expression, as well as the minutiae of court and church life.[4] Their work has close affinities with a group of manuscripts and wall paintings produced around London and Westminster for royal and aristocratic patrons (Morgan 1988: 95-96; Binski 1995: 52-89).

The miniature that illustrates the passage translated above (fol. 16v, figure 1) is a rich instance of the artist's accomplishments. The miniature divides into two scenes. On the left it depicts the return of two bishops from Rome with papal documents approving the restoration of Westminster and guaranteeing its rights and privileges. At the right, the crowned Edward and his procession of nobles encounter Guil Michel. The scene involves a fascinating series of gazes and gestures. Three nobles standing behind Edward react with quite distinct looks: a certain doubt in the bearded face at left, an evasive glance and comment by his fellow courtier, and a stare of unmasked horror from the face immediately behind the

---

4   The miniatures have been widely reproduced, and are now entirely available in the superb web site produced by the department of manuscripts at the Cambridge University Library: http://www.lib.cam.ac.uk/MSS/Ee.3.59

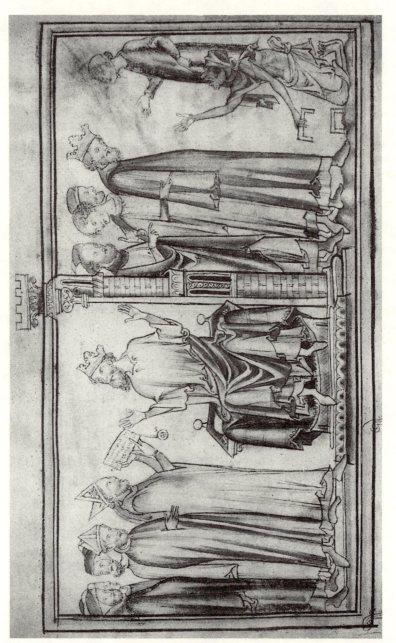

Figure 1

Figure 2

king. Hugo the Chamberlain stands behind Michel, points to him with one hand, and gestures toward the king with the other. Guil Michel himself kneels on his contorted legs and stretches one arm toward the king, while with the other he holds one of the little trestles with which he moves. While his lower body is twisted and shrunken, Michel's mouth is open in speech and his gesture is suppliant but rhetorically assertive. The image echoes his bold address to Hugo. Only Edward seems calm and (typically) static, his head bowed slightly to look frankly at the cripple.

Even more startling in this miniature filled with mitred, crowned, and robed magnates is the semi-nakedness of Michel, who has only a rag over his head and shoulders, and a loincloth tied around his waist. In his deformity and exposure, Guil Michel is by a considerable degree the most bodied presence in the entire manuscript. No other physiognomy is presented in anything like the same detail, stared at both through the description of the narrator and by the nobles and king depicted in the miniature. Not even Edith, the noblewoman with whom Edward forms a pious and chaste marriage, is so vividly described, and she of course is always decorously gowned. Yet for all Guil Michel's emphatic bodily strangeness, the line of gaze links the crowned king and suppliant cripple. The two are paired, balanced in a way reinforced by the colors of their clothing. The scrap that covers Guil Michel's head and shoulders, blue touched with red, is matched in this miniature only by Edward's blue robe and red shoes.

In the pages that follow, I want to argue that King Edward's encounter with the cripple has powerful implications for the manuscript as a whole. It is itself an episode of near-nakedness, of unnerving exposure and transformation within the broader and multiple ideological projects of the *Estoire de Seint Aedward le Rei*. Like so many stories of (re-)foundation and dynasty (consider only the defeated Aeneas and Rome, or his exiled descendant Brutus and Britain), the *Estoire* is a triumphal narrative rife with defeats and contradictions at once barely acknowledged and barely covered over. It is a text fiercely attentive to royal lineage that hinges on a virgin and childless king, concerned with legitimacy yet celebrating William the Bastard. Still, I will claim, the episode of Guil Michel propounds a kind of resolution, however uncertain and oblique, for a question so anxious it is almost unspeakable in the poem: what is the progeny of chaste kingship? In a work so preoccupied with lineage and legitimacy, where can Edward's fertility be located, and what are its means? These crippled bodies, I will claim, work with peculiar force to challenge, disrupt, and transgress secular hierarchies and identities (governmental, physiological, even sexual); yet, by insistently and even repugnantly somatic means, they translate Edward's lineage into the realm of the sacred.

The story of Edward the Confessor was put to intense but highly flexible ideological use virtually from his own lifetime. His saintliness became increasingly important to the ecclesiastical establishment, nowhere more than at Westminster, as the church struggled to establish and codify its rights after the Conquest. And his ethnicity and royal legitimacy were crucial to the Conqueror and his heirs in their efforts to construct a narrative of just dominion in England, and imagine a brief golden age they could claim to restore. Narratives, images, and physical remains – the corpse and the regalia – were all deployed toward these ends (Barlow 1992: 150-163; Baswell 1999: 128-130; Waugh forthcoming). As Paul Binski has brilliantly demonstrated, moreover, this process was at its most layered and complex in the reign of Henry III. Henry held St. Edward in special reverence, named his eldest son after the Confessor, restored and enriched Westminster as St. Edward had done, and had Edward's coronation depicted over his bed in the Painted Chamber (Binski 1995: 3-6, 52-89). Matthew Paris produced the *Flores historiarum*, an influential chronicle extracted from his own longer works, under the mingled influence of Westminster and the court; the illustrations of its manuscripts from this era emphasize coronation and the line of kingship extending back to King Arthur, especially that of Edward the Confessor.[5]

As Binski has also shown, though, the remaking of Edward the Confessor in the reign of Henry III was an eclectic and in some respects an improvised affair, for all the architectural, visual and literary monuments it has left us. There are implicit strains between Edward as a powerful king, seen in the coronation images of the *Flores historiarum* or the Painted Chamber, and Edward as a withdrawn, unworldly, and celibate visionary and miracle worker. Lurking behind these versions from the time of Henry III were earlier historical narratives of Edward as a weak king, dominated by nobles such as Earl Godwin, reigning over a divided and disordered island. This very multiplicity of representations opened the way for variance and paradox. Like Henry's elaborate restoration of Westminster itself as explored by Binski, the *Estoire de Seint Aedward le Rei* is a highly eclectic poem, an apparently loose though in fact self-conscious assemblage of genres that include genealogy, chronicle, courtly romance, hagiography, and prophecy. As with Westminster, this literary structure creates a powerful and overlapping accretion of royal themes: holy kingship, legitimate genealogy, and wonders that link and underwrite the two. It also, however, leaves open gaps and potential trajectories of readerly expectation that can pull the text in directions far from a coherent ideology of dominion. This potential expresses itself, among other ways, in the sometimes jarring transitions in the text between historical chronology and the visionary implosions of time and space that cluster toward the center of the poem.

The especially layered and finely wrought manuscript of the *Estoire*, I want to claim, is especially charged with these barely repressed instabilities, which erupt

---

5   Especially important is Manchester, Chetham's Library MS 6712, ca. 1250-1252, its decoration closely related to Cambridge Ee.3.59. See Morgan (1988: 50-51 no. 96); Binski (1995: 121-128).

repeatedly in the book itself. This book – text, images, rubrics – keeps exposing many of the political and cultural (even, I will claim, sexual) anxieties that the cult of Edward seems largely to have been intended to efface. Invasion and violent, illegitimate access to the throne are emphasized throughout, to an extent that the conquest of William the Bastard (as he is explicitly called) can seem unnervingly like an echo of the earlier Danes. Saintly kingship at its high points, further, can seem to banish secular rule, royal lineage, and their guarantor, marital heterosexuality.

The episode of Guil Michel occurs at such a structurally liminal and unstable moment, a shift in the tone and focus of the entire work. Despite the visionary episodes that bring news to Edward across uncanny distances, to this point he has been a chaste and pious but not a miraculous king, at least not in the sense of effecting marvelous bodily change. As mentioned above, however, immediately before the encounter with Guil Michel, and in an episode depicted in the same miniature, Edward's unfulfilled pilgrimage vow has been lifted from him by means of a bull from Pope Leo, its production elaborately narrated and depicted (ll. 1641-1654, fol. 14v). This arrives just after another written text, from a hermit who learned the same news in a vision of St. Peter.[6] Both texts grant Edward permission to replace his pilgrimage with the restoration of Westminster, an alternative first suggested by his alarmed nobles. It is a thick moment, supercharged with documents and vision, and instructions both papal and heavenly. It marks a departure, almost a generic transformation, from the poem's concerns with secular history, governance and courtliness (concerns that will re-emerge only around the king's deathbed) and into hagiography. Edward's own transformation toward sainthood begins here, with the cure of Guil Michel that immediately follows.

Hearing Guil Michel's message from his chamberlain Hugo, King Edward agrees to carry the cripple into Westminster, and thanks God for having chosen him for such a duty ("a teu mester", l. 1974). In undertaking this burden, though, Edward also encounters the objections of part of his court, and for the first time ignores wishes of his barons:

Li nunsavant s'en funt lur gas.	The ignorant make scorn of it.
Dïent li: 'Lessez atant!	They say to him: "Stop this instant!
Ke portez tu le las puant?	Why do you bear the stinking wretch?
De ses boces la quiture	The pus from his sores
Desent par vostre vesture,	Runs down on your vestments,
Vostre cors e robe soille	Soils your body and robes,
E gesk'as garetz vus moille'.	And stains you down to the knees."

                                                                (ll.1978-1984)

---

6   After a chronological loop back to the origins of Westminster's precursor abbey, Thorney, the narrative of documentation is reprised, almost obsessively, when Edward appeals to Leo's successor Pope Nicholas for a letter of confirmation (ll. 2324-2389). For the role of written documents in this and contemporary works, see Wogan-Browne 1994.

The danger to which the courtiers object is not explicitly a diminishment of royal dignity, but a more physiological fusion, a transfer of bodily fluids overflowing from the cripple who mounts him from the back. The flow of Michel's discharge down to the king's "garetz" (l. 1984, knees, thighs) leaves Edward's robes and body wetted across the genital area that has been, until now, so overdetermined a site of protection.

Both for the cripple and for Edward it is a moment of irreversible translation, in several senses. Not only Guil Michel, but Edward with him, move from secular space – the public road – to the sacred precincts of the high altar. Both shift from engagement and dialogue with secular to ecclesiastical officials. Both undergo bodily transformations, Edward stained and wetted, while for Guil Michel,

Atant es vus ke la char morte	Instantly, behold how the deadened flesh
S'estent, e laschent les junctures,	Swells, and the joints loosen,
S'adrescent les cuntrefaitures.	The deformities straighten out.
Li nerfs ki furent besturnee	The tendons that were turned the wrong way
En lur droit liu sunt redrescee.	Are restored to their right place.
Li rois, ja travailez e las,	The king, all worn out and weary,
Celui ki unc n'ala un pas	Puts down the man who never took a step
Devant l'auter sur les desgrez	Before the altar on the steps,
Avale, e cist asta es pez,	And he stood on his feet
E lua Deu ki l'a guari,	And praised God who has cured him,
E cist ki la sunt ofvec lui.	As do those there with him.

(ll.1986-1996)

When he puts Guil Michel down inside Westminster, King Edward is weary, "las" (l. 1991), again echoing a term that had been used, three times, in describing the cripple's body (ll. 1929, 1956, 1977). Along with Guil Michel's bodily fluids, Edward takes on an aspect of his physiological condition.

Indeed, all the somatic absences or refusals of Edward's history – the sexual chastity, immobility, and bodily languor – seem to crowd suddenly into this one episode. Here, instead, are physical effort, near-nakedness, bodies atop one another, wetness, smell, swelling limbs, fluid exchange, and finally exhaustion. Even if it is not meant as erotic, the scene with all its intimacy, moisture, and tumescence, is spectacularly dense with analogies to eroticism. Yet the result of the episode only pushes Edward toward his "mester" of sainthood. This is his first miracle cure, and a whole sequence of further cures – for scrofula and seven cases of blindness – occur soon after. The almost sexual economy of his exchange with Guil Michel begets Saint Edward's miraculous bodily lineage in those other cured bodies, most often enacted through the exchange of yet another fluid, water, with which the king has washed himself. The scene is all the more striking because it is the first time that Edward, increasingly an immobile and quiescent king – almost himself a cripple – undertakes physical labor (see Binski 1990: 344). There is a rich paradox that the only time he expends physical energy in the poem is to lift

and carry a man who can neither lift nor carry, yet who is still far more mobile
than Edward, having gone six times to Rome.

A further connection between Edward and Guil Michel, though of a different
sort, is suggested by the six-line rubricated verse summary that shares the page
with this scene and its illustration:

Li reis mut s'en humilie.	The king greatly humbles himself.
Le cuntrait porte ki l'en prie.	He carries the cripple who begs him to.
De pecchez ad li reis pardun,	The king gets pardon for his sins,
Li cuntraiz du cors garaisun,	The cripple a cure for his body,
Chescuns de eus saluz receit,	Each of them receives deliverance,
Plenerement Deu lur enveit.	God sends it to them amply.

(rubric XXIX, ll.4853-4858)

If Edward's saintliness transforms Michel's body, so Michel's six trips to Rome
provide a bodily replacement for Edward's unfulfilled vow of pilgrimage, which
until now has been commuted by the much more mediated agency of papal letters.
Only the rubricated summary introduces the notion that Edward's unfulfilled vow
leaves him in a state of sin; and only this summary aligns Michel's crippling with
some moral debility.

The illustration of Edward carrying Guil Michel (fol. 17r, figure 2) provides
yet a third account of the episode, parallel but not identical to those of the poem
and the rubric. This miniature is divided into two scenes by the body of Godriz the
sacristan. At the left, Edward carries Michel toward Godriz, bent by the weight he
carries. Michel uses his right hand to support his torso above Edward's shoulder;
with his left hand he gestures toward Godriz, or the altar, the actual site of his
cure. His torso is held away from Edward's shoulders and head, with a clear space
between them. His legs and feet trail below, useless and slack. Their bodies connect, then, only at Michel's thighs. The only other time Edward is depicted in so
intimate an embrace is on his deathbed (another explosive moment of transition),
when he is kissed and embraced by Edith (fol. 28r, left), then supported by her as
he sits up to deliver his final prophecy (28r, right); and then again on the facing
page when she half-lies across his corpse, her right arm threaded through his bent
arms (fol. 29r). Between Edward's feet and the hem of Godriz's vestment, we see
Michel's abandoned hand trestles. At right, Michel kneels at the altar, his hands
raised to the cross, roughly inverting the gesture he makes on the opposite page to
King Edward himself. Above Michel, a priest looks upward, and from his mouth
comes the phrase "Te deum laudamus", opening the hymn used to thank God for a
special blessing, often used in coronation rituals, including those depicted in the
first miniature of this manuscript.

Both the illustrations of Guil Michel practice intriguing, and I think significant evasions. Michel's body is fit, even muscled, in both images, though his legs
are realistically shrunken and twisted; the artist seems alert to his six pilgrimages

and depicts a body capable of them. There is however no visual representation at all of the running sores to which the text pays so much attention, as if the artist were unnerved by them just as the ignorant courtiers explicitly are. The crippled body is only partly effaced, though, by the omission of its suppurating wounds. Otherwise, its freakishness is rather boldly displayed, evoking the stares of the onlookers I described earlier. If that sequence of gazes performs for us the socially disruptive potential of the crippled body, the whole encounter with Guil Michel seems to open up an analogously incoherent (yet not contradictory) narrative array: text, rubric, and selective images.

The second scene, within Westminster (fig. 2, fol. 17r, right), seems to reflect a further hesitancy. There, Guil Michel's actual cure is left as visually inexplicit as his running sores. We are told, but not shown, that he walks with Godriz to the altar. Kneeling at the altar in the right-hand scene of the miniature, Michel is no more upright than he was when addressing the king from the road on the facing page. In fact, except for arm positions, the two images of Guil Michel almost mirror one another; and his legs and feet, described as straightened and whole by the poem, are hidden by the vestments of Godriz and the second priest.

His undepicted sores and his uncertainly depicted cure, even if evasive, nonetheless contribute to Guil Michel's persistent otherness in the book. He splits the narrative into a multiplicity which hovers, unresolved. His hand-trestles, hung on the wall of Westminster, are memorial objects within the narrative (ll. 2011-14), and his emphatic depiction in the manuscript is a memorial for the reader. Textually cured, visually crippled, Guil Michel enacts codicologically the anxious ambivalence of Edward's own status as worldly king or saint. If the issue of Edward's physiological sterility is seen but anxiously unspoken, his one bodily partner is cured in words but anxiously not in sight. He persists, yet in his irresolution he is an irritant. Guil Michel the cripple is a worry like Edward's sterile chastity, a challenge to category that will not fully disappear. If the poem first introduces Guil Michel within comfortable distinctions of high and low, palace and road, clothed and naked, whole and crippled, such binarism swiftly disperses in the vocabulary he shares with Edward, and their brief fusion as a single, mobile, and (incompletely) transformed being.

The cripple, as we have seen, is elaborately passed among noble, royal, and clerical hands. Guil Michel's body, at once unstable and persistent, visually arrested between crippling and cure, is the crossing point that links Edward the king and saint, and the three great social orders: the commons in the road from whom he emerges, the nobles, and the clergy. He is, in this structurally and thematically crucial scene, the somatic membrane that briefly links them as a national body. Guil Michel also helps fashion, with new intensity, the narrative and religious network among Edward himself, Rome, and Westminster – a network which previously was much more tentative and fragmentary, adumbrated in the royal vow of pilgrimage, baronial reaction, and diplomatic exchanges.

At the same time, the thematic valence of this religious triangulation helps pull the poem out of its earlier chronological mode, and into a more associative structure of sacred architecture, bodily cure, and visionary wonder. Along with this generic shift, the narrator moves away from using courtly attributes for Edward, and toward increasingly hagiological descriptions: "Le seint peisible Aedward" (l. 2513), holy, peace-loving Edward. The next major narrative moment after that of Guil Michel is a long loop backward into the prehistory of Westminster, the story of the first building of Thorney and its miraculous dedication by St. Peter himself, witnessed by a Thames fisherman.[7] When King Edward returns significantly to the story, it is in the visionary high point of the poem, where he sees the infant Christ replace the elevated host at the high altar of Westminster Abbey (ll. 2514-59, fol. 21r). And that infant Christ, the only completely naked figure in the entire manuscript, echoes the almost naked Guil Michel, and extends King Edward's accelerating occasions of entry into the sacred uncanny; he draws the rapt attention of those who see him as strongly as Guil Michel had before.

The sometimes sudden moves in genre in the *Estoire* can give the impression of an uncontrolled work, tugged merely by narrative occasion among unconsidered arenas of style and diction. This impression, as I suggest above, is wrong. In fact, the poem makes a broad sweep from chronicle to hagiography and back to chronicle, with nicely calibrated shifts in diction and tone. This description of course simplifies matters to a degree; passages of prayer, vision, and prophecy lend considerable coherence and episodic rhythm across all parts of the work. The opening "historical" section is further inflected by diction and topoi from courtly romance. The closing "historical" section, on the other hand, includes religious events, especially the opening of Edward's tomb, leading toward his canonization. The hagiographic core of the work, too, for all its puncturing of chronology and challenges to secular social order, closes with Edward's obscure death-bed prophecy, whose interpretation in the text links it specifically to the secular, royal line. Careful symmetries further structure the poem. Foreign invasions (Danes and Normans) and civil strife lead toward a triumphant coronation in each of the "historical" sections.[8] Within the narrative of Edward's emerging sainthood, the mira-

---

7   See ll. 2035-2265. This ecclesiastical prehistory, I would claim, balances and complements the dynastic prehistory of England itself that Edward had addressed, also to St. Peter, in a prayer during his boyhood exile in Normandy, a passage strikingly altered from its source in Aelred's *Vita* (ll. 738-815, cf. Aelred ch. 5.) For prayers throughout the *Estoire*, see Gouttebroze 1981.

8   The poem breaks off with Harold's burial at Waltham, hence the almost certain account of William's coronation is missing. Most pages have three columns of up to 24 lines each of the main text, usually reduced to 16 or 18 lines in the center column to make space for 6 to 8 lines of rubricated verse summary. On those pages with only a 2-column miniature (such as fol. 17r, fig. 2), though, one column may hold as many as 48 lines. Hence the missing leaf could have held as few as 124 lines ([24 + 16 + 24] x 2) or as many as 180 ([24 + 18 + 48] x

cle cures during his life (a cripple, a scrofulous lady, six blind men and a seventh with one eye) are neatly repeated by those after his death (lacking only a posthumous cure of scrofula). Such large-scale symmetries are sometimes visually reinforced locally by echoes between the two miniatures of an opening, as with the near-mirror images of Guil Michel on folios 16v and 17r.

Among these structural symmetries, the crucial one is Edward's first posthumous cure, in the first narrative episode following his death and ascent to heaven, conducted by angels who sing *Te deum laudamus*, the hymn that also marked Guil Michel's cure. At this point the poem tells of

Uns povres, nez de Normendie,	A poor man, born in Normandy,
De povere e messaisé vie,	Of poor and suffering life,
Ki de l'aumosne lu rei fu,	Who by the king's charity
Tant cum vesqui, sustenu –	Was sustained as long as he lived –
Cuntrait de membres e nerfs,	Crippled in limbs and tendons,
Li pé li sunt au dos aers,	His feet are stuck to his back.
Les meins li sunt e meins e pez.	His hands serve both as hands and feet.
A trestelez s'est apuiez.	He supports himself on little trestles.
Purpensez s'est de un e[n]gin	He figured out a contrivance
Par quei s'en va par le chemin,	By which he moves along the road,
Un auget u s'est asis	A wood trough where the wretch sits
E se trait memes li cheitifs.	And drags himself along.
Eu chemin nagge sanz flot.	He sails in the road without water.
Des grantz vertuz seint Aedward ot	He heard everyone talking
La gent tute recunter.	About the great miracles of St. Edward.
Atant s'est trait a Westmuster	Right away he drags himself to Westminster
E la vent a queuke peine.	And gets there with great trouble.
Ço fu meimes la simaine	It was the very week
Ke li rois Aedward transi	That King Edward passed
Du mund.	From the world.

(ll.3989-4008)

The technology ("engin", l. 3997) and effort of crippled motion are even more emphatic here than in the case of Guil Michel. The cripple laments the poverty he'll suffer now that "rois Aedward deboneire" (l. 4009) is dead. He prays Edward either for death or aid in his miseries, and no more finishes his prayer than he is cured, clearly a miracle to all who are there (ll. 4019-4024). Irish and Norman, both cripples are foreign to the Anglo-Saxon king, although the object of this second cure may serve to introduce the rising fortunes of Normans after Edward's death.

---

2). The final leaf, written in a different hand from that of the rest of the manuscript, narrates the opening of Edward's coffin and the replacement of his pall by one made at the command of "rois Willame" (l. 4667).

The image and the rubricated verse summary (ll. 5083-5088) on this page (fol. 29v) conflate Edward's funeral, which is never explicitly narrated in the main text, and his first posthumous cure. The miracles begin even as his body is being laid in the tomb, still uncovered. Other suppliants are shown crawling through squeezing spaces beneath the tomb. The depiction of the Norman cripple, like that of Guil Michel before, is intriguingly ambiguous. He is shown in a short blue tunic to mid-thigh, as he kneels facing left with his hands raised toward Edward's head. While the cripple is not shown rising "on his legs and his feet" ("As gambes e as peez", l. 4021), his feet are not bent backward like Guil Michel's, and there is some musculature apparent in his calves. His two hand trestles sit on the ground in front of him. In the visual structure of the manuscript, the hidden cure of Guil Michel is here revealed and completed. The two images perfectly bracket the initiation and completion of Edward's sanctity. If the first scene of cure was associated with fragile and putrescent mortal bodies, here it is depicted with the incorruptible saintly corpse (ll. 3982-3983).

The *Estoire*, as I have suggested, sets out on an ideological project to construct several kinds of stable body: the coherent body of Edward "king and confessor", the body politic of English royal dominion, the body of papal Christendom and such directly subject members as Westminster itself. Nonetheless it holds at its miraculous center profoundly if marvelously unstable bodies: those of the cripples whose cures initiate and finalize Edward's manifest sanctity. These incomplete, "othered" subjects define bodily integrity by their radical alterity, and even provide a necessary complement, a completion, to the chaste, isolated royal body. At the same time, in the key, transformative encounter with Guil Michel, Edward's own body briefly takes on an abnormal, or rather paranormal, eroticism; and in the same encounter his body virtually doubles that of the exhausted ("las") cripple whose weight he bears. What I have tried to argue is that the book's cripples enact Edward's definitive move from corruptible mortality to sanctity, yet they embody the insufficiencies, the permanent breakages, and the uncanny, queer affiliations such a move involves. This strange embrace with Guil Michel, and the descent of his fluid onto the king's ceremonial garments and his very body become, I would claim, the moment of Edward's fertility, the occasion of his saintly lineage.

References

Aelred of Rievaulx
1997   *Vita Sancti Edwardi Regis.* Trans. Jerome Bertram, FSA. Southampton UK: The Saint Austin Press.

Barlow, Frank (ed. and trans.)
1992   *The Life of King Edward who rests at Westminster, attributed to a monk of Saint-Bertin.* Oxford: Clarendon.

Baswell, Christopher
1999   "Latinitas", in: David Wallace, ed., *The Cambridge History of Medieval English Literature.* Cambridge UK: Cambridge University Press: 122-151.

Binski, Paul
1990   "Reflections on *La estoire de Seint Aedward le rei*: hagiography and kinship in thirteenth-century England", *Journal of Medieval History* 16: 330-50.

1995   *Westminster Abbey and the Plantagenets: Kingship and the Representation of Power 1200-1400.* New Haven and London: Yale University Press for the Paul Mellon Centre for Studies in British Art.

Gouttebroze, Jean-Guy
1981   "Structure et sens des textes de prière contenus dans la *Estoire de seint Aedward le rei*". In: *La Prière au Moyen Âge: littérature et civilisation* (*Sénéfiance*, vol. 10). Paris: Champion: 299-314.

Luard, H. R. (ed. and trans.)
1858   *Lives of Edward the Confessor.* London: Rolls Series.

Morgan, Nigel J.
1982   *Early Gothic Manuscripts I, 1190-1250.* (A Survey of Manuscripts Illuminated in the British Isles, 4.) Oxford: Oxford University Press.

1988   *Early Gothic Manuscripts II, 1280-1285.* (A Survey of Manuscripts Illuminated in the British Isles, 4.) Oxford: Oxford University Press.

Vaughan, Richard
1958   *Matthew Paris.* Cambridge: Cambridge University Press.

Wallace, Kathryn Young (ed.)
1983   *La Estoire de Seint Aedward le Rei, attributed to Matthew Paris.* London: Anglo-Norman Text Society.

Waugh, Scott
Forthcoming   "The Lives of Edward the Confessor and the Meaning of History in the Middle Ages".

Wogan-Browne, Jocelyn
1994   "The Apple's Message: Some Post-Conquest Hagiographic Accounts of Textual Transmission". In: A. J. Minnis (ed.), *Late-Medeival Religious Texts and their Transmission.* Rochester NY: Boydell and Brewer: 39-53.

Looking at the Sun in Chaucer's *Troilus and Criseyde*

V.A. Kolve, UCLA

"What is the sonne wers, of kynde right,   [II, 862]
Though that a man, for feeblesse of his yën,
May nought endure on it to see for bright?
Or love the wers, though wrecches on it crien?"

In *Chaucer and the Imagery of Narrative*, and in a number of essays published since, I have sought to show, one tale at a time, how Chaucer in his mature art uncovers within his fictions a range of iconographic images, rich in affiliation, that he and his first audiences knew from other literary works and the visual culture of their time. Passages that can readily be visualized with the "eye of the mind", they are central to the story and distinguished by the force and clarity of their detail. But what makes them most distinctive within late medieval poetic practice is the fact Chaucer insists so little on their symbolic dimension. That is left for the reader/listener to discover as the tale progresses, and to take thoughtful pleasure in after it is over. Though such images loom large in memory – within any given tale it is rare for more than one or two to emerge in this way – they are subsumed within a narrative style that gives prominence to setting and event, character and conversation, emotion and rhetorical address, adorned by only the occasional metaphor or simile. The prison/garden and the tournament amphitheatre in "The Knight's Tale" are examples of this kind, as is the runaway horse in "The Reeve's Tale", the rudderless ship at sea in "The Man of Law's Tale", or the carter cursing his horses in "The Friar's Tale".[1] Though embedded in the plot, either as setting or as an action the story moves to or through, the symbolic potential of these images allows the poet to suggest meanings larger and more general than those of the tale's literal fiction. I have taken a special interest in that sort of imagery, with other studies yet to come.

This essay will concern two images whose function is as large, but which are constructed on wholly different principles. Images that *insist upon* their need for non-literal interpretation, they are woven into the mimetic surfaces of the poem only by the fiction that they have been received in dreams, where the obscure and enigmatic are commonplace. In doing so, they remind us how little the other sort of image, more characteristic of Chaucer's mature practice, conforms to some of the most important teaching concerning images current in his time. That de-

---

1   See Kolve (1981 through 1997). Chapters I and II of *Chaucer and the Imagery of Narrative* (Kolve 1984) – "Audience and Image: Some Medieval Hypotheses" and "Chaucerian Aesthetic: The Image in the Poem" – develop at length the theory summarized above.

scended through handbooks written by Cicero (*De oratore*) or widely attributed to him (the celebrated *Rhetorica Ad Herennium*), up to and well beyond a treatise on the art of memory (*De Memoria Artificiali*) we reasonably attribute to Thomas Bradwardine – the fourteenth-century "Bisshop Bradwardyn" Chaucer refers to in the "Nun's Priest Tale" as an authority on free will [*CT* VII, 3242].[2] We will pay his treatise some close attention here.

In teaching the art of persuasive public speech, Rhetoric recognized that an orator, beyond skill in arrangement, delivery, invention and style, needs to remember in logical order the topics of the speech he plans to give in counsel or forum. And so a fifth branch of rhetoric taught the art of memory, in which certain assumptions about imagery, influential throughout the Middle Ages, are spelled out in intriguing detail.[3]

It taught a way of creating memory systems – first by visualizing in one's mind a well-known place or "background", usually architectural, containing several distinct locations (*loci*) within it. There, in a sequence natural to the place, usually from left to right, one could place a set of "images" invented to represent the topics of one's speech, so memorable as to be readily revisited in the mind. In two magisterial books, Mary Carruthers has shown how memory treatises of this kind reflect cultural practices deeper and more widespread than the training of "artifical" memory on its own.[4] Common to most is the assumption that images effective in this way will exhibit a certain exaggerated quality – as Bishop Bradwardine, along with many others, makes clear. I quote Carruthers' summary:

> Because the memory retains distinctly only what is extraordinary, wonderful, and intensely charged with emotion, the images should be of extremes – of ugliness or beauty, ridicule or nobility, of laughter or weeping, of worthiness or salaciousness. Bloody figures, or monstrosities, or figures brilliantly but abnormally colored should be used, and they should be engaged in activity of a sort that is extremely vigorous.[5]

---

2   A theologian at Merton College, Oxford from 1325 to 1335, he became chancellor of St. Paul's, and even for a brief time Archbishop of Canterbury, before dying of plague in 1349.

3   See Murphy (1975) and Camargo (1983) on the history and importance of rhetoric in medieval culture.

4   To give these books their full titles: Carruthers (1990), *The Book of Memory: A Study of Memory in Medieval Culture*, and Carruthers (1998), *The Craft of Thought: Meditation, Rhetoric, and the Making of Images, 400-1200*. She builds upon Frances Yates' groundbreaking *The Art of Memory*.

5   Carruthers (1990) p. 133; see pp. 130-137 for her full discussion of the treatise *De Memoria Artificiali*, translated by her (from a MS text) in Appendix C, pp. 281-288. Compare the advice given in the *Rhetorica ad Herennium* [III. xxii. 37]: "We ought, then, to set up images of a kind that can adhere longest in the memory. And we shall do so if we establish likenesses as striking as possible; if we set up images that are not many or vague, but doing something; if we assign to them exceptional beauty or singular ugliness; if we dress some of them with crowns or purple cloaks, for example, so that the likeness may be more distinct to us; or if we

Bradwardine used the zodiac to show how such images may best be invented and arranged, linking them to each other through actions that are violent, improbable, and often sexual in kind. "Suppose someone", he writes, "must memorize the twelve zodiacal signs, that is the ram, the bull, etc. So he should make for himself in the front of the first [memory] location a very white ram standing up and rearing on his hind feet, with (if you like) golden horns. Likewise one places a very red bull to the right of the ram, kicking the ram with his rear feet; standing erect, the ram then with his right foot kicks the bull above his large and super-swollen testicles, causing a copious infusion of blood. And by means of the testicles one will recall that it is a bull, not a castrated ox or a cow". (By this image we will remember Aries and Taurus.) "In a similar manner", Bradwardine goes on, "a woman is placed before the bull as though laboring in birth, and from her uterus as though ripped open from the breast are figured coming forth two most beautiful twins, playing with a horrible, intensely red crab, which holds captive the hand of one of the little ones", making him weep, while the other caresses the crab "in a childish way. Or the two twins are placed there born not of a woman but from the bull in a marvelous manner, so that the principle of economy of material may be observed. To the left of the ram a dreadful lion is placed, who with open mouth and rearing on its legs attacks a virgin, beautifully adorned, by tearing her ornate garments. With its left foot the ram inflicts a wound to the lion's head. The virgin truly holds in her right hand scales for which might be fashioned a balance-beam of silver with a plumb-line of red silk, and then weighing-pans of gold; on her left is placed a scorpion wondrously fighting her so that her whole arm is swollen, which she tries to balance in the aforesaid scales".[6] (By these images we will remember Gemini, Cancer, Leo, Virgo, Libra and Scorpio). Bradwardine goes on to fill a second "memory location" in similar fashion, completing the Zodiac's divisions, and concluding that one who holds such images in his mind can revisit the whole in whatever order he wants, forwards or backwards. Carruthers, however, emphasizes something deeper: "what is most surprising, to a puritan-formed sensibility, is the emphasis on violence and sexuality which runs through all the interaction of the figures in each scene".[7] That, she makes clear, is the very essence of the art. A wildly singular image is put in touch with others equally odd, in an interaction or display that can be readily recalled – here to remember the signs of the zodiac in their order, or (quite possibly) to use them as a primary "location system" in which to place other invented images equally startling and bizarre. As the ancients knew, and all experience confirms, what is extraordinary and extreme impresses itself upon the mind.

---

somehow disfigure them, as by introducing one stained with blood or soiled with mud or smeared with red paint, so that its form is more striking, or by assigning certain comic effects to our images ..." [etc]. p. 221.

6   Quoted from Carruthers (1990) pp. 283-284.
7   Ibid., p. 134.

Whether Chaucer knew such ideas directly, from the handbooks of rhetoric itself, we do not know. But he knew the kind of imagery such teaching produced,
for he built two of his dream-vision poems, *The Parlement of Foules* and *The
House of Fame*, around just such imaginings. In the former, the goddess Nature is
described as seated in a glade bounded by green halls and bowers, attended by
every sort of bird, arranged according to their kinds. She is imported directly from
Alain de Lille's "Complaint of Nature" [*De planctu naturae*], where her description runs to many pages:

> And right as Aleyn, in the Pleynt of Kynde,   [316]
> Devyseth Nature of aray and face,
> In swich aray men mygte hire there fynde.[8]

In the second of these poems, Chaucer presents the goddess Fame as one whose
size expands and shrinks constantly; whose ears, eyes and tongues are as numerous as feathers on a bird; and whose feet are adorned with partridge-wings, signifying the swiftness of rumor. From within her palace, built on a mountain of ice
whose one side melts in the sun, she delivers capricious justice to suppliants who
beg for good fame or bad fame, wrong fame or no fame at all. Everything about
her is artificial, in the root sense of the word:

> Y saugh, perpetually ystalled,   [1364]
> A femynyne creature,
> That never formed by Nature
> Nas such another thing yseye.

Indeed, almost everything about her has been taken from Virgil's *Aeneid* and
Ovid's *Metamorphoses*, which provide the details noted above. To visit the dream
images in these earlier poems is to gain entrance to their main attraction – the allegorical construct is, in many ways, the poem.

That is not the case with the two "strong" images that are my subject in this essay: Criseyde's dream of the eagle, Troilus's dream of the boar. I mean to give them
a "strong" reading in turn, noting first their iconic importance, being the kind of
extravagant, unnatural image favored in the rhetorical handbooks and memory treatises; and exploring, second, their iconographic affiliations, which invite thoughtful
interpretation. But the poem that encloses them is not allegorical in mode, and so
they function (like embedded images, but not "covered over" or concealed), as a
symbolic means of organizing the action of the poem as a whole. They are images
that suggest more than they present; they leave more for the auditor/reader to do.

---

8   All Chaucer quotations are from *The Riverside Chaucer*, ed. Benson, 3d ed.

Some 1750 lines into his poem – possibly the most leisurely poem about love ever written – Chaucer imagines a critic registering this objection:

Now myghte som envious jangle thus: [II, 666]
"This was a sodeyn love; how myght it be
That she so lightly loved Troilus
Right for the firste syghte, ye, parde?"

Chaucer's answer to the charge is dismissive and urbane: everything, he tells us, has to begin somewhere. But this is merely an understated way of introducing one of the most beautiful passages in his ravishing poem. In the next 261 lines, he will enter the consciousness of Criseyde as she thinks about Troilus's proffered love – an inner debate in which concern for reputation and private tranquility sometimes clouds her face as clouds cover the sun [II, 764-70]. The prospect both intrigues and frightens her, so much so that she can reach no decision: "now hoot, now cold", she chooses instead to put it out of mind, walking in the garden "for to pleye" [II, 808, 812]. Accompanied by three young women, she wanders up and down, surrendering herself to desultory conversation and the beauty of a "Trojan" song. Chaucer gives us its lyric in full.

Sung by her niece Antigone, it affirms the goodness and worth, majesty and mystery of romantic love: "... al this blisse, in which to bathe I gynne ... / This is the ryghte lif that I am inne" [II, 849]. Criseyde, hearing it as first-person testimony, asks in an offhand sort of way, "Who made this song now with so good entente?" To which Antigone replies,

"Madame, ywys, the goodlieste mayde   [II, 880]
Of gret estat in al the town of Troye,
And let hire lif in moste honour and joye".

The question of authorship is of great importance: though no name is given, the song's maker is known, and its substance reflects her life. Composed by someone like themselves – a Trojan woman apparently of similar age ("the goodlieste mayde") and of their own social class ("of gret estat") – it testifies to the pleasure of loving passionately, and to the possibility of doing so without loss of happiness or reputation. Or at least, Criseyde reflects, "so it semeth by hire song". But can there really be such bliss among lovers? "Ye, wis", Antigone replies, though not everyone is capable of it, and though no one can describe it well. If you want to know about heaven, you must ask a saint. Fiends can only report on the foulness of hell.[9]

---

9   Borthwick (1961: 228) writes about the song "as a reflector of the object both as it is and as it should be". In this sense, she argues, Antigone's song might be called a 'mirour' of love, in the tradition of the medieval literary "mirror" or *speculum*. She sees its high idealism as self-

The reassurance gained through that oblique exchange, enforced by the beauty and high idealism of the song, imprints itself upon Criseyde's consciousness, leaving her a little less afraid than before, and moving her slowly toward a kind of love-adventure she has never known. Soon it grows dusk, when "white thynges waxen dymme and donne", and her women prepare her for bed. There, in a kind of reverie, she hears a nightingale sing its " lay / Of love". It too works upon her, gladdening her heart, readying her for change, bringing her to sleep.

And then the final persuasion. In a single stanza, Chaucer invents for her a dream so bizarre and violent, sexual and surreal, that it fastens itself in the reader's memory as forcefully as it plays upon the unconscious of Criseyde:

> And as she slep, anonright tho hire mette   [II, 925]
> How that an egle, fethered whit as bon,
> Under hire brest his longe clawes sette,
> And out hire herte he rente, and that anon,
> And dide his herte into hire brest to gon –
> Of which she nought agroos, ne nothyng smerte –
> And forth he fleigh, with herte left for herte".

Though situated in a narrative poem rather than a "memory" palace invented for the purpose of remembering, the image is, as the memory treatises recommend, strange and unusual in the extreme. The action it causes us to imagine so starkly – a white eagle sets his claws into Criseyde's breast, tears out her heart, replaces it with his own, and then flies away, heart left for heart – brilliantly plays upon a theme often represented in the medieval art of love: poems and pictures in which a lover quite literally offers his lady his heart, and she rewards him with a garland or chaplet in return. Most often he does so on his knees in adoration, for this is a religion of love. Chrétien de Troyes' *Cligés*, for instance, written in the twelfth century, includes "extensive heart-swapping" – the phrase is Michael Camille's – with its heroine Fenice at one point declaring that her heart is lodged as a slave in the heart of her lover. But the theme was important in other media too, including manuscript illumination and ivory carvings meant for ladies, all as a way of idealizing (sometimes satirizing) courtly loving. Figure 1, from a French writing tablet of the 14th century, shows the lover on his knees, offering his heart like something sacred in his sleeve-covered hand; she offers him a garland in return. On the right, they walk off together, an arm around each other's shoulder, with the falcon on his wrist signifying masculine dominance reclaimed. In both wings of the diptych,

---

correcting and self-critiquing by its very nature – as do I. But I would dissent from her view (ibid.: 234) that the imagery of the eagle-dream presages evil.

Figure 1

she carries a small lap dog, a sign of fidelity in courtly art of the time.[10] As Camille demonstrates, the gift of the heart symbolizes "the greatest gift of self", and in his book, *The Medieval Art of Love*, he reproduces several examples from the visual arts relevant to the dream-image under discussion here.[11] What is novel in Chaucer's version is the substitution of an eagle for a human lover, the almost surgical violence of the exchange, and (not least) the unexpected emotional response. Criseyde realizes she felt neither fear nor pain. Medieval cognitive theory held that the memory stores not only images but their "intentions" – their likely consequence for us, which we sense intuitively, as animals do. From this alarming yet ultimately benign dream, Criseyde learns, on a level deeper than conscious thought, that there is nothing to fear in love.[12]

We will return to this dream, for it serves other purposes besides preparing Criseyde for "conversion" to love. But before we do, I want to examine Troilus's dream in Book V – another "extreme" image distinguished by "exceptional beauty or singular ugliness", so much so it is "almost a marvel". This dream, in contrast, leads to utter despair.[13]

As Troilus's trust in Criseyde is eroded by her failure to return, we've been told in a summary way that he has bad dreams – "the dredefulleste thynges / That myghte ben". [V, 248]. He dreams he is alone in a horrible place, that he has fallen into the hands of enemies, that he is falling from a great height. But then he too is granted a full-scale dream, its surprising detail addressed not just to the mind but to the "eye of the mind", to the visual imagination:

---

10 Figure 1: Writing Tablet, Anonymous, The Detroit Institute of Arts, Founders Society Purchase with funds from Robert H. Tannahill. See also Kolve (1984), pp. 441-442 n76.

11 Camille (1998: 111-119), with well-chosen color illustrations, some of them parodic. I quote (here and before) from pp. 112, 114.

12 Here is Albertus Magnus on "intentions", from his extensive treatise on memory in *De Bono*, written ca. 1245, and newly translated by Carruthers (1990: 167-280, Appendix B): "the reactions [*intentiones*] which memory stores do not exist absolutely apart from the images of particulars. . . . And so these reactions are taken in at the same time along with the images, and therefore there is no need to have special [memory] rules for them" (ibid.: 279; see also pp. 59-60). Howard (1970: 189) writes of this dream: "The eagle is Troilus, but Troilus as he exists in Criseyde's inner thoughts, made white by hope and sentiment, made violent and rapacious by expectation and fear. . . at once predatory and gentle. Perhaps indeed the eagle is love itself, Criseyde's hopeful and fearful image of it. . .". Spearing (1971: 142-147) finds in it "the authentic strangeness of a dream experience", saturated in obscure meaning. He uses medieval dream theory, along with Freud's distinction between manifest and latent dream-content, to offer a psychoanalytic reading: the (real) nightingale who sings outside her window becomes the eagle of her dream, betokening what she otherwise cannot yet admit, "a secret wish to give herself to Troilus" (p. 145).

13 I here quote from Albertus Magnus, in Carruthers (1990: 273-274). On these matters he echoes the *Rhetorica ad Herennium*, which he cites as the work of "Tully" (Marcus Tullius Cicero). Carruthers writes about the treatise on pp. 137-142.

So on a day he leyde hym doun to slepe, [V, 1233]
And so byfel that yn his slep hym thoughte
That in a forest faste he welk to wepe
For love of here that hym these peynes wroughte;
And up and doun as he the forest soughte,
He mette he saugh a bor with tuskes grete,
That slepte ayeyn the bryghte sonnes hete.
And by this bor, faste in his armes folde,
Lay, kyssyng ay, his lady bryght, Criseyde.

The shock of this vision is so great it wakes him, and leaves him certain the dream is true.

"The blysful goddes, thorugh here grete myght, [V, 1250]
Han in my drem yshewed it ful right".

It is indeed a monstrous dream. As he stumbles through a forest, weeping for Criseyde, he finds her in the embrace of a boar, sleeping in the sun, whom she kisses him again and again.

Both dreams symbolize *eros* in terms of bestiality – sex across species – breaching a barrier between animal and human that most societies hold utterly taboo. By the thirteenth century in Europe, bestiality was commonly classified as the most terrible of sins.[14] But Criseyde's dream, we notice, is paradoxically presented as acceptable. By expressing something that the poem and its readers have come to desire – the sexual union of Troilus and Criseyde – this action, which in real life would elicit horror, can expect to be read *in bono*, as a good and noble thing. The dream of the boar, in contrast, precludes sympathetic response. Readers, of course, immediately identify the boar as Diomede, whose calculated yet careless courtship of Criseyde we have witnessed with some pain. From within the story, however, it is a dream in need of interpretation. Troilus understands immediately that Crisyede has betrayed him. But what is he to make of the boar? Pandarus, always positive, suggests an honorable interpretation: the boar represents her father Calkas, "which that old is and ek hoor", embraced by her as he lies in the sun, waiting to die. "Thus sholdestow thi drem aright expounde!" [V, 1288] Forget the dream, he says. Write her a letter, instead, confessing how much you suffer and asking her true intent.

---

14 See Salisbury, "Bestiality in the Middle Ages", for a learned account of changing attitudes toward such behavior, ranging from its acceptable place in classical myth (gods in the form of animals often seduce humans), through Old Testament prohibitions, early Church penitentials, and so on. For the thirteenth century scholastics, see pp. 180-182.

And so a series of letters is exchanged, serving only to leave her intention less clear than before. Troilus meanwhile remains haunted by the dream
– it "may never come out of his remembraunce" [V, 1444] – and convinced
of two things in particular: that it was sent by Jove, and that "the boor was
shewed hym in figure" [V, 1449], as a meaningful sign. He finally takes it to
his sister Cassandra, the prophetess whose hard destiny it was always to tell
the truth and never to be believed. She interpets it historically. The goddess
Diana, in anger, once sent a monstrous boar "as gret as ox in stalle", to lay
waste the croplands and vineyards of Greece. The slaughter of that boar by
Meleager's, the Calydonian king, occasioned much envy and strife, and became a major cause of the war against Thebes, in which Tideus, Melager's
descendant, was killed. Since Tideus in turn fathered Diomede, the
identification is simple – "This ilke boor bitokneth Diomede" – and its
meaning painfully unambiguous:

> "And thy lady, wherso she be, ywis,   [V.1516]
> This Diomede hire herte hath, and she his.
> Wep if thow wolt, or lef, for, out of doute,
> This Diomede is inne, and thow art oute".

The exchange of hearts in Criseyde's dream, presented as courtly and noble,
is here reprised – "this Diomede hire herte hath, and she his" – but with a
grotesque change of partners – the white-feathered eagle replaced by a som-
nolent wild boar – and in language bluntly sexual – "This Diomede is inne,
and thow art oute". The two dream images, as strong as any Bishop Bradwardine invented for his zodiac, turn out to be oddly alike: the one is transformed into the other.

This strange kinship is no accident, for Chaucer derived both from a single dream in Boccaccio's *Il Filostrato*, the major source of his poem. There,
in Part VII, Troilo, disfigured with grief, dreams the following dream:

> "One day, all melancholy because of the broken pledge, Troilo had gone to sleep,
> and in a dream he saw the perilous sin of her who made him languish. For he
> seemed to hear within a shady wood a great and unpleasant crashing; at that,
> when he raised his head, he seemed to see a great charging boar. // And then af-
> terward he seemed to see Criseida underneath its feet, from whom it drew her
> heart with its snout and it appeared to him that Criseida was not concerned by
> such a great hurt but almost took pleasure in what the animal did, which made
> him so strongly indignant that it broke his feeble sleep". [15]

---

15 Boccaccio, *Il Filostrato*, ed. Pernicone, trans. apRoberts and Seldis, Book VII, vv. 23-24, pp.
    348-349:

Figure 2

Erasi un di, tutto malinconoso
per la fallita fede, ito a dormire
Troiolo, e 'n sogno vide il periglioso
fallo di quella che 'l facea languire:
che gli parea, per entro un bosco ombroso,
un gran fracasso e spiacevol sentire;
per che, levato il capo, gli sembiava
un gran cinghiar veder che valicava.

E poi appresso gli parve vedere
sotto a' suoi pié Criseida, alla quale
col grifo il cor traeva, ed al parere
di lui, Criseida di cosí gran male
non si curava, ma quasi piacere
prendea di ció che facea l'animale;
il che a lui sí forte era in dispetto,
che questo ruppe il sonno deboletto.

In tears Troilo summons Pandaro, his confidant and friend, to tell him of the dream, which Troilo has fully understood from the beginning: "This boar which I saw is Diomede, since his grandfather slew the boar of Calydon, if we can believe our ancestors, and ever afterward his descendants have carried the swine for a crest. Ah me, bitter and true dream!"[16] Figure 2, from a manuscript of Boccaccio's poem made in Naples, 1414,[17] shows Troilo in bed dreaming of Criseida. Lying placidly on her back, she is mounted by a boar with its snout in the air. No literal heart is shown.

From this single passage, Chaucer made a dream for Criseyde that would involve an eagle (his singular invention) in a heart-*exchange* wholly different in tone, along with a dream for Troilus, changing much that the first had left unused. Instead of the fierce animal Troilo sees charging and crashing through the woods before mounting Criseyde to root out her heart with his snout, Troilus dreams of a great boar asleep in the sun, with Criseyde lying beside him, "kyssyng [him] ay". It's a toss-up which version is the more repellent. Both undermine the courtly ethos of their poems.

Boccaccio's boar presents a genuine threat to hunters and countryside, to say nothing of the woman whose heart he tears out, though it is an experience she appears to enjoy. One recognizes in him the wild boar (*aper*) of the Bestiaries, a savage and dangerous beast. Figure 3 shows him charging a hunter's spear, tossing a dog in the air, and trampling a second hunter, who stabs him in the belly from below. It illustrates a Bestiary made in England in the 2d quarter of the 13th century, [18] whose text says of him, in part:

> The boar (*aper*) is so called from its wildness (*feritas*), substituting a *p* for the *f* ... The boar signifies the fierceness of the rulers of this world. Hence the Psalmist writes of the vineyard of the Lord: 'The boar out of the wood doth waste it, and the wild beast of the field doth devour it" [Psalm 80: 13] ... In the spiritual sense the boar means the devil because of its fierceness and strength. It is said to be a creature of the woods because its thoughts are wild and unruly.[19]

---

16   Ibid., Book VII, vv. 25, 27 (pp. 350-351):

> *Questo cinghiar ch'io vidi é Diomede,*
> *per ció che l'avolo uccise il cinghiaro*
> *di Calidonia, se si puó dar fede*
> *a' nostri antichi, e sempre poi portaro*
> *per sopransegna, si come si vede,*
> *i discendenti il porco.Oh me, amaro*
> *e vero sogno!* ...

17   Figure 2: New York, Pierpont Morgan Library MS M. 371, fol. 48v.
18   Figure 3: Oxford, Bodley MS 764, fol. 38v. Reproduced in color by Barber, *Bestiary*, p. 86. On this MS, see Morgan, *Early Gothic Manuscripts [II] 1250-1285*, cat. 98, pp. 53-55. The text is very full and furnished with pictures unusually elaborate in their iconography; London, British Library MS Harley 4751 is closely related.
19   Translated by Barber (1993: 87); in the Vulgate Bible, the quoted verse is numbered 79: 14. On Bestiaries, a class of book that will figure significantly in this essay, see McCulloch

Figure 3

(1962), Hassig (1995), Salisbury (1994); Berlioz, Polo de Beaulieu, and Collomb (1999). Clark and McMunn (1989) list all known Western medieval Bestiary manuscripts, and include a bibliography of Bestiary Studies since 1962, the year McCulloch's bibliography came to an end. Dupuis, Louis, et al. (1988) translates yet another English Latin Bestiary – Oxford, Bodley MS Ashmole 15ll – to add to those listed elsewhere in these notes; it has commentaries by Muratova and Poirion. Rowland has an essay on "The Art of Memory and the Bestiary" in Clark and McMunn (1980), and Carruthers too has speculated on its possible mnemonic function: see her *Book of Memory*, pp. 125-129.

The boar in Troilus's dream is surely meant to evoke some of this danger and wildness – that is why he's called a boar – but within the dream his physical threat is potential merely.[20] He is instead sensual, gross and, in his sleep, unwary – a condition more characteristic of the domesticated pig (*porcus*) of the Bestiaries than to its cousin the wild boar. Bartholomew the Englishman, in his great ency-clopedia *On the Nature of Things* (*De proprietatibus rerum*, c. 1230), can describe for us the pig's nature, here in his chapter on swine as Englished by John Trevisa at the end of the 14th century:

> A swyn hatte *porcus* as it were *sporcus* 'vile and defouled', as Isidorus seith *libro xii°*. And froteth and walweth in drytte and in fenne and dyveth in slyme and bawdeth him-self therwith and resteth in stynkyng place ... and therefore swyn ben accompted foule and unhoneste ... some swine ben tame and some wilde ... Tame swine ... grontyn in goynge and in liggynge and in slepynge and nameliche if they be right fatte. And swyn slepen faster in May than in other tyme of the yere.[21]

The emphasis is on filth, sensuality and sleep, in contrast to the fierceness and cruelty Bartholomew notes as characterisic of *aper*, the wild boar:

> he reseth ful spitously ayeins the point of a spere of the hontere ... And hath in his mouthe tweye crokede tuskes stronge and scharpe, and breketh and rendeth therewith cruelliche that him withstondeth ... the feeld swyn loveth wel rootes and wroteth and diggeth the erthe, and wroteth up rootes and kerveth hem with his tuskes ... And whanne that the bore is wroth he freteth and fometh at the mouth; and so he doth whan he gen-dreth with his wyf ... Also boores beth scharpe and most feerse whanne they beeth in loue ... .[22]

In medieval iconography the boar most often symbolizes wrath, and the pig lech-ery, though sometimes the boar stood in for the two together.[23] Chaucer invokes

---

20 Rowland (1971: 80) thought to wonder "why Chaucer should transfer to the eagle the active qualities of the boar and make the boar passive, slumbering through the kisses of the faithless lady". Her answer turns on differences between the two suitors, and is helpful, as far as it goes: "The eagle exchanging hearts suggests the sincere wooer, a sleeping boar a gross, indif-ferent one".

21 Trevisa, *On the Properties of Things* II, Book 18, Chap. 87, p. 1237; the author notes that all swine of the male gender, wild or tame, are commonly called "boars", a usage that may have contributed to the conflation of pig and boar noted above.

22 Ibid., II, Book 18, chap. 7, pp. 1117-1120; I quote from pp. 1118-1119. See Rowland (1971: 74-86) for a learned study of the boar, both wild and domestic, in literature and art; her *Ani-mals with Human Faces* (1973: 37-43) provides further information.

23 Rowland (1971: 77-78) surveys its symbolic relation to lechery. Marjodoc's dream of Tris-tan's adulterous love for Isolde in the *Tristan* of Gottfried von Strassburg offers a striking ex-ample: "the Steward saw in his dream as he slept a boar, fearsome and dreadful, that ran out from the forest. Up to the King's court he came, foaming at the mouth and whetting his tusks,

both in creating a dream-image to stand for Diomede as warrior and lover, perhaps taking his cue from Boccaccio, who merged the wild boar (*"gran cinghiar"*) of the dream with the pig (*"il porco"*) on the Calydonian heraldic crest, the latter being the sign that unlocks the dream's true meaning. But in Troilus's dream, we never see the wildness or terror of the boar. Diomede's nature is represented as sensual and complacent.

Just as Troilus was haunted by the fact his dream involved a boar – a creature he says was shown him "in figure" – so I think we are meant to wonder about Criseyde's dream, why it should involve an eagle. The choice, I repeat, was entirely Chaucer's own. One reason, of course, is that the eagle was thought of as royal – king of all birds / *rei de oisel*[24] – and Troilus is King Priam's son. To dream of Troilus in these terms is to acknowledge his high birth and to keep the dream courtly, even heraldic, in its register.[25] Perhaps that is all that needs to be said.

But Chaucer knew other lore about eagles, which I suggest is relevant here. In the *Parlement of Foules*, for instance, after noting their royal status, he calls attention to an even rarer quality, the fact they can gaze at the sun without flinching:

> There myghte men the royal egle fynde   [330-31]
> That with his sharpe lok perseth the sonne ...

This belief, widely promulgated in bestiaries and encyclopedias, was confirmed even by Albert the Great, whose importance as a naturalist stems in part from his willingness to test traditional claims against personal observation. In his *De animalibus* (c. 1258-62), he writes of the bird: "Soaring at great heights, it is able to gaze directly at the sun's disk, so great is its power of vision".[26] Bartholomew's

---

and charging everything in his path. And now a great crowd of courtiers ran up. Many knights leapt hither and thither round the boar, yet none of them dared face him. Thus he plunged grunting through the Palace. Arriving at Mark's chamber he broke in through the doors, tossed the King's appointed bed in all directions, and fouled the royal linen with his foam". (Gottfried, trans. Hatto [1960], pp. 219-220.)

24   A commonplace. The Anglo-Norman version is from the Bestiaire of Philippe de Thaon, quoted by Baugh (1963), p. 67 n331. In *The Parlement of Foules* the "tersel egle . . .the foul royal" [393] is followed in the wooing order by two other tersels of slightly lower degree, all seeking a certain "formel egle", the most gentle and virtuous of all Nature's birds, as their mate. [393-394, 415, 449-450].

25   Albert the Great in his *De animalibus*, composed between 1258 and 1262, subjects the tradition to closer scrutiny: "While the golden eagle is called the king of birds, it earns this title not because of any real governance over other birds, but because of the tyrannical violence of its actions; for it dominates all birds by oppressing and devouring them". [Translated in Albert the Great, *Man and the Beasts*, p. 195]. Rowland (1978: 51-57) provides an indispensable guide to eagle lore and symbolism.

26   Albert the Great, *Man and the Beasts*, p. 191.

encyclopedia, too, affirmed the bird's wondrous ability to behold "the sonne in roundenes of his cercle withouten any blenchinge of yyen".[27]

This unparalleled strength of vision, the Bestiary tells us, provided the eagle a sure means of testing the legitimacy of his offspring:

> It is also said of the eagle that it tests its young by putting them into the sun's rays while it holds them in its claws in mid-air. In this way the young eagle which looks fearlessly at the sun without harming its eyesight proves that it is the true offspring of its race. If it looks away, however, it is at once dropped, because it is a creature unworthy of so great a father ... [28]

Figure 4, illustrating a Bestiary made in the southeast of England, c. 1230,[29] shows the test underway. The eagle with two of his offspring gaze steadfastly at the sun as a third is cast away. T.H. White, in a note to his translation of a Bestiary, suggests these beliefs concerning the eagle may have been based on observation: "the upward glance toward the sun has been noticed by all falconers or austringers, as their captive, cocking his head on one side, gazes upward without a blink, generally at some other raptor ...".[30]

Being "eagle-eyed" implied other powers as well, more readily confirmed by ordinary observation:

> Its sight is so sharp that it can glide over the sea, beyond the ken of human eyes; from so great a height it can see the fish swimming in the sea. It will plunge down like a thunderbolt and seize its prey, and bring it ashore.[31]

From details such as these – the eagle's ability to see from great heights, its unflinching gaze, and its astonishing swiftness of its flight, ascending or descending

---

27 Trevisa, *On the Properties of Things* I (Book XII, chap. ii), p. 603.

28 Barber (1993: 119), translating Bodley 764; cf. White (1954: 107), translating Cambridge Univ. Library MS 11.4.26.

29 Figure 4: London, British Library MS. Royal 12. F. XIII, fol. 49. On this MS, see Morgan, *Early Gothic Manuscripts [I] 1190-1250*, cat. 64, p. 111. Another Bestiary shows the test taking place on a boat at sea, as an eagle and his two true offspring look directly the sun, disregarding the one being pushed overboard for having looked away. They are published in color by Payne, *Medieval Beasts*, pp. 61, 63. Morgan, *Early Gothic Manuscripts [II]*, fig. 159, publishes a page whose main subject (the Baptism of Christ by Christian bishops and clerks, with an angel and a devil pushing Jews out of the scene) is echoed by a smaller picture showing eagles gazing steadfastly at the sun, while another bird (the discredited eagle?) stares at the earth beneath its feet. It illustrates Guillaume le Clerc's Anglo-Norman verse Bestiary. See Cat. # 129, pp. 110-112.

30 White (1954: 107 n1).

31 Barber (1993: 118-119); cf. White (1954: 105).

Figure 4

– further claims were confidently made.[32] "It is a true fact," the Bestiary continues, "that when the eagle grows old and his wings become heavy and his eyes become darkened with a mist, then he goes in search of a fountain, and, over against it, he flies up to the height of heaven, even unto the circle of the sun; and there he singes his wings and at the same time evaporates the fog of his eyes, in a ray of the sun. Then at length, taking a header down into the fountain, he dips himself three times in it, and instantly he is renewed with a great vigor of plumage and splendour of vision".[33] Figure 5, from the same Bestiary as Figure 3 (MS Bodley 764), made in England in the second quarter of the 13th century, was probably meant to illustrate all three of these beliefs, showing us, on the left, the eagle as a remarkable catcher of fish; at the upper right, its recourse to the sun, where it purges its sight and singes its wings; and just below, its descent into rejuvenating waters.[34] (In the service of pictorial economy, the sea may represent not only the domain of fish, but the baptismal fountain water alluded to in the text.)[35] The picture begs to be seen in color, for the gold that blazes on the manuscript

---

32   Book II of the *Hous of Fame* can instruct us in other things Chaucer knew about eagles. In his dream, an eagle whose gold feathers shine so brightly it seems as though the heavens had obtained another sun, descends like a thunderbolt, seizes him in his claws, and carries him off to show him at first hand everything he might wish to know about the cosmos, on his way to the court of Fame (Book III). The eagle appears to arrive as an emissary of Truth, to save the dreamer from fantasy and illusion [493-93]. A great deal of scholarly attention has been devoted to this eagle, in contrast to the eagle of Criseyde's dream. See Koonce (1966: 126-177) for a learned account of exegetical tradition, useful whether or not one agrees with his interpretation of the poem; and Steadman, "Chaucer's Eagle: A Contemplative Symbol", for a foundational study, both philosophical and theological.

33   White (1954: 105); cf. Barber (1993: 119). Rowland (1978: 53) reproduces a two-tier illustration in which (above) an eagle is first shown flying across the sea with a fish in his claws, and then (again) rising upward toward the sun, while (below) he plunges into a well or fount of water to complete his rejuvenation. White (1954: 107 n1) notes that the 'mist' on the eyes "probably refers to the nictitating membrane" – "a transparent third eyelid hinged at the inner side or lower lid of the eye of various animals, serving to keep the eye clean and moist" (*Webster's New World Dictionary*, 2d College Edition).

34   Figure 5: Oxford, MS Bodley 764, fol. 57v. Barber, p. 118, reproduces it in splendid color. Closely related is the illustration from London, Brit. Lib. MS Harley 4751, fol. 35v, reproduced in color by Payne (1981: 62).

35   White (1954) illustrates his translation with line drawings based on illustrations in his principal MS. That shown on p. 106, arranged like the pictures under discussion here, shows the eagle descending into an abstract design almost certainly meant to represent the fountain, though no water is shown. Yapp (1982), color plate 18, p. 114-115, depicts the events separately, with water for the fish and water for the fountain into which he descends. This picture is very literal in showing the eagle singeing his wings; they are overlapped by the red rays of a burnished gold sun. The iconography of the Bestiary was settled early, and displays a remarkable consistency throughout the thirteenth century, when most of the manuscripts were made.

page, undiminished after all these centuries, announces in its own way the intimate relation a Bestiary eagle bears to the sun.

Figure 5

Chaucer too, in *Troilus and Criseyde*, will bring together images of the eagle and the sun. Not only does he ask us to think of Troilus as an eagle/lover, one who will (in the end) be granted an eagle's capacity for vision, he asks us to imagine Diomede as a boar who *sleeps* in the sun – "ageyne the bryghte sonnes hete" – even as he is being loved by Criseyde. This attention to the sun is again entirely Chaucer's own, something not present in Boccaccio's original. I think of it as another primal signifier – like the boar and the eagle, something in need of interpretation – as Pandarus's careful attention to it suggests:

> Hire fader, which that old is and ek hoor,   [V. 1284]
> Ayeyn the sonne lith, o point to dye ...

But Pandarus hasn't a clue. The key to interpreting the sun lies elsewhere, in the song in Book II that leads directly/indirectly to Criseyde's dream.

As Criseyde is quick to note, Antigone sings in first-person of the supreme happiness that can be found in love – "...thanked be ye, lord, for that I love! / This is the righte lif that I am inne". Whoever says otherwise, disparaging love as bondage or sin, is declared envious or foolish or impotent, proving only their incapacity to understand or sustain so great a thing:

> "What is the sonne wers, of kynde right,   [II, 862]
> Though that a man, for feeblesse of his yën,
> May nought endure on it to see for bright?
> Or love the wers, though wrecches on it crien?"

Shall we hold the sun at fault, she asks, because we cannot look at it directly? Shall we think the worse of love because wretches cry out against it? Through these rhetorical questions equating two great powers, Chaucer prepares us for the eagle of Criseyde's dream, an eagle who will prove its nature by gazing at the sun, while preparing also for a boar who will sleep against its light and heat.

Antigone's song, like Criseyde's dream, is something Chaucer added to *Il Filostrato*, an invention particularly his own. Its beauty is peerless, even as it rehearses many themes conventional in the love poetry of the time. Indeed, a fair number of lines are traceable (translated or half-remembered) to love lyrics by his French contemporary, Guillaume de Machaut. [36] But no one, so far as I know, has found a source for Antigone's equation of romantic love and the sun. For that Macrobius's influential *Commentary on the Dream of Scipio*, written at the end of

---

36   See Wimsatt (1977), p. 207, summarizing his earlier essay (1976), whose concluding note, p. 293 n32, omits the verses under examination here (II, 862-65) from those he finds paralleled in Machaut.

the fourth or early fifth century, will prove more suggestive by far. (It is the book Chaucer reads and summarizes at the beginning of *The Parlement of Foules*, lines 29-84.) Macrobius explains that when philosophers aspire to talk about "the Highest and Supreme of all the gods" – that which the Greeks called the Good (*tagathon*) and the First Cause (*proton aition*) – or when they wish to treat of the Mind or Intellect (*nous*), which holds "the original concepts of things" otherwise called Ideas (*ideai*) – they consciously reject all fables and fictions. To discuss things which "not only pass the bounds of speech, but those of human comprehension", they resort instead to similes and analogies:

> That is why Plato, when he was moved to speak about the Good, did not dare to tell what it was, knowing only this about it, that it was impossible for the human mind to grasp what it was. In truth, of visible objects he found the sun most like it, and by using this as an illustration opened the way for his discourse to approach what was otherwise incomprehensible.[37]

Cicero's *Dream of Scipio* – on whose text Macrobius erects his encyclopedic commentary – had used the same comparison in commenting on our inability to hear the music of the spheres:

> the sound coming from the heavenly spheres revolving at very swift speeds is of course so great that human ears cannot catch it; you might as well try to stare directly at the sun, whose rays are much too strong for your eyes.[38]

Until its last 80 lines or so, the subject-matter of *Troilus and Criseyde* is nowhere near as grand as the Supreme Good, the First Cause, or the Divine Intellect. But if a poem can be said to have a desire – an intention so deep that it animates all the rest – then the desire of this poem is to know the truth about love. It invests in that desire so much idealism and faith, grants it such ample scale, subjects it to such extreme pressure, and demands of it so many kinds of good, that it becomes a kind of testing ground for love, in which the earthly and the transcendent, the false and the true are first mixed together and then separated out, in deeply tragic ways. From its opening verses, heavy with liturgical language, in which the poet presents himself as a priest of love and addresses us as a congregation of lovers,[39] the poem does everything it can to elevate romantic love to the stature not only of

---

37 Macrobius, *Commentary*, II.14-15, trans. Stahl (1952: 85-86). Philosophers approve the use of fabulous narratives only "when speaking about the Soul, or about spirits having dominion in the lower and upper air, or about gods in general" (p. 85).

38 Chap. V of Cicero's text, printed in Macrobius, *Commentary*, p. 74; for Macrobius's explanation of this, IV.14, see pp. 199-200.

39 I have written about this aspect of the poem in my Presidential Address to the New Chaucer Society, "God-Denying Fools and the Medieval 'Religion of Love'"; Kolve (1997).

religion but of those great philosophical subjects named by Macrobius – despite his warning that they cannot be addressed directly and should not be approached through invented fictions (fable). From within its fiction the poem does indeed end badly. But in its final stanzas, with *Il Filostrato* overwritten by Dante's *Commedia*, Chaucer shows how the failure of romantic love, seen clearly, may at least give on to a view of something grander and more grounded in the real. First Troilus as a pagan, and then Chaucer as a Christian, will show us what it is like to look at the sun.

Before we reach those final moments, let me sketch briefly some of the ways the poem attempts to bring erotic love and the highest good together, as though they were, or could become, one; and how it does so in terms of vision, both metaphoric and literal, acute or grossly deceived. In its desire to uncover the full truth about love – an intention far outstripping Boccaccio's more personal and self-limiting poem – the *Troilus* places a premium upon the act of seeing, beginning with what feminist critics, chiefly with reference to film, have lately taught us to call "the gaze". [40]

We first meet Troilus in a temple at a feast honoring the Palladion, a statue whose sacred power guarantees the security and continuance of Troy. Callow and immature, he strolls about the temple with a group of young knights:

> Byholding ay the ladies of the town,   [I, 186]
> Now here, now there; for no devocioun
> Hadde he to non, to reven hym his reste ...

Inexperienced in love, he sees only its power to make fools of those caught in its snare – a vision and a judgment he will reaffirm more some 8000 lines later, near the poem's end. But first the poem must transform him into an instrument capable of testing love's limits; and for that, as with Criseyde later, nothing less than conversion will do. She will need to gaze on him twice, from her window, for the process even to begin: the first time without his knowledge, as he returns victorious from battle [II, 610-651], and again later, as he rides by in a dumbshow stage-managed by Pandarus [II, 1009-1022, 1247-1274]. (In this poem the erotic "gaze" is not inevitably gendered

---

[40] The first to have written specifically about "the male gaze" seems to have been Laura Mulvey in 1975; for that reference, and for materials more germane to this essay, see Jochens (1991: 3-29, and n1). See also Holley (1986), and especially Stanbury (1991), a subtle and rewarding essay, though limited to the way the two lovers first see each other. Hahn (2000) and Camille (2000) theorize the gaze historically. Bowers (1980) reads Criseyde's first sight of Troilus, riding on a horse, iconographically, against an earlier stanza comparing Troilus to blind "Bayard", a frisky horse who forgets he is one. Criseyde, Bowers also notes, *first* begins to fall in love by hearing Pandarus's reports of Troilus, rather than by seeing him. *Pace* Andreas Capellanus, love can enter through the ear.

male.) But Troilus is converted the instant he lays eyes on her – a young woman, dressed in widow's black, whose beauty and bright glances gladden all the crowd.

> Nas nevere yet seyn thyng to ben preysed deere,   [I, 174]
> Nor under cloude blak so bright a sterre.

This image, comparing Criseyde to a star covered by black clouds, is reprised near the end of the poem in a despairing song, the so-called *Canticus Troili* of Book V [638 ff], where he addresses her as a "sterre, of which I lost have al the light", and sees himself as a shipman sailing in darkness toward his death. But throughout the first three books of the poem Criseyde is more accurately likened to the sun, in its power to illumine, to quicken and excite. Her "sonnyssh" hair [IV. 736, 816] betokens the role she plays in the "hertes day" of her lover [V, 1405], just as the consummation of their love at the centre of the poem, 'whan lightles is the world' [III. 550] on a night of 'smoky reyn' [III. 628)], provides on its own all the light they need. At its end, Criseyde swears that the sun will fall from its sphere, and eagles will mate with doves, before she will ever prove unfaithful in love [III. 1495].[41]

Troilus, of course, is the eagle of her dream, while she for him embodies the power and mystery of love, equated with the sun in Antigone's song. And Chaucer, for a time, will sustain that symbolic equation with the full force of his poetry, steadily increasing the eagle's acuity of sight, allowing him to peer deeper into the real nature of things. Near the end of Book III, Troilus expresses in song the full dignity of their desire, the place of their love in the full structure of the universe. The hymn to love he sings there is, in fact, the third such hymn in Book III. The first, a proeme in seven stanzas spoken by the poet, celebrates the power and benevolence of Venus, as goddess and planet, with the planet chiefly in mind: "O blissful light", it begins, "of which the bemes clere / Adorneth al the thridde heven faire!" [III, 1] Though Venus's light may pale in comparison to the sun, its astrological influence is universal: "In hevene and helle, in erthe and salte see / Is felt thi myght, if that I wel descerne" [III, 8]. Forging universal law out of attraction and desire, she holds together not only the cosmos, but kingdoms and households and the union of true friends. The second hymn to love, three stanzas long, is spoken by Troilus when he first holds Criseyde in his arms, caressing her every limb and finding his "hevene" there [III, 1251]. In that song he praises Venus as goddess ("Citherea the swete") as well as planetary force ("the wel-

---

41 Windeatt (1992: 339-341) notices in the poem "a marked use of imagery of light and darkness which is not in Chaucer's source", and presents a good deal of evidence, well assessed. His book is an indispensable companion to all aspects of the poem.

willy planete!"), along with Hymen, god of marriage.[42] Goodness, harmony,
and cohesion are here derived from "benigne Love", the "holy bond of thynges", identified in the first line as "Charite" itself, a word (and virtue) central
to Christian theology. (This overlap with Christian belief is intentional, to be
set right at the end of the poem.) The third hymn [III, 1744 ff], bookends the
first, repeating and amplifying many of its claims. It is sung by Troilus to
Pandarus as part of his continual praise of Criseyde:

> And by the hond ful ofte he wolde take   [III, 1737]
> This Pandarus, and into gardyn lede,
> And swich a feste and swich a process make
> Hym of Criseyde, and of hire wommanhede,
> And of hire beaute, that withouten drede
> It was an hevene his wordes for to here;
> And thanne he wolde synge in this manere:
> 'Love, that of erthe and se hath governaunce,
> Love, that his hestes hath in hevene hye' ...,

He continues at considerable length in verses that deepen their original, Troilo's
hymn to love in the *Il Filostrato*, also (oddly enough) sung to Pandaro.[43] In Chaucer's version, Love has brought Troilus to "so heigh a place / That thilke boundes
may no blisse pace" [III, 1271], and he tells us what the view is like from there.
The erotic "gaze" has become philosophical, and what Troilus sees in these moments is too deeply derived from Boethius's *Consolation of Philosophy* ever to be
wholly repudiated by the poet. In Book III Troilus's experience of love ends in
something like mystical contemplation – we might think of it as the first "soul
journey" in the poem – and from its great height he sees many things truly.

But the light that is cast there comes not from the sun but from Venus, planet
and goddess, whose light we can gaze on without danger. And at the center of
what he thinks he sees is a fatal confusion of categories. In his eyes, Criseyde is
love, Criseyde is the sun. But Criseyde is also human and imperfect; Criseyde is
Criseyde.

When Troilus, in his ecstasy, praises love as a principle of order, he offers as
proof the way the sun each day brings forth the dawn – "his rosy day" – just as
every night the moon holds romantic lordship over night: "Al this doth Love, ay
heried be his myghtes!" [III, 1755-1757] But within the "hevene blisse" of a se-

---

42 Hymen otherwise counts for little, though as Kelly (1974) has shown, much of Book III reads
    like a Christian marriage ceremony, and the lovers, having pledged their troth in the presence
    of a witness, could (in medieval terms at least) consider themselves legally bound in a clan-
    destine marriage.
43 Boccaccio, *Il Filostrato*, Book 3, stanzas 73-89, pp. 171-179. Chaucer made use of this song
    in all three hymns noted above, amplifying the Boethian themes already present in it.

cret sexual affair, as the lovers quickly discover, the diurnal cycle, essential to all ideas of cosmic order, has no place at all. When "cruel day" breaks in upon the first night of their love, the lovers complain bitterly against night for ending too quickly, and rail against the sun for rising at all [III, 1422-70]. Criseyde calls for endless night, and Troilus curses the sun, wishing its light might be quenched forever: "We wol the nought, us nedeth no day have" [III, 1463]. Extravagant emotion of this sort is generic to the *aubade* tradition, but set against the cosmic idealism of Book III it sounds a discordant note that becomes their characteristic response, even after other nights of love:

> And day they gonnen to despise al newe,   [III, 1699]
> Callyng it traitour, envious, and worse,
> And bitterly the dayes light thei corse.

Books I through III, it has often been noted, are structurally modeled upon Dante's *Commedia*: Book I offers a lover's version of the *Inferno*; Book II, the book of hope, begins with verses literally translated from the *Purgatorio*; and Book III presents an erotic version of the *Paradiso* – but with this troubling difference. Its lovers cannot bear to look at the sun, not even as it rises on an ordinary day. Their "insight" into love requires darkness.

In the Books that follow (IV and V) their ability to "see clearly" weakens, dimmed on both sides by confusion, error and fantasy. Criseyde, in the Greek camp, regretting that she refused to run away with Troilus, blames herself for lacking one of Prudence's three eyes. She understands the past well enough, and can take the measure of the present. "But future tyme, er I was in the snare, / Koude I nat sen; that causeth now my care". [V, 744-49] Even in that, however, she is self-deceived: it is her anxiety about the future, so obsessively "foreseen", that makes her indecisive in the present. Gazing across the no-man's land standing between her and the high towers of Troy, she makes a fundamental misjudgment. She wonders whether Troilus thinks of her – remembers her – at all.

We know, of course, that he thinks of nothing else. As hope gives way to despair, he turns again to philosophy – to the very text that underlay his vision of love as the source of all order, harmony and integrity in the universe. But this time it is to put an urgent question concerning destiny and free will, and this time he gets the answer wrong. The mind has wings, Philosophy had taught Boethius, with which it can fly to the stars, join the sun in its path, ride with Saturn in his sphere. And then, when it has seen enough, it can fly "beyond the farthest sphere to mount the top of the swift heaven and share the holy light. // There the Lord of kings holds His scepter, governing the reins of the world. With sure control He drives the swift chariot ["that is to seyn, the circuler moevynge of the sonne"], the shining judge of all things". [Book IV.

Poem 1][44] But in Chaucer's Book IV, Philosophy's wings – "swifte fetheris that surmounten the heighte of the hevene" – cannot raise Troilus out of his darkness. In the course of a long and tortuous meditation [IV, 953 ff], he proves to himself that everything happens by necessity; that there is no free will.

As Criseyde's absence grows longer, what he sees, and the eyes with which he sees, grow ever more clouded and dim. He visits her palace, only to find the doors barred and the windows covered over, like a lantern whose light is quenched ("queynt is the light") [V, 543], or a shrine whose saint is missing. Increasingly he lives in the past, retelling its joys to Pandarus, and renewing his memory in places made numinous by their love: "Lo, yonder saugh ich last my lady daunce" / "And yonder have I herd ful lustyly / My dere herte laugh; and yonder pleye ...". [V, 565-575]. And on, and on. His own life comes to seem unreal to him – a fiction, he thinks, from which a book might be made [V, 585]. And often he stands at the city gate, gazing at the Greek camp and reliving the moment when she was led away. In a "fantasie" born of "malencolie" [V, 622], he becomes morbidly self-conscious, imagining himself diminished and disfigured, an object of curiosity or pity to passers-by. As evening falls on the tenth day, the day of her promised return, he stands again at the city gate, straining to catch sight of her in the dimming light – and, in one of the most painful passages in the poem, is suddenly convinced he does:

> "And Pandarus, now woltow trowen me?   [V, 1157]
> Have here my trouthe, I se hire! Yond she is!
> Heve up thyn eyen, man! Maistow nat se?"

What you see, Pandarus tells him sharply, is only a field-cart.

To mistake a field-cart for one's mistress marks a low-point, somewhere between the tragic and comic, in a poem that has invested so much in the faculty of vision, the power of the gaze. Troilus's capacity for hope has blinded him – "his hope alwey hym blente" [V, 1195] – as has his increasing despair: "He kan now sen non other remedie / But for to shape hym soone for to dye". [V, 1210] It is in that condition that he dreams of Criseyde in the arms of a wild boar.

The dream-vision, for all its horror, does not fully restore his sight, not even after Cassandra's brutal interpretation. Nor do Criseyde's evasive replies to his letters, each more equivocal than the last. Something more is needed, powerful enough to clear his eyes and force him to see the truth: "men seyen that at the laste, / For any thing, men shal the soothe se" [V, 1639-1640].

---

44   Boethius, *The Consolation of Philosophy*, IV, m. 1, trans. Green (1962: 76), with an interpolated gloss from Chaucer's own translation, *The Riverside Chaucer*, p. 441.

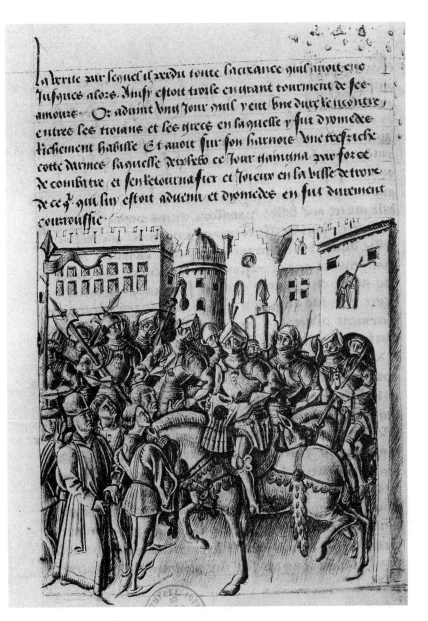

Figure 6

It comes in the form of a golden brooch – a kind of mini-sun – pinned to an heraldic coat that Deiphebus one day strips from Diomede in battle, and shows about Troy as a token of his victory. For Troilus it is a token of defeat, being the brooch she gave him on the night they first made love [III, 1370] and which he gave back to her, so that she might remember him, on the morning they were last together, just before her departure from Troy. She promised to keep it forever. Seeing it pinned to Diomede's coat-armor, Troilus knows he has lost her: "Of Diomede have ye now al this feeste!" The brooch is pictured large and resplendent in Figure 6, illustrating a French prose translation of Boccaccio's poem, made ca. 1455 or 1456, for the wife of Charles d'Orléans.[45]

This brooch – "gold and azure, / In which a ruby set was lik an herte" – serves Troilus as the sun does the Bestiary eagle: it purges his clouded vision, allowing him to see the truth. It reduces the mutual rapture experienced in Book III to little more than a dream of love, a brief episode in a history of obsession and self-deception. But it shows him, as well, that he cannot stop loving her, despite this knowledge and all this pain:

> Thorugh which I se that clene out of youre mynde   [V, 1695]
> Ye han me cast – and I ne kan nor may,
> For al this world, withinne myn herte fynde
> To unloven yow a quarter of a day!
> In corsed tyme I born was, weilaway,
> That yow, that doon me al this wo endure,
> Yet love I best of any creature!

Whether one thinks of Troilus's continuing fidelity as abject or noble – or some awful combination of the two – it is part of the mystery of love as sounded in this poem. It is both possible and terrible to love as Troilus has loved, and will go on loving. The brooch is blinding, like the sun in its full destructive power. By looking at it directly, Troilus frees himself from illusion – a good thing, no doubt. But it leaves him desirous only of death. The view comes at a price. Caring nothing for this world, he fights ferociously on the battlefield, killing many a Greek while always seeking Diomede, to kill him or be killed. But Fortune, in a final cosmic joke, will deny him even that small symmetry. In a single line of verse, "Despitously hym slough the fierse Achille". [V, 1806]

Troilus's eye of the flesh has seen as much as it can see. Rewarded for his loyalty in love, or more likely (according to Cicero's belief) for his service to the

---

45   Figure 6: Paris, Bibl. Natl. MS fr. 25528, fol. 89v. The translation is by Louis de Beauvau, sénéchal of Anjou. See Avril and Reynaud, *Les Manuscrits à peinture*, cat. # 134, p. 245, for a description of the MS. Brewer (1973: 74-91), 3d edition uniquely, publishes a generous selection of pictures from this MS, though not this one. In the *Filostrato* the brooch is simply "a brooch of gold" *'un fermaglio d'oro'* (pp. 398-399).

state,[46] Troilus's soul, released from his body, ascends the heavens, *past* the sun, to the hollowness of the eighth sphere – the sphere of the fixed stars.[47] Figure 7, illustrating Scipio's dream in a manuscript of Macrobius's *Commentary*, makes graphic the distance and liberation involved.[48]

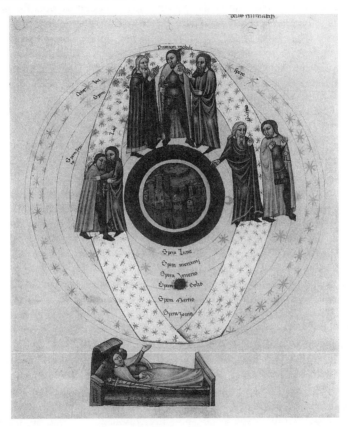

Figure 7

46 Cicero, "Dream of Scipio", Chap. II, in Macrobius, *Commentary*, p. 71: "Scipio, be persuaded of this: all those who have saved, aided, or enlarged the commonwealth have a definite place marked off in the heavens where they may enjoy a blessed existence forever".

47 Most scholars agree on counting outward, from the earth to the sphere of the fixed stars, rather than from the outermost planet (Saturn) inward, which would place Troilus in the sphere of the moon. See Windeatt (1992: 209-211) for discussion of the issue.

48 Figure 7: from Oxford, Bodley MS Can. Class lat. 257, fol. 1v, Italian, dated 1383.

At its center it shows the earth, with the warring cities of Carthage and Rome; on the left, Scipio Africanus the Younger, who will destroy Carthage, is embraced by Masinissa, King of Numidia; at the top, they are joined by Scipio Africanus the Elder, his grandfather, who once subjugated Carthage; at the right, the Scipio the Elder points to the earth; and at the bottom, Scipio in bed dreams his prophetic dream. The sun (*Solis*) is shown ablaze in the fourth sphere, counting from the center, above the spheres of the Moon, Mercury and Venus. Scipio dreams he is in the eighth sphere, here a kind of belted oval, the sphere of the fixed stars. From that place Troilus, like Scipio before him, sees the seven planets in continual motion, hears the ravishing music of the spheres, and looks down upon

> This litel spot of erthe that with the se   [V, 1815]
> Embraced is, and fully gan despise
> This wrecched world, and held al vanite
> To respect of the pleyn felicite
> That is in hevene above ...

His journey of the soul, like the flight of an aged eagle to the sun, grants him a new acuity of vision. Gazing on the brooch in Troy had cleared his eyes to the particular. Now he sees everything at its most universal, and (to our discomfort) laughs at those who mourn his death, condemning all who seek love below (now named "blynde lust") instead of raising their hearts to heaven. Everything is reduced to vanity in a world "that passeth soone as floures faire". Though the soul-journey and the backward glance are hardly a triumph or a happy ending, they do constitute a reward of sorts – a clarification if not a consolation – worthy of a pagan hero. Diomede, in contrast, "sleeps" against such knowledge even as he embraces Criseyde. The refusal to invest his heart both protects and limits him. It is not in his nature to look at the sun.

The poet finishes with Troilus's soul in two intentionally noncommittal verses:[49] "And forth he wente, shortly for to telle, / Ther as Mercurye sorted hym to dwelle" [V, 1826]. But he has not yet finished with his poem. There was uncertainty about the eternal destiny of souls born before the incarnation of Christ, and so the "hevene" Troilus experiences, possibly only briefly, is one of "pleyn felicite" (complete happiness), based upon distance and freedom from earthly cares. It is not the heaven of Christian salvation. Bestiary lore, in contrast, saw in the aging eagle's flight an image of redemption, the basic outline of which we have already noted: "When it grows old, its wings grow heavy and its eyes cloud over. Then it seeks out a fountain and flies up into the atmosphere of the sun; there its wings catch fire and the darkness of its eyes is burnt away in the sun's rays. It falls into the fountain and dives under water three times: at once its wings are restored to

---

49   Taylor (1989: 189-194) examines this with care.

their full strength and its eyes to their former brightness". But this passage from the Bestiary carries with it further teaching, unavailable within the world of Troy: "So you, O man, whose clothes are old and the eyes of whose heart are darkened, should seek out the spiritual fountain of the Lord, and lift the eyes of your mind to God, who is the fount of justice; and then you will renew your youth like the eagle".[50] It speaks of a redemption ready all along, just outside the boundaries of the Troilus story.

Having now formally dismissed Troilus from the poem – "Swich fyn hath, lo, this Troilus for love!" [V, 1828] – with or without sympathy, it is hard to tell – Chaucer advises his audience to look up and see an even greater mystery at the heart of love: the love of the god who made us, who for the sake of love redeemed us, and who, unlike earthly lovers, will never betray us.

> For he nyl falsen no wight, dar I seye   [V, 1845]
> That wol his herte al holly on hym leye.
> And syn he best to love is, and most meke,
> What nedeth feynede loves for to seke?

A paradigm shift has been made, and the eagle whose "sharpe lok perseth the sonne" [*PF* 331] is crucial to this strategy, a poetic plan in which Dante's great poem also plays a part. The *Paradiso* opens in a blaze of noon – at the Spring Equinox, with the sun directly over the equator – as Dante, still in the Earthly Paradise, discovers that Beatrice has turned about and raised her eyes to the sun: "no eagle ever / could stare so fixed and straight into such light". [*Par.* I.46-48][51] Inspired to imitate her gaze, he too stares "straight at the sun as no man could", if only briefly:

> I could not look for long, but my eyes saw   [*Par.* 1.58]
> the sun enclosed in blazing sparks of light
> like molten iron as it pours from the fire.

Though she is able to gaze at the sun continually, he is content to gaze on her – until he is drawn heavenward through the sphere of fire, whether in body or soul he is not sure, with Beatrice at his side. Figure 8, from a manuscript made c. 1445

---

50   Barber (1993: 119). The Greek *Physiologus* (Curley, trans.), dating back to the fourth century, had already drawn this allegorical lesson from a number of Scriptural texts: see pp. 12-13. The first of them proved especially important: "Your youth will be renewed like the eagle's" [Psalm 102: 5; 103: 5 in later Bibles], and is voiced in the last sentence of the Bestiary passage above.

51   I quote Dante in the translation by Mark Musa (1984), by permission of Indiana University Press. Because of space limitations, and the ready availability of the Italian text to anyone who might want to consult it, I do not print the original here.

Figure 8

for the King of Naples and illustrated by Giovanni di Paolo, shows Dante and Beatrice leaving the heaven of Venus and moving upwards toward the heaven of the sun.[52] Their further journey, across many cantos, will reveal far more than the soul journey that is awarded Troilus. A Trojan prince, living before the time of Christ, could not (in medieval belief) expect as much. But when Troilus looks down on the earth from the sphere of the fixed stars, it is the Italian poem that directs his gaze and purpose, in imitation of the way Beatrice had directed Dante's gaze before. From that same eighth sphere, in preparation for "the final blessed-ness", she had ordered Dante to look down at the vast universe beneath his feet, as a way of keeping his eyes unclouded and his vision keen:

> My vision traveled back through all the spheres,   [*Par.* 22.133]
>> through seven heavens, and then I saw our globe;
>> it made me smile, it looked so paltry there.
> I hold that mind as best that holds our world
>> for least, and I consider truly wise
>> the man who turns his thoughts to other things ...

> All seven [planets] at one time were visible: [*Par.* 22.148]
>> I saw how vast they were, how swift they spun,
>> and all the distances between the spheres;
> as for the puny threshing-ground that drives
>> us mad – I, turning with the timeless Twins,
>> saw all of it, from hilltops to its shores.
> Then, to the eyes of beauty my eyes turned.

As the canto closes, Dante turns his eyes back to Beatrice and to all the revela-tions to come, culminating (in Canto XXXIII) in a sublime vision of light, ema-nating from the Love that *moves* the sun and the other stars: *l'amor che move il sole e l'altre stele.*

The very last stanza of Chaucer's poem, translated directly from Dante's *Paradiso*, addresses the Trinity in language comparably sublime – at once veiling and making manifest the power and mystery of the Christian God:

---

52   Figure 8: London, Brit. Lib. MS. Yates Thompson 36, fol. 146. Illustrating Canto X, it is reproduced in color by Pope-Hennessy (1993: 103), who describes it so: "The Sun is a wheel of green, white and gold circles, from which golden rays descend over a panorama of hills and castellated farms" (ibid.: 102). On fol. 179, illustrating Canto XXVIII (Pope-Hennessy 1993: 165) Dante is shown looking directly at the light of God, a huge bright sphere, with a mysterious head at its center, possibly Boreas, more likely Christ. For other illustrations of the Heaven of the Sun, see Brieger, Meiss and Singleton (1969 vol. II: 454-465) and com-mentary in vol. I, 190-192; and Taylor and Finley (1997: 204-211, 241), who suggest Christ instead of Boreas, and are probably right.

Thow oon, and two, and thre, eterne on lyve,   [V. 1863]
   That regnest ay in thre, and two, and oon,
   Uncircumscript, and al maist circumscrive ...

Quell' uno e due e tre che sempre vive   [XIV, 28-30]
e regna sempre in tre e 'n due e 'n uno,
non circunscritto, e tutto circunscrive ...

Language of this kind shields us from the thing it signifies, gesturing toward
something beyond our power to see or name directly. But two stanzas a few lines
earlier, which begin by addressing the audience as "O yonge, fresshe folks, he or
she", are more characteristic of Chaucer's poem [V, 1835 ff]. They too evoke
God, but in the person of the Son, as the culmination of the poem's continuing
quest to understand the full mystery of love. The second of those stanzas discover
its highest manifestation in the death and resurrection of Christ, who "upon a
crois, oure soules for to beye, / First starf, and roos, and sit in hevene above" [V,
1843]. The mystery of love – the poem's great subject – is here absorbed into the
mystery of God, but as mediated by Christ's flesh and adjusted to the weakness of
our human vision. The false heaven celebrated in Book III is replaced by the
promise of a paradise more true, and it invites the reader/listener to see with
greater clarity than has been allowed (from within the poem) before.

The view from the eighth sphere is the longest view in the poem. But it is not
the most important. It is from *this* world that Chaucer bids us "cast up" the "visage of our hearts" to see the Son on the cross. And it is in this world that charity
emerges as the highest kind of human love. In this world at least, Troilus knows
that he cannot stop loving Criseyde, even after she has betrayed him. And Chaucer, from out of the same human condition, cannot bring himself to condemn her
either: "Men seyn – I not – that she yaf him hire herte" [V, 1050]. (In Chaucer's
English "I not" – a contraction of "I ne wot" – means simply "I do not know".)
Though in the end he will abandon her to what the books say is her story, he
knows that in the chaff rising from the threshing ground not everything can be
seen or known clearly, least of all the intentions of the human heart. Unlike Dante,
who judges with something like the eye of God, Chaucer, in the soul journey he
grants to Troilus and in his reluctance to judge Criseyde, enacts a form of Christian charity – that of a poet toward the characters of his poem. And that is perhaps
exemplary in its own right. John Wycliffe, for instance, compared the works of
charity to the strong wings of an eagle, capable of carrying us to heaven where we
shall look on a sun that "nevere schal have settynge".[53] The link between "sun"

---

53   From Wycliffe's commentary on the eagle in the Canticle of Moses, Deut. 32: 10-12, quoted
     by Koonce (1966: 131).

and "Son", unstated here but commonplace in English religious writing of the time, may furnish the deepest logic for the way Chaucer ended his poem.

Thinking about the poem in these terms reveals a structural unity that brings it closer to the *Commedia* than has perhaps been noticed before: the concluding stanzas, including the soul journey and the turn to Christ, are not as some have claimed a pious afterthought, a conventional literary reflex, or (as one distinguished critic from the '50's suggested, only half in jest) the equivalent of a poetic nervous breakdown. They are made necessary not just by the lovers' "liturgy" that opens Book I, but by Antigone's song, the dream of the eagle, and the dream of the boar, all of which Chaucer invented or made significantly his own. Their resolution, outside the Trojan story, owes much to Dante's *Commedia*, and to see the Palinode as part of the poem's trajectory from the very beginning is to see the poem whole. But the differences between the two are equally important. Where Dante ends his poem at the greatest possible distance from earth, contemplating a light much greater than the sun, Chaucer returns us from the eighth sphere to the light of ordinary day, a light in which we can look about without presumption or danger. [54] The *Troilus* ends in devotion rather than ecstatic vision, praying to Jesus and his mother out of our need for mercy. Its last word is "Amen".

For those of us not Christian, the truth-component of the Palinode – these verses invoking the redemptive love of Christ – must seem as fictive, as invented, as anything that goes before. But it is an invention (if I may) of a wholly different kind, bearing the richness and authority of an entire civilization, and it contributes something very important to the poem. I do not think Chaucer meant it to wholly overshadow all that has gone before. Proportion alone can tell us that; the poem has not been unwritten. Its interest in character and contingency, in lyric grace and urbane sophistication, along with its rich representation of our human comedy, are to be valued still, though for lack of space such things have gone largely unmentioned in this essay. But the soul journey and the Palinode must also be given their due. They contribute a kind of *gravitas* sufficient to transform Boccaccio's youthful and far less thoughtful work into something philosophic and profound. Boccaccio's love letter in verse, obsessed with his absent lady, is transformed into an epic poem on love.

---

54 *The House of Fame*, Book II, in its dream of an eagle (modeled on Dante's dream in *Purgatorio* IX. 19ff) makes a similar point. The pedantic eagle in his eagerness to teach takes "Geffrey" *too* high. Though for a while it gives him a thrilling view of fields, plains, mountains and rivers, soon they've flown so high he sees almost nothing at all. The earth has become no more than "a prikke", and the stars shine so brightly he fears they will "shenden" (destroy) his sight (1016). His incapacity and reluctance are a delectable part of the poem's comedy, but they make a serious point: what the eagle shows him (in dream) is too much for human eyes. Books, Geffrey demurrs, do that well enough at home, more safely and more comfortably.

Because Chaucer was interested in exploring love as a whole, he could not end it small as Boccaccio does, advising young men against the vanity of young women, and urging them to chose lovers more prudent and mature: women who take delight in loving; women who keep the promises they make. Nor could he send it off, in a concluding *envoy*, as though it were a letter to his lady – a Troilus kind of letter – begging her to "return here now" (his highest hope) or else command him to die. In that poetic, only the lady's "high worth" (*alta sua virtute*) can grant salvation (*mi púo render salute*).[55]

Because Chaucer's poem has asked more of love than that, it cannot end in advice so pragmatic, emotion so narrowly personal, and metaphysical confusion so great. But neither can it end in cosmic distance, cosmic dis/illusion and disembodied laughter,[56] though near the end it moves to and through those things. For beyond them there lay ready, outside the boundaries of (imagined) Troy, the redemptive love of Christ – the one truth that fully could prevail over medieval "contempt for the world". Though for some of us it is a truth culturally contingent, Chaucer and his first audiences took it to be the very ground of the real. And so it functions beautifully here, bringing to satisfactory end a very great medieval poem.

* * * * * * *

The primary texts brought together in this essay have often been mentioned in scholarship on the poem. The Riverside Chaucer, for instance, lists several of them in a single note – including the "Dream of Scipio", Bartholomew on the weakness of our human eyes and ears, Bestiary lore on the eagle, and Beatrice's ability to look at the sun. But all that is communicated, chiefly by author and title, in a note to *The House of Fame* (1015-1017),[57] not to *Troilus and Criseyde*. Brevity is proper to an explanatory note: the Riverside editors did what they should do. But notes of this kind leave undone the sort of work I have attempted here: an unpacking of what there can seem almost too compact for use, laying it out, taking pleasure in it, and speculating on what it all means, or might once have meant.

---

55 Boccaccio, *Il Filostrato*, VIII, stanzas 29-33, and IX, 5, 7, 8, pp. 410-419.

56 Steadman (1972) remains an essential study of *Troilus* and the apotheosis tradition, including contempt of the world.

57 *Riverside Chaucer*, p. 985. Norton-Smith (1974), in a few brief sentences, connects the dream-eagle with the sun in Antigone's song (p. 206). But so far as I know (I do not claim to have read everything ever written about the poem) he alone has done so. He takes the idea no further, being chiefly concerned to derive the five-book structure of the poem from the five acts of classical drama, as it was read in the schools: Plautus, Terence and especially the tragedies of Seneca, along with medieval glosses upon those texts.

The source of this essay is not that note on *The House of Fame*, nor the several that supplement it in annotations to the *Troilus* proper. It grows instead out of reading with students this poem and these related texts almost yearly for nearly forty years – the last fifteen of them at UCLA as a colleague of Andy Kelly. I offer him this essay in tribute to those years, in friendship and with high regard.

References

Albert the Great / Albertus Magnus
>   1987   *Man and the Beasts: De animalibus (Books 22-26)*, trans. James J. Scanlan. Binghamton, NY: Medieval & Renaissance Texts & Studies (vol. 47).

Avril, François – Nicole Reynaud
>   1993   *Les manuscrits à peintures en France: 1440-1520*. Paris: Flammarion: Bibliothèque nationale.

Barber, Richard
>   1993   *Bestiary: Being an English Version of the Bodleian Library, Oxford M.S. [sic] Bodley 764*. Woodbridge: The Boydell Press.

Bartholomaeus Anglicus / Bartholomew the Englishman: see Trevisa, *On the Properties of Things*.

Baugh, Albert C. (ed.)
>   1963   *Chaucer's Major Poetry*. New York: Appleton-Century Crofts.

Benson, Larry D. (ed.)
>   1987   *The Riverside Chaucer*. Third edition. Boston: Houghton Mifflin.

Berlioz, Jacques – Marie Anne Polo de Beaulieu – Pascal Collomb
>   1999   *L'animal exemplaire au Moyen Âge (V^e – XVe siècle)*. Rennes: Press Universitaires de Rennes.

Boccaccio, Giovanni
>   1986   *Il Filostrato*, ed. Vincenzo Pernicone, trans. Robert P. apRoberts and Anna Bruni Seldis. Garland Library of Medieval Literature, Series A, vol. 53. New York: Garland.

Boethius
>   1962   *The Consolation of Philosophy*, trans. Richard Green. The Library of Liberal Arts. Indianapolis: Bobbs-Merrill.

Borthwick, Sister Mary Charlotte, F.C.S.P.
>   1961   "Antigone's Song as 'Mirour' in Chaucer's 'Troilus and Criseyde'", *MLQ* 22: 227-235.

Bowers, John M.
>   1980   "How Criseyde Falls in Love" in: N.B. Smith and J.T. Snow (eds.), *The Expansion and Transformations of Courtly Literature*, pp. 141-155. Athens: University of Georgia Press.

Brewer, D.S.
   1973   *Chaucer: Third Edition, Extensively revised and with additional material.*
             London: Longman.
Brieger, Peter – Millard Meiss – Charles S. Singleton
   1969   *Illuminated Manuscripts of the Divine Comedy.* Bollingen Series 81.
             Princeton, N.J.: Princeton University Press, 2 vols.
Camargo, Martin
   1983   "Rhetoric", in: David L. Wagner, (ed.), *The Seven Liberal Arts in the
             Middle Ages*, pp. 96-124. Bloomington: Indiana University Press.
Camille, Michael
   1998   *The Medieval Art of Love: Objects and Subjects of Desire.* New York:
             Harry N. Abrams.
   2000   "Before the Gaze: The Internal Senses and Late Medieval Practices of
             Seeing", in: R. Nelson (ed.), *Visuality Before and Beyond the Renais-
             sance: Seeing as Others Saw*, pp. 197-223. Cambridge: Cambridge Uni-
             versity Press.
Carruthers, Mary J.
   1990   *The Book of Memory: A Study of Memory in Medieval Culture.* Cam-
             bridge Studies in Medieval Literature 10. Cambridge: Cambridge Univer-
             sity Press.
   1998   *The Craft of Thought: Meditation, rhetoric, and the making of images,
             400-1200.* Cambridge Studies in Medieval Literature 34. Cambridge:
             Cambridge University Press.
[Cicero]
   1954   *Ad C. Herennium: De ratione dicendi (Rhetorica ad Herennium)*, trans.
             Harry Caplan. Loeb Classical Library, vol. 1 of 28. Cambridge, USA:
             Harvard University Press.
Clark, Willene B. – Meradith T. McMunn (eds.)
   1989   *Beasts and Birds of the Middle Ages: The Bestiary and Its Legacy.* Phila-
             delphia: University of Pennsylvania Press.
Curley, Michael J. (trans.)
   1979   *Physiologus.* Austin: University of Texas Press.
Dante Alighieri
   1984   *The Divine Comedy: Volume III: Paradise*, trans. Mark Musa. Revised
             ed., 1986. Harmondsworth, England: Penguin Books.
Dupuis, Marie-France – Sylvain Louis – Xénia Muratova – Daniel Poirion
   1988   *Le Bestiaire.* Paris: Philippe Lebaud.
Gottfried von Strassburg
   1960   *Tristan ... [&] the Tristan of Thomas*, trans. A.T. Hatto. Harmondsworth,
             England: Penguin Books.
Hahn, Cynthia
   2000   "*Visio Dei*: Changes in Medieval Visuality", in: R. Nelson (ed.), *Visuality
             Before and Beyond the Renaissance: Seeing as Others Saw*, pp. 169-196.
             Cambridge: Cambridge University Press.

Hassig, Debra
    1995   *Medieval Bestiaries: Text, Image, Ideology*. Cambridge: Cambridge University Press.
Holley, Linda T.
    1986   "Medieval Optics and the Framed Narrative in Chaucer's *Troilus and Criseyde*", *Chaucer Review* 21(1): 26-44.
Howard, Donald R.
    1970   "Experience, Language, and Consciousness: *Troilus and Criseyde*, II, 596-931", in: J. Mandel and B.A. Rosenberg (ed.), *Medieval Literature and Folklore Studies: Essays in Honor of Francis Lee Utley*, pp. 173-192, 362-363. New Brunswick, N.J.: Rutgers University Press.
Jochens, Jenny
    1991   "Before the Male Gaze: The Absence of the Female Body in Old Norse", in: J.E. Salisbury, (ed.), *Sex in the Middle Ages*, pp. 3-29. New York: Garland.
Kelly, Henry Ansgar
    1975   *Love and Marriage in the Age of Chaucer*. Ithaca: Cornell University Press.
Kolve, V.A.
    1981a   "Chaucer's *Second Nun's Tale* and the Iconography of St. Cecilia", in: Donald M. Rose (ed.), *New Perspectives in Chaucer Criticism*, pp. 137-174. Norman, Oklahoma: Pilgrim Books.
    1981b   "From Cleopatra to Alceste: An Iconographic Study of *The Legend of Good Women*", in: John P. Hermann and John J. Burke, Jr. (eds.), *Signs and Symbols in Chaucer's Poetry*, pp. 130-178. Alabama: University of Alabama Press.
    1984   *Chaucer and the Imagery of Narrative: The First Five Canterbury Tales*. Stanford: Stanford University Press.
    1990   "Man in the Middle: Art and Religion in Chaucer's *Friar's Tale*", in: *Studies in the Age of Chaucer* 12: 5-46.
    1991   "Rocky Shores and Pleasure Gardens: the Poetic Landscape of Chaucer's *Franklin's Tale*", in: *Poetics: Theory and Practice in Medieval English Literature* (the J.A.W. Bennett Memorial Lectures, Seventh Series, ed. Piero Boitani and Anna Torti), pp. 165-195. Cambridge: D.S. Brewer.
    1993   "Chaucer's Wheel of False Religion: Theology and Obscenity in The Summoner's Tale", in: Robert Taylor et al. (eds.), *The Center and its Compass: Studies in Medieval Literature in Honor of Professor John Leyerle*, Studies in Medieval Culture 33, pp. 265-296. Kalamazoo: Western Michigan University Press.
    1997   "God-Denying Fools and the Medieval 'Religion of Love'", in: *Studies in the Age of Chaucer* 19: 3-59.
Koonce, B.G.
    1966   *Chaucer and the Tradition of Fame: Symbolism in 'The House of Fame.'* Princeton: Princeton University Press.

Macrobius
   1952   *Commentary on the Dream of Scipio*, trans. William Harris Stahl. (Re-
                cords of Civilization, Sources and Studies 48.) New York: Columbia
                University Press.
McCulloch, Florence
   1962   *Mediaeval Latin and French Bestiaries*. (University of North Carolina
                Studies in the Romance Languages and Literatures 33, rev. ed.) Chapel
                Hill: University of North Carolina Press.
Morgan, Nigel
   1982   *Early Gothic Manusripts [I] 1190-1250*. A Survey of Manuscripts Illu-
                minated in the British Isles, vol. 4 (in 2 parts). London and Oxford: Har-
                vey Miller and Oxford University Press.
   1988   *Early Gothic Manuscripts [II] 1250-1285*. [as above] London and New
                York: Harvey Miller and Oxford University Press.
Murphy, James J.
   1974   *Rhetoric in the Middle Ages: A History of Rhetorical Theory from Saint
                Augustine to the Renaissance*. Berkeley: University of California Press.
Norton-Smith, John
   1974   *Geoffrey Chaucer*. Medieval Authors (series). London: Routledge & Ke-
                gan Paul.
Payne, Ann
   1980   *Medieval Beasts*. New York: New Amsterdam Books, in association with
                the British Library.
Pope-Hennessy, John
   1993   Paradiso: The Illuminations to Dante's Divine Comedy by Giovanni di
                Paolo. New York: Random House.
Rhetorica Ad Herennium: see [Cicero] *Ad C. Hernennium*.
Rowland, Beryl
   1971   *Blind Beasts: Chaucer's Animal World*. Kent, Ohio: Kent State Univer-
                sity Press.
   1973   *Animals with Human Faces: A Guide to Animal Symbolism*. Knoxville:
                University of Tennessee Press.
   1978   *Birds with Human Souls: A Guide to Bird Symbolism*. Knoxville: Univer-
                sity of Tennessee Press.
Salisbury, Joyce E.
   1991   "Bestiality in the Middle Ages", in: J.E. Salisbury (ed.), *Sex in the Middle
                Ages: A Book of Essays*. pp. 173-186. New York: Garland.
   1994   *The Beast Within: Animals in the Middle Ages*. New York: Routledge.
Spearing, A.C.
   1972   *Criticism and Medieval Poetry* (2d edition). London: Edward Arnold.
Stanbury, Sarah
   1991   "The Lover's Gaze in *Troilus and Criseyde*", in: *Chaucer's 'Troilus and
                Criseyde': "Subgit to alle Poesye": Essays in Criticism*, ed. R.A. Shoaf.
                (Medieval and Renaissance Texts and Studies 104; Pegasus Paperbooks
                10.) Binghamton, NY: Medieval & Renaissance Texts & Studies.

Steadman, John M.
1960   "Chaucer's Eagle: A Contemplative Symbol", *PMLA* 75: 153-159.
1971   *Disembodied Laughter: 'Troilus' and the Apotheosis Tradition: A Reex-
         amination of Narrative and Thematic Contexts.* Berkeley: University of
         California Press.
Taylor, Charles H. – Patricia Finley
1997   *Images of the Journey in Dante's Divine Comedy.* New Haven: Yale Uni-
         versity Press.
Taylor, Karla
1989   *Chaucer Reads 'The Divine Comedy.'* Stanford: Stanford University
         Press.
Trevisa, John
1975   *On the Properties of Things: John Trevisa's Translation of 'Bartholo-
         maeus Anglicus De Proprietatibus Rerum. A Critical Text,* 2 vols. (ed.
         M.C. Seymour et al.) Oxford: Clarendon Press.
White, T.H. (ed. and trans.)
1954   *The Book of Beasts: Being a Translation from a Latin Bestiary of the
         Twelfth Century.* London: Jonathan Cape.
Wimsatt, James I.
1976   "Guillaume de Machaut and Chaucer's *Troilus and Criseyde*" in: *Medium
         Aevum* 45: 277-293.
1977   "Medieval and Modern in Chaucer's *Troilus and Criseyde*", in: *PMLA*
         92: 203-216.
Windeatt, Barry
1992   *Oxford Guides to Chaucer: Troilus and Criseyde.* Oxford: Clarendon
         Press.
Yapp, Brunsdon
1981   *Birds in Medieval Manuscripts.* London: British Library, repr. New York:
         Schocken Books, 1982.
Yates, Frances A.
1966   *The Art of Memory.* London: Routledge and Kegan Paul.

Picture credits

Lydgate: The Poet as Deviser

Gordon Kipling, UCLA

1. Are Lydgate's dramatic texts scripts?

Those who study fifteenth-century forms of English courtly spectacle often find themselves having to make bricks without much straw. One can cite a few well-known descriptions, such as the 1377 mumming in which a body of 130 variously disguised London citizens rode to visit Prince Richard at Kennington, silently played a game of "mumchance" with him (using loaded dice so that he might "win" the costly gifts they had brought), danced, and then departed (Reyher 1909: 499). Or one can ponder the significance of fifteenth-century prohibitions of mumming that seem to reflect anxieties about civil disorder: "that no manere persone ... be so hardy in eny wyse to walk by nyght in any manere mommyng, playes, enterludes, or eny other disgisynges with eny feynyd berdis, peyntid visers, diffourmyd or colourid visages in eny wise" (Welsford 1927: 38). One might even examine sixteenth-century illustrations of "disguisings" and "mummings" by Simon Bening for the evidence they may shed on fifteenth-century practices (Twycross – Carpenter 2002: 141, 165). Very little new evidence has been added to this small store of knowledge since the publication of E. K. Chambers's *Mediaeval Stage*, and for the most part, scholars in search of the fifteenth-century "disguising" and "mumming" find themselves re-examining, and re-elaborating upon, these well-known materials.[1]

Amidst this small body of material, seven of Lydgate's poems which variously describe themselves as "mummings" or "disguisings" have always held special significance.[2] For the first time, Lydgate seems to give us not just descriptions of dramatic performances but performance texts themselves. But what are the status of these texts? Many have attempted to read them as if they were theatrical scripts of some sort. According to this view, Lydgate becomes not just a poet, but

---

1 The most important modern studies of these courtly spectacles include Chambers (1903), Reyher (1909), Withington (1918-20, 2: 101-112), Welsford (1927), Wickham (1959-2002, 1: 191-228), Clopper (2001: 160-168), and Twycross – Carpenter (2002: 128-168). Almost all of these discuss virtually the same items of evidence, although the last of these is the first to discuss extensively visual materials in additional to textual evidence.

2 In MacCracken's edition (Lydgate 1934: 668-701), these are known as *The Mumming at Bishopswood*, *A Mumming at Eltham*, *A Mumming at Hertford*, *A Mumming at London*, *A Mumming at Windsor*, *A Mumming for the Mercers of London*, and *A Mumming for the Goldsmiths of London*. Throughout this essay, I will cite these Lydgate texts from Mac-Cracken's edition either by page or line numbers as seems most appropriate.

a writer of "dramas", the first English playwright to whom we can put a name. As
such, he is supposed to have invented not just texts but whole performances. Like
all playwrights, Lydgate uses a literary text to communicate his intentions to the
actors and scenery makers, and if these disappoint us in their lack of dialogue,
nevertheless they can still be recognized as somewhat primitive play scripts that
seem to be groping in the direction of authentic dialogue. "These are short scenes
in the form of dialogue or pantomimic presentations elucidated by a text in verse
which was read out before the audience", according to Walter Schirmer. "They
are thus primitive forms of stage play, and are of importance for the later history
of English drama" (Schirmer 1961: 100). Glynne Wickham similarly describes the
Mumming at Hertford as "high-spirited comedy that trembles on the brink of dialogue" (Wickham 1987: 162),[3] while Derek Forbes even more confidently calls it
"the first secular comedy in the English language" (Forbes 1998).

The trouble with this evolutionary point of view, of course, is that enough authentic play scripts remain from before Lydgate's time to testify to a widespread
and sophisticated tradition of theatrical script writing. These include, for instance,
the *Mystère d'Adam* (12th century), the *Seinte Resureccion*, the *Dux Moraud*, and
the *Pride of Life* (all 13th century), and some of these – such as the fourteenth-
century *Interludium de Clerico et Puella* – are even recognizable as comedies.
Why, then, should the Lydgate "scripts" be more "primitive" than these? Moreover, the poems which constitute the corpus of Lydgate's "dramatic" work do not
resemble scripts in some important ways.

To begin with, as Glynne Wickham points out, each of these texts is "a simple, narrative poem from which dialogue is absent" (Wickham 1959-2002, 1:
192). In summing up the traditional view of these texts, William Tydeman describes them as "*scripted* mummings, an apparent contradiction until one perceives that only a single speaker (perhaps the author) was required to recite lines,
while the other participants merely mimed before presenting the guest of honour
with a gift" (Tydeman 1994: 16). But even if these texts are intended to be declaimed (we shall examine this point further below), none of them takes the trouble to characterize the orator. John Shirley, who collected the texts of these
mummings, describes two of them as "letters" or "ballads" which are "brought by

---

3   See also Wickham (1959-2002, 3: i: 194-196) where he discusses the Hertford mumming as a
     play script, specifically a secular comedy, and then continues: "In English literature it is not
     until the end of the century, when we reach Henry Medwall's *Fulgens and Lucres* (1497) that
     we will again find this same command of secular, romantic comedy both in overall shape and
     in particular incident. That this is due to loss and destruction of scripts rather than to lack of
     them is virtually certain since these intervening decades mark the advent and rapid numerical
     growth of professional acting companies – 'the players of enterludes' – in so many noble
     households; and such companies could not have satisfied their masters if they lacked a suit-
     able repertoire of interludes to play."

a poursuyaunt", and he tells us that another was "brought and presented vn to þe Mayre by an heraude, cleped Fortune" (pp. 668, 695, 698),[4] but Lydgate's verse makes no attempt whatsoever to characterize any of the three presumed orators. He employs no heraldic turns of phrase, makes no reference to matters of heraldic interest, makes no attempt to define a distinctive personality. Only in the Hertford entertainment does he make some attempt to adjust his diction so as to characterize the "rude vpplandisshe people" and their wives who present their petitions to the king, but even here the orator who reads these petitions is given no characterization of his own (pp. 675-682).

Finally, none of the Lydgate "dramatic" texts seem very interested in prescribing stage action for the characters. The text of the *Mumming at London*, it is true, does indicate the entrances of its five main characters, but otherwise, all of the texts are completely free of stage directions, sometimes to the extent that it becomes difficult to understand the relationship between the text and the action supposedly taking place on stage. Does the pursuivant who brings the "letter" (which is how Shirley describes Lydgate's text) to the Sheriffs of London in the *Mumming at Bishopswood* actually declaim the text (pp. 668-671)? What action does the "noble princesse" May perform upon entering the hall? Does the text's reference to Orpheus, "Parnoso" and "þe lusty muses nyene" (ll. 99-105) mean that the mumming is accompanied by a spectacular Mount Parnassus pageant? Does the *Mumming at Windsor* (pp. 691-94) dramatize or merely narrate "how þe ampull and þe floure delys came first to þe kynges of Fraunce by myrakle at Reynes"? Wickham guesses that "St. Clotilda, King Clovis, St Remigius and the hermit must all have appeared in order to enact the dumbshow; and possibly God as well" (Wickham 1959-2002, 1: 206), but do they in fact appear? Why does Lydgate's "script" not make all this clear?

Lydgate's texts, I believe, cannot answer these questions because they are not scripts at all but rather *devices*. John Shirley thus twice uses this term to describe these texts: "Lo here filoweþe þe deuyse of a desguysing to fore þe gret estates of þis lande" (*Mumming at London*, p. 682) and "Nowe foloweþe nexst þe devyse of a momyng to fore þe Kyng ..." (*Mumming at Windsor*, p. 691). Shirley may not be using these terms in a very technical sense, but their use does nevertheless remind us that the word "device", when applied to literary and artistic matters, was capable of a range of meanings in fifteenth and sixteenth centuries. In many contexts, the word "device" might simply serve as a synonym for what the rhetoricians call "invention", the finding out of apt matter, the conceiving of poetic and artistic ideas. Or it might refer to a thing contrived or invented, such as a remark-

---

4   For Shirley, a bibliophile and friend of Lydgate, see Schirmer (1961: 252-253). His annotations of Lydgate's texts often give us important contextual information. I cite Shirley's annotations from MacCracken's edition of Lydgate's *Minor Poems*.

able poetic conceit, an heraldic achievement, or a machine that achieves a clever effect. Or the word might be used merely as a synonym for cleverness, as in the ubiquitous use of the phrase "quaint device" in late medieval texts.[5]

2. The practice of *devising* in the fifteenth and sixteenth centuries

In referring to Lydgate's texts as the "devices", however, I believe that Shirley may well be using the word in a more technical sense. As Geoffrey Webb points out, the word "device" can also refer to a particular kind of document, one which serves as the means by which the inventions of a "deviser" are communicated to the artisans who will execute the device described therein. Late medieval architects, artists, and poets all used such documents in the creation of works as diverse as buildings, stained glass, paintings, and tapestries (Webb 1957) – primarily works that were complex (in the sense that they required many hands to make them), material, and visual in nature.

It is important to understand, however, that such projects may well require several such documents. To take a relatively straightforward example, the glazing of the windows in King's College Chapel, Cambridge, probably required at least two sorts of devices. The first of these documents, which was apparently drawn up under the supervision of Richard Foxe, Bishop of Winchester, probably consisted of a list of the proposed subjects for each window together with the scriptures that were to accompany each scene.[6] This would have been the key document to which all subsequent devices referred. To this primary device (as we may call it), the glazer, Bernard Flower, would then have responded to this list by creating a *vidimus* or drawing of the visual design for each window, and this second sort of "device" could then be presented for approval to his patrons and could also serve to govern the painting of the glass. The process of artistic design and execution is thus shared between several people. This "devolution of the various functions of the artist in making a work of art", as Geoffrey Webb points out, is not at

---

5   See *MED*, s.v. "device", which glosses the sentence from the *Mumming at Windsor* cited in this paragraph as 'plan, design; a literary composition or device'. See also definition (4): (a) "An artistic design, a work of art; an ornament"; (b) "a heraldic design, device"; and (c) "a mechanical device".

6   A memorandum of 30 November 1515 identifies Foxe with the ultimate responsibility for the "device", which would then be communicated to the glazer, Bernard Flower: "the glasing of the great Churche there [King's College Chapel] in suche forme and condicion as my Lord of Winchester [Foxe] shal devise and commande to be doon" (Wayment 1972: 2, 123a). Since Foxe was nearly blind at this time, he could hardly have contributed much to the visual design of the windows. Wayment points out that many of the scriptures, which would have been included on the "device" along with a list of subjects, were drawn from "the second (1519) edition of Erasmus' Latin translation of the New Testament, which we know Richard Foxe to have approved of" (p. 35).

all unusual. Rather, painter, poet, sculptor, glass-painter, and tapestry worker are often conceived of as "technical experts whose business is not necessarily the creation of works of art, in the full sense of the word 'creation'; but rather the translators of given ideas into their own specialised media" (Webb 1957: 301).

Perhaps Sir Thomas More would rank as the most distinguished "deviser" in this sense. In his edition of More's English poetry (More 1931, 1: 332-335), William Rastell tells us that the young More "devysed in hys fathers house in London, a goodly hangyng of fyne paynted cloth, with nyne pageanuntes, and verses over of every of those pageauntes: which verses expressed and declared, what the ymages in those pageauntes represented: and also in those pageauntes were paynted, the thynges that the verses over them dyd (in effecte) declare, which verses here folowe". Rastell thus makes it clear that More was not merely describing a suite of painted tapestries already in existence; rather, More's text was drafted as a primary device – much like Bishop Foxe's list of subjects for the King's College Chapel windows – and it was intended to guide the painter in his work. More's device, moreover, included two kinds of information. First, he drafted a brief, verbal description of the visual scene that he wanted the painter to create:

> In the second pageaunt was paynted a goodly freshe yonge man, rydyng uppon a goodly horse, havynge an hawke on his fyste, and a brase of grayhowndes folowyng hym. And under the horse fete, was paynted the same boy, that in the fyrst pageaunte was playinge at the top and squyrge. And over this second pageant the wrytyng was thus.

More's device thus specifies those details that were important from his point of view, but it also leaves the visual design primarily to the devising of the painter, so long as the visual work includes the vital details specified by More.

What makes these details absolutely necessary is the other category of information specified in More's written device. Devices of this sort conventionally include "scriptures" as well as an indication of the visual subject matter. In most cases, the scriptures specified in such devices would have consisted of little more than a phrase drawn from the Bible, but More's scriptures are more ambitiously literary. The accompanying scripture for the second "pageaunt" thus describes "Manhod":

> Manhod I am therefore I me delyght,
> To hunt and hawke, to nourishe up and fede,
> The grayhounde to the course, the hawke to the flyght,
> And to bestryde a good and lusty stede.
> These thynges become a very man in dede,
> Yet thynketh this boy his pevishe game swetter,
> But what no force, his reason is no better.

Perhaps, as with the King's College Windows, the painter would have prepared a series of nine sketches for More's approval before undertaking the paintings, but More may just as well have regarded his own contribution to the project as completed and trusted the painter to execute the visual work without further supervision.

Primary devices of this sort were very common in the fifteenth and sixteenth centuries. They might be prepared to devise decorative and visual schemes of all sorts: paintings, sculpture, pageants. A number of devices for "Sotilties" (emblematic pastry creations) for royal banquets have been preserved. These take almost exactly the same form as do devices for emblematic pageants or paintings.[7] Consider, for instance, this "sotilte" as prescribed in a device for the coronation of Henry V's consort, Katherine of Valois (1421):

> A sotilte called pellycan on his nest with briddes And an Image of seint kateryn with a boke in hyre hande dysputing with the hethen Clerkes havyng this Reson in hyre hande Madame la Reigne ¶ The pellican answering ¶ Ceste enseigne ¶ The briddes answering ¶ Est duroy pur tenir Joy A tout gent il mette sentent.
>
> (Thomas and Thornley 1938: 117)

Or this one, taken from the very similar device for Queen Jane Seymour's sotilties (1536):

> The quenes bage garneshed and ther upon the scriptur Bound to obey and serue
> The Coronacion of our Ladie solumpni garneshed and to be crowned with the father the sone and the holy gost.
>
> (A Device for Sotilties at a Banquet for Queen Jane Seymour 1536: 22r)

As in More's poem, these devices for emblematic table decorations conventionally specify both visual subject matter (a Pelican in his nest; the Queen's badge) and suitable "resons" or "scripturs" ("Madame la Reigne"; "Bound to Obey and Serve") which the fabricator must include in constructing the finished decorations.

It must have been to draw up devices like this that Wolsey sent the poet Alexander Barclay to Guisnes in 1520 where he was "to devise histoires and convenient raisons to florisshe the buildinges and bankett-howse" that were being erected at the Field of Cloth of Gold (Nichols 1846: 83).[8] As the language sug-

---

7   Eric Ives observes that "apart from the absence of instructions about materials and colours", a
     device for sotilties "is very similar to a contract of the period for a painting or piece of sculp-
     ture" (Ives 1986: 274).

8   Geoffrey Webb observes that Barclay's task was "to provide a scheme of representational
     decoration eked out with inscriptions and mottoes rather after the kind, shall we say, of those
     Troy tapestries now in the Burrell collection. An example in which the written matters or in-

gests, they were to draw up the primary device for the wall paintings in the temporary buildings then being erected. To that end, they were to devise suitable subject matter ("histoires") and scriptures ("convenient raisons"), which the painters could use to guide them in their work. The cooperation encouraged by such "devices" necessarily recognized professional barriers between different kinds of artists and at the same time respected the differing talents of specialized artisans working independently at their own crafts.

Just how independently these artisans could work can be seen by the series of devices that were drawn up to create a series of pageants for the London entry of Charles V and Henry VIII on 6 June 1522. The primary device for the London pageants, which has been preserved among the Somers Tracts, was drawn up by a committee of the London Common Council and then approved by the Privy Council (Kipling 1992: 83-87). Like More's tapestry device and the sottie devices, this document consists of brief descriptions of the pageants which the City has agreed to erect for the occasion, sometimes mandating important details of iconography and machinery:

> Also upon the Draw-bridge shall be one Pageant of *Jason* with the Golden Fleece; because the Emperor giveth the Golden Fleece, as the King of *England* doth give the Garter.
>
> Also there shall be set, in the Likeness of the Emperor, and all the Kings that hold of the Emperor, with Crowns on their heads
>
> ...
>
> Also at the little Conduit in the *Cheap* shall be the Assumption of our Lady, as goodly as can be wrought, &c. Angels, Archangells, Patriarchs, Prophets, with the Apostles in the heavenlyest Manner. The Sun, the Moon, with the Starrs shining bright, with shall open and bow down to the Honour of Our Lady, which Voices of young Choiristers, the which shall sing most sweetly, as may be devised by Musick.
>
> (Somers 1751: 2.470-471)

Because this primary device obviously leaves much to the ingenuity and technical skill of the various artists who are charged with constructing the pageant ("as goodly as can be wrought"), and composing music for it ("as may be devised by Musick"), further secondary devices are probably anticipated in the form of drawings or musical compositions.[9]

---

scriptions have a major part can be seen in the north-eastern chapel of Long Melford church. These are the 'Histoires and convenient Raisons'" (Webb 1957: 300-301).

9   John Rastell thus appeared before the Court of Aldermen on 5 May 1522, probably with a detailed visual device and specifications, in order to win approval for his "Isle of England" pageant with its many clever – and expensive – machines. The Aldermen agreed to permit him to build the pageant he had designed, provided "that the charg*es* therof excede nott xv li" (Repertories: 4.117v). For a contemporary description of Rastell's pageant at the Stocks, see Withington (1918-20, 1: 177); for commentary, see Kipling (1998: 235-236). There was also further secondary devising in the form of heraldry. The Court of Aldermen twice directed the

While most of these secondary devices must remain hypothetical, one secondary device for the pageants – in this case a literary device – does survive. The City on this occasion commissioned the scholar and poet, William Lily, to compose scriptures for the pageants. In composing these verses, Lily clearly saw his task as quite an independent one from those who were constructing the pageantry. Just as they were devising visual matter for the pageants, so he was devising literary matter for them. But he did not work in close cooperation with them except insofar as they all were bound to respect the same primary device, the city's list of pageant subjects. For the most part, he attempted to produce verse that struck the ear as impressive but were general enough that they would not conflict with whatever visual matter the pageant builders produced.

To begin with, he thus formulated a single, generic scripture that he had emblazoned "in letters of golde / and set vp at the crosse in chepe / and at euery pagiant:"

> CArolus Henricus uiuant. Defensor uterque
> Henricus Fidei. Carolus Ecclesiæ
>
> (Baskervill 1936: 9)

Supposedly to explain what the King and the Emperor were seeing, Lily then composed several lines of Latin verse for each pageant. In fact, however, these verses explained very little. His verse for the pageant of Jason and Medea on London Bridge, for instance, is remarkable for the way that it barely makes connection with the visual iconography of the pageant:

> Letitiæ quantum Minyis præbebat Iason,
>   Aurea Phryxeæ uellera nactus Ouis,
> Letitiæ quantum tulerat Pompeius, et urbi,
>   Hoste triumphato, Scipio Romulidum.
> Tantum tu nobis, Cæsar mitissime princeps,
>   Intrans Henrici principis hospitium.[10]

Chamberlain to pay Garter King of Arms "for hys greate labours & paynes that he hath taken in & abowte the devysyng of the Pageauntes ordeygned for the Receyuyng of Themperours grace in to this Citie" (Repertories: 4.117v, 122). As Sydney Anglo points out, these payments "refer to the numberous coats of arms adorning several pageants in this series – particularly those featuring the genealogies of Henry and Charles" (Anglo 1969: 188 n. 2).

10   Richard Pynson's translation: "What great ioye was it to the people of Mynis? / What tyme the highe renowned knight Iason / Had conquered in Colchos/ the golden flis: / What ioye eke was / the tryumphe of Scipion? / And of hym Pompey / to the romayns echone / Lyke ioye to vs Charles / prince of Clemency / Is at thy comyng / with pusaunt kyng Henry" (Baskervill 1936: 11).

Lily's verse clearly assumes that the pageant will primarily be about Jason's winning of the Golden Fleece because that's all that the city's device had specified. He could not have anticipated that the pageant artists would make Medea central to the show, nor that they would indulge themselves in a pyrotechnic display. As the chronicler Hall, tells us, they chose to interpret the City's device by showing Medea as enchantress aiding Jason in some of his more colorful exploits: they thus fashioned a "fiery Dragon" and "two Bulles whiche beastes cast out fyer continually", and they constructed a "tower" in which Medea stood "very straungely and rychely appareled" (Hall 1809: 638). Lily's verse doesn't exactly conflict with the pageant's visual iconography, but it is simply not very relevant to its particular subject matter.

The verse's lack of connection with the visual iconography is not so much a mark of failure as an intended consequence of the genre in which Lyly was writing: a literary device. To modern tastes, perhaps, his verse seems pompous and empty, but pomp, after all was what he was striving for, and from Lily's point of view his verse was not empty but rather artfully generalized. Because he was creating pageant verse independently of those who were actually designing and building the individual pageants, he had to compose his verse to suit whatever visual devices and feats of ingenuity that the various pageant makers might come up with. He thus had to avoid precisely the concrete detail that one usually values in poetry. Lily's contemporaries, however, seem to have thought he did a remarkably good job at composing his pageant device. Richard Pynson, the King's Printer, published an edition of his verse as a memorial of the event (Lily 1522), and the city paid him a reward of the then remarkable sum of five pounds for his literary work. Perhaps more tellingly, the City also asked him for a copy of his verse "to thentent that they may be entred for a president herafter" (Baskervill 1936: 3). From their point of view, Lily had created the definitive model of the form.

3. Lydgate as a composer of literary devices: three case studies

Lydgate's "dramatic" texts are best seen, I think, in terms of this tradition; he, too operates as just such a "technical expert" who cooperates in the act of creation rather than acting in the more modern sense as an independent artist who takes full responsibility for the conception and execution of an entire dramatic performance. He differs from the writers of interludes, in this respect, in that he is contributing his literary expertise to a form of courtly performance that involves not only costumed performers but also spectacular pageantry. Because he is contributing to entertainments put on by courtly or civic establishments that are used to staging their own entertainments, he is probably writing his poetry to a subject matter "device" constructed by others. To see how Lydgate cooperates with such courtly and civic establishments in the creation of spectacular entertainments, we should first examine his "devising" for a variety of projects – a suite of tapestries, scriptures for banquet "sotelties", and a commemorative poem for a royal entry – all of which involve him composing suitable poetic material in response to a subject matter "device".

Perhaps the most complete example of a device from Lydgate's hand is his poem, "Bycorne and Chychevache". John Shirley's headnote describes this poem as "þe deuise of a peynted or desteyned clothe for an halle a parlour or a chaumbre / deuysed by Iohan Lidegate at þe request of a werþy citeseyn of London" (Lydgate 1934: 433-438). The repetition of "device" here suggests that Shirley is using the term in its technical sense as a set of written directions to guide the painter in executing a commission. Construed thus as a formal "device", Lydgate's poem reads very much like Thomas More's tapestry device, so much so that we may well suspect that More took his formal example for a such a composition from Lydgate. Lydgate thus combines prose iconographical descriptions with verse scriptures in the now familiar "histories" and "reasons" formula of the device. The poem thus begins with the "history" by directing the painter, "ffirst þere shal stonde an ymage in poete-wyse seying þees thre balades" (p. 433). There then follow three rhyme-royal stanzas (the "reasons") which represent the words of the "ymage" and which the painter must inscribe in this first panel of the suite of painted tapestries. Since the scene that Lydgate has in mind is complex, however, he includes some further iconographical specification between the first two stanzas of scripture: "And þane shalle þeer be purtrayed twoo beestis oon fatte a noþer leene" (p. 433).

Apparently, Lydgate's device envisions a total of six painted panels in all. Each of the separate "devices" begins with the formula, "þanne shalle þer be pourtrayhed ..." and concludes with one or more "balades" (i.e., rhyme-royal stanzas) of verse scriptures. Unlike most of Lydgate's devising work, moreover, both the descriptive material and the verse scriptures are full of sometimes graphic detail. Consider, for instance, both this direction to the painter of the fourth panel: "þanne shal be þer purtrayhed a long horned beest sklendre and lene with sharpe teethe and on his body no thing saue skyn and boone" and its accompanying scripture:

Chychevache, þis is my name,
    Hungry, megre, sklendre, and lene,
To shewe my body I haue gret shame,
    For hunger I feele so gret teene,
    On me no fattnesse wol beo seene,
By cause þat pasture I fynde noon,
þer fore I am buy skyn and boon.

(ll. 78-84)

Because he is inventing both the visual material and the scriptures, he does not have to worry about including details that may conflict with the plans of another deviser. More importantly, the composition of this device does not imply that Lydgate had any contact whatsoever with the painter who would eventually execute the "werþy citeseyn of London's" commission for a chamber of painted tapestries. The only connection between Lydgate and the painter lay through the patron, who commissioned Lydgate to produce the device on the one hand, and the painter to execute the device on the other. Once Lydgate had devised the tapestries, he had completed his task.

In composing scriptures for a trio of "sotilties" for Henry VI's coronation banquet, Lydgate worked in partnership with other devisors, and this collaboration did not permit him the same inventive freedom. On this occasion, those responsible for the feast drew up the customary "device" for the emblematic "sotiltes". Unlike the other such "devices" that we have examined, however, this one only specified the emblematic subject matter – the "histoires" – and omitted the scriptures – the "convenient raisons" – that should also be emblazoned on the design. They were omitted from the device because Lydgate had been commissioned to compose suitable "reasons" for each of the specified emblems (Lydgate 1934: 623-624).[11] The first of these thus commanded the artisans and cooks to prepare

A sotelte, Seint Edward and Seint Lowes armed in cote armours bryngyng yn bitwene hem the Kyng in his cote armour with this scripture suyng.

For this emblem the poet composed a verse scripture consisting of an eight-line stanza:

Loo here twoo kynges righte perfit and right good,
    Holy Seint Edwarde and Seint Lowes:
And see the braunch borne of here blessid blode;
    Live, among Cristen moost souereigne of price,
    Enheretour of the floure de lice!
God graunte he may thurgh help of Crist Ihesu
    This sixt Henry to reigne and be as wise
And hem resemble in knyghthod & vertue.

Two other "sotilties" follow: one showing the young King in the presence of his dead father and the Emperor Sigismund and the other showing St George and St

---

11   A number of London chronicles preserve both the device and Lydgate's verse; for a list of these, see Thomas – Thornley (1938: 418-419). MacCracken, who bases his copy-text on one of these chronicles, British Library Cotton MS Julius B. I., prints both the device and Lydgate's poem.

Denis presenting Henry VI to the Virgin and Christ child. For each, Lydgate prepared a similar stanza of verse to serve as a suitable scripture.

While it is possible that Lydgate composed both the list of subjects and the
verse scriptures, I think he did not. The list of subjects is the sort of formulaic
device repeatedly produced by the royal household throughout the fifteenth and
sixteenth centuries. Except, that is, for Lydgate's "scriptures". These do not conform to the expected formula. Such scriptures, as we have seen, conventionally
consist of one or more brief phrases ("Bound to obey and serve"), and they never
exceed a sentence at most ("Est duroy pur tenir Joy A tout gent il mette sentent").
Lydgate's verse scriptures suggest that the household was attempting something
more ambitious on this occasion. In commissioning England's most eminent poet
to provide the scriptures, they expected – and got – not just a few phrases of emblematic scripture, but stanzas of verse. Provided that the verse was reasonably
appropriate to the emblematic design, Lydgate's status as a poet and the impres-
siveness of the verse form mattered more than meaning.

Lydgate thus performs his task much in the same way that we saw William
Lily perform his. Both men are charged with devising impressive poetical material
to suit emblematic designs that had already been formulated. Because he is working as a deviser of suitable verbal material and not as a descriptive poet, it is important to see that his verse actually limits visual description, thus avoiding possible conflicts with the craftsmen who are charged with fashioning the visual material. This reluctance to make visual demands on his fellow designer thus explains
why Lydgate's verse seems so bland and free of concrete detail. The existence of
these verses, moreover, does not offer any proof whatsoever about Lydgate's
presence at court on this occasion. The planning for Henry VI's coronation (6
November 1429) evidently began in the summer,[12] so there was ample time for
the household to compose the device for sotelties, send it to Lydgate, and receive
the verse in return.[13]

On the basis of his commemorative poem, "King Henry VI's Triumphal Entry into London" (Lydgate 1934: 630-648), Lydgate has often been thought to
have devised the pageantry for the king's entry into London on 21 February

---

12   The coronation of Charles VII at Rheims in July set in motion plans for Henry's coronation.
     As Bertram Wolffe points out, the date of Henry's coronation was set "not by any English
     reasons of state, but specifically to facilitate and hasten his arrival in France, to take posses-
     sion of his French kingdom" (Wolffe 1981: 51), see also Pearsall (1997: 29) on this point.
13   In 1429, Lydgate was living in Hatfield and serving as Prior of Hatfield Regis. Located
     "three miles south-east of Bishop's Stortford, not very far from Bury but nearer London" it
     was "a small Benedictine priory in Essex which had recently been assigned as a cell to Bury"
     (Pearsall 1997: 24).

1432.[14] Lydgate's poem, it is true, includes detailed descriptions of each of the City's seven pageants. But as H. N. MacCracken demonstrated nearly a century ago, Lydgate closely modelled these descriptions on an account of the pageants sent to him by the Town Clerk, John Carpenter. Except in one significant instance, Lydgate draws all the details and, allowing for the translation from Carpenter's Latin to Lydgate's English, much of the phrasing directly from Carpenter's letter (MacCracken 1911: 97-98). For Lydgate, the letter was at the very least a useful and authoritative source of material for the commemorative poem he was writing.

What has not been realized, however, is that Carpenter's text is closely based upon the City's primary device for the pageants. The descriptions of the pageants are almost certainly a close recension of that device. As the Town Clerk of London, Carpenter would have been at the center of preparations for Henry's royal entry, and he would have had easy access to the city's pageant device.[15] For Carpenter, reference to the device would provide both an authoritative and convenient source of the information that Lydgate needed in composing his poem. The Town Clerk's letter thus describes the City's pageants in precisely the way that, as we have seen, such devices customarily do: it gives a brief verbal description of the proposed pageant and lists the scriptures that must be painted on the pageant. Consider, for example, Carpenter's account of a pageant in Cheapside. Above the

---

14 Withington thinks that "the descriptive verses which John Lydgate wrote of this royal-entry do not, it is true, prove him to be the author of this 'triumph'; but I think he may safely be so considered" (Withington 1918-20, 1: 141). Most later writers have been content to accept Withington's judgment. Schirmer takes it for granted that "Lydgate was charged with the responsibility for the official welcome given to the king on his return from France" and assures us that the poet "was responsible not only for this poem, but also for devising and planning the tableaux and scenes described" in the poem (Schirmer 1961: 139). Wickham also speaks conventionally of "Lydgate's pageant" (not just his poem) in discussing the 1432 London entry (Wickham 1959-2002, 1: 72). But see Pearsall (1997: 33-34), who thinks that "Lydgate for the most part merely versified the vivid and detailed description of the event given in an informal Latin letter from Carpenter to a brother-cleric, presumably Lydgate himself".

15 Carpenter was Town Clerk from 1417 to 1438, and was sometimes styled "secretary". He regularly corresponded on behalf of the City with the Crown, and he compiled the *Liber Albus*, a compilation of the laws, customs, privileges, and usages of the City. He was a friend of poets and an intimate of Lord Mayors of London. He was a lay brother of the convent of the Charterhouse, London, and of the fraternity of the sixty priests of London (*DNB*). For this reason, he refers to Lydgate (presumably; he does not actually name him) in his letter as "reverende frater et amice præstantissime" (Carpenter 1432), as MacCracken points out (MacCracken 1911: 77). Two years earlier, Carpenter had the verses of Lydgate's "Danse Macabre" inscribed "on the cloister walls of Pardon churchyard, attached to the chapel of the Blessed Virgin Mary at St. Paul's where Carpenter had just installed a chantry over the charnel. This became famous as 'the Daunce of Poulys,' as John Stow tells us in his Survey" (Pearsall 1970: 177; Pearsall 1997: 27).

Great Conduit ("super magnum aqueductum"), Carpenter writes to Lydgate, the
King saw:

> amoenissimum et pulcherrimum locum ad modum Paradisi consitum, stellatum floribus
> et arboribus fructiforis relucentem, et breviter omnium rerum speciositate conspicuum;
> x et cujus latere Aquilonis in civitatem Regis magni fontes vivacissime, scaturiebant
> aquas architriclinas in vinum conversas, qui gustus regious post tantam virtutum adop-
> tionem merito poterant recreare.
>
> In hoc insuper loco illi duo prædestinati cives sanctorum et domestici Dei, Ennok,
> scilicet, et Ely, congratulantes de tanti Regis adventu, portantis facem, illuminantis pro-
> priam, et dantis pacem gentibus, et, quasi desiderantes et expectantes ipsum futurum
> canonem et consortem suum, pro statu suo prospero precabantur, unus, videlicet, quod
> *Nihil proficiat inimicus in eo, nec filius iniquitatis apponat nocere ei*, et alter quod
> *Dominus conservet eum, et vivificet eum, et beatum faciet eum in terra, et non tradat il-*
> *lum in manus inimicorum ejus.* Circa vero fontes illos cuilibet litterarum oraculis incita-
> batur *ad hauriendum aquas in gaudio de fontibus Salvatoris.*
>
> (Carpenter 1432: 461-462 my italics)

Instead of reporting what the King actually saw, of course, this passage describes
what the devisers intended that the King should see. First the device sketches out
the essential details of the pageant itself: a star-strewn Paradise was to be constructed above the Conduit and filled with fruit-bearing trees. The Conduit itself
was to be employed as the fountain of this Paradise. Imitating Jesus' miracle at
Cana, the water in the Conduit must miraculously turn to wine, and all will be
invited to drink from it. Next, the device specifies only two necessary characters,
Enoch and Elijah, who must stand in this pageant Paradise to greet the King. Finally, the device concludes by specifying the three scriptures (italicized) that must
be inscribed on the pageant: Psalm 88: 23 ("The enemy shall have no advantage
over him, nor the son of iniquity have power to hurt him"), Psalm 40: 3 ("The
Lord preserve him and give him life, and make him blessed upon the earth, and
deliver him not up to the will of his enemies"), and Isaiah 12: 3 ("You shall draw
waters with joy out of the saviour's fountains").[16]

Since MacCracken has already demonstrated how closely Lydgate followed
this passage in composing his poem (the phrase "aquas architriclinas", for instance, becomes "lyke to the water off Archedeclyne" in Lydgate's poem), it is
not necessary to repeat that exercise here (MacCracken 1911: 88-92). As in his
descriptions of all the other pageants, Lydgate faithfully translates the details and
phraseology of the device into English rhyme royal stanzas, and he transcribes the
scriptures into the margins of his manuscript at the appropriate points. As Mac-
Cracken points out, however, Lydgate's description at this point also departs re-

---

16   I cite the Psalms as numbered in the Vulgate; the translations are from the Douay-Rheims
      version.

markably from his source to add considerable material not present in Carpenter's device (MacCracken 1911). If we examine these additions, we will find that they reveal a great deal about how Lydgate and the pageant artists pursued their own independent acts of devising on this collaborative project.

In the first of these additions, Lydgate introduces three entirely new characters – Mercy, Grace, and Pity – not anticipated by Carpenter's pageant device. According to Lydgate, these three "virgyns" stood at the well and "drewe wyn vp off ioye and off pleasaunce". Mercy "mynystred" wines of Temperance, Grace "shedde" liquor of Good Governance, and Pity "profered" wines of Comfort and Consolation (Lydgate 1934: 641-642). Never elsewhere in the poem does he add to the cast of characters as specified in the device. That he does so here suggests that he is uniquely reporting what he has actually seen, not merely versifying written matter.

Lydgate's addition here thus captures an important detail of the pageant maker's own devising. As in all the other devices we have examined, Carpenter's letter specifies all of the iconographical material and the characters that *must* feature in the finished pageant, but it also leaves much to the imagination of the artisans who would actually build the pageant and staff it with actors. The device, in other words, specifies the minimum necessary detail and expects that the makers will interpret the device in their own individual ways. The pageant maker here seems to have been troubled by the problem of distributing the wine to all who wished to drink. Would this not cause a dangerous and disorderly scramble? To solve this problem, he invented an orderly distribution system. Three maidens could control the distribution by drawing the wine from the fountain and offering it the crowd. At the same time, the presence of these three allegorical maidens supplied the possibility of an especially ceremonial presentation to the King and the members of his party as they approached the Conduit. It only remained to give them, and the wine they distributed, an appropriately allegorical significance modelled upon the allegory of Frère Lorens's *Somme le roi*.[17]

Every one of the pageants, of course, must have involved similar acts of inventive devising resulting in considerable departures from the device. Why does Lydgate ignore all these in his descriptions of every other pageant except this one? He certainly shows himself ready to amend Carpenter's text at the Wells of Paradise pageant; why does he not make similar amendments elsewhere? The answer, I think, is that Lydgate did not actually see any of the other pageants. He viewed the King's entry from a vantage point opposite the Great Conduit on that February day and could not view any of the other pageants. He probably could not have moved through the enforced order of the crowded London streets on that day

---

17   For a discussion of this pageant's allegory and its indebtedness to Frère Lorens, see Kipling (1998: 163-167).

to view the performances at other pageants even if he had wanted to do so.[18] As a consequence, if Lydgate was to devise a successful poem commemorating the event, he needed a written description which could provide him with adequate detail of the pageants he could not witness. Because of this departure from the device supplied to him by Carpenter, however, we have something very rare in this poem. We can not only tell that Lydgate actually was present to witness part of the show he described, we can also identify, with some assurance, the exact place that he stood to witness the event.[19]

A second addition at the same pageant also demonstrates Lydgate's aims as a deviser of a commemorative poem based upon the city's primary pageant device. In the midst of describing the Wells of Paradise pageant, Lydgate suddenly launches into an encomium on the name of the Mayor, John Wells:

> O! how thes welles, who-so take goode hede,
>   With here likours moste holsome to atame,
> Affore devysed notably in dede
>   Forto accorden with the Meirys name;
>   Which by report off his worthy ffame
> That day was busy in alle his gouernaunce,
> Vnto the Kyng fforto done pleasaunce.

To further embellish his point, the poet adds two marginal notes opposite this stanza: "The wells were for the mayor's name most proper" and "Nomen Maioris Iohannes Welles" (Lydgate 1934: 642).

In lauding the "devising" of these wells "forto accorden with the Meirys name", Lydgate surely refers here to his own ingenuity, not that of the pageant deviser. Carpenter's letter contains no hint of this conceit.[20] The pageant series seeks to dramatize the King's Christ-like manifestation to the people. The water turns to wine at the Great Conduit because the King's approach produces a Christ-

---

18 For spectators, movement between pageants was difficult. Not only were the streets crowded, but marshals preserved order and the safety of the royal procession by limiting freedom of movement as much as possible. Spectators were effectively limited to witnessing the royal entry from a single "standing" along the route. On this point, see Kipling (1998: 142).

19 MacCracken guesses that Lydgate gained his information on the three Virgins of the Wells of Paradise pageant directly from Mayor Welles to eke out the information drawn from Carpenter's letter in order to preserve the hypothesis that Lydgate throughout his poem "wrote from a description, which he himself did not compile" (MacCracken 1911: 91). I think this introduces an unnecessary complication into the process of composition.

20 Moreover, such a conceit depends upon an English pun while the pageants are all conceived of in Latin; all of the scriptures posted on the pageants are thus Latin ones. For the pun to work, wouldn't the Mayor's name have to be "Fons"?

like miracle of transubstantiation.[21] Lydgate's attempt to find a reference to Mayor Wells in the Great Conduit pageant, by contrast, suits the poem's eulogistic objectives, not that of the pageant series. Lydgate's aims are thus defined in the beginning and end of the poem. The opening of the poem thus praises the accomplishments of "The noble Meire ... / The Sheryves, the Aldermen" and "The citezenis echoon of the Citee" who had prepared this reception for their King "to yeve ensample thuruh-out the reem" (ll. 24-36). The circumstantial description of the pageants which follows functions as proof that the citizens' accomplishments. The poem then ends with a further paean of praise to "London ... Citee of Citees, off noblesse precellyng" and especially to the "noble Meir" to whom the poet offers his poem (ll. 510-537).

These passages reveal Lydgate's role not just as a poet but more particularly as a deviser. Lydgate and the pageant craftsmen were thus creating their own devices in response to the City's primary pageant device. Both were bound to observe carefully its mandated details, but provided that they remained true to the letter and spirit of those details, they were free to indulge their own independent artistry – indeed they were expected to do so. In composing a commemorative poem based on City's device, Lydgate was not an entirely free agent. He was obliged, first of all, to respect that document's prior authority. But if he could not alter the meanings of the civic device – a goal he accomplished by keeping his own description of the pageants as close as possible to Carpenter's letter – he might still add to the range of meanings which he found in it. For this reason, he found it entirely appropriate to turn the Well of Paradise pageant into a graceful compliment to the Mayor, John Wells. He was doing no more, after all, than the pageant artisan, who added three new characters to the same pageant.

4. Lydgate as a deviser of dramatic texts

Lydgate, as we have seen, not only composed formal devices but he was also skilled at writing suitable material in response to devices composed by others. Moreover, there is every reason to suppose that he may have completed many of his tasks from his writing desk at Hatfield Priory or even at Bury St Edmunds. The device convention made it possible for him to complete such apparently collaborative commissions without actually working in the company of his collaborators. Indeed, the employment of such devices suggests that the various collaborators are not often, if ever, in personal contact, that they connect with one another only indirectly and primarily through the written device. That the Lydgate canon consists of so much of this kind of work suggests that the poet was seen as a pres-

---

21 On this pageant's attempts to characterize the King as a messiah and to stage Christ-like epiphanies for him, see Kipling (1998: 143-169).

tigious and skilled composer of verbal material to accompany such visual projects as pageants, sotilties, tapestries, and – I think – mummings.

On the face of it, a verbal device for a mumming is a contradiction in terms. Shirley's headnotes describe four of the seven Lydgate texts as "mummings" (Bishopswood, Eltham, Windsor, Mercers, and Goldsmiths), but can a mumming still be a mumming if somebody speaks? I will below briefly question the common assumption that Lydgate's texts are primarily to be understood as monologues designed to be spoken by a presenter, but first I simply want to observe that Lydgate's texts seem to constitute a formal innovation. Both court and city had been performing spectacular mummings for decades without benefit of such texts, so far as we can tell. At court, in particular, what was once a traditional, domestic game became a "spectacular planned entertainment" with "theatrically-designed" costumes, pageants, music, elaborate dances, and the enactment of a fictional scenario (Wickham 1959-2002, 1: 191-228; Twycross – Carpenter 2002: 151-168). The sorts of mummings for which Lydgate was writing texts were therefore establishment entertainments in that they required a formidable establishment to afford them and to stage them. In order to produce such entertainments, the court (and to some extent the City of London) necessarily sought out and employed household servants with the necessary expertise. At court, the Wardrobe could produce costumes, Works or Tents might provide the building skills for pageants, and performers of various sorts might be found among the minstrels and the Chapel, for example.[22] In organizing all these disparate workers and performers to collaborate in the production of such a visual spectacle, formal devices would almost certainly have been drawn up.

These establishments did not require the interventions of an outside "deviser" to produce such spectacles. Rather, he was far more likely to be asked to provide textual matter on request for an entertainment being devised and organized by members of the household.[23] The headnote to the *Mumming at Hertford* offers one piece of evidence that Lydgate responded to precisely this sort of commission. John Shirley thus tells us that the Hertford mumming was "devysed by Lydegate at at þe request of þe Countre Roullour Brys" (Lydgate 1934: 675). John Brice who commissioned the text from Lydgate, was not actually the Household Controller but his chief deputy or "cofferarius regis" (Green 1976: 14-15). As Derek Forbes puts it, he was an "officer of the king's household responsible for the ordering of the hall and the meals and entertainments provided in it" (Forbes 1998:

---

22 Chambers (1903, 1: 393) points to records of the Wardrobe providing costumes for theatrical entertainments as early as 1388.

23 Both court and civic establishments had an obvious interest in ensuring that entertainments were controlled, both financially and politically. The best way to maintain these controls is to produce such spectacles from within, where such controls might be most effectively exercised.

65). In 1427, while the court was spending Christmas at Hertford Castle, he was apparently the household official chosen to organize suitable Christmas entertainments.[24] In this capacity, he commissioned Lydgate to compose a comic "bille by wey of supplicacion" of the "rude vpplandisshe" husbands and the equally comic "boystous answere of hir wyves". But why did Bryce approach Lydgate for a text? The household was perfectly capable of devising entertainments without outside intervention, and mummings did not require literary texts anyway. In these circumstances, we should be asking ourselves why Lydgate's services as a poet were required at all?

The customary answer to this question is that the courtly mumming became so artistically complex that it required verbal explanation:

> once the ceremonial mumming has become a complex artistic confection, it requires explication. If, as we assume, the mummers remain masked and retain at least a vestige of the traditional obligation to silence, they had to acquire the Presenter or Interpreter, the one person who is allowed to speak.
>
> (Twycross – Carpenter 2002: 161)

Lydgate's intervention thus comes about at the behest of a kind of evolutionary pressure which will eventually transform the mumming first into a disguising and then into a court masque.[25]

While there is much to be said for this view, I still find it highly significant that Lydgate, rather than some anonymous poet, seems to have been the first writer to devise such an explanatory text. Whatever evolutionary pressures may have been in play, I would suggest that Lydgate's reputation as England's most prestigious living poet was equally important. All seven of the dramatic texts thus date from a brief period (1427-1429)[26] when Lydgate was at the apogee of his career as a "Lancastrian propagandist and laureate poet to crown and commons" (Pearsall 1997: 28-31). During this period, as we have seen, Lydgate was repeatedly commissioned by both court and city to provide suitable poetic material for other visual spectacles. It would seem natural, at this juncture, for the devisers of

---

24 For the date of the mumming, see Green (1976: 15-16) and Pearsall (1997: 28).

25 These evolutionary dynamics were introduced by Chambers and still inform the thinking of Wickham's discussion of the mumming: "From the mid fifteenth century onwards, the word 'Mumming' is scarcely ever used to describe a courtly entertainment. The word 'Disguising' on the other hand is regularly used in this sense from then until it is superseded, as Bacon and Jonson inform us, by the word 'Mask' in the early sixteenth century" (Wickham 1959-2002, 1: 197).

26 The dating of these texts is somewhat uncertain. Since Henry and his mother were at Eltham for Christmas in both 1425 and 1428, either date is possible for the *Mumming at Eltham*. Pearsall first accepted the earlier date (Pearsall 1970: 184), but more recently has been persuaded that the latter date is "much more likely" (Pearsall 1997: 28).

yet another kind of courtly spectacle to commission Lydgate to compose suitable poetic matter to add additional luster to the performance.

But what sort of text would be appropriate to a mumming, a form of performance traditionally textless, and how was such a text to become part of the performance? John Shirley's headnotes betray a considerable interest in this problem. He thus only describes two of the Lydgate texts straightforwardly as "the devyse of a momyng" (*Windsor*) and the "deuyse of a desguysing (*London*) much as one might refer to the script of a play. He describes the Eltham text more neutrally as "a balade ... for a momyng", and since balads are usually performed texts, perhaps he means to suggest its use as a kind of script. For all the others, he describes Lydgate's poems as apparently non-dramatic texts that bear some (usually undefined) relationship to the performance. The text for the Hertford performance, as we have seen, is thus described as the texts of a petition ("bille by wey of supplicacion") and a counter-petition ("aunswere") followed by the text of a royal judgment in response. The remaining three he describes as letters: "a balade ... sente by a poursyvant to þe Shirreves" (*Bishopswood*); "a lettre made in wyse of balade ... brought by a poursuyaunt" (*Mercers*); and "a lettre made in wyse of balade ... brought and presented vn to þe Mayre by an heraude, cleped Fortune" (*Goldsmiths*). As these headnotes make clear, the texts as well as the performers enter the performance in disguise – as texts they all seem to be something other than what they actually are. At the same time, all these texts represent themselves self-consciously as texts, as actual documents used in performance.

All this textual self-consciousness may well point to the intended dramatic uses of these texts. All these varied documents – ballads, petitions, letters – may be proclaimed, declaimed, orated by a presenter. They also point, I would argue, to the limited nature of Lydgate's participation in the creation of the dramatic performances for which they are created. Why do so many of them specifically take the form of letters sent via a messenger to a recipient for whom the mumming is presented? It may well be a convenient way to introduce speech to a speechless mumming, but I think it equally probable that these texts take the form of letters because they actually are letters. If Lydgate is merely being asked to write a text for a mumming, he doesn't actually have to be present at rehearsals or even the performance. What he needs is the written device for the mumming. If all he is being asked to do is to devise a text for the mumming, then he can actually send his response to the devisers of the mumming by messenger. We need not marvel, then, that Lydgate managed to compose two of his texts in quick succession, one mumming for Mercers on Twelfth Night 1429, and another for the Goldsmiths on Candlemas night, less than a month later.

Such texts as *The Mumming at Bishopswood* (pp. 668-671) and *The Mumming at Eltham* (pp. 672-674) are thus not really dramatic texts so much as they are texts that might somehow be employed in a dramatic performance. Lydgate, however, does not take it as his business to imagine how his "balades" will be used, what action the actors will perform, or even how many characters will take part in the performance. It is hard to see how either of them could be mimed. Nor is it clear who reads these texts.[27] Does the "poursyvant" by whom the Bishopswood "balade" is "sente" also read the text to the "Shirreves" who receive it? As far as one can tell, the Bishopswood text merely introduces the Lady May to the Sheriffs, and that introduction does not properly take place until the last four stanzas of the poem. What happens, one may well ask, when she enters? Is there a dance? If so, with whom does she dance? Does she have attendants? Is she expected to do anything at all except enter? For the most part, as Lawrence M. Clopper puts it, Lydgate merely "reads" the Lady May (Clopper 2001: 161-164). She represents summer's gladness after winter's mighty violence and peace after war. If we did not know, from Shirley's poem, that it was a dramatic text, we might easily read it as a lyric in praise of summer – "Summer is icumen in" with a few political overtones.

The Eltham text, by contrast, at least specifies a basic dramatic action – the presentation of gifts – and it imagines three costumed actors – Bacchus, Juno, and Ceres – to perform it. But for the most part, he is more interested in the text as a text rather than as a dramatic script. He thus carefully crafts it into a self-conscious "balade", not only because he has composed it in rhyme royal, but also because each stanza ends "ballad style" with the repetition of the last line. Still, it is hard to imagine how even a good actor could "mime" this text very effectively. For the most part, Lydgate is content with merely "reading" the significance of the three gifts (wine, wheat, and oil) in some detail. At the end, he then asks Henry VI and his mother to accept them. Granted it serves to adorn a thoughtful moment of gift presentation, but it scarcely can be said to script an entire performance. Rather, the text serves as part of a more comprehensive program of events. It is a device in much the same way that a single pageant or a single sotiltie is a device in the context of a larger program of ceremonial events.

It is possible, of course, that these texts do not represent mummings at all but only especially heightened moments of presentation: the Lady May to the Sheriffs, symbolic gifts to the King and his mother. Or it may be that Lydgate's text is meant to serve only one part of a longer and more complex performance: a bit of verse to introduce the Lady; a ballad at the moment that the mummers present their gifts. If so, Lydgate is here working on only a portion of the device of the entire performance. He has been told who the characters are to be, what gifts are to be given, and has been asked for a verbal device to heighten the effects of the moment of presentation.

---

27 Judging by the marginal note in his edition (Lydgate 1934: 668), MacCracken seems to think that the Goddess Flora enters as a character, but as far as I can tell, she does not; she is merely referred to. The text merely tells us that Flora has "dovne sent hir owen doughter dere", the Lady May.

However one looks at it, Lydgate's text serves the performance in two important ways: it can be read and it can be presented. On the one hand, reading the text aloud transforms what would otherwise seem a brief act of presentation into high ceremony. On the other, because the text is a physical object, it can be presented much like the other symbolic gifts are presented; the letter can be physically delivered. In the form of a manuscript, the text can thus not only serve as a narrative device, but it can also serve as a means of commemorating the ceremonial presentation.

The Mumming for the Mercers of London (pp. 695-699) suggests that Lydgate's text may have played a more complicated role in the devising of the performance. Certainly John Shirley's headnote suggests a somewhat complicated situation: "a lettre made in wyse of balade by Daun Iohan, brought by a poursuy-aunt in wyse of mommers desguysed to fore þe Mayre of London" (p. 695). Were it not for this helpful description, the text might seem only a slightly bizarre narrative describing the journey of Jupiter's Pursuivant from his Lord, "whos mansy-oun is ouer þe sonnes beem" (l. 2), to London to deliver a letter to the Mayor. As the Pursuivant travels through the Gulf of Venice, we are told, the Pursuivant "saughe, as he gan approche",

> With inne a boote a fissher drawe his nette
> On þe right syde of a crystal rooche;
> Fisshe was þer noon, for þe draught was lette.
> And on þoon syde þer were lettres sette
> Þat sayde in Frenshe þis raysoun: Grande travayle;
> Þis aunswere nexst in ordre: Nulle avayle.

(ll. 57-63)

What are we to make of this curious "sight"? Wickham concludes that these enigmatic lines describe the entrance of the first of three pageant ships in which "the Mercers, disguised as Orientals (possibly the familiar Turks and Tartars of earlier Tournaments), enter the hall, ... The first ship, which let down nets and drew nothing, had written on it: GRANDE TRAVAYLE: NULLE AVAYLE". This is an ingenious suggestion, and may indeed be a "reasonable assumption", but why is there nothing whatsoever in the text to support this hypothesis (Wickham 1959-2002, 1: 201-202)? Lydgate does not even bother to employ the same rhetorical strategy which (as we shall see) the Presenter of the *Mumming at London* uses to describe something that he actually expects the audience to see: "Loo here þis lady þat yee may see" (p. 682).[28] If Lydgate's text does indeed mean to describe the entrance of a pageant ship, why does it not clearly say so?

Lydgate, I would suggest, was not trying to write a script for the Mercers, but only a device for one part of the performance. He was given a device containing a list of the pageants – three merchant ships with attached mottos – a list of the characters – Jupiter's Pursuivant, various Oriental merchants, and a brief description of the action: the first ship will cast its nets and draw nothing, the third will cast its nets and draw a full harvest. Lydgate's part in the show was to compose a verbal device to introduce the mummers. He was working, in short, as we have seen him work in such situations before, on the same project as other devisers, but independently of them. His job was to craft an impressive letter that would explain the entry of the mummers. How exactly they entered the hall was a matter for the mummers to decide. He did not have to "script" their entry, he just had to write a letter in which he "read" their entry, as Clopper puts it.

Lydgate's efforts were on crafting the letter, not on the performance of the letter, or even more generally on the performance of the mumming itself. He did not even determine who it would be who would read the letter. Presumably, since Shirley tells us that a "poursuyaunt" brought the letter, it must have been handed to the Mayor by Jupiter's Pursuivant. But he can hardly have read the letter because the letter narrates his journey to England in the third person. We might guess that Jupiter's Pursuivant was a mummer, that as a part of his mumming performance he transmitted the letter, but as a mummer he did not speak. But Lydgate's letter is frankly uninterested in such performance details.[29] Because he was crafting an introductory letter, he did not have to anticipate what followed the mummers' entry. Presumably, the mummers brought gifts to the Mayor. If so, their gifts are none of Lydgate's concern on this occasion. Mummers often play music and dance. Did these mummers do so? Lydgate's letter cannot say. Lydgate's letter, in other words, is clearly not a performance script. It is only a letter, a literary device which plays an introductory role in the mumming. The actual performance of the mumming includes and extends beyond the letter.[30]

---

28 Wickham's suggestion gains strength from the fact that the presenter eventually describes two other ships with allegorical scriptures "painted" upon their sides. But after all, the narrator may merely be indulging his audience in some colorful narration.

29 It is possible, of course, that no one read the letter aloud. Jupiter's Pursuivant, as a part of the silent mumming, may simply have delivered the letter to the Mayor and his party. Perhaps they were expected to read it silently while watching the mumming.

30 The *Mumming for the Goldsmiths of London* (pp. 698-699) raises many of the same issues as does the Mercers' mumming. It too takes the form of a letter that a herald named Fortune delivers to the Mayor. There is nothing to prevent Fortune from declaiming the letter himself in this case, but the letter does not clearly define its speaker. Like the Mercer's letter, this one serves to introduce the mummers, who are disguised as Levites and who are bearing an ark, which is the most important visual "device" of this mumming and which probably has been

The Mumming at Hertford (pp. 675-682), as many have suggested, may not be a mumming at all but rather a disguising.[31] For the first time, the text seems to comprise something like a complete performance. It is not merely an introductory device. Nevertheless, it continues to play a role in a larger theatrical performance very similar to those we have been examining. Even in this, arguably the most ambitious of Lydgate's theatrical poems, his text is once again constructed as a self-conscious literary device used for performance purposes we cannot entirely envision within a larger performance. Instead of one such literary device, the Hertford performance seems to have required three, and Lydgate crafts them not as letters but, as Shirley defines them, as "billes". These texts, moreover, are for once carefully constructed to suit the supposed characters of the petitioners. He devises a "rude, uplandish" text for the husbands, a "boisterous" one for the wives, and a tolerantly amused, official judgment for the king. It is clear that these three texts served as important devices at three moments in the performance; it is not clear, however, that they constituted the whole performance.

It is important to see that these texts are not speeches in the usual dramatic sense. The husbands present one "bille" to the King; this is answered by a second "bille" on behalf of the wives. Then follows a third bill in the form of the King's judgment. Wickham thinks that after the Presenter "supplicates to the King on behalf of six peasant-husbands", an answering petition is delivered by "one of the wives, acting as spokesman for all six".[32] But the text does not say this. Like Clopper, "I am not convinced ... that the wives speak; it is quite possible that the presenter ventriloquizes them" (Clopper 2001: 163). I would guess, in fact, that the comic effect would be greater in watching a solemn, correct court official attempting to voice the prose of "rude uplandish" men and their "boisterous" wives. Once again, I think, Lydgate is interested in crafting texts. They serve the per-

---

richly fabricated by the Goldsmiths. The ark, indeed, serves as the mummer's gift to the Mayor. Like the narrator of the Windsor mumming, the Goldsmiths narrator interacts considerably with the actors and audience. In the middle of the text, he commands the mummers to sing, but he probably means for them to sing after he has completed his narration, not as an interlude within his narration.

31 Wickham (1959-2002, 1: 204-205) distinguishes between the mumming, at which gifts were presented, and the disguising, at which they were not.

32 Wickham (1959-2002, 1: 204) thinks that for once Lydgate has divided the lines of the Hertford mumming between two speakers: a "Presenter" who "supplicates to the King on behalf of six peasant-husbands" and "one of the wives, acting as spokesman for all six", who "pleads for judgment on their side". But, as Twycross – Carpenter point out, "although one of the poems contains what looks like a direct speech from a performer, the 'aunswer of the wyves' in the Hertford entertainment, this is also a 'bill' by way of *replicatio*, which could be delivered by a representative" (Twycross – Carpenter 2002: 160 n. 44). In fact, since both husbands and wives present "bills of petition" to the King, there is no reason why the same presenter cannot declaim both.

formance as important devices – as both literary texts to be read (by someone), and as physical texts to be handled, referred to, and officially disposed of. How the actors do these things are not Lydgate's concern.

Perhaps the one mumming that resembles most closely Lydgate's other devising work is the *Mumming at Windsor* (pp. 691-694). Once again Lydgate's text serves to introduce the performance – which again seems more like a disguising than a mumming – and it can thus tell us very little about the actual performance itself.[33] The text accordingly ends as the narrator promises that "þe story" will next "here be shewed in þyne heghe presence" to the King "here sitting in þy see". For once, the mumming recounts a traditional history: "howe þampull and þe floure delys came first to þe kynges of Fraunce by myrakle at Reynes", and it does so at a politically charged moment (Christmas, 1429) when Henry VI is being prepared to travel to Rheims to be crowned King of France. To enact this history properly, however, the performers seem to have required an emblematic pageant for special effects. Two miraculous descents had to take place: an angel had to descend from heaven bringing a blue shield with fleurs-de-lys painted on it, and a dove had to descend with the golden ampulla. As a consequence, Lydgate's textual device here functions in much the same way as did his device for the sotilties at Henry's coronation banquet. The story of the fleur-de-lis provided the history, and the pageant artists had crafted a pageant to illustrate that history. In this pageant text, we see Lydgate once again crafting a literary scripture to accompany an emblematic pageant "history".

Perhaps Lydgate's *Mumming at London* (pp. 682-688) comes closest to the kind of comprehensive device for an entire performance. Lydgate's most textually ambitious theatrical device, it was composed, according to Shirley, to accompany "a desguysing to fore þe gret estates of þis lande, þane being at London", a phrase that suggests a meeting of Parliament, "almost certainly the parliament that opened on 13 October 1467" (Pearsall 1997: 28). Lydgate's text seems to adopt script-like conventions quite unlike the other textual devices we have been examining. Entrances are marked with brief stage directions: "Loo, first komeþe in Dame Fortune"; "Now komeþe here þe first lady of þe foure [Virtues], Dame Prudence"; and so on, through five successive entrances (pp. 682, 686).[34] The text

---

33 "The presentation is again extremely formal: the verses are spoken by an unnamed speaker, almost certainly Lydgate himself, and precede, not accompany, the dumb-show of the events they describe" (Pearsall 1970: 185-186). Wickham (1959-2002, 1: 205) thinks Shirley's description of this performance as a mumming in incorrect because there are "no visitation by strangers, no presentation of gifts". He also thinks it consists of a "dramatized debate", but this is clearly mistaken.

34 Although these "stage directions" may represent Shirley's editorial insertions rather than Lydgate's text, nevertheless the text, in each case, strongly indicates these entries as well: "Loo, heer þis lady in youre presence / Of poetis called is Dame Prudence, / þe which with

further specifies (ll. 316-325) such important props as Prudence's mirror, Rightwysnesse's balance, Magnyfycence's sword (though it omits to mention Attem-
peraunce's attribute). For the first time, Lydgate conceives of the narrator as inter-
acting with both the audience and the actors, if only in formulaic ways.[35] Thus,
the narrator deliberately draws the attention of the audience to the arrival of each
new character: "Seþe here þis lady, Rightwysnesse. / Of alle vertues she is
pryncesse, / For by þe scales of hir balaunces / Sheo sette hem all in gouuer-
naunces" (ll. 173-176). And at the end, the Presenter concludes the performance
by banishing Dame Fortune ("lat Fortune go pley hir wher hir list") and by com-
manding the four Virtues to sing "With al youre hoole hert entiere / Some nuwe
songe aboute þe fuyre, / Suche oon as you lykeþe best" (ll. 338-342).

Unless this text can be construed as devising only an interlude in a much larger and more complex performance, we have here, for the first time, a text that
prescribes an undeniably complete performance: it begins with the entrance of
Dame Fortune, and ends with her exit and the singing of the Virtues. It consists of
a series of presentations, much as if the Bishopswood or Eltham mummings had
been extended by accretion of other presentational episodes. But even so, Lydgate
seems to have composed a text that does not self-consciously refer to itself as a
text. For once, Lydgate is not devising a text to play a role in a performance, he is
instead devising an entire performance. Shirley's headnote describes this text as
"þe deuyse of a desguysing", and he may well be using the word in its technical
sense. If it is a device, then it is the sort of comprehensive device that governs an
entire performance, much like the primary devices for a suite of tapestries, a collection of sotilties, or a series of street pageants. Other artisans – actors, costume
makers, property fabricators – will use this text to plan their own contributions.

If we are to understand Lydgate's importance for the history of the drama,
then, we must try not to see him as some sort of evolutionary link connecting
mimed performance to true drama. Nor must we imagine that Lydgate operated as
a kind of dramaturge, flitting about the court, organizing the building of pageants,
the tailoring of costumes, the training of dancers, and the direction of actors.
Lydgate's theatrical devices, in fact, do not offer any evidence that Lydgate was
physically present for the planning or the performances. Except for the *Mumming
at London*, Lydgate seems to have provided only textual devices that serve spe-

---

hir mirrour bright, / By þe pourveyaunce of hir forsight / And hir myrrour, called provydence,
/ Is strong to make resistence / In hir forsight, as it is right, / Ageyns Fortune and al hir
might" (ll. 139-46).

35   Twycross-Carpenter 2002: 158 n. 39 suggest that "the Virtues in the 'disguising' of Fortune
and the Four Cardinal Virtues may have presented their attributes to the presiding dignitaries
of the feast: see lines 315-27". If so, then the narrator's interactions also include him com-
manding the presentation of gifts. If the Virtues do perform this action, however, it would indicate that Lydgate only thought of entrances as requiring stage directions.

cific and limited dramatic purposes. Most of these, as we have seen, have only a vague sense at best of how they were to be performed. For the most part, the over-all performances to which he contributed were contrived by others, and he left the performance details to the artistry of the actors. He may never have met those with whom he cooperated in devising these theatrical performances, and he may have attended few or none of them. He was sought out for his devices not because he was recognized to be a theatrical composer, but rather because he was re-nowned as a poet and because he had wide experience in the art of devising. It is as a deviser, then, and not as a playwright, that we will have to understand Lydgate's theatrical career.

References

Anglo, Sydney
    1969   *Splectacle, Pageantry, and Early Tudor Policy*. Oxford: Clarendon Press.
Baskervill, C. R.
    1936   "William Lily's Verse for the Entry of Charles V Into London". *The Huntington Library Bulletin* 9: 1-14.
Carpenter, John
    1432   "Letter Describing the London Entry of Henry VI", Pp. 457-463 in Henry Thomas Riley (ed.), *Munimenta Gildhallæ Londoniensis; Liber Albus, Liber Custumarum, et Liber Horn*. (Rolls Society, No. 12), vol. 3. London: Longman, Brown, Green, Longmans, and Roberts.
Chambers, E. K.
    1903   *The Mediaeval Stage*. London: Oxford University Press. 2 vols.
Clopper, Lawrence M.
    2001   *Drama, Play, and Game: English Festive Culture in the Medieval and Early Modern Period*. Chicago and London: University of Chicago Press.
"A Device for Sotilties at a Banquet for Queen Jane Seymour"
    1536   Fol. 22r. British Library, Additional MS 9835.
Forbes, Derek
    1998   *Lydgate's Disguising at Hertford Castle: The First Secular Comedy in the English Language*. Pulborough, West Sussex: Blot Publishing. Foreword by Glynne Wickham.
Green, Richard Firth
    1976   "Three Fifteenth-Century Notes". *English Language Notes* 14: 14-17.
Hall, Edward
    1809   *The Union of the Two Noble and Illustre Famelies of Lancastre and York*, Henry Ellis (ed.). London: J. Johnson.
Ives, E. W.
    1986   *Anne Boleyn*. Oxford: Basil Blackwell.

Kipling, Gordon
    1992   "'A Horse Designed by Committee': The Bureaucratics of the London
            Civic Triumph in the 1520s". *Research Opportunities in Renaissance
            Drama* 31: 79-89.
    1998   *Enter the King: Theatre, Liturgy, and Ritual in the Medieval Civic Tri-
            umph*. Oxford: Clarendon Press.
Lily, William
    1522   *Of the tryumphe / and the verses that charles themperour / & the most
            myghty redouted kyng of England / Henry the.viii. were saluted with /
            passyng through London*. London: Richard Pynson. STC 5017.
Lydgate, John
    1934   *The Minor Poems of John Lydgate: Part II, Secular Poems*, Henry Noble
            MacCracken (ed.). (Early English Text Society, OS 192). London: Ox-
            ford University Press.
MacCracken, Henry Noble
    1911   "King Henry's Triumphal Entry Into London, Lydgate's Poem, and Car-
            penter's Letter". *Archiv Für das Studium der Neueren Sprachen und Lite-
            raturen* 126: 75-102.
More, Sir Thomas
    1931   *The English Works of Sir Thomas More*, W. E. Campbell (ed.). London:
            Eyre and Spottiswoode. 2 vols.
Nichols, John Gough (ed)
    1846   *The Chronicle of Calais, in the Reigns of Henry VII. and Henry VIII. to
            the Year 1540*. (Camden Society, No. 35). London: J. B. Nichols and
            Son.
Pearsall, Derek
    1970   *John Lydgate*. Charlottesville: The University Press of Virginia.
    1997   *John Lydgate (1371-1449): A Bio-Bibliography*. (ELS Monograph Series
            No. 71). Victoria, B.C.: English Literary Studies.
"Repertories".
    1522   Vol. 4. London, Corporation of London Records Office.
Reyher, Paul
    1909   *Les Masques Anglais*. Paris: Hachette.
Schirmer, Walter F.
    1961   *John Lydgate: A Study in the Culture of the XVth Century*, Ann E. Keep
            (trans.). Berkeley and Los Angeles: University of California Press.
Somers, John, Baron Somers
    1751   *A Fourth Collection of Scarce and Valuable Tracts*. London: F. Cogan. 4
            vols.
Thomas, A. H. and I. D. Thornley (eds)
    1938   *The Great Chronicle of London*. London and Aylesbury: George W.
            Jones.
Twycross, Meg and Sarah Carpenter
    2002   *Masks and Masking in Medieval and Early Tudor England*. Aldershot:
            Ashgate.

Tydeman, William
    1994   "An Introduction to Medieval English Theatre", Pp. 1-36 in Richard Bea-
            dle (ed.), *The Cambridge Companion to Medieval English Theatre.* Cam-
            bridge: Cambridge University Press.

Wayment, Hilary
    1972   *The Windows of King's College Chapel Cambridge: A Description and
            Commentary.* (Corpus Vitrearum Medii Aevi, Great Britain), Supplemen-
            tary Volume I. London: Oxford University Press.

Webb, Geoffrey
    1957   "The Office of Devisor", Pp. 297-308 in D. J. Gordon (ed.), *Fritz Saxl
            1890-1948: A Volume of Memorial Essays from His Friends in England.*
            London: Thomas Nelson and Sons Ltd.

Welsford, Enid
    1927   *The Court Masque: A Study in the Relationship Between Poetry and the
            Revels.* New York: Russell & Russell, Inc.

Wickham, Glynne
    1959-2002   *Early English Stages 1300 to 1660.* London and Henley: Routledge &
            Kegan Paul. 5 vols in 4.
    1987   *The Medieval Theatre.* 3rd. Cambridge: Cambridge University Press.

Withington, Robert
    1918-20   *English Pageantry: An Historical Outline.* Cambridge, Mass.: Harvard
            University Press. 2 vols.

Wolffe, Bertram
    1981   *Henry VI.* London: Eyre Methuen.

Text and Meter

French Symmetry, Germanic Rhythm, and Spanish Metre[1]

Martin J. Duffell, Queen Mary, University of London

The early history of versifying in the Castilian language is, to say the least, curious and merits reappraisal and a new, more consistent, explanation.[2] The modern consensus among historical metrists is that Castilian poets did not count syllables at the very beginning of the thirteenth century, but that they rapidly adopted the practice, only to abandon it in the fourteenth, and rediscover it in the middle of the fifteenth. This vacillation is unparalleled elsewhere in Western Europe and is so far from the norm in modern Romance that the uncounted syllables that characterize Old Spanish verse are usually termed *versificación irregular* (Henríquez Ureña 1933). This label is oxymoronic, because the definition of *verse* is numerically regulated language (Lotz 1960: 135). Unregulated language is, of course, *prose*, and at the beginning of the twentieth century some great scholars declared themselves mystified as to what, if anything, was being regulated in early Castilian verse; thus Federico Hanssen called the versification of the *Poema de Mio Cid* (at least as it appears in the unique manuscript) rhymed prose (1909: 455), while Ramón Menéndez Pidal described it as primitive, irregular, and governed by unknown laws (1908: 82-83).[3]

---

1 The Ancient Greeks used the terms *symmetry* to describe the static pose of the figures in art of the Archaic period (before 480 B.C.), and *rhythm* to describe the mobile stance of those in later periods (see Richter 1987: 56-75 and 96-166). Symmetry implies that the limbs mirror one another, whereas in rhythm they contrast and balance. Modern linguistic metrics borrows from the Ancient Greeks the terms *metre*, denoting measurement, and *foot*, denoting the basic contrast (asymmetry) implied in rhythm. The Greeks called the elements in such a contrast *arsis* and *thesis*, modern writers label these elements *w (weak)* and *s (strong)*.

2 For several years Andy Kelly has urged me to pursue and publish an explanation of the changes in the metric typology of Old Spanish verse. In particular, he pointed out that the *Rimado de Palacio* must be a key text in such an enterprise, one of his many valuable insights for which I shall always be grateful.

3 Metre is the numerical regulation of language and is of several different types (see Lotz 1960, Pighi 1971: 3-64, and Preminger et al. 1974); clearly Hanssen and Menéndez Pidal were looking for only one, *syllabic* verse, and they failed to find it. The other types relevant to the present article are *accentual* and *stress-syllabic*. Traditional metrics held that the former regulates the number of accents and the latter both the number of syllables and the position of accents in the line. Modern linguistic metrics, however, has shown that it is not accent, but *prominence* that is regulated in these types of verse: syllables prominent in normal delivery because they are given greater stress than their neighbours. Note that, in languages with dynamic accent, phrasal stress renders one of two adjacent accented syllables more prominent than the other (Hayes 1995: 367-391), unless there is a distinct pause between them in delivery. I have indicated such a pause by the symbols [V] in instance (2), below.

What was obscure in 1908 is clearer to metrists in 2002, largely as a result of three developments: (1) a greater appreciation of the artistry involved in the production of some early Castilian texts (see, for example, Russell 1952 and Arizaleta 1999); (2) advances in the discipline of linguistics, particularly in the new field of metrical phonology;[4] (3) the application of modern scientific methods to metrical theory: the *transformational generative* method, derived from linguistics, and the descriptive method, which employs sophisticated statistical tools such as *probability modelling.*[5] Although a new consensus has resulted from these developments on some of the Castilian texts that puzzled metrists a century ago, there has yet to appear a holistic explanation of the mixture of syllabic regularity and irregularity that we find in medieval Castilian verse. This article is an attempt to provide one by employing all the tools currently available.

Before proceeding to my textual analysis, however, I shall discuss a fundamental hypothesis in modern metrics: the *principle of fit,* which states that metres evolve in such a way as to enable them to employ the core lexicon of the language concerned (Hanson & Kiparsky 1996: 294). They also evolve in such a way as to be a good fit for the phonology of the language concerned, since, "in John Thompson's felicitous phrase [...] meter is "language imitating itself""(Hanson & Kiparsky 1996: 325). One corollary of this is that, as phonologies change, so metres must adapt, and this is always the case when poets composing in one language imitate metres in another with a differing phonology. A clear example of the principle of fit, and one that is vital to the theme of this article, is French versification, which employs three of the most salient features of that language's phonology: *right-strength* (the right-most full syllable of words is the one with a potential for stress), *phrasal stress* (which the loss of word stress in modern French foregrounds), and *syllable-timing* (syllables are allocated equal time in delivery).[6] The combination of these three features allows French poets to create a temporal regularity, or *rhythm,* by placing a regular number of syllables between phrasal stresses (Cornulier 1996: 115).[7] As Benoît de Cornulier notes (1996: 111), the French syllabic method of versifying is a good fit only for languages with very

---

4   For an introduction to metrical phonology and the precise definition of its terms see Hogg & McCully 1987 and Hayes 1995.

5   For examples of transformational generative metrics see Hanson 1995 and Hanson & Kiparsky 1996; for statistical studies see Tarlinskaja 1976 & 1993; for probability modelling see Gasparov 1987.

6   The alternative tendency to syllable-timing is stress-timing, as in modern English, where normal delivery makes the intervals between stresses of approximately equal duration.

7   Old French had both primary and secondary word stress (Einhorn 1974: 2) and the deficit in the modern language seems to be the result of a steady weakening that occurred earlier in some dialects than in others. Mid-line accentual regulation can be detected in French verse of the ninth and tenth centuries but not in that of the eleventh; loss of word stress was complete only in the sixteenth.

weak or no word stress, and there are very few of them (he cites Japanese and, perhaps, Magyar as the only two comparable languages).

French verse is syllabic, and this may have influenced the hypothesis of Antoine Meillet (1923), that all Indo-European metrical systems have evolved from syllabic verse. M. L. Gasparov (1996: 49-54) supports this view, arguing that other types of metre were produced by linguistic changes, such as syncope, schwa-loss, and the development of stress-timing. Meillet based his hypothesis on three groups of written texts: (1) the oldest surviving Iranian verse, which is syllabic; (2) the earliest Sanskrit verse, which is regular in syllable count but has durational patterns at the line end; (3) Aeolic metres in Ancient Greek, which are regular in syllable count (although most surviving Greek verse, equally ancient, is not). Note that all these texts date from the infancy of literacy; the first two, in particular, were the products of a newly literate priesthood. It is, of course, much easier to count written syllables than spoken ones; but we can be sure that the first Indo-European verse was oral (because the borrowing of Semitic writing systems can be approximately dated). It is very likely, therefore, that illiterate speakers of a synthetic language would recognize groups of four words much more easily than groups of twelve syllables, and thus it would have been much easier for them to base long lines on the number of words.[8] In synthetic languages with word stress the number of major words equals the number of lexical stresses. The accentual folk verse found by Gasparov (1996: *passim*) in most modern European languages is thus probably directly descended from word-based oral systems rather than from syllabic ones.[9]

How Castilian and other Romance languages acquired their stress (dynamic accent) has been the subject of scholarly controversy.[10] On balance, it seems

---

8   Modern cognitive science has demonstrated that humans instinctively recognize or (*subitize*) numbers up to four (Hurford 1987: 93-95); numbers up to seven or eight (the boundary between short- and long-line verse) we can learn to recognize immediately, but only with practice (Miller 1956); larger numbers we have to learn to count.

9   Geoffrey Russom introduced the term *word-feet* to describe the structures on which Old Germanic accentual verse is based (1987: 8-24); the traditional terms for the prominence contrasts found in the verse of languages with dynamic accent are *beats* and *offbeats* (Attridge 1982: 74-144) or *upbeats* and *downbeats* (Jakobson 1960: 359-364).

10   All modern Romance and Germanic languages have a stress (dynamic) accent, as opposed to a melodic one like that of Ancient Greek (Elcock 1975: 51). The most important acoustic correlate of dynamic accent (stress) in modern English and Spanish is a shift in fundamental frequency (higher pitch); this is reinforced by greater length and increased volume (see Fry 1958, Bolinger & Hodapp 1961, Quilis 1971, and Puentes Romay 1997). The history of Latin accent is controversial: Allen argues that Classical Latin had dynamic accent (1973: 151-154); evidence in favour of this hypothesis includes the imposition of some accentual rules on Greek metres by Roman poets (1973: 166-71), the survival of passages of accentually regular folk verse (Du Méril 1843: 106-109), and the fact that Romance languages not spoken by Germanic peoples (e.g. Rumanian) have dynamic accent. Other writers, however,

likely that medieval Castilian had stress because Latin did, and that any accentual patterns found in its verse are descended from those found in Latin of various periods. Although most subsequent Spanish verse has been syllabic, some medieval Castilian verse is clearly based on regularity of accent and not syllable count. Most notably, as Juan Carlos Bayo (1999) pointed out, a large body of accentually regular folk verse has survived that is probably older than any of the texts studied in the present article. This includes the *Refranes que dizen las viejas tras el fuego* (Canellada 1980), the collection and preservation of which is attributed to the Marqués de Santillana (b. 1398, d. 1458). While many of the proverbs in this work have regularity in both the number of accents and syllable count, many others have only the former. I have emphasized both syllabification and stress in the following examples:[11]

(1)	A ca-<u>ba</u>-llo co-me-<u><u>dor</u></u>,	ca-<u>bes</u>-tro <u><u>cor</u></u>to	7F + 4F
(2)	A <u><u>buen</u></u> bo-<u><u>ca</u></u>do,	<u><u>buen</u></u> [V] <u><u>gri</u></u>to	4F + 2F
(3)	A di-<u>ne</u>-ros to-<u><u>ma</u></u>dos,	<u><u>bra</u></u>-zos que-<u><u>bra</u></u>dos	6F + 4F
(4)	A <u><u>dos</u></u> pa-<u><u>la</u></u>bras	<u><u>tres</u></u> pe-<u><u>dra</u></u>das	4F + 3F

The *refranes* are far from being the only type of medieval Hispanic verse that shows signs of accentual regulation. Other examples are the Galician-Portuguese *cantigas de amigo* (where it is combined with syllabic regulation; see Parkinson 2001), the folk songs known as *muñeiras* (see Milá y Fontanals 1893), and the *verso de arte mayor* (see Duffell 1999a and 1999b).

The Castilian language has strong word stress, full final vowels, and syllable-timing.[12] Its phonology is thus a good fit for an accentual metrics in which the

---

have argued that Classical Latin, like Ancient Greek, had a melodic accent that became dynamic in the second century A.D. (Lote 1939: 226, Norberg 1958: 87, and Elcock 1975: 51). Their evidence is some Classical descriptions of Latin accent that are suspect because they are so obviously translations of Greek definitions.

11   I have adopted a number of measures to facilitate scansion of my examples: (1) extra space between words and a wider space at the caesura; (2) hyphens to indicate separately counted syllables; (3) superscript for vowels not included in the syllable count (other than the post-tonic, or extrametrical, syllables in final strong positions). To illustrate the structure of the line in terms of my proposed verse design, I have underlined the prominent syllables in each hemistich. Double underlining indicates a major prominence (an accented syllable in a strong position), and single underlining a lesser one (a monosyllable or secondary stress in a strong position, or an accented syllable in a weak one). I have also indicated the length of hemistichs by arabic numerals denoting the number of syllables to the final stress, with a following letter: M (masculine, Sp. *agudo*) for lines with no extrametrical syllable, F (feminine, Sp. *grave*) for those with one, and E (Sp. *esdrújulo*) for those with two.

12   It should be noted that modern Peninsular Portuguese has become stress-timed; Hall 1965 argues that Old Spanish was stress-timed, the product of a 'Germanic (Visigothic) superstratum'.

number of stresses is regulated but in which they occur at irregular intervals, as in (1) to (4) above. Typically the Castilian phrase contains two or three stresses as compared with the one (final, phrasal) stress of French. An accentual line is more like the Castilian language imitating itself than is a syllabic one (although it is easier for Castilian speakers to perceive syllabic patterns than for English speakers, because syllable-timing aids their perception and Castilian phrases have always been right-strong). When Castilian poets decided to imitate French syllabic metres, however, they faced two problems: (1) irregularly occurring word stress, disrupting the temporal regularity of the phrasal stresses, and (2) post-tonic syllables at the caesura of long lines, which also interfered with temporal regularity.[13] The history of Castilian versification between 1200 and 1550 can be interpreted as the story of how poets faced and overcame these problems. I have related the second part of that story elsewhere: Duffell 1999a, 1999b, and 2000 describe fifteenth- and sixteenth-century efforts to import syllabic versification. Here, therefore, I shall concentrate on the interplay between syllable count (symmetry) and accent (rhythm) in the long-line verse of the thirteenth and fourteenth centuries.[14] The six key texts I shall use are:

(1) the *Poema de Mio Cid* (Michael 1987); the date given in the unique manuscript is according to our calendar 1207 (for the latest discussion of the date of composition see Bayo 2002);

(2) the *Libro de Alixandre* (Nelson 1973), an anonymous poem which is now believed to have been composed at the very beginning of the thirteenth century (see Arizaleta 1999);

(3) the *Milagros de Nuestra Señora* (Dutton 1971), composed by Gonzalo de Berceo, a prolific poet who we know was still alive in the early 1250s.

(4) the *Poema de Fernán González* (Geary 1987), composed at the monastery of San Pedro de Arlanza, was long believed to have been completed in 1251; more recently it has been argued that it was composed in 1276 or slightly later (see Deyermond 1991: 56);

---

13 Duffell 2000 argues that in the fifteenth century poets and audiences learned to ignore the mid-line stresses in shorter lines, thus enabling them to be composed and recognized instantly, and that two different attempts were made by the Marqués de Santillana to develop a purely syllabic long line.

14 The development of Castilian short-line verse is chronicled by Clarke 1964. She provides evidence to show that the *octosílabo* evolved into a syllabic metre only in the course of the fifteenth century (1964: 18-51). For a traditional analysis of the *octosílabo* see Navarro (Tomás) 1973, for a modern linguistic one see Piera 1980: 174-191. To Navarro it is a syllabic metre with variable rhythms, to Piera it is a trochaic metre that has lost any mid-line prominence constraints.

(5) the *Libro de Buen Amor* (Gybbon-Monypenny 1988), composed by Juan Ruiz; the first version is dated 1330 by Alan Deyermond (1971: 118), and the revised one 1343. Henry A. Kelly (1984) argues that the work may have reached its final form only in the 1380s;

(6) the *Rimado de Palacio* (Orduna 1981), composed by the chancellor Pero López de Ayala over a period between 1379 and 1403;

All of these texts include a large number of lines that have the same surface structure as the French alexandrine (their hemistichs each contain six syllables to the final stress). The first, however, represents one of the few witnesses to an earlier epic metre, and the last encapsulates a poem in *arte mayor*. I shall demonstrate that there is an essential continuity in the metrics of these texts that has gone largely unnoticed.[15]

Although the *Alixandre* may be the earlier poem, it will be helpful to begin with the *Cid*, the lines of which vary greatly in length. Alberto Montaner's analysis of the length of the *Cid*'s hemistichs shows that 20 per cent have fewer than seven syllables, 40 per cent have exactly seven, 25 per cent have exactly eight, and 15 per cent have more than eight (1993: 12). Thus at least 60 per cent of the poem's hemistichs fail to conform to any given syllable count, and in extreme instances the number of syllables in a hemistich may be four or fourteen. As Ian Michael pointed out, it is difficult to envisage that irregularity of this magnitude is simply the result of dictation and transcription error (1987: 18). The range of hemistich lengths can be seen from the following examples:

(5) los de dentro   (35a)   3F
(6) fa-bló Mio Çid   (30a)   4M
(7) tan fuer-te-mien-tre llo-rando   (1b)   7F
(8) en buen ho-ra cin-xies-tes es-pada   (41b)   9F
(9) non quie-ro fa-zer en el mo-nes-terio   (252b)   10F

A minority of lines in the *Cid* have the same syllable count as the alexandrine; for example, the fourth line of the unique manuscript:

(10) al-cán-daras va-zías,   sin pie-lles e sin mantos   6F + 6F

An even smaller minority of lines have the same syllable count as two lines (*octosílabos*) of ballad metre, for example line 30.

15 Saavedra Molina notes similarities between old Germanic verse and the *verso de arte mayor* (1946: 8-18), Clarke notes similarities between *cuaderna vía* and *arte mayor* (1964: 60-61), and Tittman argues that the latter may have been derived from the former (1969: 277-281).

(11)   as-<u>cón</u>-den-se de Mio <u>Çid</u>   ca nol' <u>o</u>-san de-zir <u>na</u>da   7F + 7F

In the late nineteenth century and in the first half of the twentieth many writers and editors argued that the text we have is the result of transcription or scribal error, and must be derived from an original in either alexandrines or *octosílabos*. These arguments are criticized in detail in Duffell 2002; they are now generally discredited.

The modern consensus on the metre of the *Cid* is that summarized by Alberto Montaner (1993: 36), who lists some of the writers identifying two metrically significant stresses in each hemistich: Navarro Tomás (1956: 60-61), Maldonado (1965), López Estrada (1982: 217-225), Pellen (1985-86), and Goncharenko (1988: 51). These two principal stresses are often reinforced in longer hemistichs by a subsidiary prominence, as in my instance (7) above. Duffell 2002 compares the line structure of the *Cid* with that of *Sir Gawain and the Green Knight* (Andrew & Waldron 1987), a well-known example of the fourteenth-century English alliterative metre. It concludes that the two poems have almost identical verse designs.[16]

The verse design of the *Cid* can be measured against Hanson & Kiparsky's five parameters (1996) as follows: (1) *position number*: eight (four in each hemistich, two *weak* and two *strong*); (2) *orientation*: the template is right-strong, weak positions preceding strong ones; (3) *position size*: strong positions may contain only one syllable (which may be followed by an optional post-tonic syllable); weak positions may contain 0-6 syllables; (4) *prominence type*: syllable strength; (5) *prominence site*: strong positions, which are constrained from containing lexically weak syllables (those adjacent to a lexical stress). Because only strong positions are constrained (5), strong syllables can occur in weak positions, producing the (subsidiary) prominences we have noted. And because the prominence type is strength (4), any type of monosyllable can occur in a strong position. This verse design is very similar to that of *Sir Gawain* as described by Andrew & Waldron 1987: 45-50.

---

16   For concise definitions of the technical terms employed by modern linguistics see Crystal, 1985. A *verse design* consists of the abstract pattern (*template*) that a poet has in his head plus the *rules* that govern the types of linguistic material that may correspond to the pattern in individual lines, or *verse instances*. Because they are abstractions, templates are described as containing *positions*, which produce a binary *weak/strong* or *strong/weak* contrast. Non-correspondence between verse instance and design is termed *tension*; two common types of tension are *substitution* (two light syllables appearing where one syllable is the norm) and *inversion* (a strong/weak combination of syllables appearing where a weak/strong one is the norm, or vice versa). *Strong* (*s*) syllables are those that the lexicon determines are more *prominent* than their *weak* (*w*) neighbours in polysyllabic words. The *closure principle* states that rules are stricter at the end of linguistic units and laxer at their beginnings (see Smith 1968).

This similarity is unlikely to be due to Germanic influence; it is more likely to be linguistically determined, a corollary of the principle of fit. Accentual metres tend to evolve in any language with strong word stress, and vestiges of such verse have survived from elsewhere in the Romance-speaking area. The three earliest surviving French poems have an accentual regularity not found in later French verse: *Sainte Eulalie*, the *Passion* of Clermont, and the *Vie de St Léger* (see Henry 1953: 6-13). Some traditional Italian folk verse is also accentually regular, and among the oldest surviving Italian texts is a *Lauda* that has a metre very like *arte mayor* (see Leonetti 1934: 119-127). Finally, Anglo-Norman and Venetian-French epics have survived that are syllabically irregular (Hills 1925). The line structure of all these poems is best explained in terms of its accentual pattern. It seems likely, therefore, that an accentual tradition of versifying existed among the (mostly illiterate) speakers of early Romance. The loss of French word-stress and the growth of literacy combined to ensure that this oral accentual verse would be superseded by the syllabic system of versifying developed in France in the eleventh century and subsequently exported to Italy and the Iberian Peninsula.

Other than the *Cid*, there remain only a very few manuscript fragments to bear witness to epic metre (see Alvar & Alvar 1991). Most of the long-line verse in my other texts is in *cuaderna vía*, the name given to monorhyme quatrains of what appear to be alexandrines, which have survived in Castilian poems of the thirteenth and fourteenth centuries. As I have noted, the alexandrine is a syllabic metre: its lines comprise two hemistichs, each of six syllables (counted to the final stress, or seven if counted according to the Spanish convention). The Latin origins of both the alexandrine and the monorhyme quatrain are explored in depth by Avalle 1962. The earliest French poem in alexandrines dates from the middle of the twelfth century, but the line of 6 + 6 derived its name, and achieved widespread popularity, from the *Roman d' Alexandre*, which appeared in Paris c.1180. This story had been told in octosyllables, decasyllables, and a mixture of metres before Alexandre de Paris produced his version entirely in lines of 6 + 6 (see Henry 1953: 88-90). In the 150 years that followed, French poets composed almost all their long-line verse in alexandrines and reworked many existing texts from other metres to meet this vogue (Kastner 1903: 144-148). Probably the first Castilian poem in the metre, the *Libro de Alixandre* was composed very soon after the French vogue began, and *cuaderna vía* dominated Castilian long-line verse over the same period as its equivalent flourished in France (by the end of the fourteenth century the dominant French long line was once again the decasyllable; see Kastner 1903: 142-144).

One difference between the thirteenth-century alexandrines of France and Castile was the structure of the strophes in which they occurred: *cuaderna vía*, as I have noted, is a monorhyme quatrain, but in France the assonanced *laisse* of irregular length, which had been the metre of *chansons de geste* since the beginning of the eleventh century, continued to be widely employed. The only other differences between French and Castilian verse in this metre were the result of the differing phonologies of the two languages. In French the only post-tonic vowel is schwa, but in Castilian full vowels occur in this position, and in *esdrújulo* words two such vowels are present. *Esdrújulos* were generally confined to the first hemistich of Castilian alexandrines; but another important difference between alexandrines in the two languages arose from the quality of their final vowels. There has always been a tendency in French for final schwas to be lost in normal speech (this loss is almost complete in modern French); from the very first, syllabically regular French verse embraced a practice called elision, whereby final schwa could be deleted before a following vowel or diphthong and thus did not contribute to the syllable count.

There is a tendency in the Romance of the Iberian Peninsula for final vowels to be deleted in normal speech (technically termed *apocope*), but how common this is has varied considerably by time and place. There is also another marked tendency in Iberian Romance, to merge adjacent vowels. This is termed *synaloepha* when it applies to word-final vowels merging with word-initial ones, and in later periods Castilian versifiers generally employed it when counting syllables. The early *cuaderna vía* poets, however, resisted this tendency and, instead, adopted the practice derived from medieval Latin verse of including all written vowels in the count. This necessitated *hiatus* between adjacent vowels in adjacent words, although synaloepha is the normal tendency in Castilian speech, and was probably also the norm in thirteenth-century folk verse (see Navarro (Tomás) 1974: 104-105).

The metrical intention of the *Alixandre*'s author is not in doubt (2a-d):

(12) mes-ter tra-yo fer-moso   non es de jo-gla-ría;
(13) mes-ter es sin pe-ccado,   qua es de cle-re-cía;
(14) fab-lar cur-so ri-mado   por la qua-der-na vía
(15) a sí-la-bas con-ta-das,   qua es grant ma-es-tría

The poet boasts of his verse art, revealing that the lines of his rhymed quatrains are based on syllable count. The two manuscripts in which the complete poem have survived, however, do not support the perfection of technique the author claims: according to the analysis by Henry R. Lang (1914), 25 per cent of hemistichs in one and 31 per cent in the other do not have 6M/F/E syllables. Modern editors attribute this irregularity to scribal error and emend the text accordingly. But, if the editors are right, the irregularity of the manuscripts shows that the copyists were ignoring syllable count, and this in itself is a remarkable thing.

An analysis of the textual variants in a contemporary French text reveals just how remarkable the errors of the Castilian scribes were. The *Chanson d'Antioche* (Duparc-Quioc 1976) is an appropriate comparison: its alexandrines, composed in the thirteenth century, have survived in nine fourteenth- and fifteenth-century cop-

ies. These nine witnesses (as compared to two or three in the case of *cuaderna vía*
texts) produce a large number of textual variants, representing 60 per cent of lines
in the poem (a much higher proportion than in any *cuaderna vía* text). But only 1
per cent of the French variants affect syllable count (most often because a monosyllable is repeated); this compares with a figure over 50 per cent for *cuaderna vía*
(I have calculated this for both early (*Alixandre*) and late (*Rimado*) examples). We
must remember that the French and Castilian poems were copied by Latin-
speaking monks educated and supervised in the same way, and in scriptoria of the
same order. This raises important questions: why were Castilian copyists, unlike
French ones, oblivious to syllable count? And how did Castilian readers and audiences recognize the syllabic regularity of the thirteenth-century originals? I shall
return to this point when I discuss the fourteenth-century rules for adjacent vowel
treatment, below.

Editors of *cuaderna vía* texts have always found it easy to add a syllable to
deficient lines: monosyllabic articles, pronouns, and adjectives abound in Castilian. Manuscript lines with too many syllables were a more difficult problem, but
this was solved in 1905 by John Fitz-Gerald, who proposed that thirteenth-century
poets had used many apocopated forms that fell out of use; later scribes saw these
apocopations and expanded these to the full forms. Most editors welcomed this
hypothesis (see, for example, Alvar 1976: 71-79); it licensed them to delete final
vowels, in addition to adding monosyllables, thus producing texts perfectly regular in syllable count. But why did later copyists expand apocopations? This is
surely further proof that they were oblivious to the regular syllable count of the
lines they copied. It also has to be said that there is a piece of pure speculation in
Fitz-Gerald's hypothesis: that thirteenth-century manuscripts, none of which have
survived, were syllabically regular. In fact we have no idea when copyists (or
readers, or audiences) lost the sense that all *cuaderna vía* lines should have 6 + 6
syllables; all that we know is that they did.

There was one important difference between the French and Castilian texts:
the strength of word stress in Castilian. The mistaken expansion of apocopations
does not change the number of accented syllables (two or three per hemistich).
When the surviving *cuaderna vía* texts were read aloud, they would have been
indistinguishable from most lines of epic metre (other than the longest and shortest). Castilian word stress usually gives strict alexandrines of 6 + 6 either an iambic rhythm (by appearing in positions 2, 4, 6) or an anapaestic one (in 3 and 6), as
can be seen from the following lines (*Milagros* 3d, 5a, 24c, 28a, & 61a):

(16)   en ve-<u>ra</u>-no bien <u>frí</u>as   en i-<u>vier</u>-no ca-<u>lien</u>tes
(17)   la ver-<u>du</u>-ra del <u>pra</u>do,   la co-<u>lor</u> de las <u>flo</u>res
(18)   a-<u>llí</u> co-<u>rre</u>-mos <u>to</u>-dos,   va-<u>ssa</u>-llos e se-<u>nno</u>res
(19)   el ro-se-<u>nnor</u> que <u>can</u>ta   por <u>fi</u>-na ma-es-<u>trí</u>a
(20)   a-<u>mi</u>-go, -<u>dí</u>-sso'l – <u>se</u>pas   qe <u>so</u> de <u>ti</u> pa- <u>ga</u>da

Both hemistichs in (16) & (17) are anapaestic, as are one third of all hemistichs in the *Milagros*. Harrison Arnold (1954: 151-152) notes that while such lines are common in the poem, extremely few of its quatrains are entirely in this rhythm. Navarro 1974: 86-88 argues that passages with this rhythm serve an expressive purpose: such a line is "slow, graceful and musical" (87). But I have analysed a large sample of such lines from the *Milagros* and concluded that most occur randomly (Duffell 1986: 116-118). All anapaestic hemistichs contain two prominent syllables (syllables carrying more accent than their neighbours), but very few iambic ones contain three. Only about 8 per cent of total hemistichs in *Milagros* have lexical stress in positions 2, 4, and 6, as in instances (18)a and (20)a above. The vast majority of iambic hemistichs have a monosyllable in one of the strong positions, as in (18)b and (20)b, or a secondary stress, as in (19)a and (19)b. The alexandrine of *cuaderna vía* is thus predominantly a line comprising two hemistichs, each with two prominent syllables, just like epic metre. Most hispanic metrists and editors have ignored this fact.

This is particularly surprising with regard to the *Poema de Fernán González*, because it has been strongly argued that this poem is a reworking in alexandrines of an earlier *cantar* in epic metre (see Victorio 1990: 13-14). The unique manuscript contains many syllabically irregular lines; for example, the following (fol. 1r, l.27; fol. 2r, l. 15: fol. 2v, l. 5; fol. 4r, l. 13):

(21) ca pre-<u>di</u>-co por su <u>vo</u>ca <u>mu</u>-cha <u>ma</u>-la sen-<u>ten</u>çia   7F + 6F
(22) Pa-<u>sa</u>-ron a [ ]es-<u>pan</u>na   con su <u>grran</u> po-<u>der</u>   6F + 5M
(23) dy-<u>xe</u>-ron los ma-<u>es</u>tros   <u>to</u>-do <u>es</u>-to non <u>va</u>-le <u>na</u>da   6F + 8F
(24) <u>to</u>-dos ves-<u>qu</u>-jan de <u>sus</u> de-<u>re</u>chos los <u>grran</u>-des & los me-<u>no</u>res   9F + 7F

Victorio 1990 regularizes all these lines: he omits "ca" in (21) and adds "el" after "su" in (22). In (23) he apocopates "vale" to "val'", and assumes synaloepha between "todo" and "esto", although elsewhere in the poem hiatus between "-o" and "-e" is the norm. In (24) he omits "todos", changes "vesquijan" to "vesquién" (disyllabic), and omits "los" before "menores". All these changes produce a line of 6 + 6 syllables, and each individual change can be defended, but it should be noted that every one of these lines, as it stands in the manuscript, is an acceptable line of epic metre. Victorio has therefore made a series of assumptions: (a) in the lost *cantar* these lines looked very much the way they do in the unique manuscript; (b) the author of the *Poema* converted them into alexandrines; (c) later scribal errors converted them back to epic metre; (d) the editor is therefore justified in changing them to how he thinks they read in the author's text. But, since this is the only version of the poem that has survived, there is another explanation of such epic lines: imperfect reworking from the *cantar* to the *Poema*. To put it simply, we do not know how regular the author's text was.

The question of poetic competence or, perhaps, intention (will to count) does not arise solely because copyists a hundred years later ignored syllable count. In the middle of the fourteenth century we find a work where it is clear that the poet himself did not care very much about it: that poet was Juan Ruiz, and his *Libro de Buen Amor* is undoubtedly (and deservedly) the most famous work employing *cuaderna vía*. Ruiz's lines in this metre are very irregular syllabically, an apparent random mixture of alexandrines, *octosílabos*, and lines of ambiguous length. The first three lines of the poem are typical:

(25)	Se-ñor Dios, q^{ue} a los jo-dí-os, pue-blo de per-di-çión	7F + 6M
(26)	sa-cas-te de cap-ti-vo, de po-der de Fa-raón	6F + 6M
(27)	a Da-niel sa-cas-te del po-ço de Ba-bi-lón	5F + 7M

While the second line in the book is a perfect alexandrine, the first is certainly not, and the third is even more interesting. Its first hemistich may be regularized by making "Da-ni-el" three syllables, but its second is one of many where the poet accepts 7M as the rhythmic equivalent of 6F syllables, instead of the usual 6M, as in (26). Note, however, that all three lines are perfectly good epic metre as they stand. Gerald Gybbon-Monypenny points out that syllabic irregularity in the *Libro de Buen Amor* is the norm, and argues that no line should be emended for metrical reasons alone (1988: 78). He concludes that Juan Ruiz probably often ignored syllable count and used the rhythm of the lines as his principal guide in versifying.

There is, thus, no doubt that at some stage in the manuscript transmission process copyists came to ignore the syllable count of *cuaderna vía* lines, and that by the middle of the fourteenth century its greatest poet had succumbed to the same accidie. We cannot, however, be sure that Castilian audiences of any period actually heard and recognized the syllabic regularity that the thirteenth-century poets set out to achieve. Since all medieval texts were composed for reading aloud, as García points out (1978: 45), readers would surely have had problems with the unpredictability of adjacent-vowel treatment in later *cuaderna vía* texts.[17] Although Clarke argues that hiatus remained the norm in Castilian verse of the late fourteenth century and synaloepha the exception (1948: 349), her own analysis of the *octosílabos* in each of the *Rimado*'s two manuscripts reveals that synaloepha gives the line a regular syllable count on 42 per cent of occasions (1948: 350-354). My own figure for a sample of López de Ayala's *cuaderna vía* in Orduna's edition is 44 per cent. To cope with this ambiguity, every reader would first have had to recognize and internalize the rules proposed by Clarke (1948:

---

17   Tittman 1969: 279 points out that applying synaloepha instead of hiatus converts some lines of *cuaderna vía* into *arte mayor*. Certainly synaloepha would make many hemistichs one or two syllables shorter and increase the proportion with triple-time rhythm.

349) and supported by Orduna (1981: 95n4). These rules state that synaloepha is permitted only when the two vowels are identical (but rarely when they are both *a*), when one of them is in an atonic monosyllable or disyllable, and when one of the vowels is either the *-o* of the first person singular or a prosthetic *e-*. The reader would then have had to anticipate the exceptions; for example, the first synaloepha is allowed and the second not in "Sant° en simpl^e unidat" (1b). Similarly we find "justo e verdadero" (6a) but "qu^e es poc^a e peligrosa" (8a) and "espaci° e logar" (19c). Such inconsistencies render the treatment of adjacent vowels in the *Rimado de Palacio* unpredictable, nor are they the only difficulties that readers faced. Orduna notes that *apocope*, *aphaeresis*, and *syncope* are used to "answer the needs of the metre", that is inconsistently and unpredictably (1981: 96).

It is, of course, relatively easy for a modern editor to manipulate these many ambiguities so as to render the majority of lines in a text regular. For a reader, with an audience waiting, it must have been quite impossible. Fourteenth-century listeners to recited *cuaderna vía* could not have appreciated the rhythm of the verse: even if they learned to ignore mid-line stresses, they would have found no temporal regularity in the final stresses of the wrongly delivered lines. The only rhythm that its intended audiences could have found in *cuaderna vía* must have lain somewhere else.

But to return to the *Rimado*, it is remarkable that, although editors have all these powerful tools for regularizing syllable count, a large number of lines still defy their efforts. García estimates that 25 per cent lines have the wrong number of syllables (1978: 43). Even Orduna is forced to confess that some lines are impossible to regularize (1981: 99). Among the many examples of lines with the wrong syllable count are the following (25a, 102b, 121b, 195c, 270b, & 902b):

(28)	<u>ju</u>-ro <u>muy</u> a me-<u>nudo</u> por el tu <u>nom</u>-bre Se-<u>ñor</u>	6F + 7M
(29)	la <u>vi</u>-ña, el <u>vino</u> <u>qui</u>-so <u>en</u>-de gus-<u>tar</u>	5F + 6M
(30)	mas <u>ti</u>-bi° e muy <u>frío</u> <u>pa</u>-ra <u>se</u> per-<u>der</u>	6F + 5M
(31)	<u>Li</u>-no e <u>Cle</u>to, que <u>fue</u>-ron <u>bien</u> u-<u>sar</u>	4F + 6M
(32)	non <u>fa</u>-gas in-<u>jurias</u> non <u>se</u>-as ca-lo-ña-<u>dor</u>	5F + 7M
(33)	que a <u>Dios</u> con-çe-<u>bir</u> o-tor-<u>ga</u>-do <u>te</u> se-<u>ría</u>	6M + 7F

In these instances, hemistichs (29)a, (30)b, & (31)a have too few syllables, while (28)b, (32)b, & (33)b have one too many. It should be noted, however, that all these hemistichs have two principal stresses, and some have a subsidiary stress, which makes them perfectly good epic metre.

The situation is made more complicated by the fact that *octosílabos* occur in the *cuaderna vía* of the *Rimado* as well as in the *coplas de arte menor* analysed by Clarke 1948. López de Ayala's long-line verse is thus, like that of Juan Ruiz, a sixes-and-sevens metre, although the chancellor sorted out the two line lengths rather better: long passages are in lines of 6 + 6, while others are in 7 + 7. García tabulates these passages to show that a change in metre usually marks a new poem, with lines of 6 + 6 also being employed for introductory and transitional strophes (1978: 47-48). Orduna, on the other hand, regards the line of 6 + 6 as the staple of the poem and the longer line as a source of variety, available for special effects, such as satire (1981: 97). He admits that there is a long passage (strophes 300-476) where the two line lengths are inextricably mixed, but argues that a change of line length usually signals a new poem.

Some of the transitions from one metre to the other, however, are very untidily managed; for example, these lines (991d, 995d, & 997d) follow a change from alexandrines to *octosílabos* in 990:

(34)	e pa-<u>la</u>-bras e que-<u>re</u>llas	a-<u>ña</u>-de[n] sin me-<u>su</u>ra	6F + 7F
(35)	pri-<u>me</u>-ro en sí <u>mes</u>-mo	<u>de</u>-ue po-<u>ner</u> es-car-<u>mien</u>to	6F + 7F
(36)	e que <u>des</u>-ta ma-<u>ne</u>ra	a <u>Job</u> po-d<u>rí</u>^a a-cu-<u>sar</u>	6F + 7M

Like instances (28) & (33), these are centaur lines, half one metre, half the other. Editors may have managed to segregate López de Ayala's two metres in their texts of the *Rimado*, but it is difficult to believe that any live performer of the lines I have quoted could have done so. Note again that, while alexandrines and *octosílabos* have to be prised apart with a crowbar, all the lines make perfectly good epic metre.

The foregoing analysis of *cuaderna vía* points to an alternative interpretation of its metre. Everyone involved in the transmission of these texts, readers, audiences, and scribes, may have perceived the verse design as a four-beat accentual one (like epic metre or *arte mayor*). In the thirteenth century poets may have counted syllables visually to produce a regularity that the oral audience could not appreciate. This would explain why, by the fourteenth century, any counting of syllables by poets seems to have been merely a tidying up after the creative event. Around 1400 Castilian poets simply gave up counting the syllables of their long lines and embraced an alternative way of making the native four-beat measure more regular. It is probably more than coincidence that this alternative, *arte mayor*, superseded *cuaderna vía* at roughly the same time as the alexandrine fell from favour in France.

Just as syllabic verse requires the prop of rhyme or assonance, so accentual verse has employed various aids to help the listener recognize the metre. In the oldest Latin and Germanic verse alliteration served as such an aid, and in thanes' halls four tugs at the strings of a harp probably served the purpose even better. At the end of the fourteenth century Castilian and English poets, independently, introduced the same new aid: regularizing the intervals between the beats. Making the majority of intervals exactly two syllables (instead of the one or three more common in normal speech) gives four-beat verse a very distinctive (triple-time) dancing rhythm. As Ker 1898 points out, this new rhythm became the rage in the verse of both languages, the similarities in their phonology temporarily overcoming the differences.[18] In Castile the new metre was known as the *verso de arte mayor* and López de Ayala employed it in strophes 818-857 of the *Rimado de Palacio*. Most modern metrists classify *arte mayor* as a stress-syllabic verse design with a template consisting of four amphibrachs: $w \, S \, w \quad w \, S \, w \quad w \, S \, w \quad w \, S \, w$ (see, for example, Clarke 1964: 51-61, Piera 1980: 95-98, and Duffell 1999a: 64-67). The wide range of syllabic and accentual variants that actually occur in the *arte mayor* of the *Rimado de Palacio* can be regarded as tension against such a design, as the following lines (838b, 829a, 831a, 834e, 833a, 825a, & 831d) illustrate:

(37)	To-le-do la grande,	lo-gar en Es-paña	5F + 5F
(38)	V Dios lo de-mande	per la su sen-tençia	4F + 5F
(39)	con grant re-ue-rrençia	V yo per-don pido	5F + 4F
(40)	e⁺non ve-o nin-guno	que⁺la quie-rᵃ a-co-rrer	6F + 6M
(41)	e con grant a-mor	des-ta con-clu-sion	5M + 5M
(42)	ca-llen di-a-leticos	e los ca-no-nistas	5E + 5F
(43)	de fa-blar do cansan	fa-blar los doc-tores	5F + 5F

The traditional analysis of these lines describes their variation from an amphibrachic norm in terms of "missing syllables", "extra syllables", and "(leftward/rightward) shifts of stress". Clarke 1964: 1-17 tabulates the frequency with which each of these phenomena occurs in the verse of a long list of poets. There is, however, another way of describing the variation found in these lines, one that makes *arte mayor* an accentual metre like the verse of the *Cid*. I shall couch such an accentual description in the terms of Hanson & Kiparsky's 1996 parametric theory. The right-strong template has eight positions; there is also a mid-line mandatory word boundary: the second and third strong positions (4 and 6) cannot be occupied by syllables of the same word. The maximum size of strong positions is one syllable (but hemistich-final ones may also contain the post-tonic syllables of a *grave* or *esdrújulo* word); the maximum size of weak positions is three syllables. The prominence site is strong positions and the prominence type is strength; thus weak syllables (those adjacent to a primary stress in the same word) are constrained from appearing in strong positions. We can observe the setting of these

---

18 Kennedy 1999 summarizes modern research into the structure of Middle English alliterative verse. It is clear that its second hemistichs, unlike those in Old English four-beat verse, are restricted in both syllable count and rhythm. Sixteenth-century *tumbling verse*, the English equivalent of Castilian *arte mayor*, is merely an extension of these restrictions to the whole line. For a late example (1579) of tumbling verse see Spenser's *Shepheardes Calendar*, 'May', 'July', and 'October' (McCabe 1999).

parameters in the instances above. While the majority of weak positions contain two syllables, position 1 in (38) and 5 in (39) are void (marked "V") and positions 1 and 5 in (40) contain two (marked "+"). Position 1 in (43) also contains two syllables and position 3 in (42) contains three, as a result of what is termed *inversion* in stress-syllabic metrics (which would regard the contents of positions 1-2 in (42) and 2-3 in (43) as having been transposed). Note that, because the prominence type is strength not stress, unaccented monosyllables and secondary stress may appear in strong positions ("la" in (38), "con" in (41), and "los" in (42)), while words like "a-le-ga-ciones" (848c) occupy both strong positions by virtue of their secondary stress (see Harris 1983: 85-86).

The reason for preferring an accentual description of Ayala's *arte mayor* is the amount of tension that has to be allowed if a stress-syllabic verse design is assumed: 15 per cent of his hemistichs are like the first of (42) and (43): they contain inversions. This figure is extremely high for such a strong form of tension; in delivery the triple-time (amphibrachic) rhythm would frequently be lost by the audience.[19] As Clarke's tables show, other Castilian poets subsequently developed the *verso de arte mayor* in different directions. Juan de Mena (b. 1411, d. 1456) favoured a stress-syllabic verse design: he significantly reduced the number of hemistichs with inversion to facilitate a triple-time delivery throughout. The Marqués de Santillana (see above) and Juan del Encina (b. 1468, d. 1529), on the other hand, tried to make their verse syllabic: they maintained the amount of inversion found in the *Rimado*, but their only exception to a line of 5 + 5 syllables was allowing a void position 1. Finally, the *arte mayor* of Juan de Padilla (b. 1468, d. ?1522) is regular in both rhythm and syllable count and his lines are almost perfectly amphibrachic. Unfortunately the demands of this ultra-regularity made his work semantically imprecise, stylistically flabby, and rhythmically monotonous.

In the middle of the sixteenth century Castilian poets abandoned the *verso de arte mayor*, the dominant metre of the fifteenth-century *cancioneros*, in favour of the Italianate *endecasílabo*. Syllabic regularity then remained the norm in Castilian versifying until the beginning of the twentieth century. Over that long period Spanish poets and readers learned how to count the syllables of short-line verse rapidly and easily, and they found in the *endecasílabo* sufficient accentual props to enable them to master longer lines, too.[20] It is, therefore, not surprising that most twentieth-century editors and critics ignored the accentual patterns that characterized Castilian long-line verse between 1200 and 1400 and sought syllabic

---

19 Lázaro Carreter 1972 argues in detail that Mena probably intended his *arte mayor* to be wrenched in delivery (for which the technical term is *recession*) so that any inversions were eliminated.

20 The *endecasílabo* has been classified as a metre transitional between syllabic and stress-syllabic (Gasparov 1987: 330-332; see also Duffell 1999a: 37-44).

ones. But, as the present article has tried to show, the accentual patterns probably meant a great deal more to audiences in that period than did the foreign fad of syllable count, which had to be reintroduced in the fifteenth century and triumphed only in the sixteenth. A four-beat rhythm, rather like that of old Germanic verse, is the constant we find in medieval Castilian verse; French symmetry, difficult to detect, and even more difficult to deliver, is the variable that obscures it.

References

Allen, W. Sidney
    1973   *Accent and rhythm: prosodic features of Latin and Greek: a study in theory and reconstruction*. Cambridge: Cambridge University Press.

Alvar, Manuel
    1976   "La apócope y la métrica", in: Manuel Alvar (ed.), 71-79.

Alvar, Manuel (ed.)
    1976   *Libro de Apolonio*, I. Madrid: Fundación Juan March and Castalia.

Alvar, Carlos – Manuel Alvar
    1991   *Épica medieval española*. (Letras Hispánicas 330.) Madrid: Cátedra.

Andrew, Malcolm – Ronald Waldron (eds.)
    1987   *The poems of the Pearl Manuscript: "Pearl", "Cleanness", "Patience", "Sir Gawain and the Green Knight"*. (2nd edition.) Exeter: University of Exeter.

Arizaleta, Amaia
    1999   *La translation d'Alexandre: recherches sur les structures et les significations du "Libro de Alexandre"*. (Annexes de Cahiers de Linguistique Hispanique Médiévale 12.) Paris: Séminaire d'Études Médiévales, University of Paris 13.

Arnold, Harrison H.
    1954   "Rhythmic patterns in Old Spanish verse", in: *Estudios dedicados a Menéndez Pidal*, V, 151-162. Madrid: Consejo Superior de Investigaciones Científicas.

Attridge, Derek
    1982   *The rhythms of English poetry*. (English Language Series 14.) London: Longman.

Avalle, D'Arco Silvio
    1962   "Le origini della quartina monorima di alessandrini", in: *Saggi e ricerche in memoria di Ettore Li Gotti*, I, 119-160. (Centro di Studi Filologici e Linguistici Siciliani Bollettino 6.) Palermo: CSFLS.

Bayo, Juan Carlos
    1999   "La teoría del verso desde el punto de vista lingüístico (el sistema de versificación del *Cantar de Mio Cid*)", unpublished doctoral thesis, University of Barcelona.

2002   "La datación del *Cantar de Mio Cid* y el problema de su tradición manuscrita", in: Alan Deyermond – David G. Patison – Eric Southworth (eds.), 15-34.

Billy, D. (ed.)
1999   *Métriques du Moyen Âge et de la Renaissance.* Paris: L'Harmattan.

Bolinger, Dwight – Marion Hodapp
1961   "Acento melódico, acento de intensidad", *Boletín de Filológía de la Universidad de Santiago de Chile* 13: 33-48.

Canellada, María Josefa (ed.)
1980   Marqués de Santillana, *Refranero.* Madrid: Editorial Magisterio Español.

Clarke, Dorothy Clotelle
1948   "Hiatus, synalepha and line length in López de Ayalas's octosyllables", *Romance Philology* 1, 347-356.

Clarke, Dorothy Clotelle
1964   *Morphology of fifteenth century Castilian verse.* (Duquesne Studies Philological Series 4.) Pittsburgh: Duquesne University Press – Louvain: Nauwelaerts.

Crystal, David
1985   *A dictionary of linguistics and phonetics.* Oxford: Basil Blackwell – André Deutsch.

Cornulier, Benoît de
1995   *Art poëtique: notions et problèmes de métrique.* Lyon: Presses Universitaires de Lyon.

Deyermond, A. D.
1971   *A literary history of Spain: the Middle Ages.* London: Ernest Benn.

Deyermond, Alan
1991   *Historia y crítica de la literatura española,* 1/1, *Edad Media: primer supplemento.* Barcelona: Crítica.

Deyermond, Alan (ed.)
2000   *Santillana: a symposium.* (Papers of the Medieval Hispanic Research Seminar 28.) London: Queen Mary and Westfield College.

Deyermond, Alan – David G. Pattison – Eric Southworth (eds.)
2002   *"Mio Cid" Studies: "Some Problems of Diplomatic" Fifty Years On.* (Papers of the Medieval Hispanic Research Seminar 42.) London: Queen Mary and Westfield College.

Du Méril, Edélestand
1843   *Poésies populaires latines antérieures au douzième siècle.* Paris: Brockhaus et Avenarius.

Duffell, Martin J.
1986   "The origins of *arte mayor*", *Cultura Neolatina* 45, 105-123.
1999a   *Modern metrical theory and the "verso de arte mayor".* (Papers of the Medieval Hispanic Research Seminar 10.) London: Queen Mary and Westfield College.
1999b   "The metric cleansing of Hispanic verse", *Bulletin of Hispanic Studies* (Liverpool) 76, 151-168.

| 2000 | "The Santillana factor: the development of double audition in Castilian", in: Alan Deyermond (ed.), 113-128. |

2000 "The Santillana factor: the development of double audition in Castilian", in: Alan Deyermond (ed.), 113-128.

2002 "Don Rodrigo and Sir Gawain: family likeness or convergent development?", in: Alan Deyermond – David G. Pattison – Eric Southworth (eds.), 129-149.

Duparc-Quioc, Suzanne (ed.)
1976 *La Chanson d'Antioche*. (Documents Relatifs a l'Histoire des Croisades 9.) Paris: Academie des Inscriptions et Belles Lettres.

Dutton, Brian (ed.)
1971 Gonzalo de Berceo, *Obras completas*, II, *Milagros de Nuestra Señora*. London: Tamesis.

Einhorn, E.
1974 *Old French: A concise handbook*. Cambridge: Cambridge University Press.

Elcock, W. D.
1975 *The Romance languages* (2nd edition revised by John N. Green.) London: Faber and Faber.

Fitz-Gerald, John
1905 *Versification of the "cuaderna vía" as found in Berceo's "La vida de Santo Domingo"*. New York: Columbia University.

Fry, Dennis
1958 "Experiments in the perception of stress", *Language and Speech* 1: 126-152.

García, Michel
1978 "La versificación", in: Michel García (ed.), 41-58.

García, Michel (ed.)
1978 Pero López de Ayala, *Libro de poemas, o Rimado de Palacio*, I (Biblioteca Románica Hispánica 4.12.) Madrid: Gredos.

Gasparov, M. L.
1987 "A probability model of verse (English, Latin, French, Italian, Spanish, Portuguese)", trans. Marina Tarlinskaja, *Style* 21, 322-358.

1996 *A history of European versification*, trans. G. S. Smith – Marina Tarlinskaja, ed. G. S. Smith – L. Holford-Strevens. Oxford: Clarendon Press.

Geary, John S. (ed.)
1987 *Historia del Conde Fernán González: a facsimile and paleographic edition*. Madison: Hispanic Seminary of Medieval Studies.

Goncharenko, S. F.
1988 *Stilisticheskiĭ analiz ispanskogo stijotvomogo teksta: osnovy teoriĭ ispanskoĭ poeticheskoĭ rechi*. Moscow: Vysshaĭa Shkola.

Gybbon-Monypenny, G. B. (ed.)
1988 Juan Ruiz, *Libro de Buen Amor*. (Clásicos Castalia 161.) Madrid: Castalia.

Hall, Robert A. Jr
1965 "Old Spanish stress-timed verse and Germanic superstratum", *Romance Philology* 19, 227-234.

Hanson, Kristin
1995 "Prosodic constituents of poetic meter", *Proceedings of the West Coast Conference on Formal Linguistics* 13, 62-77.

Hanson, Kristin – Paul Kiparsky
1996 "A parametric theory of poetic meter", *Language* 72: 287-335.

Hanssen, Federico
1909 Review of Menéndez Pidal 1908, *Revue de Dialectologie Romane* 1, 452-469.

Harris, James W.
1983 *Syllable structure and stress in Spanish: a non-linear analysis.* Cambridge MA: MIT Press.

Hayes, Bruce
1995 *Metrical stress theory: principles and case histories.* Chicago: University of Chicago Press.

Henríquez Ureña, Pedro
1933 *La versificación irregular en la poesía castellana.* (Anejos de la Revista de Filología Española 4.) (2nd edition.) Madrid: Centro de Estudios Hispánicos.

Henry, Albert
1953 *Chrestomathie de la littérature en ancien français.* Berne: A. Francke.

Hills, E. C.
1925 "Irregular epic metres: a comparative study of the Poem of the *Cid* and certain Anglo-Norman, Franco-Italian and Venetian epic poems", in: *Homenaje a Menéndez Pidal*, I, 759-777. Madrid: Hernando.

Hogg, Richard – C. B. McCully
1987 *Metrical phonology: a course book.* Cambridge: Cambridge University Press.

Hurford, James R.
1987 *Language and number: the emergence of a cognitive system.* Oxford: Blackwell.

Jakobson, Roman
1960 "Closing statement: linguistics and poetics", in: Thomas A. Sebeok (ed.), 350-377.

Kastner, L. E.
1903 *A history of French versification.* Oxford: Clarendon Press.

Kelly, Henry A.
1984 *Canon law and the Archpriest of Hita.* (Medieval and Romance Texts and Studies 27.) Binghamton NY: Center for Medieval and Early Renaissance Studies.

Kennedy, Ruth
1999 "New theories of constraint in the metricality of the strong-stress long line as applied to the rhymed corpus of late Middle English alliterative verse", in: D. Billy (ed.), 131-144.

Ker, W. P.
1898 "Analogies between English and Spanish verse (*arte mayor*)", *Transactions of the Philological Society*, 113-128.

Lang, Henry R.
1914 "Notes on the metre of the Poem of the Cid", *Romanic Review* 5, 1-30.

Lázaro Carreter, Fernando
1972 "La poética del arte mayor castellano", in: *Studia hispanica in honorem Rafael Lapesa*, I, 343-378. Madrid: Gredos and Cátedra - Seminario Menéndez Pidal.

Leonetti, Pasquale
1934 *Storia della tecnica del verso italiano*, I. Naples: Morano.

López Estrada, Francisco
1982 *Panorama crítico sobre el "Poema del Cid"*. (Literatura y Sociedad 30.) Madrid: Castalia.

Lote, Georges
1939 "Les origines des vers français", *Annales de la Faculté des Lettres d'Aix* 21, 219-415.

Lotz, John
1960 "Metric typology", in: Thomas A. Sebeok (ed.), 135-148.

Maldonado de Guevara, F.
1965 "Knittelvers "verso nudoso"", *Revista de Filología Española* 48, 34-59.

McCabe, Richard A. (ed.)
1999 Edmund Spenser, *The shorter poems*. Harmondsworth: Penguin Books.

Meillet, P. J. Antoine
1923 *Les origines indo-européennes des mètres grecs*. Paris: Presses Universitaires de France.

Menéndez Pidal, Ramón (ed.)
1908 *"Cantar de Mio Cid", texto, gramática, vocabulario*, I. Madrid: Bailly-Baillière.

Michael, Ian (ed.)
1987 *Poema de Mio Cid* (Clásicos Castalia 75.) (2nd edition.) Madrid: Castalia.

Milá y Fontanals, Manuel
1893 "Del decasílabo y endecasílabo anapésticos", in: *Obras completas*, V, 324-344. Barcelona: Álvaro Verdaguer.

Miller, George A.
1956 "The magical number seven plus or minus two", *Psychological Review* 63, 81-97.

Montaner, Alberto (ed.)
1993 *Cantar de Mio Cid*. (Biblioteca Clásica 1.) Barcelona: Crítica.

Navarro (Tomás), Tomás
1956 *Métrica española*. Madrid: Guadarrama.
1973 "Las modalidades del octosílabo", in: *Los poetas en sus versos desde Jorge Manrique a García Lorca*, 35-66. Barcelona: Ariel.
1974 *Métrica española*. (5th edition.) Madrid: Guadarrama.

Nelson, Dana Arthur (ed.)
1979   Gonzalo de Berceo, El *"Libro de Alixandre"*: reconstrucción crítica. (Biblioteca Románica Hispánica 4.13.) Madrid: Gredos.
Norberg, Dag
1958   *Introduction à l'étude de la versification latine médiévale.* Stockholm: Almqvist & Wiksell.
Orduna, Germán (ed.)
1981   Pero López de Ayala, *Rimado de Palacio.* 2 vols. Pisa: Giardini.
Parkinson, Stephen
2001   "Concurrent patterns of verse design in the Galician-Portuguese lyric", paper presented at the Thirteenth Colloquium of the Medieval Hispanic Research Seminar, London.
Pellen, René
1985-86   "Le Modèle du vers épique espagnol, à partir de la formule cidienne [el que en buena hora ...]", *Cahiers de Linguistique Hispanique Médiévale* 10, 5-37 and 11, 5-132.
Piera, Carlos José
1980   "Spanish verse and the theory of meter", unpublished doctoral thesis, University of California Los Angeles.
Pighi, Giovanni Battista
1970   *Studi di ritmica e metrica.* Turin: Bodega d'Erasmo.
Preminger, Alex – Frank J Warnke – O. B. Hardison Jr, (eds.)
1974   *Princeton encyclopedia of poetry and poetics.* (Enlarged edition.) Princeton: Princeton University Press.
Puentes Romay, José A.
1997   "Acento tonal en romance y latín: algunas implicaciones", *Moenia* 3, 503-518.
Quilis, Antonio
1971   "Caracterización fonética del acento español", *Travaux de Linguistique et Littérature* 9, 53-72.
Richter, Gisela M.
1987   *A handbook of Greek art.* Oxford: Phaidon.
Russell, P. E.
1952   "Some problems of diplomatic in the *Cantar de Mio Cid* and their implications", *Modern Language Review* 47, 340-349.
Russom, Geoffrey
1987   *Old English meter and linguistic theory.* Cambridge: Cambridge University Press.
Saavedra Molina, Julio
1946   *El verso de arte mayor.* Santiago de Chile: Prensas de la Universidad de Santiago de Chile.
Sebeok, Thomas A. (ed.)
1960   *Style in language.* Boston: MIT Press.

Smith, Barbara Herrnstein
    1968   *Poetic closure: a study of how poems end.* Chicago: Chicago University Press.

Tarlinskaja, Marina
    1976   *English verse: theory and history.* (De Proprietatibus Litterarum Series Practica 17.) The Hague: Mouton.
    1993   *Strict stress-meter in English poetry compared with German and Russian.* Calgary: Calgary University Press.

Thompson, John
    1961   *The founding of English meter.* London: Routledge & Kegan Paul – New York: Columbia University Press.

Tittman, Barclay
    1969   "Further remarks on the origins of *arte mayor*", *Cultura Neolatina* 29, 274-282.

Victorio, Juan (ed.)
    1990   *Poema de Fernán González.* (Letras Hispánicas 151.) Madrid: Cátedra.

Emendation and the Chaucerian Metrical Template[1]

Donka Minkova, Robert Stockwell, UCLA

1. The metrical template of Chaucer's iambic pentameter

The following is familiar information, to be found in roughly this form in dozens of sources from at least the time of Walter Skeat and George Saintsbury. We summarize it here, with apologies, only to establish a foundation, a base line for the more controversial discussion that follows. The metrical template of a Chaucerian line of iambic pentameter looks like this, in the most neutral terms we can suggest (eschewing notations that carry a multitude of baggage and preconceptions with them):

Da DUM	da DUM	da DUM	da DUM	da DUM	(di)
1 2	3 4	5 6	7 8	9 10	

The DUM's are called "strong syllables" and the da's are called "weak syllables". Monosyllabic words may appear freely in either position, though there is a preference for monosyllabic nouns, adjectives, adverbs, and verbs to appear in strong positions (even positions) and for function words in weak positions (odd positions). The only restriction on stressed monosyllables is that they are prohibited from appearing in the optional eleventh position; this is another way of saying that unlike other odd positions, the eleventh position must be filled (if at all) by the unstressed final syllable of a non-monosyllabic word.[2] The *only* words which have a lexically-fixed stress pattern that determines where they can fit in the line are polysyllabic (*little, women, under*, etc.). If they were recently borrowed from French they may vary between right stress (as in French) or left stress (as in earlier English). For disyllabic nouns and adjectives (*conseil, diverse, torment*, etc.) the only place where the French stress is generally preferred is in rhyme position.[3]

---

1   Andy Kelly unwittingly provided the focus of this paper by putting in our hands a copy of the 2001 *SAC* article by Jill Mann. Our original intention had been to address the occurrences of trisyllabic feet in Chaucer, and we would perhaps have stayed with that question, had Andy not directed our attention to the more pressing issues of template definition. For this, for his friendship, and for the many happy and educational hours spent on Chaucer, etymology, Latin stress, architecture, Ireland, airplane food, current TV shows, traffic school, and the wisdom of charging the net at tennis, we are grateful.

2   The "rich" feminine rhymes *nonys: noon ys* (*GP* 523-524) *Rome:to me* (*GP* 671-672), *cynamome:to me* (*MilT* 3700:3701) etc. always involve pronouns or copulas.

3   Minkova (2000: 438-439) found that initial stress on such items appears between 84%-92% in Chaucer's *Troilus and Criseyde*. The count was based on the verse-internal use of 36

The two main features that define the template of Chaucer's pentameter line are metrical alternation and a tightly restricted number of syllables per line. In addition, it is convenient to assign to this template at least one more piece of structure, called "footing". The number of feet corresponds to the number of strong syllables. Each foot ideally includes a weak syllable followed by a strong syllable; it is an iamb. Also, the line is often split in two parts by a caesura. The caesura is a syntactically-determined break which occurs commonly after position four, but also (with diminishing frequency) after positions six, five, seven, eight, and two[4]. The caesura is not a pause; rather it is normal syntactic contour phrasing. And because it is highly variable, we should not assign a specific position to it as part of the metrical template.

1.1. The significance of metrical alternation

Alternation between weak and strong syllables penetrates Chaucer's verse template so deeply that if three open-class lexical words occur in a row, presenting us with three clashing strong syllables, the middle one is demoted to metrically weak, as in (we are replacing the DUM notation for strong positions with a slash, and the *da* with an *x* in the few places where metrical weakness needs to be marked for clarity):

        x   /   x   /
He felte a coold swerd sodeynliche glyde   *KnT* 1575[5]

               /   x   /
But as a child of twelf month oold, or lesse   *PrT* 484

Conversely, three weak syllables in a row demand the promotion of the middle one:

        x / x
And prechest **on** thy bench, with yvel preef!   *WBT* 247

        x / x
Thou seist to me it **is** a greet meschief   *WBT* 248

---

types/266 tokens for the lower percentage which includes the items *fortune, honour, service.* Disregarding these items brings up the initial stress attestations to 92%.

4 Assay, and he shal fynde it that so dooth   *WBT* 942
   This knyght, of which my tale is specially   *WBT* 983
5 The example is cited in Mann (2001: 101).

1.2. Number of syllables: too few and too many

The metrical template stipulates ten syllables, with an optional eleventh, always weak. This is no arbitrary fact: it is inherited from the (hen)decasyllabic tradition on the continent, especially Italy. For the full history, see Duffell 1996, 1999-2000.

Although the template is iambic, Chaucer frequently begins his lines from the strong position of the first foot. Such lines can be of two types depending on the number of syllables per line. Lines of ten (eleven) syllables can have an inverted first foot, as in:

> /   /   /   /   /
> Daunced ful ofte in many a grene mede.   *WBT* 861

> Wedde no wyf, for noght that may bifalle.   *ClT* 84

The inversion can extend beyond the first foot, of course, as in:

> Blessynge halles, chambres, kichenes, boures,
> Citees, burghes, castels, hye toures,
> Thropes, bernes, shipnes, dayeryes –   *WBT* 869-871

Alternatively, the first foot may be missing its weak position:

> /   /   /   /   /
> Wommen may go saufly up and doun[6]   *WBT* 878
> 1   2   3 4 5 6 7 8   9

These are called "headless" or "acephalous" lines (for Chaucer the latter term is used by Saintsbury (1923: 175)). They necessarily have only nine (plus feminine) positions, having dropped the first one. As Li (1995: 238) shows, Chaucer used headless lines less and less frequently as he mastered his craft (ending at 0.7 percent, about half his early usage of 1.7%). Barney (1993: 109-110) refers to the headless lines as "a major cause of scribal activity and editorial difference". He (ibid.) estimates about 2% of headless lines in the *Corpus* ms. of *Troilus*, based on scanning the first 1,000 lines. It is said (e.g. ten Brink 1901: 215) that Chaucer himself must have been aware of the option of skipping the weak syllable of the

---

6   This is the syllabic structure of the line both in Hg and El – the two manuscripts differ only in the orthography of *women* (the Ellesmere has a brevigraph) and *down* (El has *doun*). The 1957 Robinson edition has *now* inserted after *go*, a somewhat questionable emendation in our view.

first foot, as, perhaps, evidenced by the *House of Fame* 1094 self-deprecatory banter *Though som vers fayle in a sillable*, embedded in regular tetrameter.[7] Although nominally headless lines do violate the basic syllable template, an unfilled position at the left edge of the line is common in English poetry before and after Chaucer. Headless lines are particularly frequent in Chaucer's iambic tetrameter verse, where the proportion of headless lines is as high as 9.4% of the total lines. Even a comparison with the monotonously regular Hoccleve shows that at least some of the editorial emendations, e.g. at lines 71, 96, 266 of his *Complaint* are based on headless lines.[8] Whether authorial or scribal, therefore, such headless lines in Chaucer do not constitute an argument against taking syllable count as a defining feature of his verse structure.

If the line has more than ten syllables (not counting the optional weak syllable in position eleven), then there is usually a way of accommodating the ten-syllable requirement by "slurring" – a general term favored by George Saintsbury (1923) and covering a variety of contractions: syncopation, apocope, synizesis, or elision to eliminate the extra weak syllable.

The question of whether Chaucer allows extrametrical weak syllables at the caesura remains open. On this we tend to agree with Smithers (1983), who points to the rarity of triplets, where two weak syllables appear instead of one in a weak position (creating an anapest), as being very damaging to the claim that they can, in principle, be attributed to the poet's intention rather than to textual transmission or authorial failures: "One reason for doubting in practice that the author [Chaucer] used these two rhythmic patterns [either one, or two, successive weak syllables – DM and RS] is the fact that there are relatively so few secure examples of them" (1983: 219). Li (1995) provides precise figures drawn from systematic sampling totaling 3020 lines, 10% of the Chaucerian pentameter corpus. If we project his figure of 34 in 10% of the corpus, the total of the so called "anapestic substitutions" or triplet-containing pentameter lines can be estimated at about 340. This is still a tiny proportion of the total: it suggests that Chaucer studiously avoided triplets and that Smithers' assessment is correct.

2. Jill Mann's challenge to syllable count in the *CT*

In a recent paper Jill Mann took the position (2001: 101-102) that syllable count is unimportant, that what matters is the number of stresses per line. Her position was stated in the context of assessing the metrical arguments for and against the pri-

---

7   There is a headless line in the same *Invocation: Thou shalt se me go as blyve* (HF 1106)
8   The statement is based on examining the lines cited as prompting metrical emendations on the basis of syllable count in Burrow (1999: xlvii).

macy of the Hengwrt over the Ellesmere manuscripts of *The Canterbury Tales.* Here are two statements that characterize her position:

> In discussing the "regularity" of Chaucer's meter, it is important to distinguish between a stress-based concept of verse and one based on syllable count. Although Hoccleve seems to have used an essentially syllabic meter, *Chaucer did not* (emphasis RS-DM)
>
> (2001:101)

> ...I feel considerable alarm when I find both Blake and Pearsall talking about Chaucer's verse in terms of the number of syllables, rather than the number of stresses. It is the disturbance which scribal variation causes to stress, rather than the disturbance to syllable count, which matters.
>
> (2001: 102)

Mann goes on to point out some virtues of her preference. Her first point is that "a strong stress in a weak position may be 'neutralized' by adjacent stresses," as in *KnT* 1575 and *PrT* 484, cited above. But of course three strong syllables in a row are impossible in iambic pentameter: the middle one must be demoted. This makes perfectly good sense. What it really means is that stress *alternation* is the stronger force. The verse is not "stress-based" (her phrase) but "alternation based", and alternation in turn demands a fixed number of syllables, so in fact the syllable count is fixed, which also fixes the number of feet.

Another argument that appears to go against the syllabic count concept in Mann's view is suggested by the exceptions to fixing the number of syllables at ten (plus feminine hangover): "two unstressed syllables separated by a liquid or nasal may occupy a single weak position, as in *NPT* 2853: 'Wel sik**erer** was his crowing in his logge'." The "slurring" of liquids and nasals is a phonetically easy case. In Old English /r, l. m, n/ may develop an epenthetic unstressed vowel (*wuldr—wuldor, tacn—taken*); spelling and metrical treatment testify to show the coexistence of mono-and disyllabic forms of such words.[9] In pre-Chaucerian syllable-counting verse, syncopation of syllables containing sonorants is quite common.[10] The same phenomena are widely attested in seventeenth-century verse, and, indeed, throughout the history of English versification.[11] Significantly, in our context, Hoccleve, whose loyalty to the ten-syllable line is undisputed, uses the same stratagem (Burrow 1999: xxx-xxxi).[12]

The appearance of an extra weak syllable is not limited to syncopation in the environment of liquids and nasals. Here are some tougher cases:

---

9   Campbell (1959: 150-152), Fulk (1992: 66-91).

10 Minkova (1992: 169-171).

11 See, for example Kiparsky (1977: 239-240).

12 The statement is based on examining the lines cited as prompting metrical emendations in Burrow (1999: xlvii).

```
     /    /    /            /      /      (stress positions)
Is lik-ned til-a fish-that is wa-terlees –    GP(1)180
1  2  3   45 6    7   8 9 10                  (syllable count)
```

```
       /         /          /     /    /     (stress positions)
Of a so-lemp-ne and-a greet-frater-nitee     GP 364
1    2    3    4    5   6   7 8 9 10          (syllable count)
```

In the second example the first weak position contains two weak syllables which cannot be successfully slurred (unlike the syllables – *ne and* that constitute position four). The problem in the next example (below) is similar (in the sense that there is no reasonable slur that will regularize it), but at least there is no weak syllable stranded at the onset of the line:

```
     /     /     /      /        /      (stress positions)
As wel-of this-as of o-there thyn-ges moore    WBT.584
1  2  3  4   5  6  7  8     9    10             (syllable count)
```

In addition to the statistical paucity of such lines as remarked by Smithers and confirmed by Li, it is important to note that the metrical equivalence of a single weak position and a "split" weak position is not unusual in syllable-counting verse in other periods of English. As discussed by Li (1995: 85, 236), the examples of "split" weak positions conform to a pattern of two adjacent "light" syllables, belonging to two separate words (*of a, that so, with a, was a*), etc. Out of the 34 instances recorded by Li, only a single line appears to go against this pattern:

Cometh up, ye wyves, offreth of youre wolle   *PardT* 910

However, the syllabic count of the line is easily regularized by syncopation of the inflection on *cometh*, a frequently attested adjustment: [13]

Thy gentillesse cometh fro God allone.
Thanne comth oure verray gentillesse of grace   *WB* 1162-63

---

13   Similarly *GP* 838, *KnT* 2208, etc. The ratio of *cometh* to *comth* spellings in the 1957 Robinson edition of the CT (online version made available from the University of Michigan *Corpus of Middle English Prose and Verse*) is 1:2, though admittedly the majority of the examples are of the verb in the 3rd person singular, not in the plural. On the correlation between spelling and metrical syncopation of 3rd person *cometh* and *comth* in El and HG, see Mann (2001: 93-94).

In view of this distribution, we prefer to treat the rare lines where two syllables occupy one weak position jointly, as patterns governed by a well-defined linguistic principle, similar to the principles of elision, syncopation, etc.

Returning to Mann's objection to syllable count as a defining metrical principle, let us consider this case (Mann 2001: 86). At issue is the first line of Fragment V, the Introduction to the *Squire's Tale*. Ellesmere has:

Squier-com neer-if it -youre wil-le be   *SqT* 1 El
 1 2   3   4   56   7   8 9 10

This is a straightforward decasyllabic line, perfectly iambic. Hengwrt has:

    Sire Frankeleyn com neer if it youre wille be   *SqT* 1 Hg

This is not straightforward at all. Mann asserts that it has six stresses, which means that she reads it thus:

        /   /   /   /   /   /
    Sire Fran-keleyn-com neer-if it-youre wil-le be   *SqT* 1 Hg
     1   2   3   4   5   6   78   9   10 11 12

Granted, Mann's focus in this comparison is to show that the El version is at least as good as the Hg version, and we find her general thesis fully convincing. However, the syllable count argument she uses in this instance is not watertight; she fails to seek out a legitimate scansion with five stresses – but it exists, though, perhaps, somewhat forced:

        /   /   /   /   /
    Sire Franke-leyn com-neer if-it youre-wille be   *SqT* 1 Hg
     1   2   3   4   5 6 7 8   9   10

The point is, the difficulty in scansion is caused by the extra syllables – which may, and do on her reading, require building an extra foot in order to accommodate them. But building an extra foot is the wrong move, as compared with some form of slurring to get things right. Building an extra foot is the one thing we believe Chaucer would not have done. His metrical template can only be defined as ten syllables (plus feminine syllable) arranged with alternating stress beginning weak: i.e., five iambic feet, because this template makes the right predictions for all but a tiny subset of the roughly 30,000 lines of iambic pentameter verse that he left us. Variants on the template, such as trochaic inversion, are just that: variants that provide variety by creating tension in the template – but only certain types of tension are permitted, *not* including an extra foot randomly constructed to fit in extra syllables.

As justification for our scansions of "Frankeleyn" in the lines above, we note that "Frankeleyn" is necessarily scanned disyllabically two or three times and trisyllabically two or three times in the lines below:

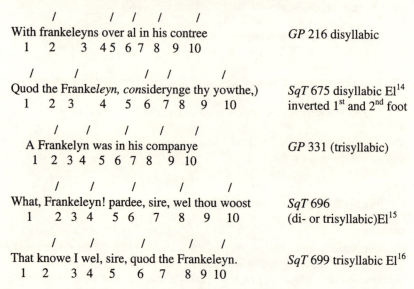

／ ／ ／ ／ ／ With frankeleyns over al in his contree 1　2　　3　45　6 7　8　　9　10	*GP* 216 disyllabic
／　　　／　　　　　／ ／　　　　　／ Quod the Franke*leyn, con*siderynge thy yowthe,) 1　2　3　　4　　5　6　7　8　9　　10	*SqT* 675 disyllabic El[14] inverted 1ˢᵗ and 2ⁿᵈ foot
／　／　　／　　／　　／ A Frankelyn was in his companye 1　234　5　6　7 8　　9　10	*GP* 331 (trisyllabic)
／　　／　　／　　　／　　　／ What, Frankeleyn! pardee, sire, wel thou woost 1　　2 3 4　　5 6　7　8　9　10	*SqT* 696 (di- or trisyllabic)El[15]
／　　／　　／　　　／ ／ That knowe I wel, sire, quod the Frankeleyn. 1　2　　3 4　5　　6　7　　8 9 10	*SqT* 699 trisyllabic El[16]

In fact, in all of the examples cited by Mann (2001: 103-104) where scribal interference/variation in one of the manuscripts affects the meter, it is a matter of syllable count: the number of stresses is unaffected. This is also true of the list of metrically relevant variations cited by her (2001: 99-100), where twelve out of thirteen patterns have to do with the presence or absence of an unstressed syllable. What she is really talking about is the possibility/option of an unfilled or a doubly-filled weak position in spite of her denials of this interpretation.[17]

14　The Hg reads: *Quod the Marchant...*
15　The Hg reads: *What Marchaunt pardee sire wel thow woost.* This suggests the possibility of disyllabic *sire* and therefore also disyllabic Frankeleyn in El.
16　The Hg reads...*quod the Marchant certeyn.*
17　The reference is to such statements as the ones cited above, or that Chaucer's pentameter line "may have nine syllables or eleven, instead of the usual ten, and that syllable count is dispensable while "...what it [the line] *cannot* dispense with is the five stresses that give it its shape and its dynamism." (2001:101). It will be clear from our exposition that the constraints on the number of syllables are crucial determiners of the rhythmic shape of the line.

Even more interesting in this regard is her list of lines where "both [Hg and El] are affected by scribal error" (2001: 106). She suggests ten corrections *metri causa,* not claimed to be new: seven of the ten were made in Robinson's 1933 edition, but the other three do not show up even in the *Riverside* Chaucer (Benson 1987).

Hise resons he spake ful solempnely	*GP* 274, El and Hg
. . . spake he . . .	recommended by JM
His purchasing myghte nat been infect	*GP* 320, El and Hg
. . . he myghte nat . . .	recommended by JM
For he hadde geten hym yet no benefice	*GP* 291, El and Hg
. . . hadde get hym . . .	recommended by JM

Mann is clearly right in assuming scribal error in all ten examples she cites, and in every instance except the inversion of *he spak* in GP 274, which affects only the stress, the correction either adds a syllable or deletes a syllable – that is, it is the deca-syllabic syllable count constraint in its purest form that is driving her approval of these emendations.

In the next paragraphs (ibid.:104-106) Mann challenges Norman Blake for in ef-fect defending imperfect lines in Hg. In particular she points out that "smoother" lines can be found both in Hg but also in El. By way of illustration: she posits that *GP* 426 Hg has six stresses, presumably assuming that *drogges* needs to scan as a disyllabic word. Here too, however, it is not stresses that are at issue: the lines in question read thus in Hg and El:

To senden hym his drogges and his letuaryes	*GP* 426 Hg
To sende hym drogges and his letuaries	*GP* 426 El

Again, Mann is certainly right about the need for finding a way to restore the metri-cality of these lines as found in Hg. Whether this is done through straightforward syllabic accommodation (syncopation) of *drogges*, or by removing *his* in Hg is irrele-vant; either way a *syllable* is removed which then has the *secondary* consequence of fixing the stresses that she is concerned about.

We don't want to belabor the point any further. As historical linguists we believe that the processes observed in modern speech and independently claimed for Middle English, such as syncopation and elision, must be taken into consideration in con-structing the metrical template of Chaucer's verse. Similarly, as historical metrists, we believe that the principles of meter applicable to verse in general, such as flexibility of the left edge of the line (headlessness), and the compression of two monosyllabic function words under one weak position (as in Kiparsky 1977, see also Youmans 1996), can be projected safely onto the Chaucerian template. Ultimately, on the issue of editorial emendation, we agree with Jill Mann that the meter, and not scribal varia-tion, should determine what the modern reader gets out of the edited verse text.

References

Barney, Stephen
   1993   *Studies in Troilus. Chaucer's Text, Meter, and Diction.* East Lansing: Colleagues Press.

Benson, Larry D. (ed.)
   1987   *The Riverside Chaucer.* Third edition. Boston: Houghton Mifflin.

Burrow, John (ed.)
   1999   *Thomas Hoccleve's Complaint and Dialogue.* EETS No. 313. Oxford: Oxford University Press.

Campbell, Alastair
   1959   *Old English Grammar.* Oxford: Oxford University Press.

Duffell, Martin J.
   1996   "Chaucer, Gower, and the history of the hendecasyllable." In McCully, C.B. and J. J. Anderson, *English Historical Metrics.* Cambridge: Cambridge University Press, 210-218.
   1999-2000 "The Craft so Long to Lerne': Chaucer's invention of the Iambic Pentameter." *Chaucer Review* 34. 3: 269-288.

Fulk, Robert
   1992   *A History of Old English Meter.* Philadelphia: University of Pennsylvania Press.

Kiparsky, Paul
   1977   "The rhythmic structure of English verse." *Linguistic Inquiry* 8, 189-247.

Li, Xingzhong
   1995   Chaucer's Meters. Ph.D. Thesis, University of Missouri, Columbia.

Mann, Jill
   2001   "Chaucer's meter and the myth of the Ellesmere editor of *The Canterbury Tales.*" *Studies in the Age of Chaucer* 23, 71-107.

Minkova, Donka
   1992   "Verse Structure in the Middle English *Genesis and Exodus.*" *Journal of English and Germanic Philology* 91: 2, 157-179.
   2000   "Middle English prosodic innovations and their testability in verse." In Irma Taavitsainen, Terttu Nevalainen, Päivi Pahta, and Matti Rissanen (eds.) *Placing Middle English in Context,* Berlin: Mouton de Gruyter, 431-461.

Robinson, F. N.
   1933   *The Complete Works of Geoffrey Chaucer.* Cambridge, Mass: The Riverside Press. 2nd Ed. 1957.

Saintsbury, George
   1923 [1906] *A History of English Prosody from the Twelfth Century to the Present Day.* Second edition. Vol. I. New York: Macmillan.

Skeat, Walter W.
   1894   *The Complete Works of Geoffrey Chaucer.* Oxford: Clarendon Press.

Smithers, G.V.
1983   "The Scansion of *Havelok* and the use of ME -en and -e in *Havelok* and by Chaucer." In Gray, Douglas and E.G. Stanley (eds.) *ME Studies Presented to Norman Davis*. Oxford: Clarendon Press, 195-234.

Ten Brink, Bernhard
1901   *The Language and Meter of Chaucer*. Second Edition. Rev. Friedrich Kluge. Transl. M. Bentinck Smith. London: Macmillan.

Youmans, Gilbert
1996   "Reconsidering Chaucer's prosody." In C.B. McCully and J.J. Anderson (eds.) *English Historical Metrics*. Cambridge: Cambridge University Press, 185-210.

Reception

A Franciscan Reads the *Facetus*

Glending Olson, Cleveland State University

The subject of this essay is a fourteenth-century friar's citation, in a commentary on Aristotle's *Nicomachean Ethics*, of a twelfth-century poem, the *Facetus: moribus et vita*, which is known primarily for its long Ovidian section advising young men on the art of pursuing women. In exploring some of the implications of what seems initially to be a surprising reference, I offer this narrowly focused study as a salute, by way of contrast, to the wide range of Andy Kelly's learning, which has given to medievalists, as the Franciscan said of the *Facetus*, *multa documenta* on topics from the philosophical to the physical.

Gerard of Odo (a.k.a. Gerardus Odonis, Geraldus Odonis, Guiral Ot, *et al.*) was born, probably around 1290, near Figeac in south-central France. He became a Franciscan friar at some unknown date, probably received his bachelor's and certainly received his master's degree in theology from the University of Paris, and for a while in the 1320s lectured there as well as in Toulouse. In 1329 he became Minister General of the Order, following upon fierce controversy between the Spiritual Franciscans and the rest of the community over the question of evangelical poverty and then even fiercer reaction to Pope John XXII's challenge to beliefs about Christ's poverty that were fundamental to the entire Order. John deposed the existing Minister General, Michael of Cesena, who had criticized the Pope's views and decisions on this matter and who continued to do so after his removal from office. In these circumstances it is not surprising that Gerard had a controversial administrative career, subject to attacks from Michael and his supporters (Ockham, among others, accused him of heresy). Nor did Gerard help himself when in 1333 he preached on behalf of John's personal interpretation of the Beatific Vision, outraging the Paris faculty of theology. Apparently a friend of the Pope's, he acted as his emissary on various matters during his years as Minister General. In 1342 Clement VI appointed him patriarch of Antioch and bishop of Catania in Sicily, where he died of the plague in 1349.[1]

A variety of Gerard's writings survive, including letters, biblical exegesis, logical treatises that have recently been edited (Giraldus 1997), a commentary on

---

1   For biography see Langlois (1927), Kent (1984: 17-34), Giraldus (1997: 1-5). For the context of controversy over Franciscan poverty see (in ascending order of respect for Gerard's performance as Minister General) Moorman (1968: 307-336), Lambert (1998: 221-269), and Nimmo (1987: 205-211, 370-382). Given the variety of possible and defensible choices of name for Gerard, I simply follow the Anglicized form used by the *Cambridge History of Later Medieval Philosophy*, which has a chapter by Georg Wieland surveying the medieval reception of the *Nicomachean Ethics* (Kretzmann *et al.* 1982: 657-672).

the *Sentences*, and a commentary on the *Nicomachean Ethics*, which survives in over a dozen manuscripts and in two Renaissance editions (Lohr 1968). Probably written during the 1320s while he was at the University of Paris, it appears to be the earliest complete commentary on the *Ethics* by a Franciscan. It takes the form of section-by-section *expositiones* of Aristotle's text, sometimes followed by one or more *questiones* on issues raised by the material in that section. Like most of Gerard's other work, the commentary has not received much detailed scholarly attention, with the exception of James J. Walsh's study exploring its influence on John Buridan's treatise on the *Ethics* (1975) and Bonnie Kent's dissertation, which focuses on Gerard's relationship to Franciscan ethical thought and to Franciscan attitudes toward Aristotle (1984).

The passage from the commentary that I want to explore here occurs in a *questio* on one of the virtues discussed in the fourth book of the *Ethics*. Aristotle analyzes these virtues as means between two extremes, one of excess and one of defect. Because human beings are social creatures, interaction with others is necessary to life, and there are virtuous and vicious ways in which one can behave in such informal, quotidian social relationships. Aristotle discusses three such relational virtues, one concerned with truthfulness and two with pleasantness. Truthfulness in the context of social communication (as opposed to truthfulness in matters of public or legal responsibililty) has to do with the honest representation of oneself; it is the mean between the extremes of boastfulness and self-deprecation. Pleasantness in social situations occurs either in the arena of jest and play or in the arena of ordinary social exchange. In playful situations, the mean is a decorous playfulness (*eutrapelia*, usually but perhaps a little too narrowly translated as "wittiness"); the vicious excess is buffoonery, doing anything to entertain or to get a laugh, and the defect is boorishness, being utterly without humor, unable either to enjoy or provide amusement. In routine social exchange, says Aristotle, the virtuous mean does not have a name, but it most closely resembles friendship in the way a person relates congenially yet honorably to others. Aristotle indicates two different terms for the excessively pleasant person – one who seeks always to please just for the sake of giving pleasure (no matter what the moral consequences) is obsequious; one who always seeks to please out of financial or self-aggrandizing motives is a flatterer. The defect in regard to this virtue is quarrelsomeness or contentiousness (Aristotle 1962: 1126b11-1128b9; for commentary on this grouping of three social virtues see Aristotle 1970: 304-05).

After his *expositio* of Aristotle's chapter on the virtue and vices in regard to pleasantness in ordinary social conversations, Gerard poses the question (*lectio* 21, q. 39) whether the mean between the extremes of *placiditas* and *discolia* is indeed a virtue (Geraldus 1482: sigs. s-s2). The first argument advanced in opposition is that if it were a discrete virtue it would have a name, but since Aristotle says the mean in this case does not have a name, it is not a virtue. In response to this and three other objections, Gerard follows the *Ethics* in maintaining that a distinct virtue exists, and he spells out why: communication with others is required for human living (here and elsewhere he cites as authority book one of Aristotle's *Politics*); unsociable behavior disrupts such communication, and obsequious behavior corrupts it by not discouraging vice; hence between these extremes there must be a virtue of properly agreeable behavior in communicating with others. In responding to the first objection Gerard argues that Aristotle said the virtue did not have a name because he knew that not everyone used the same term to describe it. Aristotle preferred the term *amicitia*, since conducting oneself according to this virtue looks very much like practicing friendship, even though it is not true friendship since there is no special affection involved; but Homer (according to the *Politics*) seems to have called it *socialitas*. Gerard's citation of these two different terms would have made his point minimally that more than one name has been given to this virtue, but he does not stop there. He develops his response into a substantial excursus on the nomenclature, both past and present, used to designate the virtue concerned with pleasantness in social exchange:

Multi autem nostri temporis vocauerunt eam affabilitatem. Est enim affabilitas prima conditio eius vt visum est, tamen non est ipsa. Fuit etiam haec virtus aliquando vocata urbanitas ad differentiam rusticatitatis, quia viuentes in vrbe sciebant grate conuiuere et colloqui, viuentes autem in rure sicut indocti ruditer et ingrate ceteris conuiuebant et colloquebantur. Vocatur etiam hodie vulgariter curialitas per eandem rationem, quia qui versantur in curiis sciunt pre ceteris gratiose conuiuere et colloqui quibuscumque. Vnde cum aliquem vocamus curialem intendimus ipsum laudare de ista virtute sicut ipsam habentem, et oppositum vocamus incurialem hominem discolum et in conuictu tediosum et onerosum. Vocata est etiam aliquando lepos vel lepiditas, quia homo dicitur lepidus cum est mollis et dulcis, gratus et acceptabilis in conuictu. Vocatur etiam per eandem rationem iocunditas et habens eam iocundus, non quidem ex eo quod ipse sit formaliter iocundus et letus sed quia talis est virtualiter, quia homines sibi colloquentes et conuiuentes reddit iocundos et letos. Sed propriissime vocata est antiquitus facetia, unde dicitur facetus medius inter discolum et placidum, et de ista commendat gallicos boetius in libro de disciplina scolarium, dicens quod venit parisius ad videndum facetos gallorum ritus, quia secundum veritatem natio gallicana super omnem nationem ad vitam facetam est prompta et magis abundat in ista gratissima facetia. Quidam autem more poetico de facetia edidit vnum libellum qui dicitur facetus, in quo dat multa generalia facetia documenta in principio, qui namque ait, "Moribus et vita si quis vult esse facetus / Me legat et discat que mea musa docet". Quod nomen vtitur Augustinus recitans cuiusdam mimi facetissimam vrbanitatem (13 de trinitate, c. 3).

(Geraldus 1482: sigs. sv-s2)

[In our time many people have called it *affabilitas* from its most apparent quality, even though it is not that. Sometimes this virtue has been called *urbanitas*, in contrast to rusticity, since those residing in cities knew how to associate with others and converse agreeably, whereas those in the country, being ignorant people, associated and spoke with others crudely and ungraciously. And it is commonly called *curialitas* for the same reason, since those who are engaged in court life know better than others how to associate and talk agreeably with all sorts of persons. So when we call someone courtly, we

mean to praise him for possessing that virtue, and we call the opposite sort of person
uncourtly, ill-tempered and annoying and burdensome in social relationships. It has also
sometimes been called *lepos* or *lepiditas*, for a person is called pleasant when he is gentle and kind, well-liked and welcomed in social gatherings. For the same reason this virtue is also called *iocunditas* and the person possessing it *iocundus*, not because he is in-
herently merry and happy but because he produces that effect, for such a person causes
people talking and congregating together to become agreeable and happy. But, most appropriately, in ancient times it was called *facetia*, and thus being *facetus* is said to be the
mean between being ill-tempered and being obsequious. In *De disciplina scholarium*
Boethius commends the French for this virtue, saying that he came to Paris to observe
the *facetus* manners of the French, for truly the French people are disposed to the
facetus life more than any other people and possess more completely that most gracious
virtue of *facetia*. Also, someone produced a little book in verse about *facetia*, which is
called *Facetus*, in which the author provides, at the beginning, much general instruction
in *facetia*. It begins: "If a person wishes to be agreeable in behavior and living, / let him
read me and learn what my muse teaches". Augustine also uses this term, recounting (in
De trinitate 13.3) a most agreeable pleasantry of a certain mime.]

Gerard deals with the three other objections in only half the space that he devotes to answering this one. The disproportion suggests some particularly compelling interest at work here, and the passage is to my knowledge totally original;
nothing in earlier medieval commentary on the *Ethics* comes close to his effort to
provide a semantic history of what he takes to be terms that designate the virtue in
regard to pleasantness in conversation. His efforts, and the social values that inform them, are worth some scrutiny. His reference to the many people who have
called this virtue *affabilitas* is an allusion to the influence of Thomas Aquinas's
commentary on the *Ethics*. Albert the Great, in his first commentary on the treatise, defended *amicitia* as a proper term for this virtue, since it consists of the ex-
terior words and deeds that manifest friendship even if not the inner feelings that
characterize true friendship (Albertus 1968-72: 279; this edition incorporates
Grosseteste's Latin translation of the *Ethics*). In his second commentary Albert
takes the same position, though he adds that in Cicero the virtue is called *gratia*
since it is the habit of living graciously, agreeably, with others (Albertus 1891:
316). Aquinas acknowledges the appropriateness of using *amicitia* but then adds
that since the virtue goes unnamed in Aristotle, it is reasonable to call it "affabilitas" (Thomas 1969: 248); during the fourteenth century *affabilitas* became, I believe, the most popular term for the virtue in academic circles and beyond, as
some later evidence will suggest. Gerard's replacement of it with *facetia* may
have something to do with his reaction to the popularity of Aquinas (canonized in
1323, very near the time the commentary must have been written) and with his
opposition, evident elsewhere in the commentary, to some of the Dominican's
ideas (Kent 1984: 624-25 and *passim*).

But more than just fraternal rivalry is at work here. Gerard clearly believes
that this virtue is not solely a matter of friendliness or affability, and his deploy-

ment of a variety of terms from both earlier and contemporary usage points to a constellation of features that he thinks constitute it. His excursus in fact creates rather than records semantic history and in the process reshapes Aristotle's nameless virtue to conform to and provide philosophical justification for a collection of medieval courtly and curial values. Aristotle's text recognizes the desirability of bringing pleasure rather than pain in social exchanges, but its principal focus is on the moral limits of such action, for example the appropriateness of one's behavior given circumstantial differences and the point at which it becomes more honorable to choose to give another person (corrective) pain rather than pleasure in order to prevent that person's subsequent misfortune. Gerard's list of terms shifts the emphasis from ethical issues to style – pleasant behavior in social situations becomes linked with urban sophistication rather than rural boorishness, the pleasingness of having a courtly and polished demeanor. His introduction of *facetia* as the most appropriate term for this virtue is the culmination of this extrapolation, for the particular kind of agreeableness associated with the term in the Middle Ages involves a complex of characteristics including graciousness, modesty, and urbanity as well as wittiness.[2]

At this point Gerard provides three historical references to help solidify what he means by *facetia* and thus what he thinks is the nature of Aristotle's virtue in regard to pleasantness in social situations. The citation of Augustine refers to a passage in which he argues that some human desires are so general that even though we do not know directly what a person is thinking we do know some of what that person wants.

> There is the story of a comedian and his witty pleasantry (illa cuiusdam mimi facetissima praedicatur urbanitas) when he promised in the theater that at his next show he would tell the audience what they all wanted. So on the appointed day a greater crowd than usual came along full of great expectations, and as the silence and suspense grew he said, so the story goes, "You all want to buy cheap and sell dear". In this saying of a frivolous comedian (in quo dicto leuissimi scenici) all found their own self-awareness expressed, and in their admiration for his telling them so unexpectedly a truth that was as plain to all of them as their own noses, they warmly applauded him.
>
> (Augustine 1991: 346; Augustine 1968: 387)

---

2   In the later twelfth century Huguccio of Pisa seems to see two different meanings for *facetus*: "curialis, urbanus, proprie de doctrina et in factis," but also "qui iocos et ludos gestis et factis commendat" (Nicholls 1985: 147-148). Similarly a gloss on *facetus* in a thirteenth-century manuscript, while citing Isidore's definition of the word as concerned with "iocos et lusus," in fact defines it more broadly as "urbanus i. curteis" (Hunt 1958: 281). For Gerard it is clear that *facetia* as verbal cleverness and playfulness is comfortably subsumed within the wider meanings of urbanity and courtliness. On the use of the term in the Middle Ages as part of the development of ideas of refined behavior see Jaeger (1985: 161-168) and Bond (1995: 122-127). Jaeger notes that a variety of works in the Middle Ages adopted *Facetus* as a title; for the also-popular *Facetus: cum nihil utilius* see Nicholls (1985: 145-148, 181-182).

This example of *facetia* seems to apply the term in a way familiar both in classical usage and in the Renaissance, where it chiefly refers to jokes, pleasantries, and anecdotes, as in Poggio's anthology, the *Liber facetiarum*, and later collections with similar titles (Speroni 1964: 1-15, 315-17). But in Aristotle wittiness *per se* is part of the virtue of *eutrapelia*, pleasantness in the arena of playful words and deeds. Gerard seems to blur the division between these virtues more than other commentators by introducing elements of wit and playfulness into his understanding of *affabilitas*, possibly because he correspondingly nudges *eutrapelia* away from purely conversational wittiness and toward more recognizably formal sorts of entertainment or performance (see Olson 1995: 198-201). Here it is not so much the performance setting "in theatro" that Gerard wants to highlight but the clever and provocative quality of the entertainer's *dictum*.

Gerard's other two examples, however, take us beyond shrewd remarks. The *facetus* manners of the French appear to encompass a social style that includes graciousness, congeniality, and sophistication. Gerard follows the usual medieval misattribution of the thirteenth-century *De disciplina scholarium* to Boethius. He is correct about its reference to the author's visit to Paris in part to observe the "facetos gallorum ritus", although he neglects to say that the context is not purely laudatory; the trip to Paris is mentioned in a chapter about the need for students to be obedient and diligent, and it reveals how many unstudious ones the author found on the streets of the city (Ducci 1967: 95-97). Gerard's selective quotation here points to a certain nationalistic or local pride that may well be part of the motivation behind his distinctive elaboration of Aristotelian *affabilitas*. His compatriot at the University of Paris, John of Jandun, writing also in the 1320s, expressed similar views of Parisian *mores* in similarly Aristotelian ways, selecting from the virtues named in the fourth book of the *Ethics* those most relevant to the observable social behavior of ordinary citizens: *mansuetudo, affabilitas, eutrapelia*, and *veritas*. The majority of Parisians, he says, appear so agreeable as a result of their affability and urbanity, and those who deviate from that virtuous mean tend to be excessively pleasing rather than impudent.[3]

Gerard's remaining instance of *facetia*, the focus of this essay, is a reference to the Latin poem known as *Facetus: moribus et vita*, which Peter Dronke has persuasively argued dates from the twelfth century (1976: 129-30). This poem

---

3   John of Jandun (1867: 54). "Plerique etiam eorum videntur decentis affabilitatis atque urbanitatis spirituali dulcedine gratiosi: qui autem ipsorum declinant a medio magis se placidos exhibent quam protervos." The agreeableness, cheerfulness, and elegance of the French were noted at least as early as the twelfth century; see the remarks of Guibert of Nogent (Bond 1995: 207) and John of Salisbury (Southern 1970: 145). Such characteristics could, of course, from another perspective be made to seem less appealing. To Petrarch the French propensity for manners and merriment was trivializing, rendering them "leves" (Wilkins 1959: 237-238).

offers advice on socially agreeable behavior, first of a general sort and then specifically addressed to people of differing *status*, both in regard to age (boys,
youths, the elderly) and profession (judges, physicians, knights).[4] Almost exactly
half of its 510 lines are devoted to advice to "juvenes" on love, with frank Ovidian
attention both to the *ars* of seduction and the *remedia* for extricating oneself from
love. This section of the poem seems to have intrigued both medieval and modern
audiences, for it circulated as a separate text in many manuscripts (see the discussion of E. J. Thiel's work in Dronke 1976: 126-28) and has tended to be the focal
point for what limited attention the poem has received over the last few decades.
There is good reason for interest in its Ovidian material, given the poem's early
date and the number of manuscripts of both the *Facetus* itself (over 30) and the
separately circulating text of its love-section (at least 25). Each of these totals easily surpasses the dozen surviving manuscripts of Andreas Capellanus's famous *De
amore*. The evidence of the more extensive circulation of the *Facetus* in the later
Middle Ages is another reminder of how modern scholarly preoccupation with
Andreas's work has distorted our perspective on the nature and status of medieval
treatises offering love-advice in Ovidian mode.[5]

Gerard's reading of the *Facetus* reminds us that its material on playing the
game of love (the metaphor is prominent throughout that section) is only a portion
of a larger whole. His reference is not just casual, and surely not just based on a
few excerpts encountered, say, in a *florilegium*. His quotation of the poem's first
two lines varies from Morel-Fatio's text in some instances but not in any ways
that distort meaning; the variations could be scribal or memorial. He indicates
quite fairly the contents of the first 32 lines ("multa generalia ... documenta")
where the advice is indeed directed to all "cupientes esse facetos" before the poem
enters into more specific counsels for people of varying *status*, starting in line 33
with the "puer" who is being brought up among clerics. Gerard could not have
known that the general precepts were only "in principio" had he not read further
than that. Whether he read substantially further, and what he might have thought
of the hundreds of lines devoted to seduction, is of course impossible to know.
Assuming he had some knowledge of the whole, his approving citation of the first

---

4   For the original with an English translation see Elliott (1977), who bases her Latin text on the
     edition of Morel-Fatio 1886, which is primarily concerned with a Catalan translation of the
     Facetus. For a fourteenth-century French translation see Morawski (1923: xxxvi-xxxvii, 81-
     112). For discussions of the poem see Dronke (1976), Elliott (1977: 27-29), and Jaeger
     (1985: 166-168).
5   Hence Andy Kelly's need several years ago to "exorcis[e]" the idea that adultery was essen-
     tial to medieval conceptions of romantic love (Kelly 1975: 31). In this regard, it is worth not-
     ing that the *Facetus* tells its young man interested in the art of love not to pursue women who
     are nuns or who are married, since it is a sin ("nephas") to dishonor them (Elliott 1977: 38, ll.
     133-136). On similarities between the *Facetus* and Andreas, see Dronke (1976: 130-131).

part of the poem and neglect of the rest may indicate the distinctly medieval kind of reading that Mary Carruthers has described, an approach to texts based on attention to those parts most relevant to oneself rather than appreciation of an objective entirety (1990: 156-88). Or it may suggest that the contextualizing of the Ovidian instruction within the *Facetus* – first as advice exclusively for *juvenes*, second as an *ars* or craft (practical rather than prudential knowledge), and third as ludic activity – provided enough layers of moral insulation that a clerical male reader would not find the love-advice so radically inconsistent with the rest of the poem as to demand dismissal of the whole.

We can know, at least, what sorts of words and actions Gerard accepts as *facetus* and thus as ethically admirable within an Aristotelian framework. Take satisfaction in nobility. Do not be deceitful, but that does not mean you should always tell the truth. Hide "crimina" with a jest. Avoid vulgar language, sure evidence of "rusticitas." Praise others rather than yourself. Do not speak either hastily or arrogantly. All this counsel in the first part of the *Facetus* is oriented to making a person "placidus" to others. Some of the advice, such as not always telling the truth, might be seen as ethically questionable, but the *Facetus* could well be thinking here of the kinds of circumlocutions that allow for conversations to stay unruffled; and the jesting concealment of "crimina" might refer to subtlety in one's reproaches of others rather than, as usually translated, to concealment of one's own crimes. Not much in these lines is clearly contrary to Aristotle's discussion of his nameless virtue, yet the text has a pragmatic focus that certainly blunts the moral edge of the way the *Ethics* approaches social pleasantness. One could argue that following the counsels of the *Facetus* might well lead to the sort of *placiditas* that is for Aristotle a vice. For Gerard, though, this poem apparently delineates what he takes Aristotle to intend. This virtue is "propriissime" named *facetia* – and in the following *lectiones* Gerard refers back to it using that term rather than *amicitia* or *affabilitas* (1482: sigs. s2, s4v, s6). *Facetia* is a social pleasantness entailing a manner that is affable, modest, witty, and urbane. To be *facetus* is not just to be friendly or agreeable; it is also to be clever, discreet, and socially polished. To be *facetus* is to be, well, Parisian.

Gerard's assimilation of Aristotelian friendliness to medieval courtly ideals and more specifically to medieval stereotypes of the city in which he was living did not remain confined to his commentary alone. As Walsh has shown (1975: 237-75), John Buridan borrowed large parts of that work in the writing of his own *Questiones* on the *Ethics*. Book IV, q. 16 asks whether *affabilitas*, which Aristotle calls *amicitia*, is a moral virtue. In posing and answering this question Buridan draws heavily on Gerard's *questio*, including his entire semantic survey printed above, omitting the Augustine reference but paraphrasing those to Pseudo-Boethius and the *Facetus*: "Et est idem facetia quod eloquentia vel decentia vel suauitas in verbis et factis, unde metrificator quidem librum quem de plurimis ad hanc pertinentibus virtutem documentis composuit; vocauit facetum" (Buridan

1968: f. 86v). [And *facetia* also refers to eloquence or propriety or pleasingness in words and deeds, concerning which a versifier wrote a book which has many teachings related to this virtue. He called it *Facetus*.] Did Buridan know the *Facetus* independently, or did he just assume from the reference and context in Gerard that it was indeed about speaking well and acting in a pleasing way? In any case, Gerard's restriction of the ethical relevance of the *Facetus* to its early general recommendations has disappeared – the entire poem is cited as instruction in *facetia* and thus instruction in Aristotle's unnamed (but now multinamed) virtue.

A few qualifications are in order by way of conclusion. I do not wish to imply that Gerard's discussion of the virtue in regard to social pleasantness loses moral focus as it expands on courtliness. In the context of the *lectio* and its following *questio* he is quite clear that pleasingness is virtuous only when directed to people's welfare ("ad eorum bonum"), and the features of *facetia* he dwells on are certainly not necessarily incompatible with that goal. Further, in Gerard's larger scheme of all the virtues, *facetia* ultimately belongs among those considered as not essential to human goodness, whereas the more important cardinal virtues are (Kent 1984: 566-82). Finally, there may be elements of a distinctly Franciscan approach to social interaction in Gerard's focus on the more performative aspects of interpersonal pleasantness. John V. Fleming has recently noted the "colourful personality" and "histrionic impulse" of the founder of the Order and his supposed reference to his followers as *joculatores Dei* (1999: 351). In Aristotelian friendliness Gerard may have seen a distant secular analogue to the love and joy so often publicly expressed by St. Francis; according to Thomas of Celano, Francis once told a depressed friar that a servant of God should always be "pleasant" and wrote to his brethren to "show themselves joyful, cheerful, and consistently gracious in the Lord" (Armstrong *et al.* 2000: 331).

Even so, Gerard's redirection of *amicitia* toward *facetia* is an intriguing intrusion of secular material into Franciscan commentary. It expands the conception of proper social gregariousness, as defined by Aristotle and reinforced by the *Ethics'* chief Dominican commentators, into the arena of courtly self-presentation. It introduces the clever and witty use of language as part of virtuous social behavior in all situations, not just overtly playful ones; it gives ethical force to politeness, discretion, geniality, urbanity. It testifies to the way in which medieval courtly values, nationalistic self-consciousness, and perhaps individual taste become intertwined with presumably detached philosophical and historical analysis. And its reference to the *Facetus* reminds us of the medieval popularity of that poem and gives some indication of the respectful way one fourteenth-century reader read at least a part of it. Gerard's excursus offers another instance of commentary telling us more about itself and its social context than about the work that prompted it.

Chaucer's Prioress, like Gerard, was also a member of a religious order who showed substantial interest in proper social pleasantness and "curteisie". She "peyned hire to countrefete cheere / Of court". She was "ful plesaunt, and amy-able of port". While she did not know "Frenssh of Parys", she spoke Anglo-French "fetisly" (GP ll. 124-140 in Chaucer 1987: 25). These lines have usually been read as part of Chaucer's satire on a nun whose secular impulses betray her spiritual superficiality, just as he elsewhere satirizes friars who use pleasantness and French phrases for purposes of greed and lust. But Gerard's expansion of Ar-istotle's *affabilitas* suggests that there were those of religious vocation who could articulate a serious defense of the propriety of social graciousness for clerics as well as layfolk. His text says nothing, of course, about Chaucer's literary inten-tions, and I do not mean to suggest that I see no satire in the Prioress's portrait. Nevertheless, the attention to *facetia* given by Gerard and adopted by Buridan within a firmly ethical framework may help illuminate a minor portion of the so-cial and semantic context within which the Prioress's portrait was created and took on meaning. In regard to her being "amyable", for example: Nicole Oresme, in his translation of the *Ethics*, notes that while there is no precise term for Aris-totle's nameless virtue in Greek, Latin, or French, it can be reasonably called "amiableté" (Oresme 1940: 264). In regard to "fetisly": the first line of the French version of the *Facetus* translates "facetus" as "faitis" (Morawski 1923: 81). Cer-tainly the semantic range of some of Chaucer's language about the Prioress's be-havior extends beyond romance and beyond La Vielle's speech in the *Roman de la rose*. Andy Kelly (2000) has recently raised questions about the ease with which some scholars have assumed that the Prioress is implicated in profits from stewhouses on property in the hands of her Priory. W. Rothwell (2001) has chal-lenged the idea that her Stratford French would have been perceived by Chaucer and his audience as a gauche, unsophisticated dialect. Perhaps we need to tread a little more carefully as well in regard to one other aspect of her portrait: the as-sumption that Chaucer could not have imagined in any way other than ironically the co-existence of the debonair and the devout. Gerard, at least, seems to have seen no incompatibility.

References

Albertus Magnus
  1891   *Commentarium in X Libros Ethicorum*. In *Opera omnia* 7. Auguste
              Borgnet (ed.). Paris: Vivès.
  1968-72   *Super Ethica Commentum et Quaestiones. Libros quinque priores*. W.
              Kübel (ed.). In *Opera omnia ... curavit Institutum Alberti Magni
              Coloniense ...* 14.1 (2 fasc.). Munster: Aschendorff.

Aristotle
1970   *L'Ethique à Nicomaque* 2.1. René Antoine Gauthier and Jean Yves Jolif (trans.). Louvain: Publications Universitaires.
1962   *Nicomachean Ethics.* Martin Ostwald (trans.). Indianapolis: Bobbs-Merrill.
Armstrong, Regis J. – J. A. Wayne Hellman – William J. Short (eds.)
2000   *Francis of Assisi: Early Documents, Volume II: The Founder.* New York: New City Press.
Augustine of Hippo, Saint
1968   *Sancti Aurelii Augustini de trinitate libri XV (libri XIII-XV).* W. J. Mountain (ed.). Corpus Christianorum Series Latina 50A. Turnhout: Brepols.
1991   *The Trinity.* Edmund Hill (trans.). Brooklyn: New City Press.
Bond, Gerald A.
1995   *The Loving Subject: Desire, Eloquence, and Power in Romanesque France.* Philadelphia: University of Pennsylvania Press.
Buridan, John
1968   *Questiones Joannis buridani super decem libros ethicorum.* Paris, 1513; rpt. Frankfurt: Minerva.
Carruthers, Mary
1990   *The Book of Memory: A Study of Memory in Medieval Culture.* Cambridge: Cambridge University Press.
Chaucer, Geoffrey
1987   *The Riverside Chaucer,* 3d ed. Larry D. Benson (gen. ed.). Boston: Houghton Mifflin.
Dronke, Peter
1976   "Pseudo-Ovid, Facetus, and the arts of love", *Mittellateinisches Jahrbuch* 11: 126-131.
Ducci, Edda (ed. and trans.)
1967   *Un saggio di pedagogia medievale. Il "De disciplina scholarium" dello Pseudo-Boezio.* Turin: Società editrice internazionale.
Elliott, Allison Goddard
1977   "The *Facetus*: or, the art of courtly living", *Allegorica* 2.2: 27-57.
Fleming, John V.
1999   "The friars and medieval English literature", in David Wallace (ed.), 349-375.
Geraldus Odonis
1482   *Expositio in Aristotelis Ethicam.* Brescia: [Boninus de Bonnis] for Bonifacius de Manerva.
Giraldus Odonis
1997   *Opera Philosophica Volume One: Logica,* L. M. de Rijk (ed.). Leiden: Brill.
Hunt, R. W.
1958   "The 'lost' preface to the *Liber derivationum* of Osbern of Gloucester", *Mediaeval and Renaissance Studies* 4: 267-282.

Jaeger, C. Stephen
    1985   *The Origins of Courtliness: Civilizing Trends and the Formation of Courtly Ideals 939-1210*. Philadelphia: University of Pennsylvania Press.

John of Jandun
    1867   *Tractatus de laudibus Parisius*, in Le Roux de Lincy – L. M. Tisserand (eds. and trans.), 32-79.

Kelly, Henry Ansgar
    1975   *Love and Marriage in the Age of Chaucer*. Ithaca and London: Cornell University Press.
    2000   "Bishop, prioress, and bawd in the stews of Southwark", *Speculum* 75: 342-388.

Kent, Bonnie Dorrick
    1984   Aristotle and the Franciscans: Gerald Odonis' Commentary on the *Nicomachean Ethics*. [Unpublished doctoral dissertation, Columbia University.]

Kretzmann, Norman – Anthony Kenny – Jan Pinborg (eds.)
    1982   *The Cambridge History of Later Medieval Philosophy*. Cambridge: Cambridge University Press.

Lambert, Malcolm D.
    1998   *Franciscan Poverty. The Doctrine of the Absolute Poverty of Christ and the Apostles in the Franciscan Order 1210-1323*, rev. ed. St. Bonaventure, New York: The Franciscan Institute.

Langlois, Charles
    1927   "Guiral Ot (Geraldus Odonis), frère mineur", in *Histoire littéraire de la France* 36: 203-225. Paris: Imprimerie nationale.

Lohr, Charles H.
    1968   "Medieval Latin Aristotle Commentaries, Authors G-I", *Traditio* 21: 163-164.

Lincy, Le Roux de – L. M. Tisserand (eds. and trans.)
    1867   *Paris et ses historiens aux XIVe et XVe siècles*. Paris: Imprimerie impériale.

Moorman, John
    1968   *A History of the Franciscan Order from its Origins to the Year 1517*. Oxford: Clarendon Press.

Morawski, J.
    1923   *Le Facet en françoys*. Poznan: Gebethner i Wolff.

Morel-Fatio, Alfred
    1886   "Mélanges de littérature catalane III. – Le livre de courtoisie", *Romania* 15: 192-235.

Nicholls, Jonathan
    1985   *The Matter of Courtesy: Medieval Courtesy Books and the Gawain-Poet*. Woodbridge, Suffolk: D. S. Brewer.

Nimmo, Arthur
    1987   *Reform and Division in the Medieval Franciscan Order*. Rome: Capuchin Historical Institute.

Olson, Glending
    1995   "Plays as play: a medieval ethical theory of performance and the intellectual context of the *Tretise of Miraclis Pleyinge*", *Viator* 26: 195-221.

Oresme, Nicole
    1940   *Le Livre de Ethiques d'Aristote*. A. D. Menut (ed.). New York: G. E. Stechert.

Rothwell, W.
    2001   "Stratford atte Bowe revisited", *Chaucer Review* 36: 184-207.

Southern, R. W.
    1970   *Medieval Humanism*. New York: Harper and Row.

Speroni, Charles
    1962   *Wit and Wisdom of the Italian Renaissance*. Berkeley: University of California Press.

Thomas Aquinas
    1969   *Sententia Libri Ethicorum*. In *Opera omnia iussu Leonis Xiii P. M. edita*, ed. Fratrum Praedicatorum, 47.2. Rome: Sancta Sabinae.

Wallace, David (ed.)
    1999   *The Cambridge History of Medieval English Literature*. Cambridge: Cambridge University Press.

Walsh, James J.
    1975   "Some relationships between Gerald Odo's and John Buridan's commentaries on Aristotle's *Ethics*", *Franciscan Studies* 35: 237-275.

Wilkins, Ernest Hatch
    1959   *Petrarch's Later Years*. Cambridge, MA: Mediaeval Academy of America.

The Imagined Chaucerian Community of Bodleian MS Fairfax 16[1]

Theresa Tinkle, University of Michigan, Ann Arbor

The last booklet of Bodleian MS Fairfax 16 begins with "The Lover's Mass", a clever erotic parody of the Christian sacrament. Drawing provocatively on the language and attitudes of the Mass, the narrator describes his reverence before the altar of Cupid, his confession and sacrifice of faith, and his prayers on behalf of fellow lovers. The "Mass" unifies sexual desire, religious devotion, and poetic craft – a familiar Chaucerian nexus, though taken here to unusual extremes. In the manuscript, a prose "Epistle" follows and recommends that all true lovers meditate devoutly on Troilus and on the "holy legende of martyrs of Cupydo" (f. 317v; Hammond 1927: 213, ll. 183-184).[2] These references credit Chaucer with key texts of the narrator's religion and locate the "Mass" firmly in the same tradition. MS Fairfax 16 is framed by poems that similarly invoke Cupid, supporting the writer's assertion of an English poetic tradition.[3] Booklet 1 includes Geoffrey Chaucer, F Prologue to the *Legend of Good Women* and *Parliament of Fowls*; Sir John Clanvowe, *Book of Cupid*; Thomas Hoccleve, *Epistle of Cupid*; and John Lydgate, *Complaint of a Lover's Life* and *Temple of Glass* (or, as this manuscript has it, *Temple of Bras*). The manuscript's final booklet begins and ends with Cupid ("The Lover's Mass", "Parliament of Cupid"). Cupid makes further minor appearances in such poems as Chaucer's "Envoy to Scogan" (Booklet II). The compilation of this manuscript (*circa* 1450) was clearly governed by a strong interest in the "matere" of Cupid, and poets' diverse responses to this subject and to each others' treatments of it provide much of the anthology's interest.[4] MS Fairfax 16, with all its rich intertextual resonances, therefore offers a stunning opportunity for us to advance our understanding of how the Chaucerians represent the masculine community within which they fashion themselves as lovers and poets, and how that community was perceived in the mid-fifteenth century.[5]

---

1   I am grateful to the friends and colleagues who commented on a draft of this essay: Andreea Boboc, Rebecca Garber, Colette Moore, Catherine Sanok, and Karla Taylor.

2   For the reader's convenience, I follow this form for citations throughout: folio citation from MS Fairfax 16, which I cite from the facsimile, Norton-Smith 1979; line (and where appropriate page) numbers from standard modern editions.

3   Norton-Smith's Introduction to the facsimile describes the manuscript and its contents (1979: vii-xxix).

4   This is consistent with Hanna's argument about the priority of thematic subjects in medieval anthologies (1996: 46-47).

5   Recent scholarship on fifteenth-century Chauceriana has tended to emphasize contrasts between the great Chaucer and his imitators, a group apparently rendered impotent by the anxiety of influence. See Spearing (1985: 88-110) for a subtly illuminating analysis of Chaucer as

That opportunity has yet to be seized, in part because the manuscript has gained only sporadic scholarly notice,[6] and in part because critical attention typically falls on the individual poems rather than on their potentially dialogic relations. Critical treatments tend, moreover, to follow one of two schools, both of which address the poems in relation to intellectual or aesthetic traditions rather than in relation to material manuscript contexts: modern exegetes advance the supposed medieval connection between Cupid and concupiscence (e.g., Lampe 1967: 49-62; Crockett 1993: 67-93); other critics emphasize the poems' courtly implications (usually reading the poems through the problematic filter of "courtly love"[7]). From the latter perspective, poems of Cupid have come to epitomize a narrow and superficial coterie activity. They serve, in Anne Middleton's influential response to Chaucer's canon, no higher or more complex cultural purpose than "reaffirming one's possession of the tastes and qualities that assure one's membership in polite society", and "celebrating the graces requisite to courtly society" (1980: 30, 48). This view of Cupid's poets has developed considerable authority in recent years. Paul Strohm persuasively supports Middleton's view of Chaucer's love visions (1982: 3-8), and Seth Lerer extends the analysis to fifteenth-century Chaucerian texts, asserting that the later poems of Cupid also affirm courtly values (1993: 31-34, 59-60, 67, 82-84). These are sensible critical responses to individual texts, yet they fail to take into account the poems' original material contexts or their intertextual relations within a specific manuscript (though Strohm and Lerer consider other manuscript evidence).[8]

The Chaucerians' Cupid is certainly a figure of "gentil" love, social exclusivity, and amatory rites of passage – a direct descendant of the great Amor Jean de Meun invented to preside over the *Roman de la Rose*, who is in turn descended from Ovid's wild boy god. Yet Cupid is not only a sign of gentility in Chaucerian verse, nor do his devotees inevitably admire court fashions in love or poetry.[9] In fact, Chaucer and the Chaucerians brought together in MS Fairfax 16 evidence a wide range of attitudes

---

the "father of English poetry", with all that title implies about the Oedipal anxiety of influence for his successors and imitators. Lerer extends this model in his "study of the post-Chaucerian literary system as a phenomenon of subjection ... Chaucer's authority subjects his readers, subjugating them into childhood or incompetence" (1993: 5). There are, however, other ways of defining father-son relations, just as there are other models for masculine relations. See, e.g., Trigg (1999) for an astute analysis of "discourses of affinity".

6   See Allen (1975: 481-482), Boffey and Thompson (1989: 280-283, 290, 303-304), Jansen (1989: 206-224), Edwards (1996: 56-58), Boffey and Edwards (1999: 167, 173, 177, 179-180).

7   Moore (1979: 621-632) offers an astute analysis of the problems with this term. Kelly (1985: 217-223 and 1986-87: 301-327) establishes the range of meanings given "amour courtois" in the originary work of Gaston Paris.

8   On material intertextuality, see Tinkle (2000: 341-377).

9   For arguments on this point, see Tinkle (1989: 92-192, 239-307) and Tinkle (1996: 112-129, 166-177, 198-210).

toward the social and literary conventions associated with Cupid. Chaucer's narrators in *Parliament of Fowls* and the Prologue to the *Legend of Good Women* describe the great god of love, but preserve a careful distance from him, refusing him the fealty he expects. Though obviously influenced by Chaucer, Clanvowe presents in his *Book of Cupid* the opposite figure – a narrator steadfastly loyal to the "gentil" values associated with the god. Hoccleve introduces further variation by adapting Christine de Pizan's *Epistre au dieu d'Amours* in order severely to critique conventional gentility; here Cupid denounces his own court. Lydgate's *Complaint of a Lover's Life* similarly challenges "polite" society by detailing the woes of an unsuccessful true lover, defeated by Cupid's preference for False Seeming. By contrast, Lydgate's *Temple of Glass* transforms amorous desire into a mystical religion of love, and "The Lover's Mass" elaborates this religion into something like a parodic Lay Folks' Mass Book. The Chaucerians' use of standard conventions – the temples and courts of love, the precedence of Venus and Cupid – gives their poems a superficial similarity. When gathered together into an anthology, however, the poems' differences and dialogic potential come to the foreground, allowing us readily to recognize the poets' constant revisions of each other. Their originality, we find, lies precisely in their novel treatment of the same conventions, and in their ability to devise seemingly endless variations on a few themes.[10]

Instead of affirming a stable code of courtly behavior, this collection insistently questions the ethics and cultural consequences of amatory conventions, revealing the degree to which courtliness is a contested value. Even a brief survey of these poems thus affirms Richard Firth Green's argument that the court of love in late medieval England is a vehicle for discussions about literature – a subject for literary debate, and a conventional motif of poetic self-fashioning (1983: 87-108). Indeed, MS Fairfax 16 (particularly the first and last books) appears less a book of polite manners than a sophisticated engagement with the literary issues that fostered the Quarrel of the Rose – still a lively debate at the time of compilation.

The English literary debate centers on two conventional motifs – the royal court and the religion of love. Although these motifs apparently have little appeal for modern readers (or so a prolonged critical silence implies), both court and religion had considerable power for the mid-fifteenth century audience of MS Fairfax 16: as Benedict Anderson suggests, these are the two primary "imagined communities" available in the time (1983: 20-28). As such, these potent symbols of masculine affiliation deserve our close attention. At the same time, a number of factors undermine these imagined communities in late fourteenth- and fifteenth-century England: the royal court is nonexistent for much of this time, and Church unity is challenged by the papal schism and spread of heterodoxy. In this age of transition, the old hierarchical orders are breaking down (they will be reorganized in the next centuries), and new

---

10 Phillips (1997: 71-97) demonstrates this brilliantly, and I am indebted to her insights.

horizontal forms of affiliation are beginning to replace them. MS Fairfax 16 allows us insight into this historical shift: the manuscript displays how writers draw on the motifs of court and religion, but it also reveals that they are re-imagining their affiliations. Ultimately, I will argue, the poems of Cupid in this manuscript represent for the mid-fifteenth century reader an imagined masculine community of vernacular English writers and readers – a pre-national (and pre-print) alternative both to the Latinate clerical brotherhood and to the Gallic court.

We might begin to understand this imagined community by turning to Chaucer, with whom the English literary conversation begins. Chaucer's narrators view the supposedly great and mighty god of love through ironic filters, continually casting doubt on his amatory and literary standards. *Parliament of Fowls*, for example, begins with a hyperbolic portrait of Cupid:

> Al this meene I be love that my felynge
> A-stonyeth soo with a dredeful worchyng
> So soore y wys that whan I on hym thynke
> Nat wote I wel wher that I wake or wynke

(f. 120r; Benson 1987: ll. 4-7).

The narrator immediately disavows this "felynge", suggesting that bookish reports of this lord are greatly exaggerated: "For al be that I knowe not love in dede / ... Yet hapeth me in bookes ofte to rede / Of hys miracles" (f. 120r; ll. 8, 10-11). Cupid undergoes a further comic lowering in the narrator's dream vision, which pictures him as a relatively powerless arrow-maker near the temple of Venus. A similar comic deflation occurs in the *Knight's Tale*, when Theseus laments the workings of "The God of love, a benedicite! / How myghty and how greet a lord is he!" (Benson 1987: ll. 1785-1786) (Though this poem is not included in MS Fairfax 16, Clanvowe begins the *Book of Cupid* with these lines.) Theseus's puissant Cupid is quickly reduced to the status of attendant lord in Venus's progress ("Biforn hire stood her sone Cupido", l. 1963). *House of Fame* ignores the lordly deity and depicts only the blind son of Venus, a child-like god no more important than Vulcan in the temple scene (f. 156r; ll. 137-138).

These are conventional images of Cupid, and yet Chaucer's juxtapositions and choices of poetic detail create new meanings. The great lord of love belongs primarily to amatory poetry; his portrait is refined and elaborated by Jean de Meun, Guillaume de Machaut, and Jean de le Mote. As Cupid appears at the opening of the *Parliament of Fowls* and in Theseus's lament, he represents this near-contemporary French poetic community, a court constituted by the audiences of books, united in their common experience of specific vernacular conventions. The narrator performs the expected reader response to this lord ("my felynge / A-stonyeth"), showing his ability to participate in that court. At the same time, he has access to Latin writers (including Cicero, Macrobius, Alan of Lille) and to philosophical as well as amatory discourses: his literary universe is explicitly larger and more various than the circle of French poets. Accordingly, he juxtaposes the amatory convention of Cupid as regal lord with an iconography drawn from medieval Latin mythography. Here Cupid typically appears as a small boy, winged, carrying a bow and arrows, and, in the later Middle Ages, often blind.[11] Instead of following either the amatory or the erudite tradition exclusively, Chaucer uses Cupid to represent his relation to a double literary lineage: he defines a vernacular poetic indebted to the authority of learned Latin traditions, and distanced from amatory Gallic conventions. In other words, Chaucer's double treatment of Cupid in *Parliament of Fowls* challenges the literary precedence of the Gallic court with the authority of the Latin schoolroom. Chaucer thus establishes an English countertradition for the god of love.

Both court and schoolroom are imagined communities – constituted through books and not bound to geographical places or contemporaneous time. In the *Parliament of Fowls*, these are communities of one: the narrator, alone with his books. This is, in fact, how a reading community would typically be conceived in manuscript culture: each book is unique, and each reader holds a different version of a work – with those differences ranging from inconsequential spelling variants to substantive content variations. The reader can think, as the Chaucer narrator does, of holding a text bound into a book; the reader cannot picture a mass of fellow readers, each holding an exact replica of the same text (that imagined community is a feature of print culture: Anderson 1983: 41-49). Chaucer's narrator does not conjure up a horizontal literary affiliation in the present; his most important affiliations (or so he represents them) are with the past and with Latin authors. The court of Cupid, then, forms only a small part of Chaucer's imagined literary community, and he diminishes that court by setting it in the broadest possible cultural context. He thereby locates his poetry between high Latin culture and the court of Cupid.[12]

The Prologue to *The Legend of Good Women* once again represents the problematic court of Cupid, but now a group of contemporary poets – French participants in the cults of leaf and flower – become the narrator's primary imagined poetic community. The narrator addresses this group directly in the dream frame:

> Allas that I ne had Englyssh ryme or prose
> Suffisant this flour to preyse a-ryght
> But helpeth ye that han konnyng and myght
> Þe lovers that kan make of sentment
> In this case oght ye be diligent
> To forthren me somwhat in my labour
> Whethir ye ben with the leef or with the flour
>
> (f. 83v; Benson 1987: F Prologue, ll. 64-72).

---

11   For discussions of iconography, see Panofsky (1939: 95-128), Tinkle (1996: 42-77).

12   My conclusion is profoundly influenced by Middleton's argument (1980: 15-56) on "enditing" as a middle way between "making" and "poetry".

The narrator seeks to enter into a partnership with experienced poets whose skill might help him compensate for the perceived poverty of English. His implicit trust in their feeling for a fellow poet and in their ready assumption of mentoring duties suggests confidence in their strong social bonds. The narrator presents himself in a submissive role, willing to glean after them in the field, yet he also asserts his own authority to command and direct the group ("helpeth ye that han konnyng"; "oght ye be diligent"). Poetry appears here a vehicle for masculine socialization – the means by which a man both shows his deference to hierarchical order and asserts his own identity. The narrator joins this literary community by fashioning himself as a lover; according to convention, he derives his authority to speak from his "gledy desire" (f. 84r; l. 105). In short, Chaucer represents erotic desire as the basis for male bonding, mentorship, and (poetic) rivalry – and as the source of masculine poetic community. Eve Sedgwick's important theoretical work, *Between Men: English Literature and Male Homosocial Desire*, argues that male bonds are masked in representations of heterosexual eroticism; consequently, she sees the critic's task as unveiling disguised forms of homoeroticism (Sedgwick 1985: 1-48). Chaucer's poem and, as we will discover, the other poems in this manuscript, suggest a radically different culture, for here heterosexual eroticism overtly constitutes male homosocial bonds.

Chaucer defines his narrator's love in vividly religious terms: he reverences the daisy as his "erthely god" whose "resureccion" he anticipates with "glad deuocion" (f. 84r; ll. 95, 110, 109). Saint Valentine presides over the ritual, and Love's company joins in the narrator's worship of this "relyke" (f. 87r; l. 321). The religious language emphasizes the intensity of the narrator's passion, the "truth" that justifies his membership in the cult. More significantly, these references complicate his self-fashioning: the new member of an elite community of lover-poets also participates in a broader and more universal community of faith. He does not rely entirely on the authority of the lover; by appropriating religious codes, he lays claim as well to a traditionally Latin and clerical authority for his vernacular "legends". By making erotic desire and sacred passion appear analogous, Chaucer creates a dynamic tension between secular and sacred communities, and between models of poetic authority. His narrator is a liminal figure, standing on the thresholds of both French coterie and Latin clerical traditions; in this position, he both draws from and displaces both traditions.

The dream of the Prologue takes this narrator into the center of Cupid's court, where Chaucer self-consciously represents him(self) as a disruptive presence. Cupid appears in the Prologue garbed in embroidered silk, wearing a solar crown, and bearing angel wings; these details signify an intimidating confluence of feudal, natural, and religious powers. His appearance strongly recalls Amor in Guillaume de Lorris's *Roman de la Rose*, the quintessential representative of courtly French traditions.[13] The great lord charges Chaucer with disturbing his court:

> And thow my foo and al my folke werreyest
> And of myn olde *servauntes* thow mysseyest
> And hynderest hem with thy translacion
> And lettest folke from hire deuocion
> To serve love thou maist yt nat denye
> For in pleyne text with-outen nede of glose
> Thou hast the *Romaunce* of the rose
> That is an heresye ayenis my lawe
> And makest wise folke fro me with-drawe

(f. 87r, ll. 322-325, 327-331).

Cupid describes the court as united under his possessive rule – he refers to "my folke", "myn olde servauntes" – until Chaucer creates division and leads the "wise folke" away. The passage makes Chaucer's English literary activity appear remarkably forceful: he makes war on the court, slanders it, and prevents the courtiers from fulfilling their sacred duties. Cupid depicts Chaucer as an outsider, but more importantly as a triumphant rival: the poet who single-handedly challenges the court of love, shows its follies, and teaches the best courtiers to defect. Cupid's charge effectively conveys Chaucer's not very subtle boast about his own impact on the literary scene. Although this Cupid has obviously stepped directly out of *Roman de la Rose*, moreover, he views that text as a "heresye". In other words, Chaucer uses Cupid, the central figure in the French court of love, to repudiate the most important text in that tradition.

Chaucer continues his challenge to the court of love by having Alceste explicitly critique its values:

> For in youre courte ys many a losengeour
> And many aqueynt totelere accusour
> That tabouren in youre eres many a swon
> Ryght aftir hire ymagynacion
> To have youre daliance and for envie

(f. 87v; ll. 352-356).

Alceste depicts the servants of Love in terms of masculine competitiveness and verbal dissimulation, as if they were so many False Seemings imported directly from Jean de Meun's *Roman de la Rose*. She defines service to the god as a deceitful performance. Chaucer uses Alceste to push coterie values into a broader cultural context and toward more ethical purposes. He significantly attributes this purpose to

---

13   For this iconography, see Tinkle (1996: 110-112).

the intervention of a feminine reader, suggesting his own desire to negotiate carefully between masculine and feminine audiences.[14] Interestingly, Alceste's position
closely resembles Christine de Pizan's in the Quarrel of the Rose, and, given Christine's close connections with the English court of Richard II, it is not difficult to see
Chaucer as one possible inspiration for her contributions to that debate. The god's
specific charge against Chaucer – that the poet spoke ill of women – in particular
anticipates Christine's indictment of Jean de Meun in her *Epistre au dieu d'Amours*
(1399).[15]

Alceste finally justifies Chaucer's poetry because it appeals to a new audience:
"Yet hath he made lewde folke delyte / To serve yow in preysinge of your name" (f.
88v; ll. 415-16). She answers the god's complaint about the loss of "wise folke" by
celebrating a new, "lewde" community of readers. Cupid and Alceste characterize
"folk" by what they read. According to Cupid, "wise folke" read the translation of
the *Roman de la Rose* and *Troilus and Criseyde* and thereafter depart from his
court. Alceste argues that "lewde folk" take up the *House of Fame, Book of the
Duchess, Parliament of Fowls*, and "many a thinge" (f. 88v; l. 430), and grow inclined to serve the god. Between Cupid's and Alceste's accounts, Chaucer slyly
claims both "wise" and "lewde" readers, both defectors from the Gallic court (it is
worth remembering that Richard II and the aristocracy favored French at this time:
Robbins 1978: 94-99) and a more general English audience. The "wise folke" represent Chaucer's coterie circle, those who appreciate his most challenging and ex-
perimental vernacular poem, *Troilus and Criseyde*. The "lewde" readers are ultimately, however, at least as important to Chaucer's conception of English poetry:
the primary meaning of "lewde" is "uneducated, ignorant", but "lewde" may also
denote low birth, a lack of sense or refinement, and a lack of sophistication (*Middle
English Dictionary* 2001: "leued"). Alceste's reference to "lewde" readers therefore
defines a broad audience of those who are who are not courtiers, not learned in the
medieval sense of the word (that is, not clerics, not Latinate), not refined or sophisticated in their literary taste. "Lewde" includes women readers. In short, the
"lewde" readers are the emerging English bourgeoisie.

Parliament of Fowls and Prologue to the *Legend of Good Women* reveal how
Chaucer situates his vernacular poetry between the powerful literary traditions represented by French courtly verse and Latin discourses (including but not restricted
to religious discourses).[16] Both poems show him in the process of inventing an Eng-

---

14   Sanok (2001: 323-354) compellingly analyzes the impact and implications of the imagined
     feminine audience.
15   Christine could easily have had knowledge about Chaucer's Prologue and other poems of
     Cupid that predate her contributions to the Quarrel. For details about Christine, the court of
     Richard II, and the Quarrel, see Willard (1984: 42-43, 73-89).
16   My argument parallels Middleton's (1980: 15-56) except that I find Chaucer declaring this
     program earlier in his career than Middleton proposes.

lish literary community, compounded from Gallic and Latinate traditions but finally separate from both. Chaucer shares with his Latin *auctores* a value for erudition and ethical content, while he borrows his secular content and ideal of masculine self-fashioning from Gallic models. These poems also disclose how Chaucer conceives of an audience that includes courtiers, clerics, and women as well as boors – a broadly English audience, not restricted to a single social class, tradition of learning, or gender. He invents, in short, a pre-national English community: Chaucer is the father of this English community because he imagined it into being. This is to some extent a masculine and elite community, based on the bonding and rivalry that occur among men who share similar experiences of erotic desire and literary pleasure; at the same time, women are included and their literary values affirmed. We discover Chaucer's influence over his successors perhaps most suggestively in their evocation of the strong male bonds that constitute their imagined literary communities. We discover the limits of his influence in the fact that their imagined communities are composed almost exclusively of men.

The court of Cupid and religion of love are central to the Chaucerians as to Chaucer, but the court remains a problematic model of masculine affiliation throughout MS Fairfax 16. For example, Clanvowe's *Book of Cupid* portrays a narrator who remains utterly loyal to the court of love, but his values are debated inconclusively by a cuckoo and a nightingale (much as Alceste and Cupid present opposing views of the court in the *Legend of Good Women*). The nightingale praises the honor, gentility, and courtesy of love's servants; while the cuckoo remarks on the sorrow, folly, and care men experience in a court that advances only untrue men. This debate challenges the wisdom of the narrator's love service. The poem ends by calling for the birds' debate to be resolved before "the quene / at Wodestok" (f. 39v; Scattergood 1965: ll. 284-285), effectively diminishing the court of Cupid by placing it in a larger cultural context. Other poems in the collection further emphasize the dubious status of Cupid's court. The knight in Lydgate's *Complaint of a Lover's Life*, for instance, critiques the court as a place of envy, lies, and, ultimately, injustice, charges that echo Chaucer's Alceste and Clanvowe's cuckoo. The lady in Sir Richard Roos's *La Belle Dame Sans Mercy* likewise denounces the masculine art of deceitful love talk, as does Cupid in Hoccleve's *Epistle of Cupid*. The concentration of these poems in Booklet I of MS Fairfax 16 enhances the force of the thematic argument and creates a context for reading the rest of the manuscript. In this book, the Chaucerians appear united in their rejection of the court as a site for poetry.

At the same time, these poets represent themselves as members of a close-knit community, defined by shared values and by the principles of masculine interdependence and fellow feeling. As the "Parliament of Cupid" puts it, "eu*er*y man in faythfull wyse / Be warnid thus that no man hinder othir / But loue hys felowe as he wer his brothir" (f. 327v; MacCracken 1911: p. 172, ll. 33-35). Here the poet acknowledges the potential for masculine rivalry in love, but admonishes men instead to cultivate mutual love and fraternal closeness. The solidarity of masculine community is represented as more important than the individual pursuit of erotic fulfillment. Lydgate's *Temple of Glass* values masculine empathy still more highly, presenting a narrator who identifies passionately with the suffering male lover of the dream vision: "for routhe of whiche his woo as I enditen / my penne I fele quaken as I writte" (f. 76r; Norton-Smith 1966: ll. 946-947). The experience of erotic desire and the suffering of unrequited love are the basis for male bonding. In Lydgate's *Complaint of a Lover's Life*, the narrator similarly insists that he writes on behalf of the knight whose complaint he records ("for this mannys sake", f. 23r; Norton-Smith 1966: l. 182) and from his own experience of the same masculine sorrow: "who that shal write to distresse / In partye nedeth to know felyngly / cause and rote of al such malady" (f. 23r; ll. 187-189). Each of these poems represents men who feel intensely for each other and give each other the pity women deny them. Indeed, the bonds between men appear more intense and potent than those they attempt to form with women.

Lydgate's *Complaint of a Lover's Life* makes his narrator's affiliation with the suffering knight an explicit model for the audience:

> yf that eny now be in this place
> that fele in love brennyng or fervence ...
> Let hym of routhe ley to audyence
> with deleful chere and sobre contenaunce
> to here this man

(f. 23v; Norton-Smith 1966: ll. 204-205, 211-213).

The narrator invites the reader to identify feelingly with the knight, to turn the memory of love's fervor into "routhe" for another sufferer, and thereby to become a fit audience for his lament. Not leaving the reader's response to chance, Lydgate explicitly teaches him how to "hear" the poem – how to participate in the new literary community. A similar passage falls near the end of Chaucer's *Complaint of Mars*, which opens Booklet I of the MS Fairfax 16. Here Mars appeals directly to the audience: "to yow hardy knyghtis of renoun / Syn that ye be of my deuisioun / ... therfore ye oght haue somme compassion / of my disese" (ff. 18v-19r; ll. 272-273, 276-277).

These repeated addresses to the reader (always imagined as a male) invite participation in the sympathetic masculine group; indeed, these poems script a consistent role for the reader in an English literary community. This effect appears central to the contemporary thematic interest of the manuscript, which thus defines for the mid-fifteenth century reader an accessible model of masculine affiliation that serves to replace the problematic model of the court. As we have seen, modern critics typically understand poems of Cupid as teaching men to fashion themselves according to the polite manners of court. In fact, however, these works teach men to conceive of themselves as part of a quite different (even a "lewde") community, an English reading audience that might include courtiers but is not exclusive to them. The reader enters into this community by participating vicariously in the homosocial bonds between men – by identifying with the masculine community of lovers, affirming their solidarity with one another, and acknowledging their strong emotional attachments to other men.

This sense of group identity depends on a specific experience of vernal love. As Clanvowe puts it,

> Ffor euery trew gentil hert fre
> that with him [Cupid] is or thinketh for to be
> ayens may now shal haue somme steryng
> other to ioy or elles to morenynge
>
> (f. 35v; Scattergood 1965: ll. 21-24).

Here a masculine elite is brought together by shared "gentil" values, and by the fiction that they feel the same "steryng" at the same time. We encounter the same myth often in the poems of Cupid, as men repeatedly encounter and sympathize with each other in their vernal excursions. The mention of May – when Chaucer's narrator goes to worship the flower in the Prologue to *Legend of Good Women* – is crucial to the literary invention of this masculine community, for the date allows readers to envision a group of men simultaneously experiencing the same feeling. The black knight in Lydgate's *Complaint of a Lover's Life* repeats the motif of a narrator surrendering to a ritualized amatory experience in May, with the date once again creating the impression that a group of men comes together annually in order to conduct a literary game.[17]

This repeated date turns the manuscript's diachronic sequence of literary exchanges into an imagined synchronic English community. Indeed, the poets' May day becomes finally analogous to the liturgical hours of prayer in the Church – a specific time that ritually constitutes an imagined spiritual community. Within this community, warm fellow feeling prevails: men identify closely with each other, feel erotic impulses together, and set aside rivalry in order to advance their peers. Such a homosocial community serves as a powerful model of affiliation during the court's late medieval decline (a decline observed but not lamented in these poems). If the court has been largely rejected in this poetic model, the Church has not. The coherent values of the poets' community – mutual love, fraternal closeness, and self-sacrifice for the good of the whole – obviously recall those of the Church. In fact, the poets' lay community exemplifies the spiritual values and social virtues that are singularly absent from many contemporary accounts of the Church, often portrayed as a divided, corrupt, and degenerate institution. The

---

17 Chaucer's poetry, in fact, offers evidence of an annual event: see Kelly's provocative argument (1986: 99-127).

imagined community of MS Fairfax 16 thus ultimately supplants both court and religion.

At the end of Lydgate's *Complaint*, the narrator's fellow feeling prompts him to pray to Venus on behalf of the lover whose suffering he witnesses and identifies with. This allusion to a religion of love enhances the narrator's ideal of masculine unity and interdependence, suggesting a brotherhood of lover-poets. In MS Fairfax 16, "The Lover's Mass" most fully develops both the religious motif and the related theme of homosocial bonding. The poet stages his scene in a church, and begins with the narrator worshipping before an altar. According to the decorum of the time, he occupies a space reserved for lay men, and the text celebrates the love that ideally characterizes this brotherhood. The scene delicately balances individual worship and participation in a larger imagined community. The narrator dramatizes his entry into the fraternal order in his initial prayer of repentance, under the heading "Confiteor":

> I speke pleynly as I fel
> Touchynge the grete tendyrnesse
> Of my youthe and my symplesse
> Of myn vnkonying and grene age
> Wil lete me han noon avantage
> To serue loue I kan so lyte
> And yet myn hert doth delyte
> Of hys seruauntys for to here
> By exaumple of hem I myghte lere
> To folowe the wey of ther seruyse
> Yif I hadde konnyng to devyse
> That I myght a seruant be
> Amongys other in my degre

(f. 314r; Hammond 1927: ll. 16-28).

Youthful erotic love attaches this man first and foremost to other men, whom he trusts to have compassion on his simplicity, ignorance, and lack of experience. The narrator pictures himself as a green boy entering meekly into the company of powerful men, respectful of the hierarchies and privileges of rank, wishing only to be a "seruant ... Amongys other in my degre". The poem's "Introibo" similarly emphasizes submissiveness: the narrator approaches the altar "Of the myghty god of love" and desires to be taken perpetually "To hys seruyse" (f. 314r; ll. 3, 11). These passages dramatize the young man's erotic socialization as a series of submissions to more powerful masculine figures; in each case, "delyte" rewards his subjection. Here, as elsewhere in the manuscript, erotic love is the occasion of homosocial bonding. "The Lover's Mass" defines these male bonds in terms of both courtly and religious codes: the humility and physical passion of a youth at court combine with the diligent fidelity of a monk. This particular combination of values makes homosociality look both intensely physical and (playfully) spiritual.[18]

At the end of his religious service, the narrator of "Lover's Mass" offers prayers for other men's erotic success, demonstrating once again the intense empathy that shapes men's bonds with each other:

> Pes concord and vnyte
> God send hem sone ther desyrs
> And reles of ther hoote ffyrs
> That brenneth at her herte sore
> And encresseth more and more

(f. 315v; ll. 107-110).

Religion ideals support this ideal of community, determining the poet's emphasis on "pes concord and vnyte". The narrator's prayers create analogies between physical desire and spiritual values: to love is to become a member of an enduring community, to adopt its values of peace and mutual support. The elite masculine group of those who feel love's "hoote ffyrs" becomes, in this representation, a universal community, who, like the religious in the Church, perform the same rituals at the same times year by year. By appropriating religious codes, the poet can reshape the ideal of an erotic homosocial community, both declaring its virtue and suggesting its ludic equivalence to the Church.

The "Epistle" that follows the "Lover's Mass" amplifies the poem's religious element. The epistle is directed "To all the holy ffraternite and confrary: of the same bretherhede And to alle hospytlerys and Relygious" (f. 316v; Hammond 1927: p. 212, ll. 147-148). As with other poems of Cupid, the address to the reader invites entry into a community shaped by familiar religious values. The narrator recounts the trials of his erotic pilgrimage and the pains of his service to the god of love. As he considers all his "worthy bretheren and predecessours in love // that ha passyd the same pilgrymage toforn" (f. 317v; p. 213, ll. 179-180), he creates a part for himself in the imagined community of love's servants. He ends by asking the reader devoutly to join this brotherhood: "Besechynge ful lowly to all yow my brethere vn to whom thys lytel Epystel ys dyrect / / That yt lyke yow of pyte amonge your devout obseruaunces to han me Recomendyd wt som Especial Memorye in your prayers" (f. 317v; p. 213, ll. 189-192). The narrator assumes once again a pose of humility, subjecting himself to the reader as he has to powerful male figures throughout the poem. This is a fresh and graceful way of asking readers (once again) to feel empathy for the male lover and intercede on his be-

---

18   Camille (1989: 308-316) persuasively explicates the tension between sacred and profane in earlier representations of Amor, though he fails to recognize the possibility of "subversive play" (313) after the thirteenth century.

half, and to envision themselves as members of this fraternal community. Like the other poems of Cupid, "The Lover's Mass" and "Epistle" define a homosocial English community, modeled on the universal brotherhood of the religious, but secular in its poetic program; a community informed by the masculine power dynamics of court, but emphasizing the delights of submission rather than the potential for rivalry.

The religious motif recurs throughout these poems, as poets write their own variations on the theme. Clanvowe, for instance, opens the *Book of Cupid* with a lover's devout description of the god's quasi-papal powers ("he can bynde and vnbynde eke", f. 35v; Scattergood 1965: 1. 9), evoking the Chaucerian model of a unified, universal poetic community. This motif enhances the poets' authority and the perceived universality of their message. As in Chaucer's Prologue to the *Legend of Good Women*, references to the religion of love throughout the manuscript create the illusion of a very broad reading community – love's laity, encompassing both "lewde" and learned. Although the Church appears a conceptually vital imagined community to these poets, it is, like the court, finally inadequate to their purposes. They therefore recreate ecclesiastical ideals and values in the context of a secular male-bonded group, a vernacular poetic community.

The poems of Cupid in MS Fairfax 16 reveal a cultural transition in progress: the hitherto dominant models of community – (Gallic) court and (Latinate) religion – do not suffice for the project of inventing an English poetic tradition; so poets borrow features from each in order to invent a new kind of imagined community, characterized by both erotic passion and moral virtue, by a pleasurable subjection to other men and an idealized trust in their brotherly good will. The English poets typically represent the court of love as a corrupt Gallic convention, a place of envy, devious rivalry, and injustice; they express no desire to fashion themselves according to its dictates. Instead, they invent a countertradition: a masculine community of lovers distinguished for their empathy. The English poems of Cupid portray men who are more concerned to promote each other than to advance themselves; in this book, the rituals of heterosexual love attach men first and foremost to each other. This masculine community is not represented as a narrow, provincial coterie, nor is it necessarily elitist. The poets of MS Fairfax 16 consistently appropriate the values of religion – peace, unity, concord, fidelity, spirituality – in order both to reform and to broaden inherited (Gallic, Latin, English) ideas of a literary community. They draw on the motifs of religion and court in order to invent a new masculine group: an English audience composed of both "wise" and "lewde" readers, united by their fervent personal bonds with one another, bonds that transcend differences of rank and even education. These poems make it possible for the reader to imagine himself part of an English community that is virile as well as virtuous, refined as a court and unified as a congregation. The English community brought to life in the poems of Cupid thus becomes for the reader of this manuscript an appealing alternative to existing models of affiliation. In sum, MS Fairfax 16 fashions an imagined community that is peculiarly English as distinct from French, a lay community but united in its devotion to shared spiritual values and ideals. In the mid-fifteenth century, with England struggling to define an identity separate from France, with a Church marked by too-obvious corruptions, this model of masculine affiliation no doubt seemed doubly welcome.

A great deal of the existing scholarship on fifteenth-century literary culture treats it as pitifully inadequate in comparison with its more glorious fourteenth- and sixteenth-century siblings. Paul Strohm focuses, for instance, on evidence of a "narrowing" in the Chaucer tradition: "Chaucer's fifteenth-century followers ne-glect his mature works of greatest formal and thematic complexity, in favor of a comparatively narrow range of *dits amoureux* and visions in the manner of conti-nental France" (Strohm 1982: 5). Strohm is far from alone in his aesthetic judg-ment of the period, and few of us would argue that the *Assembly of Gods, Sidrac and Boctus,* or *Little Book of English Policy* is superior to *Troilus and Criseyde, Sir Gawain and the Green Knight,* or *Piers Plowman.* The persistent idea of a literary decline – an autumn of the Middle Ages – nonetheless keeps us from rec-ognizing the positive cultural work texts and manuscript collections can accom-plish during this period. MS Fairfax 16 allows us to recognize the contemporary gender-specific appeal of the love visions, for these texts turn reading into an act of male-bonding, an act constitutive of community. Indeed, the poems of Cupid invent the idea of a broad-based homosocial English community, and grant the reader a place in this imagined group. We can recapture the excitement of that innovation by studying the material manuscripts and coming to appreciate the dramatic roles poets played in constituting the imagined masculine community of late medieval England.

References

Allen, Richard Green
   1975   "Crapshooting Devices in a Medieval Manuscript", *Papers of the Biblio-graphic Society of America* 69: 481-482.
Anderson, Benedict
   1983   *Imagined Communities: Reflections on the Origin and Spread of Nation-alism.* London: Verso.
Benson, Larry D. (ed.)
   1987   *The Riverside Chaucer.* 3d ed. Boston: Houghton Mifflin.
Boffey, Julia – A. S. G. Edwards
   1999   "Bodleian MS Arch. Selden.B.24 and the 'Scotticization' of Middle Eng-lish Verse", in Thomas A. Prendergast – Barbara Kline (eds.), 166-185.

Boffey, Julia – John J. Thompson
> 1989   "Anthologies and Miscellanies: Production and Choice of Texts", in Jeremy Griffiths – Derek Pearsall (eds.), 279-315.

Burgess, Glyn S. – Robert A. Taylor (eds.)
> 1985   *The Spirit of the Court: Selected Proceedings of the Fourth Congress of the International Courtly Literature Society.* Cambridge: D. S. Brewer.

Camille, Michael
> 1989   *The Gothic Idol: Ideology and Image-Making in Medieval Art.* Cambridge: Cambridge Univ. Press.

Chamberlain, David (ed.)
> 1993   *New Readings in Late Medieval Love Poems.* Lanham, New York, London: Univ. Press of America.

Cooper, Helen – Sally Mapstone (eds.)
> 1997   *The Long Fifteenth Century: Essays For Douglas Gray.* Oxford: Clarendon.

Crockett, Bryan
> 1993   "Venus Unveiled: Lydgate's *Temple of Glas* and the Religion of Love", in David Chamberlain (ed.), 67-93.

Edwards, A. S. G.
> 1996   "Bodleian Library MS Arch. Selden B.24: A 'Transitional' Collection", in Stephen G. Nichols – Siegfried Wenzel (eds.), 53-67.

Green, Richard Firth
> 1983   "The *Familia Regis* and the *Familia Cupidinis*", in V. J. Scattergood – J. W. Sherborne (eds.), 87-108.

Griffiths, Jeremy – Derek Pearsall (eds.)
> 1989   *Book Production and Publishing in Britain 1375-1475.* Cambridge: Cambridge Univ. Press.

Hammond, Eleanor Prescott (ed.)
> 1927   *English Verse between Chaucer and Surrey.* Durham: Duke Univ. Press.

Hanna, Ralph, III
> 1996   "Miscellaneity and Vernacularity: Conditions of Literary Productions in Late Medieval England", in Stephen G. Nichols – Siegfried Wenzel (eds.), 37-51.

Jansen, J. P. M.
> 1989   "Charles D'Orléans and the Fairfax Poems", *English Studies* 70: 206-224.

Kelly, Henry Ansgar
> 1986   *Chaucer and the Cult of Saint Valentine.* Leiden: E. J. Brill.
> 1985   "Gaston Paris's Courteous and Horsely Love", in Glyn S. Burgess – Robert A. Taylor (eds.), 217-223.
> 1986-87   "The Varieties of Love in Medieval Literature According to Gaston Paris", *Romance Philology* 40: 301-327.

Lampe, David E.
> 1967   "Tradition and Meaning in *The Cuckoo and the Nightingale*", *Papers on Language and Literature* 3: 49-62.

Lerer, Seth
    1993   *Chaucer and His Readers: Imagining the Author in Late-Medieval Eng-land.* Princeton: Princeton Univ. Press.
MacCracken, Henry Noble (ed.)
    1911   "Poems from the Fairfax MS 16, in the Bodleian", *PMLA* 26: 155-174.
Middle English Dictionary
    2001   http: // ets.umdl.umich.edu/m/med/ (Oct. 21, 2002).
Middleton, Anne
    1980   "Chaucer's 'New Men' and the Good of Literature in the *Canterbury Tales*", in Edward W. Said (ed.), 15-56.
Moore, John C.
    1979   "'Courtly Love': A Problem of Terminology", *Journal of the History of Ideas* 40: 621-632.
Nichols, Stephen G. – Siegfried Wenzel (eds.)
    1996   *The Whole Book: Cultural Perspectives on the Medieval Miscellany.* Ann Arbor: Univ. of Michigan Press.
Norton-Smith, John (ed.)
    1979   *Bodleian Library MS Fairfax 16.* London: Scholar Press.
    1966   *John Lydgate Poems.* Oxford: Clarendon.
Panofsky, Erwin
    1939   *Studies in Iconology: Humanistic Themes in the Art of the Renaissance.* New York: Oxford Univ. Press.
Phillips, Helen
    1997   "Frames and Narrators in Chaucerian Poetry", in Helen Cooper – Sally Mapstone (eds.), 71-97.
Prendergast, Thomas A. – Barbara Kline (eds.)
    1999   *Rewriting Chaucer: Culture, Authority, and the Idea of the Authentic Text, 1400-1602.* Columbus: Ohio State Univ. Press.

Robbins, Rossell Hope
    1978   "Geoffroi Chaucier, Poète Français, Father of English Poetry", *Chaucer Review* 13: 93-115.
Said, Edward W. (ed.)
    1980   *Literature and Society.* Baltimore and London: Johns Hopkins Univ. Press.
Sanok, Catherine
    2001   "Reading Hagiographically: The *Legend of Good Women* and its Feminine Audience", *Exemplaria* 13: 323-354.
Scattergood, V. J. (ed.)
    1965   *The Works of Sir John Clanvowe.* Cambridge: D. S. Brewer.
Scattergood, V. J. – J. W. Sherborne (eds.)
    1983   *English Court Culture in the Later Middle Ages.* London: Duckworth.
Sedgwick, Eve Kosofsky
    1985   *Between Men: English Literature and Male Homosocial Desire.* New York: Columbia Univ. Press.

Spearing, A. C.
    1985   *Medieval to Renaissance in English Poetry*. Cambridge: Cambridge
             Univ. Press.

Strohm, Paul
    1982   "Chaucer's Fifteenth-Century Audience and the Narrowing of the 'Chau-
             cer Tradition'", *Studies in the Age of Chaucer* 4: 3-32.

Tinkle, Theresa
    2000   "The Case of the Variable Source: Alan of Lille's *De Planctu Naturae*,
             Jean de Meun's *Roman de la Rose*, and Chaucer's *Parlement of Foules*",
             Studies in the Age of Chaucer 22: 341-377.
    1989   "Cupid and Venus, Chaucer and Company" [PhD Dissertation, Univ. of
             California Los Angeles.]
    1996   *Medieval Venuses and Cupids: Sexuality, Hermeneutics, and English
             Poetry*. Stanford: Stanford Univ. Press.

Trigg, Stephanie
    1999   "Discourses of Affinity in the Reading Communities of Geoffrey Chau-
             cer", in Thomas A. Prendergast – Barbara Kline (eds.), 270-291.

Willard, Charity Cannon
    1984   *Christine de Pizan: Her Life and Works*. New York: Persea Books.

Mary Shelley, Godwin's *Chaucer*, and the Middle Ages

John Ganim, University of California, Riverside

Chaucer appears unexpectedly as one of the talismanic figures in the lives of certain nineteenth- and twentieth-century writers (Trigg 2002; Ellis 2000). One such little-remarked appearance occurs right before and after one of the most famous diary entries in literary history. According to Mary Shelley's diary, Percy was reading the *Life of Geoffrey Chaucer*, as of Saturday, March 4, 1815 (Shelley – Shelley 1987: 67). It is unlikely that Mary read the book at this time herself, since she had given birth prematurely to her baby Clara on February 27 of the same year, but it is possible that Shelley read parts out loud. The entry for Sunday, March 5, indicates that Shelley finished reading the *Life of Chaucer*. The chilling entry for the next day, however, Monday, March 6, is "find my baby dead" (Shelley – Shelley 1987: 68). The entries for the next few days record her grief over the loss of little Clara. On March 13, she writes "stay at...home net & think of my little baby – this is foolish I suppose yet whenever I am left to my own thoughts & do not read to divert them they always come back to the same point" (Shelley – Shelley 1987: 70). But on Wednesday, March 15, the diary is cataloguing Shelley's reading, observing "S. has read the life of Chaucer," though it is likely that Shelley himself made the notation (Shelley – Shelley 1987: 69). A few days later, on Sunday, March 19, is one of the most famous and moving entries in her journal, "dream that my little baby came to life again – that it had only been cold & that we rubbed it by the fire & it lived – I awake and find no baby – I think about the little thing all day" (Shelley – Shelley 1987: 70). *Frankenstein* was begun in 1816 and completed in 1817, and this passage is often cited as support for the interpretation of the novel in terms of its tortured images of birth and its virtual absence of mothers. Although Mary almost certainly had read the *Life of Chaucer* or parts of it at an earlier stage, her record of it in her diary occurs at one of the most traumatic moments in a life marked by a relentless series of traumas. This is, after all, a period of Mary Shelley's life when she is surrounded by the consequences of her father's (and her mother's) most notorious ideas about personal life, ideas which in the abstracted and self-absorbed version that Percy Shelley adopted were objected to famously by William Godwin himself, who after her elopement with the future poet refused to communicate with his daughter (Sunstein 1989). These disasters formed an almost Old Testament punishment (and were seized on as such by his enemies) of Godwin, who, admittedly, had urged rational, ethical conduct uncircumscribed by official approval, not personal, emotionally driven experimentation.

We know Mary Shelley as the author of *Frankenstein* (Shelley 1831) and as a key figure in our ongoing reconsiderations of Romanticism, but almost overlooked in this new scholarly attention is the place of Mary Shelley as a writer of historical novels set in the Middle Ages, of non-fiction prose about medieval figures, and, the daughter of William Godwin (1756-1836), as a virtual student of a certain Middle Ages as defined by her father.[1] Mary Wollstonecraft Shelley does not indicate that she read *The Canterbury Tales* until 1815 and there are few mentions of Chaucer in her letters and diaries. Her diaries, by no means exhaustive, record her and Shelley's reading of *The Floure and the Leaf: Chaucer's Dream*, thought to be by Chaucer, in 1821 (Shelley – Shelley 1987: 386). *Troilus and Criseyde* was probably read by Mary in 1820 and definitely read by both in 1821. A possible allusion to *The Knight's Tale* and to *Troilus and Criseyde* may be found in *Valperga* (Shelley 1996c: 117) where at Euthanasia's Court, William Borsiere (a character from Boccaccio's *Decameron*) sings of Palomon and Arcite and of Troilus and Cressida. The allusion is obviously to Boccaccio's works, dated later than the narrative, but the emphasis is such as to suggest the reader's knowledge of Chaucer's versions. Chaucer, however, is conspicuously absent from *Frankenstein*, despite Percy and Mary's immersion in his work just before the composition of the novel. Yet her father, William Godwin, one of the godfathers of modern anarchist thought, had written one of the first major Chaucerian studies, *Life of Chaucer* of 1803 (Godwin 1803), the book referred to in the diary entries. Godwin's *Life of Chaucer* is as interesting for its sense of the uses of the past as for its interpretation of Chaucer. Mary Shelley's narrative practices, especially in her later novels, represent a debate with Godwin's idea of the ethics of history, especially as exemplified in the medieval past. This dialogue and her revisions of Godwin's medievalism are much more central to her work than any allusions to Chaucer or borrowings of Chaucerian narrative. That is, there is good reason to consider the relation, however indirectly filtered through her father's biography of the poet, between Chaucer and Mary Shelley, not least of all because of the place of this relation in the complex and ambivalent stance towards the Romantic conception of art and life that is so powerfully articulated in *Frankenstein* as well as in some of her lesser known historical novels set in the Middle Ages, such as *The Fortunes of Perkin Warbeck* (1830) (Shelley 1996a) and *Valperga* (1823) (Shelley 1996c). My argument is that aspects of Godwin's *Life of Chaucer* find their way into *Frankenstein,* and the later historical novels, even if Chaucer himself barely registers. The literary attitudes of William Godwin are both honored and struggled with in *Frankenstein* and in these medieval historical novels.

In 1793, William Godwin published *An Enquiry Concerning Political Justice* (Godwin 1793), now one of the classics of political thought, and a book that immediately became one of the touchstones of Romantic republicanism. (It was, of course, Godwin's intellectual fame that drew Percy Bysshe Shelley to visit him in

---

1   Among the most important recent studies of Mary Shelley's work other than *Frankenstein* are Mellor (1988), Walling (1972), Reiman – Jaye – Bennett (1978), Conger – Frank – O'Dea (1997), Smith (1996), Bennett – Curran (2000), and Lowe-Evans (1998). The closest thing to a classic article on Mary Shelley's historical fiction is Bennett (1978).

October, 1812, resulting in the fateful meeting with Mary the next month, and Shelley's abandonment of his wife and children and elopement with the seventeen-year-old Mary in 1814.) Government, for Godwin, was an unnecessary evil, and it would become more unnecessary by the increase in knowledge and education, which would encourage the development of private morality. The free expression of this morality in the public arena would render superfluous such oppressive institutions as private property, marriage and laws. Even the physical body would become subject to mental control, and we could theoretically thereby eradicate illness, bodily decay, and death. Godwin's ideas were tempered somewhat after his famous partnership with Mary Wollstonecraft in 1797, who dies in the same year after giving birth to Mary Shelley at the age of 38. Mary Wollstonecraft convinced Godwin of the importance of emotional as well as rational capacities. His ideas also changed as the French Revolution devolved towards Empire, and like many radical intellectuals he modified his original enthusiasm, growing simultaneously more utopian and more pessimistic. Publication of a memoir of Mary Wollstonecraft detailing her affair with Gilbert Imlay and admitting to a premarital relationship with her on his own part lost Godwin the few friends he had in polite society and even scandalized some of his radical colleagues. Marriage to Mary Jane Clairmont in 1801, and absorption of a large family (including Fanny Imlay, the daughter of Mary Wollstonecraft and Imlay, and Mary Shelley) required Godwin to increase his income, and a stream of books with sales potential culminated in the founding of a press in 1805. That is, the immediate context of the *Life of Chaucer* is created in part by a new need to reach a larger public and a somewhat more conservative turn in William Godwin's thought.

Even so, the modern reader of Godwin's *Life of Chaucer* turns to it and from it with some puzzlement. For one thing, it is as much an account of Chaucer's times as of his life, and far less than half its pages are devoted to Chaucer's own biography, and far fewer to his writings.[2] Contemporary reviews of Godwin's biography, after all, archly complained, as did Sir Walter Scott in a review, that the book "has no more title to be called a life of Chaucer, than a life of Petrarch" (Scott 1804: 440). (To Godwin's complaint that he was not allowed access to crucial private libraries, Scott replied that this was hardly a surprise given Godwin's published contempt for private property.) But it is the emphasis of the *Life of Chaucer* that is more surprising. Given Godwin's place in the history of anarchist thought, his en-

---

2   The harsh but reasonable review by Robert Southey complains, "By attempting too many things in this work, the author has failed in all," asking instead for a chronological rather than thematic account of Chaucer's life, a close examination of his use of his sources. "Instead of heaping together old information concerning the manners of the fourteenth century, because they must have produced an effect upon Chaucer, he should have endeavoured to shew what effect Chaucer produced upon his age, instead of what effect his age produced upon him" (Southey 1804: 473).

thusiasm for John of Gaunt is remarkable. Given Godwin's place in revolutionary circles, his scorn for the Revolt of 1381 is even more remarkable. The old enemy of Church and one-time atheist now finds a theatrical beauty, conducive to literary inspiration, in the Roman mass (though he remains sufficiently derogatory, ascribing its power to its appeal to the senses) to draw attacks in reviews. And given the delusionary status accorded to feudal ideals and the appeal of medieval romance in Godwin's novels, such as *St. Leon* (1799) (Godwin 1992) and *Caleb Williams* (1794) (Godwin 1970), the ascription of all literary virtues to the feudal system is apparently contradictory. Indeed, the *Life of Chaucer* is much more warmly received in anti-Jacobin circles by his old enemies than it is by his former comrades. But it also may be that the apparent contradictions of his *Life of Chaucer* are not contradictions at all, given the fact that unlike many of his Republican comrades, he never entirely endorsed the French revolution, remained skeptical of universal suffrage, and idealized the brilliant and exceptional individual, predicting the Byronic hero in his novels.

Godwin praises the dream visions and Chaucer's handling of nature in the dream visions and the early poems, and though he offers a Dryden like description of *The Canterbury Tales*, his aesthetic appreciation of the dream visions and of their sources, such as *The Romance of the Rose*, is surer and more sophisticated, even original. But the intriguing aspect of the *Life of Chaucer* is as much its politics as its poetics. From the time he publishes the biography in 1803, Godwin experiences a decline in reputation and influence so precipitous that when Shelley writes him his famous letter of introduction, the poet claims to be pleasantly surprised that Godwin is still alive and well. Beginning with the *Life of Chaucer* and running through the publication date of *Frankenstein,* and indeed, until the 1820s, when he turns again to public controversy, Godwin's output, still prodigious, consists of plays, historical novels, children's books, and educational materials. That is, the *Life of Chaucer* can be regarded in Godwin's development as a transition from his political to his more general belletristic writings (though of course there was a political and philosophical agenda to even the most forgotten of these later writings). Godwin's account of the Revolt of 1381 strongly resembles, and in fact corrects, a species of anti-Jacobin narrative, such as Burke's account of the excesses of the French Revolution. Interwoven in his condemnation of the violence and arrogance of the rebels is an understanding of the causes of their grievances. John of Gaunt is pictured as a victim rather than an agent of the historical crisis that triggered the rebellion, and Chaucer, like William Godwin, is imagined as someone who could have told us I told you so:

> If John of Gaunt had not foreseen the tumults of this period, we may well believe that Chaucer foresaw them. Not exactly in time and place; for that is not the province of human sagacity. But he saw the posture of society; he saw what was passing in the minds of men; he heard the low, indistinct, murmuring, pent up sound, that preceded this memorable crash of the elements of the moral world. He perceived the oppressed and fettered multitude shaking their chains, and noted their quick, impatient pants after

freedom and happiness. Like every good man, and every true lover of his species. it is reasonable to suppose that he sympathised in their cause, and wished them success to their aims, til he saw them conducting themselves in such a manner, as was no less destructive to themselves as calamitous to their lords, and as led to the introduction of universal ignorance and barbarism.

(Godwin 1803: 316)

Godwin's Chaucer is in fact beholden to the same social changes that incite the revolt; the same decay of the feudal system gives rise to the possibility of individual lay achievement; the same yearnings for freedom are expressed in the new aesthetic freedom of his work. The perspective of Chaucer is at one with the perspective of Godwin, but it also is at one with at least one of the many perspectives in *Frankenstein*, the Geneva republicanism of Victor himself ("I am by birth a Genevese; and my family is one of the most distinguished of that republic", Shelley 1831: 29), which he announces in his first words to the narrator (who also sympathizes with it), and which is revealed to be rife with contradictions as the novel proceeds.[3]

If the "Chaucerian" perspective is unraveled in the portrayal of Victor, misunderstood greatness, shared by both Victor and his monstrous creation, is the theme of Godwin's account of John of Gaunt's personality. Godwin's account of John of Gaunt (whom he often refers to as "the king of Castille") owes much to Lancastrian propaganda (and Protestant valorization), but also to a peculiar identification with him as a persecuted and misunderstood potential Great Man. "To the insurgents of this period, the king of Castille appears to have been particularly obnoxious... Having withdrawn from all concern in the administration of public affairs, it was to be expected that he should have escaped that odium which ordinarily attaches to the situation of the minister... The contrary of this however was evidently the case... They had calumniated his temper, and had seized or invented occasions to persuade his countrymen that he was harsh, imperious, overbearing and revengeful" (Godwin 1803: vol. 2, 318-319). Godwin portrays Gaunt as a political *naif*: "He was not skilled to court the wayward suffrage of the public voice; he was ignorant of the thousand arts by which virtues are often made to appear of twofold value" (Godwin 1803: vol. 2, 319). Gaunt is persecuted, hunted and abandoned: "He was cut off from all his friends, from all whom duty and the ties of nature instructed him to love. He was cut off from them at a season of unspeakable peril, when the king, his youthful ward, was compelled day after day to expose himself to the violence of a brutal populace, drunk with prosperity and with blood... Nor was the king of Castille only prevented from assisting, or understanding the condition of, his family and country. He was exposed to the most painful anxiety as to his own situation and the clearness of his fame" (Godwin 1803: vol. 2, 322-323). Rumors associate him with

---

3   Mary's account of the unpleasant aspects of her travels in Switzerland in *History of a Six Weeks' Tour* (Shelley – Shelley 1989) and Mary Jane Clairmont's descent from a Genevan family render Victor's assertion less noble than it might sound.

a treasonous Scottish conspiracy and as a result, the rebels are enraged against him and "one of the first outrages they committed when they entered London, was the demolition of his magnificent palace of the Savoy... It was enough that any man was reputed to be his friend to render him an object of their pursuit; they reversed his arms, obliterated his name, and proclaimed him a traitor to his country. When he arrived at Berwick, he found himself unexpectedly treated as an outlaw" (Godwin 1803: vol. 2, 324).

The language applied to John of Gaunt here is unmistakably echoed in Mary Shelley's own character portraits. Godwin portrays John of Gaunt as a Byronic hero, misunderstood and persecuted through no fault of his own, indeed, punished for pursuing what feudal society had deemed his by right. In *Frankenstein*, however, similarly persecuted figures like the monster, or self-persecuting figures like Victor, cannot escape responsibility for their circumstances; even when innocent, they are guilty, or make themselves so. If Frankenstein's monster is an embodiment of the contradictions of Revolution, he is also an anti-populist propagandist. Read through the lens of the *Life of Chaucer* with its critical, even condemnatory sympathy for the rebels, the monster is both oppressor and rebel, both agent and victim.

Of course, this is to say that John of Gaunt becomes the typical Godwinian hero, one found in Godwin's novels, though in the novels the hero is more often than not the victim rather than the upholder of feudal values. His novel *St. Leon* is about a man who is able to recover his wasted fortune through the secret of the Philosopher's Stone and related alchemical knowledge. Obsessive and self-isolating, he wanders across Europe attempting to do good with his new wealth, but finding chaos each way he turns. Godwin's immersion in Chaucer is much more direct, and if there is a link with the proto-Faustian elements of *The Canon Yeoman's Tale* in *Frankenstein* it is almost certainly filtered through Godwin's novel. Again, however, Mary Shelley underlines the theme of personal responsibility and domestic chaos, the inescapable hurting of the ones you love in personal discovery. Godwin's most famous novel, *Caleb Williams*, has as its narrative engine a failed obsession with chivalry on the part of Caleb Williams' master, resulting in the disastrous duel and coverup that occasions Caleb's fugitive status. It is probably the larger ambivalent medievalism of Godwin that made the greater impression on Mary Shelley rather than Godwin's love for Chaucer. Percy Shelley, as well as many visitors, marveled at the collection of early English writers in Godwin's library. One more peculiarity of Godwin's *Life of Chaucer* is Godwin's claim for Chaucer's place in literary history. Chaucer is compared to an English Petrarch, virtually authorizing the tradition of English literature. At the same time, Godwin elevates Chaucer, considering his rough and untutored age, to the status of Shakespeare, notably displacing Milton. Yet it is Milton to whom Mary Shelley turns for much of the rhetoric and symbolism of *Frankenstein*. The conspicuous absence of Chaucer from the web of literary references in *Frankenstein* suggests almost an intentional slight.

Nevertheless, high regard for Dante (and of Italian literature in general) is reflected in the *Life of Chaucer*, and Dante so obviously permeates the imagery of *Frankenstein*, albeit the great Romantic reinterpretation of Dante, that it hardly needs comment. Mary Shelley's residence in Italy, and the model of the Italian settings and sources of many of Shelley's and Byron's poems, as well as her father's enthusiasms, obviously shape her web of references. Yet it is important to consider how much Mary Shelley makes Italian literature her own province. Even after the depression occasioned by the death of little William in 1819, Mary Shelley expresses a deep love of Italian literature, culture, and landscape (though not the Italian people themselves, towards whom she expresses a surprisingly provincial English prejudice – as she was to reveal earlier towards the French and Swiss people she encountered in *History of a Six Weeks' Tour* [Shelley – Shelley 1989]). She found in Italy a refuge from the hostility towards herself, Shelley, and her father so pervasive in English social circles, even though she would hope against hope for much of her life for acceptance at home.

Indeed, by making herself one of the more notable interpreters of Italian literature in England, she seems to have attempted to merge exile and return. Her entries for The Cabinet Encyclopedia *Eminent Literary and Scientific Men of Italy, Spain and Portugal* include sketches of a number of Italian medieval writers (Montgomery ed., 1835). Her entry for Petrarch, for instance (Shelley 1835a) is lengthy and detailed, but it is a more or less loose review of Petrarch's life as it is recounted in his own letters and other writings. Nevertheless, it is shaped by Mary Shelley's own interests as well as by the influence of her father's *Life of Chaucer*. For here again, the life path of the individual, and the difficulties erected by political conflict, looms larger than either the creative imagination or the writings of the author. More coherent than Godwin's biography of the poet, Mary Shelley's biographical chapters nevertheless also consider the life as almost equivalent in value to the literature that justifies its recounting. Unlike her father's biography of Chaucer, however, around whom the forces of history whirl and who often seems an observer from the margins, Mary Shelley's biography of Petrarch is very much a life observed through Petrarch's eyes. The fourteenth century is marked not by its alterity, but by its resemblance to the present day, only beset by even more obstacles to a happy life. As with *Frankenstein* and the historical novels, and even *The Last Man*, biographical time is marked by a series of exiles. Written for an audience concerned with bettering itself, the chapter begins with an oddly proper sense of genealogy (admittedly drawn from Petrarch himself), "Francesco Petrarch was of Florentine extraction, and sprung from a respectable family" (Shelley 1835a: 61), echoing the opening of Victor's narrative in *Frankenstein*. Political and personal exile, unfulfilled love, and even an epiphanic value accorded to Rome, unite the lives of author, Mary Shelley, and subject, Petrarch. The Middle Ages is yet one other arena for the struggle of Mary Shelley's sense of character, between how much we are made by our circumstances and how much we make ourselves, and how much literature is the means by which we can make ourselves and rise above our circumstances. The self-described themes of Petrarch's life – unrequited passion, exile, misunderstanding, isolation, and ambition – are the constructing themes of modern (and Romantic) subjectivity, but Mary Shelley makes them peculiarly her own, reflecting her vacillation between a desire for independence and a need for acceptance. Even the defense of the passion behind the Petrarchan conceit which she offers against accusations of artificiality is unsurprising given the heightened and often formal rhetoric of her own novels. Indeed, amid the highly masculinized world of major late medieval writers, Mary Shelley curiously figures Petrarch as the closest to feminine emotional life, according to her own sentimental definitions of gender, "his disposition was frank, independent, and generous; but he was vain even to weakness; and there was a touch of almost feminine softness in his nature, which was even accompanied by physical timidity of temper" (Shelley 1835a: 107). Her account of Petrarch's translation of Boccaccio's story of Griselda from the *Decameron* is the occasion for one of Mary's few allusions to "our English poet Chaucer, who in his prologue to the story of Griselda says that he 'Learned it at Padowe of a worthy clerke,/Francis Petrarch.' Chaucer had been sent ambassador to Genoa just at this time" (Shelley 1835a: 114). Given Petrarch's place in the history of landscape and the sublime, her emphasis on his appreciation of nature is appropriate, and it is interesting how clearly she can distinguish his perspective on nature from that of the Romantic poets. At the same time, his own shuttling between Vaucluse, the Alps, Rome, and the Italian countryside is retold (from his own accounts) in ways that resemble her own divided loyalties between England and Italy and between society and isolation.

If Petrarch is pictured as one of the originary points of modern subjectivity in Mary Shelley's account, the life of Boccaccio, the following chapter in The Cabinet Encyclopedia, rather stresses the primitivism of the fourteenth century. His father's name, she points out, was formed by adding a version of his grandfather's name to form Boccaccio di Chellino, and Boccaccio himself referred to himself as Giovanni di Boccaccio da Certaldo, "such, as in the Highlands of Scotland and other places in the infancy of society, was the mode by which the Italians formed their names" (Shelley 1835b: 116). Late medieval Italy is thereby connected to Ossianic Britain. Certainly Boccaccio associates with the sophisticated court of Naples and elsewhere, but he is marked as an "imaginative youth," and his calling is sealed by a visit to Virgil's tomb and its sublime natural setting: "Nature presents her most enchanting aspect; and the voice of human genius breathing from the silent tomb, speaks of the influence of the imagination of man" (Shelley 1835b: 119). The outline of her life of Boccaccio is consonant with contemporary accounts, but she highlights a sense of poetic calling closer to Keats and Shelley than to a medieval writer, which is to say a romantic version of poetic life as medieval romance. Boccaccio then attends Petrarch's lecture on poetry presented to Robert King of Naples, and the maternal inspiration of nature, as it were, is given shape by the paternal guide represented by Petrarch. As with Petrarch, she is attentive to the development of a poetic career, from the "unreadable"

Filocolo through the more masterful *Teseide*, which occasions yet another Chaucer reference ("The subject is familiar to the English reader, as the 'Knight's Tale' in Chaucer" [Shelley 1835b: 124]). Yet Mary Shelley is convinced that Boccaccio is finally "not a poet" and his real strength is narrative. The author of *The Last Man*, in which the civilization is destroyed by plague, regards Boccaccio's description of the Black Death as his greatest achievement, although she astutely observes that it is probably not based on first hand observation of the plague in Florence. Although her comments on the *Decameron* are brief and confined to a description of the frame, her appreciation of the work as a whole is noteworthy, far from the puritanical aversion of her father from Chaucer's ribald tales. Nevertheless, she is affronted by the antifeminism of the *Corbaccio*, and regrets its composition. What is good in Boccaccio, she suggests, is his creative imagination, and what is bad is the result of the age that he lived in, by which she seems to mean a decadent court culture and irresponsible monastic and clerical institutions (such as the lack of care of manuscripts at Monte Cassino). She then details Boccaccio's scholarly efforts and literary criticism. In her portraits of both Petrarch and Boccaccio, she is as much concerned with the origin and development of the man of letters as a type in European culture as she is with aesthetic or poetic appreciation. In a sense, she applies to them the standards she applies to herself, or that Godwin would have applied to either himself or his subjects. It does not take much to highlight the many episodes of failed friendships and personal disappointments in the life of either Boccaccio or Petrarch, but the identification of Mary with their travails is obvious in the retelling.[4] In contrast to the entries by other contributors to The Cabinet Encyclopedia, which emphasize the works of their subjects, Mary's entries stress the personal qualities of her subjects, and she seems to regard their medieval settings as an almost allegorical extension of these qualities and their testing by physical and political deprivations. Read in the context of her other entries in the encyclopedia, these entries make it clear that Mary is as concerned with tracing the development of incipient ideas of Republican freedom and enlightenment humanism in Italian thought as she is with elucidating the writings of her authors or of communicating a sense of the age they lived in. As with her novels, the Middle Ages serves as an occasion rather than a setting.

Mary Shelley's place in literary history is assured by the canonical, even originary, status of her futurist and science fiction novels, *Frankenstein* and *The Last Man*. Yet she wrote two major novels (as well as a few sketches and stories) set in the Middle Ages.[5] In many novels with medieval settings, the Middle Ages is as much a character as a backdrop. This is certainly the case with Scott's novels. It is also the case with the medievalized settings and sets of Gothic novels. But with few excep-

---

4   A rare discussion of the *Lives* is available in Kucich (2000: 198-213).

5   According to Sunstein (1989: 311) the diarist Henry Crab Robinson, a member of Godwin's circle, in reaction to the 1831 republication of the novel, thought that *Frankenstein* would have been more appropriately set in the medieval period.

tions (and these are often Gothicized), Mary Shelley's Middle Ages is peculiarly abstract, even when backgrounds, buildings, and landscapes are described in detail. Two of Mary Shelley's rarely read historical novels in fact take place in something like a Godwinian Middle Ages, in which the feudal system, far from being the humane order of a Sir Walter Scott that only needs renewal, serves as a figure for oppressive associations and values which compromise the purity of individual choice and private altruism. *Valperga* was published in 1823, but Mary Shelley worked on it shortly after completing *Frankenstein*, from 1817 through 1821. Mary and her father were now on better terms, and he assisted with editorial and other suggestions, including the eventual title, *Valperga*. The son of an exiled Ghibelline family in thirteenth-century Tuscany, Castruccio grows towards a proto-Machiavellian desire for repatriation, power, and revenge. Meanwhile, his female companion Euthanasia, of Guelph heritage, espouses a Republican ideal of peace, freedom, and cooperation. Castruccio will eventually attack Valperga, Euthanasia's castle, where they once shared their idyll, even though she attempts to moderate his depredations and even though he remains in love with her. A subplot involving witchcraft and heresy touches on both of their fortunes and introduces a Gothic note into an otherwise rationally historicized narrative. That is, the Gothic version of the medieval past as nightmare contrasts with a historical romance's version of the Middle Ages as yet another arena for recognizable human passions, calculations, and political ideas and ideals. In fact, *Valperga* opens with an enlightenment disparagement of the Middle Ages and a celebration of the republican modernity glimpsed in fourteenth-century Italy: "The other nations of Europe were yet immersed in barbarism, when Italy, where the light of civilisation had never been wholly eclipsed, began to emerge from the darkness of the ruin of the Western Empire and to catch from the East the returning rays of literature and science" (Shelley 1996c: 7).

In *Valperga*, she ascribes the retrogressive dimensions of history, party loyalty, and vengeance, to the experience of war and displacement, marking Castruccio's earliest memories and eventually overwhelming the beneficent influences of an enlightened education. One of *Valperga*'s earliest and most memorable scenes is that of a pageant in Florence enacting Dante's *Inferno*; so many people crowd around to see it that the bridge of Carraia collapses, creating a scene of a living hell:

> Driven by the crowd, he at length came in sight of the Arno. It was covered by boats, on which scaffoldings were erected, hung with black cloth, whose accumulated drapery lent life to the flames, which the glare of day would otherwise have eclipsed. In the midst of these flames moved legions of ghastly and distorted shapes, some with horns of fire, and hoofs, and horrible wings; others the naked representatives of the souls in torment; mimic shrieks burst upon the air, screams and demoniac laughter. The infernal drama was acted to the life; and the terrible effect of such a scene was enhanced, by the circumstance of its being no more than an actual representation of what then existed in the imagination of the spectators, endued with the vivid colours of a faith inconceivable in these lethargic days.

Castruccio felt a chill of horror run through his frame; the scene before him appeared for a moment as a reality, rather than a representation; the Arno seemd a yawning gulph, where the earth had opened to display the mysteries of the infernal world; when suddenly a tremendous crash stamped with tenfold horror the terrific mockery. The bridge of Carraia, on which a countless multitude stood, one above the other, looking on the river, fell. Castruccio saw its props loosening, and the curved arch shake, and with a sudden shriek he stretched out his arms, as if he could save those who stood on it. It fell in with a report that was reverberated from the houses that lined the Arno; and even, to the hills which close the valley, it rebellowed along the sky, accompanied by fearful screams, and voices that called on the names of those whom they were never more to behold. The confusion was beyond description terrible; some flying, others pressing towards the banks of the river to help the sufferers; all, as himself, seized with a superstitious dread, which rebuked them for having mimicked the dreadful mysteries of their religion, and which burst forth in clamorous exclamations and wild horror.

(Shelley 1996c: 15)

Based on a historical incident, the episode nevertheless reminds readers of the descriptive powers of "the Author of *Frankenstein*" as Mary was announced on the title page, despite Godwin's marketing concerns. This is the Mary Shelley who could evoke the wildness of the mountains and the glaciers and the ice fields of the Arctic, and who could match the poet of *Mont Blanc* for auditory effects. It is also impossible to read without recalling that the author herself had experienced the horrors of similar catastrophes. Yet for all that, Mary Shelley's narrator cannot help but frame the scene as a reverse morality play, in which the audience is trapped by their own naive beliefs in what is from her perspective tantamount to superstition. The novel will in fact repeatedly express anti-Catholic sentiments disguised as enlightenment progressivism, and it is well to remember that even Godwin's celebration of John of Gaunt in the *Life of Chaucer* derives at least partly from Gaunt's place in the history of Protestant hagiography, as a protector of Wycliff. In the middle of a passage that again affirms her place in the history of horror fiction, she insists on the philosophical status of even violent accidents. In this scene, the unchannelled forces of imagination turn out to be destructive, even suicidal. Few writers are as attuned to both the powers and the dangers of imagination and belief. The border between art and life literally collapses.

This scene is a miniature lesson in Mary Shelley's medievalism, which might be termed a medievalism against itself, or, more properly, a critical medievalism. The very imaginative power of medieval culture is adapted to explore its limitations and dangers, much as *Frankenstein* framed Romantic Faustianism. The "Inferno" passage is something of an exception in the novel, the point of view of which is usually that of Castruccio, and which therefore regards landscape, setting, and description tactically (Castruccio, when he enters Valperga for the first time, observes its defensive capacity). Castruccio turns a rationalist eye to the portents beloved of the Florentines, such as the birth of cubs to their lioness mascot (Shelley 1996c: 122). Euthanasia, however, while equally skeptical, links their belief to their imaginative and aesthetic capacity, which can result in such triumphs as the *Duomo*. Occasionally, nature provides a refreshment and perhaps even a sense of regret to him as it reminds him of what his drive to power has left behind. Pageantry and local color are more often associated with Euthanasia, especially in the chapters describing her court. The other "medieval" theme to a medieval novel which is in fact minimal in its medievalizing apparatus is the subplot involving Beatrice, its other major female character.

In good Gothic fashion, the theological background of Beatrice's status as a prophet is narrated by the Bishop of Ferrara, who tells Castruccio of a heresy propounded by Wilhelmina of Bohemia, who, with a female companion by name of Magfreda, secretly preached that she was the incarnation of the Holy Spirit. Magfreda had asserted to the Bishop that "She has revealed Her will to me, and by Her command I now confide to you the treasure of my soul," confiding in him the existence of Wilhelmina's child, who is of course Beatrice (Shelley 1996c: 133). Just as Castruccio the next day hears Beatrice preach, she is arrested by the inquisition. She miraculously survives a trial by ordeal, walking unharmed over hot irons (a feat we learn later had been fraudulently engineered by her allies). This hallucinatory narrative compression also derives from the Gothic novel. In fact, each of the three main characters generates their own generic world. Beatrice's world is that of the Gothic, luridly linking mysterious sexuality, heresy, torture, and prophecy, pitting the pure but alluring female against the inquisition. Late in the novel, the nearly deranged Beatrice turns to witchcraft in a desperate attempt to woo back Castruccio, and falls mad and dying, almost unrecognized, as he passes on a road before her. Euthanasia's scenes resemble either medieval romance, such as the description of her court, or medieval allegory, such as when she engages Castruccio in long debates that link her with Prudence, Wisdom, or Peace. Towards the end of the novel, Euthanasia, serving as a sort of therapist to the near-mad Beatrice, describes the human mind in the Platonic language of allegory. But with few exceptions, Castruccio himself is firmly rooted in masculinized historical narratives, calculating, rational, and often ruthless. If he sees himself as modernizing rather than medieval, it is perhaps a further sign of Mary Shelley's oxymoronic combination of skepticism and idealism about either the possibility of progress or the value of tradition.

When Castruccio departs from Ferrara, Beatrice dreamily watches him as he rides away, "she, most unfortunate, mistakes for the inspirations of Heaven the wild reveries of youth and love" (Shelley 1996c: 146). She becomes a type of the faery lover, so central to the Romantic notion of medieval romance. Beatrice here predicts a Victorian type, to be enshrined in the poems of Tennyson and the art of the PreRaphaelites, but Mary Shelley insists on the self-delusion of Beatrice's fantasy. On the one hand, Beatrice is an eighteenth-century sentimental heroine, seduced and abandoned, both by Castruccio and her own visions. On the other hand, she is the archetypal prophetess whose vatic powers disappear with her sexual innocence. In fact, for Mary Shelley, Beatrice is a prisoner of her own medieval faith and of the past, while Euthanasia is a prophetess of what will become the *resurgimento*.

Mary Shelley also sets a later novel, *The Fortunes of Perkin Warbeck* (1830), in the fifteenth century. *Perkin Warbeck* includes a rare quotation from Chaucer, in the form of a chapter headnote (Shelley 1996a: 105), where "The Summoner's Tale's" equation of friars and devils is used to describe the Tudor assassin Meiler Tragner. As with *Valperga*, she chooses a time period or place that is not quite the site of sentimental medievalism. Instead, these are times and places that allow for the dramatization of an incipient modernity. Yet as with Godwin, the past has a double purpose, one to serve as an explanation for the failure of enlightened behavior, the other to serve as a backdrop for a moral struggle that is not specific to an historical moment. Her Perkin has a legitimate claim to be considered an heir to the throne, actually the Prince Richard, Duke of York, who, according to conventional histories, was murdered by Richard III. Eventually imprisoned and executed, Perkin-Richard's life represents a chivalric ideal played against the bloody internecine struggles of the Yorkist succession, at first providing an heroic alternative and then succumbing to the practical consequences of a chivalry lived in the real world. In *Valperga*, the typical settings of medieval historical novels were employed both to lay claim to the genre and also to critique the illusions of the female characters trapped by those settings: Beatrice's horrendous imprisonment (both internal and external) by the belief systems of the medieval past and Euthanasia's partial commitment to medieval values in her Guelph loyalties and her elaborate court festivals. The medieval settings in the earlier novel were ironically "feminized," in that they were associated with these powerfully imagined female characters, but were also symbolic of the restrictions imposed, and internalized, by a value system associated with the past. But *Perkin Warbeck*, for all its politically powerful female figures, eschews romance settings almost consciously, so that no alternative exists to a masculinized politics. Generically and stylistically, the result is an almost overwhelming emphasis on *realpolitik*, hardly leavened by the Gothic and romance elements of *Valperga*. Mary Shelley was inevitably influenced by Shakespeare's history plays and Ford's *Perkin Warbeck*. But where their works depended on a legitimate succession to order a chaotic history, she insists on emphasizing how that very chaos is occasioned by the effort to impose a legitimacy which is finally arbitrary. In questioning the national myth of the War of the Roses, Mary Shelley's *Perkin Warbeck* sacrifices its own narrative progress. It is not that the novel's form sympathetically imitates chaos and confusion; it is that Shelley's resolute refusal to accept fictions of concord is reflected in narrative entropy and abrupt conclusion rather than resolution. Mary Shelley found the late Middle Ages to be a useful site for her sense of history because its records and its contemporary chroniclers offered a similarly pessimistic historiography, even if she was critical of the values and beliefs encoded in those records.

The story of Perkin Warbeck fits perfectly into Mary Shelley's entropic view of history. After Bosworth Field, the Yorkist claims are impossible to sustain by military or political means. Perkin's role as pretender takes on the quality of a quixotic alternative history, one that might have replaced the grand Lancastrian and Tudor narrative, but which would have been unlikely to stem the inexorable rise of a centralized and absolute monarchy. Despite her condemnation of blood feuds as regressive and destructive, Shelley honors Lancastrian heroism in the novel, framing it as equal to the efforts of the Yorkists. In the chapters set in Spain, the Moors are described as every bit as brave as the Christians, and de Faro, a major figure in the novel, was born a Moor and raised by monks as a Christian. But Tudor politics are another matter. She assigns Henry and his followers the role of calculation and cunning without passion. In this sense, the novel accords a certain beauty to the waning of the Middle Ages. Bosworth Field operates as a traditional dividing line between the Middle Ages and the Renaissance, or so it was regarded in the nineteenth century. Whether Mary Shelley divided history up in this way or not, Perkin-Richard and Henry represent two fundamentally different conceptions of polity, with Richard associated with chivalry, personal loyalty, and military derring-do, and Henry with strategic deployment of diplomacy and economic blackmail, with the rise of the state and the concentration of power in the abstract status of the sovereign. Underneath this profoundly masculinized politics and narrative, however, the most vibrant consciousness (and the last word) are accorded to Richard's bride, Margaret Gordon, and his sister, Elizabeth, married to his enemy Henry VII. In their state as prisoners of fortune, misunderstood and maligned, history acquires a human form quite different from that of the masculine rivalry of the novel's chief agents.

Mary Shelley shared with her father, and probably learned from him, a dual attitude towards the Middle Ages, that its greatest achievements were inevitably intertwined with its greatest failures. In contrast to the enthusiasm of Scott and generations of antiquarian medievalists, Mary Shelley brought an objective, even rationalized perspective on the medieval past.[6] But what the novels do is to dramatize even more clearly than Godwin's novels one of the contact points between Romantic aesthetics and Romantic politics. Godwin's novels offer an almost Whiggish hope in the eventual triumph of reason and altruism, or at least the promise of an evolution towards their triumph. Mary Shelley's medievalism shares with her father's Middle Ages a fundamental duality that underlies Godwinian politics, that medieval men and women are limited and shaped by their

---

6   Curran, in the excellent introduction to his Oxford edition of *Valperga* (Shelley 1997: xvi-xviii) contrasts the medievalism of the "scholarly" Shelley with the "antiquarian" Scott, and furthermore observes that *Valperga* offers a feminist reply to the patriarchal character portraits of *Ivanhoe*. For a detailed discussion of gender politics in *Valperga*, interestingly related to Italian Romanticism, see White (2000). See also, in the same volume, Garbin (2000).

historical circumstances at the same time that they must seek to rise above them through reason and individual discovery. But in Mary Shelley it is not the chivalric Middle Ages alone or the ideals of Republican liberty which produced great art and truth, but the conflict between them, a conflict which ultimately destroys its actors, often in ironically reversed circumstances.

I have argued that Mary Shelley would have read or reread or been reminded of her father's biography of Chaucer at a critical turning point in her own life and a time when she was conceiving of the novel that would become *Frankenstein.* Moreover, she creates analogues to the most admirable figures in Godwin's historical account, and demonstrates how they are as much agents as subjects of their own predicaments. She does this partly by intersecting the heroic and the domestic and partly by taking the role of the Chaucerian artist as defined by her father to its limit. The recent revaluations of *Frankenstein* and *The Last Man* have catapulted Mary Shelley into a canonical place both in literary history and in the history of science fiction and futurist literature. I have tried to suggest here that she also deserves a place, albeit a contrary and critical one, in the history of medievalism. From her father's early and counterintuitive engagement with Chaucer, she builds a substantial alternative to sentimental and romantic medievalism in her historical novels and essays. In fact, because of her capacious reading, her unusual education, and the experience of alternating independence and dependence, exile and return, in her personal life, most of Mary Shelley's intellectual and creative positions evade traditional labels. In the case of her version of the Middle Ages, she sets up a dialogue among what we ordinarily consider an eighteenth-century disparagement, a Romantic celebration, and a Victorian ethical analysis of the value of the medieval past. It is entirely possible, and not at all reductive, to read this dialogue, as many others, as a debate with the writings and influence of her husband and her father, which is to say that in her sense of the past as in so many other aspects of her life, the personal and the political, the emotional and the intellectual, merge and collide. As with their later admirers Virginia Woolf and William Morris, the Romantics turn to the Middle Ages both for permission to carry on the great romantic and modern agenda to live one's life as a work of art – and as a retreat from the damage wreaked by such an effort. From Mary Shelley's *Frankenstein* on, Romanticism articulates and criticizes this very agenda, and this dual impulse towards experimentation and awareness of the dangers of moving beyond the limits continues through high modernism, where everywhere in the imagery of its canonical texts and figures – from Eliot's *Waste Land* onwards, is a record of the costs both of repression and experimentation.

References

Bennett, Betty T.
    1978   "The Political Philosophy of Mary Shelley's Historical Novels: *Valperga*
            and *Perkin Warbeck*", in Donald H. Reiman – Michael C. Jaye – Betty T.
            Bennett (eds.), 354-371.
Bennett, Betty T. – Stuart Curran (eds.)
    2000   *Mary Shelley in Her Times*. Baltimore: Johns Hopkins University Press.
Conger, Syndy M. – Frederick S. Frank – Gregory O'Dea (eds.)
    1997   *Iconoclastic Departures: Mary Shelley After Frankenstein: Essays in
            Honor of the Bicentenary of Mary Shelley's Birth*. Madison, NJ, London,
            Cranbury, NJ: Fairleigh Dickinson University Press, Associated Univer-
            sity Presses.
Eberle-Sinatra, Michael (ed.)
    2000   *Mary Shelley's Fictions from Frankenstein to Falkner*. Basingstoke,
            Hampshire, New York: Macmillan Press, St. Martin's Press.
Ellis, Steve
    2000   *Chaucer at Large: The Poet in the Modern Imagination*. Medieval cul-
            tures. Minneapolis: University of Minnesota Press.
Garbin, Lidia
    2000   "Mary Shelley and Walter Scott: *The Fortunes of Perkin Warbeck* and
            the Historical Novel", in Michael Eberle-Sinatra (ed.), 150-163.
Godwin, William
    1793   *An Enquiry Concerning Political Justice and Its Influence on General
            Virtue and Happiness*. London: Print. for G.G.J. and J. Robinson.
    1803   *Life of Geoffrey Chaucer, the Early English Poet: Including Memoirs of
            His Near Friend and Kinsman, John of Gaunt, Duke of Lancaster: With
            Sketches of the Manners, Opinions, Arts and Literature of England in the
            Fourteenth Century*. 2 vols. London: R. Phillips.
    1970   *Caleb Williams*. David McCracken (ed.). London New York: Oxford
            University Press.
    1992   *St. Leon*. Pamela Clemit (ed.). London: W. Pickering.
Kucich, Greg
    2000   "Mary Shelley's *Lives* and the Reengendering of History", in Betty T.
            Bennett – Stuart Curran (eds.), 198-213.
Lowe-Evans, Mary (ed.)
    1998   *Critical Essays on Mary Wollstonecraft Shelley*. Critical Essays on Brit-
            ish literature. New York, London: G.K. Hall, Prentice Hall International.
Mellor, Anne Kostelanetz
    1988   *Mary Shelley: Her Life, Her Fiction, Her Monsters*. New York: Methuen.
Montgomery, James (ed.)
    1835   *Eminent Literary and Scientific Men of Italy, Spain, and Portugal. The
            Cabinet Encyclopæia*. 3 vols. London: Printed for Longman *et al.* Vol. 1.

Reiman, Donald H. – Michael C. Jaye – Betty T. Bennett (eds.)
   1978   *The Evidence of the Imagination: Studies of Interactions Between Life and Art in English Romantic Literature.* New York: New York University Press.
Scott, Sir Walter
   1804   Rev. Godwin, *Life of Chaucer. Edinburgh Review* 3:437-452.
Shelley, Mary Wollstonecraft
   1831   *Frankenstein or, The Modern Prometheus.* London: H. Colburn and R. Bentley.
   1835a   "Francesco Petrarch", in James Montgomery (ed.), 61-115.
   1835b   "Giovanni Boccaccio", in James Montgomery (ed.), 116-149.
   1835c   "Niccolo Machiavelli", in James Montgomery (ed.), 256-312.
   1996a   *The Fortunes of Perkin Warbeck: A Romance.* Doucet Devin Fischer (ed.). London, Brookfield, Vt.: W. Pickering.
   1996b   *The Last Man.* Jane Blumberg – Nora Crook (eds.). London, Brookfield, Vt.: W. Pickering.
   1996c   *Valperga, or, The Life and Adventures of Castruccio, Prince of Lucca.* London, Brookfield, Vt.: W. Pickering.
   1997   *Valgerga, or, The Life and Adventures of Castruccio, Prince of Lucca.* Stuart Curran (ed.). Women Writers in English 1350-1850. New York: Oxford University Press.
Shelley, Mary Wollstonecraft – Percy Bysshe Shelley
   1987   *The Journals of Mary Shelley, 1814-1844.* Paula R. Feldman – Diana Scott-Kilvert (eds). Oxford and New York: Clarendon Press, Oxford University Press.
   1989   *History of a Six Weeks' Tour.* Revolution and romanticism, 1789-1834. Oxford: Woodstock Books.
Smith, Johanna M.
   1996   *Mary Shelley.* Twayne's English Authors Series. New York, London: Twayne Publishers, Prentice Hall International.
Southey, Robert
   1804   Rev. Godwin, *Life of Chaucer. Annual Review and History of Literature for 1803* 2:462-473.
Sunstein, Emily W.
   1989   *Mary Shelley: Romance and Reality.* Boston: Little, Brown.
Trigg, Stephanie
   2002   *Congenial Souls: Reading Chaucer from Medieval to Postmodern.* Medieval cultures. Minneapolis: University of Minnesota Press.
Walling, William
   1972   *Mary Shelley.* New York: Twayne Publishers.
White, Daniel E.
   2000   "Mary Shelley's *Valperga*: Italy and the Revision of Romantic Aesthetics", in Michael Eberle-Sinatra (ed.), 95-108.

Chaucer

The Disappointments of Criseyde

Edward Condren, UCLA

What kind of article does one write to honor a colleague and friend who is the finest scholar he has ever known? Professor Kelly has asked and pursued some of the most searching literary questions in his field, often for the first time: about the authorship of "Dante's" letter to Can Grande; the original Feast of St. Valentine; clandestine marriages; the images on the walls in Chaucer's dream visions; the ownership of stews in Southside; and a few dozen other subjects most of us have never thought of. Well, to honor a man able to detect an erroneous attribution in *Patrologia Latina*, where a passage by Bishop Otto of Lucca is wrongly said to be by Hugh of St. Victor, one certainly does not risk offering a piece of exacting scholarship. Rather, I shall turn to a largely overlooked passage in the Chaucerian canon that embodies the very essence of literature, thus offering a critic an irresistible invitation. By containing a possible hint of clandestine affection, here assumed to be a deeply felt emotion unannounced to a wider public, the passage touches subjects with which Professor Kelly has long been associated.

Often said to be Chaucer's most highly polished, his most completely finished work, *Troilus and Criseyde* includes near its beginning a seminal scene initiated by the one character who would otherwise seem least likely to initiate anything. Though assertive in her dealings with her immediate circle, especially with her uncle Pandarus, elsewhere Criseyde reveals a demure manner, a woman accustomed to having others make decisions for her. Yet here, at the very beginning of Chaucer's long chronicle of what may be the most important event in her life, when she is doubly vulnerable by lacking the support of an influential male and acquiring the name of a traitor's daughter, Criseyde abandons her passive nature to lay her helplessness before Hector. This sequence, in a poem of more than eight-thousand lines, remains the only act planned and executed by Criseyde herself. We assume it must take extraordinary courage for her to call on Hector and plead her case before him:

> On knees she fil biforn Ector adown
> With pitous vois, and tendrely wepynge,
> His mercy bad, hirselven excusynge.
>
> (I.110-12)[1]

---

1   All quotation from Chaucer are taken from Larry D. Benson, Gen. Ed., *The Riverside Chaucer*, 3rd edition (Boston: Houghton Mifflin Company, 1987).

This touching appeal to Troy's most formidable warrior for a clarification of her status receives in return a gracious response that would allay anyone's fears:

> "Lat youre fadres treson gon"
> Forth with meschaunce, and ye youreself in joie
> Dwelleth with us, whil yow good list, in Troie.
>
> "And al th'onour that men may don yow have,
> As ferforth as youre fader dwelled here,
> Ye shul have, and youre body shal men save,
> As fer as I may ought enquere or here."

(I.117-23)

A generous, unqualified response. But is it precisely the reaction Criseyde longed to receive when she planned this interview? The possibility that Criseyde has other hopes for this meeting, richer by far than Hector's assurance of political asylum, takes tantalizing shape in the narrator's spare report of her gratitude:

> And she hym thonked with ful humble chere,
> And ofter wolde, and it hadde ben his wille,
> And took hire leve, and hom, and held hir stille.

(I.124-26)

Line 125 intrigues us with its suggestiveness. It may, of course, merely convey the depth of Criseyde's gratitude, affirming that she would continue thanking Hector for his protection, if his demeanor implied it would be appropriate for her to do so. Yet such an innocent meaning would more likely imply the circumspect speech of a princepleaser than the heartfelt plea of a fearful widow anxious about her bodily well-being. Whatever else may be revealed of Criseyde's character, she is certainly not an oily courtesan in Book I. On the other hand, the phrase "ofter wolde" may refer only to her appearing in Hector's presence, rather than to the words she might utter on such occasions. The following conditional clause, "and it hadde ben his wille" (I.125) would then qualify how receptive Hector might be to her frequent attendance, rather than how eager he would be to hear words of indebtedness repeated obsequiously often. If Criseyde has indeed taken herself to Hector and fallen on knees before him in order to fetch a reaction to her feminine appeal, the officiousness of his response must be deeply disappointing.

Criseyde's initiative in Hector's direction concludes on a sad line, "And took hire leve, and hom, and held hir stille" (I.126). If intended, at least in part, to achieve more than official protection, her effort has come to naught. Chaucer's literary purpose, however, is brilliantly successful, for it sets in motion a quintessentially Chaucerian strategy. It establishes, first, that Criseyde's entitlements are as strong as those of anyone else in Troy. No motive, political, practical, or social, can justify using Criseyde as a bargaining chip in the later scheme to trade her for Antenor. More important for the poem's literary design, the implication that

Criseyde would welcome Hector's attentions gives deep irony to Pandarus's plan to prepare her for the news that a king's son is a secret admirer. Only designed to peak his niece's curiosity, this lengthy whetting of her appetite succeeds beyond any expectation. Finally, the subtlest reach of Chaucer's strategy flows directly from this deep irony. Hector's disappointing response to what may have been a personal overture permits Chaucer to begin charting the parallel development of affection in both the widow and the warrior from a point unencumbered by emotional connections, and to show in stark relief the similarities and differences, not only between Criseyde and Troilus, but also between women and men as they fall in love. By reminding her of her disappointment, Pandarus awakens in Criseyde a calculating strain that increases over time. The motif that begins innocently with Criseyde's courageous appeal to Hector eventually takes her from love to meretricious exchange. Let us examine this triple strategy.

I

The literal reason for Criseyde's appeal to Hector should not be minimized. Trojan anger at her father's abandoning Troy for the Greek camp daily reaches her ears, driving her "Wel neigh out of hir wit for sorwe and fere" (I.108). The depth of this anger takes palpable form when the citizens of Troy unhesitatingly reveal their eagerness to send Criseyde to the Greek camp that they might recover "so wys and ek so bold baroun" (IV.190) as Antenor. Hector's sound arguments, that Criseyde is not a prisoner (IV.179), nor is Troy accustomed to trading in women (IV.182), certainly fulfill his earlier pledge to protect Criseyde. But they fail to sway the parliament. "As breme as blase of strawe iset on-fire" (IV.184), they reach the decision that seals Criseyde's fate:

"O kyng Priam", quod they, "thus sygge we,
That al oure vois is to forgon Criseyde."
And to deliveren Antenor they preyde.

(IV.194-96)

The shock Criseyde may feel on realizing the low esteem in which Trojans hold her translates into her own poor showing for remaining in Troy. It is painfully obvious (if we may glance ahead) that her resistance to Troilus's pleas to leave Troy gains in strength, producing a crescendo that has its desired effect as his pleas become progressively weaker. He appeals first to philosophy: substance (i.e., their remaining together) is more important than accident (the means of achieving this substance). Since reliance on the *chance* of her returning to Troy presents a riskier "accident" than the *certainty* of their running away, their choice should be obvious (IV.1503-12). His next argument lowers his aim to a mercantile sense of the word "substance": they have enough money to live comfortably (IV.1513-26). His last plea, thrown out as an irrelevant afterthought following his agreement to "suffre unto the tenthe day, / Syn that I se that nede it mot be thus" (IV.1598-99), gains no sympathy at all. For her part, Criseyde parries philosophy with the weak claim that if they run away they will live to regret it, neglecting to say why (IV.1528-31). Then she offers a stronger, three-stanza hyperbolic vow to be faithful to Troilus, a sentiment Chaucer reprieved a decade later for May to speak in January's garden (IV.1534-54; cf. *CT*, IV.2188-2206). Next, she lists the certain harms that would accrue if they ran away: the folly all would see in his leaving friends for any woman; the ridicule he would suffer if peace should ever return to Troy; the public assumption that he acted from lust rather than love; the harm to her own reputation when news of their flight circulated. She concludes this litany with two more stanzas assuring Troilus of her certain return (IV.1555-96). Would these debater's rebuttals have been as energetic, we wonder, if the loved one she was asked to leave were Hector?

The literary strategy Chaucer employs here amounts to character exegesis. Hector has said she is no prisoner, that is, she is not a suitable exchange for Antenor, and that Troy does not traffic in women. But Criseyde's sustained resistance to Troilus's plan, on top of the parliament's order that she be sent to the Greek camp, has the effect of reversing Hector's argument. It does not trouble her, she implies, that she is being used as a commodity in a commercial exchange. Even more incomprehensible to readers, though apparently not to the woman herself, this failure to resist the trade makes her equivalence to Antenor disturbingly clear. When the poem acknowledges the historical fact (cf. IV.202-05) that Antenor betrays Troy, Criseyde's treatment of Troilus cannot be understood differently. The narrator's gracious attempt to reduce "how Criseyde Troilus forsook" to a mere claim that "at the leeste ... she was unkynde" (IV.15-16) cannot soften her indifference to Troilus's plea. Nor, later in the poem, can her conduct with Diomede be explained by noting the limited choices a woman has at the mercy of political forces greater than her own, nor yet by the inevitability of Diomede's power to coerce intimacy. As surely as Antenor betrays Troy, the city of his birth, Criseyde betrays Troilus, the man who loves her.

II

The seminal scene with which we began, where Criseyde's possible romantic motive in appealing to Hector is strongly hinted, helps us understand how Pandarus is able to raise his niece's expectations to an extraordinary height at the beginning of Book II. She knows that her uncle has only one interest in life, the affairs of lovers; the second sentence he utters on entering Criseyde's house asks of the book she and her ladies are reading, "Is it of love?" (II.97). Thus, when she hears directly thereafter that he could tell her something she would enjoy hearing (II.121), she pleads to hear this news. But Pandarus will not reveal it. "And whi so, uncle myn? Whi so?" (II.136) she asks. Because

"proudder womman is ther noon on lyve,
And ye it wiste, in al the town of Troye.
I jape nought, as evere have I joye!"

                                                        (II.138-40)

Now certain the news concerns her, she pretends to wander in the transparently
clear direction her next speech confirms. Affecting to change the subject, but doing nothing of the sort, she and her uncle engage in some unspecified small talk,
"Tyl she gan axen hym how Ector ferde" (II.153). Her clever segue masks the
underlying connection; it is logical she should ask after Hector, for the war preoc-
cupies the town and Hector is its greatest champion. But Pandarus has already
denied that his news concerns the war. Indeed, the information he holds exceeds
by fivefold, he says, any report of the ongoing campaign. Criseyde's inquiry after
Hector's well-being obviously turns to the subject most on her mind, the matter
that Pandarus's teasing remarks are undoubtedly awakening. She further indicates
her growing interest in learning Pandarus's news when she agrees to dance with
him, after having earlier declined, expressing shock that he should ask her, a
widow (II.113-14). At length she is so eager to hear what her uncle has to say that
she cuts off his fulsome preamble:

"Now, good em, for Goddes love, I preye",
Quod she, "come of, and telle me what it is!"

                                                        (II.309-10)

The opening words of this best-of-all-possible-sentences-she-could-ever-hear
quickens an already keen excitement:

"Now, nece myn, the kynges deere sone ...

A reader can almost feel the page pounding with Criseyde's heart-beat as this
king's son's virtues stretch leisurely across the next line:

The goode, wise, worthi, fresshe, and free ...

Criseyde must need extraordinary discipline to contain herself, especially when a
particular trait of this son, already exercised in her behalf, receives special attention in the next line:

Which alwey for to don wel is his wone ...

She cannot possibly be unaware that the figure who undoubtedly fills her dreams
will be named in the next line, the line beginning

The noble ...

                                                        (II.316-19)

When the expected name is pronounced "Troilus" (II.319), her disappointment must be crushing. Her pleasure, increasing with every word descriptive of the ideal she has had in mind, crashes on hearing the name of a different son of the same king. How great a shock this must be to Criseyde may be gauged by the next sixty-eight lines during which Pandarus fills the air with noisy words and a burst of tears (II.320-385, 326) before she breaks her silence with a single question (II.388-89), then falling silent again for another seventeen lines.

By bringing Criseyde down to the spent emotional level she reaches on learning that Troilus, not Hector, admires her in secret, Chaucer creates a critically appealing opportunity. Pandarus will soon busy himself promoting the sexual, then emotional union of Troilus and Criseyde. The expanse they must traverse, as well as the different behavioral characteristics males and females display on such a journey, are shown in greater relief if they begin their affair from the same point. Troilus's professed indifference to love, discussed below, is well established in Book I, but no parallel indifference to love may be found in the remarks or actions of Criseyde. On the contrary, her visit to Hector gives reason to suspect she would be more than receptive to the attentions of an admirer. That her stratagem does not fetch the desired response implies her regret at having planned it in the first place and her resolve to steel herself against the future, a widow resigned to living alone. That resignation, like Troilus's professed indifference to love, may be a pose. For the present, however, Chaucer has brought her back to a level equal to the indifference to love that Troilus had formerly taken habitual pleasure in showing.

III

The immediate reactions of these future lovers to the very idea of love, though beginning in vaguely similar, sudden ways in Book I for Troilus and Book II for Criseyde, develop very differently because Chaucer's sensitivity to the different stimuli that move a man and a woman governs this first phase of their respective introductions to romance. If love is something different from a mere natural impulse, but implies as well a person to whom this impulse is directed, we may accept as accurate Troilus's disdain for love when we first meet him guiding his fellow knights at the feast of Palladion. The bravado he displays there, though certainly related to love, testifies only to a young male's preoccupation with his physiology, not yet the emotion that a mature woman can arouse and eventually draw upon to lead a man to love. A proud Bayard indeed, Troilus saunters through the temple,

> Byholding ay the ladies of the town,
> Now here, now there; for no devocioun
> Hadde he to non, to reven hym his reste,
> But gan to preise and lakken whom hym leste.

                                                                    (I.186-89)

The suddenness with which his first glimpse of Criseyde stuns him, like "a lasshe ... of the longe whippe" (I.220) and a shaft that "smot, and ther it stente" (I.273), should not be understood to foreshadow the Greek warrior who will replace him later in the poem, "this sodeyn Diomede" (V.1024), whose corrupting designs on Criseyde hasten Book V to its sad end. Diomede can never be anything but sudden, as quick to spot a target of amorous opportunity as to dissemble to achieve it. The suddenness we see in Troilus shows only his first emotion, quickly concealed to catch "ayeyn his firste pleyinge chere" (I.280) and avoid an embarrassing revelation.

A more telling similarity may be drawn from this temple scene when Chaucer deftly uses the word "ascaunces". Appearing elsewhere only three times in the whole Chaucerian canon, here the word appears twice in quick succession. When a pleasing aphorism comes to Troilus's mind about blind, foolish, love-sick knights incapable of being forewarned by the folly of others, Chaucer has him strike a self-assured pose:

> And with that word he gan caste up the browe,
> Ascaunces, "Loo! is this naught wisely spoken?"
>
> (I.204-05)

Within a dozen stanzas a nearly identical remark offers a swift glimpse of Criseyde, underscoring the identical emotional levels on which their relationship begins:

> she let falle
> Hire look a lite aside in swich manere,
> Ascaunces, "What, may I nat stonden here?"
>
> (I.290-92)

Though proceeding from different traits of character, self-satisfaction in the former case, insecurity and the need to assert status in the latter, these words appear at the same emotional point in both instances, immediately after Troilus expresses pleasure at being unencumbered by romance, and shortly after Criseyde realizes that from Hector she can expect only formal protection. Chaucer has metaphorically signaled the clean slates of both his principal actors.

Torn between wishing to replace the image in his mind with the person he longs to possess, yet wanting to conceal his condition from others, Troilus can do no more than take to his bed, lament the woeful state his first glimpse of Criseyde has thrown him into, and dreamily continue creating images of her to torment his restless thoughts. Help arrives shortly. Like a genie in an Arabian tale or an allegorical image in a medieval romance, within fifteen lines of Troilus's literal prayer to God for help,

> A frend of his that called was Pandare
> Com oones in unwar, and herde hym groone.
>
> (I.548-49)

The ensuing stanzas record an artful rhetorical battle in which Troilus refuses to disclose the name of the woman whose presence has put him in his helpless state, while Pandarus refuses to cease pummeling him until that name is pronounced:

> "Thef, thow shalt hyre name telle."
> But tho gan sely Troilus for to quake
> As though men sholde han led hym into helle,
> And seyde, "Allas, of al my wo the welle,
> Thanne is my swete fo called Criseyde!"
> And wel neigh with the word for feere he deide.
>
> (I.870-75)

The parallel scene in Book II, where Criseyde learns of the adventure that awaits her, has an entirely different objective. Engineered by this same Pandarus, though in the opposite directions of a mirror image, Criseyde must wheedle from her uncle the name of her secret admirer. Pandarus yields after a convincing show of resistance. Her surprise on hearing a different name from the one she expected echoes what must have been Pandarus's surprise on hearing from Troilus the name of his own niece. But the revelation that Troilus loves Criseyde energizes Pandarus, whereas Criseyde remains inert at the disappointing news she hears. These opposite reactions to new information are not the only differences separating love's progress when viewed from Troilus's and Criseyde's perspectives. From this point forward Criseyde begins increasingly to display a quite different self-awareness from what we see in Troilus, a calculating self-consciousness that moves her closer to Pandarus's and what must be her father's character, than to the constancy displayed by Hector and Troilus.

After disclosing the name of her admirer, Pandarus prattles on for nine stanzas of ineffective argument before Criseyde collects her thoughts for a response. Her uncle speaks of lover's malady, as if it were a literal threat to life; he claims his own well-being hangs in the balance; he alleges that a beauty who is unkind to an admirer is like a worthless gem, a useless herb, a cruel taskmaster. He denies he performs a baud's service, insisting he asks only that she show Troilus more cheer than she has done in the past. Whether Criseyde believes this barrage one cannot say, but it may be doubted. In any case, when she finally has a chance, she makes a silent note of caution and voices a non-committal question:

> Criseyde, which that herde hym in this wise,
> Thoughte, "I shal felen what he meneth, ywis."
> "Now em", quod she, "what wolde ye devise?
> What is youre reed I sholde don of this?"
>
> (II.386-89)

At this point Pandarus makes his only mistake in the poem. Misreading his niece's question as a surrender to his guidance, he grants that the best course is to return Troilus's love, encouraging her to follow this advice with two stanzas that could easily have served as model for Marvell's "To His Coy Mistress". Criseyde makes no objection to the reminder that "Time's winged chariot [is] hurrying near", until he takes his argument one step too far:

> "'So longe mote ye lyve, and alle proude,
> Tyl crowes feet be growe under youre yë,
> And sende yow than a myrour in to prye,
> In which that ye may se youre face a morwe!'"

(II.402-05)

The suggestion twelve lines earlier that she become Troilus's lover produced no reaction. But here, at the mention of crows' feet, a mirror, and the word "proud" that Pandarus has already used of her, Ciseyde bursts into tears. The detached demeanor she has shown to this point suddenly vanishes, perhaps on recalling the wrinkles she noticed in some recent glance at a mirror of her own. Her quick recovery attributes her tears to Pandarus's seamy proposal, a transparent falsehood. She would have thought, she claims, that her uncle would be the very one urging her to refuse such a proposal, even if Achilles or Hector–that name again!–or anyone else were pursuing her. The breach is momentary, for she returns to the original subject within six stanzas. Her descent, however, into artifice and calculation has been irrevocably set in motion.

The love that Pandarus has helped to bring about reaches exquisite fruition in Book III. Surviving a pitifully mismanaged, ludicrous first assignation, Troilus and Criseyde eventually consummate their passion and become sincere lovers, nearly transcending time, for every reader is surprised to learn that their love, requiring fewer lines to tell than those describing the lovers' first meetings, has lasted three years (see V.8-14). The original basis of this love may be more difficult to understand, when the many sound arguments Criseyde mulls over, both for and against commencing the affair, are overshadowed by an unworthy final argument:

> And after that, hire thought gan for to clere,
> And seide, "He which that nothing undertaketh,
> Nothyng n'acheveth."

(II.806-08)

The thought itself, no more than an adage to fill an awkward silence, would scarcely call attention to itself, but for its similarity to a later remark by Criseyde's "protector" in the Greek camp. Diomede has little to recommend him. From his first sight of Criseyde he has been wondering how he might become her lover, an enterprise that needs caution. Broaching the subject of love too soon after she left Troy would be fruitless, he realizes, if she still has her heart set on someone still in Troy. And Diomede thinks he knows who that someone is. Nevertheless, he "shal fynde a meene / That she naught wite as yet shal what I mene" (V.104-05). At his second meeting with Criseyde we hear the words that startle us into recognizing how similar Diomede and Criseyde really are. While searching for some means of seducing Criseyde, Diomede speaks the identical words Criseyde spoke when she decided to receive Troilus's attentions.

> He nyst how best hire herte for t'acoye;
> "But for t'asay", he seyde, "naught n'agreveth,
> For he that naught n'asaieth naught n'acheveth."

(V.782-84)

If Criseyde's similarity to her father and her uncle is not already clearly fixed in our mind, a final remark of hers leaves no doubt that, whatever she may have been before she loved Troilus, her descent from what she knew at the height of that love is now complete. Perhaps her most painful words – painful to her as well as to us – are spoken in the course of a conversation with Diomede, before she has actually succumbed to his proposals, but after she has heard his ominous prediction that every Trojan will perish. Criseyde dissembles, perhaps in calculated self-defense, but with words that are almost too difficult to read:

> "But as to speke of love, ywis", she seyde,
> "I hadde a lord, to whom I wedded was,
> The whos myn herte al was, til that he deyde;
> And other love, as help me now Pallas,
> Ther in myn herte nys, ne nevere was."

(V.974-78)

Criseyde knows well what future generations, especially women, will say of her, yet it remains uncertain why she becomes the woman we see at the end of the poem. She is called "the ferfulleste wight / That myghte be" (II.450-51) and "sly-dynge of corage" (V.825), a streak of cowardice that could easily explain some of what readers find disappointing in her conduct. But it cannot account for all. Her unwillingness to resist being exchanged as a prisoner, her failure to return to Troy within ten days, her calculating nature, as well as her denial of love for Troilus, may present to her a less frightening alternative than the public actions she would be required to take if she remained truthful and steadfast. Whatever combination of character traits combine to produce the gracious, accomplished, intriguing, loveable, and, yes, faithless woman whom Troilus, the narrator, and every reader of the poem come to love, it is hard to deny that Chaucer began unfolding that character when he had her fall on knees before Hector and petition for his protection.

Madame Eglentyne: The Telling of the Beads

John V. Fleming, Princeton University

The defining intellectual contours of the rich bibliography of studies devoted in whole or in part to Chaucer's Prioress seem to be defined in two American essays of the early decades of the twentieth century. The first, by John Livingston Lowes, one of the early giants of the academic study of literature in this country, dealt with the issue of poetic diction in the Prioress's description in the "General Prologue" (Lowes 1910: 440-451). Lowes was particularly interested in the adjectives *simple* and *coy* in the second line of that description. He demonstrated with an impressive erudition the role of those two adjectives in the stock vocabulary of French romance, preparing us for the intuition, suggested by many other details in the description, that the Prioress finds herself caught between her religious vows and aspirations of romantic courtliness. "[Chaucer's] delicate irony – of the rare strain that has its roots in the perfect merging of artistic detachment with humorously sympathetic comprehension – is nowhere more pervasive; and the hovering of the worthy lady's spirit between 'love celestiall' and 'chere of court' is depicted with unerring art" (Lowes 1910: 440). The particular strength of Lowes's essay, and the source of its continuing suggestiveness, is its thorough command of the context of early French romance. For the Prioress is not merely a French speaker; she is to a large extent a French creation. The second of the essays to which I allude was written by an American nun, Sister Mary Madeleva, and at least partly owing to the experience and authority of its author, it has long enjoyed a particular prestige (Madeleva 1925: 3-42). It is an elegant essay in appreciation – appreciation of Chaucer's generous artistry, to be sure, but also an appreciation, by an "insider", of the aspirations of religious life. It is very much worth the reading still, though the professional Chaucerian is likely to be struck by the irony of her editor's confident praise (in 1925) of "the fortunate finality of her discussion of Chaucer's nuns" (Lehman, "Foreword" to Madeleva 1925: i). One doubts that there is any "finality" in Chaucer studies, but there certainly has been none with respect to Chaucer's Prioress. In fact there has been a virtual tsunami of scholarship and criticism devoted to the forty-five lines of the Prioress's description in the "General Prologue" and her rather gruesome tale – most of it of a considerably darker hue than Lowes's gray, let alone Sister's Madeleva's creamy white.

In a certain sense the Prioress has been abandoned by history. The subject matter of her tale, the legend of Saint Hugh of Lincoln, is a classic set piece of medieval anti-Semitism. And though the term "anti-Semitism" may have limited usefulness in the fourteenth-century English context, it has had all too real and terrible a relevance in the twentieth-century context to allow the tale to hide, as the *Merchant of Venice* and some other familiar works of English literature long hid, behind a veil of unexamined cultural assumption. No reader today can find the tale, and by extension its teller, entirely unproblematical. Even so, Madame Eglentyne has not been without her able admirers and defenders. Forty years after Sister Madeleva wrote, Florence Ridley published a beautifully balanced mono-graph, *The Prioress and the Critics*, which advances a generally sympathetic view of the nun. She admits that "The entire characterization of the Prioress is mildly satiric" (Ridley 1965: 22). But there is a definite if implicit emphasis on the "mildly", and as for her anti-Semitic tale, "The attitudes for which Madame Eglentine is condemned by the twentieth-century critics were shared by most of her countrymen, and we have no real reason for believing that those attitudes were condemned rather than shared by Chaucer himself" (Ridley 1965: 35).

It is hardly to be expected that a literary portrait so obviously founded in various sorts of ambiguities would elicit a single response or even a critical con-sensus; but a candid review of scholarship in the last four decades leaves little room for the benign and admirable Prioress of Sister Madeleva or even the Prior-ess who is the beneficiary of a kind of critical standoff or draw posited by Prof. Ridley. The destructive effects of historical analysis as deployed on the various elements of the Prioress's description in the "General Prologue" is perhaps sug-gested by the title of an important essay by an ecclesiastical historian: Richard Rex's "The Sins of Madame Eglentyne" (1995).

I have long been committed to a "Robertsonian" reading of the Prioress, by which I mean one that, as it is disposed to take her votive religious status as a mat-ter of moral seriousness, stresses the numerous apparent divergences between her ascetic profession and her actual attitudes and practice. Yet the interpretive prob-lem, though often argued from an apparently "historical" grounding, eventually returns to narrowly literary issues. Finally, perhaps, it is a matter of taste or of assessment of tone. That Chaucer satirizes his Prioress is now widely accepted. The controversy concerns the tone, the degree, the censoriousness of his satire. Is it the excoriation of vice or the almost affectionate anatomy of widely shared hu-man foible? It is to an important early Chaucerian, John Dryden, that we owe what is still the justest description of the poles of Chaucer's satirical methods. "There is still a vast difference," he wrote, "betwixt the slovenly butchering of a man, and the fineness of a stroke that separates the head from the body, and leaves it standing in its place" (1962: 2.137). Though in his satirical descriptions of sev-eral of his ecclesiastic pilgrims (monk, friar, pardoner, summoner) he does not wholly eschew the tools of the abattoir, Chaucer is on the whole a literary swordsman. He does not say of the Prioress anything quite equivalent to what he says of the Monk ("a prikasour aright" GP 189) or the Friar ("a noble post" GP 214) or the Summoner ("of his visage children were aferd" GP 628) or of the Par-doner ("a geldyng or a mare" GP 691).[1] Chaucer does not explicitly say of the

---

1   My citations from Chaucer are from Chaucer (1987).

Prioress, as he does of the Monk, that she rejected the teachings of the Benedictine *Rule*. Instead he shows her violating its precepts in an almost schematic fashion, but with an absence of rhetorical emphasis that allows critics to believe that, somehow, all that doesn't count. Here is the acme of literary surgery, the bloodless decapitation. Perhaps such an operation can be called one of "artistic detachment" and "humorously sympathetic comprehension"; but it hardly amounts to moral neutrality.

That is my belief, but neither the exposition nor the defense of my belief will be the subject of this essay. I propose, instead, by looking closely at the literary filiations of a single prominent detail in the Prioress's description, to suggest some of the fascinating ways in which Chaucer's literary imagination engaged some of the writers he most admired, and particularly Jean de Meun, the principal author of the *Roman de la Rose*. The description of the Prioress in the "General Prologue" concludes with the description of her rosary, a decidedly material emblem of a presumably immaterial devotion:

> Of small coral about hire arm she bar
> A peire of bedes, gauded al with grene,
> And theron heng a brooch of gold full sheene,
> On which ther was first write a crowned A
> And after *Amor vincit omnia*
>
> (GP 158-162).

What will concern me is the possible "meaning" of this rosary, a meaning that may perhaps emerge from the intertextual study of its possible origins and its possible posterity. But I must begin with an even smaller bit of cultural material – small and non-existent to boot.

> Hir over-lippe wiped she so clene
> That in hir coppe there was no ferthyng sene
> Of grece, whan she dronken hadde hir draughte.
> Ful seemly after hir mete she raughte
>
> (GP 133-136).

At table the Prioress exercises polite table manners. She wipes food residue from her upper lip so carefully that her lip touches her wine without leaving even a hint of emulsion, not the tiniest speck of grease on the liquid surface. Unlike her rosary, the topic of the Prioress's table manners has a well established literary maternity. It derives, distantly, from Ovid's *Ars amatoria*. Its clear proximate source is some advice offered by the most meretricious old bawd in medieval vernacular literature. In an extended passage in which *La Vieille* (the Old Woman) is prepping *Bel Accueil* (Fair Welcome) for the "old dance", she turns her attention to the importance of good table manners

> Si doit si bien sa bouche terdre
> qu'el n'i lest nule gresse aherdre,
> au mains en la levre deseure,
> car quant gresse on cele demeure,
> ou vin en perent les mailletes,
> qui nu sunt ne beles ne netes.[2]

[She ought to wipe her mouth so that no grease sticks there, especially on the upper lip; for when grease stays there, *mailletes*, which are not pretty or clean, show up in the wine.]

What is being talked about is clear enough: tiny droplets of grease against the dark surface of the wine in a drinking utensil. That is what the word *mailletes* denotes. Chaucer has "translated" *maillete* as *ferthyng*: not a farthing of grease is to be found in the Prioress's cup. This could mean a drop the size of the smallest English coin or a quantity of the value of the smallest English coin. Either way the sense in context is "not a smidgen"; but it does raise a philological question. Why does Chaucer render Jean de Meun's *maillete* ("small spot") as "farthing"? Has he mistaken the French? That he did make some mistakes of translation is certain; but my own view is that Chaucer knew French very well – how to speak it and read it, probably also how to write it. His barbed compliment about the Prioresse's own French,

> And Frenssh she spak ful faire and fetisly,
> After the scole of Stratford ate Bowe,
> For Frenssh of Parys was to hire unknowe
>
>   (GP 124-126),

which immediately precedes the problematic praise of her table manners, is offered in a condescending tone which the author could doubtless claim by right. But an expert in Romance philology has found in Chaucer's "farthing" a rare example of his misunderstanding of French, under the category of "homonymic and paronymic perturbations" (Orr 1962: 8-9). The idea advanced is that Chaucer was confusing "two similar words of different origin" – *maille* < L. *macula*, meaning a spot or blemish, and *maille* < late L. **medalia/ *medialia*, meaning a half-penny. Thus Chaucer's nice phrase "farthing of grease" was a serendipitous philological error.

It seems certain that Jean de Meun's diminutive plural form *mailletes* does mean "little spots". But Chaucer has been defended by another Romance philologist, T. B. W. Reid, who demonstrates by reference to another thirteenth-century French text that whether by pun or by phonetic collapse the two senses of *maille*

---

2   Guillaume de Lorris and Jean de Meun, *Le Roman de la Rose*, ed. Lecoy (1965-70: lines 13397-13401 [II, p. 158]). All citations of the *Roman de la Rose* come from this edition. English translations of the text are based in Dahlberg (1971), though I have frequently made slight alterations for contextual clarity.

had already come together before Chaucer's time (Reid 1964: 373-374). The text is the *Clef d'Amors*, one of the several early French versions of Ovid's *Ars amatoria*, and the specific passage is this:

> Tes levres ne soient pas ointes
> ne tes dois moilliez siqu'as jointes;
> quer se issi te contenees,
> durement blasmee en serees.
> Ainz que verre ou henap mennies
> voil je que tes levres essies,
> a la fin que dedenz ne metes
> ne parisis ne maailletes.

(La Clef d'Amors 1890: ll. 3229-3236)

Reid translates the final three lines of this passage as follows: "Before you handle a glass or goblet I want you to wipe your lips so that you do not put into it either Paris pence or little halfpence." His translation is amplified by a learned note supplied by the editor of the *Clef d'Amors*: "*ne parisis ne maaillettes*, termes qui désignent étymologiquement de petites pièces de monnaie et, par analogie, les taches rondes, les yeux que la graisse forme à la surface des liquides. Godefroy cite un autre exemple tiré du *Roman de la Rose*, mais il place à tort ce sense avant celui de: menue monnaie."[3] In other words, Chaucer's "farthing" is a mistake only to the extent that an author's witty play on words is erroneous. He probably knew a spot of grease from a five-spot as well as Hamlet knew a hawk from a handsaw, just as he probably knew the difference between *farting* (< OE **feortan*) and a *farthing* (<OE *feorthing*), yet did not hold back from confusing them with punning purpose in the "Summoner's Tale" (1967).

The *Clef d'Amors* is one of several "versions" of Ovid's *Ars amatoria* in medieval French.[4] This fact encourages us to review the Ovidian Ur-text from which all the vernacular versions eventually derive. The advice of the *Ars amatoria* is quite brief: "Carpe cibos digitis: est quiddam gestus edendi; / Ora nec immunda tota perunge manu" (3. 755-756). [Pick up your food with your fingers; there is an art of eating, too. Don't smear your whole mouth with a filthy hand.] Here we have the idea of a greasy mouth, but not of transferring grease from mouth to drinking vessel. Jean de Meun's is a translation of the idea, but not of text. The passage in the *Clef d'Amors* on the other hand does exhibit traces of Ovidian text, first in the word *ointes*, which preserves the etymon of *perungo*, then in the *dois* (*digitos*). Chaucer of course has both the *fyngres* and the *grese*; but what might be regarded as the most important part of the image, namely *leaving greasy traces in a cup*, is in neither Ovid nor Jean de Meun, except by implication. The *Clef d'Amors*, on the other hand, presents us with two different words for a drinking vessel, *verre* and *henap*.

---

3   *Clef d'Amors*, ed. Doutrepont (1890: p. 152).
4   Surveyed by Paris (1885: 455-525).

Since the *Clef d'Amors* also gives us the punning meaning of *maalletes* (as blem-
ishes and small coins) the possibility that Chaucer has actually read and used this
obscure work of French Ovidianism, as we know he used another, the *Pamphile et
Galatée* of Jehan Bras-de-Fer, becomes the stronger.[5]

Of course there is nothing in Ovid concerning the *wiping* of the mouth, a detail
that appears first among our vernacular texts in Jean de Meun. Its probable source,
as Brian Ragen has pointed out, is biblical (Ragen 1988: 295-296). Proverbs 30.20
reads thus: "Talis est via mulieris adulteræ, quæ comedit et tergens os suum dicit
'non sum operata malum'" ["Such is the path of the adulterous woman, who eats
and, wiping her mouth, says 'I have done nothing wrong'"]. As Ragen notes, the
biblical Proverbs are present in the Old Woman's speech by repeated allusions and
citations.

Without pretending to establish a paradigm I should nonetheless draw attention
to a number of points most relevant to the principal inquiry of this essay: (1) Jean de
Meun's "Ovidianism" is enriched or supplemented by his "biblicism". (2) Chaucer
in his adaptations of Jean de Meun's Ovidian imitations may complicate them with
reminiscences of other works of vernacular Ovidianism. (3) The text of the *Roman
de la Rose* plays an important role in the construction of Chaucer's Prioress; and (4)
Chaucer's "translation" of Jean de Meun may wittily exemplify "homonymic and
paronymic perturbations".

But let us proceed with, or at least towards, the Prioress's rosary. For the moment leaving aside the Prioress, there are altogether four heavily satirized ecclesiastics in the "General Prologue": in order of their descriptions the Monk, the Friar, the
Summoner, and the Pardoner. So great an impact did Jean de Meun's masterly invention of *Faussemblant* (False Seeming) as a durable type of ecclesiastical hypocrisy have on Chaucer's literary imagination that it is easy to demonstrate direct textual filiation between Jean's text and the descriptions of each of these pilgrims. In
two instances this is a truth too obvious to need further argument. The friars of the
Prologue and the "Summoner's Tale", insofar as they are separate entities, share
with the Pardoner a common textual dependence on False Seeming, as can be demonstrated by recalling several of Chaucer's more memorable lines, such as "His
purchas was wel better than his rente" (Friar GP 256) and "I wol nat do no labour
with myne handes" (Pardoner C 444).[6] Furthermore, the confessional structure of
the Pardoner's Prologue, with its repeated explicit identifications of the hypocrisy
of the speaker, closely parallels that in the confession of False Seeming to the God
of Love.

---

5   See Mieszkowski (1985: 40-60). I take tardy opportunity of citing this excellent article which
     I had not read, and consequently left uncited, when I myself mentioned in print a connection
     between Chaucer's *Troilus* and the *Pamphile and Galathée* that I had first noticed as a gradu-
     ate student in 1962.

6   Cf. *Roman de la Rose*, 11536 and 11490.

One must conclude, indeed, that so far as Chaucer's concept of both his Friar and his Pardoner are concerned, the *Roman de la Rose* is a definitive "source". False Seeming's influence on the portrait of the Monk is somewhat less direct, but at one point, in the monk's abhorrence of manual labor, it comes to the surface.

> Why sholde he studie and make hymselven wood,
> Upon a book in cloystre alwey to poure,
> Or swinken with his handes, and laboure,
> As Austyn bit? How shal the world be served?
> Let Austyn have his swynk to hym reserved!

(GP 184-188)

Here the division of work as between study and actual manual labor probably reflects the notable passage in the False Seeming medley of the *Roman* in which Jean de Meun appears to have supplemented his text with two graphic diagrams, one of a physical, the other of a "spiritual" hand.[7] There Jean uses a nice phrase to speak of the two kinds of "chivalry" with which one may defend the faith – "soit d'armes ou de letreüre" (1143) – "either with arms or by cultivation of his mind". That the Monk will neither "study" nor "swinken with his handes" covers both possibilities. The explicit citation of Augustine is also telling, since it is obvious that the Augustinian work referred to as rejected by the Monk is the *De opere monachorum*. This text was introduced to the antifraternal debate by Guillaume de Saint-Amour in the *De periculis novissimorum temporum*, and the arguments supplied by False Seeming come into the *Roman de la Rose* by that route. The Augustinian work, furthermore, is the source of an important antifraternal interpolation that was used in the translation of the Middle English *Romaunt*.[8]

That the Summoner, too, is one "of Antichrist's boys" (*des vallez Antecrit*, 11683), as False Seeming identifies himself, will hardly surprise us. The theme of an unholy collusion between the Summoner and those whose job it is for him to correct echoes one of False Seeming's themes. Furthermore there is a very witty textual evidence of the relationship in the rather extraordinary final line of the Summoner's description: "A bokeleer hadde he maad hym of a cake" (GP 668). A Chaucerian specialty deployed in the "General Prologue" is the line that seems syntactically and semiotically plausible until one really thinks about it. The Prioress herself has one such line – "Ful semely after hir mete she raughte" (GP 136) – to which I shall presently return. The poetic license of exaggeration does not cover absurdity. Perhaps we can accept that the Wife of Bath's headgear was *as large as a buckler or a target*; but we are unlikely to accept that she wore a sol-

---

7   See Lécoy's note to lines 11449-11450 (*Roman de la Rose* 1966-1970, vol. 2: 285-286). The images are graphically presented in Langlois' edition (1914-1925) and in the translation of Dahlberg (1971: p. 201).

8   See Dahlberg's notes to 11414-11491 (1971: p. 396).

dier's shield upon her head. Skeat tried to solve the problem by positing a convenient meaning of *cake* as a shield-shaped loaf of bread; but Chaucer does not say
the Summoner had a loaf that looked like a shield but that he had *made* a shield
out of a cake. I continue to believe that this is verbal reification of one of False
Seeming's metaphors, in which he counsels those who want to defend themselves
against getting into trouble with inquisitorial churchmen to make recourse to various kinds of alimentary protections.[9] The ambitions of Antichrist's boys are
hardly modest:

> Si avironnons mer et terre,
> a tout le mond avons prise guerre,
> et volons du tout ordenere
> quell vie l'en i doit mener

> (11689-11692).

> ["Indeed we occupy both sea and land. We have made war against everyone, and we
> want to prescribe everything about the life each should live."]

The suggested protection against such intrusion is bribes – bribes of food that take up
a full ten lines of octosyllables to list, but among which are *tartes ou de flaons*
(11713), that is, cakes. The deployment of such alimentary armor will not prove unsuccessful. Among those for whom such bucklers will be efficacious are priests living
in concubinage (11704). Of the Summoner Chaucer writes that "He wolde suffer for
a quart of wyn / A good felawe to have his concubyn" (GP 649-650) – lines made all
the more delicious by the slight ambiguity as to whether the Summoner is winking at
the priest's concubine or exchanging his own for a quart of wine!

What of the Prioress? I have already acknowledged a marked difference in the
tone of the satire directed against the corrupt male churchmen and that in the Prioress's portrait. Such a disparity of tonal registers was commented upon long ago by the
historian G. G. Coulton, who contrasted the Prioress's "pardonable luxuries of a fas-
tidious nature" which "stand in artistic contrast to the grosser indiscipline of the
Monk" (1908: 147). But is False Seeming there at all? Insofar as hypocrisy may be
regarded as a universal human tendency, he must be; and though he claims for his
habitat both the world and the cloister, he specializes in the latter. But there is more
explicit evidence. False Seeming describes himself as having the power of Proteus
(11151) to take whatever shape he chooses, man or woman, and he incidentally includes the specific form of a prioress (*prieuse*, 11180) among them. "Sometyme am I
prioresse" (6349), as the *Romaunt* puts it. But does False Seeming infect this particular prioress?

---

9   See Fleming (1981: esp. 133-136). I am pleased to be able to drag this reference into my
     essay as the collection in which it was printed records my first crossing of paths with my
     friend Andy Kelly, who also has an essay in the collection, and the first of many valuable op-
     portunities to learn from him first-hand.

That an important part of her portrait comes from the *Roman de la Rose* we already know. She can hardly be charged with the grosser sort of hypocrisy evident in the vicious male ecclesiastics, but she is far from an admirable representative of the religious life. Her shallow romantic sensibility and her worldly aspiration to "be holden digne of reverence" clash with an ascetic situation; I say "situation" rather than "vocation". For it is precisely a religious calling she lacks. We may imagine that, like so many medieval women, she came to the cloister out of social convenience or coercion rather than the wholly voluntary desire to take the hard vows of poverty, chastity, and obedience. A famous and beautiful essay on Madame Eglentyne, that of the social historian Eileen Power, regards her type as unassailably "historical", and Chaucer's "mellow, amused, uncondemning" satirical portait as "one more instance of the almost photographic accuracy of the poet's observation" (1924: 60). Yet as so often, I believe, Chaucer's observation of life was guided by his prior observation of books, the *Roman de la Rose* prominent among them. Jean's name for false male religion was False Seeming. Its parallel for females was "Constrained Abstinence". In the *Roman de la Rose*

> Tantost Astenance Contrainte
> vest une robe kameline
> e s'atourne come beguine
> et ot d'une large queuvrechief
> e d'un blanc drap couvert le chief.
> Son sautier mie n'oublia;
> unes *paternostres* i a
> a un blanc laz de fil pendues ...
>
>   (12014-12021).

[Constrained Abstinence straightway put on a robe of cameline and fixed herself up as a Beguine; she covered her head with a large kerchief and a white cloth, and she did not forget her psalter. She had a rosary hanging on a white thread-lace.]

It is hardly surprising that a nun would have a rosary or, indeed, that a poet composing a portrait of a nun might well describe or allude to it. It is less expected, perhaps, that a nun's rosary should be a talisman of her love-life. That is certainly the situation with regard to the rosary carried by Constrained Abstinence, and probably that with regard to Madame Eglentyne's as well.

It is of preliminary interest that in the text of the *Roman de la Rose* the nun's rosary is part of an elaborate disguise designed to make its bearer seem a more plausible *pilgrim*: "Si ont part acort devise / qu'il s'en iront en tapinage / ausinc con en pelerinage" (12010-12012) [By agreement they worked out a plan of going stealthily as though they were on a pilgrimage]. Jean goes on to say, with heavy sexual innuendo, that the rosary is a gift from a friar who, on the pretext of being a relative, makes frequent intimate visitations. In this passage the religious language of preaching and penance, two mendicant specialties, is given sexual valence. This is precisely the kind of sexual innuendo that Chaucer picks up in the portrait of his Friar who, being a "noble post", had made "ful many a marriage / Of yonge women at his owene cost" (GP 212-213).

With regard to what might be called the "lubricious gift" we have a parallel of sentiment if not an actual textual echo when Chaucer says of his friar "His typet was ay farsed ful of knyves / And pynnes, for to yeven faire wyves" (GP 233-234). It requires no particular depravity of the imagination to sense the phallic suggestion in the image of the stuffed tippet, also called a "tail" (Latin *cauda* or *penis*) of a fourteenth-century Franciscan's cowl.

Chaucer's phrase "a peire of bedes" is actually ambiguous. It identifies the Prioress's bracelet as prayer-beads, but as we know from iconographic evidence such beads could be more or less elaborate. They could be a simple string or circlet of beads. Such is the rosary that Chaucer himself seems to be holding in the well-known "Harvard portrait". Yet the ancillary textual details suggest something rather more elaborate and closer to the rosary that is normative in Catholic devotion today. If so, it would have contained fifty small beads in red coral, arranged in decades separated by (probably) six beads of larger size, and perhaps of different shape, called the *gauds*. The coral beads signaled the recitation of an "Ave", the gauds of a "Paternoster". A common vernacular name for the rosary in French and English alike was "paternoster", and the surviving London street called Paternoster Row was presumably the place where the craftsmen who made rosaries worked. The gauds on the Prioress's set of beads were green in color.

What Chaucer calls "a broche of gold ful shene" hangs from the beads, and it is of very particular textual interest. It probably hung from the circlet between the first and the sixth of the gauds. I draw this inference partly from the text and partly from the evidence of the one surviving English rosary of comparable artistic pretension. Rosaries are among the more vulnerable pieces of material religious culture, and very few have survived intact from the European Middle Ages. Most were probably quite literally used to pieces. For reasons easily apprehensible, medieval English rosaries in particular were very unlikely to have long survived the Reformation. There is, however, one quite remarkable rosary elaborately worked in gold that has survived from Yorkshire, where it historically belonged to a family named Langdale.[10] It is a happy irony that this rosary is, perhaps, the oldest surviving complete set of beads in all of Europe. The pendant on modern rosaries is almost always a crucifix, though sometimes only a cross; but the pendant on the Langdale rosary is "a large four-sided knop, rather melon-shaped with flat vesica-shaped faces about 21 x 15mm.; the whole knop is about 3 mm. long and 20 mm. wide, and weights 190.56 grains" (MacIagan and Oman 1936: 2).

Another way of saying this would be that it is "a broche of gold ful shene", for the word "broche" is sufficiently vague to denote a variety of ornaments or

---

10   Maclagan and Oman (1936: 1-22). The rosary is now in the Victoria and Albert Museum.

clasps worn at or around the neck or wrist. The OED records its plural as the translation of *monilia* in Canticum 1.9. There is of course episcopal criticism of bejeweled nuns.[11] Thus as an iconographic clue to Chaucer's satirical strategies, the Prioress's brooch may be warm, but it is hardly smoking in the fashion of the Monk's similar brooch: "And for to festne his hood under his chyn, / He hadde of gold ywroght a ful curious pyn; / A love-knotte in the gretter ende ther was" (GP 195-197).

Still the "broche of gold ful shene" will offer us what I regard as the safest path to the ideographic significance of the rosary. Yet before setting down that path it is necessary to review the various earlier attempts that have been made to find a symbolic or iconographic significance in the material construction of the Prioress's rosary – so far as that construction can be understood from Chaucer's text. Francis Manley had the happy inspiration of collating the Prioress's coral ornament with "the Coralls which thy wrist infold" in Donne's sonnet "The Token" (1959: 385-388). He shows by learned recourse to medieval and Renaissance lapidaries that coral had a complex set of associations. On the one hand it was said to have the power to ward off diabolical evil; on the other it could be used as a love-charm. "Chaucer gave his graceful lady prioress a string of beads as delicately ambiguous as everything else about her...a coral rosary would offer her double indemnity: the stones as well as the prayers would save her from temptation. But any such surface statement is qualified by the ambiguous Amor with which the beads are tagged" (1959: 388).

John Block Friedman elaborated upon Manley's findings in an article published a decade later (1970: 301-305). His contribution is useful both for its numerous medieval testimonies to the apotropaic powers of coral and for its evidence, drawn from medieval English wills, that coral rosaries were far from uncommon. Evidence from France suggests that while they were undoubtedly luxurious, coral beads were actually probably among the more modest of up-market rosaries made for the luxury trade. The inventory of the possessions of the French king Charles V has a special category for rosaries, twelve in number, none of which is made of coral. The preferred materials would appear to be gold, pearls, and jet. However there are more than a dozen other sets of prayer beads listed in miscellaneous fashion elsewhere in the inventory, and at least four of them are described as being made of coral.[12] One of the texts adduced by Manley, the Renaissance lapidary of the physician Franciscus Rueus, seems to "decry the decline in production of coral rosaries" in the sixteenth century (1959: 387).

The demonstration that coral rosaries were fairly common, of course, makes it the harder to argue convincingly that Chaucer is making a sharp symbolic allusion as opposed to an accurate social observation of the kind praised by Eileen Power.

---

11   See Kuhl (1923: 305-306).
12   See Charles V [of France] (1879: especially items 2070, 2819, 2824, and 3029).

A bead made of coral, unlike a buckler made of cake, was something of an actual, material commonplace. A similar reason makes me pause before accepting an argument, with the implications of which I am in entire agreement, that finds a definite authorial meaning in the realm of color symbolism. Despite the exuberantly polysemous nature of colors in the exegetical tradition, such an argument has been made by Richard Rex (1995: 61-68). The small bright red coral beads of the rosary are divided into their decades by larger *gauds* green in color. Materials suggested include malachite and glass. Rex first examines various possible suggestions of the color red in the verbal iconography of courtly romance, then shows that in fourteenth-century theological lore green can be associated with, among other things, hypocrisy and lubricity. "Simply by his choice of colors Chaucer transforms a well-known symbol of religious devotion into one suggestive of carnal appetite and hypocrisy" (Rex 1995: 68).

The salient features of the brooch on the Prioress's rosary are its preciousness and its decorative inscriptions. With minor exceptions which I shall adduce presently I have been unable to find detailed textual evidence that might help us to understand how remarkable or unremarkable Chaucer's lines would have seemed to an informed contemporary reader. Under these circumstances we shall perhaps do best to begin with the visual evidence of the Langdale rosary, even though it dates from perhaps a century after Chaucer's death.

The iconography of what I am calling its brooch – the large golden knop that fastens the core thread of the rosary rather in the manner of a plumb bob – is that of the Epiphany. On what was presumably meant to be the principal or outward of the four faces of the knop, incised into the gold, is a commonplace Nativity tableau. The Virgin is at the center with the Christ child on her left knee. At her right, marginalized, is a standing Joseph. Behind her, to the left, is the barn stall with the ox and the ass. Immediately above her nimbed head is a large star. Each of the other three faces of the knop displays one of the three kings. Two are crowned and standing, each holding his gift. The third, uncrowned, is perhaps kneeling or genuflecting, holding out his gift in presentation (MacIagen and Oman 1936: fig. 1, a-d). Each of the beads – the six "Pater" and the fifty small "Ave" beads, all in gold – are likewise pictorially decorated. Altogether the rosary is of a magnificence worthy of the goldsmith saint Eligius, by whom the Prioress has apparently been known to swear, and who may or may not himself feature on one of the "Ave" beads.[13] A very interesting feature of the beads is that – unlike the brooch – each has a verbal inscription identifying its pictorial subject.

This brings me at length to the possible textual dimension of rosary decoration. Each of the beads on the Langdale rosary is inscribed with what is in effect a

---

13   See Maclagan and Oman (1936: plate IV, fig. 2, 41b, and p. 9): "the first saint...s' lod-
     com'...", a bishop with what looks like a hammer, suggests S. Eligius. The inscription seems
     to read as above, but I am not sure of some of the letters."

rubric, though in this instance in black rather than in red. The Prioress's rosary-brooch is inscribed both with an emblem, a "crowned A" and a Latin sentence *"Amor vincit omnia"*. This, at least, is how I parse the lines "there was first write a crowned A, / and after *Amor vincit omnia*" (GP 161-162). It is conceivable that the lines could mean that the crowned A *is* the initial A of *Amor*; but this seems unlikely.

Rosaries must have been among the most intensely personal and intimate material objects among the possessions of a practicing medieval Christian, and it is only to be supposed that they might have been "personalized" in a variety of ways – through private and individual association, through heraldic allusion, or through the use of initials, for example. Indeed we do have archival or visual evidence of some initialed rosaries. Several of the *patenostres* in the inventory of Charles V had been in the possession of his daughters Marie and Ysabel.[14] Among them is the following (no. 807): "Item, unes autre patenostres à M M, qui furent à ladicte dame [Madame Marie de France], plaines d'ambre, a ung bouton de perles; pesant troys onces" (Charles V [of France] 1879: 111). The two majuscule letters M were obviously part of the decoration and very likely an emblem of the onomastic union of its owner with the Blessed Virgin.

The famous painted rosary beads in the Hours of Catherine of Cleves, from the early fifteenth century, present points of comparison of striking interest both to the Prioress's rosary and the gold rosary of the Langdales. This rosary is a string of beads, elaborately tassled at its two ends, rather than a circular chaplet. It lies in casual fashion around three sides of one of the versos of the book, as though upon the parchment. The Epiphany subject is somewhat eccentrically placed among the hagiographic suffrages. The beads are of bright red coral. The sumptuous illustration which it frames is of the Epiphany, with the text of an antiphon that begins "Tria sunt munera preciosa que obtularunt magi domino et habent in se divina misteria".[15]

The painting has all the iconographic elements mentioned above (including two standing kings and one kneeling one), but there is an additional witticism. Three ornaments are attached to the string of beads, a small purse, a cross, and at the top a large seven-pointed star, a huge version of the star within the miniature to which one of the magi points. The greater, marginal star echoes the lesser, internal one. The purse, which appears at the bottom of the page, is elaborately initialed in pearl-studded gold: cd [*catharina dux*].

In the notes of the *Riverside Chaucer* Florence Ridley, referring to one of Lowes' numerous influential articles, seems to suggest that the "crowned A" refers to Queen Anne of Bohemia, wife of Richard II. In fact Lowes, while advanc-

---

14   They alone of his daughters survived infancy. See Delachenal (1931, vol. 5: p. 120).

15   Reproduced in *The Hours of Catherine of Cleves*, intro. and commentaries by Plummer (1966: n. p.).

ing the probable argument that a line in the *Troilus* (I.171) does allude to Anne, notices that it would be pointless for Chaucer to have made such an allusion with regard to the Prioress (1908: 297-298n). It is on the other hand at least possible that the "A" is her own initial, as English "eglantine" starts with an "A" in several medieval Romance texts; but there is very good reason to think that it must indeed stand for "Amor" – and not as abstract noun but as personification.

What most strongly argues the likelihood that while he was framing the Prioress's portrait Chaucer definitely was meditating on ideas and images from the *Roman de la Rose* is complex textual convergence. In order to be able to appreciate that convergence, we do well to remind ourselves of the concluding narrative movement of Jean's poem: the Lover's eventually successful attempt to reach Fair Welcome. The Lover has learned from *Amis* (Friend) that the path to his goal is a pecuniary one, and no poor man can walk it. It is the road of *Trop-Doner*, Extravagant Giving (7855f). We have here, somewhat feebly allegorized, the Ovidian advice that the lover must be prepared to distribute treasure liberally – bribes for janitors and go-betweens, gifts for the beloved. No sooner does he leave his conversation with Amis than he sets out to find this path, the quickest route to the prison in which Jealousy has Fair Welcome locked up. From the point of view of the moral allegory, Jean is at this point rather heavy handed. He has his Lover say that the cynical advice of Amis is much more valuable than the advice of Lady Reason: "m'est avis, au mains de fet, / qu'il set plus que Reson ne fet" (9975-9976)[16] [it seemed to me, indeed, that he knew at least more than Reason did]. Then, like the pilgrim Dante at the beginning of the *Inferno*, he avoids the right path for the sinister, as being the quickest to his goal: "eschivant la destre partie, / vers la senestre m'achemin / por querre le plus brief chemin" (10000-10002)[17] [avoiding the right direction, I made my way to the left, to search for the shortest path].

Like Raison, though for entirely different reasons, Richese is hostile to the Lover's cause; and in the poem's final lines, after he has savored the sexual favors so ardently sought, Amant dismisses them together in a common curse (21730-21737). Temporarily checked, he wanders disconsolately through the rose-garden, where he reaffirms his commitment to Amors who, satisfied with his penance, calls a parliament of his barons to prepare a siege of the castle with the aim of freeing Fair Welcome. Surprisingly, False Seeming and Astenance Contrainte show up at this conclave, before which False Seeming makes a lengthy confession

---

16 Strubel (*Roman de la Rose* 1992: p. 537), adopting the Wife of Bath's view of *experience* and *auctoritee*, takes this to mean that while Reason may have a better grasp of *theoretical* matters, her abstract advice lacks the concrete usefulness of advice founded in Amis' *experience*. I see the episode as a flagrant reminder of the Lover's folly.

17 Cf. Rutebeuf, "La Voie de Paradis", ll. 69ff., in *Œuvres complètes* (1969, vol. 1: pp. 343-344).

of his hypocrisy. The two false religious disguise themselves as pilgrims and set off to enter the castle by fraud. It is in this context that we have the description of the nun's rosary. While ostensibly hearing Malebouche's confession, the friar in fact murders him. Then, joined by Largesce and Courtoisie (Fair Welcome's mother), they sneak into the castle and confront Fair Welcome's chaperon, the Old Woman, threatening her to coerce her cooperation. She acquiesces and sets off immediately to persuade Fair Welcome to accept Amant's love-token, a garland (*chapel*, 12601).

It is clear that the acceptance of this gift is a symbol of sexual surrender, and Fair Welcome fearfully but briefly (less than twenty lines) refuses. But accept it he does, at which moment the Old Woman laughs out loud and begins her long and very famous Ovidian speech which Chaucer brilliantly pillaged in the construction of his Wife of Bath – and for the Prioress's table manners. At its eventual conclusion, Fair Welcome agrees to see the Lover, and the old go-between sets off to arrange the meeting. The meeting takes place. Fair Welcome thanks the Lover for his *chapel* and promises to acquiesce in his sexual desires. But even as he reaches out to pluck the bud Danger leaps out from hiding to block his way. He is joined by *Paor* (Fear) and *Honte* (Shame). Furthermore the siege of the castle undertaken by Amors and his barons seems to be getting nowhere.

Once again things look bad for the Lover. Under these circumstances, Amors sends messengers to Cytherea to fetch his mother Venus. Mother and son swear a solemn oath that they will take the castle. "May I perish a miserable death," says Venus, "if I ever let Chastity dwell in any woman alive".[18] Then Nature makes her verbose confession of about three and a half thousand lines of verse, which is followed by Genius's quite remarkable and only comparatively brief (a thousand lines) words of "absolution". After that things move much more rapidly. Venus readies her bow with its flaming brand and, pausing only for a few hundred lines to recite the story of Pygmalion, a story prompted by the surprising presence of a carved image of a woman on the castle wall, fires her burning phallic bolt at the vaginal target between the image's thighs. All resistance within the castle collapses. Courtesy rescues her son Fair Welcome from the burning fortress and, citing the authority of a line of Virgil, counsels him immediately to give the Lover what he wants. Fair Welcome acquiesces immediately.

It is perhaps remarkable that, from the point of view of mere plot development, so very little can occupy ten thousand lines of Jean's poem, but as many readers have realized, his artistic strategy is not to advance the plot but to postpone it. Still, a plot *is* there. It is an allegory of the way a man achieves sexual intercourse by circumventing or overpowering the social and psychological forces that would keep the woman from him. The sexual desire that animates the man

---

18 "Male mort," dist ele, "m'aqueure, / qui tantost me puist acourer,/ se je ja mes les demourer / Chastée en fame vivant" (15800-15802).

resides as well in the woman. Her consciousness is "conflicted", as we would now say, between the antierotic forces of social norms and the frankness of her own intuitions of erotic desire as represented by the personified abstraction Fair Welcome. This is the "Fair Welcome" of the English *Romaunt* – that aspect of the woman's psyche that welcomes the sexual advance. Personification allegory can never be an entirely tidy matter, especially not in a language characterized by grammatical gender, and Fair Welcome, a "man" who has to represent a deeply feminine category, presents a case in point. I have written elsewhere about how some of the poem's illustrators faced this problem (Fleming 1969: 43-46). They imagined him as a woman, and we may too. Indeed for narrative purposes we can imagine him as *the* woman.

In his quest the Lover has adversaries and he has allies. Among the latter are False Seeming and Constrained Abstinence, and through them the Old Woman, a classical Ovidian mediator of desire. The concrete sign of the intermediation is a flowery garland, a *chapel*. This *chapel*, to which we now need to turn our attention, first enters the text at lines at 12409-12410, where the word is actually *chaplet*. The false religious half bribe half threaten the Old Woman into taking it to Fair Welcome. Here it is the collaboration between the false nun, Constrained Abstinence, and the Old Woman to which I should draw attention. We can trace certain textual parallels between them and Chaucer's Old Woman (the Wife of Bath) and his most prominent nun (the Prioress). For example, consider the wimple. There are two wimpled women in the *Roman*, and two in the *Canterbury Tales*. The Wife of Bath wears a wimple with other headgear: "Upon an amblere esily she sat, / Ywympled wel, and on hir heed an hat / As brood as is a bokeler or a targe" (GP 469-471). So also does the Old Woman: "D'un chaperon en leu de vaile / sus sa guimple ot covert sa teste" (12360-12361) [with a hood over her wimple, instead of a veil, she had covered her head]. Constrained Abstinence dresses as a Beguine in a "large queuvrechief / et d'un blanc drap covert le chief" (12015-12016) [she covered her head with a large kerchief and a white cloth]. Of the Prioress Chaucer famously wrote "Ful semyly hir wympul pynched was / Hir nose tretys, hir eye greye as glas" (GP 151-152).

These are not textual "sources", but they may be poetically intuited textual reminiscences. Nobody knows what "greye as glas" means, though numerous suggestions have been offered.[19] In fact it might just mean "no color at all", "colorless" – a possibility we might be invited to consider if we allowed into our memory the paleness of Constrained Abstinence, who "resembled...the horse in the Apocalypse that signified the wicked people...for that horse bore no color

---

19   See the note, with bibliography, in Chaucer (1987: p. 805).

upon himself except a pale, dead one."[20] There is at any rate more promise in an attempt to find meaning in "color symbolism" when it can exploit a proximate textual source than when it cannot.

Del Kolve has taught us to be alert to unexpected manifestations of Chaucer's visual imagination. An image like his "farthing of grease" may alert us to another aspect of the poet's imagination – the inspiration wrought by the convergence of the visual and the lexical. Constrained Abstinence wears a rosary – which in at least one manuscript known to me is visualized as made of coral beads[21] – that is a token of her illicit relations with a friar. Now with the collusion of a corrupt friar and an ancient bawd she acts as one of the couriers whose job it is to deliver a love-token, a *chapelet*, from Amant to Fair Welcome. It would have been obvious to Chaucer and his first readers, as it is perhaps no longer obvious to modern English-speakers, that a *rosary* and a *chaplet* are the same thing: namely, a crown of roses. In modern French, indeed, the common word for "rosary" is *chapelet*; in modern German, *Rosenkranz*. In these and other European languages the intimate connections between the *rose* and the Virgin honored by the devotion of the *rosary* are still lexically obvious. The word *rosarium* means "rose-garden"; a garland or crown made of roses is a miniature rose-garden of decorative artifice.

Two rich studies devoted to the patterns of thought underlying their connection, to the iconography of the spiritual rose-garden, and to the large body of literature devoted to its manifold themes, obviate the need to attempt an extensive demonstration for which I would in any event be unqualified: Eithne Wilkins's *The Rose-Garden Game* (1969) and Anne Winston-Allen's *Stories of the Rose* (1997). Although the devotion of the rosary grew greatly in popularity and spiritual elaboration between the thirteenth century and the Counter Reformation, its most prominent features were well established by the time of the composition of the *Roman de la Rose*. The garden imagery in Guillaume's poem immediately establishes an uneasy relationship with the paradisal Garden of Eden; and to the considerable extent that the whole poem presents an allegorical re-enactment of the Fall, the much desired rosebud in the center of the amatory *rosarium* has its inevitable adversarial associations with the Rose as the center of the spiritual one. I am not suggesting that the authors of the *Roman de la Rose* consciously or artistically built their poem around the idea of a rosary, but that they would have had no cultural means, even had they wished to, of forbidding a powerful if ambiguous thematic and iconographic association. At the very outset of his poem Guillaume de Lorris directs his work to an audience of one: "Cele por qui je l'ai empris: / c'est cele qui tant a de pris / et tant est digne d'estre amee / qu'el doit estre

---

20   "... un poi fu pale de vis./ El resembloit, la puste lisse, / le cheval de l'Apochalipse [Apoc. 6:8], / qui senefie la gente male,/ d'ypocrisie tainte et pale; / car cil chevaus seur soi ne porte / nule coleur, fors pale et mort" (*Roman de la Rose*, 12036-12042).

21   Oxford Bodleian Library, MS e Musaeo, 65, fol. 95r. See Friedman (1970: 304n).

Rose clamee" (41-44) [she for whom I have undertaken the work is one so precious and so worthy to be loved that she ought to be called Rose]. The old idea in
the French criticism is that Guillaume was in love with a girl named Rose, whom
he sets out to seduce ("win" being the critic's word of choice) through poetic
means. I continue to see in these lines a courteous dedication to the Virgin.

Hardly less troublesome in its possible ambiguity is the name of the Prioress.
Though it is notoriously difficult to make sound botanical identifications on the
basis of the plant names that appear in old texts, we must make some attempt at
least to understand why the Prioress "was cleped Madame Eglentyne". That the
eglantine is the sweet-briar is very probable, though Milton, in some lines in
"L'Allegro", seems to think they are distinct: "Through the sweet-briar or the
vine, / Or the twisted eglantine" (47-48). What has not been commented upon,
perhaps, is that the sweet briar is a *rose*. Its botanical name, indeed, is the *rosa
eglanteria*. It is also to be noted that the eglantine itself was, according to some
traditions, the plant used in the construction of one of the most famous of all
flowery garlands. The first usage of "eglantine" adduced by the OED – they cannot use Madame Eglentyne, presumably, as she is a prioress and not a plant – refers to the mocking crowning of Jesus Christ as reported in the first English version of Sir John Mandeville. After saying that Christ's cross was made of four
different kinds of wood, Mandeville recites, with nonchalant incoherence, the legend of the three seeds buried beneath Adam's tongue, seeds from which sprang
the trees from which the cross was made. It is perhaps as a parallel to these three
trees that there were three separate crownings of Christ during his passion,
confusingly presented as four. The most celebrated of these featured a prickly
garland, which, although called a "crown of thorns", was actually made of "jonkes
of the see that is to sey rushes of the see that prykken als scharpely as thornes"
(Mandeville 1919: 8). This is the famous relic, part of which is in Constantinople,
and part in the Sainte Chapelle of Paris. But Jesus was first crowned, immediately
upon his arrest, with the thorns of the *albaspina*, whitethorn, which grew in the
garden where he was captured. Then, in the garden of Annas, he was once again
crowned with, this time "a swete thorn that men clepeth Barbarynes" (Mandeville
1919: 9). Next he was taken to the garden of Caiphas where "he was crouned with
Eglentier". Finally he was brought before Pilate, and there he was tormented with
the *real* crown of thorns, that made of sharp sea rushes, which he kept upon his
head while he was on the cross (*ibid*).

Hence while eglantine may have associations with secular romance, it has
them no less interestingly with sacred romance. Madame Eglentyne has perhaps
fallen under too much suspicion with regard to the former, and been granted too
little leeway with regard to the latter. For her name is the name of if not *the* rose at
least a *rose*. As such it inevitably invites association with the female "rose" *par
excellence*, the Blessed Virgin Mary, an association prominent in the onomasticon
of all Catholic countries, as well as latent in such popular songs as "Rose Marie"
and "My Wild Irish Rose". The Prioress's introduction to her tale suggests the

kind of intimate self-identification with the Virgin that the regular recitation of the rosary is meant to induce.[22]

The history of the religious chaplet is well traced in the studies to which I have referred; but the meaning of the chaplet which Amant sends to Fair Welcome can hardly be described as "religious". The "secular" chaplet, in European culture and religion, considerably antedates the "religious" chaplet. The Latin words for the thing are *corona* and its diminutive *corolla*. These are the festal head-decorations familiar in the amatory poems of Propertius, Catullus, and others. There is another word, *sertum/serta*, which usually refers to the garlands which festooned altars and the like; but the two often merge in poetic expression. The particular purpose of the *corolla* was the pledge or promise of love, and this role is abundantly evident in the amatory iconography of medieval manuscript illumination, carved ivories, and the like. A frequently cited verse in the Book of Wisdom (2:8, "coronemus nos rosis antequam marcescant; nullum pratum sit quod no pertranseat luxuria nostra", "Let us crown ourselves with roses before they fade") fixed the rose-chaplet in particular as an emblem of youth's thoughtless pursuit of pleasure. In what is perhaps the best known poetic expression of the "Carpe diem" theme in English, Herrick's famous "Gather ye rosebuds", the idea is still preserved in its moderated and Anglican form. The forces of the god of Love very much want Fair Welcome to accept the *chapel*, because to accept it is a sign of the final sexual surrender.

The motto on the Prioress's rosary – *Amor vincit omnia* – has been called "proverbial"; but like so many things that are "proverbial", it has a classical literary source, in this instance in the *Eclogues* of Virgil (10.69). Yet if to call it "proverbial" is merely an abdication, to call it a citation of Virgil *tout court* is somewhat inexact. Virgil's line is *Omnia vincit Amor*, Chaucer's its reverse, *Amor vincit omnia*. There are perfectly good prosodic reasons for Chaucer's formulation. Even for Chaucer some choices must have been based on the need for a rhyme; and he probably wanted the rhyme of the "crouned A" in emphatic final position. Furthermore, reversing the line gave him not merely a rhyme but smoother iambs. Chaucer's line does, however, reproduce perfectly, "pleynly save oure tonges difference", the Virgilian line as it appears in the concluding passage of the medley of the *Roman de la Rose* to which I have drawn attention.

> Por Dieu, ne refusez tel offer,
> biau douz filz, ainz la recevez
> par la foi que vos me devez
> et par Amors qui s'an efforce,
> qui mout is a mise grant force.
> Biau filz, Amour vaint toutes choses,
> toutes sunt souz sa clef ancloses.

---

22 See Frank (1979: 346-362).

Virgiles neïs le conferme
par santance courtaise et ferme;
quant *Bucoliques* cercheroiz,
"Amors vaint tout" I trouveroiz
"et nous la devons recevoir."
Certes il dit et bien et voir;
en un seul ver tout ce nous conte,
n'i peüt conter meilleur conte.

(21297-21306)

[For the love of God, sweet son, do not refuse his offer, but rather receive it by the faith you owe me and by Love who impels it and who has given it such great power. O fair son, Love conquers everything; everything is held by his key. Even Virgil confirms this idea in a powerful and courtly saying. When you look through the *Bucolics* you will find that "Love conquers all" and that "we should welcome Love." Indeed, he spoke well and truly when he tells us all this in a single line; he could not tell a better tale.]

As so often Jean de Meun is quite explicitly echoing the words of Guillaume de Lorris, who had begun the book by saying "Ce est li Romanz de la Rose, / ou l'art d'Amors est tote enclose" (37-38) [It is the *Romance of the Rose*, in which the *Art of Love* is wholly enclosed].

No small part of Jean's wit in this passage is to validate twenty thousand lines of Ovidianism with a single line of Virgil! Jean reminds us that "Amors" is a personification, not an abstract noun, and helps us to see a richer meaning in the idea of "enclosure"; for teachings of love are not merely "contained" in the book, they are locked or held there "close". Such enclosure is that of the *clu* of the *trobar clu* – hermetic verse whose truths lie hidden in the shadows of allegory until they may be freed by the mental exertions of an alert reader or teacher. What is *closed* must be *glosed*. It is this hermeneutic or interpretive sense that the anonymous author of the thirteenth-century *Clef d'Amors*, echoing Guillaume de Lorris, gives to the title of his work.[23]

We do not need to suppose that Chaucer knew the *Bucolics* well or even knew them at all. The passage in Jean de Meun is self-sufficient and self-contained, a rare instance in his poem of a textual citation together with its scholarly footnote. It is still worth recalling the tone and vocabulary of the tenth eclogue. "Love" the affection is treated as a disaster, a madness, a calamity. Love the god is cruel and harsh. The famous line "Omnia vincit Amor, et nos cedamus Amori" – "Love conquers all, and let us, too, surrender to Love", a line almost always quoted out of its context – is far from joyous, affirmative, or carniva-

---

23 "Icest livre que j'ai sommé/la clef d'amors sera nommé;/quer par lui porra l'en ouvrir/les ars d'amours et descouvrir", *La Clef d'Amors* (1890: p. 9, ll. 169-172). Steadman, who wants to believe that the Prioress is from a house dedicated to Saint Leonard, a saint useful for people needing to be unshackled or unchained, suggests that we should understand *vincit* as meaning "binds" or "chains" (1963: 351–353).

lesque. On the contrary, it is somber, pessimistic, and resigned. Though Virgil was not a "love poet" as Ovid was, his medieval readers nonetheless not unreasonably found in him a rejection of sensuality that well accorded with the ascetic ethic.[24]

It is a well-established article of belief in discussion of the Prioress that "Amor vincit omnia" is irresolutely ambiguous. Does it refer to *caritas* or to *cupiditas*, to "celestial love" or to "courtly love"? – or does it fall with graceful indeterminacy somewhere along the lengthy axis separating such poles? Most of Chaucer's recent readers are happy to accept ambiguity as a terminal literary good, but according to classical and medieval rhetorical theory alike, ambiguity, the "enemy of truth", is in large part a result of the absence of a sufficient clarifying context.[25] We are in a position to adduce at least some of the relevant context here. Chaucer was not merely a reader of the *Roman de la Rose*, but its translator; but even if no *a priori* assumption were justified, we would still be able to adduce literally hundreds of examples of the French poem's textual influence, beginning with the "Book of the Duchess", continuing through the *Troilus*, and in a certain sense culminating in the *Canterbury Tales*.

Jean de Meun gives us a picture of a nun who carries a rosary. Chaucer gives us a picture of a nun who carries a rosary. These data in themselves have no significance beyond the facts that there were lots of nuns in the Middle Ages, and that nuns are not unlikely to have rosaries; but they do not stand alone. There is other contextual data. The rosary carried by Jean's nun is a satirical emblem of a carnal love that belies a hypocritical ascetic appearance. We are not told where the Prioress got hers, but one is allowed to pose the question. Jean de Meun's nun is in important narrative commerce with the Old Woman. Chaucer's nun is in important textual commerce with the Old Woman, from whom she has learned her Ovidian table manners. A rosary means (1) a rose-garden, and (2) a string of beads. Lexically these two disparate things merge in the word *chapelet*. The *Roman de la Rose* is a poem that allegorizes the arena of sexual desire as a rose-garden. The specific token of sexual intermediation within the poem is a *chapelet*. Chaucer's nun's rosary is marked with an inscription, in Latin but reproducing exactly the French syntax of Jean de Meun's earlier translation of it, which is the authoritative culmination and seal of the narrative medley which features Jean's nun, Jean's nun's rosary, and the table manners exhibited by Chaucer's Prioress have been taught to Fair Welcome by the Old Woman who is on a mission to deliver a gift

---

24 See O'Meara (1968: 307-326). Nicholas Trivet, O.P., whose glosses to Boethius appear in Chaucer's translation, in his Virgilian commentary stresses the "incendiary" qualities of love in his explanation of the lines "Æthiopum versemus ovis sub sidere Cancri. / Omnia vincit Amor: et nos cedamus Amori": "Est enim Æthiopia calidissima regio per quam status amantium significavit, ut dicit consequenter: *omnia vincit amor*, [etc.] Quasi diceret: amore urimur, ex quo non possumus aliquid." See Trivet (1984: 187).

25 See, e.g., Augustine (1975: caps 8 and 9).

Fair Welcome by the Old Woman who is on a mission to deliver a gift from the Lover, a *chapelet*. We have here the evidence of commodious convergence.

Then there is the larger ideographic context of the *Roman de la Rose* itself. That it is about sex none of its readers is likely to dispute. Extensive research into that poem over many years has convinced me, however, that Jean's essential originality, and probably also his great literary success, lay not in his interest in sex but in the context in which he explored his theme. The *Roman de la Rose* permanently established biological sex as a philosophical and "scientific" subject of weight and dignity. Jean's method – which like so many pioneering breakthroughs in literary history must seem in retrospect rather obvious – was to orchestrate a confrontation between Love and Reason, between Ovid, the greatest poetic authority on the erotic, and Boethius, the greatest poetic authority on the philosophical. In the immediate social context in which he lived and worked – a medieval male, clerical, intellectual world – the argument for philosophical restraints on sexual desire overlapped and merged with a powerful body of Christian ascetic theology.

Among Jean's own most conspicuous literary teachers was the philosophical ascetic poet Alain de Lille. In one of his two very famous poems, the *De planctu Naturae*, Alain had already imitated the genre of the *Consolatio Philosophiæ* in his attack on what he regarded as "unnatural" sexuality. Following the influential anthropology of Saint Paul in the first chapter of the Epistle to the Romans, which identified idolatry and homosexuality as violations against human nature apprehensible as such to all rational beings without recourse to a special theological revelation, Alain dramatized and allegorized the Pauline idea in a literary episode in which Genius, in the context of hearing the confession of Nature, "excommunicated" sodomites from Nature's community. Though Alain's principal aims were doubtless philosophical and theological, his poem was probably not wholly divorced from social reality. It is virtually certain that in the social context in which he wrote, his poem was in part an attack on widespread sexual irregularities in the religious communities of his day, and an implicit defense of traditional Christian ascetic teaching, with its insistence on the necessity of votive chastity. In the *Roman de la Rose*, into which Jean de Meun imported Alain's literary tableau of Nature's confession to Genius, there is a truly revolutionary increment of the argument. In Jean's poem Genius receives his burlesque episcopal authority from the god of Love and his mother Venus, who install him as their bishop. Jean's Genius excommunicates not merely homosexuals but all those who abstain from natural (heterosexual) intercourse as well. His target is necessarily votive Christian ascetics – that is, all the clergy, monks, and nuns of Latin Christendom!

False Seeming and Constrained Abstinence are for Jean de Meun allegorical emblems of a contested doctrine of religious celibacy. They pretend to be what they are not. Their association is nastily suspect. The very name of "Constrained Abstinence" posits a conflict between an institutional ascetic requirement and an unwilling heart. The two false religious are recruited by Amors and Venus, and they have an important connection with the Old Woman. It is their mission, successfully achieved, to persuade the Old Woman to take the *chaplet* to Fair Welcome. Now if we look at those characters on the Canterbury pilgrimage who have obvious textual filiations with False Seeming and the Old Woman, we shall in every case find in the Chaucerian texts echoes of the intellectual context of the *Roman de la Rose*. This is most flamboyantly obvious with regard to the Wife of Bath, an obvious lineal descendant of the Old Woman, and her professional colleague on the faculty of the Academy of the Old Dance. We do not get ten lines into her Prologue before we confront the explicit exegetical arguments of Jerome's *Adversus Jovinianum*, a text of great polemic wit and rhetorical power absolutely central to the discussion of clerical celibacy. The discussion of Christian "perfection" – with "perfection" being defined entirely in terms of the degree to which one abstains from sexual intercourse – dominates the first long section of the Wife's Prologue. One of the principal aspects of the hypocrisy of the Friar and the Pardoner, who share in the literary paternity of False Seeming, is sexual. The Friar has arranged the marriages of many a young woman, and the Pardoner will have his jolly wench in every town.

Whatever else is unresolved in the critics' evaluation of the Prioress, there is a consensus nearing unanimity that she is a woman imperfectly matched in temperament to an ascetic life. We may bracket or avoid the question of whether Chaucer *condemns* her for her want of religious zeal, or indeed whether he has any point of view at all concerning the matter. But we cannot fail to see that he *portrays* her in this fashion. The life to which she seems to aspire is a "courtly" life. The idea of "courtliness" appears lexically twice in her portrait. She "peyned hir to countrefete cheere / of *court*, and to been estatlich of manere" (GP 139-140). Earlier we had been told that "In *curteisie* was set ful muchel hir lest" (GP 132). The vocabulary of "courtliness" is very slippery, very hard to pin down against a moral grid. In fact there is a good deal of slipperiness in her description altogether, so that, for example, the lexicographers and glossators have had to find a meaning of the word "conscience" nowhere else attested to in Chaucer (in about forty other uses of the word) to avoid what might otherwise be a troubling irony in the exercise of her "conscience" on dead mice and dead puppies.

When we examine the "courtesy" on which her desire is fixed, it, too, is puzzling. Is it the "courtesy" that the Knight, too, loved, along with chivalry, truth, generosity, and honor? Or perhaps the "courtesy" which should convince Nicholas to remove his paws from Alison's haunchbones, or inhibit Absalon from passing the collection plate to good looking women? We may find a clue to Chaucer's meaning once again in context. The line "In *curteisie* was set ful muchel hir lest" comes in the midst of the description of her table manners and seems, indeed, to refer especially to them. The line is the sixth in the ten lines devoted to that subject. But the Prioress's table manners are those taught by the Old Woman to Fair Welcome. Fair Welcome's mother is named Courtoisie; and this Courtoisie is nearly rabid in her enthusiasm for the Lover's sexual mission. It is this Courtoisie who quotes with approval the "courteous" maxim (*santance courtaise*, 21300) of Virgil,

"Amors vaint tout", the word-for-word re-Latinization of which is "Amor vincit omnia".

Poetical satire works in part through an author's ability to make words do more or less than on first glance they seem to do. I think that the word "courtesy" is for Chaucer such a word, but it is hardly the only one. The final line of the passage concerning the Prioress's table manner is "Ful seemly after hir mete she raughte" (GP 136). This is supposed to mean "She reached for her food in a very polite manner". If it means that, or only that, it is a boring anticlimax to what is otherwise a spirited treatment of a subject; but it probably does not mean that, or just that. In the first place one would reach for one's food before one was careful not to drop any from her mouth; reaching would also logically go with the line she "ne wette hir fyngres in hir sauce depe" (GP 129). Next, though "meat" in Chaucer can refer to particular food, it more often means food in general, and sometimes means a meal without reference to what the meal consists of. In its other appearance in this passage, the initial line, "At mete wel ytaught was she with alle" (GP 127), that is what it has to mean. She had been well instructed – and we know from whom! – as to how to behave at table. Next, the phrase "reach after" is not idiomatic modern English, and I can find no evidence that it was idiomatic Middle English. Next, all other times that Chaucer uses "after" with "meat" it is clearly in a temporal sense, meaning after the meal. Next, nowhere else in Chaucer does the word "raughte" mean "reached" in the sense of a human agent literally extending an arm for something, as opposed to long tresses reaching the ground or tall trees reaching the sky.

I suspect that once again Chaucer is indulging his weakness for "homonymic and paronymic perturbation", as he did with his "farthing of grease". Although the MED is here silent, there is good reason to suspect word-play. The OED gives two definitions for the verb "reach". The first is the commonplace. The second, now vanished, is to cough violently, to hawk, cough up, spew, or noisily clear one's throat – that is, to *wretch*. In this instance the Old English sources of Chaucer's Middle English "homonymic and paronymic perturbations" are the verbs *reccan* (with its preterite *reahte*) and *hræcan* (preterite *hræhte*). A philologist long ago offered this suggestion, but polite readers were not yet prepared to discover the Rabelaisian in Chaucer, and it seems to have died for lack of a second (Drennan 1914: 136). I think the suggestion would be of the milder form of eructation, burping or belching, or the hawking brought on by a hiatal hernia. If one can *cough* "with a semy soun", as Absalon does in the "Miller's Tale", one can presumably *wretch* "ful semily" as well. We may recall that Chaucer twice jokes about mendicant eructation in the "Summoner's Tale".[26]

---

26   At l. 1770 the friar announced his arrival at Thomas's house by saying "Deus hic!" – an alarmingly inflated version of the prescribed Franciscan greeting "Pax huic domui." Then, at l. 1935, after downing a toothsome snack of parodic amplitude, in the process of contrasting

It is only in such textual hints and innuendos, for which there is nothing like an overt suggestion in the Prioress's description, that this nun could herself be suspected of the often flagrant sexual immorality so copiously attested to in medieval historical records, and prominently displayed in the satirical folios of the *Roman de la Rose*. The very fact that Chaucer has made her portrait using in part Jean's old bawd and in part his false nun, however, should encourage us at least to remember the intimate connection between bawds and nuns in the tradition of ecclesiastic satire. The most famous such connection is doubtless to be found in the Spanish *Libro de Buen Amor*, attributed to Juan Ruiz, the Archpriest of Hita, who is also its fictive narrator-hero. It is a work clearly related in spirit both to Jean de Meun and to Chaucer, of the latter of whom Juan Ruiz was the contemporary.

In the *Libro de Buen Amor* the old bawd famously has the name Trataconventos, the "Convent-Trotter", with the implication being that convents are indeed one of the principal sites of her activity. In this poem, nuns are repeatedly recommended for their admirable qualities as lovers. In a memorable comic medley of the poem Trataconventos does her best to fix the Archpriest up with a nun, Doña Garoza.[27] The numerous thematic connections between Doña Garoza and Madame Eglentyne have been nicely catalogued by Graciela Daichman (1986: 115-160).

There are adumbrations of convent-trotting in the *Roman de la Rose*. After offering the Old Woman the Lover's bribes – which include, incidentally, a brooch (*fermaill*, 12398) – False Seeming muses silently to himself about how the Old Woman had better cooperate, since it might be possible to get to Fair Welcome anyway, when her back was turned. It is *where* that back would be turned that is of interest in the present context: "Une heure alissiez au moutier, / vos i demouraste mout ier" (12471-12472) [You might have gone for an hour to the convent, where you stayed so long yesterday]. She might go for an hour to the *moutier*, where she spent such a long time yesterday. (Like Chaucer, Jean is full of witty rhymes.) Struble translates *moutier* as *l'eglise* but *moutier* derives from *monasterium*, a house of religious of either sex, and I think that Dahlberg correctly captures Jean's innuendo with modern English *convent*. And what we might call the Old Woman's professional pace, as she sets off on her mission to Fair Welcome, is a *trot*: "La vielle illeuc point ne sejorne, / le trot a Bel Aqueull retorne" (12511-12) [The Old Woman stayed there no longer, but to Fair Welcome at a trot].

In one of the famous critical essays of the last century, "Tradition and the Individual Talent", T. S. Eliot fixed our attention on an essential feature of the classical tradition in European poetry: its perennially fecund union of an admired common literary legacy with the unique sensibility of particular genius. Chaucer, in common with all great poets comfortable with an inherited literary tradition, is chiefly re-

---

the Jovinian secular clergy with the abstemious friars, he thus imagines the former reciting the forty-fifth "psalm of Davit" : "Lo, 'buf' they seye, '*cor meum eructavit*'!"

27 Ruiz (1974, vol. 2: pp. 179-186, stanzas 1332-1347).

markable for the manner in which he responds to admired models as opposed to the fact that he has them. The kinds of textual filiations that have concerned me in this essay cannot determine our understanding of Chaucer's Prioress, but if their apparent implications are to be denied or overruled, the procedures of determination should be informed and transparent. The "debate" surrounding Chaucer's attitude to Madame Eglentyne – as to so much else – has been in effect a contest for privilege between a criticism founded in a supposed appreciation of the poet's geniality and generosity of spirit, and one founded in an awareness of the supposedly determinative meaning of historical facts and iconographic patterns.

The terms of the contest are unlikely to change, but they demand renewed scrutiny and adjustment. We need to attend to such clues as have survived the corrosive operations of time – remembering that a clue is a thread or woven chain that may lead us through historical and philological mazes from something we know to something we want to know. Some of the oldest and simplest rosaries were textile, weavings knotted or knopped, and there is a strong thematic link between the rosary and the usually feminine task of spinning.[28] And the later Middle Ages saw a profusion of "literary" rosaries in which the participial relationship between *textus* and *texere* (to weave) is clearly apparent.[29] In this regard we may end with one final bead in the textual chain of the Prioress's "paire of bedes".

At the end of the *Confessio Amantis*, Venus, in dismissing old John Gower from the fray of Love, invests him with a parting gift:

> ...and to the queene [Venus]
> I fell on knes upon the grene,
> And tok my leve forto wende.
> But sche, that wolde make an end,
> As therto which I was most able,
> A Peire of Bedes blak as Sable
> She took and heng my neck about;
> Upon the gaudes al without
> Was write of gold *Por reposer*
>
>   (8. 2899-2907)[30]

Here the reminiscence of Chaucer's lines comes in the context of the poet's awareness of a much greater debt to Jean de Meun. Like Chaucer, Gower paid to Jean the high compliment of inventive imitation. The *Confessio Amantis* takes as its central conceit the confession to Genius, and as its central character Jean's Lover (Amans), submerged in the fictive persona of the narratorial "John Gower". The mood of the last book of the *Confessio Amantis* is that of a palinode, a rejection of eroticism. Such a palinode is common in the medieval Ovidian tradition;

---

28   See Wilkins (1969: 94-99).
29   See Winston-Allen (1997: esp. 31-64).
30   Gower (1901, vol. 3: 465).

its absence from the *Roman de la Rose* was one of Jean's most daring ironies. Whether because of his incremental wisdom, or simply because he is too old to cut the mustard any more, the Lover is given his *congé*. We may compare the motto on old Gower's rosary with that on the rosary of Madame Eglentyne. The one proclaims Love's all-conquering power, the other the freedman's repose after long captivity. "This have I for thin ese cast," says Venus, "That thou nomore of love sieche." He is on orders to vacate the arena of Love and "go ther vertu moral duelleth", to the secular monastery of his library in fact, where, we must speculate, he will pursue wisdom in his old books and in the telling of his beads.

References

Augustine
    1975   *De dialectica*, B. Darrell Jackson (ed.), Jan Pinborg (trans.). Dordrecht: D. Reidel.

Charles V [of France]
    1879   *Inventaire du mobilier de Charles V, roi de France*, Jules Labarte (ed.). Paris: Imprimerie Nationale.

Chaucer, Geoffrey
    1987   *The Riverside Chaucer*, L. D. Benson (ed.). Boston: Houghton Mifflin.

La Clef d'Amors
    1890   Auguste Doutrepont (ed.). Halle: Max Niemeyer.

Coulton, G. G.
    1908   *Chaucer and His England.* London: Methuen.

Daichman, Graciela
    1986   *Wayward Nuns in Medieval Literature.* Syracuse: Syracuse University Press.

Delachenal, R.
    1920-1931   *Histoire de Charles V.* 5 vols. Paris: Picard.

Drennan, Charles M.
    1914   "Chaucer's Prioress, 'C.T.,' Prol. 136: 'Ful semily after hir mete she raughte'," *Notes and Queries*, ns 11 vol. 9: 136.

Dryden, John
    1962   *Of Dramatic Poesy and Other Critical Essays*, George Watson (ed.). London: Dent.

Fleming, John V.
    1981   "Chaucer and the Visual Arts of His Time", in Donald M. Rose (ed.), 121-136.
    1969   *The Roman de la Rose: A Study in Allegory and Iconography.* Princeton: Princeton University Press.

Frank, Hardy Long
    1979   "Chaucer's Prioress and the Blessed Virgin", *Chaucer Review* 13: 346-362.

Friedman, John Block
      1970   "The Prioress's Beads 'of Smal Coral'", *Medium Ævum* 39: 301-305.
Gower, John
      1901   *The Complete Works of John Gower*, G. C. Macaulay (ed.). 3 vols. Ox-
                  ford: Clarendon.
Guillaume de Lorris – Jean de Meun
      1914-1925   *Le Roman de la Rose par Guillaume de Lorris et Jean de Meun*, Ernest
                  Langlois (ed.). 5 vols. Paris: Firmin-Didot.
      1966-1970   *Le Roman de la Rose*, F. Lécoy (ed.). 3 vols. Paris: Champion.
      1992   *Le Roman de la Rose*, Armand Strubel (ed.). Paris: Livre de Poche.
      1971   *The Romance of the Rose*, Charles Dahlberg (trans.). Princeton: Princeton
                  University Press.
Kuhl, Ernest P.
      1923   "Notes on Chaucer's Prioress", *Philological Quarterly* 2: 305-306.
Lehman, B. H.
      1925   "Foreword", in Madeleva 1925 (q. v.).
Lowes, John Livingston
      1908   "The Date of Chaucer's *Troilus and Criseyde*", *PMLA* 23: 285-306.
      1910   "Simple and Coy. A Note on Fourteenth Century Poetic Diction", *Anglia*
                  33: 440-451.
Maclagen, Eric – C. C. Oman
      1936   "An English Gold Rosary of about 1500", *Archæologia* 85: 1-22.
Madeleva, Mary
      1925   *Chaucer's Nuns and Other Essays*. New York: Appleton.
Mandeville, Jehan de
      1919   *Mandeville's Travels, Translated from the French of Jean d'Outremeuse*,
                  P. Hamelius (ed.). EETS, 153. London: Kegan Paul.
Manley, Francis
      1959   "Chaucer's Rosary and Donne's Bracelet: Ambiguous Coral", *Modern
                  Language Notes* 74: 385-388.
Mieszkowsky, Gretchen
      1985   "Chaucer's Pandarus and Jean Brasdefer's Houdée", *Chaucer Review* 20:
                  40-60.
Milton, John
      1940   *The English Poems of John Milton*, Charles Williams – Walter Skeat
                  (eds.). London: Oxford University Press.
O'Meara, John
      1968   "Virgil and Augustine: The Roman Background to Christian Sexuality",
                  Augustinus 13: 307-326.
Orr, John
      1962   *Old French and Modern English Idiom*. Oxford: Blackwell.
Paris, Gaston
      1885   "Chrétien Legouais et autres traducteurs ou imitateurs d'Ovide", *Histoire
                  littéraire de la France*, vol. 29: 455-525.
Plummer, John (ed.)
      1966   *The Hours of Catherine of Cleves*. New York: G. Brazillier.

Power, Eileen
    1924   *Medieval People.* New York: Houghton Mifflin.
Ragen, Brian Abel
    1988   "Chaucer, Jean de Meun and Proverbs 30.20", *Notes and Queries* 233: 295-296.
Reid, T. B. W.
    1964   "Chaucer's 'Ferthing of Grece'", *Notes and Queries* 209: 373-374.
Rex, Richard
    1995   *"The Sins of Madame Eglentyne" and Other Essays on Chaucer.* Newark: University of Delaware Press.
Ridley, Florence
    1965   *The Prioress and the Critics.* Berkeley: University of California Press.
Rose, Donald M. (ed.)
    1981   *New Perspectives in Chaucer Criticism.* Norman: Pilgrim Books.
Ruiz, Juan
    1974   *Libro de Buen Amor.* 2 vols. Madrid: Espasa-Calpe.
Rutebeuf
    1969   *Œuvres complètes de Rutebeuf*, E. Faral – J. Bastin (eds.). 2 vols. Paris: Picard.
Steadman, John M.
    1963   "The Prioress' Brooch and St. Leonard", *English Studies* 44: 351-353.
Trivet, Nicholas
    1984   *Commentario a las Bucólicas de Virgilio*, Aires Augusto Nascimento – José Manuel Díaz de Bustamante (eds.). Santiago: Universidad de Santiago de Compostela.
Wilkins, Eithne
    1969   *The Rose-Garden Game: The Symbolic Background to the European Prayer-Beads.* London: Gollancz.
Winston-Allen, Anne
    1997   *Stories of the Rose: The Making of the Rosary in the Middle Ages.* University Park: Pennsylvania State University Press.

The Cook, the Miller, and Alimentary Hell

Matthew Brosamer, Mount St. Mary's College

Robyn and Roger both have mouths that gape in a particularly repellent manner, so much so that numerous critics over the past several generations have been reminded of the hell-mouth, with its enormous demon-head yawning wide to receive the souls of the damned. The Miller's mouth "as greet was as a greet forneys" (I, 559),[1] and the Manciple is so appalled at the foulness of the Cook's mouth and breath that he exclaims, "Hoold cloos thy mouth, man, by thy fader kyn! / The devel of hell sette his foot therin!" (IX, 37-38) Given the ubiquity of the hell-mouth image in medieval iconography, there seems little reason to doubt that Chaucer had it in mind when describing the two pilgrims. However, there are broader implications of Chaucer's hell-mouth imagery to be addressed. Specifically, I believe that a hell-mouth necessarily implies a hell-stomach, and further that there is an abundance of material in Chaucer's writings that calls for a consideration of hell in its full alimentary signification.

That the entrance to hell was a mouth – for the Latin Middle Ages, anyway – is beyond dispute. This is particularly the case with regard to the visual arts; manuscript paintings bear abundant witness to the prevalence of the image, and a brightly painted hell-mouth often served as the *locus* of Hell in productions of vernacular plays.[2] It would be a mistake, though, to understand the hell-mouth as simple iconographic shorthand for hell or its threshold. The way into hell was through the mouth of a toothy infernal creature, but what is inside? A typical image now is of a hell more or less like Dante's – a systematic locus of punishment, complete with geography, hierarchy, and various other aspects of order. It is possible (though in my view, unlikely) that Chaucer shared this notion, but for our present purpose there is one demonstrably certain aspect of Chaucer's hell that is rarely mentioned in Dante: its smell. A hell that takes up the full range of associations implied by the hell-mouth would be pervasively and malodorously vile, because it would exist within the gut of a devil. Such, I believe, is the hell envisioned by Chaucer.

The hell of Chaucer draws on a number of sources,[3] but none is more important than *De miseria condicionis humane* (1195) of Lotario dei Segni (later Pope Inno-

---

1   This and all other citations from Chaucer's works are taken from Benson (ed.) 1987.

2   See Chambers (1903: 86, 137, 142), Rossiter (1950: 64). Of course, not all medieval plays involved hell, and not all of those that did featured hell-mouths when performed, but it was a relatively common practice. Henslowe had a hell-mouth in his prop closet, and religious plays on the continent featured increasingly opulent hell-mouths well into the seventeenth century.

3   Best summarized in Spencer (1927: 177-200).

cent III). A work of unremitting gloom by modern standards, this treatise survives in a remarkable 671 manuscripts, and was translated into a number of vernacular languages (Lewis 1978: 5). Chaucer knew it (it is a major source for the *Pardoner's Tale* and the *Man of Law's Tale*, and in the Prologue to *The Legend of Good Women* Chaucer lists an English translation of *De Miseria* among his works), and it also directly influenced many of Chaucer's other sources. It therefore demands close scrutiny.

De Miseria is divided into three parts, each dealing with a different order of misery suffered by mankind. Part One involves the simple misery of living in a fallen world, expressed in terms of man's relationships with the forces that affect his life. The material world, his own body, human society, the natural world, and contingent circumstance are all corrupting, violent, and loathsome. Part Two treats of sin, inasmuch as it makes man's life miserable. Part Three discusses the misery of the afterlife; the last judgment is described at some length, but the torments of hell receive far more attention.

No attempt is made in *De Miseria* to alleviate the overwhelming sense of doom and pessimism that pervades the work. Even at the end of Part Three, where a hint of possible salvation might be expected, we find nothing but a catalogue of the agonies that await the damned. The work ends with the following sentence: "There shall be weeping and moaning, wailing and shrieking, grief and torment, gnashing and shouting, fear and trembling, labor and pain, fire and stench, darkness and anxiety, anguish and harshness, calamity and want, distress and sorrow, oblivion and confusion, tortures and pains, bitterness and terrors, hunger and thirst, cold and heat, brimstone and fire burning forever and ever".[4] The insistent physicality of this passage is characteristic of the treatise as a whole; misery itself may be a state of mind and spirit, but its causes are firmly rooted in a hostile world of violence, disease, decay, and mischance. Moreover, the bodily misery of this world stems both from man's vulnerability to misfortune, and from sin: "Pride inflates and envy gnaws, avarice stimulates, anger inflames, gluttony chokes, lechery destroys, lying binds, murder corrupts".[5] As might be expected, the sins committed in the world by the damned are reflected in the nature of their punishments in hell. All sin is appetite, and the appetites that were fed in life are denied in the afterlife, while insatiable worms feed with immortal vigor on the once-pampered flesh. The opening chapter of Part Three is entitled "De Putredine Cadaverum", but the point is that human

---

4   "Ibi erit fletus et gemitus, eiulatus et ululatus, luctus et cruciatus, stridor et clamor, timor et
     tremor, labor et dolor, ardor et fetor, obscuritas et anxietas, acerbitas et asperitas, calamitas et
     egestas, angustia et tristicia, oblivio et confusio, torciones et punctiones, amaritudines et ter-
     rores, fames et sitis, frigus et cauma, sulphur et ignis ardens in secula seculorum" (Lewis
     1978: 232-233).
5   "Superbia inflat et invidia rodit, avaricia stimulat, ira succendit, angit gula, dissolvit luxuria,
     ligat mendacium, maculat homicidium" (Lewis 1978: 122).

flesh, borne of and fed by concupiscent appetite, is as rotten in life as in death: "For man is conceived of blood made rotten by the fire of lust; in the end worms stand by his body like mourners. Alive, he brings forth lice and tapeworms; dead, he will beget worms and flies. Alive, he produces dung and vomit; dead, he produces rottenness and stench. Alive, he fattens one man; dead, he will fatten many worms".[6] The images of stink and consumption here are palpable, and the connection of stench and putrefaction with sin is all too clear; man is born in a corrupt state, and this moral corruption is the source of all subsequent decay, both physical and spiritual. Saints, on the other hand, remained incorrupt after death, and the odor of the bodies was invariably sweet.

Much of Lotario's imagery was taken directly from scripture, where one finds numerous references to the torments the damned will suffer after death. Fire is the dominant motif, but it must be noted that brimstone is often coupled with fire as a component of divine retribution, both on earth (as in the case of the destruction of Sodom and Gomorrah) and in the afterlife, where those who "adore the beast and his image... shall be tormented with fire and brimstone" (Rev. 14: 9-11).[7] Brimstone was known for two noteworthy qualities: first, it was "the stone that burns" (hence its name – "brim" and "burn" are cognates); and second, it stank when it burned. The unpleasant smell of sulfur in brimstone was, it would seem, part of the punishment. That Chaucer was aware of this idea is confirmed in the *Parson's Tale*, where we find in the discussion of *luxuria* the following: "Now lat us speke thanne of thilke stynkynge synne of Lecherie that men clepe avowtrie of wedded folk; that is to seyn, if that oon of hem be wedded, or elles bothe. Seint John seith that avowtiers shullen been in helle, in a stank brennynge of fyr and of brymston - in fyr for hire lecherye, in brymston for the stynk of hire ordure" (X, 840-841).[8] The Parson refers here to Rev. 21: 8, where a host of malefactors is consigned to eternal punishment in a pool of fire and brimstone. The Parson's gloss on the text, though, makes the distinction between fire and brimstone significant on two levels. Fire both symbolizes and punishes lechery, in that its blazing heat, linked to lechery in life only through metaphor, becomes the actual instrument of punishment after death. This is the *contrapasso* of Dante – and indeed, of the *Visio Pauli* and even of Vergil – and is as such part and parcel with the received Western tradition of how punishment in

---

6   "Conceptus est enim homo de sanguine per ardorem libidinis putrefacto; cuius tandem cadaveri quasi funebres vermes assistent. Vivus, gignit pediculos et lumbricos; mortuus, generabit vermis et muscas. Vivus, producit stercus et vomitum; mortuus, producit putredinem et fetorum. Vivus, hominem unicum inpinguat; mortuus, vermes plurimos inpinguabit" (Lewis 1978: 205-207).

7   All scriptural citations are from *The Holy Bible* 1971.

8   He continues with this image when condemning those who frequent brothels, "thilke harlotes that haunten bordels of thise fool wommen, that mowe be likned to a commune gong, where as men purgen hire ordure" (X, 885).

hell works. The brimstone operates in the same way, but the quality that serves in both its symbolic and punitive dimensions is its smell. Brimstone burns, it is true, but its fire is indistinguishable from that of the pool of fire. Its function is to stink, and in so doing both to punish and to signify. The word "ordure" completes the olfactory image, in that it supplies an excremental element that had long associations with *luxuria*. The idea that all sins are connected, and that sinning in one manner renders the sinner more susceptible to temptation in another, was a commonplace of moral theology. Gluttony and lust, however, were thought to have a special affinity (both being sins of the flesh, or incontinence, as opposed to sins of the spirit), and it was frequently observed that the proximity of the genitals to the belly (or anus) was no accident.[9]

The belly was as foul-smelling as what emerged from it, and thus the words "stynk" and "ordure" are fairly applied to the sin of adultery, both in the symbolic and physical senses. The passage from the *De Miseria* quoted above now makes better sense; if "man is conceived of blood made rotten by the fire of lust", then sexual ardor produces rottenness – and presumably, the accompanying smell. Misbegotten in such a manner, man naturally produces dung and vomit while alive, because the sin that corrupted his engendering likewise corrupts his digestive functions.[10] And thus stink pervades all; the first chapter of the *De Miseria* returns to this theme regularly in the space of one page: "Man... becomes fuel for the fire, food for worms, a mass of putridness... Man is conceived in the heat of desire, in the fervor of the flesh, in the stench of lust: what is worse, in the blemish of sin... He will become fuel for the inextinguishable fire that always flames and burns; food for the immortal worm that always eats and consumes; a mass of horrible putridness that always stinks and is filthy" (Lewis 1978: 94).[11] Thus, everything that man is or does on earth (insofar as it is sinful or tainted by original sin) exhibits the very

---

9   The idea is at least as old as Tertullian. In his *De ieiunio aduersus psychicos*, he wrote: "monstrum scilicet haberetur libido sine gula, cum duo haec tam unita atque concreta sint, ut si disiungi omnino potuissent, ipsi prius uentri pudenda non adhaerent" (Reifferscheid – Wissowa 1890: 274). ["Lust without voracity (*gula*) would certainly be considered a monstrous phenomenon; since these two are so united and concrete, that, had there been any possibility of disjoining them, the pudenda would not have been affixed to the belly itself rather than elsewhere" (Thelwall 1995: 103)].

10 It is perhaps of note that when Chaucer lists his works in the Prologue to the *Legend of Good Women*, he gives the title of his translation of the *De Miseria* as "Of the Wreched Engendrynge of Mankynde" (LGW G, 414). By using "engendrynge" instead of "condicioun", he responds to Lotario's insistent emphasis on mankind's corrupt beginnings, from the moment of conception.

11 "Homo... [f]it cibus ignis, esca vermis, massa putredinis... Conceptus in pruritu carnis, in fervore libidinis, in fetore luxurie: quodque deterius est, in labe peccati... Fiet cibus ignis qui semper ardet et urit inextinguibilis; esca vermis qui semper rodit et commedit immortalis; massa putredinis qui semper fetet et sordet horribilis" (Lewis 1978: 95).

qualities of corruption and stink that will engage his attention in hell, should he arrive there. I have suggested that in Chaucer this corruption and stink has an alimentary dimension, and it is to this notion that we will now turn.

That hell was foul-smelling was evidently somewhat proverbial with Chaucer; for example, he memorably refers to hell as "stink eterne" in "An ABC" (56). A more detailed picture is presented in the *House of Fame*, where the wind-god Eolus blows upon a trumpet of brass that is "fouler than the devel" (HF 1638). Its foulness is indeed diabolical, because it is the trumpet of slander, and it works as quickly and malignantly as the vice itself. The sound travels "[a]s swifte as pelet out of gonne / Whan fyr is in the poudre ronne" (HF 1643-1644), and from the trumpet's end emerges a repellently multicolored smoke that "stank as the pit of helle" (1653). The reference to gunpowder is entirely appropriate here; slander does indeed travel quick as a shot, but as a hellish stink it should smell like hell, and Chaucer suggests that it does. The connection is not explicitly stated, but it seems unlikely that the stink of hell and burning gunpowder – primary ingredients of which are sulfur and saltpeter – would be brought up at the same time by accident. Saltpeter was obtained from the dung of horses and cattle, and brimstone was both notably smelly and hellish by connotation; Chaucer has the Canon's Yeoman say of alchemists the following:

> Men may hem knowe by smel of brymstoon.
> For al the world they stynken as a goot;
> Hir savour is so rammyssh and so hoot
> That though a man from hem a mile be,
> The savour wole infecte hym, trusteth me.
>
> (VIII, 885-889)

The fire of the Canon's alchemical furnace is fed with hellish brimstone; he stinks. That his smell is "rammyssh" and infectious adds to the infernal picture, with images of bestial heat and corruption. For Chaucer, therefore, the stink of hell and the stink of brimstone are very close indeed. But the picture in the *House of Fame* contains a final detail that requires our attention. The color of the smoke that comes from Eolus's trumpet is likened to that produced by melting lead, which emerges "al on high fro the tuel" (HF 1649). A *tuel* is a chimney-hole, but it is also an anus. Both meanings of the word, given the malodorous topic at hand, must surely be intended. Why an anal pun in the context of a description of the stink of hell? Because hell is a belly, a gut – and the stink of hell is the stink of the bowels.

This symbolic relation between the entire alimentary system and hell is amply attested in Chaucer's works. In the *Legend of Good Women*, there is a reference to Aeneas coming "to paradys / Out of the swolow of helle" (LGW 1103-1104). "Swolow" is usually glossed as "mouth", but the action of swallowing is surely invoked as well, with the implication that the metaphor of eating goes beyond the entrance to hell. Food goes to the belly, after all. Similarly, in the *Tale of Melibee* Dame Prudence notes that "the avaricious man is likned unto helle, that the moore it swelweth the moore desir it hath to swelwe and devoure" (VII, 1617). In the description of the Summoner in the *General Prologue*, we read that "[p]urs is the ercedekenes hell" (I, 658). Hell is here a bag, an image that brings to mind the Pardoner's exclamation: "Oh wombe! O bely! O stynkyng cod, / fulfilled of dong and of corrupcioun!" (VI, 534-535) Here we are back with Lotario dei Seigni, and his jaundiced view of the human digestive apparatus; the gut is a filthy sack, a bag of excrement. Also of note is the antifraternal joke in the Prologue of the *Summoner's Tale*. The swarm of friars lives within Satan's "ers", and the reader is thereby provided with concomitant images of sin, hell, and stink – all localized inside Satan, that is, between his "ers" and his mouth. The joke ends here, but the overriding image does not; the *Summoner's Tale* is, from beginning to end, a vast elaboration on this joke, a confusion of bellies and bowels, appetites and stinks – all pointing straight to hell.

Friar John is an energetic promoter of his order, extolling at considerable length the ascetic virtues upon which it was founded, while at the same time failing to practice them. An unrepentant hypocrite, he is not perturbed by the vast gulf separating his words and deeds. This portrait is informed by a large body of traditional antifraternal satire, which in the main saw friars as greedy, hypocritical, dissimulating, and given to leading lives of gluttonous leisure.[12]

Friar John, as a mendicant friar and as a *lymytour*, was authorized to go about within a certain district begging for alms, by which his convent maintained itself. John compares the friars' supposed poverty to the wealth of the monastic and secular clergy: is it not better to give to the poor friars, who are in greater need? Among the many fraternal virtues about which John boasts, the first is fasting:

> We lyve in poverte and in abstinence,
> And burell folk in richesse and despence
> Of mete and drynke, and in hir foul delit.
> We han this worldes lust al in despit.

(III, 1873-1876)

The friars, then, are especially holy men whose prayers are the more efficacious thereby. Thomas, John's beleaguered prey, would be wise to leave them a legacy (John argues), so that this influence might be brought to bear on lessening his time in purgatory. This posture is of course a sham; John's profession of abstinence ("The body is ay so redy and penyble / To wake, that my stomak is destroyed" [III, 1846-1847]) is a lie, as he wheedles any kind of food he can from the people in his region (see III, 1746-1750). He even mincingly requests rich and delicate food of Thomas'

---

12 Extensive discussions of the antifraternal elements in the *Summoner's Tale* may be found in Fleming (1966: 688-700), Szittya (1986: 231-246), and Plummer (1995: 44-50).

wife: "Have I nat of a capon but the lyvere, / And of youre softe breed nat but a shy-vere, / And after that a rosted pigges heed" (III, 1839-1841). He also exhibits sins commonly associated with *gula* – namely, lechery and wrath. His conduct with Tho-mas' wife is at best overfamiliar (he kisses her, and they banteringly discuss Thomas' unwillingness to render the marital debt), and his reaction to Thomas' bequest is one of fury. The dramatic irony implicit in his rage, a rage immediately following his lengthy discourse on the wickedness of wrath, is surely intended, as is the emphasis in his sermon on the connection between wrath and drunkenness. In view of John's manifest hypocrisy, it seems likely that his denunciation of drunkenness implies ha-bitual overindulgence on his part; it may perhaps also be a dig at Huberd, who "knew the tavernes wel in every toun" (I, 240).

The comeuppance received by John at the tale's conclusion may also be seen as a commentary on his gluttonous habits. As was noted above, scatological imagery was regularly employed in condemning *gula*, and farting should be seen here in this light – witness the fart of Glouton in *Piers Plowman*. The anus is the end of the gut oppo-site the mouth, and its distasteful associations serve to emphasize the foulness of mouth-related sins. This was made clear to the Friar in the Prologue to the *Sum-moner's Tale*, who "hadde his fille" (III, 1700) after seeing the vision of friars swarm-ing about Satan's "ers", and it was made clear to Friar John both in the initial be-stowal of Thomas' gift, and more elaborately in its final division amongst his breth-ren. Hints at this connection abound in the *Summoner's Tale*; John's reference to the "fundement" of his cloister, a costly building whose funding takes food from the mouths of the poor, foreshadows his eventual discomfiture at Thomas' "fundement", and his groping about for the hoped-for treasure recalls his searching queries about the various kinds of food he might obtain. But it is the interview of John with the lord of the village, and the subsequent conversation of the lord with Jankyn, his squire and *kervere*, that finally compel the reader to see the fart's bestowal and distribution fully as an indictment of the friar's gluttony.

At the outset, one should note the near-constant references to food, eating, taste, etc., that permeate this scene. First, John's anger at Thomas' insult is such that he "grynte with his teeth" (III, 2161). This image is associated not only with anger, but with the act of consumption frustrated; John departs from Thomas' house with none of his appetites satisfied, and so chews emptiness.[13] The lord of the village (who is eating his dinner) is initially sympathetic to the obviously distressed friar, and praises him in terms of food and taste: "Ye been the salt of the erthe and the savour" (III, 2196). Upon considering the conundrum of how to divide a fart, he again uses the word "savour": "Who sholde make a demonstracion / That every man sholde have

---

13   Other pertinent texts are Matthew 22:13 (the parable of the wedding guest, who is cast from the marriage feast into the darkness, there to wail and gnash his teeth), and the confession of Wrath in *Piers Plowman*, whose frustrated appetite is illustrated by a related image - he pro-ceeds to confession "nippynge his lippes" (C VI 104) (Pearsall 1978: 114).

yliche his part / As of the soun or savour of a fart?" (III, 2224-2226) Given the repetition of the word, and in its two senses of "taste" and "smell", it seems evident that we
are meant to link them: eating with smelling, gluttony with farting. Seemingly (and
perhaps sarcastically) amazed at the logical difficulties manifested by the problem,
the lord's solution is to throw up his hands, and suppose that Thomas is possessed by
the devil; he tells John, "Now ete youre mete, and lat the cherl go pleye; / Lat hym go
honge hymself a devel weye!" (III, 2241-2242) Now John has come full circle; he
approached Thomas' house in search of a meal, and he has now found one. But the
devil has been invoked, the odor of the fart lingers over the gathering, and the friar's
appetite is as polluted as the gift he received.

Jankyn's solution to the problem of the division of the fart has occasioned as
much scholarly attention as the antifraternal satire in the tale (summarized in
Plummer 1995: 46-48), and the image of the fart distributed through the spokes of a
wheel is now held to be a parody of the descent of the Holy Spirit at Pentecost. What
has not been recognized is the continuance of themes related to food and *gula* into
this last portion of the tale, and into the images and ideas associated with both the real
Pentecost and its parody in the tale. The account of Pentecost in Chapter 2 of the Acts
of the Apostles contains much in the way of such themes; the Holy Spirit descends
upon the apostles in the form of tongues of fire, and their subsequent preaching is
taken by onlookers to be a sign of drunkenness. Further, this preaching is effective,
and many are brought into the Church; note that their communal meal-taking is mentioned twice, in verses 42 and 46. To compare this account with the final section of
the *Summoner's Tale* is to see not simply a parody of Pentecost, but an inversion of
the sacramental meals described there. Szittya (1974: 19-46) is surely correct in asso-
ciating Jankyn's reference to "the firste fruyt" (III, 2277) with the custom of offering
the first fruits of the harvest as an offering to the Lord, but I think the association goes
beyond harvest offerings. Levitical tradition also demanded that the firstborn male
child be offered to the Lord (needless to say, not as a burnt sacrifice); such was the
reason for Christ's presentation at the temple by Mary and Joseph. This was naturally
taken by hosts of patristic and medieval exegetes as a figure for the sacrifice on the
cross, and hence for the Eucharist. At the last supper Christ's body was divided and
eaten; in Jankyn's scheme, the fart will be divided and smelled. This is an elaborate
joke, to be sure, but one that is thematically and imagistically consonant with the tale
as a whole. In the end, the *Summoner's Tale* is an exploration of greed as tainted appetite, with the stink of the bowels as a governing metaphor. It is surely no accident,
too, that the devil is twice referred to immediately before Jankyn's solution is proposed. As an inversion of Pentecost, the division of the fart is by definition diabolical,
but its signification is fundamentally rooted in what a fart *is*: a sulfurous odor identical to the stink of hell. The corruption of the devil is his stink, and he wishes it to
spread.

The offense of flatulence is not confined to its smell; farts are also loud, and it
must be remembered that John's task is to divide not only the "savour" of the fart, but

also its "soun". It has long been observed that the "wind" of the divided fart is an inversion of the "mighty wind" (Acts 2: 2) from heaven that accompanied the arrival of the Holy Spirit at Pentecost. So it is, but it must be further observed that hell was, by tradition, a very noisy place.[14] This noise was of two kinds: there was a continuous strong wind, and hell's inhabitants were quite vocal, often maniacally so. The windiness of hell is part of its unpleasantness; the blast of wind is variously hot and cold, but it is always fetid. The vocal noise in hell is typically irrational; it is either tormented wailing, or an expression of the bestial cruelty (and despair) of demons. The widow and her daughters of the *Nun's Priest's Tale* "yolleden as feendes doon in helle" (VII, 3389) when their cock is carried off by a fox; the comparison is humorous, but quite apt, and those who find the appearance of daun Russell reminiscent of the devil will find it still more so. The noise is not only cacophonous, but bootless – they do not catch the fox, and the farm is left in a general uproar. The noise of flatulence is therefore hellish in two senses; it is a loud and noxious wind, and it is, quite literally, the opposite of rational speech: it is meaningless sound, emanating from the mouth's opposite.

What, then, of the mouths of Roger and Robyn? The basic facts are these: they drink to excess, they speak churlishly, and they gape in such a way that many readers are reminded of the hell-mouth. To proceed beyond this, we must consider what they do and say in light of the frames of reference described above. We will begin with the fact of their drunkenness. The Miller's Prologue describes his drunken interruption of the Host as follows:

> The Millere, that for dronken was al pale,
> So that unnethe upon his hors he sat,
> He nolde avalen neither hood ne hat,
> Ne abyde no man for his curteisie,
> But in Pilates voys he gan to crie,
> And swoor...

(I, 3120-3125)

Drunkenness, like farting, is related to nonsensical speech, though as a cause rather than a symbol. The Miller's drunkenness causes him to speak like an actor playing the role of Pilate; such a performance would involve a great deal of ranting and raving. The Cook's inebriation causes him to lose the faculty of speech altogether; when the Manciple abuses him for being drunk, he becomes extremely angry, but his condition prevents him from saying a word. The ability to speak temperately and rationally is, it seems, something of a moral barometer; the devils in hell, Pilate, Robyn, and Roger are all one in that they cannot do so.

14　See Spencer (1927: 192-193) for medieval examples of this. For Vergil, too (and hence Dante), hell was full of wailing and screaming, with iron gates crashing and trumpets blaring – in short, it was a noisy city, but the raucous tumult was vain and without purpose.

The account of the Cook's drunkenness in the Prologue of the *Manciple's Tale* is the most extensive and detailed description of a character's inebriation to be found in the *Canterbury Tales*. While the Miller can scarcely remain on his horse, the Cook actually falls off his mount, and must be put back in his seat with "muchel care and wo" (IX, 54). The Host wonders what he has been doing all night:

> What eyleth thee to slepe by the morow?
> Hastow had fleen al nyght, or artow dronke?
> Or hastow with som quene al nyght yswonke,
> So that thow mayst nat holden up thyn heed?

(IX, 16-19)

The Manciple is more censorious, and abuses him in detail for his drunkenness, his repulsive physical appearance, and his bad breath:

> For, in good feith, thy visage is ful pale,
> Thyne eyen daswen eek, as that me thynketh,
> And, wel I wot, thy breeth ful soure stynketh:
> That sheweth wel thou art nat wel disposed.
> Of me, certyn, thou shalt nat been yglosed.
> See how he ganeth, lo, this dronken wight,
> As though he wolde swolwe us anonright.
> Hoold cloos thy mouth, man, by thy fader kyn!
> The devel of hell sette his foot therin!
> Thy cursed breeth infecte wole us alle.

(IX, 30-39)

It is at this point that the Cook becomes so angry that he falls from his mount. This catalogue of ills might easily have come from any one of a number of patristic or medieval treatises, sermons, or other such writings on the physical disabilities brought about by drunkenness. But his stench, as foul and infectious as the vapors of hell, is not simple halitosis; rather, it emanates from the internal excremental corruption that *gula* engenders. The author of the *Fasciculus morum* makes this connection clear: "For too much wine leads to the body's ruin. The body ruins whatever one puts into it, just as a bad container gives the liquid poured into it a bad smell, as one can experience clearly by its aftertaste; Joel 2: 'Mourn, all you who drink sweet wine; for it is cut off from your mouth'. For that reason the mouth of a glutton reeks worse than the biggest dungheap, according to Revelation 9: 'The smoke of the bottomless pit arose as the smoke of a great furnace'" (Wenzel 1989: 629).[15] The bottomless pit is of course hell. The Manciple's

---

15 "Nam per nimiam gulam vini adquiritur corporis corrupcio. Nam corpis corrumpit quicquid infunditur, sicut vas corruptum liquorem reddit fetidum aliquatenus ei infusum, quod per exitum gustus aperte probatur; Ioelis 2: 'Ululate qui bibitis vinum in dulcedine; perit enim ab ore vestro'. Inde enim est quod plus fetid os gulosi quam maximus fimarius, iuxta illud

implication that there was something hellish about the Cook's gaping mouth now makes perfect sense. The mouth of a glutton is like the mouth of hell, but his stomach is the "pit" of hell proper, with all the malodorous and diabolical associations that come with it. On the same topic, the author of the *Fasciculus morum* writes: "Notice that it is literally true that a person who gets drunk at night has bad breath the next morning. Therefore he can be compared to a sepulcher, after the words of the Psalm: 'Their throat is an open sepulcher'. Notice also that a man's body can be called an absolutely worthless and ugly piece of land. For other pieces of land are given dung so that they may produce fruit; but when the land of man's body, in contrast, has been given the most dainty food, it produces no fruit but dung, and in fact, the more precious the food is, the more vile what goes down the privy" (Wenzel 1989: 639).[16] Here we have imagery of the dead employed as well; the significance of the image lies not only in the equation of sin and death, but in the stench and corruption associated with corpses. The Pardoner takes up the sepulchral image, warning, "For dronkenessse is verray sepulture / Of mannes wit and his descrecioun" (VI, 558-559). This certainly applies to Roger, as his speech and reason are corrupted to the point of insensibility. He has become like an animal, as have the fallen men and angels who inhabit hell.

The Cook's professional shortcomings also conform to this model quite readily. In the Prologue of the *Cook's Tale*, the Host needles him with playful but pointed accusations that he sells adulterated and spoiled food:

> For many a pastee hastow laten blood,
> And many a Jakke of Dovere hastow soold
> That hath been twies hoot and twies coold.
> Of many a pilgrym hastow Christes curs,
> For of thy percely yet they fare the wors,
> That they han eten with thy stubbel goos,
> For in thy shoppe is many a flye loos.

> (I, 4346-4352)

Such complaints about commercial food service are well documented throughout Chaucer's England, and the repeated promulgation of new laws regulating food

---

Apocalipsis 9: 'Ascendit fumus putei abissi ut fumus fornacis magne'" (Wenzel 1989: 628). Written by an English friar in the early fourteenth century, this text contains the sort of material that might have been heard (adapted and translated for the occasion) from the pulpits of English churches in Chaucer's lifetime.

16 "Et nota ad litteram quod qui de sero se inebriat os habet fetidum de mane. Et ideo bene sepulchro comparatur iuxta illud Psalmi: 'Sepulcrum patens est guttur eorum'. Nota eciam quod caro hominis potest dici terra pessima et fetidissima. Ceteris autem terris apponuntur stercora ut fructificent, set econtra terra corporis hominis appositis cibariis delicarissimis nichil fructificat nisi stercora, et quanto preciosiora sunt cibaria, tanto ad secessum perveniencia sunt viliora" (Wenzel 1989: 638).

preparation and punishing offenders is evidence of a continuing problem.[17] It is such concerns, I think, that are behind the description of the Cook in the *General Prologue* as having a "mormal", or ulcerated sore: "But greet harm was it, as it thoughte me, / That on his shyne a mormal hadde he" (I, 386-387). While it is true that such afflictions were thought to spring from dissolute habits,[18] the fact that the Cook's "mormal" is mentioned in the midst of an account of the many kinds of elaborate dishes he can prepare implies that another association is also meant: that his food is as diseased as his flesh.[19] Flies buzz about his shop, bringing corruption to what should be pure and healthy, but he himself performs this same function through his culinary alchemy. As the Pardoner says:

> Thise cookes, how they stampe, and streyne, and grynde,
> And turnen substaunce into accident
> To fulfille al thy likerous talent!
> ...
>
> But, certes, he that haunteth swiche delices
> Is deed, whil that he lyVeth in tho vices.

(VI, 538-540, 547-548)[20]

Thus the Cook's food is twice-adulterated; it is literally diseased, but it is also designed to appeal to an appetite diseased by repletion and the quest for novelty. What the Parson says of the proud could easily be applied to what the Cook does to his food, and to the tastes of his customers: "Thilke manere of folk been the flyes that folwen the hony, or elles the houndes that folwen the careyne". (X, 441) Corruption and rottenness, as we have seen, are what hell is all about; the Cook purveys contaminated wares, just as he himself is inwardly corrupt through drunkenness, and the hell that will receive him will be as unsavory as his food and his breath.[21] His gaping mouth (especially if he eats his own food!) leads to a hell-

---

17   An excellent account of the means by which dishonest food purveyors in Chaucer's London sought to increase profits by selling adulterated and/or spoiled foods may be found in Cosman (1976: 67-91). See also Drummond – Wilbraham (1958: 31-48) and Tannahill (1973: 160-166).

18   Curry (1960: 47-52) concludes that the Cook's sore is *malum mortuum*, "a species of ulcerated, dry-scabbed apostema produced by corruption of the blood of natural melancholia or sometimes of melancholia combined with *salsum phlegma*". The medical authorities cited by Chaucer generally confirm that this disease, which is often localized on the shins, is caused by improper diet, intercourse with diseased women, and strong wine.

19   For many readers, the "mormal" (a sore that oozes pus) of line 386 is a bit too close for comfort to the "blankmanger" of the following line.

20   This text may derive from the *De Miseria* (2,17,5-14). The source text forms a part of the chapter *De gula*, and Lotario's statement that the preparation of such elaborate dishes was both an instance of gluttony and an incitement to it is echoed by the Pardoner in his sermon.

21   For the iconography of hellish cooks and cooking devils, see Kolve (1984: 260-263).

ish interior indeed, and if the *mormal* is any indication, the worms are already at work.[22]

Returning to the Miller, we note that his condition seems to be a little better than that of the Cook in the Prologue of the *Manciple's Tale*. He remains on his horse (barely), and there is nothing wrong with his ability to speak. But what of his mouth? If it is as large "as a greet forneys", then we may safely assume that it is both huge and gaping, and whether one takes "forneys" to mean "furnace" or "cauldron", there is every reason to associate his mouth with the mouth of hell.[23] He can also reasonably be associated with other men who, like the Cook, have made a hell of their own bellies, and his drunkenness (along with his presumably fetid breath) is only part of the reason for this. The various attempts (summarized in Andrew 1993: 464-478) to associate millers generally with devils (in particular) or wickedness (in general) are not much help here; this is the fourteenth century, and there are no dark satanic mills. The behavior of this particular miller, though, signifies quite a lot, especially insofar as he tells a tale whose plot hinges so fundamentally on alimentary inversion.

As we have seen, the medieval homiletic tradition emphasized that for the drunkard, stinking breath was in fact a larger issue than simple morning-after halitosis, in that it involved the other end of the alimentary system as well. The Pardoner exclaims:

> Allas, a foul thyng is it, by my feith,
> To seye this word, and fouler is the dede,
> When man so drynketh of the white and rede
> That of his throte he maketh his pryvee
> Thurgh thilke cursed superfluitee.

(VI, 524-528)

A drunken miller with a gaping, hellish mouth, telling a tale of rough-hewn adultery whose main olfactory image is that of the fart, and which features a misdirected kiss and a red-hot plowing implement forced into someone's anus, might suggest the devil and hell to a medieval reader for several reasons. There is of course the old idea that devil-worship involved the misdirected kiss as an oath of fealty. More important, to my mind, is the fact that the tale associates the sexual and the scatological so closely. Long a staple of the fabliau genre, this association was (as we have seen) taken quite seriously by moral theologians and homilists

---

22 This is no exaggeration. Skin diseases, appalling by modern standards, were widespread in the Middle Ages, and the infestation of open sores by worms was not uncommon.

23 The Parson is instructive here. On the "five fingers" of the sin of lechery, he notes: "The fourthe fynger is the kissynge; and trewely he were a greet fool that wolde kiss the mouth of a brennynge oven or of a fourneys. / And moore fooles been they that kissen in vileynye, for that mouth is the mouth of helle" (X, 855-856).

since the days of the early church; by emphasizing the proximity of the organs of generation and excretion, they were able to indicate in a particularly vivid manner the debased nature of human sexuality.

Whether or not the *Miller's Tale* has a didactic element, the comedy of the tale depends on the reader's ability to lay aside traditional moral norms; old John the carpenter is a *senex amans*, and so, in the world of the fabliau, is quite rightly cuckolded. With cleverness and credulity replacing virtue and vice as opposing moral norms, we see that Absolon violates these norms to an absolute degree, and his comically exaggerated diabolical associations serve to amuse rather than terrify. A laughably inept lover, he plays the part of Herod (presumably in a local production of a mystery cycle) in an effort to win Alisoun's affections. The absurdity of this effort is evident; Herod was a character so notoriously unsympathetic as to be a joke in Chaucer's day. He tries to kill the infant Jesus, and rages uncontrollably. Moreover, he dies in a truly repellent state; in a tradition extending back to Josephus,[24] his bowels began to rot and ulcerate within him, and his genitals putrefied, producing worms. This death was often portrayed in enthusiastically vivid detail on stage. This is not the sort of role that makes women swoon. His punishment for this ineptitude is to be subject to the very inversion of rightly ordained human sexuality that Christian tradition so vehemently emphasized. For moral theologians, the contamination of human sexuality by sin was symbolized by the physical proximity of the organs of reproduction and elimination. For Absolon, the symbol became a manifestly physical reality.

The layers of inversion embodied by the episodes of the misdirected kiss and the fart are as obvious as they are numerous, but for our purposes several points are worth noting. Absolon initially seeks genital intercourse, but will settle for a kiss. He gets his kiss, but on the end of Alisoun opposite the mouth, which is in turn so close to his original goal that he feels her "berd". He hopes to find sweetness with her and in her mouth, a sweetness he anticipated by putting breath-freshening herbs under his tongue. The sweetness of his mouth was therefore a "berd" in itself, covering (one assumes) Absolon's bad breath. This false sweetness is then itself corrupted by Alisoun's "ers", just as the Cook's meretricious foods are themselves corrupted by the flies and uncleanliness of his shop. These are inversions within inversions, but the end result is a "savour" that takes the reader inside the body; this is the very stink of licentiousness (and hell) which homilists described with such relish. Something similar happens in the episode of the fart; Absolon expects one anus and gets another (an inversion of person and gender), and is moreover punished again with a hellish stink. He expects to sear

---

24 *Jewish Antiquities*, XVII, 6, 5. This recalls the punishment of King Antiochus, as described in the *Monk's Tale*: "thurgh his body wikked wormes crepte, / And therwithal he stank so horribly / That noon of al his meynee that hym kepte... Ne myghte noght the stynk of hym endure" (VII, 2616-2620).

the orifice by which he was humiliated, but is instead humiliated anew by another. His revenge is reminiscent of how devils torture the damned; confronted with the odor of hell, he quite naturally follows through with the act of a punishing demon, an act that confronts and ratifies hell as necessarily interior. An angel brings a hot coal to the lips of Isaiah, cleansing him of his iniquity, but Absolon brings a hot coulter to the "ers" of Nicholas, which is a bit like bringing coals to Newcastle. This brings into a new light his response to the misdirected kiss, when he swears, "My soul bitake I unto Sathanas" (I, 3750), and visits the suggestively nocturnal smithy of the blacksmith Gervys.[25] By calling upon and submitting himself to Satan, he violates again the moral precepts of the fabliau, where killjoys are always punished. Satan provides him with his revenge, but it is on the wrong person, and the stink remains.

The Miller, in telling this tale, gives utterance to all it describes and implies – it comes from within, and emerges through the great "forneys" of his mouth. Like our own world, the world of the fabliau is not hellish, but neither is it entirely free from hell's dominion. There is one entrance to hell, but as long as there are drunkards and *goliardeys*, it will have many mouths, and as many bellies.

Images are important in Chaucer, because they define the experiential boundaries of what he describes; we read and (it is hoped) understand, but images appeal to the senses as well as the intellect. The image of the hell-mouth is vivid and arresting, but as a strictly visual image it is incomplete. The medieval players of the mystery cycles were aware of this; it was impractical to build an entire hell on stage, but a hell-mouth was all that was needed. Smoke emerged from the mouth, symbolizing not only the fires of hell, but its reek. Pots and pans were banged offstage to portray the infernal clamor of the damned. Hell was what was inside; the mouth led to a throat, and the throat to a belly, where the misdirected appetites of sinners were punished by the alimentary inversions of hell. Chaucer's Cook and Miller both embody such appetites, and their gaping mouths are, both literally and figuratively, only entrances.

---

25   On the satanic associations of Gerveys and his smithy, see Reiss (1970: 115-124).

References

Andrew, Malcolm (ed.)
  1993   *A Variorum Edition of the Works of Geoffrey Chaucer, Vol. II: The Can-
            terbury Tales: The General Prologue, Part 1B: Explanatory Notes.* Nor-
            man and London: University of Oklahoma Press.
Benson, Larry D. (ed.)
  1987   *The Riverside Chaucer.* Boston: Houghton Mifflin.
Chambers, E.K.
  1903   *The Medieval Stage.* Vol. 1. London: Oxford University Press.
Cosman, Madeline Pelner
  1976   *Fabulous Feasts: Medieval Cookery and Ceremony.* New York: George
            Braziller.
Curry, Walter Clyde
  1960   *Chaucer and the Medieval Sciences.* 2nd edition. New York: Barnes and
            Noble.
Drummond, J.C. – Wilbraham, Anne
  1958   *The Englishman's Food: A History of Five Centuries of English Diet.*
            Revised edition. London: Jonathan Cape.
Fleming, John V.
  1966   "The Antifraternalism of the *Summoner's Tale*", *JEGP* 65: 688-700.
The Holy Bible, Translated from the Latin Vulgate
  1971   [1749-1752 Challoner revision of the Douay-Rheims version.] Rockford:
            Tan Books.
Josephus
  1998   *Jewish Antiquities, Books XVI-XVII.* Vol. 11. Ralph Marcus – Allen Wik-
            gren (trans.). Loeb Classical Library 410. Cambridge, Mass.: Harvard
            University Press.
Kolve, V.A.
  1984   *Chaucer and the Imagery of Narrative: The First Five Canterbury Tales.*
            Stanford: Stanford University Press.
Lewis, Robert E. (ed. and trans.)
  1978   *De miseria condicionis humane*, by Lotario dei Segni. Athens, Georgia:
            University of Georgia Press.
Pearsall, Derek (ed.)
  1978   *Piers Plowman by William Langland: An Edition of the C-Text.* Berkeley
            and Los Angeles: University of California Press.
Plummer, John F. (ed.)
  1995   *A Variorum Edition of The Works of Geoffrey Chaucer, Vol. II, Part 7
            (The Summoner's Tale).* Norman and London: University of Oklahoma
            Press.
Reifferscheid, A. – Wissowa, G. (eds.)
  1890   *De ieiunio aduersus psychicos.* CSEL Vol. 20, Part 1. Vienna: C.
            Geroldi.

Reiss, Edmund
   1970   "Daun Gerveys in the *Miller's Tale*", *Papers in Language and Linguistics* 6: 115-124.
Rossiter, A.P.
   1950   *English Drama from Early Times to the Elizabethans*. London: Hutchinson's University Library.
Spencer, Theodore
   1927   "Chaucer's Hell: A Study in Mediaeval Convention", *Speculum* 2: 177-200.
Szittya, Penn
   1974   "The Friar as False Apostle: Antifraternal Exegesis and the *Summoner's Tale*", *Studies in Philology* 71: 19-46.
   1986   *The Antifraternal Tradition in Medieval Literature*. Princeton: Princeton University Press.
Tannahill, Reay
   1973   *Food in History*. New York: Stein and Day.
Thelwall, Sydney (trans.)
   [1995]   *The Ante-Nicene Fathers*. Vol. 4. Peabody, Massachusetts: Hendrickson Publishers, Inc.
Wenzel, Siegfried (ed. and trans.)
   1989   *Fasciculus Morum: A Fourteenth-Century Preacher's Manual*. University Park and London: Pennsylvania University Press.

The Shipman's Tale: Merchant's Time and Church's Time, Secular and Sacred Space

Eric Jager, UCLA

Since its first appearance over forty years ago, Jacques Le Goff's now famous distinction between "merchant's time" and "church's time" has been widely cited as a working hypothesis – and, sometimes even as a foregone conclusion – for the study of late medieval culture. According to Le Goff, late-medieval society experienced a new awareness and conception of time, "merchant's time", that was distinct from time as understood and experienced in religious terms, or "Church's time". Le Goff maintained that the shift from Church's time to merchant's time was associated with an increased awareness of "measured time", related in turn to the spread of public time-keeping devices, or clocks (Le Goff 1960).

In recent years, Le Goff's thesis has been scrutinized and even revised. In one noteworthy study, Gerhard Dohrn-van Rossum acknowledges the importance and value of Le Goff's thesis while emphasizing its originally *provisional* (or heuristic) status and cautioning against what he sees as its often premature or simplistic application. Citing the evidence of merchant's diaries, ledgers, and other writings from the fourteenth and fifteenth centuries, Dohrn-van Rossum concludes that while "merchant's time" is a distinguishable concept and experience in the later Middle Ages, it does not necessarily correspond as closely to "*measured* time" as has often been assumed. But Dohrn-van Rossum also sees the need for further study: "... independent of the history of 'measured time' we still need to ask whether, and if so *how, the temporal aspects of commercial activity and commercial rationality came to consciousness in the Late Middle Ages*, and whether it is not likely, therefore, that in the group of those most affected by this [i.e., merchants], 'time' became a topic of special interest" (1996: 230, my emphasis).

The Shipman's Tale, a fabliau about a merchant, his wife, and a monk in Chaucer's *Canterbury Tales*, hardly constitutes historical evidence of actual mercantile practice in the way that a merchant's account books and records would. But this comic tale does put a monk and a merchant into conversation about – and competition over – time, suggesting a practical distinction between "merchant's time" and "church's time". The tale also raises questions about the nature, measurement, and value of time, satirizing the monk and the merchant for often confusing the two distinct temporal orders to which they supposedly belong.

To borrow Dohrn-van Rossum's terms, the Shipman's Tale also provides some clues as to how "the temporal aspects of commercial activity and commercial rationality came to consciousness in the Late Middle Ages", and as to how "in the group of those most affected by this [i.e., merchants], 'time' became a topic of special interest. This tale of mercantile life also contains some references to measured time per se. More importantly, however, it illustrates the late-medieval growth of a certain kind of time-consciousness among the mercantile class, including the notion of time as something that can be measured, lost, or turned to profit, and as virtually a commodity to which a person's worth, identity or reputation might be closely linked.

* * *

Like a Hollywood movie plot, the Shipman's Tale can be summed up in a single sentence: "A monk borrows money from a merchant to buy sex with the merchant's wife, who repays her husband in the same coin". But in adapting this version of the folktale known as "The Lover's Gift Regained", Chaucer enriches the tale with lively dialogue, domestic details, humorous ironies, and rounded characters who engagingly fill out their stock roles--cuckolded husband, adulterous wife, and lustful monk.

As a satire of the monied middle classes and the clerics who pray *for* them even as they prey *on* them, the tale is replete with the language of money and commerce. The opening lines establish the economic vocabulary to which everything else in the world of the tale is reduced – terms such as *riche*, *richely*, *dispence*, *worth*, *paye*, *worshipe*, *waste*, *cost*, and *gold* (VII. 2-19; Benson 1987, further references parenthetical by fragment and line number). Although all of these terms initially refer to money or material wealth, in the course of the tale they are applied to everything else, including even time and space.

At first, the monk might seem to embody a needed spiritual counterpoint to the worldly values of the merchant. The two men are old friends who hail from the same village and are bound together, we are told, in eternal brotherhood – "knyt with eterne alliaunce" (VII. 40). But the real bond between monk and merchant is actually more worldly and temporal – a love of food, drink, and pleasure, including the sexual favors of the very same woman.

Indeed, the monk, Daun John, whose name happily anticipates that of Don Juan, is almost more worldly than the merchant himself. He even *resembles* the merchant in being a kind of traveling businessman, for like the monk portrayed in the General Prologue, he is an "outrider" whose job it is to inspect the granges and barns controlled by his religious house, which were a major source of its income. In a sense, then, the monk himself is on a business trip when he makes a three-day stopover in St. Denis to visit the merchant, who is preparing to travel to Bruges on business of his own (VII. 53-61).

For the first two days, the monk and the merchant eat, drink, and "pleye" (VII. 73) with apparently no conflict between merchant's time and church's time. On the third day, the merchant "up ariseth" (VII. 75) and goes to his counting house – his home office – to do his accounts. This would seem to be merchant's time, although with a hint of Church's time in the coy reference to a resurrection. There he occupies himself with his accounts, "reken[ing] with hymself", consulting his "bookes", and calculating his earthly "tresor" – terms whose satirical double meanings hint that the moral economy is not his most immediate concern, despite the many devout oaths that flavor his conversation throughout the tale (VII. 78, 82, 84).

Chaucer leaves the merchant in his counting house, counting out his money, and turns to the monk. He marks the transition from one place to the other, and perhaps as well one sort of time to another, by a noticeable rhyme, saying that the merchant worked "for the meene tyme" until "it was passed pryme" (VII. 87-88). Prime, originally one of the hours of monastic prayer, has a religious connotation. In Chaucer's day, according to the *Middle English Dictionary*, "prime" could mean anywhere from sunrise, about six o'clock in the morning, to as late as 9 AM (s.v. *prime*). Whatever its exact denotation here, it marks a specific hour.

"Meene tyme", on the other hand, where *mene* derives from OF *moien* (ModF *moyen* 'middle'), refers to time not as a moment but as a duration, an interval, even a period of what Le Goff and Dohrn-van Rossum call "measured time". The way the merchant shuts the door of his counting house so as not to be disturbed while doing his accounts "in the mean time" hints at the mercantile notion of time as money – and money, time – a notion that becomes quite explicit as the tale proceeds.

It is tempting to speculate whether a term that means essentially "middle time" might have had a special relevance for merchants, the middlemen of the economy, but the term's usage as recorded in the *Oxford English Dictionary* (s.v. *mean time*, *meantime*) and the *Middle English Dictionary* (s.v. *mene-time*) applies equally to secular and religious matters, to judge by the illustrative quotations.

Yet Langland, closely contemporary with Chaucer, does use the phrase "mean time" in *Piers Plowman* in a speech by Haukin, a representative of the "active life" and a merchant, to indicate the period during which a merchant awaits the profits on his investment, when religious exercises fail to distract him from anxiety about his business affairs. Now repenting of his lifelong devotion to money, Haukin confesses:

> Worst of all was when I had sent my apprentices overseas, to barter goods or exchange money in Bruges or in Prussia; for in the interval of waiting (ME: *in the mene tyme*) neither Mass nor Matins, nor any kind of diversion, could comfort me; and though I performed penances and said Paternosters, my mind was always on my goods ...
> (B-Text, Passus 13.44; trans. Goodridge, 163)

The repentant merchant even points his moral with a scriptural quotation – "For where your treasure is, there will your heart be also" (Matt. 6.21) – as if to contrast the two realms of time and the two realms of treasure. So perhaps in Chaucer the "mean time" points to the merchant's preoccupation with temporal things and the cash value of time in particular.

In any case, with the mention of "pryme" the tale turns to the monk, who upon rising goes into the garden and walks about saying his "thynges" (VII. 91), a term that here means prayers but later will take on other meanings. Soon afterwards he encounters the merchant's wife, also taking an early morning garden walk, and the two begin a long, intimate *tête-à-tête*. Among other things, the merchant's wife complains to the monk of her husband's miserly ways, pointing suggestively toward her dissatisfaction with how he pays the marriage debt as well. "[H]e is noght *worth* at al / In no degree the value of a flye", she says, for example (VII. 170-71, my emphasis).

The obvious subtext for this equation of marriage, sex, and money is the Pauline marriage "dette" of sexual obligation earlier invoked by Alison of Bath (III. 130). As for her own sins, the merchant's wife confesses merely to a financial embarrassment. Sunday next she must pay a clothing bill of one hundred francs, a debt she cannot repay on her own and that she dares not mention to her husband. Hearing of her plight, the sympathetic monk is only too glad to help, and he offers to lend her the money himself. Quickly the two strike a bargain, as the merchant's wife promises to "paye" back the monk "at a certeyn day" (VII. 190). The form of this "payment" becomes clear as the two seal the bargain with a kiss and a tight embrace, and Chaucer neatly sums up the equation of business with pleasure in his famous rhyme on "frankes" and "flankes" (VII. 201-202).

The merchant and his wife are material people living in a material world where nearly everything is reduced to its cash value – sex, marriage, friendship, religion, even time itself. So it is no surprise that the worldly monk should turn his religious accessories – a portable sundial and a pocket-sized prayerbook – into tools of personal advancement that help to point up the tale's rampant confusions of time and space – or place. His sundial ("chilyndre", VII. 206) is supposed to tell him the hours of prayer, but he uses it instead to tell meal times – that is, to break his obligatory fasts. As for his prayerbook ("portehors", VII. 135), once he has finished his morning devotions, he solemnly swears on it to assure the merchant's wife that he will never betray her secrets. Church's time, as represented by a device designed to tell the canonical hours, thus gives way to a more secular time-consciousness if not exactly what we might call measurable "merchant's time". At the same time, the sacred space of the open prayerbook is snapped shut to become a prop in a business deal.

The merchant's wife, delighted at her secret bargain with the monk, goes and knocks on the counting-house door to announce to her husband that lunch is served. In this truly liminal scene, which takes place at a doorway and marks yet another plot transition, the secular and the sacred worlds collide. Or, rather, the two collapse into one, as Chaucer suggests through a series of satirical double-edged references:

> "*Quy la?*" quod he, "Peter! It am I",
> Quod she; "What, sire, how longe wol ye faste?
> How longe tyme wol ye rekene and caste
> Youre sommes, and youre bookes, and your thynges?"
>
> (VII. 214-17)

Obviously, *thynges* have changed their meaning here from "prayers" to money or other material objects. The semantic shift seems apposite, since the medieval Church made a profitable business of accepting money for prayers. But

Chaucer was hardly a proto-Protestant, and the wordplay is probably meant to satirize the monk's own personal failings as an officer of the Church rather than a wider, systemic abuse. The point is that the monk's "thynges", in the final analysis, are no different from the merchant's.

There is more. The wife's oath – "Peter!" – obliquely reminds us that Saint Peter, heaven's gatekeeper, keeps the treasures of heaven, upon which human hearts should be set, rather than upon earthly things. And the wife's mention of fasting also points two ways: to forgoing food because of the press of worldly business, and to forgoing it as a religious exercise, with a hint that the active life of self-advancement may have unsuspected affinities with the contemplative life of self-mortification.

The merchant, annoyed by his wife's interruption, offers a short sermon on the difficulties and risks of his business. Then he reminds her of his plans to depart the next day for Bruges, counseling her to "kepe oure good", and assuring her that she has "ynough" (245) until his return (VII. 243, 245). By "good" he means of course their material wealth rather than their moral good, although he has no idea of how she will play fast-and-loose with both of these during his absence. And, like "thynges", the word "ynough" is now circulating promiscuously in the tale, another term of quantity or value that marks the mercantile reduction of everything to its material worth or cash equivalent.

Church's time and merchant's time, secular and sacred space, meet again in the scene that follows:

> ... hastily a messe was ther seyd,
> And spedily the tables were yleyd,
> And to the dyner faste they hem spedde,
> And richely this monk the chapman fedde.
>
> (VII. 251 – 54)

"Richly" – but of course. Having eaten the merchant's food, the monk is about to borrow some of his money to purchase some sex from his wife.

After lunch, the double-dealing monk ensures that he gets the best side of both bargains by making a secret deal with the merchant as well. After softening him up with some advice about travel and diet, Daun John asks to borrow a hundred francs "for a wyke or tweye" (VII. 271.) Here the monk makes no pretense of operating according to Church's time, and his mention of "a week or two" even hints at his appreciation of the fact that, for the merchant, time is money, and money time. The offered reason is that he has to buy some "beestes" (VII. 278) for his religious house, a sexual joke that goes right past the unsuspecting merchant.

The merchant takes the monk's request for a temporary loan as his cue to preach another sermon about the hardships of being a businessman. (The merchant's repeated sermonizing, normally the monk's domain, is yet another way that the characters confuse the sacred and the secular.) To a merchant, money is like a "plogh" (VII. 288), he says, unwittingly improving on the monk's sexual joke. The merchant also makes three references to time and money:

> My gold is youres, *whan* that it yow leste ...
> We may creaunce *whil* we have a name,
> But goldlees for to be, it is no game.
> Paye it agayn *whan* it lith in youre ese ...

(VII. 284, 289-91)

That is, the merchant tells the monk he will gladly lend him the money *whenever* he likes, but he stresses that merchants may obtain credit ("creaunce") only *as long as* they maintain a good reputation, and he reminds the monk to pay him back the borrowed money *when* he can.

"Creaunce", of course, is another double-edged term that satirically points to religious belief as well. Earthly treasure apart, treasure is stored up in heaven by means of this other sort of "creaunce". But here time, credit, and value are all measured in strictly mercantile terms, where merchant's time is less a precisely measured interval (although "one or two weeks" puts a pretty well-defined limit on the period of the loan) than a well-calibrated awareness or consciousness of how time affects the merchant's identity and his credit-worthiness, his "name" and his "creaunce".

After this catechism, the merchant fetches the money, offers the monk a drink, and then the monk returns to his abbey, while the merchant goes off to Bruges. (Upon returning from Bruges, the merchant takes out a loan that he must make good on by "reconyssuance" [VII.330] – "recognizance", where personal worth and social reputation again depend on one's credit rating. His wife's earlier promise to repay the monk's loan "at a certeyn day" [VII.190], suggests a similar outlook on the relation of time to money.)

The next Sunday, the monk returns in the merchant's absence and spends a night in "myrthe" with the merchant's wife (VII. 318), leaving behind the merchant's hundred francs. The monk's abuse of the seventh day – a quintessential form of Church's time – in order to commit the seventh sin, and to break his vow of chastity, scarcely needs comment.

A few days later, the merchant returns home, greets his wife, and then leaves again to secure a large loan against his expected profit. Afterwards he pays a visit to his friend the monk to inquire after his health and also hint at the debt he owes. Picking up the hint, Daun John says he has already returned the hundred francs to the merchant's wife. Slightly embarrassed about the misunderstanding, but still in a good mood because of his successful business trip, the merchant goes home and merrily beds his wife.

But when he asks for still more sex after a night of love-making, she replies, "Ynough!" (VII. 380), clearly replying to her husband's earlier remark, before his trip, about leaving her "enough" money. Suddenly reminded of his accounts, the merchant chides his wife for not having told him of the monk's repayment. But she denies the monk's story, saying that she has already spent the money, thinking it was a present from her husband to her. Besides, she adds, you have other debtors who are more in arrears than myself,

> For I wol paye yow wel and redily
> *Fro day to day*, and if so be I faille,
> I am youre wyf; score it upon my taille.
>
> (VII. 414-16, my emphasis)

In this ultimate equation of marriage, sex, and business, the Shipman's Tale improves upon even Alison of Bath's very liberal interpretation of the marriage debt, not least of all by innovatively adding an installment payment plan, as suggested by the wife's promise to pay back her husband "from day to day". Time, money, and sex here become virtually synonymous. In response to his wife's appeals, the merchant accommodatingly "forgives" her (VII. 425), where this word has a double sense, financial and religious, although in this denouement both mercantile and moral values are trumped by sex.

* * *

As already suggested, the Shipman's Tale correlates merchant's time and Church's time with secular and sacred space. The main action of the tale takes place in three distinct parts of the merchant's house: counting house, garden, and bedroom. Each of these spaces is associated with a different sort of production: (1) commercial, (2) natural or agricultural, and (3) sexual or reproductive. In addition, the garden has religious overtones as a typological space that could represent temptation, redemption, or both.

All three domestic spaces are settings for specific personal transactions as well. The merchant and his wife speak through the counting-house door; the monk and the wife converse in the garden; but the bedroom does double-duty, since there the wife has sex with *both* her husband and the monk. The tale thus involves a violation or confusion of domestic space, where the values of the bedroom and the counting house become confused, and the garden – with its tempter in the form of a monk – loses its redemptive possibilities. Or instead we might say that the tale simply makes *explicit* and then pursues to one possible logical conclusion the monetary basis of marriage in the Middle Ages, the fact that the marriage debt had been turned from a spiritual metaphor into an economic reality.

Chaucer's satire of the rising middle class, its growing worldliness, and even the Church's attraction to merchant's time, space, and values, has an analogue in the history of the well-known Quinten Massys portrait (c. 1500), "The Banker and his Wife" (sometimes entitled "The Moneychanger and his Wife"). In this portrait, the woman is holding a prayerbook, which clearly embodies sacred things and religious devotion and provides a spiritual counterpoint to the worldly values represented by her husband's balance, coins, and other symbols of the secular life and the world of business.

In some later copies of this painting, however, another artist replaced the prayerbook with *an account book*, thus turning a religious symbol into a secular one, and turning the couple into an embodiment of a wholly secular life. "The religious component of the picture has disappeared entirely", as monetary reckoning replaces moral reckoning (Silver 1984: 212). Painted about a century after Chaucer wrote the Shipman's Tale, this portrait suggests the definite – if hardly inevitable – way in which merchant's time, space, and values triumphed over those of the Church during the late Middle Ages, and the growing awareness among merchants that the value of time, whatever its ultimate relation to eternity, could be measured in more worldly and strictly economic terms.

References

Benson, Larry D. (ed.)
  1987   *The Riverside Chaucer*. 3d ed. Boston: Houghton Mifflin.
Dohrn-van Rossum, Gerhard
  1992   *History of the Hour: Clocks and Modern Temporal Orders*. Trans. Thomas Dunlap. Chicago: The University of Chicago Press, 1996.
Langland, William.
  1886 [1979] *The Vision of William concerning Piers the Plowman in Three Parallel Texts, together with Richard the Redeless*. Ed. Walter W. Skeat. 2 vols. Oxford: Oxford University Press, 1886. Rpt. 1979. Trans. J. F. Goodridge. *Piers the Ploughman*. Harmondsworth: Penguin, 1959. Rpt. 1982.
Le Goff, Jacques
  1980   "Merchant's Time and Church's Time in the Middle Ages". Trans. Arthur Goldhammer. (Orig., "Au Moyen Âge: Temps de l'Église et temps du marchand", 1960). In *Time, Work, and Culture in the Middle Ages*, translated by Arthur Goldhammer. Chicago: The University of Chicago Press, Pp. 29-42, 289-93.
Middle English Dictionary
  1952-2001 Ed. Hans Kurath, Sherman M. Kuhn, Robert E. Lewis. Ann Arbor: University of Michigan Press.
The New Oxford Annotated Bible with the Apocrypha
  1977   Ed. Herbert G. May and Bruce M. Metzger. New York: Oxford University Press.
The Oxford English Dictionary
  1989   2nd ed. Ed. J. A. Simpson and E. S. C. Weiner. 20 vols. Oxford: Oxford University Press. Online version, 1992.
Silver, Larry
  1984   *The Paintings of Quinten Massys with Catalogue Raisonné*. Montclair, N.J.: Allanheld & Schram.

Hagiography

Ansgar, Pragmatic Visionary

George Hardin Brown, Stanford University

H. Ansgar (*heiliger Ansgar*) and H. Ansgar (Henry Ansgar) share more than a name. Our honorand, whom I have long cherished as a friend and eminent medievalist, embodies many of the splendid qualities of his namesake, St. Ansgar (Anskar, Anscharius), the ninth century Apostle to Scandinavia.[1] Like Andy, the monastic missionary bishop was highly intelligent, a persistent idealist and pragmatic realist, a quietly determined and wise administrator, a practiced and principled politician, and a dedicated teacher of both students and the public (*magister scolae et doctor populi*, Rimbert 1884: 26). Like Andy, Ansgar was a bookman: he loved books, read and copied books, wrote books, used books in his classroom and on his missions, always carried books with him, collected books and formed libraries, and rescued books from marauders. Charismatic and visionary, he transformed his dreams into an active apostolate (Wood 2001: 127-129; Dutton 1994: 51-54; Berschin 1986: 343; Lammers 1965: 541-558). A primary goal in all his missionary work was education of the young. He influenced many people's lives, as Andy has done is his years as scholar, professor, and Director of the Center for medieval and Renaissance Studies at UCLA.

St. Ansgar was blessed in his biographer, St. Rimbert, who succeeded him as archbishop of Hamburg-Bremen and who modeled his own episcopate and apostolate on Ansgar (Wood 2001: 132-135).[2] Rimbert included in his biography a number of Ansgar's own accounts and reports. With a Latin style admirably direct and readable if distinctly postclassical, Rimbert presents his hero's career in a fascinating and carefully structured historical account that he intersperses with visionary narrative (*huic operi interserere delegimus*, Rimbert 1884: 20). It is likely, as Ian Wood has affirmed, that an account of the history of the missionary legation that Ansgar provided late in life to Louis the German to support the unification of the dioceses of Hamburg and Bremen served as a factual and accurate basis for Rimbert's *vita Anskarii*; to it Rimbert added the visionary material (Rimbert 1884: ch. 41; Wood 2001:126). Though himself strongly influenced by Ansgar's visionary reports, as a hagiographer Rimbert was troubled that his subject despite all his visions was not renowned for miracles and wonders. Ansgar's

---

1   My references to the Latin edition of the *Vita Anskarii* will be to that by Waitz 1884, to the English translation, to that by Robinson 1921, except where indicated otherwise.

2   While intending no disrespect for the saints, I shall in this essay dispense with the title "Saint" for brevity's sake and to avoid an implied hagiographic stance. I have also consulted the excellent introduction and facing-page German translation of Ansgar's biography by Werner Trillmich, used by Wood.

life by Rimbert, like those of Ansgar's abbots Adalhard and Wala by Paschasius Radbertus, is devoid of thaumaturgy (Ganz 1990: 103-120). Like Adalhard and Wala, Ansgar was exemplary because of his life of dedicated service, not because of posthumous miracles. Rimbert also had to deal with the fact that Ansgar's greatest visionary revelation, namely that he would suffer martyrdom, remained troublingly unfulfilled. Although Ansgar aided the ill, he lay no claim to the miraculous. Instead, he remarked to Rimbert, "Were I worthy of such favor from my God, I would ask that he would grant to me this one miracle, that by his grace he would make of me a good man" (Rimbert 1921: 121). Andy too may seem to have worked miracles as Director of the Center and as a prolific scholar, but he too, I dare say, would first wish to be known as "a good man". That he is such a man of dedicated service, we are witnesses.

When Ansgar was born in Picardy in 801, Charlemagne was reigning as emperor; when Ansgar died in 865, he had benefited from the patronage of Charles's son Louis the Pious (d. 840), and suffered under the division of the empire by Louis's sons. After the treaty of Verdun in 843, when Ansgar was fully engaged in his work, the empire was divided into three parts by Louis's sons, Charles the Bald, Louis the German, and Lothar. During their reigns the political and religious situations frequently changed, and Ansgar had to make the best of the unstable situation. He experienced notable setbacks also because the areas where he missionized were repeatedly overrun by warring factions, often by pagan chiefs. How did this monk survive the nasty maneuverings of these squabbling kings and the frequent disappointments in the missionary field? After a glance at his training, let us trace his career, highlighting some of its major points.

At the tender age of five, shortly after the death of his mother, Ansgar was presented as an oblate to the monastery of Corbie (*Corbeia*). Although in the high Middle Ages monasteries no longer received oblates at such an early age, during the early Middle Ages children from age five to nine were regularly donated by their parents or relatives as offerings to serve God in monastic life (Quinn 1989: xv, 106). The Venerable Bede, who was himself given by his relatives as an oblate at age seven to the monastery of Wearmouth-Jarrow, expressed one prevalent view that an early formation in the religious life allowed youth to live more uncorrupted by the world than those who entered later (Bede 1983: 112-113) Ansgar's contemporary, the Carolingian encyclopedist Rabanus Maurus, an oblate at age nine, wrote a celebrated treatise defending the practice (*Liber de oblatione puerorum contra eos qui repugnant institutis beati Patri Benedicti*. PL 57.419-40; Quinn 1989: 108-109; 139).

Ansgar was fortunate to have begun his monastic life at the abbey celebrated for its powerful prelates, its fine school, and great library. A royal foundation near Amiens, Corbie had been founded by Balthild and her son Chlothar III between 657 and 661. Balthild had requested Abbot Waldebert of Luxeuil to provide the first abbot, Theudefrid, who came accompanied by a great number of monks. The original rule, a *regula mixta*, combined the rules of Benedict and Columbanus, but after the Carolingian reforms of Benedict of Aniane, Corbie became, like the other monasteries of the empire, Benedictine. During the Carolingian period Charlemagne's cousins, Adalhard and Wala, were abbots of Corbie, often opposing royal policies. Even more important to the history of medieval culture as well as to Ansgar's education was Corbie's eminence as scriptorium and library. It was here under Maurdramnus (abbot 771-781) that Caroline minuscule, which Italian humanists thought classical roman, developed. More manuscripts have survived from that library than from any other early monastery (Ganz 1990; Héliot 1957).[3]

Rimbert suggests that as a child Ansgar was not particularly fervent, but in a vision the Blessed Mother told him that if he wanted to be reunited with his mother he had to reform his life. That and the death of Charlemagne in 814 brought about a conversion in him (Rimbert 1884, 1921: ch. 2). Since the abbey church was dedicated to St. Peter and a separate building housed a chapel honoring St. John the Baptist, it is not surprising that Saints Peter and John appeared to him on the night of the Feast of Pentecost in another dream that proved momentous for his future career. After undergoing a purgation that in the dream lasted three tortuous days, he was escorted to the heaven of the Book of Revelation. There in the midst of the saints the divine majesty said to him, "Vade, et martyrio coronatus ad me reverteris" ["Go and return to me crowned with martyrdom"] (Rimbert 1884: 23; 1921: 33). This mandate, though never fulfilled, proved a major motive for Ansgar's life, and was at least indicative of a force running contrary to monastic stability, as we shall see.

Having become an exemplary monk with his training completed, Ansgar was appointed *magister* not only of the internal community but also of externs, the laity. The latter he taught outside the monastery in order to preserve the monastic rule of cloister, but it is significant in the light of his vision of Saints Peter and John that on his way to and from class he stopped to pray in the chapel of the Baptist (Héliot 1957: 27).

In 823 Ansgar was among those delegated to establish a sister foundation at Corvey on the Weser (*Nova Corveia*), where for a time he continued the cenobitic life in peace, studying, teaching, and writing. However, an event occurred which,

---

3   As David Ganz notes, "The Maurdramnus minuscule is the earliest datable example of Caroline minuscule and is an excellent and superbly balanced script. Over sixty manuscripts in this script survive. They include copies of elaborate multivolume works, and a wide range of patristic texts, together with collections of grammatical treatises which trained monks in how to read Latin. Also present are works by court theologians; this testifies to the importance of Adalhard's abbacy, and the fruits of his friendship with Paul the Deacon and Alcuin. Other texts in Murdramnus script are copies of volumes in Charlemagne's court library" (Ganz 1990: 12). Most of the manuscripts are now housed in the Bibliothèque nationale in Paris and the Russian National Library in St. Petersburg.

though partially prepared for by his visions, utterly changed his life. In the summer of 826 the Danish petty king (Old Norse *smákonungur*, German *Teilkönig*) Harald Klak was living in exile in Louis the Pious's court, seeking the emperor's aid in overthrowing his rivals (Rimbert 1884: cap. 6; Adam 1977: 21-22; Ermoldus 1884: lib. IV). According to Rimbert, Louis persuaded Harald "to accept the Christian faith because there would then be a more intimate friendship between them, and a Christian people would more readily come to the aid of his friends if both were worshippers of the same God" (Rimbert 1921: 38). It is clear that Louis was following his father Charlemagne's policy of uniting the nations within the Church for the political purpose of integrating them under his imperial authority, and Harald in need of imperial support opted for Christianity. Louis sought from the assembled clerics a missionary to accompany Harald and his band. Greeted with an underwhelming response from the clergy out of fear of the Northmen, Louis was pleased that Abbot Wala finally "stood forth and said to the emperor that he knew a monk in his monastery who burned with zeal for true religion and was eager to endure suffering for the name of God" (Rimbert 1921: 39-40). Ansgar, fully aware of the Realpolitik by his official position in a royal abbey under prince-abbots, nonetheless eagerly accepted the invitation, with the blessing of Abbot Wala, to work for the conversion of the Danes.

We must stop to query what first appears a totally laudatory act on Ansgar's part but then on reflection involves at least a repudiation of a monastic vow. By leaving the monastery to enter the world as a missionary, Ansgar, a professed Benedictine, was violating the Benedictine Rule of stability, *stabilitas loci*, a solemn vow.[4] The fact that his abbot, Wala, volunteered Ansgar as a candidate for the mission, permitted another monk, Autbert, an officer in the community from the nobility and a friend of Ansgar, to accompany him, and gave his blessing on the enterprise, only complicates the issue for both subjects and superior. This is not a pseudo-problem fabricated from hindsight, since in the words of the Benedictine professor of Canon Law, Bernard Austin Sause, the vow of stability "is monasticism's identifying feature" (*New Catholic Encyclopedia* 1967: 9.1021; Haas 1985). In later Canon Law religious superiors would be given the power to allow "secularizartion" (after 1918 called "exclaustration" *New Catholic Encyclopedia* 5.762-3) of a monk for a just cause, but that does not address the central issue. The essence of monasticism is retreat from the world; the essence of the missionary episcopate is apostolate in the world. So, after vowing to God to remain in the cloister, how could Ansgar be justified in leaving it even for a good cause?

---

4   On St. Benedict's insistence on *stabilitas loci*, see Regula Benedicti 4.78, 58.17 and the explanation in *RB 1980*, 463-65.

Ansgar's biographer is clearly aware that this is a genuine problem and attempts to deal with it in the chapter preceding the narrative of Ansgar and Autbert's commissioning. There he tries to explain "qua occasione a loco stabilitatis suae huc secesserit, et cum apud vos Deo oblatus sit ibique oboedientiam promiserit, quo instinctu cuiusque rei dispositione ad has partes emigraverat atque ad episcopatus officium apud nos sublimatus sit" ["for what motive he left from the position of stability, and since he had offered himself to God in your midst and there promised obedience, by what impulse and circumstance he was elevated to the office of bishop among us" (Rimbert 1884: 26, my translation). Adam of Bremen resolves the issue by an apt aphorism, saying that Ansgar was "foris apostolus, intus monachus" ["on the outside an apostle, on the inside a monk"] (Adam 1917: 37). The real justification for Ansgar's leaving the cloister, besides his own visions and conscience, is precedent. And of course the precedents were numerous and unassailable.

Pope St. Gregory the Great, himself a monk, had been sent on diplomatic duty to Constantinople by Pope Pelagius II, and he himself became bishop of Rome and Head of the Church despite his desire to return to solitary life. However, for Gregory "the monk is bound to God by the 'chain' which is Christ; he no longer needs the iron chain binding him to his home" (Straw 1988: 76). Furthermore, although Gregory wrote the earliest biography of St. Benedict (Gregory 1967), he was not a Benedictine nor did he subscribe to the Benedictine rule of stability. He saw monks as available and suitable for every type of work in the Church. By preferring monks over clerics in his appointments, he attempted to purify the Church from secular corruption (Straw 1988: 5). For the development of monastic missions in northern Europe the powerful impetus was Gregory's sending Augustine, prior of Gregory's own monastery of St. Andrew, with his monastic companions in 597 to convert the Anglo-Saxons.

Henceforth, the tradition was established in Anglo-Saxon England that most prelates, for example, Paulinus and Chad, were monastic, and Bishop Wilfrid, who for a time missionized both on the Continent and England, was responsible for constituting the Benedictine Rule as official in his diocese. The Irish foundations at Iona and Lindisfarne likewise appointed monks as missionary bishops, among whom most famous were the Irishman Aidan and the Anglo-Saxon Cuthbert. Irish monastic missionaries precede the Anglo-Saxon monks on the Continent, and Ansgar's own monastery of Corbie was founded, as we have noted above, by monks form the Irish foundation of Luxeuil. However, the direct lineage of monastic bishops can be most directly traced to the Anglo-Saxon missions in Francia. The monk Ecgberht, who had lived in Ireland and ardently desired the conversion of the Germanic peoples he considered cousins of the English, sent a number of pupils, including Wihtberht, Willibrord, and Swithbert and the two Hewalds. The Northumbrian Willibrord was joined by the West Saxon Boniface (Wynfrith), the most famous of all the Anglo-Saxon missionaries. Boniface in turn drew a number of Englishmen, such as Wynnebald, abbot of Heidenheim, and Willibald, bishop of Eichstätt. They were followed by two Northumbrians, Leofwine (Lebuin) and Willehad. The latter preceded Ansgar himself as bishop of Bremen (787-9) (Lapidge, *Blackwell Encyclopaedia* 1999: 318-19;Wood, *Missionary Life* 2001: part 2).[5] The spiritual bond between the Northumbrian Willehad and his Continental successor Ansgar is especially manifest by the fact that Ansgar while archbishop of Hamburg-Bremen wrote *The Miracles of St. Willehad* (*Acta Sanctorum* 1910: 847-851).[6] With such precedents and with such an urgent call to proselytize the peoples of the North, Ansgar seemed justifiably and rightfully dispensed from the vow of monastic stability in order to dedicate himself as a second Paul to the Gentiles. Many another religious has been dispensed from a vow taken at one point with full assent but voided at another for just cause.

Having received his apostolic commission, Ansgar embarked on a courageous and frequently thwarted missionary career. Ansgar accompanied Harald Klak on his return to Denmark. Rather, Harald accompanied Ansgar. Although Louis had provided Ansgar and Autbert with "ministerialia ecclesiastica" for the journey, including writing cases (*scrinia*), tents, and other equipment, Harald provided nothing. Arriving in Cologne, the local prelate, Bishop Hadebald, "had compassion on their needs and presented them with a good boat in which they might place their possessions and in which there were two cabins" (Rimbert 1921: 43). Harald liked the accommodations and took over one of the cabins for himself. On arrival in Denmark Ansgar set to work with Autbert among the natives and "searched for boys whom they might endeavor to educate for the service of God" (Rimbert 1921: 44). Just as Pope Gregory the Great had purchased English slave boys in order to train them in the Christian faith, and Boniface and Lull had similarly done in their mission areas, so Ansgar repeatedly did likewise in each of his missions. Although conversion was pitched primarily to the local ruler and his society, education of the young was the hope of the future. However, after two years' joint industry, Ansgar's noble companion Autbert fall ill and, after returning to Corvey, died (Rimbert 1884: ch, 8). Then the mission itself died. For in 827 Harald Klak was driven out of Denmark again, and pagan rule resumed (Kurze 1895: 173).

---

5   On Ansgar's authorial relationship to Willehad, see below, p. 10.
6   Ansgar names himself as author in the preface to the *Virtutes et Miracula S Willehadi* in, *Acta Sanctorum*, Novembris, t. 3, pp 847-851; MGH Scriptores 2, 384-390; see *Lexikon für Theologie und Kirche*, I. 716; Berschin: (1991: 341). The Life of St. Willehad, *Vita S. Willehadi*, MGH SS II, 379-84, written a decade earlier (850) was in the nineteenth century falsely ascribed to him. Ansgar, we are told by Rimbert, also composed a collection of prayers, called *Pigmenta*; but a work by that name that was ascribed to him also in the nineteenth century is not his. See Berschin 1986: 349-50.

This melancholy event in Ansgar's career exemplifies the Achilles' heel of the early medieval conversion procedure. Ever since Gregory the Great and the Augustinian mission to England at the end of the sixth century, missionaries put most of their effort into converting the local ruler and his queen, with the warranted surmise that, with the ruler and his court converted, the people would follow suit, at least eventually. However, when the newly converted ruler was either defeated in battle, exiled, killed, or turned apostate, the whole Christian enterprise collapsed. Bede's *Ecclesiastical History* is replete with examples for England. There are many examples from the Continent as well, but none more poignant than Ansgar's. In his case, every time he embarked on a new missionary effort either in Denmark or Sweden, a Viking attack or an internecine struggle disposed of his sympathetic host, and the country and people then reverted to paganism (Andersson 1985: 67-70; Wood 1987: 58-59).

Undiscouraged, Ansgar in 829 once again generously answered the call to serve as a missionary in Scandinavia, this time in response to a Swedish legation at Louis's court, telling him that "there were many belonging to their nation who desired to embrace the Christian religion, and that their king so far favored this suggestion that he would permit God's priests to reside there" (Rimbert 1921: 45). As a confirmation of his calling, Ansgar received another dream vision, in which the Lord told him, "Go, and declare the word of God to the Swedes" (Rimbert 1921: 46). As a substitute for the deceased Autbert, the prior Witmar served as his companion and fellow-laborer. On their journey north they fell among pirates, who robbed Ansgar and his entourage of everything, including some forty precious books. As a result, "some were disposed to turn and go back, but no argument could divert God's servant from the journey" (Rimbert 1921: 48). Having reached Birka on Lake Mäleren, the port of Sigtuna and a great trading center, they worked among the Christian captives and, with the help of Herigar, a Christian counselor to the king, worked among the natives for six months before returning to report to Louis.

Ansgar was then appointed to the new see of Hamburg, and was given Torhout in Flanders as a support station and retreat. He traveled to Rome to receive the pallium of an archbishop, and the pope charged him with the mission to the Danes, Swedes, and also Slavs, a task he was to share with Ebo, archbishop of Rheims, who sent his nephew Gauzbert to missionize Sweden (Rimbert 1884, 1921: chs.11-14). While bishop of Hamburg Ansgar redeemed boys from captivity; some he trained personally and others he had trained for God's service at Torhout (Rimbert 1884, 1921: ch. 15). Later, when the empire was divided among Louis' three sons, Ansgar lost the economic and spiritual supply station of Torhout. He also lost the boys whom he had sent to be Christianized and formed for the apostolate. Ansgar could do nothing to prevent Charles the Bald from handing over Torhout to a certain Raginar (Rimbert 1884, cap. 21). However, Ansgar did not let this injury pass without revealing his chagrin.

In a vision which he had soon afterwards, he appeared to have come to a certain house and to have found there King Charles and Raginar. It seemed to him that he reproached them in regard to these boys and said that he had arranged to train them for the service of Almighty God and not to act as servants to Raginar. When he said this, it seemed to him that Raginar lifted his foot and kicked his mouth, and when this happened he thought that the Lord Jesus Christ stood by him and said to the king and to Raginar, "To whom does this man whom ye treat so shamefully belong? Know that he has a Master and because of this you will not go unpunished". When he said this they were terrified and affrighted, whereupon the bishop awoke. The divine vengeance which overtook Raginar showed how true was the revelation. For a little later he incurred the displeasure of the king and lost the monastery and everything that he had received from the king, nor did he ever regain his former favor.

(Rimbert 1921: ch. 26)

Soon even greater setbacks to Ansgar's apostolate occurred. In 845 Viking pirates attacked and sacked Hamburg and his residence. Ansgar only had time to collect a few sacred relics before escaping without even a cloak. His church and his entire library, including a glorious bible that the emperor had given him, were consumed by flames. "But by none of these things was our holy father distressed". He simply repeated the words of Job, "the Lord gave, and the Lord has taken away" (Job 1.21; Rimbert 1921: 58). With Hamburg in ruins, Ansgar was appointed to the see of Bremen in 847, making him missionary archbishop of Hamburg and bishop of Bremen, It was not just the Vikings and the secular powers that gave him grief. The archbishop of Cologne, Gunthar, who claimed Bremen as a suffragan, challenged Ansgar's episcopal plurality. Nonetheless, the two dioceses were amalgamated, with Pope Nicholas I settling the dispute definitively in Ansgar's favor in 864 (Rimbert 1884, 1921: ch. 23).

Undeterred by the pagan onslaughts, and inspired by another powerful vision, Ansgar resumed missionary work in Denmark (Rimbert 1884, 1921: ch. 25). He formed a good relationship with King Horic I, only to experience another disastrous setback when the king was killed in 854. During the civil war the mission of course suffered. But the next ruler to emerge, Horic II, also formed good relations with Ansgar, with the result that a mission and church was founded at Ribe (Rimbert 1884, 1921: ch. 33). With the constant Viking raiding and internecine struggles, Ansgar and his missions were never totally at peace, but from his station in Bremen he continued to travel and work even as old age weakened his efforts.

As bishop of Bremen Ansgar was not only a preacher but also a scholar. Rimbert commented, "Furthermore, the large manuscripts that are with us and which were copied out and marked by his own hand, witness to his zeal and his desire to intensify his devotion and love to God" (Rimbert 1921: 109-110). One of the books he composed was the little work mentioned earlier, *Virtutes et Miracula Sanctri Willehadi*. By recording the spate of miracles done for poor and simple women at his predecessor's tomb, Ansgar not only associated himself with the founding monastic bishop but also with his flock who, like him, were constantly suffering the threat of pagan destruction. Hamburg had been ravaged in 845 but Bremen too was attacked in 858. Like the apostle Paul, Ansgar for himself was well able to endure persecution and even the obliteration of many of his missionary efforts, but he was greatly concerned for his demoralized Christian community and wished by relating God's providential care for humble and needy women to call attention to his continued presence in their midst (Wood 2001: 132).

Ansgar died in 865. Despite all the vicissitudes and setbacks of his career and of his missions, he emerged as victor. In his youth he had been trained by royal politicians as well as learned churchmen, Adalhard and Wala; he had earned respect as teacher and tutor; he was prepared to work with petty kings and their warring tribes even while other clerics looked upon the whole Scandinavian enterprise as hopeless and too dangerous. With longsuffering and forbearance, he maintained his honor and dedication. In the face of enormous odds and repeated obliteration of his missions in Scandinavia and the destruction of his church, library, and residence in his episcopal city, he soldiered on. He courageously and realistically faced every challenge; his visions provided him with courage and purpose. Others would have given in to disappointment and defeat at the apostolic reversals he repeatedly encountered, but throughout his career he remained squarely realistic and truly idealistic. His only disappointment was that he had not died a martyr. However, Rimbert insisted in his biography, that Ansgar really was one, because a martyr is a "witness", and there could prove no better witness to Christ and his gospel than the assiduous discipleship Ansgar so ardently lived (Rimbert 1884, 1921: ch. 42) This dedicated monk well deserved the title "Apostle to the Scandinavians". He also merits honor as the patron and namesake of Henry Ansgar Kelly, whose own generous nature and assiduous career we now celebrate.

References

(1910) *Acta Sanctorum*. Novembris, Tomus Tertius. Bruxelles, Socios Bollandianos.

(1967) *New Catholic Encyclopedia*. New York, McGraw-Hill.

(1993) *Lexikon für Theologie und Kirche*. Freiburg im Breisgau, Herder.

(1844) *Patrologiæ cursus completus [PL, Series Latina]*. Ed. J-P. Migne. Paris, J-P. Migne.

(1981) *RB 1980: the Rule of St. Benedict in Latin and English with Notes*. Ed. Timothy Fry. Collegeville, Minn., Liturgical Press.

Adam of Bremen
  1959 *History of the Archbishops of Hamburg-Bremen*. Trans. Francis J. Tschan. New York, Columbia University Press.

Adam von Bremen
1917 *Hamburgische Kirchengeschichte.* Ed. B. Schmeidler. 3rd ed. Hannover, Hahn.

Andersson, T.M.
1985 "Heathen Sacrifice in Beowulf and Rimbert's Life of Ansgar". *Medievalia et Humanistica: Studies in Medieval and Renaissance Culture* 13: 65-74.

Bede
1969 *Bede's Ecclesiastical history of the English People.* Ed. Bertram Colgrave and R.A.B. Mynors. Oxford, Clarendon Press.
1983 *In Tobiam; In Proverbia; In Cantica Canticorum.* Corpus Christianorum Series Latina 119B. Ed. David Hurst. Turnholt, Brepols.

Berschin, W.
1986, 1991 *Biographie und Epochenstil im lateinischen Mittelalter.* Vol. 3. Stuttgart, A. Hiersemann.

Dutton, P.E.
1994 *The Politics of Dreaming in the Carolingian Empire.* Lincoln, University of Nebraska Press.

Ermoldus
1884 *In Honorem Hludiwici Libri IV.* Monumenta Germaniae Historica. Poetae Latini Aevi Carolini. Ed. E. Duemmler. Berlin, Weidmann. 2: 4-79.

Ganz, D.
1990 *Corbie in the Carolingian Renaissance.* Sigmaringen, Thorbecke.

Gregory the Great, Pope
1967 *The Dialogues of Gregory the Great. Book Two: Saint Benedict.* Trans. Myra L. Uhlfeder. Indianapolis, Bobbs-Merrill

Haas, W.
1985 "Foris apostolus – intus monachus. Ansgar als Mönch und 'Apostel des Nordens'". *Journal of Medieval History* 11(1): 1-30.

Héliot, P.M.L.
1957 *L'abbaye de Corbie, ses églises et ses bâtiments.* Louvain, Bureaux de la Revue Bibliothèque de l'Université.

Kurze, Friedrich (ed.)
1895 *Annales Regni Francorum.* Monumenta Germaniae Historica, Scriptores, In Usum Scholarum 6. Hannover, Hahn.

Lammers, W.
1965 "Ansgar, Visonäre Erlebnisformen und Missionsauftrag". *Speculum Historiale. Geschichte im Spiegel von Geschichtsschreibung und Geschichtsdeutung.* Ed. C. Bauer, L. Boehm and M. Müller. Freiburg, München, Alber: 541-558.

Lapidge, Michael (ed.)
1999 *The Blackwell Encyclopaedia of Anglo-Saxon England.* Oxford; Malden, Mass., Blackwell.

Quinn, Patricia A.
1989   *Better Than the Sons of Kings: Boys and Monks in the Early Middle Ages.* New York, P. Lang.
Rimbert
1856   *Leben der Erzbischöfe Anskar und Rimbert.* Trans. J. C. M. Laurent Berlin, W. Besser (F. Duncker).
Vita Anskarii. Ed. G. Waitz. Monumenta Germaniae Historica. Scriptores Rerum Germanicarum. Hannover, Hahn.
1921   *Anskar, the Apostle of the North. 801-865.* [London], The Society for the Propagation of the Gospel in Foreign Parts. Ed. and trans. Charles Henry Robinson.
Straw, C.E.
1988   *Gregory the Great: Perfection in Imperfection.* Berkeley, University of California Press.
Trillmich, Werner (ed. and trans)
1961   *Quellen des 9. und 11. Jahrhunderts zur Geschichte der hamburgischen Kirche und des Reiches.* Darmstadt, Wissenschaftliche Buchgesellschaft.
Wood, Ian N.
1987   *"Christians and Pagans in Ninth-Century Scandinavia". The Christianization of Scandinavia: Report of a Symposium Held at Kungälv, Sweden 4-9 August 1985.* Ed. Birgit Sawyer, P. H. Sawyer, Ian Wood. Alingsås, Sweden, Viktoria Bokförlag. 36-67.
2001   *The Missionary Life: Saints and the Evangelisation of Europe, 400-1050.* Harlow, England; New York, Longman.

Uncertain Peregrinations of the Living and the Dead: Writing (Hagiography) as Translating (Relics) in Osbern Bokenham's Legend of St. Margaret

Margaret Bridges, University of Bern

Latinitas, raptus, travelling writers, travelling saints (dead or alive); what does violence done to the object of one's veneration have to do with displacement of foot and hand, with hagiography and with translation from Latin into the vernacular? How does the trope of the writer as traveller (through Italy) coincide with the travels of the dead saint's relics (through Italy)? These questions are rhetorical only insofar as they signal that the present study situates itself at a crossroads where many of the scholarly and personal preoccupations of our honoree and friend intersect. I consider myself fortunate indeed that our peregrinations allowed us to travel some of the way together, as the result of a fortuitous meeting at a place where scholars' paths converge. Although I do not wish to labour the parallel between the community of scholars and the communion of saints, I cannot help wondering what a meeting between St. Ansgar (whose peripatetic career led him from Poitiers, via Hamburg and Bremen to pre-conversion Denmark and Sweden) and the "oriental" St. Margaret (whose relics could be described as widely travelled) might have yielded, had that been allowed to take place. But that was not to be: St. Ansgar lived at a time when relics were just beginning to be transferred as part of the processes of Christianization of Northern Europe and the Franks' progressive political domination of the West[1] whereas the cult of St. Margaret, which allowed her relics to circulate widely, is not evidenced in the West before the ninth century. Although the fifteenth-century Austin friar whose work I shall be considering was – by his own account – the author of a number of (lost) lives of male saints, Henry Ansgar's namesake seems not to have been among them.[2] So I turn to a legendary of female saints, specifically that of my own namesake, for my reflections on travel, translation and hagiography. If these reflections single out the figure of St. Margaret, it is essentially because the posthumous travels of other saints in this legendary are rudimentary and fail to exploit to the same degree the ambivalence inherent in the concept of translation.

---

1 Geary 1994: 167.
2 The first chapter of his *Mappula Angliae* refers to a number of English saints whose lives Bokenham claims to have "compiled" from the *Legenda aurea* "and of other famous leg-endes". He specifically names Chad, Felix, Edward and Oswald (quoted in Serjeantson 1939: xvii).

In spite of the dedication of a handful of scholars, from the late nineteenth-century Carl Horstmann to "our own" Sheila Delany[3], we "know" little more of Osbern Bokenham, whose extant works include a *Mappula Angliae* and a compilation of female saints' lives generally referred to as the *Legendys of Hooly Wummen*[4], than we can gauge from his self-representation in these two works. Both of these figure the author as a translator. To the former work – a translation (dated roughly 1440) of the "Descriptio Britanniae" with which Ranulph Higden had prefaced that part of his *Polychronicon* dealing with the history of Great Britain[5] – Bokenham added "a short epiloge excusatorie of the translatours rudnesse". His apology for using the "englyssh tounnge" is not just grounded in the assertion of the inferior eloquence and the "natyff rudnesse of my modur-tounnge" – inscribing the translator's project in the traditional affirmation of the superiority of Latin over the vernacular language (as well as in the abjection of the mother!) – but extends to a representation of himself as an inveterate native-language user who is unable to escape the "infected and cankyred" constraints of the linguistic environment in which he was brought up from childhood:

> ... alle-be-hit that this seyde tretis be not so convenyently nor so eloquently expressid & spokyn yn englyssh tounnge as the excellence of the auctours latyn stile requirithe. For, certenly, the natyff rudnesse of my modur-tounnge hathe so infectyd & cankeryd my speche & my language wyt the barbarisme of the soyle the wych I haue be fostryd & brought forthe yn of youthe, that y neyther may ner can other thynge vttryn ne shewyne then hit hathe been vsyd & acustomyd to, [...] syche savour as the newe shelle takithe, when hit is eldder hit kepythe.
>
> (the introduction to Mary Serjeantson's edition of the *Legendys of Hooly Wummen* , Serjeantson 1939: xvi).[6]

To this representation of the translator as old and linguistically impaired, Bokenham adds a categorical refusal to occupy the position of author:

---

3   Delany (1992: xiv-xvi) mentions two other works tentatively associated with Bokenham, one of them a translation of Claudianus's *De Consulatu Stilichonis*, the other a "Dialogue at the Grave" recounting the genealogy of Joan of Acre. Bokenham scholarship today owes a great deal to Delany's 1992 translation of the *Legendys* and her exciting *Impolitic Bodies* (1998); thanks to these two works, Bokenham's hagiography (whether or not it is read against Chaucer's *Legend of Good Women*, as Delany suggests) has been relocated (or translated) from its earlier philological context to the critical context afforded by the study of the gendered body politic.

4   The title by which this work is referred to is derived from lines 5038-5040, in which Bokenham listed the lives he had already written by the time he was working on his prologue to the life of Mary Magdalen.

5   The chapter headings of Higden and his anonymous fifteenth-century translator refer to "Great Britain otherwise called England," an equivocation not retained by John of Trevisa, whose (Latin!) heading refers to Britannia only (Higden 1865: 2-3).

6   Middle English thorn has been transcribed throughout this paper as th.

I of no thynge seyde there-yn chalenge ne desire to be holdyn neythur Auctour ne asser-
tour, ne wylle aske no more but to be holdyn oonly the pore compilatour & owte of
latyne in to ynglyssh the rude & symple translatour.

(Serjeantson 1939: xvi-xvii)

Whether or not we consider Bokenham's stance to be a function of his "Chaucerian" identity[7], the denial of authority/authorship, which in Chaucer seems more
often than not to be an ethical question associated with the problematics of responsibility, is of course here also a renunciation of the ability to "master" the
discursive object. For in the course of its translation, the master discourse constituted by Higden's eloquent and excellent "long and laborious work" is reduced to
a "tretis", a diminutive excerpt[8], a "little map". As such, Bokenham perceives
translation as a process which involves excision, elision, and maltreat-
ment/impairment – to mention but some of the forms of violence done to the es-
teemed "original" or "master" text.

His self-styled "late" work – the *Legendys* are repeatedly represented by their
compiler/translator as the labour of an old bespectacled man close to death – adds
its own variations to the motif of translating as an exhausting and imperfectly controlled process which does violence to the object of its veneration. Leaving aside
for the present purpose the many other ways in which the text's hagiographical
subjects embody violence towards an author figure[9], and in which the author embodies himself in this text, I propose to focus on those passages in which Bokenham, through his extended use of the trope of the writer as traveller, foregrounds
the process of writing, or translating, as a physical activity subject to accident, and
of uncertain conclusion. Since the translation of the relics of one of the saints in
his compilation is evoked in surprizingly similar terms, this is also a reflexion on
the approximation of one mode of translation to another. It is an approximation
that is inherent in the polysemous word itself. In the most basic, etymological
sense of the term, the fourteenth-century Middle English loanword "transla-

---

7   As a reader of the prologue to *The Canterbury Tales* and of the *Legend of Good Women*,
    Bokenham would be exposed to Chaucer's problematization, even denial, of his authorial
    status.

8   I believe Bokenham is using the term "tretis" in sense (b) cited by the Middle English Dic-
    tionary, inasmuch as he is referring to a "chapter, section or portion, etc. of a work" (MED,
    1048).

9   As for instance when Christine tears a lump of flesh out of her flanks and tosses it into her
    father's face (lines 2467-2474) or when the same saint spits a piece of her mutilated tongue
    into the face of her tormentor, blinding him and taunting him verbally with her miraculously
    preserved – or perhaps "translated"- power of speech (lines 3070-3082). I would like to ac-
    knowledge an unpublished petit mémoire by Nadine Barreiro of the University of Geneva for
    her comparison of Christine to Philomela, who translated the experience of rape from the po-
    tentially oral medium of the spoken complaint (of which she was deprived when Tereus cut
    out her tongue) to the artistic medium of her tapestry (Barreiro 2002: 12 et passim).

cioun"[10] designated the transfer of persons and (discursive or non-discursive) objects from one site or context to another: what may appear to be a trope or metaphor – a figure for which coincidentally the Latin rhetorical term was "translatio" – is in fact merely a function of the word's ubiquity.[11] It is essentially with the interplay of two of the word's multiple meanings that I am here concerned: that which is proper to hagiography and that which is properly linguistic. Slipping in and out of story time, Bokenham refers to his hagiographical text as "translacyoun", and to himself as its "translatour", in nine of the thirteen Lives comprising his Legendary. Most of these references occur in brief colophons and consist of conventional requests for the saints' intercession; many of them implicitly (by mentioning the labour involved) or explicitly refer to the time of writing.[12] Five of the Lives refer to the (mostly uneventful) "translacyoun" of the saints' remains from their original place of burial, for the most part cursorily. Only two Lives provide contexts for both uses of the term: those of St. Faith (lines 3986-4020 and 4021-4034), and of St. Margaret, discussed below. Finally, it is only in the latter that both the author's self-representation as translator and the translation narrative itself are elaborated in terms which underscore the parallels between linguistic and hagiographic translation.[13]

In the case of the translation of a saint's relics, the term designates the process whereby the remains of a saint were transferred from their tomb (or shrine) to a new tomb or shrine; from the tenth century onwards the fixed stages of what became a ritual process – usually consisting of *inventio*, *adventus*, *elevatio* and *depositio* – were prescribed and described in *ordines* (Heinzelmann 1979: 43-62 et passim). The displacement of the relics might involve relatively close points of departure and of arrival (say within the same community, when architectural restoration and innovation led to the building

---

10   Displacing earlier vernacular transitive verbs of motion like "awendan" (used by Aelfric), the verb "translaten" is first found in *Cursor Mundi*, from the beginning of the fourteenth century; the noun seems not to be attested before the final quarter of the century.

11   For a succinct overview of the multiple, context-bound definitions of the Latin term "translatio", see Ashley and Sheingorn 1996: 30-31.

12   The colophon to the legend of St. Katherine mentions the "dayis fyue" it took to translate the work (line 7367). Implicit in the references to the labour involved in translating, is the question of authorial merit. The colophon to the Life of St. Agnes is especially interesting for the way Bokenham ascribes the laboriousness of translating from St. Ambrose's original to his "straunge" and "vnkouth" enditing (lines 4718-4720).

13   I do not include the legend of St. Katherine here, because when the body of St. Katherine is removed by angels from her place of execution to Mt Sinai, where it effects miracles, Bokenham does not use the term "translacyoun", but "take up" and "carry"; this miraculous translation – as it is referred to in line 7346 - is followed by a colophon in which the author of "this short translacyoun" appeals to the Saint on behalf of her two namesakes among his patrons (lines 7363-7376).

of new shrines and the consecration of new churches). It might also involve a geographical redistribution of the saint's remains across immense distances as part of the process that Peter Brown has described as "pilgrimage in reverse": instead of the people coming *ad sanctos*, the saints come to the people, or rather to the bishops and abbots who held (or wished to hold) ecclesiastical control over the sacred. Since "saints by their physical presence were a primary means of social integration, identity, protection and economic support for the communities in which they were found" (Geary 1994: 171) there was a great deal to be gained by possessing their relics, which were widely dispersed by three principal circulatory mechanisms, gift, theft, and commerce (Geary 1994: 194-214). Translation narratives, as opposed to the translations themselves, would often be part of the process of explaining how a saint came to be "present" in a particular location, however remote from the saint's original place of burial. The discursive representation of translation rationalizes the saint's "unlikely" presence by relating the journey of the relics as one that occurs of the saint's own volition: the saint controls the process whereby his or her relics are discovered, authenticated and removed, preferably by abduction or theft, since a saint worth his or her sanctity would be too precious to his or her original community to be given away or sold, and too powerful to allow himself or herself to be abducted without consent. The process whereby a new community or new location is chosen as the saint's preferred site of worship is of course also controlled by that most valuable of commodities, the saint's relics, whose value is confirmed and increased by its very circulation. In the words of Geary (1994: 214) "acquiring the relic gave it value because it was worth acquiring [...]. Circulation thus created the commodity being circulated, although to survive as a commodity it had to continue to meet the high expectations raised by the mode of its creation". Although many of these features mark the narrative of the translation of St. Margaret's relics, I shall be foregrounding only those which reflect the ambivalence of the concept of translatio.

In her brief article subtitled "Translation as Theft" Florence Bourgne touches upon some points of convergence between the linguistic and hagiographic concepts of translatio in Bokenham's work. In the course of her examination of the translation of saints' lives as "an authoritative, historical and spatial transfer of knowledge" (1996: 53), she privileges the dragon episode from Margaret's passion in order to relate the "realism" of the text (specifically evidenced in Bokenham's use of a reified Cross, as opposed to a sign of the Cross) to what she calls actualisation of spatial reunion between believers and the objects of their cult through relic worship (1994:62). The liberties taken by the translator in "inventing" rather than translating certain features of his source-texts are interpreted by Bourgne as evidence that Bokenham is engaged in a form of theft: he has smuggled a "real" Cross into the plot (1994:

59). Moreover, in the course of its translation the episode undergoes a process of self-authentication comparable to that evidenced by furta sacra. Finally, she points to Bokenham's colophons as evidencing the translator's need of receiving the saint's benediction before he can complete his translation – a clear parallel to the the notion that the saint controls the process of her own circulation. Not once does Bourgne dwell on the extended narrative of the translation of St. Margaret's remains[14], or the startling *interiectio ex parte poetae* that separates the "life and passion" from the translation narrative. It is to this hiatus established by the poet's leap into "real time" – his time, the time of writing – that I now turn.

In the form of "real time", authorial presence – if that is what we may call Bokenham's self-representing mode – is all-pervasive, if not downright invasive, in, around and about the first of his legends. Lines 1-336 (the prologues, general and onomastic) and countless references to the story-teller's difficult art that interrupt the narrative of St. Margaret's vita (e.g. lines 365-370, or 407-420) are followed by 70 lines (869-938) reverting to the time of writing (a time which may, of course, be a fiction). In between the "amen" concluding the prayer for the intercession of the saint, whose martyrdom and transportation to heaven have just been reported, and the date (AD 908) with which the translation narrative proper begins, the narrator turns to his addressee to "aske leyser & space/ Of reste a whyle" (879-880). This addressee, whose identity has been constructed in the prologue as the *sone*, *fadyr* and *frend* to whom Bokenham directs his work, is also represented as being part of the author's "real" world. Here he is constructed as an authority by virtue of the author's prefatory promise to consign to him the life, passion and translation narrative of St. Margaret (lines 201-225 and 869-877). Reference to the addressee at this point sustains the fiction that the translation narrative cannot be written without his consent for deferral. Developing the trope of the writer as peregrinus, Bokenham refers to the weariness that makes him incapable of japing and playing, talking, singing and making cheer:

> And now of you I aske leyser & space
> Of reste a whyle, for certeynly
> Euene as a pilgrym so fare now y,
> That feyntly walkyth be the weye,
> And neythyr lyst to iape ner pleye,
> Ne talke ne synge ne make no cher,
> Til to his herberwe he gynne drawe ner.

>   (lines 878-884)

---

14 She does, however, briefly point to the analogous "posteriority" of translation narratives, which come "*after* the legend or story the translator is using, exactly as the *translatio*, which tells of the peregrinations of the saint's remains, follow the 'lif and passioun' in the time sequence" (1996: 53).

Although the term was available in both senses as of the fourteenth century, it will be for later authors/ compilers to avail themselves of the word "travayl" to designate both their labour of writing and the travel that they undertake vicariously through writing (the Elizabethan author-compiler-translator Richard Hakluyt comes to mind).[15] Bokenham here embodies himself as a reflex of the Chaucerian pilgrim, whose tale-telling is a function of his mental and physical condition – which in turn is subject to refreshment. Writing both as a function and form of travel cannot be performed in a spirit of travail, but is attached to the principle of leisure. The propriety of mood may be as questionable here as it is at times in *The Canterbury Tales*, but the similitude soon develops into one of the writer as a frail, old man in need of physical aids such as spectacles and a sharpened pen:

> Ryht so, as I seyde, it faryth be me;
> For sykyr myn handys gynne to feynte,
> My wyt to dullyn, and myn eyne bleynte
> Shuld be, ner helpe of spectacle;
> My penne also gynnyth make obstacle,
> And lyst no lengere on paper to renne
> For I so ofte haue maad to grenne
> Hys snowte vp-on my thombys ende,
> That he ful ny is waxyn unthende;
> For euere as he goth he doth blot,
> And in my book makyth many a spot,
> Menyng therby that for the beste
> Were for vs bothe a whyle to reste,
> Til that my wyt and also he
> Myht be sum craft reparyd be.
>
>   (lines 894-908)

These lines plead for a restoratory respite which is not just a request for the extension of a deadline – though they may be that also. Especially interesting is their attribution of volition to the pen, which no longer "lyst" to run on paper in a way that is reminiscent of the attribution of volition to the relics of St. Margaret in the process of her translation: when the saint's relics grow unbearably heavy upon their arrival at Beucasa's house, the translation process is thought by its agents (who are also "translators") to have arrived at the saint's chosen resting place.[16] Between line 920 (which signals nine days of "time-out": "Now I am free/ Nyne dayes heraftyr for to pleye me") and line 921 (which signals the resumption of the labour of writing at Michaelmas) the narrator has inserted a gap that foregrounds the vulnerability of the writing

---

15 See further on this subject Bridges (in press).
16 The appropriately named Beucasa, comfortably installed in a beautiful house he has no intention of leaving, will be coerced by life-threatening storms into allowing his domicile to be transformed into a church that "houses" the saint (lines 1352-1379).

hand whose pilgrim's progress is subject to the accidence and contingency of illness and exhaustion. In the following translation narrative, the intra-diegetic translator's illness and death will prevent his designs from being fulfilled. Furthermore, Bokenham has already said he visited Margaret's shrine not out of design, but as the accidental effect of heavy rain ("... from Rome homward ageyn/ Whil I was taryed wyth greth reyn/ Thys blyssyd virgyne I dede visyte", lines 117-119). The author slips out of his self-representational mode and resumes his narrative with a passage that both serves as a formal conclusion to the "interiectio ex parte poetae" (it ends with a prayer to the saint and with an "Amen", like the legends themselves) as it serves as prologue to the translation narrative proper, which can now begin:

> Now myhilmesse day is come & past,
> To acomplyse I wyl me hast
> The promys wych that I behyht
> Of my cunnynge aftyr the myht.
> That is to seyne, whow & whan,
> Fro whens, & wheder, & be what man,
> And also fyrst be what occasyoun,
> Of seynt Margarete the translacyoun
> From Antyoche was maad into Italye.
> And in this processe that I not fayle
> Of the treuthe, I lowly beseche
> Hym that treuthe is & treuthe doth teche,
> The lord that syt a-boue the skye,
> That he in treuthe vouchsaf to gye
> On-to the lande of the virgyne swete
> And blyssyd martyr, seynt Margerete,
> Bothe my wyt & eek my pen.
> I prey eche treuman to seyn Amen.

(Lines 921-938)

The prayer for divine guidance to the land of the virgin martyr constructs the trope of the hagiographer as traveller. His translation narrative will take both writer and saint from the East (Antioch) to the West (Italy) on a journey which also, incidentally, mimics the itinerary of "translatio studii", or the transfer of knowledge from a classical linguistic medium to a vernacular one.[17]

The story of "how, when, from whence, whither, by what man and by what occasion" (my translation of lines 925-927) the saint was translated from Antioch to Italy is complex, long and open ended. It is complex inasmuch as the author refers to two discrete translations: the saint's enshrinement at Montefiascone in AD 1405 is evoked as her "secunde translacyoun" in line 1387, but her body – not to mention her body parts – has (have) arguably been described as having been

---

17   As was pointed out by Bourgne, although she didn't associate the East to West movement of the transfer of knowledge with the East to West movement of Margaret's relics.

translated at least twice already (at "Palantes" and at "Ruuyllyan"). It is long in-asmuch as the 460 lines of translation narrative (from which the authenticating miracles at the tombs have been elided for sake of brevity!)[18] cover a "story time" of some 500 years – not to mention their implicit extension into the writer's own time by the prefatory reference to the presence of the saint's foot in a priory near his birthplace, the heel and big toe of which were in a Reading convent (lines 135 – 143). The story of their translation remains a suggestive blank that readers fa-miliar with the whereabouts of other relics of this widely travelled saint are no doubt incited to fill with further translation stories. For this narrative, like the saint's posthumous journey, is as indeterminate as it is open-ended. There is sim-ply no knowing when and where the saint's translation – and the translation of her translation – will end. It certainly did not end where the intra-diegetic translator, abbot Austin *of* Antioch but *from* Pavia, intended it to end, as he lamented when illness forced him to stop and start on his journey northwards from Brindisi, via Rome, to his destination in Pavia. The red flux (from which, the onomastic pro-logue had told us, St. Margaret was especially empowered to deliver him)[19] led Austin to halt first in Sutri, where his donation of one of the saint's ribs contrib-uted to the consecration of the new church of the Victory of the Virgin (lines 1102-1103), and then at a monastery of St. Peter at Pallantes, where he donated the body of St. Margaret and the head of St. Euprepia to the monastery in which he died. There is nothing final about his death as far as the saint's translation is concerned, however, since the latter continues independently of her translator's agency and of his designs.[20] Both Austin and the saint herself seem to control the process of translation uncertainly. For a while it even appears as though the saint's relics are powerless to manifest any design of their own when their resting places – at which the mandatory miracles are said to have occurred – are devastated by war and the passage of time (see especially the evocation of the desolation of Pal-lantes – in lines 1184-1190 – followed by the translation of the relics to Rovigli-ano, which itself becomes a wilderness in the course of lines 1205-1211).

Among the points of analogy between the journey of the saint's relics and that of her hagiographer is the fact that the compiler of the legendary starts and stops as part of his work of compilation. Every legend has a beginning and an

---

18 "Ther god wrowt/ Manye grete miraclys, as I wrytyn haf see./ Albe-it for hast that I reherce hem nowt,/ Or for to other thyngys I wold spede me,/And also to eschewyn prolixyte" (lines 1177-1181).

19 See lines 284-285 of the onomastic prologue. This apparent indifference of the saint towards the translator of her relics is but one of the ways in which her translation occupies an equivo-cal position between unauthorized theft and consenting abduction.

20 St. Margaret is not seen to manifest volition or intervene herself until five centuries after her original translation, when she appears in a vision to direct operations leading to an *inventio* and a *depositio* that are fraught with obstacles (and as many miracles).

ending, marked by a prologue and a colophon respectively, but every beginning
and ending is a relative one, since the former follows upon an ending (that of the
previous legend), and the latter precedes a beginning (of the next legend). Moreover the compilation as a whole has no general prologue or clearly marked conclusion: the legendary begins with the prologue to the legend of St. Margaret and
concludes with the colophon to the legend of St. Elizabeth. The hagiographer's
project may be recorded in the list of legends of folio 193 recto, but that too may
be considered to be open-ended, for Bokenham suggests time and again that the
individual legends grew out of requests by patrons – most notably in his prolocu-
tory to the legend of St. Mary Magdelen, where Bokenham lists eight works he
had compiled before the Countess of Eu commissioned a ninth legend, that of
Mary Magdelen (lines 5035-5046). Who is to say whether Bokenham (or, indeed,
the collection itself) will encounter new patrons susceptible of demanding that
new legends be added to this work of uncertain finality? Even the concluding
colophon (listing the translator's name and provenance, the scribe's name, the
date, price and recipients of the transcription) must be considered a mark of uncertain finality, compiled as it is by four different hands (see Serjeantson 1938: 289).

Other forms of indeterminacy and contingency mark both the processes of
hagiographical and linguistic translation. Reluctantly forgoing the opportunity to
elaborate on them in detail, I will here restrict myself to staking out areas of investigation and will express myself mainly in the interrogative mode. Firstly, there is
the indeterminate identity of the relics themselves: just exactly whose relics are
being translated is a surprizingly perplexing question to have to be be asking of a
narrative genre where one expects a straightforward correlation between the saint
being celebrated and the relics being translated. Alongside the body of St. Margaret, we find the head of St. Euprepia, the body of St. Felicity and the ribs of Saints
Como and Damian occasionally sharing in moments of *inventio* and *depositio*.
How are we to read their coextensive circulation, culminating in their sharing of
one and the same sacred space, which is that of the reliquary? Is this community
of saints' bodies to be understood as an analogous to the common hagiographical
corpus, in which most saint's lives, passions and translations read like most other
saints' lives, passions and translations? We would then, here as elsewhere in this
work, be in presence of a sophisticated mechanism of "mise en abyme" reflecting
not just on the process of writing hagiography, but also on the nature of its sub-
jects-objects.

Another indeterminate feature of the narrative that reflects the nature of *translatio* concerns the mode of authentication associated with *inventio* as the discovery of something – an enclosed and inscribed body – that was always already
there. Its translation is initiated as a result of secret or privileged knowledge that is
authentic because of the way in which it has been transmitted. Just as the abbot

Austin locates the relics of St. Margaret in the devastated wilderness of Antioch[21] as the result of knowledge accidentally acquired when hearing a dying monk's confession; and just as the assistance solicited from two laymen, who help him remove the entombed relics, requires dissimulation and utmost secrecy (the inscribed silver casket containing precious relics is enclosed in a plain wooden box, "that of tresore shuld no suspycyoun be", line 1069), so the hagiographer has learned the details of how St Margaret's relics came to be in Montefiascone firsthand from the monks whose community houses the virgin's relics – which he visited as a result of accident (heavy rain forced him to seek shelter) and not out of design. In his prologue he had described the divulgation of his "simple treatise" as a venture fraught with difficulties that could only be overcome by dissimulation and secrecy ("that men shul not muse/ To haue of me ony suspycyoun", lines 224-225). Do these parallels, grounded in the uncertain legitimacy of the translation of relics, allude to the uncertain legitimacy of linguistic translation from an original, classical context (Antioch for St Margaret, De Voragine for Bokenham's Latin source) into the world of tyrants, warriors and deceptive Trebbiano wine (evoked, for example, in lines 114-116), the world of incompetent rhetoricians speaking in their rough and rude mother tongue (so despised by envious, capacious and subtle Cambridge wits that Bokenham begs his friend Thomas de Burgh to dissimulate his identity in lines 196-225)? Is Italy (and beyond Italy, England) a worthier place for the saint to reside than the oriental wilderness, which in the fifteenth century was subject to Muslim rule? Does plain English provide a better linguistic medium for the mixed (male and female, religious and lay) communities of readers desiring to perpetuate the cult of St Margaret than does the language of universities and rhetorical treatises? These are but a few of the many difficult questions that the extraordinarily forceful presence in his own text of Bokenham the peripatetic hagiographer raises. It would of course take nothing less than the generosity and extraordinary critical skills of our friend and honoree to take us some way towards formulating satisfactory answers.[22]

---

21 Antioch is devastated as a result of internal political strife, related in considerable detail in lines 939-978.

22 Grateful thanks to Elizabeth Aldrich Kaspar and to Donka Minkova for their helpful queries and comments on this paper.

References

Ashley, Kathleen and Pamela Sheingorn
    1996   "The Translations of Foy: Bodies, Texts and Places". In: Ellis and Tixier 1996, 29-49.

Barreiro, Nadine
    2002   Unpublished "petit mémoire"."Be ye tunglees? The Image of the Tongue in Chaucer's Legend of Philomela and Bokenham's Lives of Saint Christine and Saint Katherine". Université de Genève.

Bokenham, Osbern.
    1939   *Legendys of Hooly Wummen*. See Serjeantson.
    1887   *Mappula Angliae*. See Horstmann.

Bourgne, Florence
    1996   "Translating Saints' Lives into the Vernacular: Translatio Studii and Furta Sacra". In Ellis and Tixier, 50-63.

Bridges, Margaret
    In press   "The Reinvention of the Medieval Traveller as Cultural Colonization in Hakluyt's *Principall Navigations, Voyages, Traffiques and Discoveries of the English Nation*". In *Berichten-Erzaehlen-Beherrschen*, edited by Susanna Burghartz for the series *Zeitsprünge* (Frankfurt/M).

Brown, Peter R.L.
    1983   *The Cult of Saints: Its Rise and Function in Latin Christianity*. Chicago: University of Chicago Press.

Delany, Sheila (trans.)
    1992   *Osbern Bokenham. A Legend of Holy Women*. Notre Dame: University of Notre Dame Press.

Delany, Sheila
    1998   *Impolitic Bodies: Poetry, Saints and Society in Fifteenth-Century England. The Work of Osbern Bokenham*. New York and Oxford: Oxford University Press.

Ellis, Roger and René Tixier (eds.)
    1996   *The Medieval Translator. Traduire au Moyen Age*. Cardiff Conference on the Theory and Practice of Translation in the Middle Ages; Conques, France, 1993. Turnhout: Brepols.

Geary, Patrick
    1978   *Furta sacra. Thefts of Relics in the Central Middle Ages*. Princeton, N.J.: Princeton University Press.
    1994   *Living with the Dead in the Middle Ages*. Ithaca and London: Cornell University Press.

Heinzelmann, Martin
    1979   *Translationsberichte und andere Quellen des Reliquienkultes*. Typologie des Sources du Moyen Age Occidental. Turnhout: Brepols.

Higden, Ranulph
    1865   *Polychronicon Ranulphi Higden Monachi Cestrensis.* Ed. Churchill Babington. Rerum Britannicarum Medii Ævi Scriptores (Rolls Series) 41, Volume 2. London: Her Majesty's Stationary Office.

Horstmann, Carl (ed.)
    1887   Osbern Bokenham: Mappula Angliae. *Englische Studien* 10.

Lewis, Robert (ed.)
    1993   *Middle English Dictionary: T.* Ann Arbor: University of Michigan Press

Serjeantson, Mary S. (ed.)
    1939   *Legendys of Hooly Wummen by Osbern Bokenham.* EETS. o.s. 206. London: O.U.P.

Joachim's Infertility in the St. Anne's Legend

Anita Obermeier, University of New Mexico[1]

In her 1999 poem, "Guenever Prays for a Child", Wendy Mnookin has the desperately childless Guinevere entreat St. Anne for help in her quest for fertility. Anne is the perfect choice because, like Guinevere, she herself once suffered from barrenness. But who is this Anne? Much medieval devotional and modern scholarly energy has been spent on St. Anne, the apocryphal mother of Mary.[2] Scholars have called her a polysemous medieval symbol that can serve dynastic aspirations, elevate married over celibate life, and shore up the developing doctrine of the Immaculate Conception. Anne's story first appears in the *Protevangelium Jacobi* (*The Gospel of James*), one of the infancy narratives of the second century.[3] Her character is patterned after the barren matriarchs of the Old Testament who finally conceive after long spells of infertility; subsequently, she becomes the medieval icon of fecundity.

Hardly any scholarship focuses on Joachim, her husband, maybe because both medieval art and text privilege Anne over him, endorsing a matrilinear genealogy of Christ that begs this examination of Hebrew, late-Antique, and medieval notions of fertility, sterility, and gender. A series of texts, from Old Testament parallels, to the *Protevangelium*, to Jacobus de Voragine's *Legenda Aurea* (*Golden Legend*) (ca. 1260) and Osbern Bokenham's *Legendys of Hooly Wummen* (*A Legend of Holy Women*) (ca. 1443-1447), illustrate how medical, philosophical, and theological views deal with Joachim's admission of sterility, which marginalizes him in the conception of Mary. Because Joachim's infertility is an object of curious interest in the Middle Ages, we must take a tour through theories of fertility and sterility in the Bible as well as in ancient and medieval culture.

The Old Testament boasts a number of barren women whose main goal is to produce a male heir for their spouses. Some of the legalistic texts of the Old Testament claim that barrenness is a "punishment for sin", but these passages date mostly from the 8th-century BCE exile period (Callaway 1986: 16). The

1   I would like to express my gratitude to the Research Allocation Committee at the University of New Mexico for funding part of this research project. Many thanks to Robert E. Bjork and Leslie Donovan for expertly and kindly commenting on drafts of this essay. I am also grateful for the student assistance offered by the Institute for Medieval Studies at the University of New Mexico, and to Spring Robbins and Sam Waters for providing this research support.

2   See Ashley and Sheingorn (1990), Brandenbarg (1987 and 1995), and Dörfler-Dierken (1992). For additional bibliographical references, see Ashley and Sheingorn (1990: 62-68).

3   For a full scholarly edition, see Amann (1910).

other examples can be found primarily from Genesis through Kings, featuring Sarah, Rebekah, Rachel, Samson's mother, Hannah, and the Shunammite woman. Striking similarities exist among these women characters: the barrenness is not attributed to any wrongdoing or explained other than through Yahweh's closing their wombs; all, but one, do something to alleviate their barrenness – such as providing a maid servant to the husband – and all, but one, conceive at the favor of Yahweh; except for the Shunammite woman, all others give birth to important male children in biblical history, often the favorites of their parents (Callaway 1986: 17, 27). While many scholars attribute this motif of barrenness to folk sagas, Mary Callaway has shown that the barrenness of the first three women is an addition by the Yahwist redactor for a particular purpose, and the latter three are midrashic commentary by the Deuteronomist historian (1986: 30, 32).[4]

Yahweh's command in Genesis 1: 28, "Be fruitful, multiply, fill the earth and subdue it",[5] stylizes him as a fertility god. The subsequent frenzy for fertility, especially in Genesis,[6] can be explained by the fact that Yahweh is competing with the indigenous Canaanite fertility god Baal and the goddesses Asherah, Astarte, and Ishtar.[7] Callaway argues that "the stories of the women whose wombs were opened and closed according to Yahweh's will were part of the monotheizing theology of the Yahwist" (1986: 32), essentially antidotes to the allure of pagan fertility cults.[8] The barren Genesis matriarchs Sarah, Rebekah, and Rachel, for whom motherhood traditionally is the defining ingredient of a woman's personhood (Ozick 1994: 89), serve to make Yahweh's point to his people. Sarah first tries to alleviate her infertility with the legal custom of providing Abraham with a concubine, a wife of secondary status, whose child would be considered Sarah's. The slave girl Hagar conceives and

---

4   Callaway defines midrash as "a thread which runs through the warp and woof of the history of the people of God. Its forms are altered in different ages, and it takes on characteristics from its milieu, but always its aim is constant" (1986: 9): midrashic exegesis seeks to validate "tradition from scripture," to find "ways of attaching contemporary custom and belief to the sacred text" (Metzger and Coogan 1993: 307-310).

5   All quotations and citations from the Bible are taken from *The New Jerusalem Bible* (1985).

6   See Miles (1995: 26-84).

7   Callaway compares this to other ancient near Eastern texts: "Of the three Ugaritic epics extant, the Legend of Krt and the Legend of Aqht are concerned with the problem of obtaining heirs. In the first, Krt is left a widower and childless by the catastrophic deaths of his wife and children. In the second, Dnil gives oblations to the gods and lies on a couch of sackcloth because he has no son. In both stories, Baal intercedes for the men before El, and provides a wife 'who will bear seven sons' for Krt and life-breath with which the invigorated Dnil will impregnate his wife" (1986: 13).

8   Some scholars argue that the Yahwist, the writer of the Gospel of Luke, and the author of the Song of Songs could have been women.

promptly becomes conceited: now "her mistress counted for nothing in her eyes" (Gen. 16: 4). After this humiliation, Sarah conceives Isaac by the favor of Yahweh. In Rebekah's case, Isaac prays to Yahweh as fertility god "on behalf of his wife, for she was barren. Yahweh heard the prayer, and his wife Rebekah conceived" (Gen. 25: 21). For Leah and Rachel, the competition between two wives becomes more complicated by the addition of the concubines Bilhah and Zilpah, highlighting the importance of childbearing in ancient near Eastern cultures (Gen. 30). In 1 Samuel, the Deuteronomist historian uses this competition between fertile and sterile wife in a midrashic way to compose Samuel's birth narrative.

Through the inclusion of the barren women in Judges, Samuel, and Kings, the biblical authors construct intertextual ties back to Genesis and foreshadow Luke's Gospel and the *Protevangelium*. For instance, Samson's angelic annunciation prefigures Gabriel's annunciation of Jesus: Manoah's "wife was barren; she had borne no children. The Angel of Yahweh appeared to this woman and said to her, 'You are barren and have no child, but you are going to conceive and give birth to a son'" (Judges 13: 2-3). This statement, followed by prescriptions of a nazirite lifestyle,[9] is the most elaborate pronouncement by Yahweh on fertility in the Old Testament. Just as Abraham and Sarah, who hosted Yahweh at Mamre, are promised a son, so does the Shunammite woman receive this promise from Elisha (2 Kings 4: 8-17). Both promises ensue as rewards for hospitality.

The closest Old Testament parallel to the St. Anne's Legend is the story of Hannah, Samuel's mother, who is more eager than Sarah, Rebekah, or Rachel, to become a mother. Both Hannah's and Anna's names mean "grace". It can be argued that the author of the *Protevangelium* selected the parallel to Hannah to provide a typological connection (Ashley and Sheingorn 1990: 6). Hannah relives Rachel's predicament as the favorite but childless of Elkanah's two wives. Like Sarah, who is first snubbed by and subsequently mistreats her servant Hagar – who bears Ishmael for Abraham – Hannah first suffers at the hands of her taunting rival Peninnah. But then she takes matters into her own hands by going to the sanctuary at Shiloh to pray for a son, whom she consecrates to Yahweh (1 Samuel 1-2: 11); this is the first time a Biblical mother decides her child's future *ab utero*. Marcia Falk points out that Hannah is also the first non-priestly Hebrew person to pray in a sanctuary, qualifying her as a "symbol for rabbinic Judaism" (1994: 98). Her perseverance and faith are re-

---

9   A nazarite lifestyle required that the person "abstain from the fruit of the vine and other intoxicants, avoid defilement by contact with a dead body (even that of a close relative), and not allow a razor to cut the hair" (Metzger and Coogan 1993: 552), every one of which Sampson violated.

warded with the birth of Samuel.[10] This faith and reward theme is created by
the Deuteronomist, as Callaway argues: "it is 'midrash' on the barren matriarch tradition ... which made the old story of Samuel's birth into a story of
hope for Israel in exile, [and] was to alter the shape of [that] tradition permanently" (1986: 56).

The barren matriarch tradition, especially the story of Hannah, and its
changes continue in the *Protevangelium*,[11] when Anna repudiates herself and
receives rather mild criticism from her maid, Euthine, that God had closed
Anna's womb. Anna laments: "I will mourn my barrenness ... Woe is me! Who
gave me birth? What sort of womb brought me forth? For I was born a curse
among the children of Israel. I was made a reproach, and they derided me and
banished me out of the Temple of the Lord my God" (*PRT* 1984: 385, 386).
Actually, the *Protevangelium* never shows Anna suffering this kind of treatment, but the author does have her invoke Sarah and her son Isaac.

Although Anna and Joachim seem to stand in a long line of infertile Old
Testament couples, as well as the initially barren New Testament parents of
John the Baptist – Elizabeth and Zecharia[12] – the biblical stories always portray "barren women rather than childless men" (Callaway 1986: 16).[13] The
onus of infertility is clearly put on the wombs of the Old Testament wives;
husbands are never "blamed" for infertility – usually showing their sexual
prowess by fathering children with other women. It is at this juncture that the
Protevangelium and its subsequent reincarnations – which in their titles stress
either the birth of the Virgin Mary or the life of St. Anne – depart from the Old
Testament models. Like Hannah, Joachim goes to the temple, where he is
harshly attacked and severely humiliated for his childlessness: "Reuben stood

---

10   In her praise song after her vindication, Hannah seems to refer to Peninnah: "my mouth de-
     rides my foes ... / Do not keep talking so proudly, / let no arrogance come from your mouth,
     / for Yahweh is a wise God, / his to weigh up deeds ... / the barren woman bears sevenfold /
     but the mother of many is left desolate" (1 Sam. 2: 1, 3, 5). In the *Protevangelium*, Anna
     demonstrates a similar sense of triumph and vindication: "'I will sing a sacred song to the
     Lord my God, because he considered me and took away from me the reproach of my ene-
     mies; and the Lord my God gave me a fruit of his righteousness, one yet manifold before
     him. Who will report to the sons of Reuben that Anna gives suck?'" (1984: 387)
11   All subsequent parenthetical references to the *Protevangelium* are abbreviated *PRT*.
12   In Luke 1, Zecharia is visited in the temple by the angel Gabriel, who announces the birth of
     John the Baptist in a nazirite fashion. Elizabeth professes great relief at her own pregnancy,
     since the humiliation she suffered in public is now gone.
13   Of the four canonical gospels, only two contain an infancy narrative of Christ. Neither the
     Gospel of Mark nor the Gospel of John includes infancy material. In an attempt to satisfy
     Hellenistic curiosity about the childhood of heroes, Matthew adds a birth story. Luke adds a
     more developed infancy narrative of Jesus and the connected new birth narrative of John the
     Baptist.

up against Joachim, saying, 'It is not permissible for you to bring your offerings first, for you did not produce offspring in Israel" (*PRT* 1984: 385). This
repudiation so dismays and shocks Joachim that he checks the temple records
to see if he really is the only Israelite failing to father offspring. While the
temple records compound Joachim's repudiation, the gospel writer juxtaposes
a reference to Abraham's belated fruitfulness, undoubtedly as a sign of hope
and foreshadowing in the story. Nevertheless, Joachim decides not to return to
Anna, but pitches his tent in the desert for forty days – at best an unorthodox
way to increase his fertility.

The *Protevangelium* is written in the Greek Septuagint tradition, in which
this blaming of Joachim flies in the face of Old Testament precedents. Even in
the close parallel of Samson's birth narrative, Hannah suffers through the
situation alone, since her otherwise fertile husband, Elkanah, and father of
multiple children by Peninnah, does not understand her preoccupation with
producing a son. These Biblical passages are not explicit about whether the
women conceive through intercourse with their husbands or through divine
intervention alone.[14] The mechanisms are not explained, since the biblical
writers are priestly historians uninterested in the specifics of procreation, but
the method is generally obstructionist, in that the women's womb is closed and
therefore prevents the semen from entering the uterus. Even if the women are
blameless, it is implied that male sperm is always abundant and viable but
foiled by the closed womb.

Most ancient and medieval notions of sexuality, fertility, and gender re-
volve around the nature of semen, offering diverse opinions on conception
theory and sex determination.[15] The basic but ubiquitous procreational notion
is encapsulated in the agricultural analogy of seed and semen,[16] through which
the man contributes form and soul, and the woman is vessel or soil. This view
of conception considers the male as active and the female as passive.[17] The

---

14 Tamar's case is not included here because she is not technically barren, since her first hus-
    band is killed by Yahweh, and the second one spills his seed on the ground. Because Judah
    withholds his third son out of fear that he, too, will die, Tamar goes through an elaborate
    scheme dressing up as a prostitute to snare Judah himself on the side of the road. She does
    conceive by him (Gen. 38). Ruth and Orpah are in effect also childless, since when their hus-
    bands die, they had been married for ten years. Ruth eventually marries Boaz and "when they
    came together, Yahweh made her conceive and she bore a son" (Ruth 4: 13). This passage
    shows that at the time of intercourse, Yahweh, the fertility god, intervenes on her behalf.
    Tamar is an ancestor of Ruth, whose son, Obed, will be the grandfather of David.

15 For an overview, see Cadden (1993).

16 McElvaine argues that women probably invented agriculture (2001: 83) and might therefore
    have been the unwitting creators of this equation.

17 For discussion on how this myth is still upheld even in modern scientific dialogue, see Martin
    (1996).

Bible is no exception to that. Yahweh refers to both Noah's and Abraham's seed. In Genesis 38, Onan spills it on the ground to avoid impregnating his brother's widow, Tamar. Both Leviticus and Deuteronomy employ the metaphor often, identifying male sexual organs as the source of fertility. Because there is "no Jewish medicine in the sense that we speak of an Egyptian or a Greek medical science" (Preuss 1978: 4), we need to turn to Hellenistic medical thought, which influenced the Jewish and early Christian worldview.[18]

In the Hellenistic world, pre-Aristotelian medical writers espoused various incongruous theories for the generation of semen. One such theory focuses on the ancient Persian triad of seed/brain/marrow, but within that framework one set of authors champions the premise that semen originates from the brain; another group asserts that semen springs from spinal marrow (Lesky 1950: 10-11). Other authors were convinced that semen from the right testicle produced males, and from the left, females; or that incubation on the right or left side of the womb had the same results (Preus 1977: 66). Empedocles adds the idea that procreation is tied to the generation of heat (Lesky 1950: 31-38). Hippocrates[19] then posits a two-seed model, where both the male and female contribute seed, mostly trying to explain why children can also resemble their mothers. Therefore, each person has both male and female seed; the sex of the child is determined by whose seed is stronger (Hippocrates 1952: 31-34). Furthermore, Hippocrates favors a pangenetic source for semen, arguing that it is generated in the entire body.[20]

Aristotle, in his work the *Generation of Animals*, is critical of most of the premises espoused by the writers before him. He opposes pangenesis (1984: 1: 20, 1131)[21] and endorses the hematological theory,[22] in which blood undergoes thermal transmutation to become semen: "woman is as it were an impotent male, for it is through a certain incapacity that the female is female, being incapable of concocting the nutriment in its last state into semen owing to the coldness of her nature" (1984: 1: 20, 1130). Aristotle is consistent on hematology when he asserts that menstrual blood "is a residue ... analogous in females to the semen in males" (1984: 1: 19, 1128). This menstrual blood, however, is the mere nutritive material for the life- and form-generating male semen, for the female is "a mutilated male, and the menstrual fluids are semen, only not

---

18 For a discussion of the medical ideas recorded in the Talmud from 200 to 600 CE, see Preuss (1978), Rosner (1977), and Snowman (1974).

19 Although it is now accepted that the writings in the Hippocrates corpus cannot all be attributed to Hippocrates of Cos but to a group of writers, I use the singular for convention's sake.

20 For more information on Hippocrates, see Grensemann (1982) and King (1998).

21 All citations of Aristotle's *Generation of Animals* contain book and chapter, as well as the page number in this particular edition.

22 See also Héritier-Augé (1989).

pure; for there is only one thing they have not in them, the principle of soul" (1984: 2: 3, 1144). With this assertion, Aristotle solidifies the following gendered binaries: male/female correspond to form/matter, active/passive, pure/impure, strong/weak, with soul/without soul. He sums up his notions with the statement that being male is "better and more divine" (1984: 2: 1, 1136).[23]

According to Aristotelian gender theory, Joachim is responsible for providing the life giving semen. The *Protevangelium*, however, exonerates him with the typical Old Testament explanation that Yahweh had closed Anna's womb. Why then did the gospel writer even bring up this egalitarian-sounding double reproach strategy? Certainly, the story provides ancestry for Mary in Old Testament fashion through patterns of famous barren couples that bring forth important people in Hebrew history, but Joachim's admission of infertility is actually the beginning of a literary and later pictorial trend that marginalizes him in the conception of Mary – perhaps in a parallel strategy used in relation to his son-in-law Joseph – to de-emphasize the staining quality of male semen and to bolster the developing doctrine of the Immaculate Conception.

During the forty-day separation of the couple in the *Protevangelium*, both Joachim and Anna are visited by angels.[24] The angel visits Anna first, telling her that she "will conceive and give birth, and [her] offspring shall be spoken of in the whole inhabited world" (*PRT* 1984: 386), essentially rendering Joachim invisible. In the nazirite vein of both Samson's mother and Hannah, Anna offers her unborn child to the service of God, adding the interesting parenthetical comment, "whether male or female" (*PRT* 1984: 386). Old Testament matriarchs would not have been considering a daughter at all. Here, of course, femaleness is prized since the *Protevangelium* anachronistically lays the groundwork for Mary and Jesus, the teleological endpoints of Christian salvation history. The angel's visit to Anna stands in grammatical contrast to Joachim's visit. The angel tells Joachim, "behold, your wife Anna is pregnant" (*PRT* 1984: 386). If Anna is already pregnant before Joachim returns from his forty-day stay in the wilderness, then is this conception a foreshadowing of Mary's conception of Jesus? After all, Anna's conception of Mary is the much debated Immaculate Conception, Mary's conception without sin.

While the Aristotelian and Augustinian cult of sperm reigns supreme in antiquity and the Middle Ages, male semen is also considered the defiling factor of virginal women. Even Chaucer's Monk in *The Canterbury Tales* mentions "mannes sperme unclene" (1985: l. 2009). The only way someone could escape the transmission of original sin is not to be conceived with man's sperm

---

23   For further information on Aristotle's procreation theories, see Connell (2000), Davis (1997), Horowitz (1976), Morsink (1982), Pomata (1995), Tress (1992), and Tuana (1995).

24   In the Old Testament, angels are generally taken to be synonymous with Yahweh. In the New Testament, and as angel lore develops, angels are considered separate entities from God.

(Journet 1958: 44). *The Catholic Encyclopedia* cryptically explains that Mary's "body was formed in the womb of the mother, and the father had the usual share in its formation" (Immaculate Conception). Although the *Protevangelium* is as enigmatic about the actual conception mechanism as the canonical scriptures, it implies conception happens when Joachim finally returns home. Another entry in *The Catholic Encyclopedia* also asserts the physical engendering of Mary by Joachim: "According to Ephiphanius it was maintained even in the fourth century by some enthusiasts that St. Anne conceived without the action of man. This error was revived in the West in the fifteenth century" (St. Anne). Some of the controversy about the Immaculate Conception has to do with chronology, as it is the grammatical gap in the *Protevangelium* that has given rise to the notion of the Immaculate Conception. Was Mary conceived with original sin but then sanctified by God *in utero* and born sinless, or was she already conceived without sin? The answers to these questions fill volumes and go beyond the scope of this essay.[25] But this ambivalence surrounding sexuality and sperm touches the theories about Mary's conception and helps to privilege Anne over Joachim.

In the *Protevangelium*, the ensuing birth of Mary is a great joy to the couple, and every privilege is lavished on her. Mary's salvific importance contrasts sharply with Aristotle's claim that a health deficiency in the parents' fluids is the cause of Mary's sex: "those of a moister and more feminine state of body are more wont to beget females, and a liquid semen causes this more than a thicker; now all these characteristics come of deficiency in natural heat" (1984: 4: 2, 1186). As Robert Con Davis phrases it: "the person of too little semen, whether male or female" is in essence "an infertile male" (1997: 45). We can see then how prevailing gender notions have to be adjusted to elevate Mary to her exalted position. Further feminine privileging manifests itself in Joachim's choice of ten female lambs to be sacrificed to God when the angel tells him of the pregnancy. Usually, sacrificial animals in the Old Testament are male, and the other animals that Joachim offers to the priests are, too. But the sacrifice of the female lambs to God foreshadows Mary's consecration to his service.

Although numerous Latin and vernacular versions of the St. Anne's legend[26] exist after the *Protevangelium*, Dominican Friar Jacobus de Voragine's[27] widely popular *Legenda Aurea* (ca. 1260) contains the most famous account.

---

25 For further information on the medieval controversy surrounding the Immaculate Conception, see D'Ancona (1957), Haney (1981), Horst (1987), Mildner (1939), and O'Connor (1958).

26 The St. Anne legend was especially prominent in England, Germany, and the Netherlands.

27 There are 800 extant Latin manuscripts of the *Legenda Aurea* and several hundred later vernacular versions. For more discussion on its dissemination, see Reames (1983).

"The Birth of the Blessed Virgin Mary" in the *Legenda Aurea* presents a combination of saint's life and patristic commentary, giving detailed explanations about the missing Davidic pedigree of Mary and Jesus,[28] when, as Voragine puts it, "Joseph ... had nothing to do with the conception of Christ" (1995: 149). The author expands certain familial levels, such as providing Anna with a sister named Hismeria who will be Elizabeth's mother. Furthermore, after Joachim's death, Voragine has Anna marry two more times. Through this so-called *trinubium*, Anna will produce Mary Cleophas and Mary Salome, who will engender half of the apostles and the Holy Family Kinship.

Voragine remakes the *Protevangelium* to reflect his own and contemporary theology. In the *Protevangelium*, Joachim is called prosperous, representing the Old Testament favor of Yahweh to the patriarchs, whereas in the *Legenda Aurea*, Joachim and Anna are exceedingly charitable by giving a third of their wealth to the poor – substantially more than the required 10 percent tithe – reflecting medieval emphasis on almsgiving. Both parents promise to dedicate their offspring to the temple before Joachim suffers his rebuke there, now with some intensifying twists: "When the priest saw him, he angrily ordered him away and upbraided him for presuming to approach the altar of God, declaring that it was not proper for one who was subject to the Law's curse to offer sacrifice to the Lord of the Law, nor for a sterile man, who made no increase to the people of God, to stand among men who begot sons" (Voragine 1995: 151). The passage's more codified theology demonstrates theological changes through the millennium that separates these two texts: therefore, the rejection of Joachim coming from an angry priest, is now linked to an unexplained scriptural curse, where the former fertility God Yahweh has turned to an impersonal Lord of the Law; the term *sterile* is actually applied to Joachim; and the requirement is narrowed to male offspring.

Despite this harsher treatment of Joachim, other aspects of the text favor him.[29] This favoring can be attributed to Aristotle's privileging of male over female. Voragine makes Joachim, not Anna, the first and primary audience for the angel's annunciation. The Yahwist position outlined by Callaway is still evident, as the angel informs him that closed wombs are used by God to demonstrate his divine generosity vis-à-vis human carnal desire. Furthermore, the reference to carnal desire demonstrates the impact of Augustine's theology of original sin, the sin transmitted through sex and semen. Contrary to the Old Testament examples, Voragine evokes sin and punishment. In the *Protevan-*

---

28 Voragine uses the terms "seed of David" and raising "up seed to his brother" (1995: 149).

29 Thomas of Hales' mid-thirteenth-century version of *The Lyf of Oure Lady* provides the angel's annunciation only to Joachim, while Anna's role is minimized (1985: 34-39).

gelium, Joachim is identified with Abraham, but here Voragine lists the sterile matriarchs again.

In a noteworthy editorial comment, the angel calls the priestly charge of infertility "wrongly put upon" Joachim (1995: 152). Sterility is safely back with the woman, in the oxymoronic epithet of the "unfruitful mother" Anna (Voragine 1995: 152). Oddly enough, though, Anna's self-repudiation has been totally eliminated from the text. Her lament simply focuses on not knowing the whereabouts of her husband. These strategies reveal Voragine's Dominican bias because the Dominicans opposed the doctrine of the Immaculate Conception. Therefore, the angel uses the future tense to announce the couple's pregnancy.

Furthermore, the *Legenda Aurea* represents Aristotelian views, whose longevity results from scholastic thinkers like Albert the Great and his pupil Thomas Aquinas, whose works anchored his ideas of sexuality and gender into medieval philosophy and theology.[30] Aquinas reasserts the formula of woman as "matter" and man as "form", as "the semen's active power is a kind of impression derived from the begetter's soul ... therefore a certain matter really assumes the form of human nature by the semen's power" (Aquinas 1970: 1a. 119.1). One wonders then, if such prominence is bestowed on the male in the process of medieval conception, why women, the mere vessels, are the ones accused of sterility. One can argue that when the soil is poor, the seed cannot take root, but the problem also lies in the fact that the pseudo-biologist philosophers Aristotle, Albert, and Aquinas were considered the primary authorities.[31]

Augustinian monk Osbern Bokenham's *Legendys of Hooly Wummen*[32] contains the most remarkable version of the St. Anne's legend, the "Vita Sanctae Annae Matris Sanctae Mariae" ("Life of Saint Anne, the Mother of Mary"), a fifteenth-century *Legenda Aurea* remake that quite contradicts it. The reason that Bokenham puts Anne in the title and the center of the legend might stem from the fact the Anne's prominence has continuously increased during the Middle Ages culminating in the 1500's. While both the *Protevangelium* and Voragine tell the story from the couple's infertility to the birth of Jesus, Bokenham focuses on Anne and Joachim, with only one hundred lines out of ca. 2,100 lines devoted to Mary until her presentation at the temple.

Bokenham starts the life with a reference to Anne's womb that carries Mary. The narratological order within the legend definitely changes with the theological positions expounded in the individual versions. Bokenham inserts

---

30 See Aquinas (1972: 3a. 31-32) for his inclusion of Aristotle's views.
31 See Jordan (1988).
32 See also Delany's translation of the legends (Bokenham 1992).

all kinds of biblical and theological commentary, but it is his use of the word "seed" that is most illuminating. He identifies the couple's twenty-year wait for a child as "of here seed no fruht grew" (1938: l. 1661). Their seed has produced neither male nor female offspring. This reference to both their seeds implies that Bokenham no longer follows Aristotle and Aquinas but the second-century physician Galen. The ancient physicians Hippocrates and Galen purported a more modern and egalitarian gender and conception model. Galen, in his work *On Semen*, draws on Hippocrates' two-seed model, refutes some of Aristotle's views on semen,[33] and adds his own theories. Still trying to explain why some children look like their mothers, Galen states that "it is necessary that the female also produces semen" (1992: II 1.73). Galen actually found the ovaries and identified them as the source of female seed, although he had not really discovered the *ovum*, but only a whitish slime he observed in the fallopian tubes. This two-seed model is not yet a completely egalitarian affair, as Galen asserts, "for even if the female most certainly produces semen, and generative semen at that, yet it is by no means more abundant or more generative than the male semen. Therefore the female semen should always be ruled and indeed defeated, and the male should prevail over it" (1992: II 2.2-3).[34]

Because of this two-seed model, Bokenham's Joachim suffers greater humiliation than before. He is now rebuked by Bishop Issachar, whom Bokenham identifies as Anne's father, as a "bareyn and frutles" man (1938: l. 1684). Since the rebuke now comes from Joachim's father-in-law, it assumes a more personal note and sharper edge because Issachar's own line is threatened. Only if Joachim gets absolution from this legal and scriptural curse and has "fecundyte" (Bokenham 1938: l. 1698) shall his gifts be acceptable.

Here the angel first appears to Anne, then to Joachim, and once more to Anne. Although the angel promises Anne that the fruit of her body will be greatly revered, Anne's guilt returns, along with her unsympathetic maid servant. The servant tells Anne that God has made her barren and taken her husband: "'Wenyst þu these myscheus I might redresse? / Nay, nay!'" (Bokenham 1938: ll. 1815-6). The maid's vehemence of denial sounds like a throwback to the Old Testament where a female servant might be expected to bear children for her mistress, which is now impossible since the husband had disappeared.

Joachim's conversation with the angel highlights the problematic semantic equation of male sperm and agricultural seed. He complains that "The seed is lost which I haue sowe" (Bokenham 1938: l. 1832), echoing Galen who observes that females who void semen do not become pregnant (1992: I 1.4).

---

33 For further information on Galen's procreation theories, see Boylan (1986), Connell (2000), Preus (1977), and Tuana (1995).

34 See Giles of Rome (1243-1316), who vehemently denies female seed any generative power (Hewson 1975).

Joachim further bemoans his lack of manhood and progeny, concluding that "syth in my felde no fruht may fynde, / To telyn it lengur it were but veyne" (Bokenham 1938: ll. 1837-8). Joachim clearly rejects intercourse in this passage, shouldering great blame for the continued infertility.

Sheila Delany argues that Bokenham's St. Anne's legend, while far from being decisive, leans more toward the maculist position because of the Augustinian order's theological allegiance (1998: 84-85). Indeed, medical detail increases as he gives us an exact nine-month timeframe for the pregnancy after the couple's reunion. While my main point is not to argue for or against a maculist or immaculist position, I do perceive Bokenham to favor Anne over Joachim. He uses present tense in the angel's announcement, "For a doughter she hath" (1938: l. 1887) in place of the future tense in the *Legenda Aurea*. The angel instructs Joachim to hurry home to his wife, "For blessed is hyr seed, whos dowghter shal be / Modyr of blysse euerlastynge, perde" (Bokenham 1938: ll. 1894-5). Such an emphasis on her seed is highly unusual, since women's contribution is usually referred to as the fruit; even the Hail Mary describes Jesus as the fruit of Mary's womb. The female seed, combined with the asexual kiss at the Golden Gate – which has been so often iconographically fixed in artists' paintings[35] and interpreted by medieval theologians as the point of Mary's conception – as well as the angel's pronouncement that Mary shall be filled with the holy ghost from her mother's womb (Bokenham 1938: l. 1891-2) strongly suggests that Joachim's contribution is diminished, if not eradicated.

Four explanations offer themselves for Bokenham's choice to single out Anne's seed in its generative function. First, the mention of Anne's seed evokes Galenic conception theory. Galen attributes sex determination to a struggle between the male and female semen. This struggle would always end in favor of the stronger male semen; however, "the female semen received the power from the menstrual blood as a contribution to its strength ... For since the semen of the female is congenial to it, (the menstrual blood) increases and strengthens the substance and power of that semen rather than that of the male semen" (Galen 1992: II 2.23-24). Consequently, since Mary is female, according to Galen's theory, Anne's seed aided by her menstrual blood prevailed over Joachim's seed.[36]

Second, A. I. Doyle has suggested that the Arundel manuscript of the *Legendys of Hooly Wummen* was copied for the Franciscan nuns of Aldgate and Denny (ctd. in Edwards 1994: 157). Since the Franciscans were the major pro-

---

35   See Mayberry (1991).
36   Fifth-century Talmudic commentary also mentions a two-seed model that resembles Aristotle's encompassing the generative male semen and the nutritive blood of the woman (Rosner 1977: 175-177).

ponents of the Immaculate Conception, maybe Bokenham also favored Anne to please his Franciscan audience. Third, Delany's assertion that the Augustinian order opposed the Immaculate Conception is not completely correct. The order did oppose it until the mid-fourteenth century, but then switched camps and sided with the Franciscans (Balic 1958: 222-3). Fourth, the theory of the Immaculate Conception, in essence, tries to erase the stain of original sin, which Augustine claims gets propagated through the male semen during sex. Making the conception of Mary asexual or more like the conception of Jesus, divinely orchestrated, would solve this problem of the tainting male seed. Late medieval and early Renaissance artists seem to agree with this uncharacteristic privileging of the female over the male. They paint Anne centrally, both in St. Anne's Trinity pictures, where an adult-sized Anne holds both baby Mary and Jesus on her lap, and the St. Anne Holy Kinship pictures,[37] where Anne occupies the central spot among her extended family, with her three daughters who all produce important New Testament men, while the husbands are all situated around the edges, even separated by walls or dividers (Figure 1).

Figure 1   Follower of the Master of Saint Veronica, Holy Kinship. Cologne, Wallraf-Richartz-Museum, Inv. Nr. 59. Ca. 1405 to 1420. Photo Nr. 143 950: Reprinted with permission from the Rheinisches Bildarchiv, Cologne.

---

37   For St. Anne's images, see Arnold (1993), Ashley and Sheingorn (1990), Brandenbarg (1987), D'Ancona (1957), and Haney (1981).

The veneration of Anne flourished especially in the fifteenth and sixteenth centuries, to the point where some critics complain that Anne has exceeded Mary in popularity. Although Jan van Denemarken (d. 1545) writes a separate but commensurate life of St. Joachim, he could not rival his more popular spouse (Brandenbarg 1987: 105). Her meteoric rise in these two centuries may be tied to the immaculist controversy. The feast of the conception of Mary is first evident in eleventh-century England, mostly because of the devotion of the Winchester monks. Hence, the mid-twelfth-century Winchester Psalter contains an illumination of the annunciation to Joachim (Haney 1981: 111), reminiscent of the annunciation to Zecharia. In England, the feast was established in 1130. For the next three hundred years, a theological controversy raged about the Immaculate Conception. In 1439, the Council of Basle declared it doctrinal, and in 1476, Pope Sixtus IV "adopted the feast for the entire Latin Church" (Immaculate Conception). Bokenham wrote during those contentious times when theological opinions were divided. Some argue that Mary was conceived naturally, but some Middle English stanzaic versions of Anne's life show Anne conceiving without spouse, most likely in an analogy to her daughter Mary. In the first stanzaic *Life of St. Anne*, this non-sexual conception is most evident. Anne exclaims this message after the kiss at the Golden Gate and before the couple returns home:

> I was a wedow in my lyfe,
> Now loue I god I am a wyfe;
> Lo goddes help ay es nere.
> Barren I was & I ne wyst how,
> Bot se I haue consawed now
> & flerfore make gud chere.

(1928: ll. 272-76)

All the St. Anne's legends, including the New Testament stories of Elizabeth and Mary, are literary commentaries on the Old Testament stories. Each story is non-static and vibrantly adjusts to and reflects medical, philosophical, and theological concerns of its time. In that framework, Joachim becomes marginalized because, as the Biblical stories move closer to Mary and Jesus, the traditional female infertility notion turns into a fertility notion. Mary is, in essence, too fertile too soon, as she is pregnant when she marries Joseph. Since these concepts are intertwined with medieval theological fears of sexuality,[38] and we are dealing with the birth of a divine being in Jesus, the powerful human male seed is now a tainting substance. Anne's and Mary's fertility and male infertility trade places, mar-

---

38   It is interesting to note that the non-sexual conception of Jesus is put in the genealogy of David, which contains Tamar and Ruth, both of whom employ questionable sexual strategies in making sure that the line of David continues.

ginalizing the men. In essence, Anne, especially through her *trinubium* and super-charged fecundity, has returned us to Genesis and the pinnacle of fertility cults. Thus, the medieval Anne can be viewed as an ancient fertility goddess in her own right, where fruitfulness is firmly in control of a woman, as Mnookin portrays Guenever praying to Anne for a child:

St. Anne
You knew emptiness,
        the years
Of hollow longing.
Your prayers were answered.
Answer mine now.

(1999, ll. 1-6)

References

Amann, Émile
  1910   *Le Protévangile de Jacques et Ses Remaniements Latins*. Paris: Letouzey
          et Ané.
Aquinas, Thomas
  1970   *Summa Theologiae*. M. J. Charlesworth (ed. and trans.). Vol. 15. New
          York: Blackfriars.
  1972   *Summa Theologiae*. Roland Potter (ed. and trans.). Vol. 52. New York:
          Blackfriars.
Aristotle
  1984   *Generation of Animals. The Complete Works of Aristotle*. Jonathan Bar-
          nes (ed.). Vol. 1. Princeton, NJ: Princeton University Press. 1111-1218.
Arnold, Klaus
  1993   "Die Heilige Familie: Bilder und Verehrung der Heiligen Anna, Maria,
          Joseph und des Jesuskindes in Kunst, Literatur und Frömmigkeit um
          1500", in *Maria in der Welt: Marienverehrung im Kontext der Sozialge-
          schichte 10. – 18. Jahrhundert*. Claudia Opitz *et al.* (eds.), 153-174. Zu-
          rich: Chronos.
Ashley, Kathleen – Pamela Sheingorn (eds.)
  1990   *Interpreting Cultural Symbols: Saint Anne in Late Medieval Society*.
          Athens and London: University of Georgia Press.
Balic, Carlo
  1958   "The Mediaeval Controversy over the Immaculate Conception", in Ed-
          ward Dennis O'Connor (ed.), 161-212.
Bokenham, Osbern
  1938   *Legendys of Hooly Wummen*. Mary Serjeantson (ed.). London: Oxford
          University Press.

1992   *A Legend of Holy Women*. Sheila Delany (trans.). Notre Dame, IN: University of Notre Dame Press.

Boylan, Michael
1986   "Galen's Conception Theory", *Journal of the History of Biology* 19.1: 47-77.

Brandenbarg, Ton
1987   "St Anne and Her Family. The Veneration of St Anne in Connection with Concepts of Marriage and the Family in the Early-Modern Period", *Saints and She-Devils: Images of Women in the 15th and 16th Centuries*. 101-128. London: Rubicon Press.
1995   "Saint Anne: A Holy Grandmother and Her Children", in Anneke B. Mulder-Bakker (ed.), 31-65.

Büchmann, Christina – Celina Spiegel (eds.)
1994   *Out of the Garden: Women Writers on the Bible*. New York: Fawcett Columbine.

Cadden, Joan
1993   *Meanings of Sex Difference in the Middle Ages: Medicine, Science, and Culture*. Cambridge: Cambridge University Press.

Callaway, Mary
1986   *Sing, O Barren One: A Study in Comparative Midrash*. Atlanta: Scholars Press.

Chaucer, Geoffrey
1985   "The Monk's Tale", in *The Riverside Chaucer*, Larry Benson (ed.). 3rd ed. Boston: Houghton Mifflin, 240-52.

Connell, Sophia M.
2000   "Aristotle and Galen on Sex Difference and Reproduction: A New Approach to an Ancient Rivalry", *Studies in History and Philosophy of Science* 31.3: 405-427.

D'Ancona, Mirella Levi
1957   *The Iconography of the Immaculate Conception in the Middle Ages and the Early Renaissance*. New York: College Art Association of America.

Davis, Robert Con
1997   "Aristotle, Gynecology, and the Body Sick with Desire", in Lori Hope Lefkovitz (ed.), 35-57.

Delany, Sheila
1998   *Impolitic Bodies: Poetry, Saints, and Society in Fifteenth-Century England–The Work of Osbern Bokenham*. Oxford: Oxford University Press.

Dörfler-Dierken, Angelika
1992   *Die Verehrung der heiligen Anna im Spätmittelalter und früher Neuzeit*. Göttingen: Vandenhoeck & Ruprecht.

Edwards, A. S. G.
1994   "The Transmission and Audience of Osbern Bokenham's *Legendys of Hooly Wummen*", in A. J. Minnis (ed.), 157-67.

Faher, M. *et al.* (eds.)
1989   *Fragments for a History of the Human Body*. New York: Zone.

Falk, Marcia
1994 "Reflections on Hannah's Prayer", in Christina Büchmann – Celina Spiegel (eds.), 94-102.

Galen
1992 *Galen on Semen: Edition, Translation and Commentary.* Phillip de Lacy (ed.). Berlin: Akademie Verlag.

Grensemann, Hermann
1982 *Hippokratische Gynäkologie.* Wiesbaden: Franz Steiner Verlag.

Hales, Thomas of
1985 *The Lyf of Oure Lady: The ME Translation of Thomas of Hales' Vita Sancte Marie.* Sarah M. Horrall (ed.). Heidelberg: Carl Winter Universitätsverlag.

Haney, Kristine Edmondson
1981 "The Immaculate Imagery in the Winchester Psalter", *Gesta* 20.1: 111-118.

Héritier-Augé, Françoise
1989 "Semen and Blood: Some Ancient Theories Concerning Their Genesis and Relationship", in M. Faher *et al* (eds.), 159-75.

Hewson, M. Anthony
1975 *Giles of Rome and the Medieval Theory of Conception: A Study of the De formatione corporis humani in utero.* London: Athlone Press.

Hippocrates
1952 *On Intercourse and Pregnancy.* Tage U. H. Ellinger (trans.). New York: Henry Schuman.

Horst, Ulrich
1987 *Die Diskussion um die Immaculata Conceptio im Dominikanerorden.* Paderborn: Ferdinand Schöningh.

Horowitz, Maryanne Cline
1976 "Aristotle and Woman", *Journal of the History of Biology* 9.2: 183-213.

"Immaculate Conception"
2002 *The Catholic Encyclopedia Online.* http://www.newadvent.org/cathen/07674d.htm 12.2.2002

Journet, Charles
1958 "Scripture and the Immaculate Conception: A Problem in the Evolution of Dogma", in Edward Dennis O'Connor (ed.), 3-48.

Jordan, Mark D.
1988 "Medicine and Natural Philosophy in Aquinas", in Albert Zimmermann (ed.), 233-246.

Keller, Evelyn Fox – Helen E. Longino (eds.)
1996 *Feminism and Science.* Oxford: Oxford University Press

King, Helen
1998 *Hippocrates' Woman: Reading the Female Body in Ancient Greece.* London and New York: Routledge.

Lefkovitz, Lori Hope (ed.)
1997 *Textual Bodies: Changing Boundaries of Literary Representation.* Albany, NY: State University of New York Press.

Lesky, Erna
1950 *Die Zeugungs- und Vererbungslehren der Antike und ihr Nachwirken.* Wiesbaden: Franz Steiner Verlag.

The Life of St. Anne
1928 *The Middle English Stanzaic Versions of the Life of St. Anne.* Roscoe E. Parker (ed.), 1-89. London: Oxford University Press.

Lupack, Alan – Barbara Tepa Lupack (eds.)
1999 *Arthurian Literature by Women.* New York: Garland.

Martin, Emily
1996 "The Egg and the Sperm: How Science has Constructed a Romance Based on Stereotypical Male-Female Roles", in Evelyn Fox Keller – Helen E. Longino (eds.), 103-17.

Mayberry, Nancy
1991 "Conception in Medieval and Renaissance Art, Literature, and Society", *Journal of Medieval and Renaissance Studies* 21.2: 207-224.

McElvaine, Robert S.
2001 *Eve's Seed: Biology, the Sexes, and the Course of History.* New York: McGraw-Hill.

Miles, Jack
1995 *God: A Biography.* New York: Alfred A. Knopf.

Metzger, Bruce M. – Michael D. Coogan (eds.)
1993 *The Oxford Companion to the Bible.* New York and Oxford: Oxford University Press.

Mildner, Francis M.
1939 "The Immaculate Conception in England up to the Time of John Duns Scotus", *Marianum* 1: 86-99.

Minnis, A. J. (ed.)
1994 *Late Medieval Religious Texts and Their Transmission: Essays in Honour of A. I. Doyle.* Woodbridge, UK: D. S. Brewer.

Mnookin, Wendy
1999 "Guenever Prays for a Child", in Alan Lupack – Barbara Tepa Lupack (eds.), 345.

Morsink, Johannes
1982 *Aristotle on the Generation of Animals: A Philosophical Study.* Washington, D.C.: University Press of America.

Mulder-Bakker, Anneke B. (ed.)
1995 *Sanctity and Motherhood: Essays on Holy Mothers in the Middle Ages.* New York and London: Garland.

The New Jerusalem Bible
1985 New York: Doubleday.

O'Connor, Edward Dennis (ed.)
1958   *The Dogma of the Immaculate Conception: History and Significance.*
Notre Dame, IN: University of Notre Dame Press.

Orland, Barbara – Elvira Scheich (eds.)
1995   *Das Geschlecht der Natur: Feministische Beiträge zur Geschichte und Theorie der Naturwissenschaften.* Frankfurt am Main: Suhrkamp.

Ozick, Cynthia
1994   "Hannah and Elkanah: Torah as the Matrix for Feminism", in Christina Büchmann – Celina Spiegel (eds.), 88-93.

Pomata, Gianna
1995   "Vollkommen oder verdorben? Der männliche Samen im frühneuzeitlichen Europa", *L'Homme* 6.2: 59-85.

Preus, Anthony
1977   "Galen's Criticism of Aristotle's Conception Theory", *Journal of the History of Biology* 10.1: 65-85.

Preuss, Julius
1978   *Biblical and Talmudic Medicine.* Fred Rosner (trans. and ed.). New York and London: Sanhedrin Press.

Protevangelium Jacobi. The Other Bible
1984   Willis Barnstone (ed.), 385-92. New York: HarperCollins.

Reames, Sherry L.
1985   *The Legenda Aurea: A Reexamination of its Paradoxical History.* Madison, WI: University of Wisconsin Press.

Rosner, Fred
1977   *Medicine in the Bible and the Talmud: Selections from Classical Jewish Sources.* New York: Ktav Publishing House.

Snowman, J.
1974   *A Short History of Talmudic Medicine.* New York: Hermon Press.

St. Anne
2002   The Catholic Encyclopedia Online
http://www.newadvent.org/cathen/01538a.htm 12.2.2002

Tress, Daryl McGowan
1992   "The Metaphysical Science of Aristotle's *Generation of Animals* and its Feminist Critics", *Review of Metaphysics* 46: 307-341.

Tuana, Nancy
1995   "Der schwächere Samen: Androzentrismus in der Aristotelischen Zeugungstheorie unter der Galenschen Anatomie", in Barbara Orland – Elvira Scheich (eds.), 203-223.

Voragine, Jacobus de
1995   *The Golden Legend: Readings on the Saints.* William Granger Ryan (trans.). Vol. 2. Princeton, NJ: Princeton University Press.

Zimmermann, Albert (ed.)
1988   *Thomas von Aquin: Werk und Wirkung im Licht neuerer Forschungen.* Berlin: Walter de Gruyter.

Lay Piety and Christian Diversity

A Pig for *Samhain?*[1]

Joseph Falaky Nagy, UCLA

As I write, Hallowe'en is around the corner, and, along with my Celticist colleagues scattered across the US, I look forward with a combination of weary amusement and exasperation to the inevitably shallow reports in newspapers and on television having to do with the origins of the celebration of Hallowe'en (including trick-or-treating) and its supposedly "Celtic" origins. If reporters and researchers in the popular media did their homework properly, they would find plenty of scholarship (such as Hutton 1996: 360-385 and Tuleja 1994: 82-90) arguing convincingly that there is no evidence of a direct link between the establishment of the church's feast days of All Hallows and All Souls at the beginning of November and anything particularly Celtic, nor any compelling evidence for seeing as specifically Celtic any modern-day American customs associated with Hallowe'en, such as mischief committed on the eve of the day, children's dressing up in costume, or begging for treats.

In fact, the data collected by folklorists and ethnologists show that in northern European rural traditions (and not just in Ireland or other areas where Celtic traditions persist), already in the middle ages, early November signaled, in social terms:

(1) The definitive conclusion of the harvest and other outdoor activities.
(2) A time for taking stock of resources and prospects for survival during the winter – a task that often included the slaughtering of animals and consuming or preserving their meat.[2]
(3) The homecoming of those who had been away, including members of the community who had been tending the cattle or sheep in summer pastures.
(4) The beginning of a period of a more secluded, indoor life, punctuated by bouts of intensified social activity outdoors, weather permitting.

The concern with the supernatural which often marks northern European observances and beliefs relating to early November is to a significant degree a function of the *liminal* nature of the season, or, I should say, this time between seasons. The presence of the dead among the living as honored or feared guests, another feature of the folklore of early November, is doubtless connected to the sense of

---

1   This paper is dedicated to that fine Irishman Henry Ansgar Kelly, who has taught us to be wary of popular explanations of seasonal customs.
2   November is known as "blood" or "slaughter month" in various Germanic traditions (Walsh 2000: 633).

"return" that permeates this time, and also to the conclusion of the harvest, a social activity that can evoke memories of the dead even in cultures on the other
side of the world from Europe (see for instance Malinowski 1948: 171-190). And
the supposed opportunity for prognostication and especially for finding out about
one's future marriage partner, which constitutes another common trait of the
northern European observance of November, can be explained as a prudent collective drawing of attention to the outcome of relationships contracted by young
people and their families during the "outdoor" months, relationships that might
well receive further sanction during the winter months to come or in the spring
that lies beyond.

There is a special Irish reflex of this November complex, called *Samhain* (as
spelled in Modern Irish; in earlier Irish orthography it is *Samain*). In his authoritative book on *Early Irish Farming* (which is about far more than just farming),
Fergus Kelly[3] gives the following description of this institution, attested in early
medieval Irish literature as well as in the folklore of the Irish countryside as it was
studied in the nineteenth and twentieth centuries:

> The festival of *Samain* at the beginning of November marks the start of winter. It fea-
> tures prominently in early Irish mythological literature as a time when the barriers be-
> tween the natural world and the Otherworld are removed, and many tales deal with en-
> counters at *Samain* between mortals and the fairy people. *Samain* is a time for public
> assembly (*óenach*) and feasting (*feis*). The main dish at such feasts seems to have been
> the *banb samna* 'the piglet of Samain'.

>   (Kelly 1998: 461)

Kelly's description is refreshingly free of the misreadings and over-readings of
the evidence on Samhain that characterize not only popular but even many learned
surveys of Celtic tradition. This baggage of speculation includes the automatic
assumption that Samhain is a reflex of a pan-Celtic festival roughly congruent
with our date of November 1, and the same as the *Samon-* mentioned in the
Gaulish Coligny Calendar (Rees and Rees 1961: 84-89);[4] that Samhain marks the
beginning of the "Celtic" year; and that there obtains a special connection between Samhain and some particular pagan Irish divinity or other. The enthusiasm
that produces such speculations (often presented as facts) among scholars and
popularizers alike, while usually hindering more than helping scholarly inquiry, is
nonetheless understandable in light of the remarkably liberal attitude of many
medieval Irish *litterati* toward the recording – or in some cases the confabulation

---

3   Professor Kelly of the School of Celtic Studies of the Dublin Institute for Advanced Studies
     is no relation to the honoree.
4   The study of this artifact attracts its own set of possibly misleading assumptions, such as that
     it represents "druidic" calendrical tradition.

– of traditions that seemingly derive from before the coming of Christianity, and that pertain to a non-Christian and non-classical world view.

Kelly in his description includes the human, social aspect of Samhain as it is noted in our medieval sources – it is said by one of these to be a time of feasting and assembly, of seven days' duration (Dillon 1953: 1; Gantz 1981: 155) – but also mentions its more famous, supernatural aspect. The night before Samhain is a time when the *síde* 'otherworldly dwellings' are said to be open, and contact between worlds consequently more likely. Kelly also emphasizes the general *seasonal* (as opposed to any specific *calendrical*) significance to Samhain. Even folk tradition as recent as the last century recognizes it as one of the "quarter days" marking the change of seasons – the other three being St Brigit's Day (February 1, once known as *Imbolc*), May 1 (still known as *Bealtaine*), and, on or around August 1, *Lúnasa* (Ó Duilearga 1981: 317).

While giving "just the facts, ma'am" about Samhain in the passage quoted above, Kelly makes an observation that, given what our sources tell us, is surprisingly rare in the scholarly discussion of November 1: namely, that the celebration of Samhain features or even centers on the slaying of a pig specially raised for this occasion, and feasting upon its meat. In her 1961 study of Samhain, Françoise Le Roux, a scholar of the "mythological literature" that Kelly mentions in passing, similarly noted the importance of the pig in the festivities that took place on the eve of November 1 (Le Roux 1961: 494-499). Her reading of the evidence tilts toward a view of the sacrificed pig as a sacred animal, a status that swine probably did enjoy in pre-Christian Celtic traditions (O'Rahilly 1947: 122-123; Ní Chatháin 1979-1980; Ford 1990), and the sacrifice as connected to the pre-Christian worship of the god Lug and to the Feast of Tara, an institution of questionable historicity (Binchy 1958: 127-138). There is, however, little account taken by her of the practical aspects of pig slaughter and consumption at this time of year, when in many European folk cultures a portion of the livestock is traditionally slaughtered, especially weaker members of the herd that are unlikely to last through the winter, and animals that have little value other than as sources of meat, such as pigs (Danaher 1972: 232; Lucas 1960: 15-16).[5] Le Roux, moreover, while noting the *banb samna* (specifically as mentioned in the glossary compiled by the sixteenth-century legal scholar Domhnall O'Davoren: Stokes 1904: 366), is surprisingly skimpy in her references to instances of Samhain-tide pig-feasting in medieval Irish narrative literature, which not infrequently uses early November as the time frame for one or more events of the story being told.

---

5   The medieval English poet John Gower says in *Confessio Amantis* concerning November, "Thanne is the larder of the swyn" (Book 7, line 1166). G. C. Macaulay glosses the line thus: "Then the swine are killed and the larder, or bacon-tub, comes into use" (Macaulay 1901: 525). I thank my colleague Donka Minkova for this reference.

The Irish sources besides O'Davoren that Le Roux cites as indicating the consumption of pigs at Samhain – the day, month, or season – include the seventh-century Life of St. Columba by Adomnán, who in a grim tale of saintly revenge seems to refer to a custom of slaying and consuming a pig fed on the crop of acorns that becomes available in the fall (2: 23; Sharpe 1995: 172-173); the late Old Irish/early Middle Irish (ninth-tenth-century) saga text *Scéla Muicce Meic Dathó* "News about Mac Dathó's Pig" (Thurneysen 1935; Gantz 1981: 180-187), which features a contentious feast centered on a gigantic swine raised and slaughtered for the occasion; and the twelfth-century tale of a king's downfall, *Aided Muircertaig meic Erca* "Death of Muircertach mac Erca," in which the ill-fated king and his company are fed on magically created swine by a supernatural female who is intent on seducing Muircertach (Nic Dhonnchadha 1964: 12-13, 22).

In fact, these are hardly the only and certainly not the strongest traces of the Samhain pig to be found in the literature. Adomnán, writing in Latin, does not specifically mention Samhain or the month of November, nor does the text of *Scéla Muicce Meic Dathó*. *Aided Muircertaig meic Erca* does, but considerably after the mention of the production and consumption of the magical swine, and it is not at all clear from the text whether the latter episodes took place during the period of Samhain mentioned. Still, while Le Roux may have been casual in her summoning of evidence, she was correct in making the connection between Samhain and swine. I supply the following references to pig-eating that specifically place it on Samhain or Samhain Eve, passages from medieval texts that Le Roux may have had in mind and could have used in her argument, to considerable effect.

(1) In the late Middle-Irish eleventh- or twelfth-century text *Macgnimartha Finn* "Boyhood Deeds of Finn," the young poet-hero happens upon the communities of two twin *síde* 'otherworldly dwellings, mounds', the Dá Chích Anann "Paps of Anu" hills in Co. Kerry, exposed on the eve of Samhain. He sees a great fire in each of the supernatural residences and overhears the following exchange between a denizen of the one and a denizen of the other: "'Are you well-mannered?' – 'Well indeed – is there anything to be brought from us to you?' 'If something is brought to us, something will be given in return for it',, (*Is maith bar suabais-si? Maith em. . . In mbertar ni uaine duib-si? Dia tardtar dino duin-ne sin, berthar ni daib-si tar a eisi*). Then a person emerges out of one of the hills carrying to the other a kneading trough (*losat*) that holds a (presumably slain) pig (*muic*),[6] a calf (*laeg*), and a bunch of garlic (*dlocht*

---

6   The pig word is modified in the text by *slainsi*, seemingly a noun in the genitive. Thomas O'Rahilly suggested emending this to *sláinge*, thus relating the pig to the *mucc shlánga/mucc shláinge*, a (species of?) creature mentioned in various texts pertaining to Finn (O'Rahilly 1947: 123; Nagy 1985: 56-57). I would translate the expression as "pig of health" (cf.

crema) "[for] the day of Samhain" (*dia samna sin*). After he witnesses this transaction, Finn throws a spear into the *síd* and serendipitously (or magically) hits and slays the person who had slain the poet Oircbél, Finn's colleague for whom he had been seeking revenge (Meyer 1882: 202-203; Nagy 1985: 166-70; Oircbél had been slain by otherworldly forces on the eve of the previous Samhain). Clearly, we have here a tableau of Samhain feasting, in which pork serves as a main course, alongside veal. One of the more curious details in this episode is the use of a kneading trough to transport the meat. This unusual practice perhaps indicates a connection between the slaying of the *banb samna* and the harvesting of grain, and a commingling (as it were) of meat and cereal, a motif that reappears in data presented below.

(2) In the tenth-eleventh-century Middle Irish saga *Togail Bruidne Da Derga* "Destruction of Da Derga's Hostel," the ill-fated king Conaire finds himself in a guest house where all signs point to his impending doom, including the presence of a sinister-looking woman, Cailb, who recites a list of her several alternative names, a sign of her supernatural provenance. The first name she gives is *Samain* (Knott 1936: 17). Also boding ill for Conaire is the attendance of two other outlandish guests, one of them a swineherd of the *síd*. Fer Caille, the other, is said to be roasting a whole pig that is alive and squealing, while the swineherd is tending to the roasting of a head of a pig, still squealing (Knott 1936: 11, 35, 40-42). While the *Togail* itself does not specify the time when the feast in Da Derga's hostel took place, a *dindshenchas* (placename) text from the eleventh or twelfth century asserts that the feast and the ensuing destruction of those attending took place on Samhain Eve (Stokes 1894: 331).

(3) The incidents in in *Scéla Muicce Meic Dathó*, particularly the feast of the gigantic swine raised on great quantities of milk and poison (the latter symbolizing the deadly frenzy that the pig arouses among the guests, vying to win the hero's portion of the meat), may in fact be relevant to our topic, if this text is taken in conjunction with one from the *dindshenchas* tradition (eleventh or twelfth century) that places the feast at the time of Samhain (Gwynn 1924: 194; also in Thurneysen 1935: 24).

(4) In the *Cath Maige Tuired* "Battle of Mag Tuired" text, specifically in the earlier of two recensions, which dates to to the late Old Irish/early Middle Irish period (ninth-tenth centuries), the story is told of an epochal face-off between

---

sláin(t)e 'health, well-being'), following Standish Hayes O'Grady's rendering of it as "prophylactic pig" (O'Grady 1892[2]: 158), and would compare this pig name to that of another Finn-related pig, *Béo* 'Living' (see below).

two of the primeval population groups of Ireland: the Túatha Dé Danann "People of the Goddess Danu," whom the literary tradition presents as the primary pantheon of pre-Christian Ireland, and the Fomoire, a demonic race that perennially haunts Irish pre-history and its settlements as configured in literary tradition. The muster of the Túatha in anticipation of the battle (in which they will triumph) takes place on the day before Samhain, and the battle itself, presumably, on Samhain (Gray 1982: 46). To spy on the Fomoire and delay them while his forces gather, Lug, the leader of the Túatha, sends the Dagda (a character whose epithet means "Good God") to the camp of the Fomoire to gather information about them. The enemy, in order to poke fun at the Dagda, who is known to be inordinately fond of *litiu* 'porridge', cook a great quantity of it, using milk and flour (*men*), and flavoring it with whole goats, sheep, and swine. The *litiu* is poured into a pit, and, in a nightmare version of a guest's plight, the Dagda is told to eat it all, and that if he does not, he will be slain. The guest, however, rises to the challenge, with the help of an instrument that the text describes thus: "Then the Dagda took his ladle, and it was big enough for a man and a woman to lie in the middle of it. These are the bits that were in it: halves of salted swine and a quarter of lard" (*Gabois íer sin a léig, 7 ba himaircithe go tallfad lánomain ina lige foro láur na léghie. It é didiu m[ír]ionn fordu-rauhotar inde: lethau tindei 7 cethromthu bloinge*: Gray 1982: 46-47). Tellingly, the bits of meat and fat that are dredged out of the pitful of porridge with the Dagda's spoon are all pork, seemingly the preferred meat for Samhain. It is combined here with milk (as in the case of Mac Dathó's milk-fed pig)[7] and flour (which perhaps along with milk we would expect to find in a *losat* 'kneading trough', the vessel containing the pig and calf in the *Macgnimartha Finn* text). The *potpourri* nature of what the Dagda is served is reminiscent of the traditional food most typically prepared and consumed at Samhain in Irish rural communities of the recent past, *colcannon* (anglicized from *cál ceannan* 'white-headed cabbage'), a combination of potato, cabbage, and butter and/or milk. Additional nonedible items, especially a ring, were added to this harvest composition, potato and cabbage having replaced grain in the diet of most Irish workers of the land since the late eighteenth century. The finding of the ring or the other items concealed in the colcannon constituted a holiday game, licensed play with one's food, that could presage important events in the player's future, especially marriage (Ó Súilleabháin 1942: 346; Danaher 1972: 218-227). Perhaps the curiously gratuitous sexual element to the description of the size

---

7   Cited by Le Roux (1961: 492) is a medieval Irish quartet of quatrains on the quarter days, in which Samhain is said to be a time for meat (*carna*), tripe or goat (*cadla*), and dairy products, particularly buttermilk and butter; nuts and ale are also mentioned (Meyer 1894: 49).

of the Dagda's ladle (big enough to hold a couple) is meant to evoke an earlier medieval version of this custom and belief. In any event, it does foreshadow what happens next in the story of the Dagda's Samhain Eve adventure, an encounter with a woman who engages in a spectacular bout of sex with him (Gray 1982: 46-48).

The reader may have noticed that colcannon, unlike the Dagda's dish, contains no meat. Here the effect of the overlay of Christian tradition becomes apparent, since with the establishment of the feast day of All Saints on November 1 in western Christendom, abstinence from meat on October 31 became the custom and rule. This development did not drive the pig out of Samhain altogether, however. The mention in a mid-nineteenth-century source of a "Muck Olla" (cf. *mucc* 'pig')[8] who is rampant in east County Cork on Hallowe'en, and whose followers in costume went about collecting his tribute (Hackett 1852-1853: 308-309; Danaher 1972: 213-214), may be a clue to an Irish parallel to a Welsh folk tradition centered on this date, according to which the monstrous *Hwch Ddu Gwta* 'Black Curtailed Pig' roams the countryside on *Nos Calan Gaeaf* 'the Eve of the Calends of Winter', looking for unwary victims heading home from the bonfires that are set that night (Rhys 1901[1]: 225-226; Jones 1930: 148-149; Owen 1987: 123-124). This particular Welsh association of Hallowe'en and scary pig, attested only in folk tradition and nowhere in medieval Welsh literature, offers some of the strongest available evidence for cognate fall traditions in Ireland and Celtic Britain (Wales). Other fearsome pigs are perhaps indicated in the following lines from a Welsh folksong sung by cross-dressing boys and girls out late at night on Hallowe'en, verses that not only highlight the feeding of, not the feeding on, pigs, but leave unnervingly unsaid just what it is they are to eat: "It is one o'clock/It is two o'clock,/It is time for the pigs to have dinner" (*Mae'n un o'r gloch/Mae'n ddau o'r gloch,/Mae'n bryd i'r moch gael cin(i)o*: Jones 1930: 149).[9]

---

8   *Pace* Kevin Danaher (1972: 213-214), who proposes *macalla* 'echo' (literally 'son of the cliff') as the Irish behind "Muck Olla." William Hackett, the source for the description of the Muck Olla custom, clearly understands it to be a pig (Hackett 1852-1853: 307). I gratefully acknowledge Máirín Ní Dhonnchadha's having made Hackett's survey of "porcine legends" available to me.

9   Incidents of pigs, including domesticated swine, killing and even feeding on humans are not unknown in medieval Irish literature (Kelly 1998: 154-155, 180). In the so-called Tripartite Life of St. Patrick, a boy eaten by pigs is resurrected through the power of the saint, after the child's bones are collected per Patrick's orders (Mulchrone 1939: 119-120; Stokes 1887[1]: 199). An epic-size pampered pig in the Middle Irish text *Fled Bricrenn* "Bricriu's Feast" is prepared over the seven years of its life for his début in the dining hall by being fed on milk-and cereal-based porridge in the spring; fresh curds and milk in the summer; nuts and wheat grain in the fall; and meat with broth during the winter (*Ata torc secht m-bliadan and; [or ro boi] orc becc, ní dechaid inna béolu acht littiu lemnachta ocus menadach i-n erroch, ocus fírcroith ocus fírlemnacht issamrud, eitne cnó ocus fírchruithnecht hi fogomur, ocus feóil ocus enbruthe hi gemrud*: Henderson 1899: 8).

Irish swine that "n'ont rien de comestible ou de sympathique," as Le Roux put it (1961: 493), are also to be found in medieval Irish literature, in an onomastic episode from the Middle Irish saga *Cath Maige Mucrama* "Battle of Mag Mucrama" that explains the name *Mag Mucrama* as *Mag Muc(c)-rímae* 'Field of Pig-Counting'. It was here, says our text, that Medb the queen of Connacht attempted to count the number of pigs in a herd that had escaped out of the Cave of Crúachan (a portal for sinister supernatural forces in medieval Irish tradition). This herd, in the destructive wake of which neither grain nor grass nor leaf grew for seven years, had proven to be impossible to count, or to slay, on account of their restless movement. Medb, however, succeeded in counting them, but then the tabulation was nearly upset by a spare pig that jumped over her chariot. The quick-witted queen grabbed the animal's shank, yet, with the momentum of its leap, the pig managed to escape, leaving its leg and entire skin in Medb's hand (O Daly 1975: 48). The prominence of pigs, the breakdown of the boundary between worlds, the concern with protecting crops present and future, and even the challenge of counting or measuring the seemingly innumerable or immeasurable (compare the seemingly limitless porridge served the Dagda, which, however, he manages to encompass within his belly, or the ritual attempts to predict the future that are associated with Samhain) – all these themes in the story of the naming of Mag Mucrama would make it a fitting Samhain tale indeed, but the text does not give it a temporal setting (nor do the *dindshenchas* versions of the same tale: Stokes 1894: 470; Gwynn 1913: 382-384). And yet the prominent motif of stripping in the story of Medb's count finds its strongest intratextual parallel in the account of the fate of the Munster king Ailill Ólomm, from whose ear a *síd* woman tears off the skin after he rapes her (hence his epithet *ó-lomm* 'naked ear') on Samhain eve. This violent encounter occurs while Ailill is trying to protect a hill that every November experiences a devastation similar to that which the pigs from the Cave of Crúachan inflict on field and forest.[10] A similarly tantalizing coincidence of an overt Samhain episode and an adventure involving destructive swine takes place in the *Macgnimartha Finn*, a text already mentioned. Here, the young hero Finn, several incidents before he overhears the otherwordly conversation on Samhain Eve, slays a monstrous pig ravaging Munster. The creature, called *Béo* 'Living', thus provides a name for Slíab Muicce 'Pig Mountain' (anglicized *Slieve Muck*) in Co. Tipperary, and its head is given by Finn as a bride-price to a smith, whose daughter Finn marries (Meyer 1882: 200-201; Nagy 1985: 147-148). It is perhaps significant that the girl's name is *Cruithne*, which may be related to the ethnonym *Cruithne* 'Picts', but more likely, given the narrative scenario of the land being rescued from a destructive pig, is a reflex of *cruithnecht* 'wheat'. Such "bad," formidable pigs might seem quite removed from the unresisting pigs to be eaten at Samhain, but of course what makes these

---

10   On these and other, non-seasonal instances of the motif of stripping in *Cath Maige Mucrama*, see Ó Cathasaigh 1981.

swine bad, big, and numerous is their frenzied rooting up and eating everything in sight, a destructive propensity recognized in medieval Irish law tracts (Kelly 1998: 142-143) that fattens them up and makes them all the more desirable to humans as food.[11]

It would appear that in Ireland, following the period after most of the texts discussed above were composed, the edible if not the monstrous *banb samna* migrated from the beginning of November, which became inhospitable to the eating of meat, to a saint's celebration that in other parts of medieval Europe became not only the focal point of the traditional pre-winter slaughter of livestock but also an autumnal counterpart to Mardi Gras, a time to consume meat and other foods and drink. This is the day, or rather the eve of the day, commemorating the death of St. Martin of Tours, November 11 in the church calendar, which in Frankish custom came to mark the beginning of the austerities of Advent (Walsh 2000: 632). The cult of St. Martin was imported to Ireland early on in the course of its Christianization (Gwynn 1966), and the popularity of the saint, as made manifest in legends about his death and customs having to do with his feast day, remained strong in rural Ireland (except for areas in the southwest and the northeast) down to the twentieth century (Morris 1939; Ó Súilleabháin 1957).

Folk tradition, in the form of various sayings, exhibits a keen awareness of the connection between Samhain and St. Martin's Day, for instance: "Nine nights and a night without counting/From the night of the cabbage" – or, as a variant has it, "night of apple-chewing" – "to the night of the slaughter," or, "night of bone-chewing" (Ó Súilleabháin 1957: 253, 261).[12] And tradition (or the saint himself – "No saint in Heaven is more strict than Martin" [*Níl aon naomh ins na Flaithis is géire ná Mártan*], another saying goes) dictates that the slaughter must take place *before* November 11, between November 1 and 10, and not after it, as if to keep the blood-letting on the Samhain side of the saint's feast (Ó Súilleabháin 1957: 254). Dispensing with the sacrifice to St. Martin, the marking of the domestic space and members of the family

---

11   According to *dindshenchas* tradition, Léna, the man who raised Mac Datho's pig, was slain by it in the course of transporting the animal to the feast. During the trip Léna took a nap, and the pig buried him alive while it was rooting. Léna, however, had the last laugh, since the pig died as well, impaled on the tip of Léna's sword, which stuck out from the ground (Stokes 1895: 63; Thurneysen 1935: 23-24).

12   The "night without counting" (a rendering of the corresponding section in the Irish version of the saying, *oíche gan áireamh*, which could also be translated "a night outside the count": Ó Súilleabháin 1942, 343, 347; Ó Súilleabháin 1957: 253) intriguingly echoes the extra pig that nearly ruins Medb's count in *Cath Maige Mucrama*, and more generally reflects the theme of (im)measurability that haunts traditions about Samhain.

While he does not take note of St. Martin's Day, Jack Santino in his study of Hallowe'en in Northern Ireland points out that with the shift from the Julian to the Gregorian calendar in Ireland in the mid-eighteenth century, November 11 came to be known as "Old Halleve" (Santino 1998: 70, 88-98).

with the animal's blood, or the consuming of it in his honor, constitutes an invitation
to disaster and to a loss of livestock and human life as well, according to folk belief
exemplifed in an English-language saying: "The man who will not skin for Martin
will have many occasions to skin during the following year" (Ó Súilleabháin 1957:
254).

In those parts of rural Ireland where the tradition of celebrating St. Martin was
kept up, usually the sacrificed animal was a fowl, but other animals could be substi-
tuted, especially if they were sick, or animals could be mortgaged to the saint, with
the promise that they would be sacrificed before St. Martin's Day of the following
year. Pious legends have been recorded in which the devotee of the saint sacrifices a
highly prized animal, pet, or even a child for want of anything else to sacrifice and
subsequently is rewarded by the saint, or the sacrificed victim is miraculously recov-
ered (Ó Súilleabháin 1957: 253-254). Pigs seemingly do not figure in these modern
customs of animal sacrifice, but then the rural population of early modern Ireland,
particularly in the west, could rarely afford to raise pigs.

Earlier, literary sources, on the other hand, note the killing of a special pig on St.
Martin's Day, a young fattened female called a *lupait*, which is equated with the *banb
samna* (Kelly 1998: 85; Stokes 1904: 407). A hagiographic text of late Middle or
Early Modern Irish provenance traces the custom of the sacrifice of a pig to Martin to
St. Patrick, who established it as tribute to his monastic mentor (Stokes 1887[2]:
560).[13] Moreover, while modern Irish folk tradition may have had to find a substitute
for pork on St. Martin's Day, it continued to celebrate the connection between pigs
and St. Martin and his feast with a remarkable legend according to which these animals were originally created at the saint's suggestion out of the flesh or fat of Martin
himself (Ó Súilleabháin 1957: 259; 1970: 268). Variants of this legend, which juxta-
pose the saint's use of his own person with another demonstration of his power,
namely, making a green tree grow out of a piece of dough cast into the fire, sustain
the linkage between pork and vegetation that we have already noticed in earlier Samhain traditions (Ó Súilleabháin 1957: 259). Indeed, the gap between the saintly flesh
or fat and the piece of dough is perhaps even narrower. Although there is no prece-

---

13   Henry Morris notes that the late fifteenth-manuscript preserving this anecdote also includes a
     copy of the *Scéla Muicce Meic Dathó*, which may have "suggested to [the scribe] to explain
     the killing of a sheep on St. Michael's festival [another anecdote in the manuscript] and the
     killing of a pig at Martinmas" (Morris 1939: 233). Morris also offers the following in connec-
     tion with the St. Martin's feast: "Why a pig? Because, in my opinion, it was then the com-
     monest small domestic animal, and in size it could be accommodated to the size of the family
     party" (Morris 1939: 233).

     The medieval Irish were not alone in slaughtering pigs for St. Martin's Day. My col-
     league Shirley Arora informs me that the assocation also obtains in Spanish tradition, as wit-
     nessed in the saying, *A cada puerco le llega su San Martin*, "To every pig comes his own St.
     Martin['s Day]," that is, everyone has to face adversity sometime (Campos and Barella 1993:
     296).

dent whatsoever in the hagiographic tradition that grew up around the figure of St. Martin in late antiquity and the middle ages for these peculiar Irish developments, Irish folklore insists that St. Martin was a miller, or that he died a martyr's death after being thrown into a mill (Ó Súilleabháin 1957: 258).[14]

As with the study of any long-lived folkloric tradition, there is plenty left to discover about the pig at Samhain. For instance, some application of Frazer's model of the "Corn-Spirit" is probably appropriate here, given the connection between the *banb samna* and the harvest (Frazer 1922: 532-536). Also worthy of investigation are the possible seasonal backgrounds to some fearsome pigs mentioned in medieval Welsh literature: the sow Henwen 'Old White One', whose whiteness offers a contrast to the blackness of her later-attested swinish colleague, the Hwch Ddu Gwta, and who is said to have given birth to a grain of wheat, a grain of barley (each of which produced the best strain of grain of its kind grown in Wales), a bee, a wolf cub, an eagle chick, and a kitten, but no piglets (Bromwich 1991: 44-54);[15] and the Twrch Trwyth 'Kingly Boar', the hunting of whom is coupled with the growing of crops in preparation for a wedding feast, in the list of tasks set for the hero Culhwch, his cousin Arthur, and Arthur's men in the earliest extant Arthurian tale, *Kulhwch ac Olwen* "Culhwch and Olwen" (Bromwich and Evans 1992: 21-28; Ford 1977: 137-144).[16] On the other side of the Irish Sea, there remains the mystery of the sister of Patrick's, a saint in her own right, named Lupait (Latinized as *Lupita*), who according to medieval hagiographic tradition is slain by her enraged brother when he learns that she has broken her vow of celibacy and born a child (Nagy 1997: 247-250). It would be useful to explore whether her story represents another recycling of the hardy figure of the *banb samna*.[17]

---

14 A similar equation between flesh and flour is drawn in the Second Branch of the medieval Welsh Mabinogi, where the fierce Welsh hero Efnisien squeezes to death Irish warriors hidden in bags and then poetically commemorates them as *amryw blawd* 'a form of flour' (Thomson 1961: 13; Ford 1978: 69).

15 The connection between swine and (the sowing of) grain that is adumbrated in this remarkable account of Henwen's progeny may have an Indo-European resonance. Compare the ancient Greek autumnal festival of the Thesmophoria, during which the remains of pigs (animals sacred to Demeter, the goddess of grain and its cultivation) were ritually mixed together with the seed to be sown (Nilsson 1940: 24-25).

16 No indication is given in the text of the time of year when the hunt for the Twrch Trwyth took place, but "in the classic [medieval] French treatises the boar season is said to run from the Feast of the Holy Cross (14 September), or from Michaelmas, when they were high in flesh, to St Andrew's Day (30 November), when they joined the sows for mating" (Cummins 1988: 97).

17 There is also the tantalizing case of the Early Modern Irish poem, which has received virtually no critical attention, about a (sacrificed?) pig the death of which is fulsomely lamented, but which is at the same time mocked mercilessly as a poor morsel (Quin 1965).

References

Binchy, D. A.
  1958   The Fair of Tailtiu and the Feast of Tara. *Ériu* 18: 113-138.
Bromwich, Rachel (ed. and trans.)
  1991   *Trioedd Ynys Prydein: The Welsh Triads*. 2nd ed., with corrections. Car-
              diff: University of Wales Press.
Bromwich, Rachel – D. Simon Evans (eds.)
  1992   *Culhwch and Olwen: An Edition and Study of the Oldest Arthurian Tale*.
              Cardiff: University of Wales Press.
Campos, Juana G. – Ana Barella (eds.)
  1993   *Diccionario de refranes*. Rev. ed. Madrid: Espasa Calpe.
Cummins, John
  1988   *The Hound and the Hawk: The Art of Medieval Hunting*. London: Wei-
              denfeld and Nicolson.
Danaher, Kevin
  1972   *The Year in Ireland*. Cork: Mercier Press.
Dillon, Myles (ed.)
  1953   *Serglige Con Culainn*. Mediaeval and Modern Irish Series 14. Dublin:
              Dublin Institute for Advanced Studies.
Ford, Patrick K. (trans.)
  1977   *The Mabinogi and Other Medieval Welsh Tales*. Berkeley, Los Angeles,
              and London: University of California Press.
Ford, Patrick K.
  1990   A Highly Important Pig. In *Celtic Language, Celtic Culture: A Fest-
              schrift for Eric P. Hamp*, A. T. E. Matonis and Daniel F. Melia (eds.),
              292-304. Van Nuys, CA: Ford and Bailie.
Frazer, Sir James George
  1922   *The Golden Bough: A Study in Magic and Religion*. Abbr. ed. New York:
              Macmillan.
Gantz, Jeffrey (trans.)
  1981   *Early Irish Myths and Sagas*. Harmondsworth: Penguin.
Gray, Elizabeth A. (ed. and trans.)
  1982   *Cath Maige Tuired: The Second Battle of Mag Tuired*. Irish Texts Society
              52. Naas, Co. Kildare: Irish Texts Society.
Gwynn, Aubrey, S. J.
  1966   The Cult of Saint Martin in Ireland. *Irish Ecclesiastical Record* 105: 353-
              364.
Gwynn, E. J. (ed. and trans.)
  1913, 1924 *The Metrical Dindshenchas*, Vols. 3, 4. Todd Lecture Series 10-11. Dub-
              lin: Hodges, Figgis.
Hackett, William
  1852-1853   Porcine Legends. *Transactions of the Kilkenny Archaeological Society*,
              303-311.

Henderson, George (ed. and trans.)
1899   *Fled Bricrend: The Feast of Bricriu.* Irish Texts Society 2. London: Irish Texts Society.

Hutton, Ronald
1996   *The Stations of the Sun: A History of the Ritual Year in Britain.* Oxford: Oxford University Press.

Jones, T. Gwynn
1930   *Welsh Folklore and Folk-Custom.* London: Methuen & Co.

Kelly, Fergus
1998   *Early Irish Farming: A Study Based Mainly on the Law-Texts of the 7th and 8th Centuries AD.* Early Irish Law Series 4. Dublin: Dublin Institute for Advanced Studies.

Knott, Eleanor (ed.)
1936   *Togail Bruidne Da Derga.* Mediaeval and Modern Irish Series 8. Dublin: Dublin Institute for Advanced Studies.

Le Roux, Françoise
1961   Études sur le festiaire celtique. *Ogam* 13: 481-506.

Lucas, A. T.
1960   Irish Food before the Potato. *Gwerin* 3: 1-36.

Macaulay, G. C. (ed.)
1901   *The Complete Works of John Gower,* Vol. 3. Oxford: Clarendon Press.

Malinowski, Bronislaw
1948   Baloma; The Spirits of the Dead in the Trobriand Islands. In *Magic, Science and Religion, and Other Essays,* 149-274. Garden City NY: Doubleday.

Meyer, Kuno (ed.)
1882   Macgnimartha Find. *Revue celtique* 5: 195-204.
1894   *Hibernica Minora, being a Fragment of an Old-Irish Treatise on the Psalter.* Anecdota Oxoniensis, Mediaeval and Modern Series 8. Oxford: Clarendon Press.

Morris, Henry
1939   St. Martin's Eve. *Béaloideas* 9: 230-235.

Nagy, Joseph Falaky
1985   *The Wisdom of the Outlaw: The Boyhood Deeds of Finn in Gaelic Narrative Tradition.* Berkeley, Los Angeles, and London: University of California Press.
1997   *Conversing with Angels and Ancients: Literary Myths of Medieval Ireland.* Ithaca NY, and London: Cornell University Press.

Ní Chatháin, Próinséas
1979-1980   Swineherds, Seers, and Druids. *Studia Celtica* 14-15: 200-211.

Nic Dhonnchadha, Lil (ed.)
1964   *Aided Muircertaig meic Erca.* Mediaeval and Modern Irish Series 19. Dublin: Dublin Institute for Advanced Studies.

Nilsson, Martin
1940   *Greek Folk Religion.* New York: Columbia University Press.

Ó Cathasaigh, Tomás
  1981   The Theme of Lommrad in Cath Maige Mucrama. *Éigse* 18: 211-224.
O Daly, Máirín (ed. and trans.)
  1975   *Cath Maige Mucrama: The Battle of Mag Mucrama.* Irish Texts Society
            50. Dublin: Irish Texts Society.
Ó Duilearga, Séamus
  1981   *Seán Ó Conaill's Book: Stories and Traditions from Iveragh,* Máire
            MacNeill (trans.). Dublin: Folklore of Ireland Society.
O'Grady, Standish Hayes (ed. and trans.)
  1892   *Silva Gadelica: A Collection of Tales in Irish with Extracts Illustrating
            Persons and Places.* 2 vols. London: Williams and Norgate.
O'Rahilly, Thomas F.
  1946   *Early Irish History and Mythology.* Dublin: Dublin Institute for Ad-
            vanced Studies.
Ó Súilleabháin, Seán
  1942   *A Handbook of Irish Folklore.* Dublin: Folklore of Ireland Society.
  1957   The Feast of St. Martin in Ireland. In *Studies in Folklore in Honor of Stith
            Thompson,* W. Edson Richmond (ed.), 252-261. Bloomington: Indiana
            University Press.
  1970   Etiological Stories in Ireland. In *Medieval Literature and Folk Studies:
            Essays in Honor of Francis Lee Utley,* Jerome Mandel and Bruce A.
            Rosenberg (eds.), 257-274. New Brunswick, NJ: Rutgers University
            Press.
Owen, Trefor
  1987   *Welsh Folk Customs.* New ed. Llandysul: Gomer Press.
Quin, E. G. (ed. and trans.)
  1965   Truagh truagh an mhuc. *Hermathena* 101: 27-37.
Rees, Alwyn – Brinley Rees
  1961   *Celtic Heritage: Ancient Tradition in Ireland and Wales.* London:
            Thames and Hudson.
Rhys, John
  1901   *Celtic Folklore: Welsh and Manx.* 2 vols. Oxford: Clarendon Press.
Santino, Jack
  1998   *The Hallowed Eve: Dimensions of Culture in a Calendar Festival in
            Northern Ireland.* Lexington: University Press of Kentucky.
Sharpe, Richard (trans.)
  1995   *Adomnán of Iona, Life of St. Columba.* London: Penguin.
Stokes, Whitley (ed. and trans.)
  1887   *The Tripartite Life of Patrick, with Other Documents Relating to That
            Saint.* 2 vols. London: Her Majesty's Stationery Office.
Stokes, Whitley (ed. and trans.)
  1894   The Prose Tales in the Rennes Dindshenchas. *Revue celtique* 15 (1894):
            272-336, 418-484.
  1895   The Prose Tales in the Rennes Dindshenchas. *Revue celtique* 16 (1895):
            31-83, 135-167, 269-312.

Stokes, Whitley (ed.)
1904   O'Davoren's Glossary. *Archiv für celtische Lexikographie* 2: 197-504.

Thomson, Derick S. (ed.)
1961   *Branwen Uerch Lyr.* Mediaeval and Modern Welsh Series 2. Dublin: Dublin Institute for Advanced Studies.

Thurneysen, Rudolf (ed.)
1935   *Scéla Muicce Meic Dathó.* Mediaeval and Modern Irish Series 6. Dublin: Dublin Institute for Advanced Studies.

Tuleja, Tad
1994   Trick or Treat: Pre-Texts and Contexts. In *Halloween and Other Festivals of Death and Life*, Jack Santino (ed.), 82-102. Knoxville: University of Tennessee Press.

Walsh, Martin W.
2000   Martinmas [November 11]. In *Medieval Folklore: An Encyclopedia of Myths, Legends, Tales, Beliefs, and Customs*, Carl Lindahl, John McNamara, and John Lindow (eds.), 632-666. Santa Barbara, Denver, and Oxford: ABC-CLIO.

Marriage, War, and Good Government in Late-Fourteenth-Century Europe: The *De regimine principum* Tradition in Langland, Mézières, and Bovet

Michael Hanly, Washington State University/CNRS-UMR 8589, Paris

> Quer vecy tres perilleux temps,
> Nombre de quatorze cens ans,
> Au dit commun de maint crestiens,
> Juifz, Sarrazins et payens,
> Ou vous verrez fieres nouvelles.
> Les premisses n'en sont pas belles,
> Quant l'eglise est ainsy noire
> Et les Sarrazins ont victoire ...[1]
> [For behold, a very perilous time,
> The number of fourteen hundred years,
> As say many Christians,
> Jews, Saracens and pagans,
> When you will see portentous things.
> The omens are not good,
> When the Church is so sullied,
> And the Saracens are victorious ...]

Commonplaces about historical periods beg to be interrogated from time to time, and we're all inspired by the kind of thing Andy Kelly has done for us so many times: he'll advance a sequence of arguments made compelling by erudite research, and thereby demand either a questioning of received ideas, or a complete reversal of traditional thinking on the matter at hand. If I were to follow his lead, however, it would not be in any attempt to defend the European fourteenth century against its customary assessment as acme of disaster, because in this case, all the nasty things people have been saying are true. A devastating pestilence marked its midpoint; at the third quarter's close began a forty-year split in the Papacy; and as the new century approached, the obstinacy of an old war and fear of failure in a new one provoked despairing millenarian prophecies like the one above. The time was so beset with troubles that it seemed to many that God must be displeased with Christianity. In the West, while England and France were enmired in an endless and debilitating struggle, Europe's eastern frontier was vexed by the encroachment of an expansionist Islam. After victories at Crécy in 1346 and at Poitiers ten years later, the English had seen their French territorial conquests confirmed by the Treaty of Brétigny in 1360. Over the next generation,

---

1   Bovet in press (ed. Hanly): ll. 27-34. Further citations of the text and translation of this work are taken from Bovet in press. All other translations, unless otherwise noted, are mine.

however, the disciplined combat policies of France's Charles V turned the tide, and by 1380 his armies had conquered back almost all the land that had been ceded to the English at Brétigny. In the 1380s and 1390s, both countries suffered under the unstable leadership of boy kings, and the war continued in fits and starts. The commons on both sides called for an end to the fruitless expense, and both governments debated whether a return to battle or a continuation of periodic truces would be the better course. Along with deliberations over the lawfulness of Christian nations making war on each other came a growing recognition that open conflict with soldiers of another faith could come one day soon, for the Ottoman Turks had overrun the Serbs at Kossovo Polje in 1389, had taken Bulgaria by 1393 and Wallachia by 1395, and had crushed a combined Western force at Nicopolis in 1398. Amid the ongoing hostilities between the two greatest Christian nations, the voices of many in the West as well as the East clamored for a military effort to defend Christianity's borders. The seeming indirection among the most powerful European rulers incited many writers in this period to offer learned and urgent advice to their sovereigns, oftimes in the form of poetry.

This essay will compare the work of three contemporary writers who confront the upheaval of their times by engaging a pair of apparently divergent issues: warfare and matrimony. All three authors deal with war, just and unjust, and consider it both index of human fallenness and tool of God's judgment; all three perceive Christian marriage as embodying the divine order that should prevail in society; and all three consider their proclamations essential to the well-being of Western nations, an imperative for their rulers. This conviction that righteous leadership in the highest places would be needed to restore Christianity to the path from which it had wandered locates the arguments of these three in the *De regimine principum* tradition, the genre of learned commentary intended to be a "Mirror for princes".[2] Indeed, two of the three not only intended their works for the consumption of aristocratic or even royal readers, but actually presented those leaders with copies of the texts. I will consider first William Langland's pronouncements on war, and then those of Philippe de Mézières and Honorat Bovet, and will conclude with a consideration of their views on marriage. This first topic will necessitate a painfully brief outline of some major statements regarding medieval concepts of the just war.

Regarding the law or right to go to war (*jus ad bellum*), Saint Augustine concurs with classical authors who find that battle is only justified when peace is its goal: "Bellum geritur ut pax acquiratur" (1887: *PL* 33, col. 856).[3] Peace, for Augustine, is the natural state of existence for humankind; war, in general, is an

---

2   A useful historical summary of the genre is given by Gilbert 1938: 3-15.
3   Echoed in Augustine 1900: *PL* 41, col. 637, *De civitate Dei* 19.12: "Pacis igitur intentione geruntur et bella." For many of the details in this review I am indebted to Yeager 1987: 97-121. See also Russell 1975: 16-26.

evil, an absence of good and can be a tool of God's justice, a punishment for sin (Augustine 1900: *PL* 41, col. 640). As instrument of God's loving castigation, however, the Christian soldier must fight as a *pacificus*, so that the conquered might learn the usefulness of peace (Augustine 1887: *PL* 33, col. 856). Augustine could thereby condemn all aggressive wars, leaving room only for war to defend one's homeland. From the writings of Augustine were drawn what became commonly accepted as the three requisite conditions of hostilities that could be carried forth without sin: first, the authority of a prince to declare the war, a provision that prohibited killing during private quarrels; second, proper cause, which for Augustine was that of self-defense alone; and third, proper intention, which for Augustine had to be the restoration of peace. Saint Isidore of Seville offers a fundamental alternative to the arguments of Augustine: he holds that war can be waged, after a warning, for the recovery of lost property or lands or to compensate for particular transgressions (Isidore 1911: 2.18.1). Isidore thereby emphasizes the nature of the provocation – and not the more basic, personal motivation (peace) that he found in Augustine – and thus expands the possibilities for the just war. This view of things is made even more influential by theologians and canonists, notably Gratian, whose *Decretum* depends heavily upon the arguments of Isidore.[4] In a nutshell, then, Isidore and Gratian emphasize the wickedness of an enemy as the principal justification for war, while Augustine holds that the inclination of the heart must rule. Those who wished to make war in the later Middle Ages always seemed to be able to justify themselves through the writings of the greatest Christian scholars.

The most important English poets of the fourteenth century commented on the morality of war in their poetry, among them William Langland. His allegorical dream-vision *Piers Plowman* suggests that society could not depend on knights to make peace: it is clear that they are driven by selfish gain, and not to be trusted with the solemn responsibilities of governance. Even though *Piers Plowman*, unlike the works by the other two figures under consideration here, contains no overt dedication or other evidence of participation in the genre, in several sections of the poem Langland is clearly writing in the *De regimine principum* tradition. As Anna P. Baldwin has noted, the poet describes the ideal attributes of advisers to the prince, figures of momentous importance to the governments of England and France at a time that saw both nations beset by strife between ineffective kings and grasping royal councils. "For Langland", argues Baldwin, "as for other writers within this genre, the counselor who acts and speaks with truth (loyalty and honesty) is the one whom the king should trust" (1988: 78). The many voices in Langland's text advance arguments that can be seen as condemning both the Anglo-French war and the prospective conflict between Christendom and Islam.

---

4   Keen 1965: 63-81, cited in Yeager 1987: 101 n. 15.

Early in all of the three versions of his poem,[5] the poet describes an English royal court dominated by the character Meed, which name means "Reward" and can be taken to represent a system based on bribes and political favors. She is countered by another allegorical figure, holy Conscience, who seeks to steer the wavering king toward the path of truth.

The two clash memorably on the subject of war. Lady Meed berates Conscience for having counseled the king to make peace with his enemy and thereby abandon his designs at ruling France, the richest realm on earth: "Cowardly thow, Conscience, conseiledest him thennes – / To leven his lordshipe for a litel silver" (3.206-207).[6] Conscience, on the other hand, can be seen as representing the political positions documented by the Treaty of Brétigny: the English must renounce the throne of France, and keep the peace (Baldwin 1988: 76-77). Langland's A-Text, from around 1370, seems to hold out some hope that Edward III's heir would correct the mistakes of his father and embark upon a policy of peace. However, by the time of the B-Text, after Richard II had come to the throne in the late 1370s, all such optimism has vanished (Lowe 1997: 92). In this version, Langland's speakers put their faith only in the coming reign of Christ, who will usher in a new age; at that time, as Conscience observes in passus 3, Reason will rule (3.285), swords will be converted into plowshares, and, seemingly in response to this internal correction, both Jews and Muslims will convert to Christianity:

> Batailles shul none be, ne no man bere wepene,
> And what smyth that any smytheth be smyte therwith to dethe!
> *Non levabit gens contra gentem gladium &c.* [Nation shall not lift up sword against nation]
> And the myddel of a moone shal make the Jewes torne,
> And Sarsynes for that sighte shul synge *Gloria in excelsis &c* –
> For Makometh and Mede myshappe shul that tyme ...
>
> (3.323-325, 327-329)

Bad things, therefore, will befall both Meed and Mohammed, because once Christianity has reformed itself at the Savior's appearance, two manifestations of its corruption and disarray – graft and Islam – will cease to exist.

Langland continues his consideration of interfaith relations in passus 15, when the narrator, Will, hears a discourse by the character Anima on the function of Christian charity in the world, and on the contemporary Church's failure to practice that virtue. Anima holds that everyone, including Muslims and Jews, can be saved through faith in God. Making war on other religions never enters into this discussion. Anima does not curse the Saracens, and even demonstrates some sympathy for them, drawing parallels between their faith and Christianity, saying,

---

5   A.3.176-208; B.3.189-207; C.3.234-264.
6   All citations of the text of *Piers Plowman* are taken from Langland 1995.

... As clerkes in Corpus Christi feeste syngen and reden
That *sola fides sufficit* [faith alone suffices] to save with lewed peple –
And so may Sarsens be saved, scribes and Jewes.
Allas thanne! but oure looresmen lyve as thei leren us,
And for hir lyvynge that lewed men be the lother God agulten.
For Sarsens han somwhat semynge to oure bileve,
For thei love and bileve in o [Lede] almyghty,
And we, lered and lewed, [bileveth in oon God] –
Cristene and uncristene on oon God bileveth.

(15.387-395)

Anima complains that although many bishoprics bear titles "in the lands of the unbelievers", their bishops are shirking their duty to convert the pagans who inhabit these territories; Christ, after all, is the good shepherd, and considers the Saracens among those who should be saved (15.490-498). Anima adds that since Muslims and Jews are monotheistic and have much biblical tradition in common with Christians, it should be easy to convert them:

And sith that thise Sarsens, scribes and Grekes
Han a lippe of oure bileve, the lightloker, me thynketh,
Thei sholde turne, whoso travaile wolde to teche hem of the Trinite ...
For alle paynymes preieth and parfitly bileweth
In the [grete holy] God, and his grace asken,
And make hir mone to Makometh, hir message to shewe.
Thus in a feith leveth that folk, and in a fals mene ...

(15.500-502, 503-506)

Rather than call for crusade, Anima enjoins these "Prelates of Cristene provinces" (15.608), such as the absentee bishops of Bethlehem and Babylonia (to name only two), to exert themselves to bring the teachings of Christianity to the provinces named in their titles.[7]

A text as complex as *Piers Plowman* can hardly be reduced to being called an "anti-war" or "pacifist" text; nevertheless, nothing in any of the discourses by diverse speakers can be taken as support for war, either between nations or between faiths. Furthermore, the doctrinal message of many passages is strongly conciliatory rather than provocative. War was for Langland a condition of human existence in the age awaiting the coming of Christ; his poem shows a certain resignation in acknowledging war's existence and its consequences in the postlapsarian world, but nowhere sees it as an instrument of the faith. Unlike the other two authors we will examine below, who to varying extents dedicated their careers to reformist programs, Langland's writings suggest instead that, given the failure and

---

7   The bishoprics *in partibus infidelium* named in passus 15: l. 493, "Of Nazareth, of Nynyve (Nineveh, Assyria), of Neptalym (Nephthali, land of Judah) and Damaske (Damascus)"; l. 509, "Bethleem and of Babiloigne."

futility of human efforts at reform, one must look instead to eschatology. Richard Emmerson puts it best: "It is ... only at the end of time – as a result of supernatural intervention not of ecclesiastical reformation or any human agency – that such redemption can be accomplished. This is the hallmark of orthodox apocalypticism, the tradition of *Piers Plowman*" (1993: 47).

Any study of international conflict in the fourteenth century must consider Philippe de Mézières (1327-1405), the worldly ambassador and advocate of war against Islam (Keen 1983: 57) who was foremost among the intermediaries between the French and English courts in the 1380s and 1390s (Palmer 1972: 187). Philippe's crusading ideology developed over the course of a long political career in Europe and the Middle East. After almost thirty years in the service of Western powers in Cyprus and Venice, he returned to the kingdom of France in 1373 and appealed to King Charles V for help in mounting a new campaign against the Muslim rulers of the Levant. Charles declined, perhaps in light of France's reconquest of much territory the English had held since Brétigny, victories that could be attributed to his conservative military policies. The king likely could not envision a truce, much less a *passagium* to the Middle East, at a time when war with England – conducted at last on his terms – was paying such dividends. The king did however put the former Chancellor of Cyprus on the royal council, award him a pension, and make him tutor to his son and heir. Once again at the center of power, Philippe devoted his attention to the growing threat to Western territories posed by a militant Islam, whose expansion into eastern Europe would remain his fixation during the last stage of his career.

After the death of Charles V in 1380, Mézières continued to serve as tutor and advisor to the young Charles VI, and to pressure French and English leaders to commit to the cessation of hostilities he believed must precede any crusade. During a truce with England in 1384, Philippe made his influence known in a series of Anglo-French parleys, and took advantage of the lull in the war to preach peace between the two Christian nations. Having long envisioned an ideal Christian military brotherhood that would lead any campaign against the enemies of the faith, at this time Philippe composed a second redaction of the *Nova religio passionis*, the "rule" for his Order of the Passion of Jesus Christ, and enlisted its first members from the French and English aristocracy.[8] In 1388, when Charles began his personal rule, the young king appears to act in the spirit of his tutor by making a truce with England, and by expressing his fervent desire to end the Schism and call a new "holy war" for the elimination of the Saracen menace. Mézières's literary texts proclaim the same message. In his dream vision *Le songe du vieil pelerin*, composed in 1389 and dedicated to King Charles, the narrator calls for a

---

8   Paris, Bibliothèque Mazarine manuscript 1943, fols. 45 r°-101 r°. See Molinier 1881 and Hamdy 1964.

permanent peace between France and England and the partnership of the two nations in the re-conquest of the Holy Land (Mézières 1969: 2.292-296). At the French king's request, in 1395 Mézières wrote and sent to Richard II the *Épistre au roi Richart*, an allegorical exhortation that condemned schism and war and called for a combined crusade under the leadership of the two monarchs. This union was to be cemented by the marriage of the recently widowed Richard to Charles VI's young daughter, Isabelle. Philippe's plans seemed to be coming to fruition when the two were married in June 1396, but the overwhelming defeat of the united Christian forces at Nicopolis in September of the same year effectively ended any hopes for further crusade against Islam, and led to his retirement from the political arena (Jorga 1896: 497-513).

The reform envisioned by Philippe de Mézières, unlike that imagined by Langland, is set firmly in the *seculum*. For Philippe, the crusade will be the instrument of the Lord in punishing the infidel, and regaining for His church on earth the lands where Christ wrought the redemption of humankind. Although he nowhere invokes canon law or other authorities on the issue – unlike his contemporary Bovet, Philippe's taste is more for theological allegory than for learned citation – his crusade falls ostensibly under the rubric of quest to recover territories that have been "lost", in this case, the Holy Land. His Order of the Passion, having once made peace between Christian nations and assembled those forces in humility and righteousness (Mézières 1969: 2.292), will convert "les scismatiques et les infidelx, Tartres, Turcs et Juifz et Sarrazins, a la vraye foy de l'eglise de Romme par saintes predicacions, par doulx exemples, par la sainte escripture et doulces ammonicions, et aux obstinez et rebelles par las sainte espee de ma suer Bonne Adventure, en delivrant vaillament et devotement la sainte cite de Hierusalem et la Terre Sainte, et en soubmectant le monde a la saincte obeissance de la vraye croix ..." ["... the scismatics and the infidels, Tartars, Turks, Jews, and Saracens to the true faith of the Church of Rome through holy sermons, by sweet examples, through the Holy Scriptures and sweet admonitions, and the obstinate and rebellious through the holy sword of my sister Good Adventure, valiantly and faithfully liberating the holy city of Jerusalem and the Holy Lands, and placing the world under the obedience to the true cross ..."] (Mézières 1969: 2.296). Seven years later, in the *Épistre au roi Richart*, Philippe reiterates this proposition, with reference to the success of Charles V's military strategy after Brétigny: during sixty years of war, says his narrator, the English knights have been transformed into a cruel iron goad which has punished sin at God's command throughout France and Spain, although little conquered territory remains to the "Noirs Sengliers" ("Black Boars": Richard II's warlike uncles, father, and grandfather).[9]

---

9   Mézières had already described the English royalty as "Black Boars" in his *Songe* (1969: 11.395-403).

Their loss of these acquisitions is also God's will, since France should be for the French, Spain for the Spaniards, and so on. This fact is proclaimed so that the knights of France and England "de cy en avant doye laissier le dit office du dit aguillon de fer, ainsi poingnant comme dit est dessus, encontre les anemis de la foy, pour satisfaire a Dieu des grans maulx qui ont este fais par le dit aguillon" ["may henceforth abandon the task of the iron goad which, as already stated, has pierced so deeply their Christian brothers, and by the command of God and the two Kings turn their weapons against the enemies of the Faith, to make recompense in the sight of God for the great evils which they have wrought"] (Mézières 1975: 14-15, 87).

The inconsistency evident in the parallel clamoring to sow love, friendship, and peace between Christians and then raise the Holy Sword against infidels seems never to have occurred to Philippe; all other concerns, including logic, become subsumed under his overpowering zeal to chase the Muslims from Jerusalem. We will see a similar lack of circumspection in his pronouncements on marriage below. From the time he was a young man at the court of Cyprus, Philippe de Mézières remained devoted to the proposition that war against the unbeliever and re-conquest of *la Terre Sainte* were the only solution to the problems besetting the Christian West, the greatest of which was the Anglo-French war; his was a "war to end war". This was the counsel he offered two kings of France, fervently and unceasingly. His political imagination concerned itself fundamentally with that which lay outside Christianity: even though he demanded tactical and theological reforms of the Western military as the first step toward his supreme goal, his vision was directed ultimately toward external objectives. The third figure I mean to consider here looks at the same events and issues as Philippe, but calls for quite another response from the West.

The Benedictine monk Honorat Bovet (ca. 1350-ca. 1410) was a Doctor of Decrees and a diplomat who served both royal and papal courts in the last quarter of the century.[10] In works composed between 1389 and 1398, Bovet, like the two authors we have already considered, examines the deleterious effects of war in his time. While still employed by the Angevins in Provence in 1389, Bovet composed a treatise on international war, the *Arbre des batailles*, which he dedicated to Charles VI, and intended as advice for that king. He continued to address his petitions to the king in his last work, the *Apparicion maistre Jehan de Meun* (1398). In this dream vision, the shade of the celebrated poet and social critic Jean de Meun appears and utters dire prognostications for a world full of "iniquity, / Of cheating, of falseness" (Bovet in press: lines 23-24). He urges Bovet's dreaming narrator to speak out, "So as not to let [the world] perish" (l. 25). And so the narrator takes on this mission, directly and urgently admonishing the king – through a

---

10 For details on Bovet's life and works, see Hanly 1997 and Hanly – Millet 1996.

member of his royal council – to reform the kingdom, because the future of the world is at stake: "Car sans amender nostre vie, j'ay paour que Dieux ne nous aydera, et sy doubte que les Sarrazins durement ne griefvent crestianté, se autrement nous ne retournons a la mercy, pitié et misericorde de Dieu; car tout appertement il est adviz qu'il soit courroucé contre son pueple, par especial quant il nous a osté la tres clere lumiere de sainte Eglise et laissié prendre tel avancement aux ennemis de nostre foy" ["Because without reforming our lives, I fear that God may no longer help us, and thus fear that the Saracens may grievously afflict Christianity, unless we return to the grace, the worship, and the mercy of God; because it is quite clearly apparent that he is angry with his people, especially seeing how he has taken from us the bright light of Holy Church and allowed so much progress by the enemies of our faith"] (Bovet in press: prose lines 28-33).

His attitude toward interfaith warfare, however, is quite distinct from that of his French contemporary. Far from calling, as does Mézières in all his extant writings, for a crusade against Islam, Bovet insists that war shall not be made against the unbelievers, and his *Arbre des batailles* is considered "a turning-point in the history of crusading propaganda" (Atiya 1934: 123). Bovet's approach is based on his conviction that all of the problems facing Christianity – schism, war, and militant Islam – had resulted from sinfulness and disunity, and that only through internal reform could true concord be achieved within and without Christian society. This conviction that the faiths might reunite after reform calls to mind Langland's vision of converted Muslims during Christ's coming reign: "And Sarsynes for that sighte shul synge *Gloria in excelsis*" (3.327). Indeed, Bovet's *Apparicion maistre Jehan de Meun*, written in the aftermath of Nicopolis, maintains that interfaith combat would be useless, and that only internal reform would bring about the conditions that would lead to the conversion of the Muslims, who are not the enemies of Christianity but rather a part of its flock gone astray, a gross physical manifestation of its corrupt spiritual condition. One of the speakers in Bovet's poem insists that these conditions clearly show the triumph of wickedness, for it is the devil who

... tousjours par division
Fait perdre le tant noble don
De paix, d'amour et de concorde,
Pour lequel tout bien se discorde.
Par division vient toute guerre,
Par division pert seigneur terre,
Par division laissent seigneurs
Les petis, moyens et greigneurs ...
Regardes com par division
A mis l'Eglise turbacion;
L'estat grant et merveilleux
A mis en fier cas perilleux

(Bovet in press: 165-172, 179-182)

[... always, through discord,
Causes peace to be lost, that noble gift,
Peace and love and concord,
And for all things to split quite asunder.
From discord comes all wars,
Through discord lords lose their lands,
Through discord, lords abandon their people,
The little, the middling, and the great ...
Behold how discord
Has thrown the Church into confusion;
Its grand and wondrous standing
Has been reduced to a terrible, dangerous state.]

Christianity must look inward and clean its own house first; only then will external conflict and discord end. Christians have no right to take away from those peoples, good or bad, to whom God has given gifts; they cannot, and ought not constrain or force unbelievers to convert; finally, according to the Decrees, the Pope has no right to issue indulgences for war against the Saracens, except in the case of the recovery of Jerusalem (Bovet 1883: pt. 4, ch. 2, ll. 85-88). Bovet, therefore, can be seen as disagreeing with Mézières on the prospect of all-out war against Islam; he would concur with him, however, that canon law offers some sanction for the prosecution of a war to re-conquer the Holy Land, a provision with which Langland – although the Englishman does not broach the topic directly – would likely oppose. These authors may differ in their responses to what they see around them, but all three can be seen reacting to an era in which it seemed everything was falling apart, microcosm and macrocosm, from the leadership in church and state to relations between family members. We will now turn our attention to the second topic considered by these three writers in their efforts to advise their earthly leaders: matrimony.

If William Langland would part with Mézières over the righteousness of war against Islam, he would, however, find much in common with Philippe and with Honorat Bovet on the topic of Christian marriage, which all three see as having a broader symbolic value. As M. Teresa Tavormina has argued, Langland saw marriage and family life as a "kindly similitude" – a natural metaphor – that "reflects and transmits a divine exemplar of community" (1995: i), embodying the harmonious celestial order that should also prevail in Christian society. As Wit proclaims in passus 9, marriage is of divine origin, and embodies Christ's presence on earth: "thus was wedlok ywroght, and God hymself it made; / In erthe the heven is – hymself was the witnesse" (9.117-118). Matrimony and married life are not central concerns for Langland in the way that such things as salvation, truth, and justice are; he uses them, instead, as ways of illustrating those crucial matters, "from the right use of temporal goods ... to the ideal ordering of society ..." (Tavormina 1995: xii). His first major treatment of matrimony occurs in the episode early in the poem: a suitable marriage partner is sought for Meed, a process that concludes with her being put on trial at Westminster before the king.

The king banishes her wicked allegorical associates (Falseness, Deceit, Simony, *et al.*) but shows some clemency to Meed herself, even offering to marry her to his councilor Conscience, a knight who has "come lately from abroad" ("cam late fro biyonde", 3.110). But Conscience will have nothing of this union, since in his judgment Meed gives herself indiscriminately to any taker:

> Crist it me forbede!
> Er I wedde swich a wif, wo me bitide!
> For she is frele of hire feith and fikel of hire speche,
> And maketh men mysdo many score tymes ...
> Wyves and widewes wantounnesse she techeth ...
> For she is tikel of hire tail, talewis of tonge,
> As commune as the cartwey to [knaves and to alle],
> To monkes, to mynstrales, to meseles in hegges.
>
> (3.120-123, 125, 131-133)

In this part of the poem, Meed not only represents the system of illegal and immoral payments that Langland saw as detrimental to all of society, secular and ecclesiastical, but also betokens the primacy of marriage as both institution and symbol in that society. Tavormina (1995: 36) holds that "Meed is predicated precisely on the matrimonial metaphor: what man would want a wife whose sexual morals are so corrupt that she even lies with lepers, who teaches wives and widows to be as promiscuous as herself?" In choosing to stage this betrothing and trial at the king's court and to involve in it one of the king's principal councilors, Langland again enters into the *De regimine principum* tradition: the dramatic representation of the scene, in this context and with these characters, clearly signals the writer's expectations of those who govern. The king, Langland suggests, must not be swayed by bribes or favors, and must instead allow himself – and his kingdom through him – to be ruled by Reason, whose reign Conscience prophecies later in the same passus (3.285). As Anna Baldwin observes, Reason and Conscience "insist that [the king] will not be loved by his subjects until he once again becomes the agent of justice in his kingdom ... It was in fact a maxim of the 'Mirror for princes' literature that the king's principal function was the dispensing of justice, often called Truth, as it is in *Piers Plowman*" (1988: 81). Christian marriage is the earthly simulacrum of God's celestial order, and Meed's union with Conscience or any other man would represent a perversion of that institution. As Tavormina argues,

> The alliance poses a fundamental threat to the kingdom; Meed's indiscriminate availability to any cause, even false and wrongful ones, makes the acceptance of her *maistrye* extremely hazardous to a well-ordered realm. The marriage metaphor allows Langland to express his outrage at the workings of Meed in powerful terms, likening them to abuses of a sacramental bond of feudal faith and duty, and of sexual propriety – abuses that are blasphemous, treasonable, and obscenely scandalous.
>
> (1995: 41)

By the end of passus 4, Meed's petition has been denied, and the king has sworn to punish the malefactors and allow her no further influence in the proceedings. Even if no actual punishment is announced for Meed, the needed reforms have been effected, and the sacrament of matrimony has served to frame the discussion of a crucial political issue.[11]

Also significant in broader ways is Langland's condemnation of marriages that have been arranged for the financial advantage of the families, and without the consent of the partners. The condemnation of this tyrannical practice serves as an admonition to rulers by all three writers: just as God has endowed humankind with free will, and just as wedded people who live truly ("Trewe wedded libbynge folk", 9.108) are not coerced into marrying, neither should the king practice or countenance despotism in matters of state. In passus 9, the character Wit condemns such forced unions, which begin with avarice and later become the cause of much unhappiness and sin. Just as Cain, in medieval legend, was cursed because of his conception during a time of penitence (9.121), so are contemporary marriages doomed if entered upon for the wrong reasons:

> And thus thorugh cursed Caym cam care upon erthe,
> And al for thei wroghte wedlokes [Goddes wille ayeins];
> Forthi have thei maugre for hir mariages [men that marie so now] hir children.
> For some, as I se now, soothe for to telle,
> For coveitise of catel unkyndely ben wedded.
> As careful concepcion cometh of swiche mariages ...
> For goode sholde wedde goode, though thei no good hadde ...
>
> (9.153-158, 160)

Wit goes on to decry the practice of matching young brides with dissipated old husbands – "To yeven a yong wenche to any olde feble" – reasoning that the only fruit to be produced will be foul words (3.163-168). Tavormina (1995: 93) points out that "Because of *covetise*, contemporary parents ignore the natural – and thus divine – law that like should wed like. Instead, they arrange loveless marriages that can only yield 'carful conception'". Wit's instructions imply parallels between relationships in the microcosm (the Christian family) and in the macrocosm (the king's "household"): commercial ambition can never be the sole basis for any marriage, or for any affair of state, either. This passage can therefore be seen as directed not only to the poem's dreaming narrator, Will, but to a second audience as well, the Christian ruler, who receives an important piece of political advice. Wit concludes,

---

11   Tavormina 1995: 37: "Far more important than the particulars of Meed's punishment is the fact that Reason and Conscience will now help rule the kingdom."

Forthi I counseille alle Cristene coveite noght be wedded
For coveitise of catel ne of kynrede riche;
Ac maidenes and maydenes macche yow togideres;
Wideweres and wodewes, wercheth the same;
For no londes, but for love, loke ye be wedded,
And thanne gete ye the grace of God, and good ynough to live with.

(9.173-178)

As Tavormina notes, "Wit's comments on marriage, real and metaphorical, do not operate in isolation", and recall the previous Meed scenes in passus 3 and 4: "Like Meed's union with False, such marriages are arranged 'by the fadres wille and the frendes conseille,/ And ... assent of hemself' (9.115-118), but hardly with the approval of God or Holy Church" (1995: 108).[12] This exercise of power that denies free choice and exploits the sacrament of matrimony for financial gain teaches both the *paterfamilias* and the *familia regis* about the proper use of power. Langland's advice to rulers is offered in a more circuitous fashion than those of his contemporaries, but must nevertheless be considered as representing an equally sincere call for action.

Philippe de Mézières's attempt to influence international events by fomenting marriage seems fitting, given the prominence of matrimony as a theme in his extant writings. His obsession with the reconquest of Jerusalem is consistent with his interpretation of the sacrament, since for Philippe the physical city of Jerusalem represented the reign of God on earth just as human marriage represented the union of God and humankind. The figurative element always plays a role in his discussions of matrimony. As a gift to the wife of a friend, in the late 1380s he composed the *Livre de la vertu du sacrament de mariage*,[13] a four-part treatise on matrimony. In the third section, Mézières echoes a concern raised by Langland's Wit and by Bovet in his *Apparicion maistre Jehan de meun* (see below) insisting upon the necessity of free will in marriage (1993: 244, ll. 19-21); he goes on to blame coerced marriages for a number of social problems, notably the Hundred Years War itself: "... pour la consequence des mariages susdiz la grant guerre de France principaument a esté commencie et jusques cy poursuivie, dont tant de maulz sont avenuz que ne se porroit escripre" ["... such marriages were the main cause that the great war in France was started and continued until now, from which so much evil has come that it could not be written down"] (Mézières 1993: 245, ll. 5-7). He goes on to declare (245 l. 14-246 l. 12) that marriages arranged for the purpose of cementing alliances between warring nations should be avoided whenever possible, since these alliances themselves have been the cause of wars and other discord. At this point Mézières seems to be operating from a position very close to Langland's: free will is essential in marriage, and to deny it is to encourage unhappy unions and even greater social ills.

---

12   See also the discussion of the function of proxies in Kelly 1975: 212, 225-228.
13   Mézières 1993 (ed. Williamson).

In the final section of the *Livre de la vertu du sacrament de mariage*, however, we see the two diverge: while Langland remains mostly in the realm of the mystical and symbolic and only occasionally ventures into topical commentary, for Philippe, the political world is all. Here he inserts his translation of Petrarch's Latin rendering of the story of Griselda, in which the woman's patient sacrifice is likened to Christ's: human marriage is seen as a reflection of Jesus's marriage with his Church, a union only accomplished through the Passion. In the *Épistre au roi Richart* of 1395, he wishes the King a wife as virtuous and patient as the famous Griselda described in the story by Petrarch, the poet laureate.[14] The unquestioning female obedience described here is consistent with medieval tradition,[15] and so cannot be taken as contradicting his previous condemnations (in the *Livre*) of marriages for alliance or of the lack of free will in such unions. However, as in the case of his pronouncements on war, the single-mindedness of Philippe's commitment leads him into adopting some inconsistent positions. We must recall that his primary goal in writing the *Épistre* was the arrangement of a marriage between Richard II and Charles VI's eight-year-old daughter Isabelle, who was quite likely not asked her opinion at any time during the negotiations. As was the case with other militarist ideologues in this time, Philippe's devotion to crusade could drive him simultaneously to instigate peace between Christians and war with the infidel. That same goal here causes him to reverse his position on free will in marriage: while promoting a union that would exploit a mere child's inability to oppose it, he cites a tale whose female protagonist is herself denied voice and agency. In this last year of his career in government, Philippe would once more invoke the metaphoric significance of the Griselda story in seeking to have his way in the outcome of events.

In the same year as the *Épistre au roi Richart*, there appeared a verse drama on the topic of the patient Griselda; the text is called the *Estoire de Griseldis*, and is preserved in a single manuscript.[16] The manuscript does not bear the name of an author, but it seems beyond a reasonable doubt that this play is the work of Philippe de Mézières.[17] The *De regimine principum* theme is again quite prominent here: an inexperienced marquis must make an important decision, and is guided by his councilors, five knights who are given speaking parts in the play. Special status is assigned to the fifth of these, the *Quint Chevalier*, an aged and prudent adviser to the prince. Philippe does not greatly alter the overall plot of the Griselda story for the purposes of his play, which likely was intended for performance in both England and France at the time the

---

14 Mézières 1975: 115: "Or pleust a Dieu ... il vous vousist ottroier et mander une tele espouse et compaingne comme il fist au marquis de Saluce, apelee Griseldis ... selonq la cronique autentique ... escript par le solempnel docteur et souverain poete, maistre Francois Petrac ..."
15 Kelly 1975: 11, 293-294.
16 Paris, Bibliothèque Nationale de France fonds français 2203, dated 1395.
17 See the comments on authorship by Craig (ed.) in the most recent edition of the play (Mézières 1954: 4-6).

author was calling for the royal marriage and the crusade.[18] Significant, however, is the fact that the speaking parts that deal most directly and eloquently with the effort to convince the young ruler to marry – a clear reference, in this context, to the proposal then before King Richard II – are delivered by this venerable, respected diplomat, the *Quint Chevalier*. In this guise, he seems a surrogate for Mézières himself, and an analogue to *Piers Plowman*'s Conscience, a defender of the common weal and advocate of virtuous royal behavior, who, like Mézières, is a knight who has "come lately from abroad". The *Quint Chevalier* is extolled as "Un chevalier a ancien / En ceste court, bon catholique / Et qui aime le bien publique, / Saige, de droit naturel senz, / S'a plus veü qu'homs de ceenz. ..." ["A knight, for many years / a member of this court, a good Catholic, / And who loves the common good"] (Mézières 1954: 232-236). His task is to convince the Marquis – who advances several arguments, mainly frivolous, in defense of his desire to remain single – that marriage will not only bring him peace and happiness, but, more significantly, will safeguard his land and people. In his longest oration, the *Quint Chevalier* lauds matrimony for its beneficial effects on the body politic:

> Ha! sire, ne regardez pas
> A la paine ne au soussy.
> Maint sont marié, Dieu mercy,
> Qui moult vivent joyeusement
> Et sont de bon gouvernement
> Pour eulz et pour le bien publique ...
> Et aussi moult desavenant
> Est a prince de hault paraige
> De finer ses jours sanz lignage
> Avoir procreé de sa chair,
> Auquel est refuge et repair
> Le commun peuple de sa terre.

(Mézières 1954: ll. 378-383, 424-429)

> [Oh! my lord, do not consider
> The pain or the worry involved.
> Many are married, thanks be to God,
> Who live quite joyously
> And who conduct themselves well,
> Both for them and for the common good ...
> And it is also most disadvantageous
> For a prince of noble blood
> To end his days without an heir
> Having been engendered from his flesh,
> In which resides refuge and security
> For the common people of his land.]

---

18 Craig (Mézières 1954: 14) mentions but does not document a tradition that has the play being performed in 1395 in the presence of Charles VI, to whom a copy of the text is presented.

This pious mentor urges his protégé to better himself by taking on the responsibility of marriage and parenthood, since this reform in his own household will promote concord and stability in the country as a whole. The correspondence between dramatic action and political imperative here seems clear: the young ruler (Richard II, although previously married, is still only 28 in 1395) should follow the advice of his aged councillor, and marry, for the good of his realm. Is the *Quint Chevalier* a *Doppelgänger* for Philippe de Mézières? The fictive nobleman shows many affinities, in character and in tactics, to the real-life knight who came back to Paris in 1373 to spend twenty-three years pursuing his perennial objective, a quest that produced nothing but a brief marriage and an ill-starred crusade. His career may have ended in failure and despondency, but Mézières nevertheless had the satisfaction of seeing his labors compensated at least occasionally with successes or with honors. The same cannot be said for his contemporary and fellow Frenchman, whose rewards were never commensurate with his exertions.

Like Philippe de Mézières when he composed the *Épistre au roi Richart* in 1395, Honorat Bovet must have felt three years later that time was running out on his chances to bring about change in the West. Barely eighteen months after the French court heard the news about Nicopolis, he directed his pleas for reform to what he hoped would be a receptive audience, dedicating copies of a new poem to three members of Charles VI's inner circle: Louis, Duke of Orleans; his associate and fellow royal councillor, Jean de Montaigu; and Louis's wife, Valentina Visconti, who was very close to the king.[19] Drawing upon the two major elements in his professional experience, the courtly and the academic, Bovet presents his *Apparicion maistre Jehan de Meun* in a fashionable form, the dream vision in vernacular verse. He then appeals to his readers' aristocratic self-regard by attaching more than seventy Latin notes – most citing canon law or scripture – to the margins of the poem's two extant presentation copies. As noted above in the discussion of Bovet's perspectives on war (p. 334), Jean de Meun himself appears in the narrative. He assembles a panel of four speakers, all culled from the "margins" of Parisian society in 1398: a Jew, a medical doctor, a Dominican friar or "Jacobin", and a Muslim nobleman, the *Sarrazin*.[20] This diplomat claims to have been sent

---

19 For the political context at the court of France, see Autrand, "Le temps des Marmousets" (1986: 189-203).

20 Medical doctors were under fire at this time because they yet to cure Charles VI of the mental illness he had been experiencing for six years. Jews has been banned from the Kingdom of France since 1394, because of imputations of usury in their money-lending. The "Jacobin" is a Dominican friar; his order had been maligned since 1387 when one of its members, Juan de Monzon, began to preach that the doctrine of the Immaculate Conception was heretical. As for the Sarrazin: barely eighteen months had passed since Paris heard the news of the defeat of the Western army and massacre of most European survivors by Bajazet at Nicopolis, so this Turk would have been an object of great hatred and fear in the West at this time.

by his leader – Bajazet, the victor at Nicopolis – to gather intelligence about Christian society in advance of an invasion. He dominates the discussion for more than six hundred lines, offering a harsh and wide-ranging critique of Christian society, a harangue whose main points are largely seconded in an equally long speech by the Jacobin. The *Sarrazin* chides his interlocutors notably on the subject of matrimony, a sacred institution that can be seen as an index of Christian corruption at the end of the fourteenth century. Both Mézières and Bovet consider respect for the sacrament of matrimony to be essential to the maintenance of harmony in the state and, by extension, in the world as a whole; both use the contemporary degradation of Christian marriage as a means to criticize leaders and suggest reforms.

In Bovet's *Apparicion*, Jean de Meun – who serves as moderator for the assembled speakers – demands that the *Sarrazin* deliver an honest appraisal of the Christians he has observed during his fact-finding expedition. The Muslim first expresses astonishment at finding that so many marriages, arranged solely for the acquisition of land or title, begin with parental coercion rather than the partners' free will. Bovet would consider many arranged marriages to be a form of "tirannye", a transgression he finds responsible for many of the ills being suffered by the West in his day. For Bovet, "tirannye" embraces such offenses as the abuse of power by royal officers (ll. 783-816), by jailers (ll. 817-828), and by the Church itself, whose oppression of Eastern dissidents had led centuries before to the rise of Islam (ll. 1134-1194). The *Sarrazin* tells his Christian counterparts:

> ... ne gardés bien mariage,
> Ains la ou sont plus de parage,
> Sourvient souvent melancolie
> Telz qu'ilz seront toute leur vie
> Sans estre jamaiz bons amis.
> Se l'un vit mal et l'autre pis ...
>
> (Bovet in press: ll. 771-774, 779-780)

> [You do not respect your marriages,
> But instead, among the higher levels of society,
> They come quite often to grief,
> Since they will spend their entire lives
> Without ever having been good friends.
> So one's life is bad, the other's is worse ...]

Bovet's speaker here only implies what Langland and Mézières make manifest, that aristocratic families' arrangement of marriages for financial gain leads to unhappiness for the couple and instability for the society at large. He maintains – as does Langland (9.117-118, cited above) – that matrimony is a sacred institution made by the almighty, and implies that disrespect for this sacrament cannot but incur divine wrath. This arrogant commodification of the sacrament represents a disregard for God's law and an indifference toward His retribution, and is emblematic of broader corruption in Christianity. And this is not the only abuse of matrimony that becomes apparent to the *Sarrazin* during his investigation, since high-born people not only coerce their children into marriages to acquire lands and money, but divorce each other readily for the same reason. As his discourse continues, the *Sarrazin* condemns divorce, which is to the institution of marriage what *division* is to the body politic: "Par division pert seigneur terre", says Bovet's narrator (see passage cited above, ll. 165-172, 179-182); "Regardés com par division / A mis l'Eglise turbacion". *Division* is found responsible for many of the evils then troubling Christendom; in this context; divorce must be seen as a sub-category of that iniquity, and therefore a scourge akin to both the war between France and England and the papal schism. What he has seen leads the *Sarrazin* to infer that Christians in general have little regard for matrimony: "Vecy mandement de loy / Que vous ne gardés se bien poy (ll. 779-780); "Here is a commandment of the law / That you hardly keep at all").

Later on in the poem, the Jacobin concurs with the *Sarrazin*'s analysis, observing that

... les Françoys sont trop aprins
De deffaire les mariages.
Par ma foy, c'est bien grant dommages
Que deffaire tel sacrement,
Car Dieux le fist premierement
Et bien haultement demonstroit
Comment ce sacrement amoit,
Quant de vierge sainte et pure
Vint prendre humaine nature;
Avec Joseph sans nul oultrage
L'a donnee par mariage.

(Bovet in press: ll. 1473-1483)

[The French are too well-versed
At dissolving their own marriages.
By my faith, it is truly pernicious
To undo such a sacrament,
Because God made it in the beginning,
And most resolutely demonstrated
How He loved this sacrament,
When, from a virgin, holy and pure
He came to take human nature upon himself;
To Joseph, without blame,
She [the Virgin] was given in matrimony.]

Divorce debases this sacrament, which is meant to serve as a perpetual remembrance of Christ's incarnation, and thereby of human salvation. French wickedness has clearly incurred God's displeasure; Bovet sees his day's events as chastisement for these wrongs, and fears even worse things to come. Assuming once again the role of royal adviser, Bovet calls upon the king to purify his realm by punishing those responsible for this divine disfavor, in this case *parvenus* who seek to improve their status through divorce. The Jacobin declares that

> ... se ly roys estoit bien fiers
> De chastoyer seulement le tiers
> De ceulx qui rompent mariage,
> Pour quant qu'ilz fussent de parage,
> Les povres auroient leurs fames
> Avecquez eulx sans nulz diffames.
> Mais pour ce que de sy grant vice
> L'en n'en fait par rigueur justice,
> Aussy legier com de frommage
> Prent on femmes de mariage.

　　　　　　　　　　　　　　　　(Bovet in press: ll. 1484-1493)

> [... if the king were stern enough
> To punish only a third
> Of those who divorce
> Because they aspire to being aristocrats,
> The poor would have their wives
> With them, without any dishonor.
> But because this heinous crime
> Is not punished rigorously through our courts,
> As lightly as taking a piece of cheese
> Does one take a woman in matrimony.]

If his appraisal of current morality seems rather bleak for the most part, the narrative of Bovet's *Apparicion maistre Jehan de Meun* expresses some hope that Christianity will embrace the reforms his speakers so urgently promote. Jean de Meun and the Jacobin, who begin by mistrusting and insulting the *Sarrazin*, end by treating him with a certain amount of respect, a development suggestive of the interfaith reconciliation longed for in Bovet's and Langland's texts. The Jacobin even feels confident enough to allow that

> Dieu vueille, tost viengne par droit
> Une refformacion bien noble ...
> Il pourra bien venir un jour.

　　　　　　　　　　　　　　　　(Bovet in press: ll. 1415-1416, 1419)

> [God willing, soon will come, under the law,
> A just and equitable reformation ...
> It could truly come one day.]

Such high hopes seem to call for an epilogue, and it likely comes as no surprise that things did not work out quite the way these authors had wanted. Bovet's pleas seem to have fallen on deaf ears; his message might have simply been lost in the chaos of a court that had no real leader but many rapacious contenders, and which was now panicked by enemies at home and abroad. France certainly did not undertake the reforms Bovet had preached, and war and schism both continued until well after his death in 1410. What is more, his position in Paris was apparently revoked shortly after his allies at court received presentation copies of the *Apparicion*, a text that survives in a mere four manuscripts. Bovet's *Arbre des batailles* would bring him renown, but only later, a half-century after his death, when the war with England would finally end. As for Philippe de Mézières: he held more important offices and had a much greater impact on the period's events than did Bovet, but he also never saw his plans succeed in full; the last work he leaves us, *L'épistre lamentable*, records his isolation and despair.[21] Of William Langland's fate, finally, we know nothing; as for his aspirations, we know only what he tells us in his poem, and after six hundred years the cosmic event in which he placed his faith still has not occurred. His French contemporaries Bovet and Mézières hoped, perhaps naïvely, that they might be agents of change in the world, but Langland seems to have put no faith in the ability of human institutions to bring about reform. Instead, he urged his fellow Christians and their rulers to reject sin and embrace virtue while they waited for the return of the one whose reign alone would bring peace and justice. Theirs was an era that somehow could not bring itself to esteem the voices of sanity and moderation, that habitually found war and destruction more expedient than dialogue – an era not terribly unlike our own. We can only hope that in the retinue of today's leaders are people daring enough to oppose the customary rush to hostility, and that time has invalidated Bovet's fatalistic summation: "the world takes for a fool the man who seeks to write of new things".[22]

---

21 Brussels, Bibliothèque de Bourgogne 10486; published incompletely in Kervyn de Lettenhove (ed.) 1872.

22 Bovet in press: prose lines 111-112: "... le monde tient pour nice tout homme qui vueille escripre nouvelles choses."

References

Alford, John A. (ed.)
1988   *A Companion to "Piers Plowman"*. Berkeley: University of California Press.

Atiya, Aziz S.
1934   *The Crusade of Nicopolis*. London: Methuen.
1938   *The Crusade in the Later Middle Ages*. London: Methuen.
1962   *Crusade, Commerce and Culture*. Bloomington, IN: Indiana University Press.

Augustine, Bishop of Hippo
1887   "To Boniface", in *Opera omnia* 7, *Patrologia cursus completus: Series Latina*. J.-P. Migne (ed.), vol. 33, col. 856. Paris: Garnier.
1900   *De civitate Dei* 19:13, in *Opera omnia* 7, *Patrologia cursus completus: Series Latina*. J.-P. Migne (ed.), vol. 41, cols. 640-642. Paris: Garnier.

Autrand, Françoise
1986   *Charles VI: la folie du roi*. Paris: Fayard.

Baldwin, Anna P.
1988   "The Historical Context", in John A. Alford (ed.), 67-86.

Bovet, Honorat
1883   *L'arbre des batailles d'Honoré Bonet*, Ernest Nys (ed.). Brussels: Muquardt.
in press   *"L'Apparicion maistre Jehan de meun": A Critical Edition with English Translation*. Michael Hanly (ed. and trans.). Tempe, AZ: Medieval & Renaissance Texts and Studies (MRTS).

Emmerson, Richard C.
1993   "'Yernen to rede redels?': *Piers Plowman* and Prophecy", *Yearbook of Langland Studies* 7: 27-76.

Gilbert, Allan H.
1938   *Machiavelli's "Prince" and its Forerunners: "The Prince" as a Typical Book "De regimine principum"*. Durham, NC: Duke University Press.

Hanly, Michael
1997   "Courtiers and Poets: An International Network of Literary Exchange", *Viator: Medieval and Renaissance Studies* 28: 305-332.

Hanly, Michael – Hélène Millet
1996   "Les batailles d'Honorat Bovet: essai de biographie", *Romania* 114: 135-181.

Hamdy, Abdel Hamid
1964   "Philippe de Mézières and the New Order of the Passion, parts 2 and 3", *Bulletin of the Faculty of Arts of Alexandria University* 18: 1-104.

Isidore of Seville
1911   *Etymologiarum sive Originum libri XX*. W. M. Lindsay (ed.). 2 vols. Oxford: Clarendon Press.

Jorga, Nicolae
   1896   *Philippe de Mézières et la croisade au XIVe siècle.* Paris: Bouillon.
Keen, Maurice H.
   1965   *The Laws of War in the Late Middle Ages.* London: Routledge and Kegan
             Paul.
   1983   "Chaucer's Knight, the English Aristocracy and the Crusade", in V. J.
             Scattergood – J. W. Sherborne (eds.), 45-61.
Kelly, Henry Ansgar
   1975   *Love and Marriage in the Age of Chaucer.* Ithaca, NY: Cornell Univer-
             sity Press.
Langland, William.
   1995   *The Vision of Piers Plowman: A Critical Edition of the B-Text Based on
             Trinity College Cambridge MS B.15.17.* A. V. C. Schmidt (ed.). 2nd ed.
             London: J. M. Dent.
Kervyn de Lettenhove, H. (ed.)
   1867-1877 *Œuvres de Froissart.* 25 vols. Brussels: V. Devaux.
Lowe, Ben
   1997   *Imagining Peace: A History of Early English Pacifist Ideas, 1340-1560.*
             University Park, PA: Pennsylvania State University Press.
Mézières, Philippe de
   Ca. 1384 *Nova religio passionis.* Paris, Bibliothèque Mazarine, manuscript 1943,
             fols. 45 r°-101 r°.
   1395   Paris, Bibliothèque Nationale de France, manuscript fonds français 2203.
   1872   *L'épistre lamentable et consolatoire,* in Kervyn de Lettenhove (ed.)
             1867-1877, vol. 16: 444-523.
   1954   *L'Estoire de Griseldis.* Barbara M Craig (ed.). Lawrence, KS: University
             of Kansas Publications. [University of Kansas publications. Humanistic
             studies, no. 31].
   1969   *Le songe du vieil pèlerin.* G. W. Coopland (ed.) 2 vols. Cambridge, Eng.:
             Cambridge University Press.
   1975   *Letter to King Richard II: A Plea Made in 1395 for Peace between Eng-
             land and France.* G. W. Coopland (ed.). Liverpool: Liverpool University
             Press.
   1993   *Le livre de la vertu du sacrament de mariage,* edited from Paris, Biblio-
             thèque Nationale français 1175. Joan B. Williamson (ed.). Washington:
             Catholic University of America Press.
Molinier, Auguste
   1881   "Description de deux manuscrits contenant la Règle de la *Militia Pas-
             sionis Jhesu Christi* de Philippe de Mézières", *Archives de l'Orient Latin*
             1:335-364.
Palmer, J. J. N.
   1972   *England, France and Christendom, 1377-99.* Chapel Hill, NC: University
             of North Carolina Press.

Russell, Frederick H.
    1975   *The Just War in the Middle Ages*. Cambridge, Eng.: Cambridge University Press.

Scattergood, V. J. – J. W. Sherborne (eds.)
    1983   *English Court Culture in the Later Middle Ages*. London: Duckworth.

Tavormina, M. Teresa
    1995   *Kindly Similitude: Marriage and Family in "Piers Plowman"*. Cambridge, Eng.: Boydell and Brewer.

Yeager, R. F.
    1987   "'Pax poetica': On the Pacifism of Chaucer and Gower", *Studies in the Age of Chaucer* 9: 97-121.

"I xal excusyn þe & ledyn þe & bryngyn þe a-geyn in safte": Liturgy and Authority in *The Book of Margery Kempe*

Terri L. Bays, University of Notre Dame

In the Spring of 1433, Margery Kempe obtains permission from her confessor to accompany her daughter-in-law from Lynn to Ipswich and back. No sooner have they left Lynn, however, than Margery begins receiving a series of divine commands to go overseas. When she protests that she has neither permission from her confessor nor provision for the journey, God insists, saying, "I bydde þe gon in my name, Ihesu, for I am a-bouyn thy gostly fadyr & I xal excusyn þe & Ledyn þe & Bryngyn þe a-geyn in safte" (227.4-6).[1] With no little reluctance – and no little resistance from her daughter-in-law – Margery consents.

As I will show, Margery's account of her journey overseas arranges its participants in a manner that evokes the liturgy of a Corpus Christi procession. The object of this paper is to follow H. A. Kelly's valuable practice of concentrating on scenes of liturgical life and to explore the consequences of those scenes for our overall reading of Margery's account. In particular, I will focus on the way Margery uses the imagery commonly associated with Corpus Christi processions to convey her assertions of extra-ecclesial and extra-political authority in the face of both clerical and political opposition. In making such assertions, Margery identifies the "body of Christ" found present in His people with the body of Christ venerated at the altar. As a result, she challenges her readers to demonstrate the same degree of devotion to the one body as they already, and rightly, give to the other.

Structurally speaking, I will begin by discussing some textual reasons for thinking that Corpus Christi is the liturgical reference point for this section of Margery's tale. I will then focus on three issues which this Corpus Christi orientation allows Margery to raise: the devotion which should underpin clerical prerogative, the social responsibility which should accompany social position, and the spiritual communion which should transcend political boundaries. With regard to each of these issues, Margery uses Corpus Christi imagery to contrast the reality played out in her experience with the ideal performed in the liturgy. In response to that contrast, Margery combines a call for the reform of social institutions with a re-envisioning of the position she inhabits within those institutions.

---

1   This and all further citations of *The Book of Margery Kempe* refer to Kempe (1940) unless otherwise noted.

Let us begin with some textual indications that the feast of Corpus Christi is our liturgical reference point. Two are particularly worthy of note. The first, and the most readily apparent, is the conjunction of the journey's timing – which has Margery arriving at her destination within the octave of Corpus Christi – with the object of her journey – to venerate the holy blood of Wilsnack. The second, and the more striking, is Margery's mode of conveyance – which is usually processional and always providential.

First: the timing of the journey. Margery takes leave of her confessor "in tyme of Lenton" (226.28), and puts out to sea at the end of Passion Week – i.e., the week before Palm Sunday (229.11-15). She reaches Norway on Good Friday, and there she stays until Easter Monday, when she once again sets sail (230.31-231.14). She reaches Danzig shortly thereafter and remains there for five or six weeks, during which time she takes leave of her daughter-in-law. We expect Danzig to be the turning point of the journey, and, despite the ingratitude of her daughter-in-law, Margery "enyoyid" herself so much in Danzig that she "purposyd to abydyn þer þe lengar tyme" (231.31-32). God has other plans, however, and admonishes Margery to leave Danzig. He provides her with an escort home by way of Wilsnack and its miraculous, blood-sprinkled hosts.

Thenceforth the focus shifts away from Margery's maternal responsibility to her daughter-in-law and towards her filial responsibility to God. When Margery quails at the dangers of traveling to Wilsnack through a country at war with her own, God reproaches her, "yf þu loue me, þu xalt not dredyn to gon wyth me wher-þat-euyr I wil hauyn þe. Dowtyr, I browte þe hedyr, & I xal bryngen þe hom ageyn in-to Inglond in saf-warde" (233.26-33). Margery thus is still outward bound when she leaves Danzig. Only after she reaches Wilsnack during the octave of Corpus Christi does Margery describe herself as being on the journey "hom in-to Inglond" (238.5).

Margery reaches Wilsnack during the "Vtas of Corpus Cristi" (235.24), referring to the feast and the eight days which follow it. She mentions this timing three times in a short space. First, she reaches the end of her strength "on Corpus Cristi Euyn" (234.21), and has to be carried the rest of the way to Wilsnack in a wain. Next, having seen the miraculous blood, she travels on toward Aachen and, "for that it was wyth-inne þe Vtas of Corpus Cristi", venerates the exposed sacrament at a house of Friars Minor (235.4-32). Finally, once her companions have become displeased with her weeping adoration of the sacrament, she only manages to retain their company until "þei comyn at a good town in þe Vtas of Corpus Cristi" (235.32-236.7), at which point they desert her. Here, then, we notice a conjunction between her insistence upon the timing of her arrival – the Octave of Corpus Christi – and the object of her journey – to view the miraculous, bleeding body of Christ. Margery further emphasizes this conjunction by accounting for the hardship she suffers: her escorts desert her because they are unwilling to tolerate her immoderate devotion to the body of Christ.

The second element orienting this journey around the feast of Corpus Christi is the means by which Margery is "browte hedyr". Up until now, Margery has been quite sparing in her references to vehicular transportation on land.[2] At this point, however, she begins to mention such transport with some frequency. Repeatedly, she draws our attention to her age and infirmity, describing herself as "a woman dys-ewsyd of going & also abowtyn iij scor зer of age" (234.18-19), and accompanied by much younger, more able-bodied companions who inevitably want to travel with more haste than she can muster. She follows this up by noting, again and again, how God provides transportation just when she is at the point of dropping from exhaustion and sickness. In each of these vehicular interventions, the divine travel agent seems to favor the wain.[3]

"Wain" may simply be Margery's word for any "two or four-wheeled vehicle",[4] and the significance of the divinely provided vehicle may therefore lie purely in its providential provision. It is still worth noting that "wayn" is also the word the *Wyclif Bible* repeatedly uses for conveyance of the Ark of the Covenant. So, for example, King David returns the Ark of the Covenant to Jerusalem in a wain. When the oxen drawing this wain stumble, Uzzah presumes to steady the Ark and is struck dead in punishment. As the wain enters Jerusalem, David dances before it, drawing the scorn of his wife Michal.[5]

This Wycliffite use of "wain" does not directly link Margery's conveyance with the feast of Corpus Christi. Indeed, direct reference to a Corpus Christi-type *feretrum* would make literal sense only if Margery were dead or severely disabled, since its mundane counterpart is a bier.[6] Even so, Margery's oft-mentioned wains join their scriptural counterparts in expressing concern for the human presumption involved in undertaking to carry God. As we soon shall see, Margery's wains appear precisely where others presume to control her devotion. They arrive with providential alacrity, and they take Margery where the divine will would have her go – will she, nil she. In thus fulfilling God's promise, not only to lead Margery but also to bring her again in safety, Margery's wains invert the biblical image of God's body being carted around

---

2   While seasickness and fear provoke many references to various types of ship, there is only one earlier reference to a cart (full of thorns with which the speaker wishes Margery to be burnt 28.30), and a few isolated references to a horse (118.27, 30) or an ass (67.17).

3   Wains are provided for Margery four times between Stralsund and Calais, and she often mentions the same wain more than once in recounting an incident. See 234.32, 235.15, 238.14, 239.24-39.

4   See *Middle English Dictionary* 2001: wain (n.(1)a.

5   II Kings (II Sam.) 6: 3-4 in *Wyclif Bible* (1999) vol. 2: 105. See also I Kings (I Sam.) 6: 7-14 (vol. 2: 57) and Numbers 7: 3-10 (vol. 1: 215), though the *wains* in this last example are for the tabernacle rather than for the Ark itself.

6   Further complicating matters is the question of Margery's access to written culture in general. This has been addressed extensively in other places, including Lochrie (1991: 101-109), Staley (1994: 32-33), and Tarvers (1996: 111-124).

by his people. Or, perhaps more deeply, they draw the reader to a renewed vision of that image: Margery herself is, after all, a part of the body of Christ. The wains, however divinely dispatched, are driven by people whose communal progress to the shrine and back is punctuated by opportunities for blessing.[7] At the heart of this procession, the wains bear Margery as the instrument of benediction.

This renewed vision provides the focus for the remainder of my paper. By situating her journey within the octave of Corpus Christi, and by re-envisioning her journey as a Corpus Christi procession with her own body in the place of honor, Margery draws our attention to several issues concerning the treatment she receives from her fellow Christians. As I have said, I will address three of these here: one concerning clerical prerogative, one concerning the conflation of lay piety with wealth, and one concerning the binding power of territorial boundaries. I will argue that Margery draws attention to these issues, not so much to undermine the social framework set up by the Corpus Christi model, as to call social reality into conformity with the liturgical implications of the feast.

Let us start with the issue of clerical prerogative. Here we immediately notice a discrepancy. On the one hand, due reverence preserves to the priesthood the right to handle the body of Christ, and the canons appoint serious punishment to those priests who handle the body with negligence or disrespect (Lyndwood 1968: III.25, pp. 247-248). On the other hand, a serious lack of reverence marks that same priesthood's handling of Margery. This lack of reverence becomes particularly evident immediately after Margery and her guide have seen the miraculous hosts at Wilsnack.

At this point, we are still within the octave of Corpus Christi, and the processional aspect of the occasion is emphasized by the indication that Margery and her guide are traveling in wains "wher was meche concowrs of pepil" (235.6-7). Meeting up with a monk and some chapmen, they continue "in falaschep to-gedyr" until they come to a house of Friars Minor, where the thirsty men bid Margery go in and get some wine:

> Sche seyd, "Serys. ȝe xal haue me excusyd, for yf it wer an hows of nunnys I wolde al redy gon, but for-as-meche þei arn men I xal not gon be ȝowr leue". So went on of þe chapmen & fette to hem a potel of wyne. þan cam frerys to hem & preyid hem þat þei wolde comyn & seen þe blisful Sacrament in here chirche, for it was wyth-inne þe Vtas of Corpus Cristi, & it stod opyn in a cristal þat men myth se it yf þei wolde.
>
> (235.17-25)

Margery's juxtaposition of the thirst for wine with the exposition of the sacrament works on at least two levels. First, it draws attention to the appetites of the men. They reach a religious house within the Octave of Corpus Christi, but the wine they seek is

---

7   Corpus Christi Processions commonly involve stopping at "stations" where, after a versicle, response and prayer, the priest blesses the environs by making a large sign of the cross with the consecrated host. See Wordsworth (1901: 95) and Rubin (1991: 247-255).

the ordinary stuff of taverns, not the blood of their most precious savior. The friars must come out and ask them to come in and see – "yf þei wolde".

Second, the juxtaposition indicts the men for their thoughtless treatment of Margery. As Margery herself notes (235.18-20), their choice to send her on their errand shows disregard both for her age and for the male community her unaccompanied female presence would disrupt. The fact that she must assert the primacy of her modesty over their convenience does not recommend too highly the protection their presence was supposed to provide for her.

Disregard for Margery quickly converges with disregard for the sacrament. Earlier, Margery's tears of devotion reward her obedience to the Divine will. They are lost while she hesitates to obey the command to go overseas (226.30-36) and restored when, having consented to the journey, she witnesses the raising of the cross on Easter Day (231.5-10). Now, when the men agree to go in to see the sacrament, Margery says that she:

> thowt sche wolde se it as wel as þei & folwyd aftyr, þow it wer aȝens hir wille. &, whan sche beheld þe preciows Sacrament, owr Lord ȝaf hir so mech swetnes & deuocyon þat sche wept and sobbyd wondyr sor & not myth restreyn hir-self þerfro. þe monke was wroth & al hir felaschip for sche wept so sor, &, whan þei wer comyn a-geyn to her waynys, þei chedyn hir & rebukyd hir, clepyng hir ypocrite & seyd many an euyl worde vn-to hir. Sche for to ex-cusyn hir-selfe leyd Scriptur a-geyn hem, versys of þe Sawter, "Qui seminant in lacrimis" & cetera "euntes ibant & flebant" & cetera, & swich oþer. þan wer þei wel wroþar, & seyd þat sche xulde no lengar gon in her cumpany, & procuryd hir man to forsakyn hir.

(235.27-236.1)

Here then, the subordination of Margery's concern for modesty to her adoration of the sacrament receives divine approval but human derision. The virulence of the monk's accusation of hypocrisy suggests that he senses a rebuke in Margery's devotion, a suggestion that he too should give the cup of salvation precedence over the "potel of wyne" which Margery was to have fetched.

Certainly Margery herself gives precedence to the sacrament, and this may add to the monk's anger. In entering the house of friars, "þow it wer a-ȝens hir wille", Margery demonstrates toward God the obedience which she denied to the monk and his companions. As a person living under a vow of obedience, the monk should be Margery's champion in this matter. The fact that she names him as her most ardent detractor suggests that his own sense of obedience falls shy of the mark. As a result, the monk is "wel wroþar" when Margery accounts for her tears by citing the Psalter, an expression of obedience, the chanting of which his own rule prescribes.

The juxtaposition of Margery's suffering obedience with the raising of the cross on Easter also contributes to her identification with the Passion of Christ. Sara Beckwith examines this identification from the standpoint of the personal, mimetic responses to the Passion Margery experiences on Mount Calvary and elsewhere (1986: 48-51). Beckwith describes this identification as "both a demonstration of her self-abnegation and, by a typically Christian inversion, a laying claim to a different kind of power" (1986: 49).[8] Following Beckwith, but shifting our attention from the Passion to Corpus Christi, we can see that claim to power even more clearly. The processional collect encourages identification with Christ's body when it bids God to grant us "so to venerate the sacred mysteries of Thy Body and Blood, that we may ever perceive within us the fruit of Thy Redemption".[9] Margery's participation with the body of Christ, therefore, extends beyond the Passion, and embraces the idea that the body – lifted up from its passion and carried through the midst of the people – has the power to bless.

Thus, in his escalating wrath, the monk attempts to withdraw her devotion from the body of Christ exposed upon the friars' altar. Because he eventually succeeds in separating Margery from her escort, he also withdraws honor and succor from the body of Christ manifest in Margery's person in the midst of the company. Others mistreat Margery for the importunity of her tears, but in the context of Corpus Christi, the monk's fault is magnified by the striking contrast it presents between the liturgical model and the pastoral reality.

This contrast grows more stark once the monk has persuaded Margery's guide to desert her. On parting, Margery asserts her belief that "God xal ordeyn for me & bryngyn me forth as he wole hym-selfe" (236.22-23), but as night falls, she worries about her seemingly defenseless state. As if to emphasize her vulnerability: "þer cam priestys to hir, þer sche was at oste, of þat cuntre. þei clepyd hir Englisch sterte & spoken many lewed wordys vn-to hir, schewyng vnclenly cher & cuntenawns, proferyng to ledyn hir a-bowtyn yf sche wolde. Sche had mech drede for hir chastite & was in gret heuynes" (237.28-33). These hostile advances confirm Margery's continual fears of sexual violation. Consider also that the priests' lewd offer to lead her about if *she* wills mocks the assertion of faith she has just made. Should she not, after all, be able to turn herself over to the clergy, treating them as instruments of the God to whom she entrusts herself? The priests' mockery of Margery's person and her faith indicates the potential for divine ordination and human execution to diverge.

For God does send Margery help, if not from expected sources. Commanded in her soul to go to the local church, Margery meets "a cumpany of powr folke" that happens to be going to Aachen. Her lack of a better escort is all the persuasion they ask before receiving her into their midst:

---

8   See also Staley (1994: 29-37).
9   "Deus, qui nobis sub sacramento mirabili, passionis tuae memoriam reliquisti: tribue, quaesumus, ita nos corporis et sanguinis tui sacra mysteria venerari, ut redemptionis tuae fructum in nobis iugiter sentiamus. Qui vivis et regnas in saecula saeculorum" (Wordsworth 1901: 95).

&, whan þei comyn to any towne, sche bowte hir mete & hir felaschep went on beg-
gyng. Whan þei wer wyth-owtyn þe townys, hir felaschep dedyn of her clothys, &, sit-
tyng nakyd, pykyd hem. Nede compellyd hir to abydyn hem & prolongyn hir jurne &
ben at meche mor cost þan sche xulde ellys a ben. Thys creatur was a-bauyd to putte of
hir cloþis as hyr felawys dedyn, & þerfor sche thorw hir comownyng had part of her
vermyn & was betyn & stongyn ful euyl boþe day & nyght tyl God sent hir oþer felaschep. Sche kept forth hir felaschep wyth gret angwisch & disese & meche lettyng vn-
to þe tyme þat þei comyn to Akun.

(237.17-30)

We can contrast here the "vn-clenly cher" of the clothed clergy with the hygienic na-
kedness of the verminous poor. Margery is preserved by fearing the one, and bitten for
fearing the other. Second, we can notice that the clergy bid Margery to procure for
them, while the poor do their own begging. There is no pretense here that the fellowship of the poor is optimal – aside from the vermin, there are delays and costs to be
considered. But the contrast does indicate the moral deficit at which the clerical account
is running.

Now at first, these contrasts may seem to reflect outright anticlericalism. But by
recalling the Corpus Christi orientation that Margery gives to her journey, we enable
ourselves to distinguish Margery's specific criticism of the clergy from various forms
of simple anticlericalism. Margery is not arguing that the clergy should be ousted from
their privileged place at either the altar or the monstrance. Rather, she is suggesting that
the stance that the clergy assume at the altar and at the monstrance should – by way of
habituation – lead them to adopt a similar stance toward the people on the street. For
Margery, pastoral care of the people of God becomes a natural extension of eucharistic
devotion – "quamdiu fecistis uni de his fratribus meis minimis mihi fecistis" (Matt.
25:40).

So much, then, for the issue of clerical prerogative. Let us turn now to an issue
concerning the relationship between lay piety and wealth. Margery's fellowship with
the poor, when viewed within the context of a Corpus Christi procession, exposes gaps
between liturgy and everyday social practice. As we shall see, Margery's experience
with the wealthy makes those gaps even more apparent. On the one hand, the festal
liturgy honors the wealthy layfolk with proximity to the body of Christ. On the other
hand, everyday social practice honors wealthy layfolk by segregating them from the
importunity of the poor. On Margery's view, such a situation is untenable. If liturgical
proximity to the body of Christ is to indicate, and thus to perpetuate, power, it must be
matched by an equal proximity to and service of that same body in the world.

As for the liturgy of the procession itself, Miri Rubin describes it as a performance
permeated with the iconography of power:

The centre of the procession was the most ornate, the most densely decorated; and it included people whose rank was reflected and enhanced by proximity to the holiest of ho-
lies. The eucharist could not be handled by a lay person, so its receptacle was always
carried by priests, but the canopy and flags around it were carried by layfolk, as if they
were invented for this very end.

(Rubin 1991: 225)

As the daughter of a Mayor of Lynn, Margery would have had ample occasion to observe the delicate weighing of secular and sacred interests in the logistical project of assigning places in this kind of procession. Desiring as she did to be "worshepd of þe pepul" (9.27), Margery herself may have angled for pride of place in her youth. Thus, at sixty, she is well positioned to note such angling in others.

We have seen such angling give way before necessity in Margery's experience with the poor, who offer her such service and proximity that she comes to share their vermin. Contrast this with the behavior of a "woschepful woman of London, a wedow wyth meche meny wyth hir" (238.1-2). This woman encounters Margery in Aachen and grants Margery "al hir desyr, & dede hir etyn & drynkyn wyth hir, & made hir ryth good cher" as they wait to see Our Lady's smock and the other relics shown on the feast of St. Margaret (238.3-7). Margery hopes this woman will escort her back to England, but, once the feast is over, the woman speeds out of town, leaving Margery behind. Despite the evasion, Margery catches up and tries again, going "to þe worshepful woman, wenyng to a be receyuyd wyth a rith glad cher. & it was euen ryth contrary; sche fonde rith schort cher & had rith scharp langage, þe worschepful woman seying to hir, 'What wenyst þu for to gon wyth me? Nay, I do þe wel to wetyn I wyl not medelyn wyth þe'" (240.6-12). So, for reasons left largely to our imagination, this "worschepful woman" does Margery honor in the time of preparation for the feast of St. Margaret of Antioch. Devotion to St. Margaret – not only Margery's namesake but also the patroness of her parish in Lynn – is one explanation that presents itself. Another possible explanation for the generosity of the "worshepful woman" is the need to perform charitable actions in spiritual preparation for devotion to the relics.

But, whatever the explanation for this generosity, once that feast is over and the relics have been put away, the woman will "medelyn" with Margery no longer. When, despite every effort, the woman is forced to share a boat with Margery from Calais to Dover, Margery is granted the grace to avoid seasickness. This allows Margery to tend to the woman, who, in having "most of þat passyon & þat infirmite" (242.25), may have learned something about the benefits of extra-ceremonial caretaking.

Again, the contrast between the occasion-oriented kindness demonstrated by this woman and the everyday accommodation of the poor does not suggest that one make a habit of seeking succor from the poor rather than the rich (there is, after all, the issue of vermin). What it does suggest is that the rich, like the clergy, are failing to live up to the model they enact in their liturgical roles. The rich claim the honor of sheltering the body of Christ as it travels in liturgical processions. On certain liturgical occasions, they may even claim the honor of sheltering Margery's body for Christ's sake. Having taken such places of honor on feast days, they should not then abandon Christ's body as they travel through the ferial world. To some degree, this is merely a matter of noblesse oblige. At a deeper level, however, it involves a basic faithfulness to the implications of the liturgy in which the rich so willingly – and so prominently – play a part. In addition, the charitable consent to "medelyn" with the likes of Margery brings with it the real possibility that this burdensome creature will – by enacting her *own* role as the body of Christ – prove a blessing in return.

This brings us to our final issue, concerning the relationship between the body of Christ, on the one hand, and the boundaries articulated by merely political forces, on the other. In order to see this issue in a liturgical context, let us start by returning to Miri Rubin's account and consider the range of political themes a processional route might express. Although scholars have become accustomed to thinking of Corpus Christi processions as merely "beating the bounds" of the local community:

> the more complex the processing body and the more inclusive the procession, the more varied the narrative unfurled on the processional way which framed the social act. Itin-eraries fall into two main categories, those *demarcating* territories, and those *linking* them. The former is by far the commonest: it was used to trace village boundaries, and in urban processions to mark spheres of influence, seats of particular families. . . . In England the *linking* type is more common, and in the urban sphere, it sewed with a pro-cessional thread the periphery to the centre, the parishes to the cathedral, the suburbs to the market place.
>
> (Rubin 1991: 267-268, emphasis hers)

Thus, while a processional route can, and clearly does, articulate *some* relation-ship among the areas through which it passes, there are many kinds of relationship it can so articulate. In adapting this understanding of processional dynamics to Margery's itinerary, therefore, we should be neither too hasty nor too rigid in our categorization. The processional context raises issues of linking and demarcation without favoring the one or the other.

Back home at St. Margaret's, Lynn, Margery herself notes some tension be-tween linking and demarcating types of itinerary in the Ascension procession. Extending our initial account of these dynamics to an understanding of temporal and cosmic as well as political realms, we can see the use to which Margery puts such tension:

> On þe Holy Thursday, as þe sayd creatur went processyon wyth oþer pepil, sche saw in hir sowle owr Lady, Seint Mary Mawdelyn, & þe xij apostelys. And þan sche be-held wyth hir gostly eye how owr Lady toke hir leue of hir blysful Sone, Crist Ihesu, how he kyssed hir & alle hys apostelys & also hys trewe louer, Mary Mawdelyn.
>
> (174.12-18)

For Margery, then, the Ascension procession links the temporal realms of past and present as Christ, the twelve apostles, Mary Magdalene and the Virgin Mary join Margery and the "oþer pepil" of her parish.[10] The intimacy of Christ's kiss emphasizes the immediacy of the connection.

---

10 The idea of tethering her mystical experiences to items on the liturgical calendar is not origi-nal to Kempe, but was available in many of the devotional works that served as her explicit

That being said, the Ascension is a leave-taking liturgy, and in witnessing that kiss Margery is painfully aware of the "partyng" necessitated by the apparent distance between heaven and earth. She continues, noting that:

> it was a swemful partyng & also a joyful partyng. Whan sche beheld þis sygth in hir sowle, sche fel down in þe feld a-mong þe pepil. Sche cryid, sche roryd, sche wept as þow sche xulde a brostyn þer-with. Sche myth not mesuryn hir-self ne rewlyn hir-selfe, but cryid & roryd þat many man on hir wonderyd. But sche toke non heed what ony man seyd ne dede, for hir mende was ocupyid in owr Lord. Sche felt many an holy thowt in þat tyme whech sche cowde neuyr aftyr.
>
> (174.18-27)[11]

Margery's awareness of the demarcation between heaven and earth thus occasions her transcendence of social norms of measure and rule, her heedlessness of mortal words and deeds, and her engagement in thoughts that exceed normal earthly capacity. Thus, though the procession beats the boundaries between heaven and earth, its demarcation only fuels Margery's desire to overcome those boundaries and link the two regions.

With this context in mind, let us now consider Margery's procession through the Low Countries and back home again to England. Here we see a similar dynamic at work, only now the political and spiritual "spheres of influence" align themselves less neatly. In Danzig, Margery identifies her journey to Wilsnack as transnational, not only because it takes her from England, but because the "iij Oostys & Precyows Blood ben þer on-to þis day had in gret worschip & reuerns & sowt fro many a cuntre" (232.13-14). She thus begins in what we might read as a linking mode, asserting that these many countries are united in common worship.

As at Ascension, however, there is tension between this spiritual linking and a more political impulse towards demarcation. In this case, the impulse is supplied by Margery's escort, who promises both to take her to Wilsnack and to come "wyth hir tyl sche wer in þe costys of Inglond þat sche myth han good felaschep of hir nacyon" (232.20-22). He presents this return to "hir nacyon" as more comforting than her time among co-worshippers of other nations, and the reader is all the more inclined to accept his assessment in light of Margery's continual (and not entirely ill-founded) anxiety when she is among strangers.

---

and implicit models. So, for example, Nicholas Love, whose *Mirror of the Blessed Life of Jesus Christ* is thought to have strongly influenced Kempe's contemplative method, translates for his readers some advice from the pseudo-Bonaventuran *Meditationes Vitae Christi* to contemplate the events of Jesus' life, not only according to the days of the week, but also according to the themes of the liturgical year. See Love (1992: 13.20-27).

11 Margery has a similar, yet more subtle experience during a Corpus Christi procession in Lynn, responding to another woman's suggestion that they "folwyn þe steppys of owr Lord Ihesu Crist" by withdrawing to a house and crying out "I dey, I dey" (107.31-35). *Imitatio Christi*, indeed.

Compare, then, the man's assessment with Margery's experience. As she re-calls, this comforting, political identification with one's "nacyon" soon proves an obstacle to worship. Margery and her escort find themselves without permission to leave Danzig and go to Wilsnack, "for sche was an Englisch woman" (232.25). Because of political tensions between the Teutonic Order of Prussia and the English Government, she has "gret vexacyon & meche lettyng er sche myth getyn leue of on of þe heerys of Pruce for to gon þens" (232.25-28). In the long run, it is a mer-chant of Lynn who comes to her aid, acquiring for Margery the permission to go where she wants. The point, then, is not to dispense altogether with regional loyal-ties. The point is to note that these loyalties – and other people's demarcation of the boundaries between nations – hinder Margery at least as much as they help her.

Not long after this incident, nationalism again becomes an issue. Having left Stralsund behind, Margery and her escort go forth on foot and in great dread, ex-periencing, as Margery reports, "many perellys" (233.15). While warfare presents a potential threat, the only peril Margery actually depicts is that posed by the fear of her guide, who

was euyr aferd & wold euyr a forsakyn hir cumpany. Many tymys sche spak as fayr to hym as sche cowde þat he xulde not forsakyn hir in tho strawnge cuntreys & in myddys of hir enmyis, for þer was opyn werr be-twix þe Englisch & þo cuntreys. þerfor hir drede was meche þe mor, & euyr a-mong owr Lord spak to hir mende, "Why dredist þe? þer schal no man don non harm to þe ne to non þat þu gost wyth. þerfor comforte þi man & telle hym þer xal no man hurte hym ne harmyn hym whil þat he is in þi cum-pany".

(233.16-25)

Clearly, a reversal has taken place here. The guide, having threatened to desert Margery because he fears himself endangered by her Englishness, now proceeds un-der the transnational protection God has afforded her.

Now, none of this should suggest that Margery discounts the danger of traveling through a land with which her country is at war: as we have noted, she is accosted by priests "of þat cuntre" who call her "English sterte". Even so, Margery takes refuge in this particular instance with "þe good wife of þe hows" (236.34). Presumably this woman is also "of þat cuntre", yet she treats Margery with considerable kindness.

Nor are all the English as helpful to Margery as was the merchant of Lynn: it is, after all, a "worschepful woman of London" who refuses to travel with her.[12] Without belaboring this point, we can recognize a contrast between Margery's fellow English – who provide uneven charity at best – with those "whech had neuyr seen hir be-forn" (241.27-28) – who often provide her with security and shelter, comfort and clothing,

---

12 In fairness, she also meets a "monke of Inglond, þe whech was to-Rome-ward" (237.32), and she finds that meeting a comfort "in-as-mech as sche had a man þat sche cowde vndirston-den" (237.33-34).

meat and drink. That some should accept while others revile her is a common characteristic of Margery's account. That the division between the two should so closely "beat" political boundaries, that Margery's political allies should prove her spiritual opponents, is less common. By the time Margery returns to London, met by the reproof "A, þu fals flesch, þu xalt no good mete etyn" (243.20-21), we have seen just what comfort one's fellow nationals can – and cannot – offer.

Reviewing Margery's sojourn in the Low Countries, then, we can recognize two sets of oppositions between spiritual and political methods of categorization. The first set involves a series of linkages. On one side we see political forces attempting to cut Margery off from her destination on account of the conflict between England and the Teutonic Order. On the other side we see spiritual forces driving her onward to Wilsnack so that she may join with other devotees from many different lands. The second set involves demarcation. Here, political wisdom defines "Margery's people" as her fellow English, while spiritual wisdom defines them as those, of any nation, who either give her aid or receive it from her. By upholding spiritual authority in these confrontations with political authority, the processional dynamic of Margery's journey calls us to reconsider the values by means of which we claim the comforts of home.

What, then, are we to make of Margery's return? The structure of Margery's itinerary requires us to consider this question in two parts. The first deals with her return to the English soil of London.[13] The second deals with her return to Lynn. In these two homecomings, we see the issues of the journey finally come to fruition.

First, then, Margery's "false flesh" (243.21) returns to London from the hardships of her journey to Wilsnack and meets with considerable reproach for her presumed hypocrisy. Yet she processes through the midst of her people, offering them correction "throw þe spirit of charite" and with regard "neiþyr for her ʒiftys, ne for her mete, ne for her drynke" (245.5, 11-12). Disregarding the comfort her fellow English might provide for her, Margery provides her fellow English with words which "profityd rith mech" those with ears to hear (245.12).

This charitable exchange further associates Margery with the body of Christ. Having said her piece, Margery comes to church, where God rewards her "for sche suffyrd scornys & repreuys for hys sake" and promises her "ful mech grace in þis lyfe & aftyr þis lyfe to hauyn joy & blysse with-owtyn ende" (245.14-18). In this imitation of Christ's passion, Margery attains considerable grace. As in the Ascension procession, she responds to the articulation of boundaries by promptly exceeding them. Here she is so comforted "þat sche myth not mesuryn hirself ne gouerne hir spirit aftyr hyr owyn wyl ne aftyr discrecyon of other men, but aftyr þat owr Lord wolde ledyn it & mesuryn it hys-self in sobbyng ful boistowsly & wepyng ful plenteuowsly" (245.20-23). This type of excess, leading to reliance upon divine rather than human measure, holds the potential for unifying the peo-

---

13   For a different reading, focused on political implications, see Staley (1994: 165-170).

ple of God. The "comown pepil" demonstrate this potential, as, having "magnifijd God" (245.28-29) in Margery, they imitate the Virgin Mary's response to the In-carnation: the assent through which all human flesh is united with the divine.

Not everyone in London shares this response, however, and Margery suffers "ful mech slawndyr & repref, specyaly of þe curatys & preistys of þe chirchis in London. þei wold not suffyr hir to abydyn in her chirchys, & þerfor sche went fro on chirch to an-oþer þat sche xulde not ben tedious on-to hem" (245.24-28). Here we see a num-ber of issues at work. We first notice the contrast between the layfolk who welcome Margery and the clergy who find her "tedious". Looking more closely, we notice that this clerical opposition overcomes parochial boundaries, propelling Margery from church to church. In the resulting procession, Margery "beats the bounds" of London, uniting those who have "good trost þat it was the goodness of God" (245.29-30) which fueled her devotion.

Taking up the second part of our question, let us now follow Margery home to Lynn. After the rejection Margery experiences from the London clergy, we are likely to take the hermit's warning – that Margery "xal fyndyn but lityl frenschep" (247.13) on her return to Lynn – as a matter of course. How, then, shall we understand this crisis of friendship – exemplified by the hostile reception Margery gets from her con-fessor? Unlike so many of the confrontations Margery recounts, the confessor's re-proach provokes no protestations of innocence, no theological riposte. The incident, and incidentally the whole narrative portion of the *Book*, ends instead with what may seem an emotionally flat statement: "owr Lord halpe hir so þat sche had as good loue of hym & of oþer frendys aftyr as sche had be-forn, worschepyd be God. Amen" (247.27-29). Having beaten the bounds of her spiritual territory, Margery finds that those bounds no longer truly bind her. Having met with no more, and often consid-erably less, comfort in her homeland than she has abroad, Margery invests less in that particular notion of belonging.

Nevertheless, to state simply that Margery's relationship with her homeland has changed does not fully account for what has happened here. Returning to Margery's Lammas Day reunion with the hermit who first led her out of Lynn, we note that she welcomes him with joy, recognizing in his arrival a providential symmetry: "I trust owr Lord sent ȝow hedyr, for now I hope as ȝe led me owt of Lynne ȝe xal bring me hom a-geyn to Lynne" (247.2-4). The procession must end its bounds-beating journey where it began, and, in Margery's return, it fittingly employs the same ministry by which it once arranged for her departure. Margery's acceptance of this arrangement involves considerably less striving than have many of her changes of escort.[14] Like-wise, what at first appears to be Margery's indifference towards her confessor's anger may just be a belated recognition that his anger will abate through no action of hers.

---

14   Cf., for example, her struggles to obtain a guide to Aachen once John has abandoned her (236.25-237.19), not to mention her adventures with the "worschepful woman of London" (238.1).

At the end of the day, then, we must still assess the significance of all Margery's bounds-beating. To do so, we should begin by recalling the means by which Margery crosses the various boundaries she encounters. Throughout her procession, Margery has found those boundaries – between England and the Low Countries, between rich and poor, between layfolk and clergy – surmountable only after she has allowed herself to be carried across them. In this sense, her final welcome to the hermit really *reenacts* the drama of Lammas Day,[15] marking her release from the chains of self-determination that have hampered her movement along the way. "This creature", who began by starting not one but two businesses, who struggled that she might "sauyn þe worschyp of hir kynred what-so-euyr ony man seyd" (9.24-25), must finally relinquish control. In doing so, she allows herself to be borne about like the common burden she increasingly portrays her vocation as being, a burden shared among the various members of the community, as are the blessings it evokes.

Margery's self-consciousness with regard to the burden her gifts impose upon others is something we often hesitate to attribute to Margery herself, preferring instead to consider her either too absorbed (whether in genuine devotion or in mania)[16] to realize how hard her behavior is to take, or too adamantly self-assertive to care.[17] Taking a page from Lynn Staley, though, we must remember that it is Kempe herself who informs us of Margery's importunity (1994: 11). After all, an account of a preoccupation with self, progressively overcome, would only further her *Book's* generic aspirations.[18] In order for "this creature" to recount the process by which she learns to depend upon her creator, she must first account for her earlier attempts at independence.

We find, then, that we need both notions – that of the divine ability to transgress temporal boundaries, and that of Margery's growing ability to accept her own dependence – to understand Margery's appropriation of Corpus Christi imagery.

---

15 Lammas Day commemorates St. Peter's release from his prison chains. Staley (1994: 169) also notices the significance of this liturgical occasion. Cf. Lochrie's citation of Richard Methley's Lammas Day rapture (1991: 215).

16 On devotion, see for example Collis (1964: 9-10, 132-133, 148-151) and Dickman (1980: 156-172). On mania, see for example Thurston (1936: 570), Allen (1940: xiv), Goodman (1978: 347-358), Howard (1980: 35), Weissman (1982: 211-217), and Partner (1991: 43-65). While the latter interpretation has lost much of its popularity since the publication of Staley (1994), it has not dropped out of circulation. Witness Holloway (1998: 151-153), Lawes (1999: 151-152), Farley (1999: 6-19), and Donnelly (2002).

17 Here any number of authors delight in what Staley calls Margery's "breathtaking dissociation from her community that places her beyond the reach of male authority" (1994: 114). See also, for example, Feinberg (1989: 132-141), Lochrie (1991: 191-198), and Beckwith (1986: 36-37 and 1992: 176-197).

18 Diehl (1996: 265-284) has an interesting discussion of the degree to which Margery's "court[ing of] heresy prosecution" (279) provides her with an audience for her spirituality which a woman out of orders normally would not be able to attract.

The imagery she appropriates is centered around the transformation of the divine, first into a human body and thence into the bread which mortals can display and carry and even eat. Margery inverts this equation, emphasizing God's provision of the means through which others carry her. Even after this inversion, she retains in her text an implication of the human soul's participation in that very divinity, by which it was created and of which it is the image.[19] Her obtrusive gifts of devotion – to the Incarnation and to the Transubstantiation of Christ – are indeed a burden, but they are a burden the community should be honored to bear.

Let us stop and take stock. We have seen that Margery orients her journey around the feast of Corpus Christi, and we have seen how she uses this orientation to address three issues: clerical prerogative, lay piety, and territorial boundaries. Stepping back and looking at the three of them together, we find that each concerns the proper role of established institutions. By situating herself in the place of processional honor, Margery grants herself a position from which she may not only criticize these institutions but bless them.

So, for example, if Margery be the body of Christ, then the clergy's treatment of her discloses a priority given to comfort and decorum over devotion. Should the clergy revise these priorities, they gain an ally in their ministries of correction. Similarly, the wealthy laity display holy-day piety, but pack up their devotion and leave at the close of the day. Should they choose to extend the time they spend with the likes of Margery, they stand to benefit not only from prayers but also from more temporal services. As for territorial boundaries, while they may have a hold on Margery, they have none on the body of Christ. By seeking to unite rather than divide the peoples of God, political units gain the grateful prayers – rather than the fearful imprecations – of the sojourner.

All of this indicates that Margery's liturgical orientation is not without institutional consequences. Where worldly institutions neglect the societal responsibilities to which they have laid a liturgical claim, the faithful must subordinate the authority of those institutions to the authority of God. Where political boundaries interfere with the movements of devotion, God will provide for the faithful.

That being said, to read Margery's journey only as a divinely ordained transgression of boundaries is to miss at least some of the point. Margery envisions her journey as a procession, a corporate act whose nature is reflected in her allusions to the companies and crowds she joins on the road. Processions set forth a model of community as it *should* be, but all too often is not. In this case, the processional model is of a community that upholds the body of Christ *both* on the altar *and* on the road. By invoking this model, Margery calls her fellow Christians not to desert the community and its institutions, but to renew the entire community's understanding of itself.

---

19   See Beckwith (1986: 41-48) for a discussion of the role played by the "resemblance and dissemblance of the soul to God" (43) in medieval theological writings.

References

Aers, David (ed.)
  1986   *Medieval Literature: Criticism, Ideology and History.* New York: St.
          Martin's.
Allen, Hope Emily
  1940   Preface. *The Book of Margery Kempe.* S. B. Meech and H. E. Allen
          (eds.). EETS o.s. 212. London: Oxford UP. liii-lxviii.
Beckwith, Sarah
  1986   "A Very Material Mysticism: The Medieval Mysticism of Margery
          Kempe", in David Aers (ed.), 34-57.
  1992   "Problems of Authority in Late Medieval English Mysticism: Language,
          Agency and Authority in the *Book of Margery Kempe*", *Exemplaria* 4.1:
          171-199.
Carruthers, Mary J. – Elizabeth Kirk (eds.)
  1982   *Acts of Interpretation: The Text and its Contexts, 700-1600.* Norman OK:
          Pilgrim Books.
Collis, Louise
  1964   *Memoirs of a Medieval Woman: The Life and Times of Margery Kempe,
          the Apprentice Saint.* New York: Crowell.
Dickman, Susan
  1984   "Margery Kempe and the Continental Tradition of the Pious Woman", in
          Marion Glasscoe (ed.), *The Medieval Mystical Tradition in England: Pa-
          pers Read at Dartington Hall, July 1984.* Cambridge: D.S. Brewer.150-
          168.
Diehl, Kari Schoening
  1996   Licensing the Word in Late-Medieval England: Strategies of Censorship
          and Evasion. [Unpublished doctoral dissertation, UCLA.]
Donnelly, Colleen
  2002   "Menopause and Life as Imitation of Art in *The Book of Margery
          Kempe*", [Unpublished paper delivered at The Thirty-Seventh Interna-
          tional Congress on Medieval Studies at Western Michigan University in
          Kalamazoo, MI.]
Farley, Mary Hardiman
  1999   "Her Own Creature: Religion, Feminist Criticism, and the Functional
          Eccentricity of Margery Kempe", *Exemplaria* 11.1: 1-21.
Feinberg, Nona
  1989   "Thematics of Value in *The Book of Margery Kempe*", *Modern Philology*
          87: 132-141.
Goodman, A.E.
  1978   "The Piety of John Brunham's Daughter, of Lynn", *Studies in Church
          History* 1: 347-358.
Holloway, Julia Bolton
  1998   *Jerusalem: Essays on Pilgrimage and Literature.* New York: AMS Press.

Howard, Donald
    1980   *Writers and Pilgrims: Medieval Pilgrimage Narratives and Their Poster-
            ity.* Berkeley: University of California Press.
Kempe, Margery
    1940   *The Book of Margery Kempe.* S. B. Meech and H. E. Allen (eds.). EETS
            o.s. 212. London: Oxford University Press.
Lawes, Richard
    1999   "The Madness of Margery Kempe", in Marion Glasscoe (ed.), *The Medieval
            Mystical Tradition: Exeter Symposium VI.* Cambridge: D.S. Brewer. 147 -167.
Lochrie, Karma
    1991   *Margery Kempe and Translations of the Flesh.* Philadelphia: University
            of Pennsylvania Press.
Love, Nicholas
    1992   *The Mirror of the Blessed Life of Jesus Christ.* Michael G. Sargent (ed.).
            New York: Garland.
Lyndwood, William
    1968   *Provinciale, seu Constitutiones Angliae.* Farnborough, Hants, UK: Gregg.
Middle English Dictionary
    1952-2001 Hans Kurath – Sherman H. Kuhn – Robert Lewis (eds.). Ann Arbor:
            University of Michigan Press.
Partner, Nancy F.
    1991   "Reading *The Book of Margery Kempe*", *Exemplaria* 3.1: 29-66.
Rubin, Miri
    1991   *Corpus Christi: The Eucharist in Late-Medieval Culture.* Cambridge:
            Cambridge University Press.
Staley, Lynn
    1994   *Margery Kempe's Dissenting Fictions.* University Park, PA: Pennsyl-
            vania State University Press.
Tarvers, Josephine K.
    1996   "The Alleged Illiteracy of Margery Kempe: A Reconsideration of the
            Evidence", *Medieval Perspectives* 11: 111-124.
Thurston, Herbert
    1936   "Margery the Astonishing", *The Month* 168: 446-456.
Weissman, Hope Phyllis
    1982   "Margery Kempe in Jerusalem: *Hysteria Compassio* in the Late Middle
            Ages", in Mary J. Carruthers – Elizabeth Kirk (eds.), *Acts of Interpretation:
            The Text and its Contexts, 700-1600.* Norman OK: Pilgrim Books, 201-217.
Wordsworth, Christopher
    1901   *Ceremonies and Processions of the Cathedral Church of Salisbury.* Cam-
            bridge: Cambridge University Press.
Wyclif Bible
    1999   Published as *King Henry's Bible, MS Bodley 277: The Revised Version of
            the Wyclif Bible.* Conrad Lindberg (ed.). 2 vols. Stockholm: Almquist and
            Wiksell.

Christian Diaspora in Late Medieval, Early Modern Perspective: A Transcription of the Treatise *Decem nationes Christianorum*

Thomas Hahn, University of Rochester

The small treatise *Decem nationes Christianorum* (*The Ten Christian Nations*) is perhaps the most compact and self-contained instance of a genre of writing that originates in Europe in the twelfth century. As an account of Christian diaspora – inventorying the particularities of belief and practice that delineate separate versions or "nations" of Christianity – it is unusual in traveling on its own, rather than as an incorporated part of a larger "orientalist" history. Moreover, though it likely originates in the late fourteenth or early fifteenth century, and survives in some fifteen different prints issued before 1516, no medieval manuscript of the text has been identified. *The Ten Christian Nations* draws indirectly upon propaganda and activities associated with the Crusades, upon intensified commitment to missionary enterprises, and upon a heightened self-consciousness of European or Western identity, defined through contrast with a variety of "others" at the frontiers of Christendom. Though apparently seldom read since the sixteenth century, and little known even to modern scholars, *The Ten Christian Nations* nonetheless offers a revealing and representative insight into momentous and distinctive processes associated with what Robert Bartlett and others have called "the making of Europe": the development, across the high and late Middle Ages, of a territorially unified culture, which, on the one hand, fostered overseas expansion and economic hegemony, but, on the other, triggered internal divisions and conflicts (in the form of nation states, ethnic divisions, religious schism, and so on).[1] In its vision of an inclusive Christianity riven by competing creeds, languages, and liturgies, *The Ten Christian Nations* underscores the changing function of religion in relation to individual, national, and transnational identities, and it provides a popular, capsule view of the condition of Christianity on the eve of the Reformation.

The Ten Christian Nations ultimately derives from the orientalist preoccupations of twelfth- and thirteenth-century European writers. Massive alteration in the extent and nature of intercultural exchange in contact zones – notably in the Middle East, but in Iberia, the North, and the far East as well – had pressed western European intellectuals towards broader engagement with Muslims and other non-Christians. Though conventionalized portrayals and stereotypes remained in circula-

---

[1] Bartlett (1993) offers a revisionary account of received, traditional understandings of medieval identities, whose classic expression is perhaps Southern (1953). Recent works that offer complementary perspectives include Bartlett – MacKay (1989), Phillips (1988), and Abu-Lagod (1989).

tion, many of the new accounts reflected genuine "fieldwork", in first-hand accounts produced by missionaries, soldiers, or their followers; the needs of religious administrators and military strategists for accurate information generated investigations, translations from Arabic, analyses, and descriptions that correspond to modern notions of "area studies" and ethnography. One of the characteristic reactions to this recognition of religious diversity was to seek new ways to imagine a universalized Christendom, whether through world conquest, missionary fervor, Christian ecumenism, or the quest for ultra-Islamic Christians – that is, co-religionists in the Far East who would allow Latins to outflank their Muslim rivals – as in the accounts associated with Prester John.

This reformulation of Christianity's claims as catholic and universal paradoxically encouraged acknowledgment of the diversity of doctrine and ritual within both historical and contemporary Christian communities or "nations". John of Würzburg seems to have composed the first systematic account of Christian diaspora (1160-1170), labeling each of the distinct sects as "nationes".[2] William of Tyre, one of the foremost chroniclers of European activities in the Middle East, equates *secta* and *natio* in his description of the *orientales nationes* of Christians (1184). James of Vitry, Bishop of Acre, writing in the early thirteenth century, helped reduce the number of separate Christian churches to about ten, and his work established *natio* as the default term of identity for each denomination.[3] The use of *nationes* in the title of the present treatise, *The Ten Christian Nations*, therefore reflects conventional use of a word whose charged meaning changed markedly over the late Middle Ages, and whose significance has changed even more drastically over the last half millennium.[4] While the modern nation-state and these late medieval Christian *nationes* differ fundamentally as cultural formations, it seems crucial to acknowledge that they share a historical and discursive linkage that originates in relations of

---

2   In her fundamental study of European Orientalist writings on Christian sects, von den Brincken (1973: 3-4) surveys the variety of sects and territories associated with non-Roman Christianity for John (Johannes) of Würzburg.

3   Von den Brincken (1973: 4-5) discusses William (archbishop of Tyre, died *ca*. 1185) and James (bishop of Acre, died 1240).

4   "The birth of the nation" as a political entity, and, indeed, the very nature of *nation*, remains a controversial issue in political theory and history, as Hardt – Negri (2000: 93-113) demonstrate in their survey of arguments. The conflicts of temporal and spiritual claims, and of state (defined through established rights of sovereignty and jurisdiction) and nation (defined "organically" through descent, territory, and so on) generated voluminous argument in the Middle Ages, which in itself evidences an intensifying "sense of nationhood"; see, for example, Canning (1988: 351-352) and Dunbabin (1988: 480-482). In characterizing the use of *nation* in the treatise, I have borrowed (Anderson 1991) the now familiar phrase "imagined community" (together with the ethnographic arguments that lie behind it). I have elsewhere (Hahn 1999: 84-91) argued for the emergence of *nacioun* as a self-conscious term of English identity in thirteenth- and fourteenth-century vernacular writing.

church and state, spiritual and temporal domains, and of language and territory as features of group identities.

The Ten Christian Nations draws upon the account of Christian diversity made standard in James of Vitry, and rehearsed in many other medieval writings.[5] On the one hand, the tracts reassembled long-familiar materials and incorporated established facts from synodal decrees; on the other, they reflect the new "ethnography", adducing new details that James, for example, had garnered as a bishop in the Latin Middle East. Such data was mediated not only by the escalating consciousness of non-Christians in the world, but also by official discourses within Christendom such as Canon Law, whose practitioners were deeply concerned with how to name and judge disparities of belief, and by expanding apparatuses for dealing with heresy. As perhaps the latest medieval report on Christian diaspora, *The Ten Christian Nations* participates in the nexus of forces – literacy, institutional regulation, enforced social ranks and territorial identities – that engenders a "persecuting society"; at the same time, however, in tone and content it stands apart from the aggressive dynamic of inclusion/exclusion that marks Christian confrontation with internal heresy.[6]

The Ten Christian Nations offers a brief, self-contained, and surprisingly non-judgmental overview of religious diversity. It presents coexistent varieties of Christianity that are at once competing (in terms of creeds and doctrines, practices, alliances, hierarchies, interrelations) and quite separate (in terms of local cultures, geopolitics, languages, social formation and group identity). Its compacted profiles characterize each *natio* definitionally – in terms of theological formulations, liturgies, sacred and spoken languages – rather than dogmatically or through contrast with orthodoxy; in this way they sidestep issues of coercive conformity to the Roman Church. Though it explicitly refers to the Jacobites, Nestorians, and Maronites as heretics, the treatise does not propose effecting reform or reconciliation by force; instead, in its last lines, it deplores the failure of communication *within* Christendom and the pope's ineffectuality as a supreme head of the church, and it implicitly endorses the convocation of general councils. In effect, *The Ten Christian Nations* presents religion as a differential and negotiated identity, powerfully shaped by cultural and regional influences, and subject to change through institutional intervention and bureaucratic policy. It stands as striking evidence of a growing awareness among late medieval intellectuals that Europe, Christendom, the West exist as

---

5   See von den Brincken (1973) for a comprehensive survey. Rogers (1962: 73-86) presents a detailed (though partial) publication history of *The Ten Christian Nations* and the texts it traveled with, as well as a survey of polemical and ecumenical contacts and motives that produced such writings.

6   Moore (1987) connects the processes of heresy prosecution with the growth of state powers and the isolation of "deviants" (sectarian, sexual, infected, criminal) from the twelfth century. Stock (1983) links the growth of institutions and communities dependent on writing to the formation of hegemonic and dissident groups with self-conscious, articulated identities.

imagined communities delimited by arbitrary borders, drawn and preserved not simply through physical incursion and defense, but through self-description, area studies, and other accounts of shared values and practices.

The precise origins of *The Ten Christian Nations* remain unclear. None of the scholars who have discussed the tract have cited a surviving manuscript copy, and it has not been edited or even reprinted since the early sixteenth century.[7] The detailed descriptions of eastern Christians that it sets out parallel in certain features the fantastic portrayals of exotic Christians in works such as *The Letter of Prester John* (written by a westerner in the twelfth century, and surviving in more than two hundred manuscripts).[8] The profiles provided in *The Ten Christian Nations* perhaps resemble more closely the detailed, often hostile accounts of "foreign" Christianities presented in the "Mongol histories" of writers such as John of Plano Carpini (*ca.* 1247) and William of Rubruck (1255), or in the missionary writings from the Near and Far East of John of Monte Corvino (1290 and later) and Ricoldo of Monte Croce (after 1300).[9] These reports deploy close observation in service of knowing the other – Nestorian, Armenian, Georgian, Indian Christians – and of recuperating them to the same. Their "data" found their way into synthetic portrayals and apologetics, such as Thomas Aquinas's *Summa contra gentiles* (1272-1276, which renders other Christians, as well as Jews and pagans, Gentiles) and Raymond Martin's more combative *Pugio adversus Mauros et Judaeos* (1278). Raymon Lull incorporated these materials to radically different effect in *The Book of the Gentile and the*

---

7   Von den Brincken (1973: 6) mentions the "Traktat über die Zehn christlichen Nationen", but without date or citation of an edition or manuscript; Rogers (1962: 81-83 and see index) discusses *Treatise on the Ten Christian Nations and Sects of Christians* and its contents, and lists some of the fifteenth- and sixteenth-century editions (186-188). Westrem (2001) presents a richly detailed account and edition of Witte's *Travels* against the background of medieval travel literature. In providing meticulous descriptions of the editions of the *Itinerarius* (ten of which include the Latin text of *The Ten Christian Nations*), Westrem (2001: 84-103) indirectly offers an invaluable publication history of the treatise, including notice of three manuscript copies of *The Ten Christian Nations* (in codices accompanying Witte's *Itinerarius*); all, however, are hand-written versions made after the printed texts of the treatise (2001: 294-298). Even more useful in tracking the publication history of *The Ten Christian Nations* is Westrem (1985: 394-462), which contains extensive bibliographic information (analytic, descriptive, historical) on each of the ten prints that includes the treatise, much of which does not appear in Westrem (2001).

8   Slessarev (1959) presents a facsimile of a French print of the *Letter* published about 1500, a translation, and extensive introductions and notes. For more recent scholarship, and a reprint of the nineteenth-century edition of the Latin *Letter*, see Beckingham – Hamilton (1996).

9   For translations of writings by John of Plano Carpini and John of Monte Corvino, see Dawson (1959: 2-72, 224-231); for William of Rubruck, see Jackson – Morgan (1990); excerpts from Ricoldo appear in Yule (1913-1916: 1.255-56, 3.260). Neill (1964: 120-139) provides a general account of these writings. Rubiés (2000: 49-53; 51) discusses the motives and patterns of Latin missionaries, who "sometimes found the culture of their declared enemies more congenial than that of Eastern Christian groups".

Three Wise Men (1274-1276), an imaginative colloquy in which a Gentile listens to a Jew, Christian, and Saracen explain their faiths, on the proviso that "each [should] be free to choose his own religion" (Bonner 1993: 167; 97-98).[10] Lull's later *Book of the Five Wise Men* (1294) stages an exchange among Roman, Greek, Nestorian, and Jacobite Christians for the benefit of a "Saracen" who wishes to discover which is the true Christian faith (Bonner 1993: 80, n. 22). This array of theological, polemical, and fictional descriptions makes clear the depth of engagement and the breadth of the repertoire possessed by European intellectuals engrossed in questions of global diversity and diaspora.

Exotic, satiric, or expansionist fantasies in vernacular writings deploy the same strategies of representation as *The Ten Christian Nations*, reproducing Oriental believers who are at once Same and Other, real and in the realm of the imaginary. Works such as Marco Polo's *Travels* (in French, about 1300; see Yule: 1929; Larner: 1999), *Mandeville's Travels* (in French, *ca.* 1360; see Higgins: 1997), and Philippe de Mezieres' *Dream of the Old Pilgrim* (French, 1389; see Coopland: 1969) expressly appropriate the concrete particularities of Oriental Christians into their narratives. Polo mentions direct dealings with Greek, Jacobite, Nestorian, Georgian, and Indian Christians, while Philippe's allegorical *Dream* invokes strange eastern Christians as one feature of his fantasy of Western world rule. In *Mandeville's Travels* (which offers accounts of eight of the "nations" named in the treatise), on the other hand, Christian diaspora furnishes yet another opportunity for the narrator's characteristic gambit of rendering difference comprehensible while sustaining estrangement: the first-person vernacular "author" mediates the details of diversity through his own experiences, allowing the reader to make sense of strangeness through designated cultural contexts, or to suspend judgment entirely in a manner akin to that of *The Ten Christian Nations*. In other ways, however, the two works stand in direct contrast to one another: *Mandeville's Travels* begins as a vernacular text, is "retro-translated" into Latin, and becomes one of the most popular writings in late medieval and early modern Europe; *The Ten Christian Nations* begins in Latin, is translated into English, and, after a flurry of editions, subsides into obscurity. Different as they are, however, *Mandeville's Travels* and *The Ten Christian Nations* participate in, and articulate, a tension between religious and secular claims, and an emergent consciousness of national, European/Christian, and global identities that in many ways constitute the most lasting legacy of this transitional period.

---

10 *The Book of the Gentile and the Three Wise Men* survives in medieval Latin, French, and Spanish translations; Bonner (1993) offers an abridged English version. Lull offers a universalist perspective, whereby one of the wise men proclaims, "What a great good fortune it would be if ... we could all – every man on earth – be under one religion and belief, so that there would be no more rancor or ill will among men, who hate each other because of diversity and contrariness of beliefs and of sects!" (Bonner 1993: 90).

The Ten Christian Nations likely took its present form in the period between the appearance of *Mandeville's Travels* (*ca.* 1360) and the treatise's first issue as a printed text (1490). In its usage of the term *natio* to designate units of difference and diaspora, *The Ten Christian Nations* agrees not only with literary works like *Cursor Mundi* and *Mandeville's Travels*, but with other established uses, as in describing the *nationes* attending various European universities.[11] *Natio*, when used in the treatise in relation to the Greeks, Indians, Georgians, or Mozarabic Christians, assuredly does not carry anything like the meaning of "national religion", or even "national church" as it might in modern historiography; even less does it evoke the powers of the state, as in raising taxes, waging war, or enforcing law. Nonetheless, *The Ten Christian Nations* demonstrates a complex and coherent investment in notions of alliance and community: in particular, its accounts of discrete groupings that make up a diaspora – a comprehensive but broken grouping – repeatedly and implicitly depend on ties that go far beyond the literal meaning of *natio* as an accident of birth.[12] These ties notably include spoken language as both a marker and a medium of communal identity; sacred, book, and liturgical languages – "unnatural", anti-vernacular media – as ritual and symbolic bonds of a congregation; defined religious practices as palpable, shared features of collective meaning; conscious beliefs and stated commitments as prerequisites for membership in the group; explicit social organizations and hierarchical allegiances (usually to a patriarch) that give form to the community; and territorial location, not merely as a feature of local place (Syria, Armenia), but also as part of regional geopolitics (the relations between the Georgians, the Greeks, and the Muslims). In all these ways, the individual descriptions presented in *The Ten Christian Nations*, however compacted, articulate a crucial and historically distinctive version of imagined community, not simply as this applies to the Oriental Christians of the diaspora, but perhaps even more as it reflects back upon, and helps to create, an increasingly self-conscious and continuously changing set of religious, national, social, and commercial identities within Europe.

The Ten Christian Nations survives in some fourteen printed editions, dating from about 1490 to 1515. The majority of these take their place as a supplement to

---

11   For the self-conscious use of *nation* in English works of the thirteenth and fourteenth centuries such as *Cursor Mundi*, see Hahn (1999: 84-91). Authorities and students continually negotiated the conventionalized use of "nationes" to designate sub-groups at the University of Paris, so that language and origin did not naturally determine affiliation; the "natio anglorum", for example, included students from Germany but not from the Low Countries in the thirteenth century. At Oxford after 1274 the northern and southern English "nationes" became a single *natio*, mimicking the resonance of the word in contemporary literary, legal, and historical contexts. See Rashdall (1936: 1.311-320, esp. 318-320: 3.57-58).

12   Hardt – Negri (2000), Canning (1988), Dunbabin (1988), and Hahn (1999) provide commentary on the medieval and early modern meaning of *nation*, and the controversies surrounding the term in current political theory.

the *Itinerarius* or *Travels* of John Witte de Hese, a cleric of Utrecht who seems to have composed his book, in Latin, between 1389 and 1392.[13] The *Travels* offers a relatively brief first-person account of a journey to Jerusalem and the Holy Land, followed by an account of fantastic adventures in Ethiopia and India, including the land of Prester John. An early printer – perhaps Johann Guldenschaff of Cologne, whose edition (*ca.* 1490) forms the basis for the text presented here – seems to have decided that *The Ten Christian Nations* would make a suitable factual appendix to the *Travels*, and each of the other nine surviving reprints of Witte's book included the treatise. Two editions of a quite different pilgrimage account – Pietro Giorgio Tolomei's *Translatio miraculosa ecclesie Beate Virginis Marie de Loreto* (*ca.* 1505, 1516), which describes the shrine of the Virgin's house in Italy – also append *The Ten Christian Nations* as a conclusion. Finally, one edition of George of Hungary's refutation of Islam includes a text of *The Ten Christian Nations.*[14]

The only surviving vernacular version of *The Ten Christian Nations* appears in the small English book, *Of the newe landes*, printed in Antwerp by the Dutch printer Jan van Doesborch (*ca.* 1510).[15] Van Doesborch seems to have relied upon one of the printed editions in producing his own translation, in a heavily Dutch-inflected Early Modern English dialect. His inclusion of *The Ten Christian Nations* in this book, where it appears as the third of four separate works, moves it far from religious pilgrimage and polemic. Van Doesborch's volume begins with a short excerpt from *De novo mundo*, a composite account of the New World attributed to Vespucci. A substantive account of the voyage of Balthasar Springer around Africa to India in 1505-1506 follows; Springer, who was an agent for German merchants, sailed with a Portuguese captain.[16] The *Letter of Prester John*, the longest text in the collection, forms the final narrative, and *Of the ten dyverce Cristeden* precedes as the third text. Van Doesborch had earlier published separate Dutch versions of the first three works in *Of the newe landes*, and in making the English book he seems both to have gone back to these Dutch publications, and also to have consulted other Latin and French versions to fill out or bolster his translations. There is no record that van Doesborch ever published a Dutch (or Latin) version of *The Ten Christian Nations*, though as an active printer in Antwerp he must have had easy access to the Dutch editions of John Witte de Hese, all of which appended the Latin text of the treatise.

---

13 Westrem (2001) has produced an exacting study of this book, its author and backgrounds, and the forms in which it survives.

14 For bibliographic details, see the Checklist of Editions.

15 Arber (1885) reliably transcribes *Of the newe landes*; for a facsimile, see D'Andrade – Randles (1960). An edition, with introduction, facing page facsimile, and extensive notes by Thomas Hahn is forthcoming (2003).

16 For a reproduction of the German text and its illustrations, together with a study of publication history, see Schulze (1902).

Van Doesborch's inclusion of *The Ten Christian Nations* in *Of the new landes*, like its inclusion in John Witte of Hese's *Travels*, reinforces its linkage to late medieval and early modern preoccupations with religion as a source of unity and divisiveness, and with regional and global differences and identities. Van Doesborch's small book combines the most up-to-date reports on non-Christians in Africa and the Far East (Springer's account was first printed in 1509) with recent sensational accounts of cannibals in the Far West (the Vespuccian *De novo mundo* appeared in 1505, and was issued in some twenty-five separate editions by 1520); to this fresh news he joins the fantastic portrayal of Oriental Christians from the *Letter of Prester John* (twelfth century). His ambitions that this mass-produced, vernacular chapbook should reach as broad and popular audience as possible are underscored in the woodcuts that he introduced to it: this small volume of forty-eight pages contains thirty illustrations. Strikingly, *The Ten Christian Nations* contains the fewest illustrations of any of the four works that make up the volume, perhaps because it is the most factual and least graphic of these texts.

In the course of the twenty-five years that span Europe's encounter with the New World and the Reformation, *The Ten Christian Nations* appeared in at least fifteen separate editions. Approximately eighty-five copies of these prints survive today; the low and high estimates for average print runs during this period suggest that at least three thousand, and perhaps as many as nineteen thousand copies of the tract reached the hands of readers in Germany, the Netherlands, England, and Italy during this quarter century.[17] This publication history suggests that the treatise filled a felt need for printers, and found a market with diverse readers. Yet it would be difficult to specify just what appetites *The Ten Christian Nations* whetted or satisfied: it never appears by itself, and though it appears in the company of pilgrimages, guide books, travel writing, and anti-Islamic polemic, it is none of these things. As an account of religious belief and practice, it seems to share more with ethnography than with apologetics. Moreover, in attempting to cover the "divisions" of Christianity, it shows itself an interstitial text, inhabiting and defining gaps rather than smoothing them over. Its exposition of differences within contemporary Christendom articulates a consciousness of diversity and commonality that resonates with current debates over the causes and nature of the Reformation.[18] *The Ten Christian Nations*, for all its summary character, gives dimension to a site that lies between the nominally unified Christian Middle Ages and the explicitly sectarian post-Reformation world. As a convergence point where forthright religious concerns confront newly mobilized identities – doctrinal, pious, geopolitical, commercial,

---

17   Watt (1991: 11-14, 42 ff.) discusses print runs for sixteenth-century ballads and chapbooks.
18   As a conscious reaction to genuine discord within Christianity, the treatise presents counter-evidence to the powerful and controversial contention (Duffy 1992) that the Reformation in England was the result of abrupt political intervention, rather than the final development of a long process.

fantastical – the treatise points up the overlaps and discontinuities that render "medieval" and "modern" at once indispensable and unreliable as historiographical markers.

* * *

The text presented here of *The Ten Christian Nations* takes as its basis the earliest surviving print of this treatise, published in Cologne by Johann Guldenschaff in 1490. I have examined copies of several of the other surviving editions as well, and these have confirmed that virtually no substantive variants mark the early prints; each new edition reproduced the established text. I have for purposes of comparison included textual notes indicating differences between the Cologne edition of 1490 and the edition published at Antwerp by Govaert Bac (1497-1499). The purpose of the textual notes is to demonstrate how closely the prints agree, or to call attention to peculiarities in the text; it does not in any way presume to be a critical edition. The comparisons presented in these notes reveal that differences between the editions are of minor stylistic importance, and do not materially alter content or expression. Likewise, the modern English translation I present here is intended to be serviceable, allowing non-specialists to make sense of the Latin text, and enabling specialists to make their own analyses. This introductory study aims not to say the last word on *The Ten Christian Nations*, but, on the contrary, aspires to provide incentives for further study and editorial work.

*

De Decem nationibus Christianorum orientalium

Notandum quod gentes Christianorum dividuntur in decem nationes, videlicet in Latinos, Grecos, Indos, Jacobitas, Nestorinos, Moronitas, Armenos, Georgianos, Surianos, et Mozarabes.

Prima natio

Latini habent imperatorem Alamanie et reges multos, videlicet reges Castelle, Aragonie, Portugalie, Navarie, et isti sunt de natione Hyspanica. In natione Gallicana est unus rex Francorum et multi duces et comites. In natione vero Ytalie est rex Cecilie, rex Neapolitanus, et multi duces et comites et marchiones ac etiam communitates magne, videlicet Venetiarum, Florentie, Senarum et Janue. In Germanica autem natione preter imperatorem qui debet esse Almanus sunt reges multi, videlicet rex Anglie, rex Scotie, rex Hungarie, Bohemie, Polonie, Dacie, Frisie, Suedie, Norwegie, Dalmatie, et multi marchiiones, langravii, duces, et comites, etc. Item in insula Cipri rex Cipri. Omnes predicti sunt obedientes ecclesie Rhomane.

Secunda natio

Greci habent parriarcham Constantinopolitanum, archiepiscopos, episcopes, abbates etc. in spiritualibus. In temporalibus vero imperatorem et duces et comites etc. Pauci tamen numero sunt nunc, quia Agareni et Turci occupaverunt et invaserunt maximam partem Grecie. Et isti non obediunt ecclesie Rhomane, et habent errores multos; qui sunt condemnati per ecclesiam, quia dicunt quod spiritus sanctus non precedit a filio, sed a patre solum, et quod non est purgatorium etc.

Tercia natio

Indi sunt quorum princeps est presbiter Johannes, huius potestas et numerus excedit omnes Christianos. Nam habet sub se septuaginta duos reges. Et quondam dictus dominus rex presbiter Johannes equitat semper facit portari ante se crucem ligneam. Quando tendit ad bellum facit portari duodecem cruces de auro et lapidibus preciosis factas pro vexillo. In illa terra est corpus beati Thome apostoli in maxima veneratione.

Quarta natio

Jacobite dicti sunt a Jacobo heretico discipulo patriarche Alexandrini. Hii in partibus orientis occupant magnam partem Asie, et terram Mambre que est propinqua Egypto, et terram Ethiopie usque ad Indiam, plus quam quadraginta regna. Hii circumciduntur et baptisant cum ferro ignito. Caracterem crucis imprimunt in frontibus et in aliis partibus corporis, ut in pectore vel in brachiis. Hii confitentur soli deo et non sacerdotibus Iudeorum et Agarenorum. Hii dicunt in Christo esse tantum naturam divinam. Aliqui eorum loquuntur lingua Caldaica, aliqui linga Arabica. Alii vero aliis linguis secundum diversitatem nationum. Isti fuerunt condemnati in consilio Cedcii.

Quinta natio

Nestorini a Nestorio heretico sic dicti, qui fuit Constantinopolitanus episcopus. Hii solum in Christo ponunt duas personas, unam divinam, aliam vero humanam. Et negant beatam Mariam esse matrem dei, sed bene hominis iesu. Hii utuntur lingua Caldaica in suis scripturis, et conficunt corpus Christi in fermento. Hii inhabitant Tartariam et maiorem Indiam, et sunt multi in numero. Terra eorum continet tantum sicut Almania et Ytalia. Isti heretici fuerunt condemnati in tercia synodo Ephesina et fuerunt divisi ab ecclesia Rhomana et permanserunt in pertinacia.

Sexta natio

Moronite a quodam heretico Morone dicti sunt. Qui unum intellectum et unam voluntatem in Christo tantum ponunt. Hii habitant iuxta Lybiam in provincia Fenice in magno numero. Viri bellatores in preliis edocti et experti.

Specialiter utuntur arcubus et sagittis. Hii more Latinorum campanis et eorum episcopi anulis mitris et baculis pastorialibus utuntur. In Scripturis littera Caldaica et in vulgari Arabica utuntur lingua. Hii aliquam fuerunt sub obedientia Rhomane ecclesie. Nam eorum patriarcha interfuit consilio generali Lateranensi celebrato Rhome sub Innocentio tercio. Sed postea recesserunt ab ecclesia Rhomana. Hii primo fuerunt condemnati in synodo Constantinopolitano. Et postea venerunt ad obedientiam Rhomane ecclesie. Et iterum reversi sunt ad suam opinionem in quo perseverant.

Septima natio

Armeni habitant in regno Armenie prope Anthiochiam. Hii proprium ydeoma et linguam commune omnibus habent et scripturas sanctas et officium ecclesie cantant et dicunt in vulgari lingua ita quod ab omnibus secularibus, viris et feminis intelligantur. Habent suum primatem quem vocant catholicum, cui obediunt velut pape cum magna devotione et reverentia. Quadragesimam ieiunant cum magna devotione in qua non comedunt pisces nec bibunt vinum. In diebus tamen veneris comedunt carnes.

Octava natio

Georgiani a beato Georgio (quem habent in preliis in patronum) dicti sunt, et habitant in partibus orientalibus, et est populus multum pulcher, fortis, et deciciosus. Medis, Parsis, et Assyriis (in quorum confinibus commorantur) valde formidolosi. Et utuntur lingua greca. Utuntur quoque sacramentis more Grecorum. Clerici habent coronas rotundas in capitibus rasas, seculares vero quadratas. Quando veniunt ad sanctum sepulchrum non soluunt Sarracenis tributum. Et ingrediuntur Iherusalem cum vexillis erectis, quia Sarraceni timent. Eorum femine ununtur armis sicut viri; barbas et crines etiam habent sicut viri. Utuntur pilleis altis in capitibus ad altitudinem cubiti. Quando scribunt Soldano statim dat eis quod petunt.

Nona natio

Suriani dicuntur a civitate Sur que est eminentior civitas in Suria vel Assyria. Hii untuntur in sermone vulgari lingua Sarracenica. In scripturis divinis et officiis misse lingua Greca. Habent episcopos et consuetudines Grecorum servant, et eis obediunt in omnibus. Conficiunt in fermento et habent opiniones Grecorum contra Latinos. Hos sequuntur aliqui Christiani qui in terra sancta vocantur Samaritani. Conversi primo tempore apostolorum, sed non bene ipsi sapiunt in catholica fide.

Decima natio

Mozarabes hii fuerunt olim multi numero, in partibus Affrice et Hyspanie, sed modo sunt pauci. Sunt etenim dicti Mozarabes quia modos Christianorum de Arabia in multibus tenebant. Isti utuntur in officiis divinis lingua Latina, et obediunt ecclesie Rhomane et prelatiis Latinorum. Conficiunt in azimo ut Latini.

Sed in multis discrepant a Latinis, quia cum dies naturalis dividitur in viginta quatuor horas diei et noctis, tot officia habent sive horas et psalmos ac hymnos ac certas orationes habent et nimis prolixas quas non dicunt more Latinorum. Nam et quod Latini dicunt in principio ipsi dicunt in fine vel in medio. Sacramentum eucharistie dividunt aliqui in septem partes, aliqui in decem. Et est hec natio valde devota. In matrimonio vero non coniunguntur nisi personis sue gentis sive nationis; inter quos femina amisso primo marito nunque coniungitur alteri, sed permanet in castitate perpetua.

Causa vero tante divisionis inter Christianos fuit quod antiquiis temporibus Christiani fuerunt astricti ne celebrarent consilia generalia. Ideo insurgentibus hereticis in diversis mundi partibus non fuit qui remedium apponeret. Secunda causa fuit negligentia summorum pontificum quia non curaverunt nuncios mittere ad Christianos in erroribus positos. Quia si hoc fecissent, multos aut omnes ad unam fidem et obedientiam Rhomane ecclesie reduxissent.

*

Decem nationes Christianorum
Textual Notes

I have used as the base text for this transcription *Itinerarius Johannis de Hese ... Tractatus de decem nationibus Christianorum ...* Cologne: Johann Guldenschaff, *ca.* 1490. Readings from this text (designated "C", for Cologne) are cited in italic; alternate readings are given from *Itinerarius Iohannis de Hese ... Tractus [sic] de decem nationibus Thristianorum [sic] ...* Antwerp: Govaert Bac, 1497-1499; readings from this imprint are designated "A". I have not recorded non-substantive spelling variations, such as *y* for *i*, or non-significant changes in phrasing or word order. I have modernized some features of the printed editions, capitalizing proper names, and supplying punctuation whose absence might be confusing for a modern reader. I have expanded common abbreviations (ampersand for "et", superior strokes indicating nasals like "n", case terminations such as "ibus" and "us") silently.

Prima natio Latini habent. A: Prima Natio est Latinorum qui habent. For each group C provides a rubric, which A incorporates into the first sentence of description.

Alamanie. A: Almanie.

Aragonie. A: Arragonie.

isti sunt de natione. C: istos in natione. I substitute A's reading as more grammatically regular.

Gallicana. A: gallica.

et comites et marchiones. A: comites marchiones.

ac etiam. A: ac.

Bohemie: A: rex Boehemie.

langravii. A: Lantgravii.
et comites. A: Comites.
ecclesie Rhomane. A: Rhomane ecclesie.
Secunda natio Greci habent. A: Secunda Natio est grecorum qui habent.
et duces et comites. A: duces comites.
invaserunt. A: innaserunt.
et quod non est purgatorium etc. A: Etiam dicunt quod non est purgatorium.
Tercia natio Indi sunt quorum. A: Tercia Natio est Indorum quorum.
Huius potestas et numerus. A: cuius potestas.
dominus rex presbiter. A: dominus presbyter.
in maxima veneratione. A: in magna veneratione.
Quarta natio Jacobite dicti sunt a Jacobo heretico discipulo patriarche Alexandrini. A: Quarta Natio est Jacobitarum a Jacobo heretico discipulo patriarche alexandrini iacobite dicti sunt.
Asie, et terram. A: Asye terram.
Hii dicunt. A: et dicunt.
Isti fuerunt. A: Et isti fuerunt.
Quinta natio Nestorini a Nestorio heretico sic dicti, qui fuit Constantinopolitanus episcopus. A: Quinta Natio est Nestorinorum, a Nestornio heretico qui fuit Constantinopolitanorum episcopus. Sic dicti Nestorini.
beatam Mariam. A: beatam virginem Mariam.
in fermento. Fermentum occurs frequently in the Vulgate bible for leaven or yeast; holydays such as Passover required unleavened bread. The Roman church (differentiated here from the Nestorians) prescribed unleavened bread for the sacrament of the altar, and *fermentum* often came to designate the eucharistic bread.
Isti heretici. A: Et isti heretici.
in tercia synoda. A: tercia synoda.
Sexta natio Moronite a quodam. A: Sexta Natio est Moronitarum. Moronite a quodam.
recesserunt. A: recesserunt ab ecclesia Rhomana.
condemnati in synodo. A: convicti in synodo.
redierunt ad obedientiam. A: venerunt ad obedientiam.
ad suam opinionem in qua perseverant. A: ad propriam eorum opinionem in qua perseverant hodierno tempore. *perseverant* is the last word on the page in C, and the final phrase (to the present time) may have been omitted for lack of space.
Septima natio Armeni habitant. A: Septima Natio est Armenorum qui habitant.
secularibus viris et feminis. A: secularibus tam viris quoque feminis.
Velut pape. A: sicut nos pape.
Octava natio Georgiani a beato Georgio (quem habent in preliis in patronum) dicti sunt. A: Octava Natio est Georgianorum, a beato Georgio quem habent in preliis in patronum dicti sunt Georgiani.
coronas rotundas in capitibus rasas. A: coronas in capitibus eorum rotundas.

Nona natio Suriani dicuntur a civitate Sur. A: Nona Natio est Surianorum, sic dicit Suriani a civitate Sur.

officio misse. A: officiis misse.

Conversi primo. A: Primo conversi.

Decima natio Mozarabes hii fuerunt. A: Decima Natio est Mozarabii. Hi Mozarabes.

Isti utuntur. A: Hi utuntur.

in azimo ut Latini. The Vulgate bible frequently uses *azymus* (an exact transliteration of the Greek adjective) for "unleavened", though it is otherwise a rare word.

hymnos ac certas. A: hymnos certasque.

permanet. A: manet.

*

The Ten Christian Nations
Translation

Note that the Christian peoples are divided into ten nations, namely the Latins, Greeks, Indians, Jacobites, Nestorians, Moronites, Armenians, Georgians, Syrians, and Mozarabic Christians.

The First Nation

The Latins have the Emperor of Germany (the Holy Roman Emperor), and many kings, namely the King of Castile, of Aragon, of Portugal, and of Navarre, and these are from the nation of Spain. In the nation of Italy there is the King of Sicily, the King of Naples, and many dukes, counts, and marquis, and many city-states, such as Venice, Florence, Sienna, and Genoa. In the nation of the Germans, however, besides the Emperor (who ought to be a German) there are many kings, including the King of England, the King of Scotland, the King of Hungary, of Bohemia, of Poland, of Dacia, of Frisia, of Sweden, of Norway, of Dalmatia, and many marquis, landgraves, dukes, and counts, and so on. Also, in Cyprus there is the King of Cyprus. All of these aforementioned give obedience to the Church of Rome.

The Second Nation

The Greek Christians have the patriarch of Constantinople, archbishops, bishops, abbots, and so on in the spiritual realm. In the temporal sphere, on the other hand, they have the emperor, and dukes and counts and so on. They are however few in number now, for the Muslims and Turks have occupied and invaded the greatest part of Greece. And these are not obedient to the Church of Rome, but hold to many errors; they have been condemned by the church, for they say that the Holy Ghost does not proceed from the Son, but from the Father alone, and that there is no purgatory, and so on.

The Third Nation

The Indians are those whose prince is Prester John, whose power and number exceed all other Christians. For he has under him seventy-two kings. And when the said lord, the priest-king John, rides forth he always has carried before him a wooden cross. When he advances to war he has borne as a standard twelve crosses made of gold and precious gems. In that country is the body of Saint Thomas the Apostle held in greatest reverence.

The Fourth Nation

The Jacobite Christians are so called from the heretic Jacob, a disciple of the patriarch of Alexandria. Situated in the East, these people have settled in a great part of Asia, along with the land of Mamre next to Egypt, and the land of Ethiopia all the way to India, in all more than forty kingdoms. They circumcise and baptize with a burning sword. They seal the symbol of the cross on the forehead and on other parts of the body, as on the chest and arms. They make confession to God alone, and not to the priests of the Jews or the Muslims. They say that in Christ there is only a divine nature. Some of them speak the Chaldean (Aramaic) language, others speak Arabic; still others speak other tongues, reflecting the diversity of these peoples. They were condemned at the Council of Chalcedon.

The Fifth Nation

The Nestorians are so called after the heretic Nestorius, who was Bishop of Constantinople. They exclusively believe in the two persons of Christ, one divine, the other human. They also say that holy Mary is not the mother of God, but properly of Jesus the man. They use Chaldean (Aramaic) in their sacred writings, and consecrate the body of Christ with leavened bread. They live in Tartary and India the Great, and are great in number. Their land stretches as far as Germany and Italy combined. These heretics were condemned at the third Council of Ephesus and were separated from the Church of Rome, but they persevered in their contumacy.

The Sixth Nation

The Moronites are so called after a certain heretic, Moron. They hold that there is only one mind and one will in Christ. They live near Lybia, under the rule of Venice, in great numbers. As warriors, they are experienced and well trained in battle, especially in deploying bows and arrows. They follow the Latin rite in the ringing of bells at mass, and their bishops use rings, miters, and pastoral staffs (croziers). In their sacred writings they use Chaldean (Aramaic), but they speak Arabic. They were once under obedience to the Church of Rome. Their patriarch attended the Lateran general council, celebrated at Rome under Pope Innocent III. Afterwards, however, they separated from the Church of Rome. They were first

condemned at the Synod of Constantinople. And afterwards they again returned to
obedience to the Church of Rome, but again they reverted to their own belief, in
which they still persevere.

The Seventh Nation

The Armenian Christians live in the kingdom of Armenia, near Antioch. They
possess their own language and speech, common to all, and they sing and speak
their sacred writings and the offices of the church in the spoken language, so that
these things are understood by all lay people, men and women both. They have
their own primate, whom they call universal (catholic), to whom they are obedient
as if to the pope, with great devotion and reverence. They fast during Lent with
great devotion, during which they do not eat fish nor drink wine, though they eat
flesh on Fridays.

The Eighth Nation

The Georgian Christians are so called after Saint George, whom they regard
as a patron saint in battle. They live in the East, and are a beautiful, strong, and
splendid people. To the Medes, Persians, and Assyrians, within whose borders
they have remained, they are fearsome. They use the Greek language, and follow
the Greek rite in the sacraments. Their clergy have round crowns shaved into their
hair; lay people have square ones. When they visit the Holy Sepulchre, they are
not accustomed to pay the Muslims tribute. And they proceed to Jerusalem with
their banners unfurled, since the Muslims fear them. Their women practice arms
just like the men; they also have beards and curly hair like the men. They wear tall
hats over their hair, a cubit in height. When they write to the Sultan, he immediately gives them whatever they ask.

The Ninth Nation

The Syrian Christians take their name from the city of Sur, which is the out-
standing city of Syria or Assyria. In ordinary speech they employ the Saracen
tongue. In their sacred writings and the offices of the mass they use the Greek
language. They have bishops and they hold to services in the Greek rite, and are
obedient to them in all things. They consecrate the Eucharist with leavened bread,
and maintain beliefs in accord with the Greeks and against the Church of Rome.
Some of these Christians follow those who in the Holy Land are called Samari-
tans. They first converted to Christianity in the time of the apostles, but they are
not well versed in the Catholic faith.

The Tenth Nation

The Mozarabic Christians were once many in number, in regions of Africa
and Spain, but now there are few. Mozarabic Christians are so called because they
practice the observances of Christians from Arabia in many respects. They use the

Latin language in their sacred ceremonies, and they obey the Church of Rome and the Latin bishops. They consecrate the sacrament of the altar as do the Latins. But they also depart in many respects from the Western Church: as when the natural day is divided into twenty-four hours of the day and the night, they have this many offices, or hours and psalms. Also, they have hymns and other prayers, extremely diffuse, which they do not say according to the practice of the Latins. For what the Latins say at the beginning, they say at the end or in the middle. Some of them divide the sacrament of the Eucharist into seven parts, others into ten. In addition, this is an exceptionally devout nation. Finally, in the sacrament of matrimony, they do not mix except with people of their own kind or nation; among them a woman, once her first husband has died, does not wed another, but persists in perpetual chastity.

The source of this profound division among Christians was that from ancient times Christians were prohibited from partaking in general councils. As a result, there was no one who might bring a remedy to heretics rising up in various parts of the world. A second cause was the inattentiveness of the supreme pontiffs, because they did not take care to send emissaries to Christians who had fallen into error. Had they done this, they would have brought back many or all to the one faith and obedience to the Church of Rome.

References

Abu-Lagod, Janet L.
    1989   *Before European Hegemony: The World System, 1250-1350.* New York: Oxford University Press.
Anderson, Benedict
    1991   *Imagined Communities: Reflections on the Origin and Spread of Nationalism.* Revised Ed. London: Verso.
Arber, Edward
    1885   *The First Three English Books on America.* Birmingham: privately printed.
Bartlett, Robert – Angus MacKay (eds.)
    1989   *Medieval Frontier Societies.* Oxford: Clarendon.
Bartlett, Robert
    1993   *The Making of Europe: Conquest, Colonization, and Cultural Change, 950-1350.* Princeton: Princeton University Press.
Beckingham, Charles F. – Bernard Hamilton (eds.)
    1996   *Prester John, the Mongols and the Ten Lost Tribes.* London: Variorum.
Bonner, Anthony (ed. and trans.)
    1993   *Doctor Illuminatus: A Ramon Llull Reader.* Princeton: Princeton University Press.

Burns, J. H. (ed.)
1988   *The Cambridge History of Medieval Political Thought*. Cambridge: Cambridge University Press.

Canning, J. P.
1988   "Introduction: Politics, Institutions and Ideas", in Burns (ed.), 341-366.

Coopland, G. W. (ed.)
1969   Philippe de Mezieres, *Le Songe du Vieil Pelerin*. 2 vols. Cambridge: Cambridge University Press.

D'Andrade, M. Freire – W. G. L. Randles (eds.)
1960   *Of the newe Landes of Ye People Founde by the Messengers of the Kynge of Portyngale Named Emanuel ... Printed by John of Doesbrorow [Antwerp], (C. 1515)*. (Facsimile.) Lisbon: [no publisher].
[1998]   [Reprinted No place indicated [?Lisbon]]: O Mundo do Livro.

Dawson, Christopher
1966   *Mission to Asia*. New York: Harper.

De Decem nationibus Christianorum orientalium
Ca. 1490   *Itinerarius Johannis de Hese ... Tractatus de decem nationibus Christianorum ...* Cologne: Johann Guldenschaff.
1497-1499 *Itinerarius Iohannis de Hese ... Tractus [sic] de decem nationibus Thristianorum [sic] ...* Antwerp: Govaert Bac.

Duffy, Eamon
1992   *The Stripping of the Altars: Traditional Religion in England, c.1400-c.1580*. New Haven and London: Yale University Press.

Dunbabin, Jean
1988   "Government", in Burns (ed.), 477-519.

Hahn, Thomas
1999   "Early Middle English", in Wallace (ed.), 61-91.

Hahn, Thomas (ed.)
2003   *Of the Newe Landes*. America Observed, Vol 1. Woodbridge, UK, and Rochester, New York: Boydell and Brewer.

Hardt, Michael – Antonio Negri
2000   *Empire*. Cambridge: Harvard University Press.

Higgins, Iain Macleod
1997   *Writing East: The "Travels" of Sir John Mandeville*. Philadelphia: University of Pennsylvania Press.

Jackson, Peter – David Morgan (eds.)
1990   *The Mission of Friar William of Rubruck*. Hakluyt Society, Second Series 173. London: Hakluyt Society.

Larner, John
1999   *Marco Polo and the Discovery of the World*. New Haven and London: Yale University Press.

Moore, R. I.
1987   *The Formation of a Persecuting Society*. Oxford: Basil Blackwell.

Neill, Stephen
1964   *A History of Christian Missions*. Harmondsworth: Penguin.

Phillips, J. R. S.
1988   *The Expansion of Medieval Society*. New York: Oxford University Press.

Rashdall, Hastings
1936   *The Universities of Europe in the Middle Ages.* F. M. Powicke – A. B. Emden (eds.), 3 vols. Oxford: Oxford University Press.

Rogers, Francis M.
1962   *The Quest for Eastern Christians: Travels and Rumors in the Age of Discovery.* Minneapolis: University of Minnesota Press.

Rubiés, Joan-Pau
2000   *Travel and Ethnology in the Renaissance: South India through European Eyes, 1250-1625.* Cambridge: Cambridge University Press.

Sander, Max
1941   *Livres à figures italien depuis 1467 jusqu'à 1530.* 6 vols. New York: G. E. Stechert.

Schluze, Franz.
1902   *Balthasar Springers Indienfahrt, 1505/06.* Strassburg: Heitz & Mündel.

Slessarev, Vsevolod
1959   *Prester John, The Letter and the Legend.* Minneapolis: University of Minnesota Press.

Southern, Richard W.
1953   *The Making of the Middle Ages.* New Haven and London: Yale University Press.

Stock, Brian
1983   *The Implications of Literacy.* Princeton: Princeton University Press.

von den Brincken, Anna-Dorothee
1973   *Die "Nationes Christianorum Orientalium" im Verständnis der lateinischen Historiographie, von der Mitte des 12. bis in die zweite Hälfte des 14. Jahrhunderts.* Cologne, Vienna: Böhlau Verlag.

Wallace, David (ed.)
1999   *The Cambridge History of Medieval English Literature.* Cambridge: Cambridge University Press.

Watt, Tessa
1991   *Cheap Print and Popular Piety, 1550-1640.* Cambridge: Cambridge University Press.

Westrem, Scott D.
1985   A Critical Edition of Johannes Witte de Hese's *Itinerarius*, the Middle Dutch Text, an English Translation, and Commentary, Together with an Introduction to European Accounts of Travel to the East (1240-1400). [Unpublished Ph.D. dissertation, Northwestern University.]
2001   *Broader Horizons: A Study of Johannes Witte de Hese's "Itinerarius" and Medieval Travel Narratives.* Cambridge: Medieval Academy of America.

Yule, Sir Henry (ed. and transl.)
1913-1916 *Cathay and the Way Thither: Being a Collection of Medieval Notices of China.* Hakluyt Society Second Series 33, 37, 38, 41. London: Hakluyt Society. 4 vols.

Yule, Sir Henry – Henri Cordier (eds.)
1929   *The Travels of Marco Polo.* 3 vols. London: John Murray.
[1993]   [Reprinted 3 vols. in 2. New York: Dover.]

Author Index

Subject Index

Studies in English Medieval Language and Literature

Edited by Jacek Fisiak